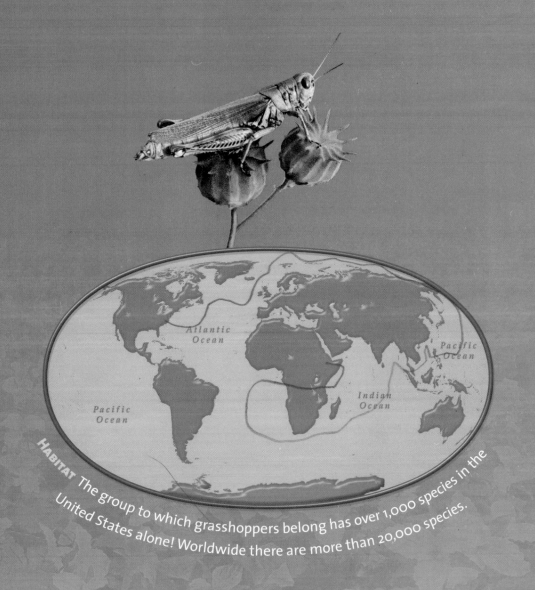

HABITAT The group to which grasshoppers belong has over 1,000 species in the United States alone! Worldwide there are more than 20,000 species.

CHARACTERISTICS Most grasshoppers have two pairs of wings—one a hard body covering, the other used for flight.

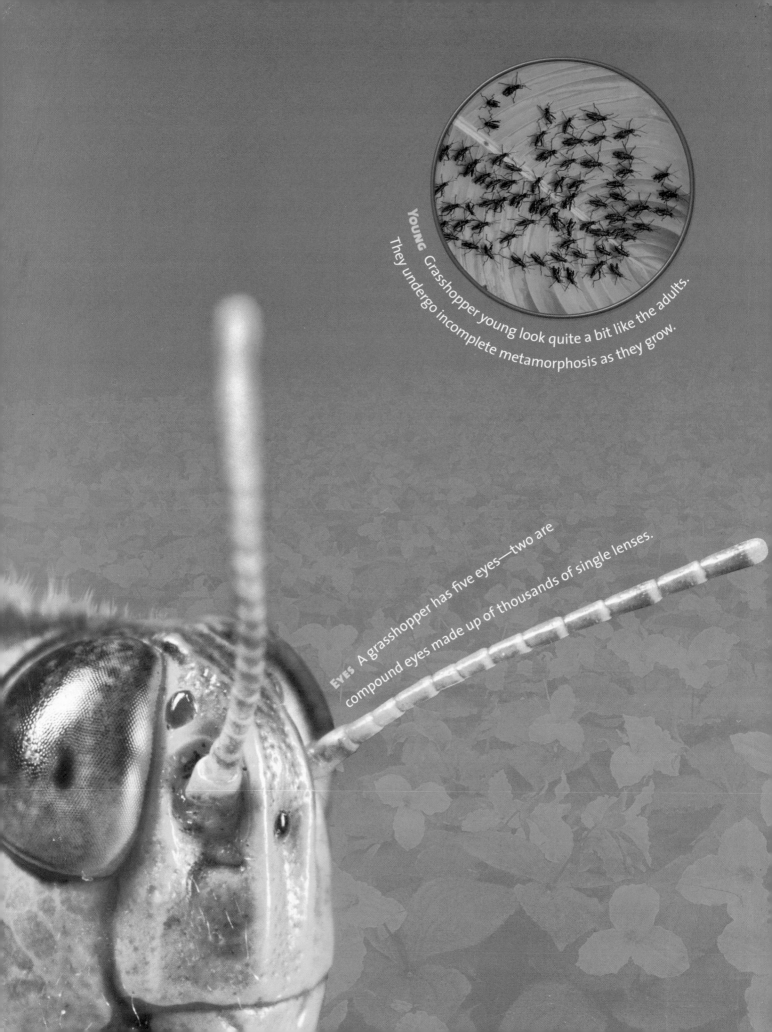

YOUNG Grasshopper young look quite a bit like the adults. They undergo incomplete metamorphosis as they grow.

EYES A grasshopper has five eyes—two are compound eyes made up of thousands of single lenses.

Science

Grasshopper

Harcourt
SCHOOL PUBLISHERS

Orlando   Austin   New York   San Diego   Toronto   London

Visit *The Learning Site!*
www.harcourtschool.com

Grasshopper

Consulting Authors

Michael J. Bell
Assistant Professor of Early Childhood Education
College of Education
West Chester University of Pennsylvania

Michael A. DiSpezio
Curriculum Architect
JASON Academy
Cape Cod, Massachusetts

Marjorie Frank
Former Adjunct, Science Education
Hunter College
New York, New York

Gerald H. Krockover
Professor of Earth and Atmospheric Science Education
Purdue University
West Lafayette, Indiana

Joyce C. McLeod
Adjunct Professor
Rollins College
Winter Park, Florida

Barbara ten Brink
Science Specialist
Austin Independent School District
Austin, Texas

Carol J. Valenta
Senior Vice President
St. Louis Science Center
St. Louis, Missouri

Barry A. Van Deman
President and CEO
Museum of Life and Science
Durham, North Carolina

Senior Editorial Advisors

Napoleon Adebola Bryant, Jr.
Professor Emeritus of Education
Xavier University
Cincinnati, Ohio

Robert M. Jones
Professor of Education Foundations
University of Houston-Clear Lake
Houston, Texas

Mozell P. Lang
Former Science Consultant
Michigan Department of Education
Science Consultant, Highland Park Schools
Highland Park, Michigan

LIFE SCIENCE

UNIT A: Understanding Living Things

UNIT B: Interactions in Ecosystems

EARTH SCIENCE

UNIT C: Exploring Earth

UNIT D: Cycles on Earth and in Space

PHYSICAL SCIENCE

UNIT E: Matter and Energy

UNIT F: Forces and Machines

Science Spin
Weekly Reader

Technology
Raising the *Kursk*, **620**

People
Making Cars Safer, **622**

Science Spin
Weekly Reader

Technology
The Wright Stuff, **646**

People
Designing Fun, **648**

References

Preparing for Science

Vocabulary

scientific method
hypothesis
independent variable
dependent variable
pan balance
spring scale
microscope

Plasma b

What happens when

Push the red bu
around its surfa

Elec

he plasma ball?

move your hand

What do YOU wonder?

These students are visiting a science museum with their class. They are interested in a plasma ball. What is plasma? What is a plasma ball? Why do sparks jump from the small ball to the outer glass ball? You will discover ways to find the answers.

What Methods Do Scientists Use?

Fast Fact

Writing It Down! This marine biologist is studying an artificial coral reef. Corals will colonize shipwrecks and other structures that are sunk to encourage reef growth. The scientist is gathering data about the numbers of organisms the reef is attracting. In the Investigate, you will gather data from another type of scientific activity.

Reaction Time

Materials ● **meterstick** ● **clipboard** ● **paper**

Procedure

1. Work with a partner. Have your partner hold the meterstick vertically near the end marked 100 cm. Hold your index finger and thumb about 5 cm apart on either side of the 0-cm mark.

2. Have your partner let go of the meterstick. As soon as you see your partner's fingers open to let go of the meterstick, snap your fingers shut to catch it.

3. Note the cm mark where your fingers snapped shut. Record that mark.

4. Complete Steps 1–3 two more times.

5. Change places with your partner, and repeat Steps 1–4.

Draw Conclusions

1. How far did the meterstick fall each time before you or your partner caught it?

2. Did your reaction time improve with more trials? Why or why not?

3. Inquiry Skill What can you infer about the movement of nerve signals from your eyes to your brain and from your brain to your fingers?

Step 2

Step 3

Investigate Further

What do you think the results might be if your partner counted "Three, two, one, go" before letting go of the meterstick? Test your hypothesis.

Reading in Science

VOCABULARY
scientific method p .4
hypothesis p. 4

SCIENCE CONCEPTS
▶ what the scientific method is
▶ how the scientific method is used

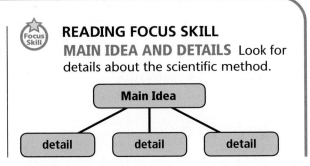

READING FOCUS SKILL
MAIN IDEA AND DETAILS Look for details about the scientific method.

Main Idea
detail | detail | detail

Methods Scientists Use

In ancient Greece, scientists thought the best way to solve a problem was to think about it. A Greek scientist would not do experiments or other kinds of research. For the past several hundred years, though, scientists have used another approach. Their accepted, organized way to address a problem is called the **scientific method**. The general scientific method is seen clearly in experiments. There are variations of this method that are used in field studies and observational investigations.

The first step of the scientific method is to make observations and ask questions. For example, Sam was helping his mother put away groceries. He noticed the items labeled as antibacterial disinfectants. He wondered if all such products are about the same. He called his friend Noah, and they talked about a question they could ask. They decided on this question: Are all antibacterial disinfectants equally good at killing bacteria?

The next step of the scientific method is to form a hypothesis. A **hypothesis** is a scientific explanation that you can test. The boys hypothesized that the disinfectants are equally effective in killing bacteria.

The boys continued with the scientific method by planning and conducting an experiment. If they had been studying something like stars or ancient plants, they would have tested a hypothesis by making a model or by making detailed observations.

They decided to ask their science teacher to help them set up an experiment using petri dishes (small glass lab dishes) and live bacteria. She began by helping them with another step of the scientific method, identifying and controlling variables. The variable they would test was the different disinfectants the bacteria would be exposed to. The control would be a dish with no disinfectant. Each of the other dishes would receive a different brand of disinfectant.

Sam, Noah, and the teacher prepared four petri dishes with agar (a material on which bacteria can grow). The boys put different disinfectants

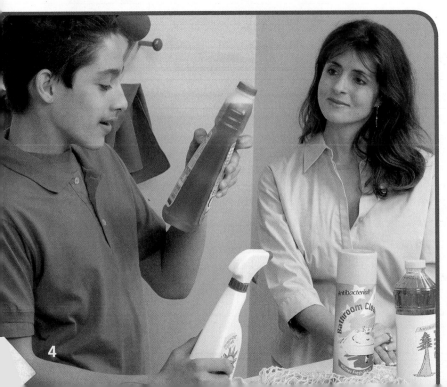

◀ **Both Sam and his mother wondered why there were so many different antibacterial products on the market.**

4

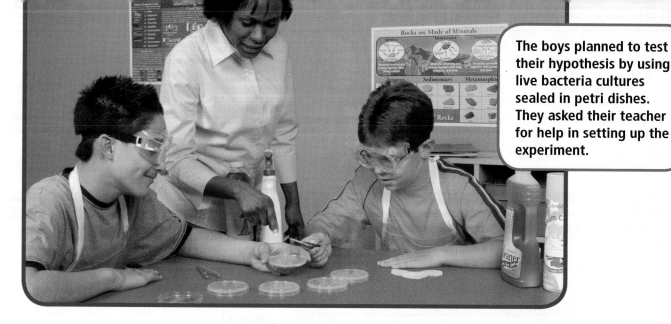

The boys planned to test their hypothesis by using live bacteria cultures sealed in petri dishes. They asked their teacher for help in setting up the experiment.

on three paper disks that would go into the different dishes. No cleaner would be on the disk for the control dish A. The teacher smeared bacteria on the agars in four dishes and sealed them with the paper disks inside.

The boys gathered and recorded data. When a disinfectant on a disk kills bacteria, a clear area appears around the disk. The boys measured such areas through the tops of the sealed dishes. They displayed the data in the table shown here. When there was no clear area around a disk, they recorded "No Change."

The next step was to interpret the data. They saw that Disinfectant B didn't kill bacteria as well as the others. Disinfectant D killed the most bacteria.

The scientific method includes not only interpreting the data but also drawing a conclusion based on the data. The boys concluded that their hypothesis was not supported. Different brands of disinfectant don't work equally well.

Believe it or not, this was a successful experiment. Sam and Noah learned something

they didn't know before. They now have evidence that some disinfectants work better than others.

Of course, the boys wondered why some work better than others. They thought the cleaners were just batches of different chemicals. Maybe the boys will set up an experiment to test the different chemicals. This is the final step of the scientific method—using results to plan more investigations.

The boys wrote a detailed report of their investigation so they could communicate their results. That way, other scientists can repeat the experiment. If others get the same results, the boys' findings are probably valid.

MAIN IDEA AND DETAILS What is the scientific method?

(Focus Skill)

Disinfectants	Day 1	Day 4	Day 8	Day 12	Day 16	Day 20
A	No Ch.	No Ch.	No Ch.	No Ch.	No Ch.	No Ch.
B	No Ch.	No Ch.	1 mm	2 mm	3 mm	5 mm
C	No Ch.	1 mm	3 mm	4 mm	5 mm	7 mm
D	1 mm	2 mm	2 mm	5 mm	7 mm	10 mm

Sam and Noah wrote their report on a computer and made the report available online. Now they can communicate with others interested in the same topic. The boys included the data they collected. ▶

Tina and Joe raised these tadpoles, or young frogs, from eggs. Now they're returning the animals to a natural habitat. Their teacher is with them to help with the release.

Experiments Versus Investigations

An experiment is a good way to test a hypothesis. You can control and manipulate variables, and you have control groups for making comparisons.

However, it's not always possible to manipulate variables. Sometimes you have to design an investigation to test a hypothesis without doing an experiment. Your investigation would involve making detailed observations and keeping careful notes. For example, if you wanted to test a hypothesis about an ecosystem, you might observe the ecosystem that's in a terrarium or aquarium.

There are also times when you can't observe something directly. It might be too big or too small. It might be hidden or very far away. It might just be too dangerous. For example, a hurricane is both too big and too dangerous for most people to observe directly.

In cases such as this, you can often construct a model. That's what the people who crash-test cars do. After all, they can't put a person in a car that's going to crash. So they put crash-test dummies in cars instead. A crash-test dummy is a model of a human being. Studying how well the dummy is protected in a crash provides

information about how well protected a person would be.

What about hurricanes? You can't make a model of a hurricane out of common materials! However, people can make models of hurricanes with computers. Weather centers have computer programs that build such models and produce data like the results of real hurricanes. Scientists use model hurricanes to help them predict the paths of real ones.

 MAIN IDEA AND DETAILS How can you test a hypothesis when you can't manipulate variables?

Construct a Model

To study classroom attendance, you could count the number of people in your classroom every day. But it would take a long time to collect enough data that way. Instead, ask your teacher for information on how many students were absent on each of the past 30 school days. Organize the data into a chart, table, or graph as a model for classroom attendance. What are your findings?

1. **MAIN IDEA AND DETAILS** Copy and complete the graphic organizer.

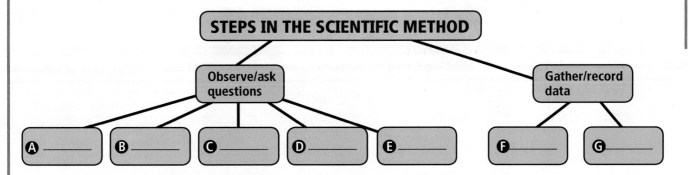

STEPS IN THE SCIENTIFIC METHOD

Observe/ask questions

Gather/record data

Ⓐ _____ Ⓑ _____ Ⓒ _____ Ⓓ _____ Ⓔ _____ Ⓕ _____ Ⓖ _____

2. **SUMMARIZE** Write three sentences that tell what this lesson is mainly about.

3. **DRAW CONCLUSIONS** If you formed a hypothesis about the formation of volcanoes, how could you test it?

4. **VOCABULARY** Use each vocabulary term in a sentence.

Test Prep

5. **Critical Thinking** According to legend, Galileo dropped two metal balls of different weights from a tower to find out whether heavier objects fall faster than lighter ones. But the two balls fell at the same speed. Was Galileo's experiment a failure? Explain.

6. Which is **NOT** a part of the scientific method?

A. interpret data   **C.** record data

B. observe   **D.** take a guess

Links

 Writing

Expository Writing

Write a careful **description** of what you did during the Investigate at the beginning of this lesson. Be sure to describe the place where you worked, the objects you used, and the procedure you followed.

 Math

Display Data

Part of making a graph is deciding which type of graph is best for displaying your data. Take your data from the Investigate at the beginning of this lesson, and display it in an appropriate graph.

 Social Studies

The Time Before Science

The scientific method has been around for only a couple of hundred years. Research the science of an earlier period, such as ancient Greece or the Renaissance. Write a report describing investigations of that period.

 For more links and activities, go to www.hspscience.com

What Are Science Inquiry Skills?

Fast Fact

Now You See Them, Now You Don't The tracks of light in this photo are the tracks of subatomic particles. They're constantly whizzing around and through us, but we can't observe them directly. In the following Investigate, you'll observe only some things directly and then will make inferences from your observations.

A Mixing of the Waters

Materials   • 2 beakers   • dropper   • stirring rod
                • water   • blue food coloring

Procedure

1. Put the same amount of water in each beaker. Put several drops of blue food coloring into one beaker and stir it.

2. Half-fill the dropper with the blue water. Carefully squeeze a single drop of blue water into the beaker of clear water.

3. Observe the beaker of clear water. Record your observations.

4. Repeat Step 3 every 5 minutes for a half hour.

Step 2

Draw Conclusions

1. What did you observe when the drop went into the clear water? What did you observe a half hour later?

2. Inquiry Skill What can you infer about the water in the beaker you observed?

Step 3

Investigate Further

Would drops tinted different colors behave differently? Plan and conduct a simple investigation to find out.

Reading in Science

VOCABULARY
independent variable p. 12
dependent variable p. 12

SCIENCE CONCEPTS
▶ what the inquiry skills are
▶ how to use inquiry skills

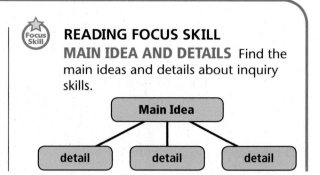

READING FOCUS SKILL
MAIN IDEA AND DETAILS Find the main ideas and details about inquiry skills.

Main Idea

detail   detail   detail

Inquiry Skills

Many things in science are really straightforward. For example, inquiry skills are skills that help you during an inquiry—they help you find things out. You use many of these skills in everyday life. You'll use them even more in science.

Observe When you observe, you use your senses to gather information about something. You usually look, but you might also use your senses of hearing, smell, and touch. (Using taste can be dangerous.) You might use these senses directly or through tools and instruments designed for gathering information.

▲ Tools can help you observe things by increasing or extending the power of your senses.

Classify/Order Objects or events can often be organized into categories based on one or another specific feature.

Infer Sometimes your observations tell you what you want to know. Other times, you have to infer. When you infer, you take the information you observed and use logical reasoning to come to a conclusion.

Compare When you compare, you find ways that two or more objects or events are the same. You also find ways they are different.

Predict Predicting is not guessing. When you predict, you use patterns you've observed and your own experience to say what you think will happen in the future.

▲ A meteorologist uses the data gathered from many sources to predict what the weather may be. This kind of map shows the data.

Use Numbers Whether you estimate or measure, your result is going to be a number. As a scientist, you'll record numbers, compare numbers, change them, and display them.

Use Time/Space Relationships Which flower blooms longer? Which molecules are farther apart? In what order should you perform the steps of a procedure? Time relationships and space relationships are a basic part of science.

10

Sometimes it's OK to estimate, but it's usually better to measure with a tool to be exact. Exact numbers can be used to make graphs.

Measure How tall is the doorway to your classroom? You can guess or estimate the answer. But when you measure, you get an exact, precise answer. Height, temperature, volume, brightness, saltiness—just about anything can be measured.

Interpret Data When you observe, measure, and estimate, all the information you gather is called data. You might use data as the basis for a prediction. You may be able to infer something from your data. Or you might decide you don't have enough data and need to collect more.

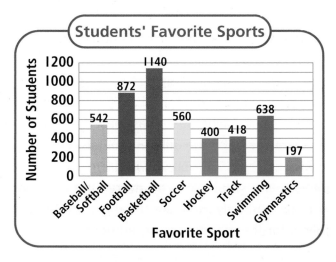

Students' Favorite Sports

Number of Students vs. Favorite Sport:
- Baseball/Softball: 542
- Football: 872
- Basketball: 1140
- Soccer: 560
- Hockey: 400
- Track: 418
- Swimming: 638
- Gymnastics: 197

Hypothesize To hypothesize is to make a hypothesis. In the previous lesson, you read that a hypothesis is simply a statement that you think is true and that can be tested. The last part is important: a hypothesis can be tested. To you, the statement "Cranberry juice is better than orange juice" may be true, but it can't be tested scientifically. "All disinfectants kill bacteria equally well" is a statement that can be tested. Once you have a hypothesis, you can perform an investigation to find out if the hypothesis is supported.

Plan and Conduct a Simple Investigation Here's where you put it all together. When you plan and conduct an investigation, you use all the inquiry skills you've just read about and more.

The previous lesson was about methods in planning and performing an investigation. Now you'll focus on inquiry skills in an investigation.

 MAIN IDEA AND DETAILS Name three inquiry skills.

▲ Iodine causes a change in color when it comes in contact with starch. What do you think the hypothesis behind this investigation might be?

Inquiry Skills in Action

Identify and Control Variables This is one of the most important parts of setting up an investigation. A specific example might make it easier to understand.

Imagine you are planning an investigation. You know that rubbing a steel paper clip in one direction along a magnet will magnetize the paper clip. You've read somewhere that temperature can affect magnetism. So you form this hypothesis: "Chilling a magnetized paper clip will demagnetize it." Now you want to test your hypothesis.

The first thing you do is to identify the variables. The **independent variable** is the factor you change in order to see its effect. In this case, you will change the temperature to compare a chilled paper clip with an unchilled

paper clip. The independent variable is temperature.

The **dependent variable** is the factor being measured. Because you want to find out if chilling affects the magnetism of a paper clip, the dependent variable is magnetism.

A simple experiment should test only one independent variable at a time. Everything else has to be kept exactly the same. You also need a control, which is a standard for comparison. For example, what would happen if you chilled a brass paper clip and compared it to an unchilled steel paper clip? If you found a difference, you wouldn't know whether it was caused by the temperature or by the different metals.

Experiment When you perform an experiment, you have to do everything carefully and methodically. Here are steps you might follow for the magnetism experiment.

1) Take two identical paper clips. Stroke each one in the same direction along a bar magnet 20 times.

2) Scatter some loose steel staples on a tabletop. Hold each paper clip about 1 cm above the staples. If any staples stick to one or the other of the paper clips, count them. Record your observations.

3) Leave one paper clip on the tabletop. This is the control. You won't do anything with it right now.

4) Place the other paper clip in a freezer. Wait half an hour, and then remove it.

5) Compare the chilled paper clip to the control paper clip by repeating Step 2.

If the chilled paper clip attracts fewer staples the second time, you might think that chilling

affected its magnetism. But if the control paper clip also attracts fewer staples the second time, you'd probably guess that magnetized paper clips simply lose some of their magnetism over time. Look at the data table. What can you conclude? It's a good idea to repeat your experiment several times to verify your data.

 MAIN IDEA AND DETAILS How many variables should you have in an investigation?

It's important to keep precise, detailed records of whatever you observe during an investigation. ▶

Number of Staples Attracted		
	Trial #1 before chilling	Trial #2 after chilling
control paper clip	25	22
chilled paper clip	23	24

It helps to communicate your findings to others.

More Inquiry Skills

Use Models As you read in the previous lesson, you might use a model to investigate something that is too big, too small, hidden, too far away, or too dangerous to be manipulated in an experiment. Sometimes you might use a model someone else has constructed, such as a computer simulation. Sometimes you might have to construct a model yourself.

Draw Conclusions This is the last step of an investigation. Once you have collected and interpreted all your data, you have to draw a conclusion. The conclusion should state whether or not your hypothesis was supported.

Communicate Once you have come to a conclusion, you communicate your findings to other scientists. If other people perform exactly the same procedure you did but get different results or come to a different conclusion, then you know you need to rethink your hypothesis or your experiment's design.

 MAIN IDEA AND DETAILS Why would you want to communicate the results of an investigation you did?

Communicate Your Observations

Observe someone doing a simple task (such as combing hair, folding a sweater, tying a shoe, or putting on a coat). On paper, record the steps that the person took in doing the task. Give the paper to a classmate, and ask him or her to follow the steps. Is your classmate able to do the task? Why is it important to record the steps of a procedure accurately?

1. **MAIN IDEA AND DETAILS** Copy and complete the graphic organizer. You can add and fill in several new boxes branching off the box in the center.

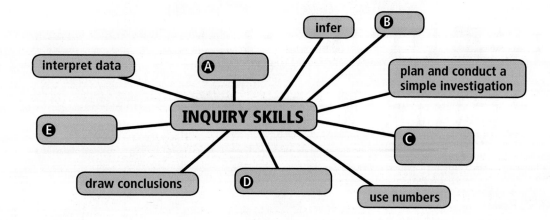

2. **SUMMARIZE** Write one sentence that tells what this lesson is mainly about.

3. **DRAW CONCLUSIONS** You've been testing a 30-cm (12-in.) model of a new car engine. What inquiry skill must you use to apply your results to the real engine?

4. **VOCABULARY** Use both vocabulary terms from Lesson 2 in a single sentence.

Test Prep

5. **Critical Thinking** You want to find out which brand of plastic wrap works best. What would be your independent variable? Your dependent variable?

6. What is the first inquiry skill you should use before planning an investigation?
   A. draw conclusions   **C.** identify variables
   B. hypothesize   **D.** measure

Links

Writing

Narrative Writing

A great scientific breakthrough can make a good story as well as contribute to science. Write a **story** about a scientist who uses inquiry skills to solve a problem.

Math

Compute a Percent

Look back at the table on page 13. Find the number of staples attracted by the control paper clip. By what percentage did the number decrease from Trial 1 to Trial 2?

Art

Arts and Sciences

A person's skills are often helpful in more than one area of life. Imagine you are a famous sculptor. Which of the inquiry skills you read about might you use when designing and executing a sculpture?

For more links and activities, go to www.hspscience.com

What Are the Tools of Science?

Fast Fact

Laser Lab What is a laser? The word stands for light amplification by stimulated emission of radiation. Lasers were first developed in the early 1960s. The scientists who worked on them didn't know they would come to be used in many industries such as communications and medicine. The scientist in this lab is continuing to research laser technology. In the Investigate, you will research the properties of drop prints.

Making Drop Prints

Materials
- water
- cup
- dropper
- red food coloring
- stirring rod
- white construction paper
- metric ruler

Procedure

1. Fill the cup about halfway with water. Add two drops of red food coloring, and stir to mix it. Rinse the dropper with clean water. Then fill it halfway with red water.

2. Place a sheet of white construction paper on a table. Hold the ruler vertically with the 0-cm end on the paper.

3. Place the tip of the dropper at the 3-cm mark. Carefully squeeze one drop out of the dropper, and let it fall on the paper.

4. Use a pencil to carefully draw around the print, or mark, made by the drop. Measure the width of the print on the paper. Record your observation.

5. Repeat Steps 2–4 four times, holding the tip of the dropper at 6 cm, 9 cm, 12 cm, and 15 cm.

Draw Conclusions

1. Did you notice a pattern in the widths of the drop prints? If so, what was it?

2. **Inquiry Skill** What conclusion can you draw about the relationship between height and print width?

Step 3

Step 4

Investigate Further

Do you think the material on which you dropped the water affected the print width? Test your hypothesis.

Reading in Science

VOCABULARY
pan balance p. 18
spring scale p. 20
microscope p. 21

SCIENCE CONCEPTS
▶ what some of the tools used in science labs are
▶ how to use science tools

READING FOCUS SKILL
MAIN IDEA AND DETAILS Look for the names of different kinds of tools.

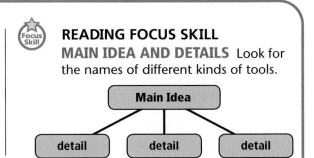

Tools of Science: Measuring Tools

A metric ruler is simply a ruler that's marked in centimeters. It's usually about 30 cm (12 in.) long.

A metric tape measure is useful for measuring large objects or distances. It's marked in centimeters and meters.

A **pan balance** is used to find the mass of an object. The metal objects at the right are gram masses. The smallest is 1 g, the mid-sized are 5 g, and the largest is 10 g. To use the balance, you place an object in the left pan and add masses to the right pan until the two pans balance. The mass of the object is equal to the sum of the masses in the right pan.

Tools for Measuring the Volume of a Liquid

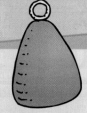

Volume: The Indirect Way

What is the volume of a gram mass? You could measure it, but its irregular shape makes that difficult. How could you find the volume of a gram mass by using a graduate and some water (and the gram mass itself, of course)?

A graduate is usually marked (or "graduated") in milliliters. Its shape makes it useful for finding the volume of small amounts of liquid. If you look closely at the top of the liquid in a graduate, you'll see that the liquid curves slightly upward at the edges. You take a reading by looking at the curve's lowest point.

A beaker is another device you can use to measure liquids. Be sure to choose the size that will meet your needs.

You can find the approximate volume of a liquid by pouring the liquid into a measuring cup. The measuring cup you use in cooking is probably marked in cups and ounces. The measuring cup you'd use in a science lab is marked in liters and milliliters.

500 mL

400 mL
±5%

300

200

No. 1060

Other Measuring Tools

You may already be familiar with using a thermometer to measure temperature. The thermometers used in a science lab are marked in degrees Celsius. Water freezes at 0°C (32°F) and boils at 100°C (212°F). Does that mean a Celsius degree is larger or smaller than a Fahrenheit degree? ▶

A **spring scale** is usually marked in units called newtons (N). You don't use a spring scale to measure mass. You use it to measure force. You attach something to one end of the scale and pull on the other end. The scale tells you how much force is being used.

Sometimes you have to examine something small or a small part of something. A hand lens makes small things look bigger.

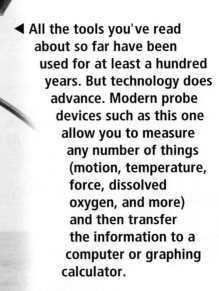

◀ All the tools you've read about so far have been used for at least a hundred years. But technology does advance. Modern probe devices such as this one allow you to measure any number of things (motion, temperature, force, dissolved oxygen, and more) and then transfer the information to a computer or graphing calculator.

◀ It's hard to look at a living thing by using a hand lens—the thing might just crawl away! A magnifying box keeps it in one place and makes it look larger, too.

A **microscope** makes very small things look larger. Some things are so small, you can't even see them without a microscope. Many microscopes have several lenses, so you can adjust how much they magnify something. ▶

Some of the things you use in a lab are too dangerous to touch. Others are too small to grasp without damaging them. In either case, a pair of forceps can help you grab what you want to grab. ▲

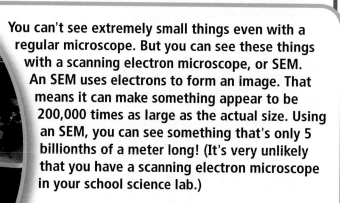

You can't see extremely small things even with a regular microscope. But you can see these things with a scanning electron microscope, or SEM. An SEM uses electrons to form an image. That means it can make something appear to be 200,000 times as large as the actual size. Using an SEM, you can see something that's only 5 billionths of a meter long! (It's very unlikely that you have a scanning electron microscope in your school science lab.)

 MAIN IDEA AND DETAILS What kinds of tools will you be using in your science lab?

Safety in Science

Investigations and experiments are a large part of the study of science. So it's very important to know and follow safety procedures in the science lab. Here are some tips about lab safety, as well as examples of safety symbols you might see.

Think It Through Before you do anything in an investigation, read all of the steps and picture yourself doing each one. If you have any questions, ask your teacher.

Spot It If there are safety symbols on the page, make sure you know what they mean.

Get It Out of the Way If you have long hair, tie it back. If you're wearing long sleeves, roll them up.

Keep It Clean Keep your work area neat and organized. You're less likely to make mistakes that way.

Watch It! Wear safety goggles whenever you're instructed to. If you get something in your eye, tell your teacher immediately.

Don't Eat It Never taste anything you're using in the lab.

Don't Short Circ-It Be especially careful if you're using an electric device. Keep the device away from water. Arrange the cord so that no one will trip over it. Never pull on the cord to remove the plug from an outlet; grab the plug itself. (These are good things to remember at home, too.)

Report It If you spill or break something or get cut or hurt, tell your teacher immediately.

Leave It the Way You Found It When you're done investigating, clean everything up and put it away. Wipe up your work area, and then wash your hands with warm, soapy water.

 MAIN IDEA AND DETAILS What is the first thing you should do when you are performing an investigation?

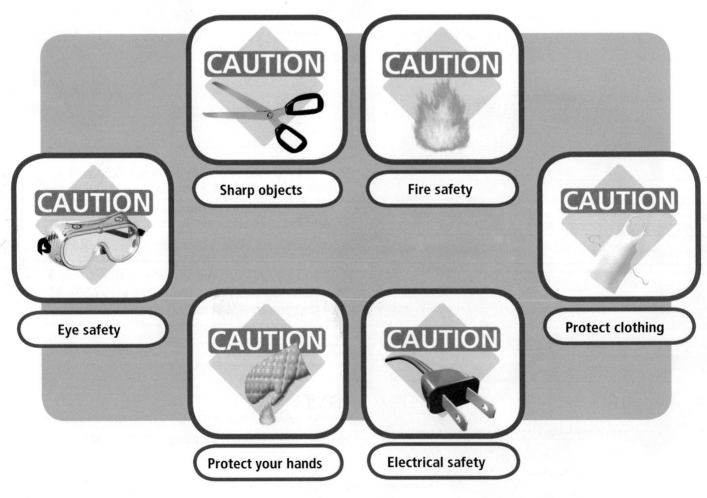

Sharp objects

Fire safety

Eye safety

Protect clothing

Protect your hands

Electrical safety

Focus Skill

1. MAIN IDEA AND DETAILS Copy and complete the graphic organizer.

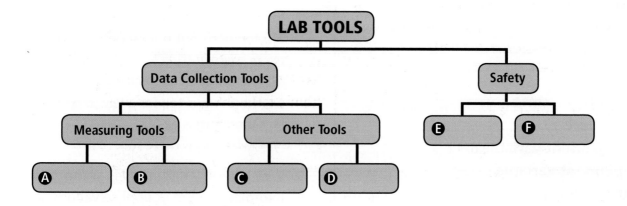

LAB TOOLS

Data Collection Tools — **Safety**

Measuring Tools — **Other Tools**

Ⓐ Ⓑ Ⓒ Ⓓ Ⓔ Ⓕ

2. SUMMARIZE Write one sentence for each main section in this lesson to tell what the section is about. (The main sections begin on pages 18 and 22.)

3. DRAW CONCLUSIONS If you wanted to study a single grain of sand, what two tools could you use?

4. VOCABULARY Write a dictionary definition for each vocabulary term.

Test Prep

5. Critical Thinking If something is too small to be seen with a hand lens or with an ordinary microscope, can it be seen with a scanning electron microscope? Explain.

6. Which of the following is **NOT** a data collection tool?

A. hand lens   **C.** knife

B. graduate   **D.** thermometer

Links

Writing

Expository Writing

Do you know how to use a hand lens? Find and read a set of instructions. Then use the information to write a **how-to paragraph** in your own words.

Math

Angles

What kind of angle is formed by the legs of a pair of forceps?

Language Arts

Word Origins

The word *microscope* comes from two Greek words. Find out what they are. Then write three other English words that come from each of the Greek words.

 For more links and activities, go to www.hspscience.com

Review and Test Preparation

Vocabulary Review

Use the terms below to complete the sentences. The page numbers tell you where to look in the chapter if you need help.

scientific method p. 4
hypothesis p. 4
independent variable p. 12
dependent variable p. 12
pan balance p. 18
spring scale p. 20

1. You might use a _____ if you want to measure the mass of an object.

2. The most important thing about a _____ is that you must be able to test it.

3. You change the _____ to see what effect, if any, it has on other factors.

4. The _____ is an accepted, organized way to find an answer to a problem.

5. You might use a _____ if you want to measure the amount of force you are exerting.

6. The _____ may or may not change when the other variable changes.

Check Understanding

7. Which of the following tools might you use to examine a tiny flower?
   A. a hand lens
   B. a graduate
   C. a meterstick
   D. a scanning electron microscope

8. **MAIN IDEA AND DETAILS** Why might you investigate something by making careful observations but not by performing an experiment?
   F. The thing is too small to handle easily.
   G. The thing is too far away to work with.
   H. Observing is easier.
   J. Observing is more fun.

9. Which inquiry skill involves taking information from your observations and using logical reasoning to come to a conclusion?
   A. classify/order
   B. infer
   C. hypothesize
   D. predict

10. **MAIN IDEA AND DETAILS** Which inquiry skill involves stating what you think will happen, based on patterns you've observed and your own experience?
    F. infer
    G. draw conclusions
    H. identify variables
    J. predict

11. What scientific lab tool is this?
    A. a beaker
    B. a graduate
    C. a measuring cup
    D. a pan balance

12. Which of the following enables you to see the smallest details?
    F. a hand lens
    G. a magnifying box
    H. a regular microscope
    J. a scanning electron microscope

13. Which method would you use to investigate this lizard?
    A. construct a model
    B. make detailed observations and keep careful notes
    C. perform an experiment
    D. use a model that someone else constructed

14. What must you always do before you start an experiment?
    F. make notes
    G. get some scientific tools
    H. tie back your hair and roll up your sleeves
    J. wash off the desktop

15. What is the first step of the scientific method?
    A. test your hypothesis
    B. observe and ask questions
    C. experiment
    D. draw conclusions

16. What must you always do before you carry out an investigation described in this book?
    F. assign variables
    G. hypothesize
    H. read all of the steps in the investigation and picture yourself doing each one
    J. clean everything up, put everything away, wipe down your work area, and wash your hands

Inquiry Skills

17. You want to find out how temperature affects the electric output of batteries. You're going to chill some batteries, freeze some others, heat some, and leave one as a control. Identify the **independent** and **dependent variables** in your experiment.

18. Predict what would happen if you had more than two **independent variables** in an experiment.

Critical Thinking

19. How is keeping your lab area neat and organized a safety issue?

20. Suppose you observe something strange and have some questions about it. You form a hypothesis and plan and conduct a simple investigation.

    Part A If your investigation does not support your hypothesis, was the investigation a failure? Explain.

    Part B If your investigation does not support your hypothesis, what would you do next?

Understanding Living Things

LIFE SCIENCE

⊙⊙⊙ Lied Jungle at the Henry Doorly Zoo

TO: cameron@hspscience.com

FROM: mario@hspscience.com

RE: Omaha, Nebraska

Dear Cameron,
What is one of the most wondrous places to explore a multitude of living things? The rain forest, of course! We usually don't have the chance to see a rain forest in Nebraska. But, thanks to the Lied Jungle, we can experience the sights, sounds, plants, and animals that inhabit three of the world's most diverse rain forests. This part of the zoo exists not only to fascinate visitors. It was also made to call attention to the fact that rain forests are disappearing from the Earth at an alarming rate. Maybe we can make a difference.
Your pal,
Mario

Yellowstone National Park

TO:	mel@hspscience.com
FROM:	alec@hspscience.com
RE:	Wyoming, Montana, Idaho

Dear Mel,

We visited Yellowstone Park, and were surprised to see a beautiful, green forest. In 1988, a wildfire burned 793,000 acres of the park. But, as days passed, after an autumn rain put out the fire, a rebirth of the forest began. The fires proved helpful to both plants and animals. Before the fire, the seeds of lodgepole pines were sealed inside the cones by resin. The heat from the fires released them. A beautiful rebirth of the lodgepole forest is now underway. Wildlife has feasted on insects housed in fallen trees. Some species once unknown to the area are now living at Yellowstone. The great fire helped to prove that forests sometimes need fire to be restored.

Write back.

Alec

Experiment!

Cell Responses All living things are made of cells that respond to changes in the environment. How do cells respond when they come in contact with different chemicals? Plan and conduct an experiment to find out.

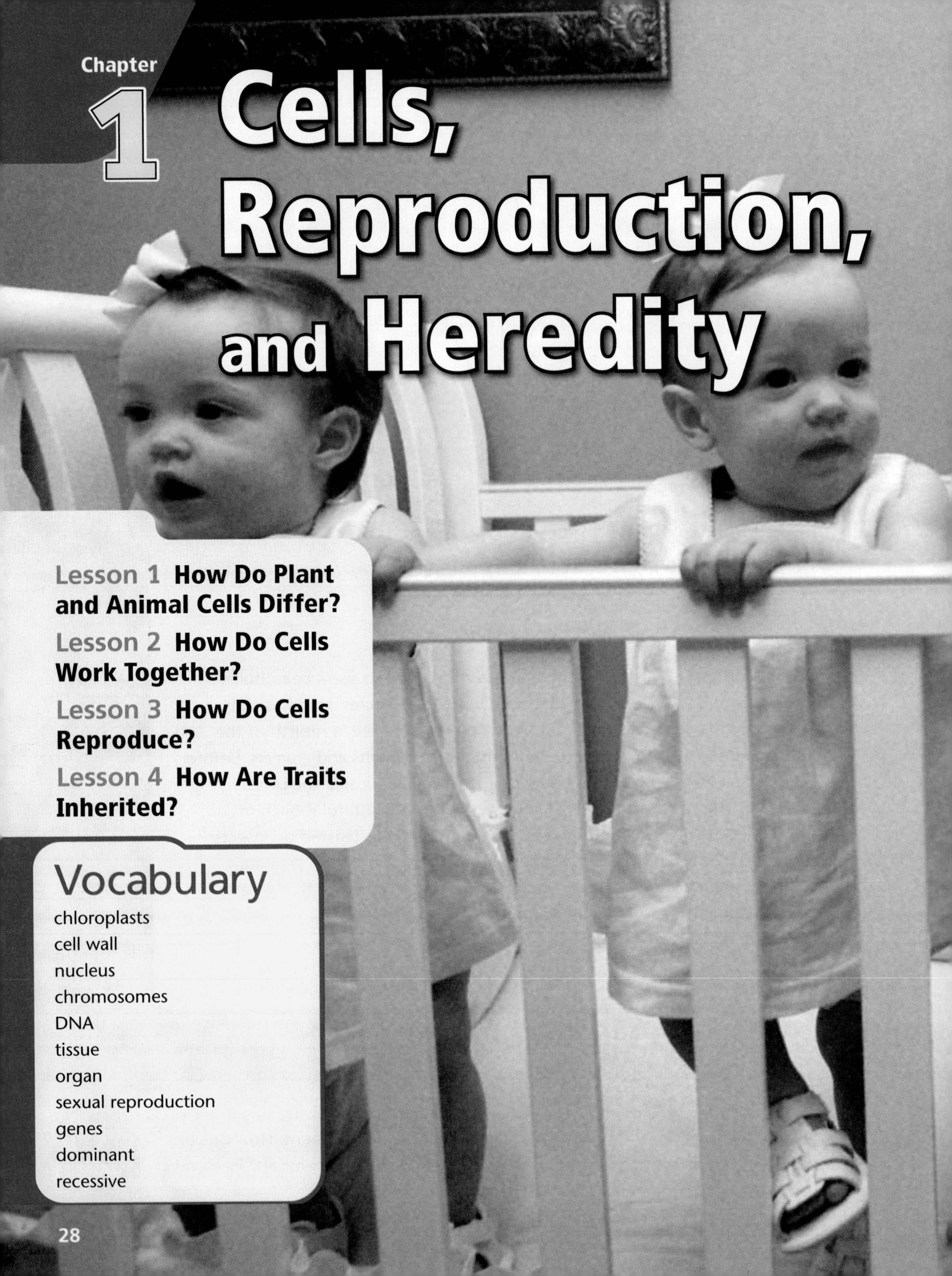

Cells, Reproduction, and Heredity

Vocabulary

chloroplasts

cell wall

nucleus

chromosomes

DNA

tissue

organ

sexual reproduction

genes

dominant

recessive

What do YOU wonder?

Quintuplets in humans are very rare. They occur only once in every 47 million births! Quintuplets are usually not identical. What similar and different traits do you observe among these quintuplets? What do you think causes them?

How Do Plant and Animal Cells Differ?

Fast Fact

Life's Blood Blood cells travel through your body all the time. Red blood cells have hemoglobin that enables them to carry oxygen to the body and return carbon dioxide to the lungs. Blood cells are produced in bone marrow. In the Investigate, you will learn more about cells.

Plant and Animal Cells

Materials
- plastic mixing spoon
- lemon gelatin powder
- boiling water
- mixing bowl
- 2 small plastic bags
- plastic sandwich box
- 2 plums
- ice cubes
- orange sections
- grapes
- 2 twist ties

Procedure

1. Make models to observe the differences between plant cells and animal cells. Use the spoon to mix the gelatin powder with boiling water and several ice cubes in a mixing bowl. Allow the liquid to cool. **CAUTION: Boiling water can burn you! Use care when near it!**

2. Place a plastic bag in the sandwich box. Pour in half of the cooled liquid. Add one plum, several orange sections, and several grapes. Tie the bag shut, and allow the mixture to set.

3. Fill the other plastic bag with the other half of the cooled liquid. Add orange sections and one plum. Tie the bag shut. Allow the mixture to set.

4. When both mixtures have set, remove them from the plastic bags.

5. Compare your model cells. Then compare them to the plant and animal cells shown here. Which of your cells is more like the unknown cell? What do you think it is?

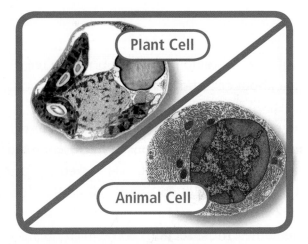

Plant Cell

Animal Cell

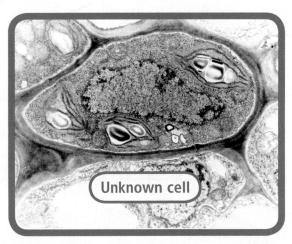

Unknown cell

Draw Conclusions

1. What similarities and differences did you observe between your two models? Which looks like the plant cell photo and which like the animal cell?

2. **Inquiry Skill** One model cell has a kind of part that the other does not have. Based on what you know about plants and animals, infer what function that part might have.

Investigate Further

With classmates, try to fit several "cells" of each type together. What differences do you observe about how the cells of each type fit together? What can you infer about how each cell is protected?

Reading in Science

VOCABULARY

chloroplasts p. 34
cell wall p. 34
nucleus p. 35
chromosomes p. 35
DNA p. 36

SCIENCE CONCEPTS

▶ what the cell theory is
▶ how the parts of the cell function

READING FOCUS SKILL

MAIN IDEA AND DETAILS Look for details about animal and plant cells.

```
              Main Idea
        /        |        \
   detail     detail     detail
```

The Cell Theory

If there were no pictures or books to tell you about cells, how would you know they existed? Before the microscope was invented, no one had any idea about such things as cells. In 1665, Robert Hooke built a microscope that magnified things 30 times. He looked through it at a thin piece of cork and realized that the cork was made up of very tiny boxlike sections. He named these sections *cells*, which means "small compartments" in Latin. The photo below shows what Hooke saw in the cork.

Ten years later, Anton van Leeuwenhoek (LAY•vuhn•hook) built a microscope that magnified objects 300 times (300X). With this new, more powerful microscope, Leeuwenhoek discovered a world of one-celled organisms in pond water.

Almost 200 years went by after Hooke's discovery and Leeuwenhoek's studies of microscopic organisms before scientists began studying cells in detail. At first, they thought that only plants had cells. As better microscopes were developed, they noticed

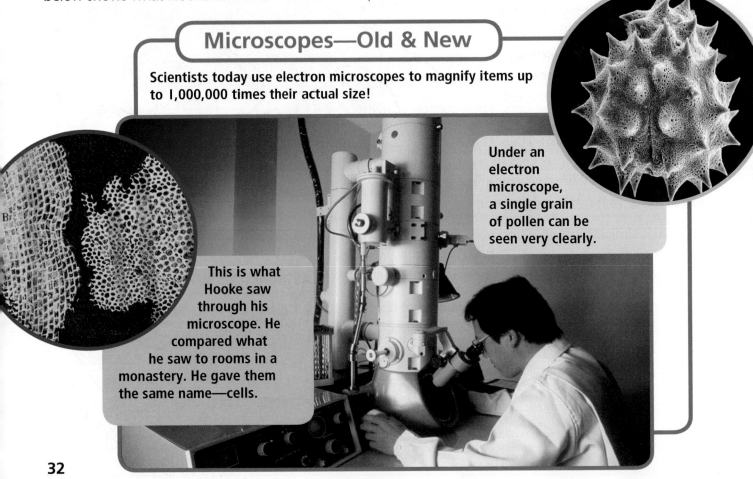

Microscopes—Old & New

Scientists today use electron microscopes to magnify items up to 1,000,000 times their actual size!

This is what Hooke saw through his microscope. He compared what he saw to rooms in a monastery. He gave them the same name—cells.

Under an electron microscope, a single grain of pollen can be seen very clearly.

that every living organism they studied had cells. By the late 1800s, scientists had developed a three-part theory about cells.

The first part states that *cells are the building blocks of all living things.* In other words, all living things are made up of cells. Some organisms have only one cell, while others have many. In addition, the parts of a living organism, such as its hair, skin, or leaves, are made of different kinds of cells with different functions. A human has hundreds of kinds of cells. The photographs on this page show some of the kinds of cells in plants and animals.

The second part of the theory states that *all life processes take place in cells.* The energy in food is released in cells. Growth and reproduction take place in cells.

The third part of the theory states that *new cells are produced from existing cells.* Living things begin life as a single cell. This single cell divides into two cells. Each new cell also divides into two cells. After a certain point, the cells begin to specialize and take on different functions. Cell division is what causes you or any other organism to grow. Your body constantly produces new cells to replace cells that die. Your skin, for example, produces new skin cells as the old cells die and fall away.

⭐ **MAIN IDEA AND DETAILS** What are the three parts of the cell theory?

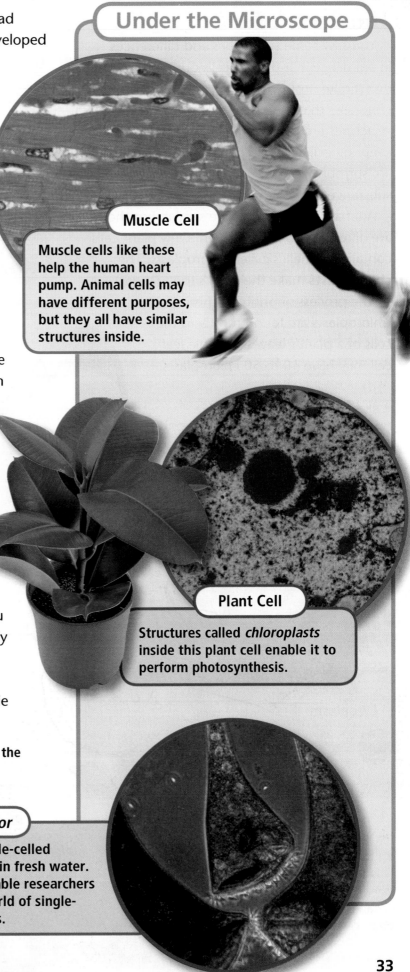

Under the Microscope

Muscle Cell

Muscle cells like these help the human heart pump. Animal cells may have different purposes, but they all have similar structures inside.

Plant Cell

Structures called *chloroplasts* inside this plant cell enable it to perform photosynthesis.

Stentor

Stentor is a single-celled organism found in fresh water. Microscopes enable researchers to observe a world of single-celled organisms.

The Parts of a Cell

You saw some similarities and differences in animal cells and plant cells during the Investigate. Inside both types of cells are structures that perform specific functions. These structures are called *organelles*. Organelles help keep the cell alive and healthy. The organelles are surrounded by *cytoplasm*, a clear, jellylike substance that holds them in place.

Animal and plant cells are similar, but there are differences between them. Only plant cells contain organelles called chloroplasts. The **chloroplasts** make the plant's food (sugar) by the process of photosynthesis. Chloroplasts are found mostly in the cells of a plant's leaves. A single leaf cell may have 40 to 50 chloroplasts.

A plant cell also has a **cell wall**, a stiff outer layer that surrounds and protects the cell and gives it shape. Animal cells don't have cell walls, but both plant and animal cells have a cell membrane that holds the cell material inside. This membrane also controls what substances enter and leave the cell. Both plant and animal cells have organelles called *vacuoles,* which store nutrients and wastes. In animal cells, vacuoles are very small. In plants, one large vacuole takes up most of the cell. Vacuoles are much bigger in

▼ Inside the leaves of this plant are many cells that contain chloroplasts.

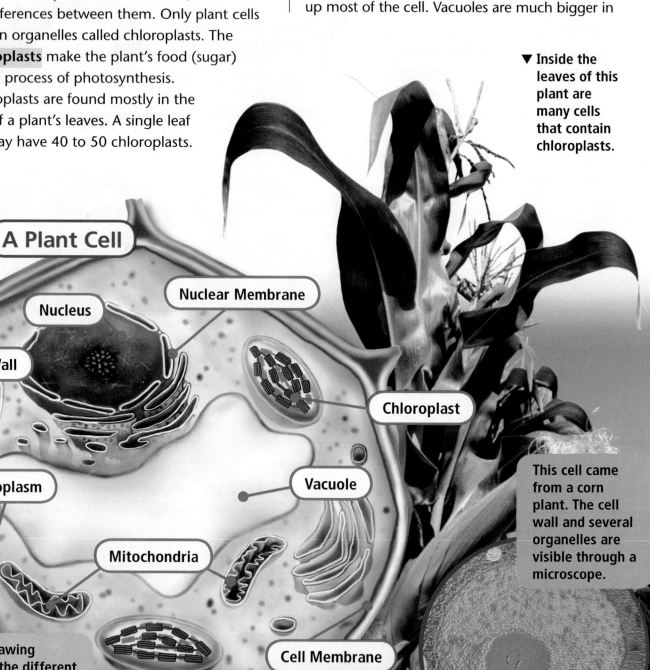

A Plant Cell

Nuclear Membrane

Nucleus

Cell Wall

Chloroplast

Cytoplasm

Vacuole

Mitochondria

Cell Membrane

This cell came from a corn plant. The cell wall and several organelles are visible through a microscope.

This drawing shows the different organelles found in plant cells.

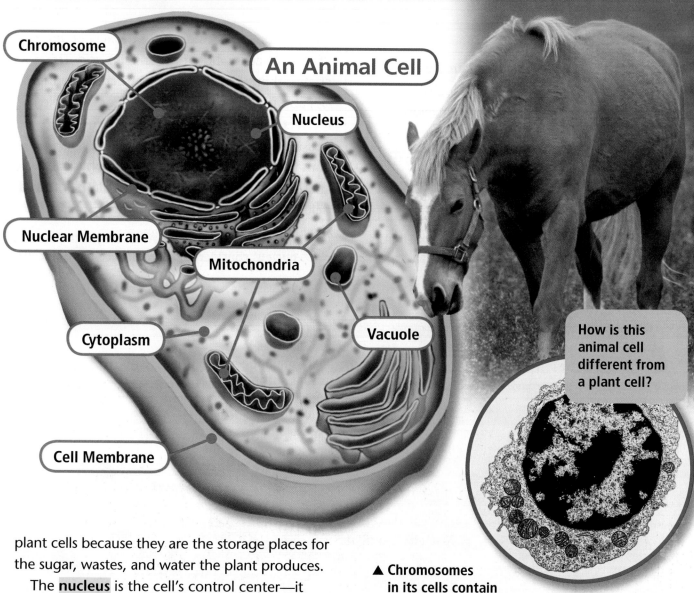

An Animal Cell

- Chromosome
- Nucleus
- Nuclear Membrane
- Mitochondria
- Cytoplasm
- Vacuole
- Cell Membrane

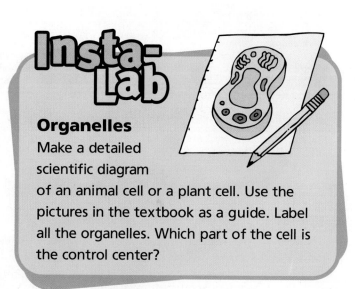

How is this animal cell different from a plant cell?

▲ Chromosomes in its cells contain the information that determines how the horse looks.

plant cells because they are the storage places for the sugar, wastes, and water the plant produces.

The **nucleus** is the cell's control center—it directs all of the activities that take place inside the cell. The nucleus contains **chromosomes**, the structures that carry an organism's genetic information. They also control activities within the cell. The nuclear membrane surrounds the nucleus and holds it together.

Cells also contain bean-shaped organelles called *mitochondria* (my•toh•KAHN•dree•uh). Food and oxygen combine in the mitochondria to release the food's energy, carbon dioxide (CO_2), and water (H_2O). This process is known as *respiration.* The energy released during respiration enables a plant or animal to complete all its cell activities.

 MAIN IDEA AND DETAILS What are the functions of different organelles in plant and animal cells?

Insta-Lab

Organelles
Make a detailed scientific diagram of an animal cell or a plant cell. Use the pictures in the textbook as a guide. Label all the organelles. Which part of the cell is the control center?

The Nucleus

The chromosomes in the nucleus contain instructions for all cell activities. It wasn't until the electron microscope was developed in the 1930s that scientists could study chromosomes in living cells and watch them divide. They found that before cells divide, the chromosomes are copied so that each new cell receives all the chromosomes it needs to function. Chromosomes are made up of DNA and proteins. **DNA** stands for *deoxyribonucleic* (dee•AHKS•ee•ry•boh•noo••KLAY•ik) *acid.* This chemical provides detailed instructions to the cell about every function of life. For example, it directs the cell to divide to make more cells and to perform various other activities. DNA contains the codes that determine physical characteristics such as flower color in plants and hair color in humans.

 MAIN IDEA AND DETAILS Why is the nucleus considered the control center of a cell?

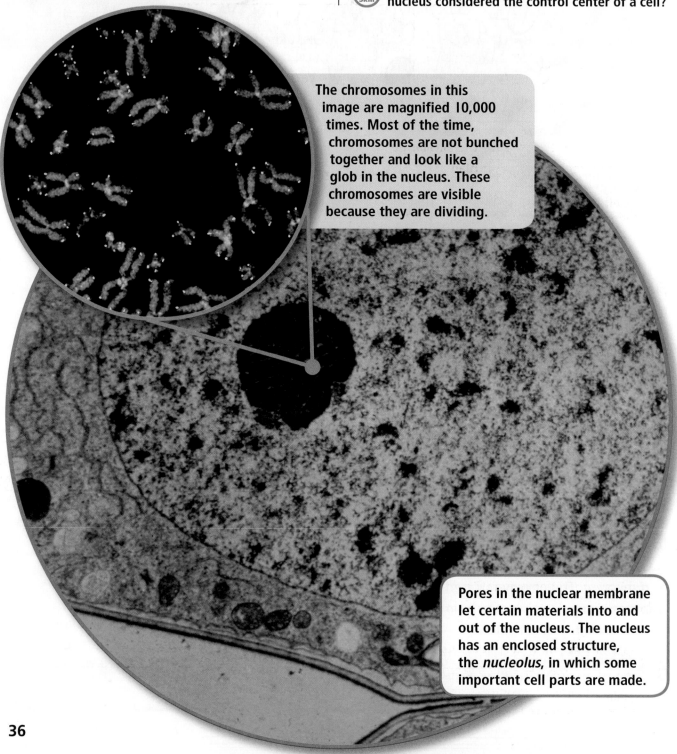

The chromosomes in this image are magnified 10,000 times. Most of the time, chromosomes are not bunched together and look like a glob in the nucleus. These chromosomes are visible because they are dividing.

Pores in the nuclear membrane let certain materials into and out of the nucleus. The nucleus has an enclosed structure, the *nucleolus*, in which some important cell parts are made.

1. MAIN IDEA AND DETAILS Draw and complete this graphic organizer.

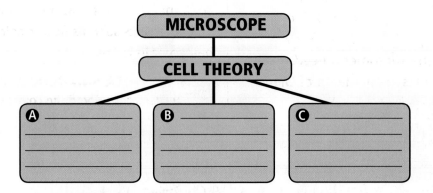

MICROSCOPE

CELL THEORY

Ⓐ _____

Ⓑ _____

Ⓒ _____

2. SUMMARIZE Summarize the similarities and differences between plant cells and animal cells.

3. DRAW CONCLUSIONS Compare what takes place in chloroplasts with what takes place in mitochondria.

4. VOCABULARY Use the words in the vocabulary list to order the parts of a plant cell from the inside out.

Test Prep

5. Critical Thinking Explain why a food that is claimed to make a person taller can't do this.

6. Which does the nucleus of a cell contain?
 A. chloroplasts
 B. chromosomes
 C. food
 D. oxygen

Links

Writing

Expository Writing

Write a **newsletter article** for third graders in which you describe the cell theory. Tell about the scientists who discovered cells and about the development of microscopes, beginning with Hooke's.

Math

Solve a Problem

A typical animal cell has a diameter of 0.001 mm. Find how many animal cells would fit across the diameter of a penny. A penny has a diameter of 2 cm.

Social Studies

Make a Time Line

Research the contributions of Schleiden and Schwann to the cell theory. Then make a time line showing the events that led to the development of the theory. Start the time line at 1665.

 For more links and activities, go to **www.hspscience.com**

How Do Cells Work Together?

Fast Fact

Get Your Nectar Here! Flowers have specialized cells to attract insects to pollinate them. Some cells form bright petals, and others produce chemical scents. Insects can't resist the combination! In the Investigate, you'll model another example of cells working together.

Modeling Lungs

Materials
- balloon
- 2-L plastic bottle with the bottom cut off
- 30-cm circle cut from plastic shopping bag
- masking tape
- rubber band

Procedure

1. Push the closed end of the balloon through the mouth of the bottle. Stretch the open end of the balloon over the top of the bottle.

2. Fold the 30-cm circle in half twice. Twist about 2.5 cm of the folded corner, and secure it with a short piece of masking tape to make a handle.

3. Cover the open bottom of the bottle with the plastic circle so the handle is on the outside of the bottle. Secure the plastic tightly to the bottle with the rubber band. There should be some slack in the plastic.

4. Gently push and pull on the handle to move the plastic in and out. Record what you observe.

5. Hold the bottle so its mouth is near your cheek, and move the surface of the plastic in and out. Record your observations.

6. Put your hands at the bottom of your ribs, and take a deep breath. Observe how your body moves.

Draw Conclusions

1. Compare your model with the second picture, and explain which parts of the model represent the lungs, chest cavity, and diaphragm (DY•uh•fram).

2. **Inquiry Skill** From your observations, what can you conclude about how your diaphragm moves in your body?

Step 1

Step 3

Investigate Further

Investigate how mucus in lungs affects breathing. Add a teaspoon of water to the balloon. Push and pull on the plastic. How do you think mucus affects the amount of air that can be inhaled?

Reading in Science

VOCABULARY
tissue p. 40
organ p. 42

SCIENCE CONCEPTS
▶ how cells are organized in multicellular organisms
▶ what functions organs and systems perform

READING FOCUS SKILL
SEQUENCE Look for ways in which organisms are organized.

Specialized Cells and Tissues

You have learned that all living organisms are made up of cells. A cell is the smallest unit of any organism. Single-celled organisms have only one cell. Multicellular (muhl•tee•SEL•yoo•ler) organisms are more complex. They are made up of many kinds of cells that have different functions. Plants and animals are multicellular. A leaf cell has many chloroplasts, so it can make food. A muscle cell has many mitochondria, so it can release a lot of energy. Muscle cells and leaf cells are specialized cells. They have specific functions. Look at the pictures of cells on this page. See how they are specialized to perform certain functions.

Specialized cells with similar structure and function form a **tissue**. Tissues are the next level of organization above cells in both plants and animals.

There are four

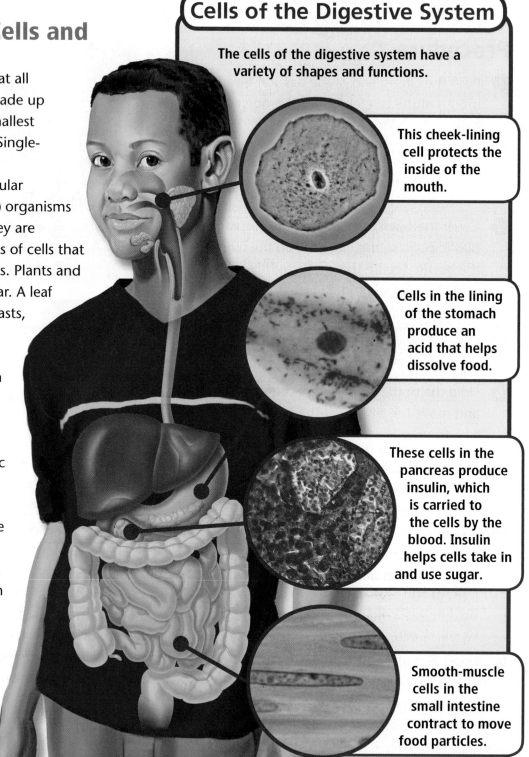

Cells of the Digestive System

The cells of the digestive system have a variety of shapes and functions.

This cheek-lining cell protects the inside of the mouth.

Cells in the lining of the stomach produce an acid that helps dissolve food.

These cells in the pancreas produce insulin, which is carried to the cells by the blood. Insulin helps cells take in and use sugar.

Smooth-muscle cells in the small intestine contract to move food particles.

40

A Closer Look at Digestion

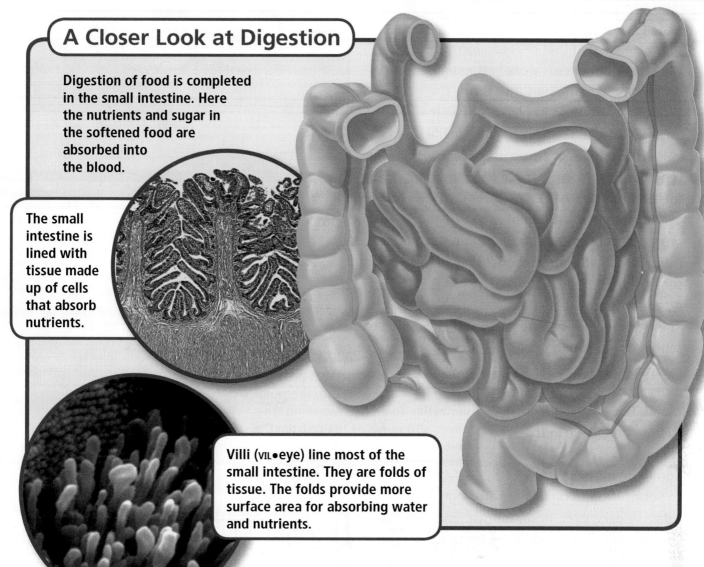

Digestion of food is completed in the small intestine. Here the nutrients and sugar in the softened food are absorbed into the blood.

The small intestine is lined with tissue made up of cells that absorb nutrients.

Villi (VIL•eye) line most of the small intestine. They are folds of tissue. The folds provide more surface area for absorbing water and nutrients.

tissue types in the human body: epithelial (ep•ih•THEE•lee•uhl) tissue, connective tissue, muscle tissue, and nerve tissue.

Epithelial tissue contains cells that are packed tightly together. Your outer layer of skin is epithelial tissue. The lining of your air passages is, too. Epithelial tissue lines your internal organs, helping them to carry out their functions while protecting the other tissues in the organ. Connective tissue adds support and structure to the body, fills spaces, and stores fat. Blood, bone, cartilage, and fat cells all form connective tissue. If you squeeze the top of your outer ear, you can feel the cartilage.

Muscle tissue is like elastic. Its job is to contract and relax. There are three types of muscle tissue. Skeletal muscle moves the bones of the skeleton when directed by the brain to do so. Smooth muscle does involuntary movements such as breathing. Cardiac muscle contracts to move blood around the body.

Nerve tissue is found in the brain, the spinal cord, nerves, and sensory receptors. Nerves send messages to and from the brain and the spinal cord. Some messages are controlled by the brain. But some messages that go through the spinal cord are reflexes. When you touch something hot, a message is sent to your spinal cord and it sends a signal back to muscles that move your hand. This happens before the message goes to your brain that there is pain.

 SEQUENCE List the steps of how tissues help your hand move when you touch a hot stove.

Organs

You've learned that cells can form tissues. You've seen how cells work in the digestive system and what tissues they form. The next level of organization in plants and animals is an organ. An **organ** is a structure made up of at least two types of tissues that work together to perform a specific job in the body.

There are many different organs in your body. You probably already know about some of them. The brain is often compared to a computer. The heart works like a pump to send blood through your body. Blood vessels are like pipelines that transport blood. Lungs enable you to breathe to take in the oxygen your cells need. Some organs help you react to your surroundings. These are your sense organs—ears, eyes, nose, tongue, and skin. All the organs in your body work together to keep you healthy.

The digestive system includes several organs. Each organ has its own job. The job of the stomach, for example, is to break down food into smaller units that cells can take up. The main job of the small intestine is to absorb nutrients from the food.

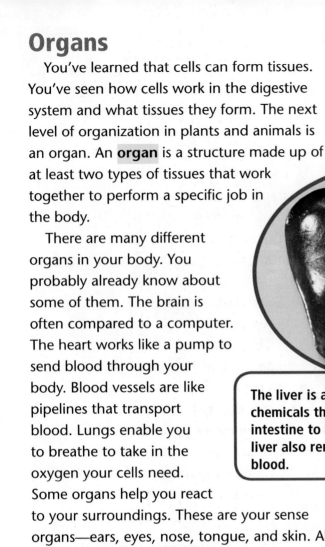

Organs of the Body

The liver is an organ that produces chemicals that flow into the small intestine to help in digestion. The liver also removes toxins from the blood.

The pancreas is an organ covered with connective tissue. Inside the pancreas are tissues that produce enzymes that aid digestion.

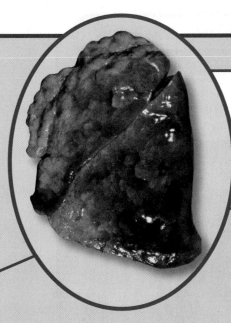

Lungs are organs that supply oxygen to and remove carbon dioxide from the blood. Lungs are made up mainly of epithelial tissue and connective tissue.

The heart is an organ that is mostly made up of muscle tissue. The heart is surrounded by connective tissue, contains nerve cells, and is covered with epithelial tissue. All the tissues in the heart work together so the heart can pump blood through the body.

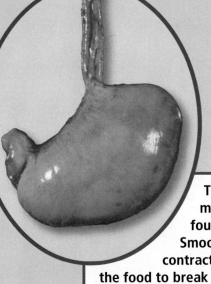

The stomach is made up of all four kinds of tissue. Smooth-muscle tissue contracts, squeezing the food to break it into smaller pieces. Epithelial tissue covers the inner and outer surfaces of the stomach.

This diagram shows many of the major organs in the body. All of them are made of tissues. Many organs are made of all four of the main types of tissues. Most organs are protected and supported by connective tissue. Organs also get messages from the brain by nerve tissue, and they move through the action of muscle tissue. For instance, muscle tissue in the heart makes it beat, and nerve tissue signals the heart to pump faster when more oxygen is needed. Your eyes are protected by epithelial tissue. They have connective tissue for support and structure, nerve tissue to deliver their messages, and muscles to move them. All these tissues work together so that the eyes can see and send messages to the brain. Organs that help with digestion, such as the liver and pancreas, also receive signals from the brain.

 SEQUENCE Describe the levels of organization from cells to organs.

What's Working?
Jump rope for 1 minute. When you stop, notice how your body feels. Make a list of organs you can feel working. Compare your list to your classmates' lists. What organs do you think are working when you exercise?

Organ Systems

You've been studying examples of how organs work together to perform a particular function. Plants and animals are very complex. Their needs are met by organs working together in systems. An organ system is a group of organs that work together to perform a specific function.

For example, the digestive system processes everything you eat. You take a bite of food, and your teeth, tongue, and salivary glands begin to break it down. Enzymes in saliva start digestion of some foods. Muscles pass the food down the esophagus to the stomach. The stomach squeezes the food, breaking it into smaller pieces. Stomach acid and enzymes turn the food into a creamy liquid that can be moved into the small intestine. Chemicals from the liver and pancreas flow into the small intestine. The food is further digested, and its nutrients are absorbed, along with water, through the wall of the small intestine into the blood. The waste, or food parts that the body can't use, is sent into the large intestine, where more of the water as well as vitamins and minerals are absorbed. The waste is then eliminated, or passed from the body.

Another organ system in humans is the respiratory system. When your diaphragm contracts you inhale, and air is pulled in through your nose. The air passes down the trachea and into your lungs. When your diaphragm relaxes you exhale, and the air moves up the trachea and out through your nose. In the lungs, oxygen from the air moves into the blood. Carbon dioxide from the blood moves into the air and is exhaled.

Each cell in your body needs oxygen. The circulatory system transports oxygen-rich blood cells throughout your body. Blood also carries the nutrients and other substances your body needs.

The skeletal and muscular systems work together to provide support and movement for the body. The integumentary (in•teg•yoo•MEN•ter•ee) system includes the skin, hair, and nails, which cover and protect

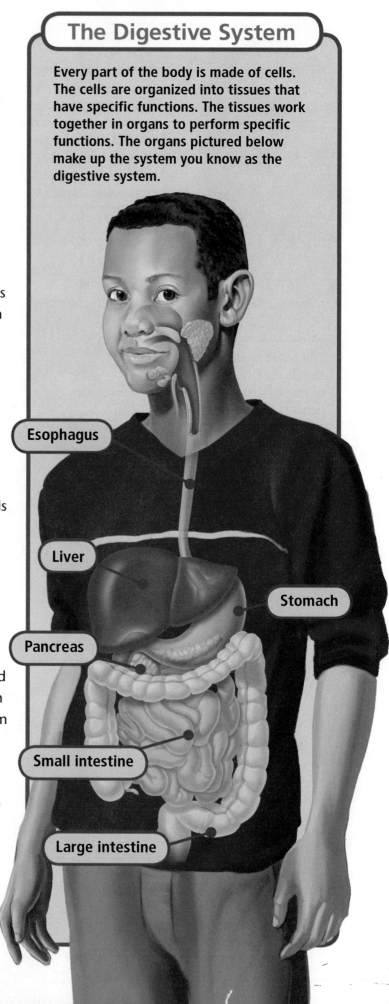

The Digestive System

Every part of the body is made of cells. The cells are organized into tissues that have specific functions. The tissues work together in organs to perform specific functions. The organs pictured below make up the system you know as the digestive system.

Esophagus

Liver

Stomach

Pancreas

Small intestine

Large intestine

44

the body. The excretory system removes wastes from the blood. The reproductive system produces a new generation of individuals. The endocrine system makes and sends chemicals called *hormones* to help control body activities.

You may not have thought about it before, but plants have organs and organ systems, too. Roots, stems, and leaves are some of a plant's organs. Like animal organs, they are made of specialized tissues, which are made of cells. For example, inside the stem of many plants are tissues called *xylem* (ZY•luhm) and *phloem* (FLOH•uhm), which transport water and nutrients. They are covered with epithelial tissue. The stem is the whole organ.

Plants have a root system and a shoot system. The root system anchors the plant in the ground. It absorbs nutrients and water and moves them throughout the plant. If necessary, the root system can store food. Stems and leaves are the two organs that make up the shoot system. Stems support the plant and have tubes that conduct water, minerals, and nutrients to all parts of the plant. Branches, leaves, and flowers grow from the stems. Leaves make food. Veins in the leaves connect with conducting tubes throughout the plant.

 SEQUENCE Describe the path of a blood cell as it leaves the heart until it returns to the heart.

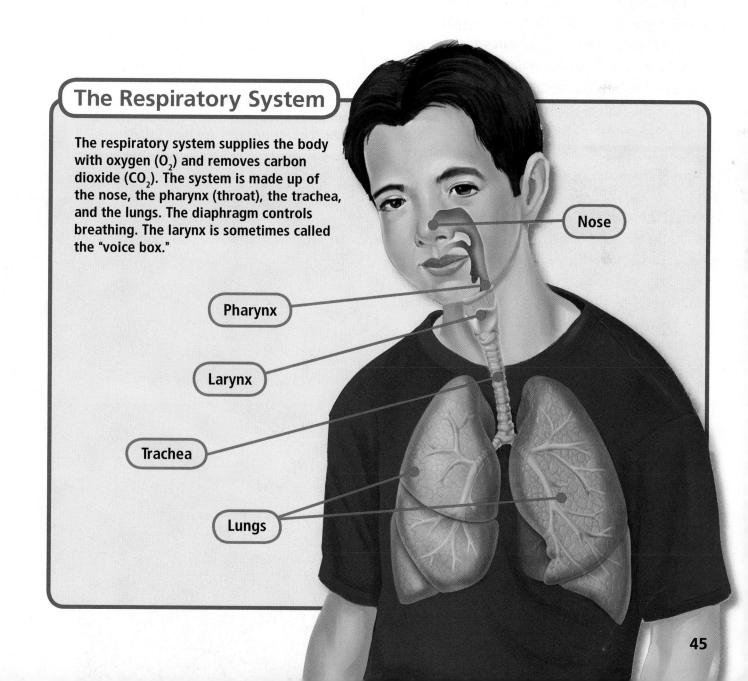

The Respiratory System

The respiratory system supplies the body with oxygen (O_2) and removes carbon dioxide (CO_2). The system is made up of the nose, the pharynx (throat), the trachea, and the lungs. The diaphragm controls breathing. The larynx is sometimes called the "voice box."

Nose

Pharynx

Larynx

Trachea

Lungs

The Organism

You are an organism. So is your dog or cat. So are the trees that grow in your yard and the birds that fly over your house. What exactly is an organism? An organism is a complete living thing that relies on cells for life functions.

In any multicellular organism, groups of cells make tissues. Two or more tissues make an organ. All the organs in an organ system work together. All the organ systems in an organism also work together. They all make up the organism.

In the human body, every cell needs oxygen and nutrients. Every cell needs to get rid of carbon dioxide and other chemicals it can't use. The respiratory system delivers oxygen to red blood cells. These blood cells, which are part of the circulatory system, carry oxygen throughout the body. They also collect carbon dioxide to be given off when you exhale. The circulatory system also carries nutrients from food to each cell. First, though, the food needs to be broken down into a form the body can use. The digestive system takes care of that.

What helps the heart to pump blood, the stomach to break down food, and the skeletal muscles to move bones? All the systems help one another. No system or organ can work well alone. Each system needs the support of the other systems to work at its best.

Humans are very complex multicellular organisms. If one system fails to do its job, the entire organism will be affected.

 SEQUENCE List in order the levels of organization in the human body.

> Marathon runners use more than just their muscular and skeletal systems to run races. Their respiratory systems provide the large amounts of oxygen that the runners need. Which other systems are they using?

1. **SEQUENCE** Complete the graphic organizer to show how the human body is organized.

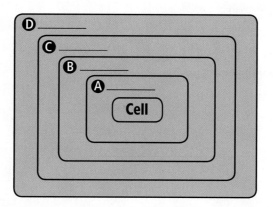

D _____
C _____
B _____
A _____
Cell

2. **SUMMARIZE** Use the graphic organizer to tell what this lesson is about.

3. **DRAW CONCLUSIONS** Which body system do you think is the most important? Explain your choice.

4. **VOCABULARY** Finish the following relationship by using vocabulary words: *Cell* is to _____ as _____ is to *system*. Then make up your own relationships.

Test Prep

5. **Critical Thinking** When you are busy and tired, why does it help to stop and take a deep breath?

6. Which type of body part is the stomach?
   A. cell
   B. organ
   C. system
   D. tissue

Links

Writing

Narrative Writing
Trace the path of a cracker as it travels through your digestive system. Write a **story** that tells what happens to the cracker along the way. Illustrate the story with a diagram and arrows showing the path.

Math

Display Data
Measure your heart rate by counting how many times your heart beats in 10 seconds. Multiply by 6 to figure beats per minute. Measure your heart rate while resting, while walking, and while running. Make a bar graph showing the different rates.

Health

Make a Menu
Use library and Internet resources to find the latest information about eating a healthful diet. Use what you learn to plan a healthful menu for a week of school lunches.

For more links and activities, go to www.hspscience.com

How Do Cells Reproduce?

Fast Fact

Let's Split This is a fluorescent micrograph of animal cells splitting during cell division. Growth happens in any organism because of cell division. In the Investigate, you'll see how new plant cells are produced as a plant grows.

How New Cells Are Made

Materials ● **MicroSlide-Viewer** ● **microslide of onion root tip**

Procedure

1 Place the slide of the onion root tip on the MicroSlide-Viewer. The slide shows cells in different stages of cell division.

2 Adjust the focus so that you can see the cells clearly.

3 Move the slide around so that you can observe different cells.

4 Observe and draw a cell that does not appear to be dividing. Label it *At Rest.*

5 Identify cells that are in different stages of division, and draw at least four different stages.

6 Order the stages of cell division by numbering your drawings 1 to 4.

Draw Conclusions

1. In the cells you observed, how could you tell which ones were dividing?

2. Which part of the cell seemed to get larger before the cell split?

3. Inquiry Skill How did you decide the order of the stages in cell division?

Step 4

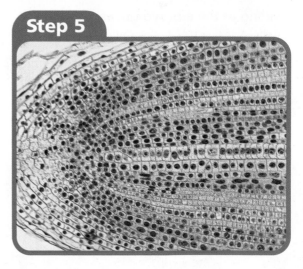

Step 5

Investigate Further

Use a MicroSlide-Viewer to observe single-celled organisms dividing, or look for pictures in reference books or on the Internet. How does cell division in a single-celled organism compare with division in the cells of the onion root tip?

Reading in Science

VOCABULARY
sexual reproduction p. 50
genes p. 51

SCIENCE CONCEPTS

▶ how DNA controls life activities

▶ how cells divide to make new cells and to make reproductive cells

 READING FOCUS SKILL
SEQUENCE Look for stages in mitosis and meiosis.

How Organisms Grow

A paramecium is a single-celled organism. It reproduces by making an exact copy of its genetic material and then dividing. The offspring gets all of its traits, or characteristics, from this one organism. This is called *asexual reproduction.*

Most animals reproduce sexually. In **sexual reproduction**, an egg cell and a sperm cell unite to form a single cell. This is called *fertilization.* That single cell divides until an embryo is formed. Cells continue dividing as the embryo grows.

When a fertilized egg cell begins to divide, it forms a ball of identical cells. After each of these cells divide many times, they become specialized and form tissues.

Cell Division

1 An organism starts life as one cell. The single cell has information that controls how the organism will develop.

2 Growth begins when the cell divides and becomes two cells.

3 In the next stage of growth, both cells divide. Now the developing organism has four cells.

4 Each of the four cells then divides. At the eight-cell stage, the organism looks like a ball. From here on, cells divide at different rates.

5 Most of an organism's cells continue to divide over its lifetime. However, the cells no longer divide at the same rate. Some cells don't divide at all.

Understanding a Growth Chart

Many Great Danes reach their full growth of about 100 lb (45 kg) at about 2 years. The graph shows one Great Dane's growth. Describe the growth. When did it level off?

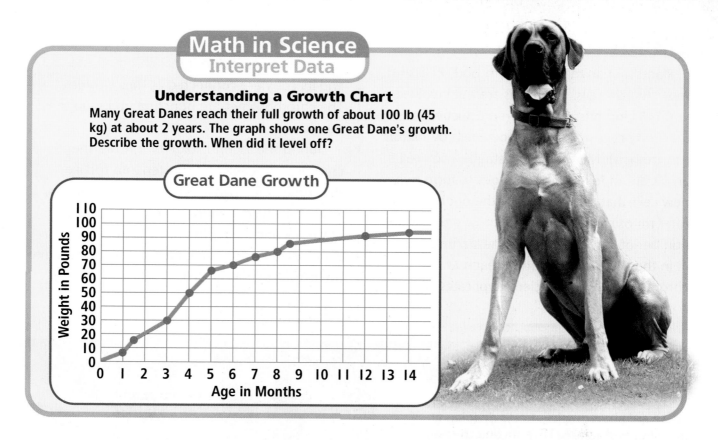

Great Dane Growth

As the embryo develops, tissues combine to form organs and organ systems.

Flowering plants reproduce in a similar way. They, too, have sperm cells and egg cells that combine to form embryos. An embryo develops inside a seed. It stays inactive until conditions are right for it to grow. At that time, the seed opens and cell division begins again in the embryo. It continues until a new plant develops.

DNA controls the way cells become specialized. Amazingly, every cell in your body has a copy of the DNA that was contained in your original cell. DNA is divided into many genes. **Genes** are pieces of DNA that carry all the information passed from parents to their offspring. Your genes control how you look, how you grow, and how your body functions.

SEQUENCE What happens within a fertilized egg, from the time it is a single cell to the time it forms tissues?

Chromosomes

Humans have 23 pairs of chromosomes, or 46 in all. Each parent contributes one chromosome to each pair. Children get half of their chromosomes from their mother and half from their father.

DNA looks like a long, twisted ladder. Scientists call its shape a double helix.

The nucleus contains chromosomes, threadlike packages of DNA and protein.

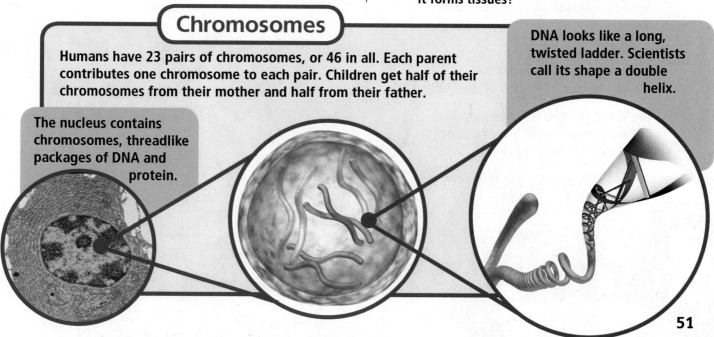

Mitosis

Plants and animals have both body cells and reproductive cells. Body cells are not involved in producing offspring, but reproductive cells are. Body cells make more body cells by *mitosis* (my•TOH•sis). Mitosis has six stages. Each cell in an organism follows these stages to form two new cells that are identical to the original cell. After mitosis, the two new cells have the same number of chromosomes as the starting cell.

In the first stage of mitosis, each chromosome in the nucleus duplicates itself. Now the cell has two of each of its chromosomes. Each original chromosome and its copy are connected at their centers. The chromosomes are bunched up inside the nucleus.

During the second stage of mitosis, the chromosomes coil and shorten into rodlike structures. Meanwhile, outside of the nucleus, long fibers have begun to form. At the end of the second stage, the nuclear membrane dissolves, allowing the paired chromosomes into the cytoplasm of the cell.

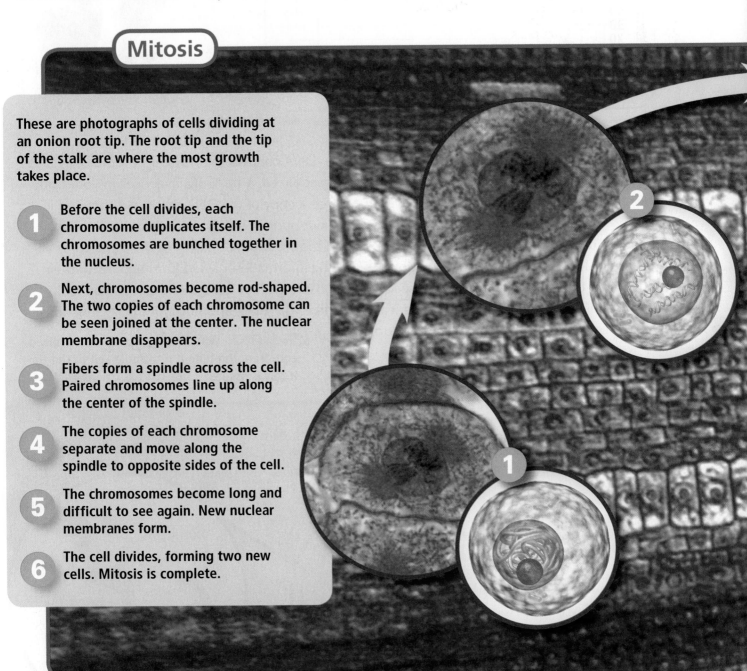

Mitosis

These are photographs of cells dividing at an onion root tip. The root tip and the tip of the stalk are where the most growth takes place.

1. Before the cell divides, each chromosome duplicates itself. The chromosomes are bunched together in the nucleus.

2. Next, chromosomes become rod-shaped. The two copies of each chromosome can be seen joined at the center. The nuclear membrane disappears.

3. Fibers form a spindle across the cell. Paired chromosomes line up along the center of the spindle.

4. The copies of each chromosome separate and move along the spindle to opposite sides of the cell.

5. The chromosomes become long and difficult to see again. New nuclear membranes form.

6. The cell divides, forming two new cells. Mitosis is complete.

The long fibers now form a network that reaches across the cell. A fiber attaches to each chromosome pair. During the third stage of mitosis, the fibers help to position the joined chromosomes in the center of the dividing cell.

During the fourth stage, the two copies of each chromosome separate. The attached fibers shorten as the members of the chromosome pairs move to opposite ends of the cell.

Now the dividing cell has two identical sets of chromosomes, one at either end of the cell. A number of things happen during the final stages of mitosis. The network of fibers breaks down. The chromosomes begin to uncoil, and a nuclear membrane forms around each set of chromosomes. In the center of the cell, the cell membrane starts to form. If the cell is a plant cell, a cell wall also begins to form. The membrane eventually reaches across the cell, dividing it in two.

Mitosis is now complete. Each new cell has exactly the same DNA. These cells can soon divide by mitosis themselves.

Focus Skill **SEQUENCE** **What has to happen before a cell can divide?**

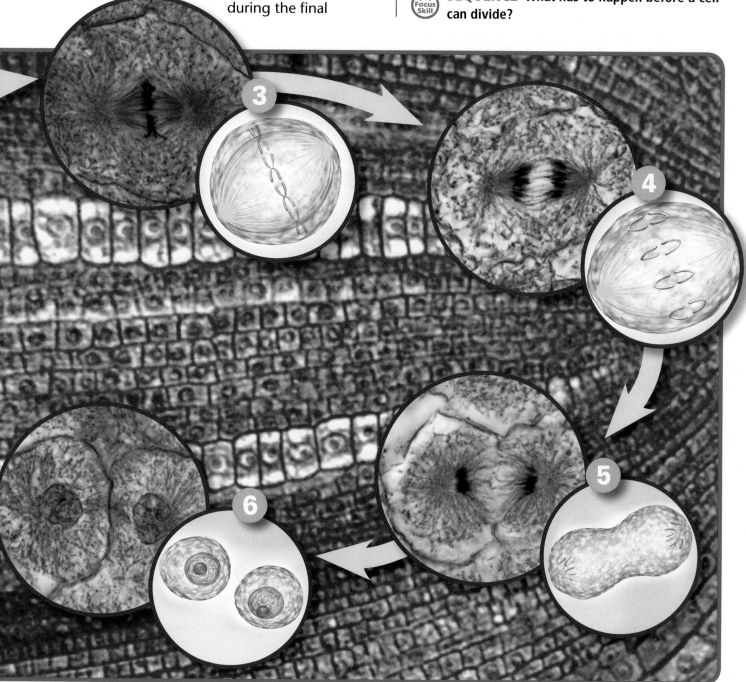

Meiosis

Reproductive cells are produced by *meiosis* (my•OH•sis). Reproductive cells are responsible for reproduction in many plants and animals. Human body cells have 46 chromosomes—23 pairs. Human reproductive cells—sperm in the male and eggs in the female—have only 23 chromosomes. When a sperm cell unites with an egg, the two join and form a cell with a complete set of 46 chromosomes. One chromosome of each pair comes from the male, and one comes from the female.

Meiosis includes two cell divisions. Before a cell divides, chromosomes are copied, resulting in two of each. The copies remain attached at their centers and the two chromosomes of each pair come together.

Each group of two chromosomes, each containing two copies, separates, and the two chromosomes of each pair move to opposite sides of the cell, and the cell divides. Each new cell has half the chromosomes of the original cell but two copies of each.

Each cell then divides again. In the second cell division, the two copies of each chromosome separate and move to opposite sides of the cell. Each of the four reproductive cells that are produced has half the original number of chromosomes and only one copy of each.

To better understand the stages of meiosis, study the diagrams on these pages.

 SEQUENCE How does meiosis make four cells with 23 chromosomes from one cell with 46 chromosomes?

Divisions in Meiosis

Meiosis occurs in more stages than mitosis. First, the chromosomes are duplicated. Then they are divided two times. In meiosis, one cell becomes four cells.

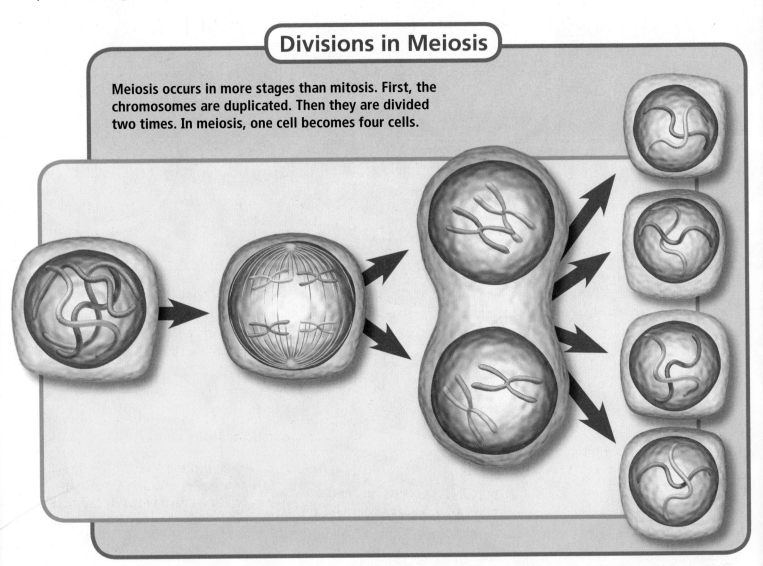

These photographs show a cell from the anther of a lily. The cell is dividing to become a male reproductive cell inside a pollen grain.

1 In the first stage of meiosis, each chromosome is copied, and the copies remain attached.

2 The joined chromosome strands come together with the other members of their pairs.

3 The paired chromosomes line up along the spindle.

4 The doubled chromosomes in each pair are drawn to opposite sides of the cell.

5 The cell divides. The two copies of each chromosome remain joined. The two new cells each have half the chromosomes of the original.

6 Another division begins in each of the new cells. The chromosomes do not duplicate themselves before this second division.

7 Spindle fibers cross each cell. The double-stranded chromosomes line up.

8 The two copies of each chromosome separate and move to opposite sides of the cells.

9 A new nuclear membrane forms around each group of chromosomes, and the cells divide. Now there are four cells, each with one-half the original number of chromosomes.

Genetic Variations in Organisms

Asexual reproduction occurs through mitosis. New cells produced by mitosis have genetic material that is identical to that of the original cell. This means that there is no genetic difference between a parent organism and its offspring.

But with sexual reproduction, there are genetic differences, or variations, between parents and offspring. Genetic variation is a result of meiosis. During meiosis, similar chromosomes from each parent may exchange DNA. These chromosomes are then randomly distributed among the reproductive cells. When a sperm and egg unite, they produce an organism with a unique genetic makeup. The new organism has only half its genes from each parent, so it is not identical to either parent. It is one of a kind.

Some traits, however, are more likely than others to show up in offspring. You'll learn about this in the next lesson.

 SEQUENCE Which part of meiosis makes it possible for offspring to vary?

Insta-Lab

Variations in Cats' Coloring

Observe the photograph of the cats. Look for similarities and differences in their coloring. How are the cats alike and different? How might genetic variations help explain these differences?

Cats are known for looking very different from their parents. These are calico kittens. They came from the same mother and father. ▼

1. SEQUENCE Draw and complete the graphic organizer.

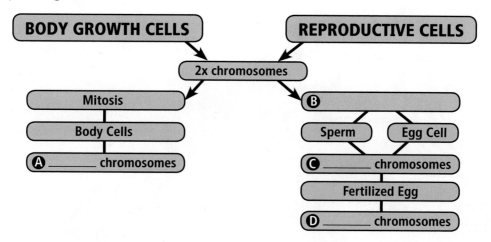

BODY GROWTH CELLS   **REPRODUCTIVE CELLS**

2x chromosomes

Mitosis

Body Cells

Ⓐ _____ chromosomes

Ⓑ

Sperm   Egg Cell

Ⓒ _____ chromosomes

Fertilized Egg

Ⓓ _____ chromosomes

2. SUMMARIZE Use the graphic organizer to describe the main differences between mitosis and meiosis.

3. DRAW CONCLUSIONS If reproductive cells were made by mitosis instead of meiosis, what would happen when a sperm cell and egg cell joined to make a new cell?

4. VOCABULARY Explain why genes are important in sexual reproduction.

Test Prep

5. Critical Thinking In what situations might the genetic variations that result from sexual reproduction be better than asexual reproduction?

6. Which of the following is **NOT** true of a gene?
   A. can't be copied
   B. determines traits
   C. comes from parents
   D. is a piece of DNA

Links

Writing

Expository Writing

Some animals are endangered—their numbers are so small that the species may become extinct. Do research on some of the breeding programs being used to increase the populations of endangered species, and write a **report** on what you learn.

Math

Solve a Problem

The cells in developing mammal eggs divide at first about every 24 hours. How many cells does a developing mammal egg have 7 days after fertilization? 10 days after?

Health

Sickle-Cell Anemia

Use library and Internet resources to research sickle-cell anemia. Which populations are affected by this disease? How do people get it? Can anything be done to cure it? Write a short report in which you tell how your findings relate to this lesson.

 For more links and activities, go to www.hspscience.com

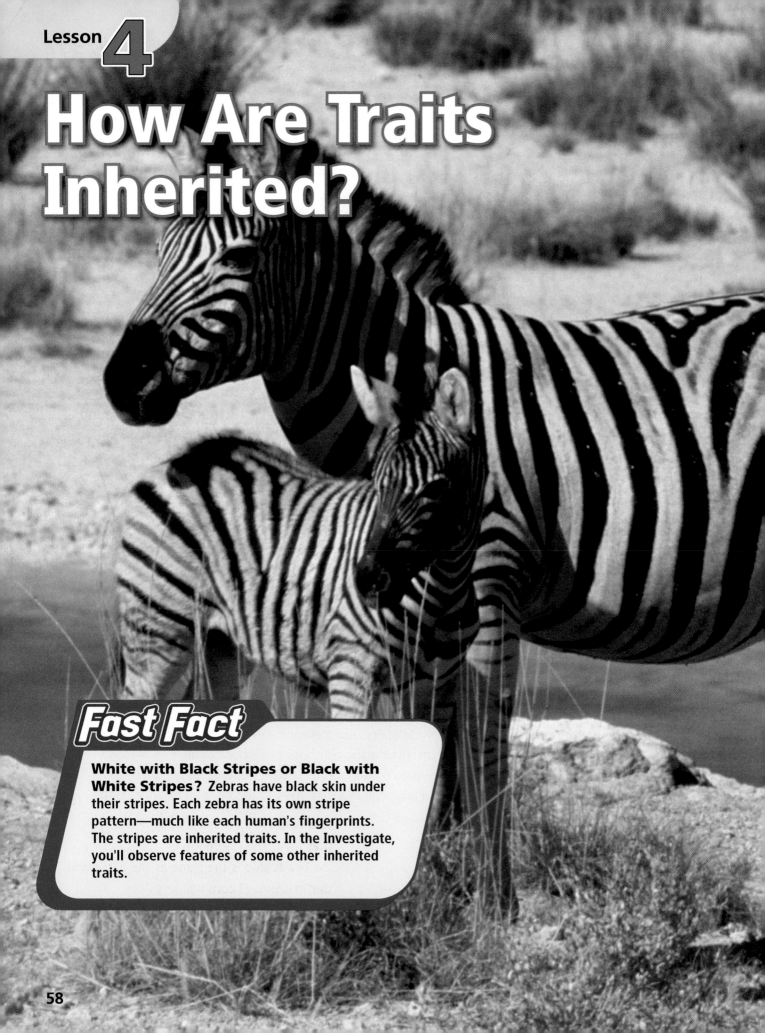

How Are Traits Inherited?

Fast Fact

White with Black Stripes or Black with White Stripes? Zebras have black skin under their stripes. Each zebra has its own stripe pattern—much like each human's fingerprints. The stripes are inherited traits. In the Investigate, you'll observe features of some other inherited traits.

Seed Color in Corn

Materials ● ear of purple-and-white corn

Procedure

① Observe the photograph of purple-and-white corn. Each kernel is a separate fruit with a seed inside. Predict the colors of kernels on corn grown from these seeds.

② Observe the ear of corn. It was grown from a seed of a corn plant that had purple kernels. Estimate the number of purple kernels and the number of white kernels.

③ Count the purple kernels and white kernels, and record the totals.

④ Find the ratio of purple kernels to white kernels.

⑤ Share your results with the class.

⑥ Add to find the total number of white kernels and the total number of purple kernels for the whole class. Then use those numbers to find the ratio of purple kernels to white kernels for the whole class.

Draw Conclusions

1. How did the class's results compare with your results?

2. Form a hypothesis about why using the class's ratio as a final result is better than using just one person's ratio.

3. Inquiry Skill Based on the ratio of purple kernels to white kernels, what can you infer about the trait for purple kernels? For white kernels?

Step 1

Number of Kernels of Corn	
Purple	**White**

Investigate Further

Toss two coins 20 times, and record how they land. The likelihood of both landing on the heads side is the same as the likelihood that a kernel of corn will be white. Hypothesize why there are more purple kernels than white on an ear of corn.

Reading in Science

VOCABULARY
dominant p. 62
recessive p. 62

SCIENCE CONCEPTS
▶ how traits are inherited from two parents
▶ how dominant and recessive genes affect the inheritance of traits

READING FOCUS SKILL
CAUSE AND EFFECT Look for causes of the results of Mendel's experiments.

| cause | → | effect |

Mendel's Experiment

Gregor Mendel was an Austrian monk. He loved to walk around the monastery garden and observe plants and wildlife. He observed that some plants look similar and some look very different. He wondered how traits are passed on from one generation to another. He began studying pea plants to find out.

Mendel chose to study pea plants for two reasons. First, pea plants have very distinctive traits. For example, the peas in Mendel's garden were either round or wrinkled. The stems were either tall or short. The second reason is that pea plants are self-pollinated, so Mendel could control how they were fertilized.

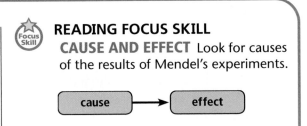

This bee is gathering nectar. In the process, some pollen collects on the bee's legs. When the bee visits another flower, pollen from its legs sticks to the stigma of that flower, fertilizing it.

Flower Parts

Most flowers have both male and female reproductive cells. In many flowers, the female stigma is higher than the male anthers. This ensures that pollen from a flower will not be transferred to its own stigma.

Stigma

Anther

Many other plants are cross-pollinated. That is, insects and birds carry pollen from one plant to another. In that way, the pollen from one plant fertilizes others. Peas, however, have closed flowers and pollen fertilizes eggs in the same flower. Because of this, Mendel could control which pollen fertilized which flower.

In one experiment, Mendel took pollen from a pea plant that had purple flowers. Using a paintbrush, he put the pollen on the stigma of a pea plant with white flowers. He also put pollen from a plant with white flowers on the stigma of a plant with purple flowers. When the plants produced seeds, Mendel planted them and waited to see what traits the new plants had.

When Mendel started his experiments in the mid-1800s, people thought that the traits of plants blended in the offspring. For example, they thought that a purple flower that got pollen from a white flower would result in lavender flowers. Or would the result be purple-and-white flowers?

Mendel cross-pollinated pea plants for many years. He recorded how many of each type of plant were produced in each generation. There were no lavender flowers. Instead, he got three times as many plants with purple flowers as plants with white flowers. He tested for six other traits, but his results were always the same: he would get three times as many plants with one trait as with the contrasting trait.

Mendel published his ideas in 1865, but most people ignored them. Today, though, Mendel is considered the father of genetics (juh•NET•iks). Genetics is the study of heredity.

CAUSE AND EFFECT What caused Mendel to choose pea plants for his experiments?

Mendel's Experiments

The flowers on a pea plant are self-pollinating. Because the anthers and the stigma are enclosed in the petals, pollen in a pea flower falls on its own stigma. In addition, the anther is above the stigma, ensuring that the pollen will fall on the stigma.

Types of Peas

It's easy to see the difference between wrinkled and round peas. And yellow peas are easy to distinguish from green peas. Mendel investigated these traits.

Mendel noticed that pea plants had either all purple flowers or all white flowers. He wondered what would happen if he crossed a white-flowered plant with a purple-flowered plant.

Dominant and Recessive Factors

The diagram below shows the results of some of Mendel's experiments. No matter what traits he looked for or how often he looked for them, the results were the same. The plants in the first generation had only one kind of trait. The traits of their offspring, the second generation, always had a ratio of 3:1. One-fourth of those plants had the trait that wasn't seen in the first generation. For example, after Mendel pollinated a purple plant with pollen from a white plant, the result in the first generation was all purple plants. When those purple plants were allowed to self-pollinate, they produced three-fourths purple plants and one-fourth white plants.

Mendel knew that seeds are produced by sexual reproduction. In other words, male and female reproductive cells join to make seeds that carry information from both parents. Mendel called the information for a trait a factor. He concluded that every plant has two factors for a characteristic—one factor from the female and one from the male. One of these factors stays hidden in the first generation, but that factor is seen, or expressed, in the second generation. Mendel reasoned that some factors are "stronger," or **dominant**. Other factors for a pair of traits are "weaker," or **recessive**. If an offspring has either one or two dominant

 Science Up Close

Mendel's Discoveries

The first generation is cross-pollinated. Mendel knew that the tall parent plant had two tall factors and the short parent plant had two short factors. What happened to the short-plant factors in the first-generation offspring? Why do the short plants show up again?

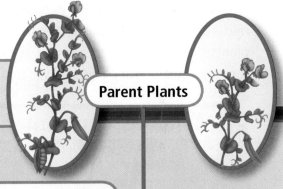

Parent Plants

Tall and short plants were cross-pollinated.

Seeds from the cross-pollinated parent plants were planted.

First Generation

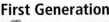

Second Generation

Seeds from the self-pollinated first generation were planted.

 For more links and activities, go to **www.hspscience.com**

factors, the trait will show up. The other trait of the pair will show up only if an offspring has two recessive factors.

Which trait is dominant—tall or short? Mendel had pollinated the plants himself. One parent was short, and one was tall. He knew that the first-generation plants

People inherit both dominant and recessive traits. Attached earlobes are a recessive trait. Which factors could the girl with the detached earlobes have?

Some traits don't show up in the first generation. You may look more like your grandfather than your father.

There are more people in the world who have dimples than there are people who don't have them. Which do you think is dominant?

all had to have a genetic factor from each parent. He couldn't tell that by looking at them, however. Only the tall-plant trait was expressed. In the next generation, the plants had a mix of traits. The tall plants needed only one factor for tallness. Can you tell what factors a short plant had? It couldn't have a factor for tallness, so it must have had two for shortness. Mendel concluded that the trait that always expresses itself is dominant. The trait that needs two factors for it to be expressed is recessive.

Let's look at this another way. Scientists use initials to stand for traits. Suppose the factor for tall stems is represented by T. The factor for short stems is represented by t. A plant with two T factors, or TT, will have tall stems. A plant with two t factors, or tt, will have short-stemmed plants. A plant with one T factor and

A cleft chin is dominant. The child without a cleft chin must have two factors for that trait. Do both the mother and the father have the recessive factor for that trait?

one t factor, or Tt, will have tall stems but ¾ of its offspring will have tall stems and ¼ will have short stems.

 CAUSE AND EFFECT What caused Mendel to conclude that the factor for tallness is dominant?

Genes and Inheritance

Mendel's "factors" for inheritance are what we now call genes. You learned earlier in this chapter that genes are small segments of DNA that carry information passed from parents to their offspring. Genes have instructions for making specific proteins. They determine the structure, development, and function of body cells, tissues, and organs. The sequence of all the gene segments on human DNA has been identified. Scientists have found that there are about 35,000 genes on human DNA.

Genes from different parents combine randomly during sexual reproduction. As a result, there are many possible variations in offspring.

You've seen examples of dominant and recessive traits. But traits aren't limited to appearance. Some people inherit an ability to play sports well or to paint well. Some people have personality traits different from other family members. The traits expressed in grandparents or great-grandparents can skip the parents and still appear in their offspring.

 CAUSE AND EFFECT From whom do you get your dominant and recessive traits?

Insta-Lab

Can You Roll Your Tongue?

Find out how many of your classmates can roll their tongues and how many can't. First, predict whether the ability to roll the tongue is dominant or recessive. Figure out the ratio of those who can to those who can't. Based on the ratio, which trait is dominant?

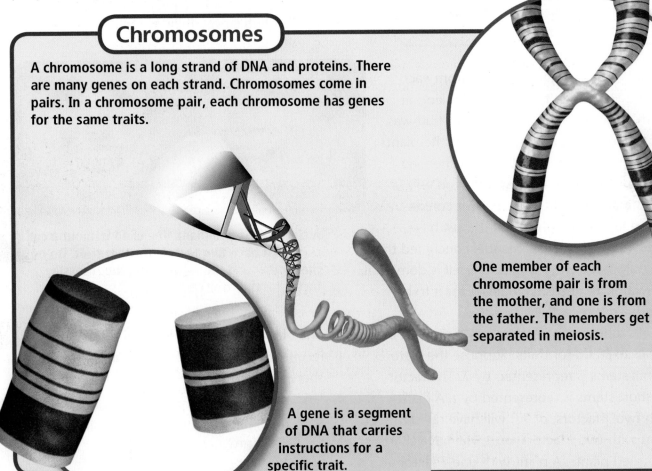

Chromosomes

A chromosome is a long strand of DNA and proteins. There are many genes on each strand. Chromosomes come in pairs. In a chromosome pair, each chromosome has genes for the same traits.

One member of each chromosome pair is from the mother, and one is from the father. The members get separated in meiosis.

A gene is a segment of DNA that carries instructions for a specific trait.

1. CAUSE AND EFFECT Draw and complete the graphic organizer.

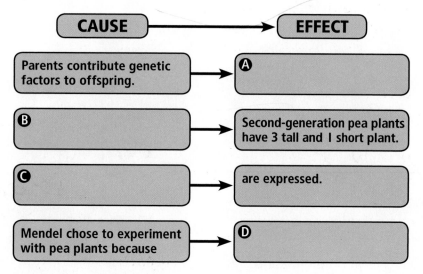

CAUSE	→	EFFECT
Parents contribute genetic factors to offspring.	→	Ⓐ
Ⓑ	→	Second-generation pea plants have 3 tall and 1 short plant.
Ⓒ	→	are expressed.
Mendel chose to experiment with pea plants because	→	Ⓓ

2. SUMMARIZE Use the graphic organizer to summarize how traits are inherited and expressed.

3. DRAW CONCLUSIONS Horses are bred to be big and strong. Describe the steps you would take to produce a big, strong horse.

4. VOCABULARY Use the lesson vocabulary terms in a sentence that illustrates their meanings.

Test Prep

5. Critical Thinking How can you explain the fact that a friend's younger sister is the only one in her family for two generations who doesn't have dimples?

6. Which trait is always expressed?
   A. a dominant one
   B. one from the father
   C. one from the mother
   D. a recessive one

Links

Writing

Expository Writing

Inherited traits are especially interesting in twins. Research the formation of fraternal and identical twins. Write a **report** for the class that tells how traits are passed from parents to identical or fraternal twins.

Math

Determine Probability

Human males have an X chromosome and a Y chromosome. Females have two X chromosomes. A sperm carries either an X or a Y. Every egg carries an X. What is the probability that an offspring will be female?

Social Studies

Hello, Dolly!

Use library or Internet resources to research the cloning of Dolly the sheep. What were the reactions to the news? What were the pros and cons that people expressed? Write a summary of what you find.

 For more links and activities, go to **www.hspscience.com**

Red Alert

Plants have amazing powers. Some plants are used as medicines that save lives. Some plants are used to build homes. Now, some plants are being used to locate hidden explosives.

Scientists in Denmark have developed a plant that may someday be used to detect buried land mines, which kill or injure about 25,000 people each year.

Hidden Danger

Land mines are explosives planted just below the surface of the ground, usually during a time of war. The explosives remain active for years after the fighting ends. The hidden mines explode when people step or drive on them.

The most common way to find mines has been to lie on the ground and poke the dirt with a stick. Another way is to use dogs or a metal detector. Each of these methods works, but the work can be very dangerous.

Now, a simple weed, called *thale cress,* may warn people of the danger underfoot when they simply look at the color of the plant. The trick lies in the genes of a watercress plant. Genes determine the makeup of all living cells.

Changing the Genes

During colder weather, such as in autumn, plants become stressed and turn red or reddish. To turn thale cress into a mine-detecting plant, scientists changed the genes of the plant. This change allows the plant to turn red only if triggered by certain soil conditions.

In this case, those conditions involve the presence of nitrogen dioxide—a poisonous gas

▲ Stressed cress!

Seeds Without Doubt

Under the scientists' plan, low-flying airplanes would spray the laboratory-made seeds onto suspected minefields. Within weeks, the seeds would sprout into plants that give a "red alert" if mines are present in the ground.

found in land mines. When the roots of the plant are exposed to the gas, the plant sends a signal to its leaves, telling them to turn red. The color change usually happens within 3 to 6 weeks after the roots sense the gas. With this simple change, scientists hope to save the lives of thousands of people every year.

Think About It

1. What causes the leaves of the altered thale cress to change color?
2. Why do you think governments would want to use the mine-detecting plant?

Spin In Find out more! Log on to www.hspscience.com

Double Trouble?

Two-headed snakes develop in the same way conjoined twins do. A snake embryo begins to split into identical twins, but only partially splits. An embryo can cease splitting at different points in its development. As a result, a snake can be divided at different places on its body.

Hunter York found this out when he was playing in his father's backyard. The Kentucky boy used a stick to pick up the 21-cm-long (8 1/2 in.), two-headed black king snake.

Hunter's dad left the reptile with a herpetologist, or reptile expert. "We couldn't force-feed it because we didn't know which head eats," said his dad. One scientist said that Hunter's find was very rare, since only about one of every 10,000 snakes has two heads.

Quick and Easy Project

Water Movement in Cells

Materials
- potato cut into several equal-size pieces
- metric ruler
- metric measuring cup
- spoon
- salt
- 4 L distilled water
- 2 bowls
- plastic wrap

Procedure

1. Measure and record the size of one piece of the potato.
2. Mix 60 mL of salt into 250 mL of distilled water, and pour the salt water into one of the bowls. Add half of the potato pieces.
3. Put 250 mL of distilled water into the other bowl. Add the rest of the potato pieces.
4. Cover the bowls with plastic wrap, and set them in a cool place. Be sure both bowls are sealed with the plastic wrap. Do not open the wrap for the whole time of soaking.
5. After several days, pour off the water from each bowl. Measure and record the size of one potato piece from each bowl.

Draw Conclusions
How are the potatoes soaked in salt water different from those soaked in plain water? What could explain the difference? What can you infer about how water moves in or out of cells?

Design Your Own Investigation

Male or Female?

Design a game or an investigation to find the chance of an offspring's being either male or female. Use two coins. Put pieces of masking tape on both sides of the coins. Mark one coin with an *X* (female) on one side and a *Y* (male) on the other side. Mark the second coin with an *X* (female) on both sides. Explain your findings.

Review and Test Preparation

Vocabulary Review

Use the terms below to complete the sentences. The page numbers tell you where to look in the chapter if you need help.

√ **chloroplasts** p. 34   **tissue** p. 40
√ **cell wall** p. 34   √ **organ** p. 42
√ **nucleus** p. 35   √ **genes** p. 51
√ **chromosomes** p. 35   **dominant** p. 62
√ **DNA** p. 36   **recessive** p. 62

1. A structure containing at least two different types of tissues that work together for a common purpose is an _____ .

2. A trait that is expressed even when only one gene for it is present is _____ .

3. Linear pieces of DNA and protein are _____ .

4. Photosynthesis takes place in the _____ .

5. Chromosomes are contained in the _____ .

6. A trait that needs two factors in order to be expressed is _____ .

7. Instructions for specific traits are carried by factors that are now called _____ .

8. A stiff outer structure that protects a plant cell is a _____ .

9. Instructions for all body activities are found in a chemical known as _____ .

10. Cells grouped together that have the same structure and function form a _____ .

Check Understanding

Write the letter of the best choice.

11. Which kind of cell is shown below?

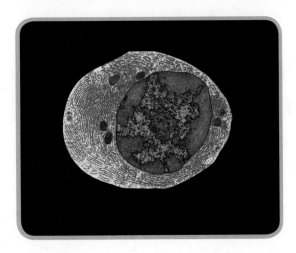

    A. animal
    B. meiosis
    C. mitosis
    D. plant

12. Which of these parts is **not** included in the human digestive system?
    F. muscles
    G. stomach
    H. tissues
    J. xylem

13. **CAUSE AND EFFECT** 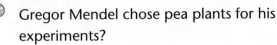 Which is one reason Gregor Mendel chose pea plants for his experiments?
    A. They don't have seeds.
    B. They have purple flowers.
    C. They are self-pollinated.
    D. They are tall.

14. **MAIN IDEA AND DETAILS** Which statement is part of the cell theory?

   F. Animal cells are different from plant cells.

   G. Cells are the building blocks of all living things.

   H. Cells perform special tasks.

   J. Dominant traits are always expressed.

15. How many cells would be in a developing frog after four divisions?

   A. 4 cells

   B. 8 cells

   C. 16 cells

   D. 32 cells

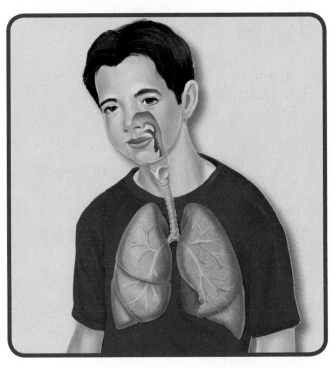

16. Which major organs are pictured above?

   F. arteries

   G. heart

   H. lungs

   J. stomach

Inquiry Skills

17. How does the number of chromosomes in a human body cell compare with the number of chromosomes in a human reproductive cell?

18. If there are three times as many students who have dimples as there are students without dimples, what can you infer about the trait for dimples?

Critical Thinking

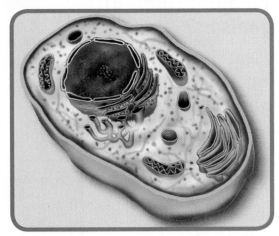

19. Suppose you were able to add chloroplasts to animal cells. Predict how this might change an animal's behavior.

20. The digestive system is an important part of the body. Animals need to eat food in order to carry out life processes.

   Part A Describe the path of a bite of food as it travels through the digestive tract. Tell what happens to the food in each organ.

   Part B Which other organ systems are involved in digestion? Pick two of those systems, and explain their roles in digestion.

Classifying Living Things

Lesson 1 **How Are Organisms Classified?**

Lesson 2 **What Are the Major Groups of Organisms?**

Lesson 3 **How Do Scientists Name Organisms?**

Vocabulary

classification
adaptation
fungus
protist
genus
species

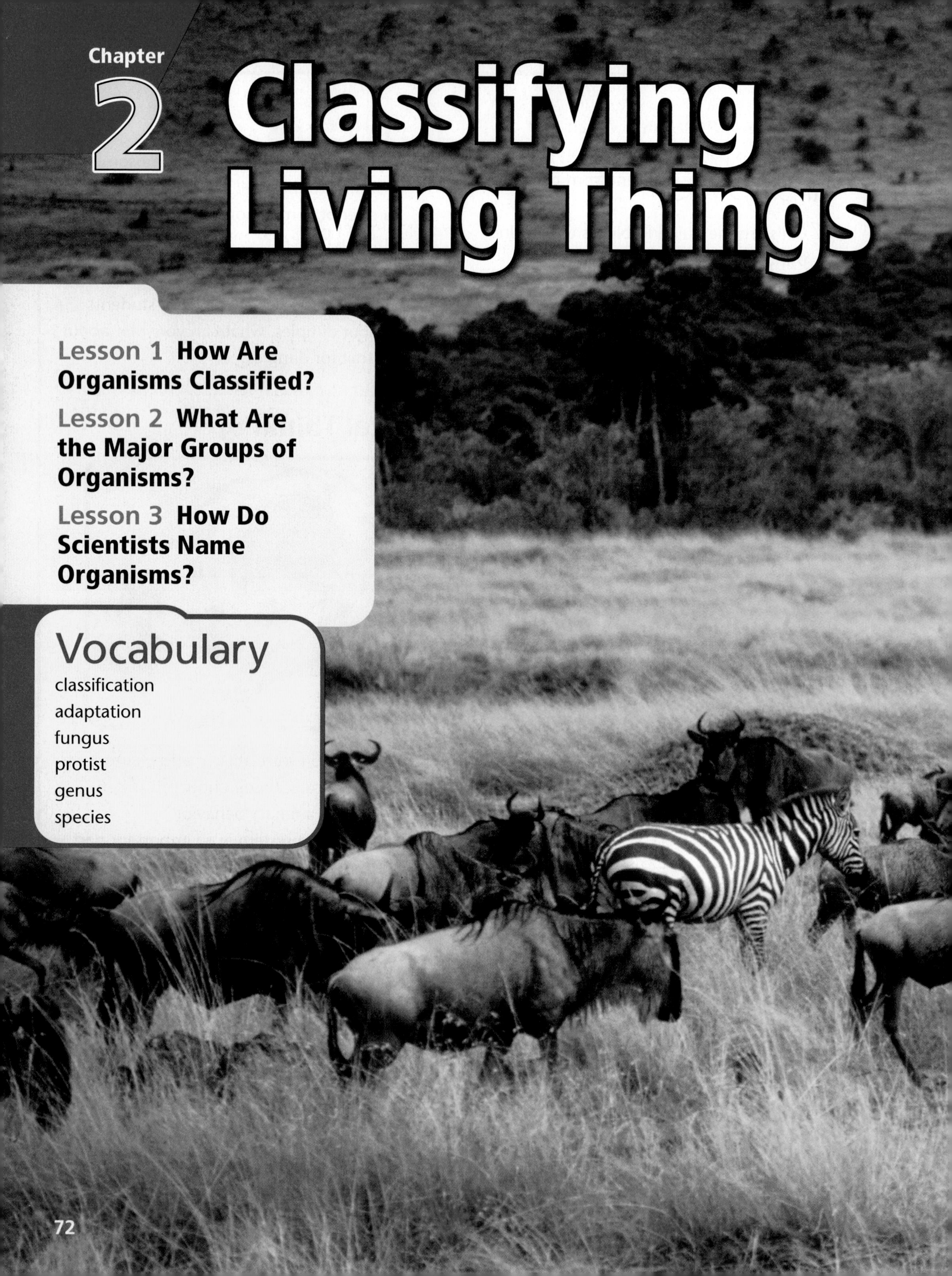

What do YOU wonder?

The Serengeti National Park is home to more than 1.3 million wildebeests; 200,000 zebras; 1500 lions; 1000 elephants; 280,000 Thompson's gazelles; 25,000 buffalo; 72,000 topi; 32,000 Grant's gazelles; 8500 giraffes; 10,000 elands; and many species of birds, insects, and grasses. How do you suppose all these animals live together in this area? Where do they get food and water?

How Are Organisms Classified?

Fast Fact

Coral Diversity The coral reefs in Florida are home to about 1 million different kinds of living things. Scientists classify these organisms into groups to make them easier to study. In the Investigate, you will model how to classify living things.

Classifying Beans

Materials • bag of mixed beans

Procedure

1. Pour the beans from the bag, and observe them carefully.

2. Make a list of the characteristics, or qualities, that you observe about the beans. Use all of these characteristics to classify, or sort the beans into as many different groups as possible.

3. Draw a table like the one shown. In it, record the characteristics of each group of beans. Draw a picture of one bean from each group. Give the group a name. Then write a short description of the bean's characteristics.

Draw Conclusions

1. Compare your results with the results of your classmates. How many different ways did your class find to classify the beans?

2. What characteristics did you use to classify the beans? What characteristics did your classmates use?

3. Inquiry Skills Scientists classify living things to show how they're similar and how they're different. Why do you think it's important for all scientists to use the same characteristics to classify living things?

Step 1

Step 3

Picture of Bean	Name of Group	Characteristics of Bean

Investigate Further

Choose a different set of objects, such as shells. Classify them according to their characteristics. How do you think your classification system is like the one you used for the beans? How is it different?

Reading in Science

VOCABULARY
classification p. 76

SCIENCE CONCEPTS
▶ how classification systems were developed
▶ how living things are classified

READING FOCUS SKILL
MAIN IDEA AND DETAILS
Look for details about how classification is helpful.

Main Idea

detail   detail   detail

Why Living Things Are Classified

When you need a book from the library, how do you find it? First, you look in the card file or on the computer. This tells you where to find the book. Then, you go to a certain area of the library. You know that similar books are placed together. This makes them easy to find. You can find fiction books in one place and nonfiction books in another place. The placing of things into groups of similar items is called **classification**.

Just as libraries classify books, scientists classify living things. So far, they have classified over 2 million different kinds of organisms. This

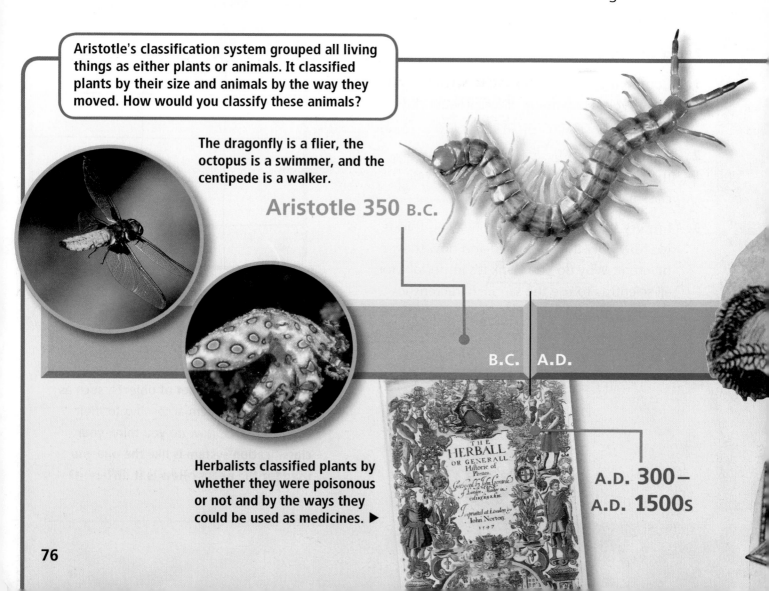

Aristotle's classification system grouped all living things as either plants or animals. It classified plants by their size and animals by the way they moved. How would you classify these animals?

The dragonfly is a flier, the octopus is a swimmer, and the centipede is a walker.

Aristotle 350 B.C.

B.C.   A.D.

Herbalists classified plants by whether they were poisonous or not and by the ways they could be used as medicines. ▶

A.D. 300–
A.D. 1500s

makes relationships among living things easier to study. Classification helps scientists correctly identify organisms and understand how living things are related to one another.

There are many ways to classify living things. It's important for scientists to agree on one system. When they discuss an organism by scientific name, they can be certain that they're talking about the same organism.

Classification systems change as scientists discover new information. Over the years, scientists have developed new technologies, such as high-powered microscopes, to study organisms in greater detail. Studying the DNA of organisms also helps scientists classify organisms and determine differences between them.

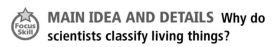 **MAIN IDEA AND DETAILS** Why do scientists classify living things?

Insta-Lab

Grab and Group!
Gather 25 small items from your classroom. How might you group them? Make up your own classification system. Make a table that shows how you classified the items. Which groups does your table show as having items that are most closely related?

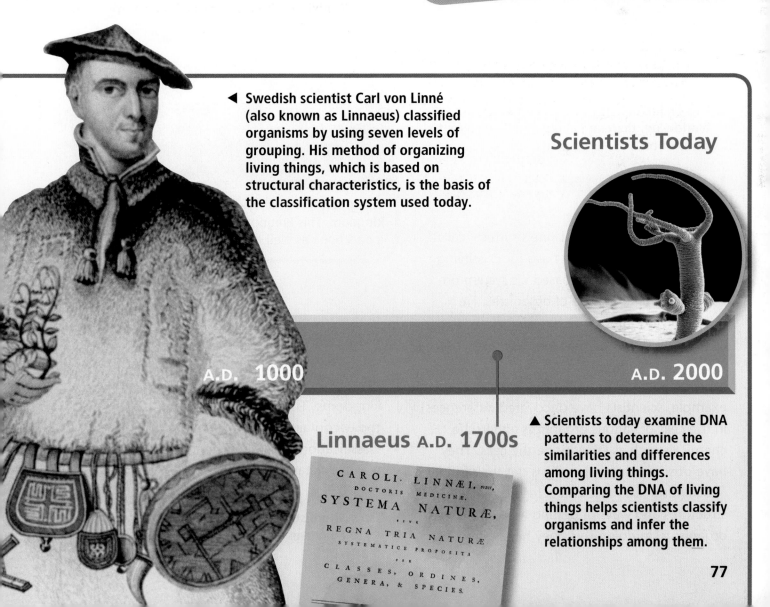

◄ Swedish scientist Carl von Linné (also known as Linnaeus) classified organisms by using seven levels of grouping. His method of organizing living things, which is based on structural characteristics, is the basis of the classification system used today.

Scientists Today

A.D. **1000**

A.D. **2000**

Linnaeus A.D. **1700s**

CAROLI. LINNÆI, *suec,*
DOCTORIS MEDICINÆ,
SYSTEMA NATURÆ,
sive
REGNA TRIA NATURÆ
SYSTEMATICE PROPOSITA
per
CLASSES, ORDINES,
GENERA, & SPECIES.

▲ Scientists today examine DNA patterns to determine the similarities and differences among living things. Comparing the DNA of living things helps scientists classify organisms and infer the relationships among them.

77

◄ Euglenas have chloroplasts, as plants do, but they can also move, as animals do. It would have been tricky to classify the euglena by using one of the early classification systems!

◄ Bacteria belong to one of two kingdoms of single-celled organisms.

▲ This orchid belongs to the plant kingdom. Worldwide, there are about 25,000 different kinds of orchids.

The green tree snake belongs to the animal kingdom. This kingdom includes animals without a backbone as well as those with a backbone.

How Living Things Are Classified

Today we still use von Linné's system, called the Linnaean system, as a basis for classifying living things. Von Linné based his system on structural characteristics of organisms. He divided living things into two kingdoms, the animal kingdom and the plant kingdom.

Since von Linné's time, scientists have used other characteristics to classify organisms. For example, scientists have discovered differences in the cells of various organisms and in the chemicals such as DNA inside the cells. They have observed how organisms get their food.

Scientists use these characteristics—cell structures and ways of getting food—to classify organisms. In doing this, they have found that many living things are different from most plants and animals. Because these living things do not fit in either the animal or the plant kingdom, scientists have added other kingdoms. The system many scientists use today contains six kingdoms. However, the classification system will continue to change as our understanding of living things changes.

 MAIN IDEA AND DETAILS How did scientists conclude that more than two kingdoms were needed?

1. MAIN IDEA AND DETAILS Draw and complete this graphic organizer.

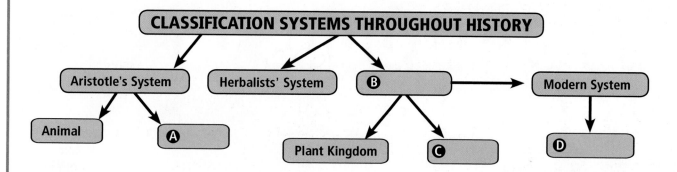

CLASSIFICATION SYSTEMS THROUGHOUT HISTORY

Aristotle's System → Animal, A

Herbalists' System

B → Modern System

B → Plant Kingdom, C

Modern System → D

2. SUMMARIZE Use the graphic organizer and lesson concepts to write a brief paragraph about the history of the classification of organisms.

3. DRAW CONCLUSIONS What might happen if all scientists did not use the same classification system to describe living things?

4. VOCABULARY Write your own definition for the vocabulary term.

Test Prep

5. Critical Thinking What modern technology helps scientists compare organisms and assign them to groups? How?

6. How do scientists classify organisms?

  A. by their structures

  B. by their scents

  C. by their heights

  D. by their weights

Links

Writing

Descriptive Writing

Write a **paragraph** to describe how confusing your life would be if some common items—such as clothes or food items in stores— were not classified.

Math

Use a Calculator

Some scientists estimate that Earth has as many as 80 million kinds of organisms. Calculate the percent of organisms that have yet to be identified if this is true.

Language Arts

Carl von Linné

Carl von Linné invented a *nomenclature*, or naming system, for living things. Use library or Internet resources to learn more about his nomenclature. How did he use it to change his own name?

 For more links and activities, go to www.hspscience.com

What Are the Major Groups of Organisms?

Fast Fact

Magnificent Macaws In both Central America and South America, the scarlet macaw has red and yellow feathers. In Central America, it also has blue feathers. In South America, it has some green feathers. Scientists disagree about whether the birds should be classified separately. In the Investigate, you will develop your own classification system.

Classifying into Levels

Materials • paper and pencil

Procedure

1 Make a table, and record all of the foods you could have eaten for breakfast. Also record the foods you would like to eat for lunch and dinner.

2 Now classify the foods. Begin by starting lists of two or three large groups of foods that are alike. Write a description of each group.

3 Classify the foods in the large groups into smaller and smaller groups, or levels. The foods in each smaller group should be alike in some way. Write a description of each group.

4 Stop classifying when you have sorted all of the foods into groups with two or fewer items.

Draw Conclusions

1. What features did you use to classify the foods?

2. Compare your classification system with a classmate's system. How are your systems alike? How are they different?

3. Inquiry Skill It is important for scientists to agree on a set of rules for classifying living things. As a class, discuss the different systems that were developed by individual students. Then decide which system would be the best to use. What features did you use to decide?

Step 1

Step 3

Investigate Further

Choose another group of objects or organisms. Classify the items into several levels. Then write a brief explanation of your classification system.

Reading in Science

VOCABULARY
adaptation p. 82
fungus p. 84
protist p. 85

SCIENCE CONCEPTS
▶ how living things are grouped, get food, and reproduce
▶ what the kingdoms of organisms are

READING FOCUS SKILL
COMPARE AND CONTRAST Look for ways in which the members of each kingdom are alike and different.

alike ——— different

Plants

Think about walking in a park in spring. The color you are most likely to notice is green. It's all around you—under your feet and over your head, in sidewalk cracks and on the walls of buildings. It comes from the living plants around you.

The plant kingdom includes a wide variety of organisms, from tiny mosses to giant trees. Plants have cells with walls and a nucleus that contains DNA. Plant cells also have *chloroplasts*, structures that help the plants make their own food.

Scientists group plants by the way they reproduce and by their structures—roots, stems, flowers, and leaves. Scientists also look at the adaptations of plants. An **adaptation** is a feature of an organism that helps it survive in its environment.

One adaptation some plants have is vascular, or tubelike, tissue that moves water and nutrients through the plant. The presence or absence of vascular tissue is used to classify plants into two main groups.

 COMPARE AND CONTRAST How are vascular and nonvascular plants alike? How are they different?

This pine tree is part of a group of plants called conifers. It has vascular tissue and reproduces from seeds formed in cones. ▼

This plant is one of more than 200,000 species of flowering plants. It has vascular tissue and reproduces from seeds formed by flowers.

Mosses don't have vascular tissue, and they don't make seeds. These plants live in or near water and require water to reproduce.

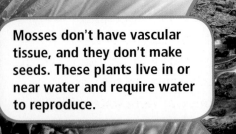

82

Diversity in the Animal Kingdom

The circle graph shows the different groups that make up the animal kingdom. Which group of animals has the most members? The fewest? About what percent of all species of animals are mammals?

This tamarin has characteristics common to all mammals. It has fur, bears live young, and produces milk for its young.

This sea creature looks like an alien life form! It's really an animal. It is one of more than 9000 species of animals related to jellyfish.▼

Mammals: 4000
Sponges: 5000
Sea stars, urchins, and related animals: 6100
Jellyfish and related animals: 9000
Minor groups: 9300
Segmented worms: 12,000
Roundworms: 12,000
Flatworms: 12,200
Other vertebrates: 38,300
Other noninsect arthropods: 50,000
Spiders and related animals: 73,400
Mollusks: 50,000
Insects: 751,000
Total number of identified animal species: 1,973,400

Animals

Like plant cells, animal cells have nuclei that contain DNA. Unlike plant cells, however, animal cells do not have walls or chloroplasts. These are the main differences between animal cells and plant cells.

How do scientists identify nearly 2 million different kinds of animals? They start by determining whether an animal has a backbone.

Animals with a backbone are *vertebrates*. Vertebrates are further classified into groups based on their body coverings and on the ways in which they breathe and reproduce. There are five major groups of vertebrates: fish, amphibians, reptiles, birds, and mammals.

Animals without a backbone are *invertebrates*. About 97 percent of all animals are invertebrates.

Scientists classify invertebrates by whether their cells form tissues, how many kinds of tissues their cells form, whether they have a body cavity, and what type of body cavity they have. They also look at the type of body symmetry animals have, the type of digestive system they have, how their embryos develop, and whether their bodies are segmented.

 COMPARE AND CONTRAST How are animals different from plants?

Yeast is a fungus that reproduces from just one cell. A small portion of the "parent" cell pinches off to form a new yeast cell.

This mushroom is an extremely poisonous fungus, but you can't tell by looking at it. Never touch or taste any mushroom you find in your yard or in the wild.

The mold *Penicillium* kills bacteria.

Fungi

A **fungus** is an organism whose cells have walls but no chloroplasts. Most fungi feed on decaying tissues of other organisms. A few kinds of fungi cause disease in living things. Fungi were once classified as plants. As scientists learned more about fungi, however, they realized that these organisms belong in a separate kingdom.

Scientists classify fungi by their shape, size, and way of reproducing. They also consider whether a particular fungus is made up of one cell or many cells. Yeasts, which cause bread to rise, are single-celled fungi. Most other fungi have many cells. Examples are mushrooms and the bracket fungi that can be seen on tree trunks in forests. Fungi can also be classified by their habitat, the way they live, and their cell structure.

COMPARE AND CONTRAST How are fungus cells like plant cells? How are they different?

Insta-Lab

Make Spore Prints

Spores are reproductive cells produced by some kinds of plants and fungi. In a mushroom, the spores are in the underside of the cap. Remove the stem from a mushroom. Place the mushroom cap, with the spore side down, on a sheet of white paper. Leave it overnight. The next day, carefully remove the cap from the paper. Observe the pattern left by the spores. Why do you think mushrooms are found in a variety of places?

Protists

Have you ever seen an *amoeba*? Maybe you've seen pictures of a little shoe-shaped cell called *Paramecium*. These are two examples of another major group of organisms called protists. **Protists** are microscopic organisms that may have characteristics of plants, animals, or fungi. You can imagine how these organisms would have confused scientists in Aristotle's day if they had known about them! Most protists are single-celled. Each cell has a nucleus that contains DNA.

Scientists often classify protists by whether they are more like plants, more like animals, or more like fungi. They group the plantlike protists mainly by their color. They also consider the types of materials protists use to store food. The cells of plantlike protists have chloroplasts, enabling them to make their own food.

Scientists group animal-like protists by their shape and size and by the way they move. The amoeba is an animal-like protist that has no cell wall and no definite shape. It moves on *pseudopodia*, or "false feet." These false feet form when cytoplasm flows against the cell membrane. Another animal-like protist, the paramecium, uses hairlike parts called *cilia* to "swim."

The *slime molds* make up most of the group of funguslike protists. Their cells have walls, but they contain no chloroplasts. They have some of the characteristics of fungi. Scientists group funguslike protists mainly by their shape and by their reproductive structures.

 COMPARE AND CONTRAST How are protists, plants, animals, and fungi similar?

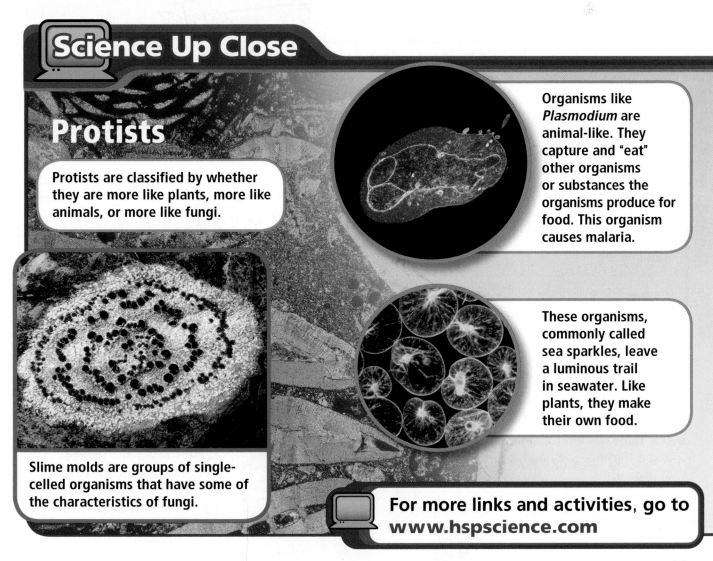

Science Up Close

Protists

Protists are classified by whether they are more like plants, more like animals, or more like fungi.

Slime molds are groups of single-celled organisms that have some of the characteristics of fungi.

Organisms like *Plasmodium* are animal-like. They capture and "eat" other organisms or substances the organisms produce for food. This organism causes malaria.

These organisms, commonly called sea sparkles, leave a luminous trail in seawater. Like plants, they make their own food.

For more links and activities, go to **www.hspscience.com**

Bacteria

Bacteria differ from the members of the other kingdoms in one important way: Their cells have no nucleus. In the past, scientists grouped all bacteria into one kingdom. Today, scientists divide bacteria into two kingdoms. One kingdom includes bacteria that live in very harsh environments—such as those that live in hot springs. The other kingdom includes all the other bacteria.

Bacteria live almost everywhere, from deep-ocean vents on the ocean floor to the snows of Antarctica. There are more bacteria on Earth than any other kind of living thing. There are even some bacteria that live inside the human body and help the body's processes. Most bacteria are harmless or even helpful. Very few cause disease.

One way scientists classify bacteria is by the way they get energy. Some need oxygen to survive, while others are killed by oxygen. Some bacteria make their own food. These include *cyanobacteria*, which are the blue-green bacteria that make up the green scum on ponds. Scientists also classify bacteria by their size and shape.

 COMPARE AND CONTRAST How do bacteria differ from other organisms?

Bacteria can thrive in almost every environment. Bacteria living in these hot springs cause many of the beautiful colors you see.

The Kingdoms of Living Things

Kingdom	Description	Described Species
Plantae	multicelled, cell walls, nucleus, make their own food, cannot move	about 270,000
Animalia	multicelled, no cell walls, nucleus, eat food, most can move	more than 1,500,000
Fungi	mostly multicelled, cell walls, nucleus, take in food, cannot move	about 70,000
Protista	mostly single-celled, some have cell walls, nucleus, take in food or make their own food, many can move	about 80,000
Monera/Bacteria (2 kingdoms)	single-celled, cell walls, no nucleus, take in food or make their own food, some can move	about 5000

▲ This table summarizes the similarities and differences among the kingdoms of organisms.

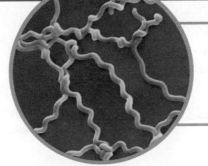

Scientists use the shapes of bacteria as one way to classify them. Bacteria that have a twisted shape are called spirochetes.

1. **COMPARE AND CONTRAST** Draw and complete this graphic organizer.

KINGDOMS OF LIVING THINGS		
Kingdom	**Number of Cells**	**Features of Cells**
Plants	**Ⓐ**	Cell walls, nucleus, chloroplasts
Animals	Many cells	**Ⓑ**
Ⓒ	Mostly many cells, some single-celled	**Ⓓ**
Protists	**Ⓔ**	Some have cell walls and chloroplasts
Ⓕ (2 kingdoms)	Single-celled	Cell wall, no nucleus

2. **SUMMARIZE** Use the graphic organizer to write a summary of the kingdom system of classification.

3. **DRAW CONCLUSIONS** What can an organism's classification tell you about it?

4. **VOCABULARY** Use lesson vocabulary and concepts to construct a crossword puzzle.

Test Prep

5. **Critical Thinking** Why do scientists classify living things?

6. Which kingdom is made up only of organisms that have no cell walls?
   A. animals   **C.** fungi
   B. bacteria   **D.** plants

Links

Writing

Descriptive Writing

Write a humorous **description** of what it would be like to carry out your activities if you did not have a backbone. What problems would you face? What benefits would you enjoy?

Math

Compute Percents

Use the data in the Interpret Data feature to calculate the percent of Earth's total number of animal species each group represents.

Health

Fungus Pharmacy

Use library or Internet resources to learn how the antibiotic penicillin was discovered. Write a short report to share your findings with the class. Put the report in the media center as a part of a display.

 For more links and activities, go to www.hspscience.com

How Do Scientists Name Organisms?

Fast Fact

Run for Your Life! The largest alligator ever recorded was found in Louisiana and was 5.38 m (19 ft 2 in.) long. An alligator can run as fast as 38 km/hr (23 mi/hr) for short distances. How do you think scientists can tell this animal apart from other similar animals like crocodiles and caimans? In the Investigate, you will use a classification key.

How to Use a Classification Key

Materials
- bean classification system from Lesson I Investigate
- bag of mixed beans
- paper and pencil

Procedure

1. Use the classification system you developed in the Investigate on page 75. Look closely at the characteristics you used to group the beans.

2. Look at the table you made and at the names of the groups you identified. Another name for the table is a key. Take a few beans from the bag and try to use your key to place the beans.

3. Give your bean classification key to several classmates. They should take a few beans from the bag, and use your key to identify the beans and place them into groups.

4. Use a classmate's key, and try to identify a few beans, using his or her key.

Draw Conclusions

1. Compare your key with those of classmates. How were the keys similar? How were they different? Were some keys easier to use than others? Explain your answer.

2. Why might a key be more useful than a set of pictures of organisms?

3. **Inquiry Skill** When scientists classify organisms, they gather and record data carefully and precisely. Why might scientists want to avoid using terms such as *small*, *big*, *heavy*, and *light* in a key?

Step 1

Step 2

Investigate Further

Choose another group of objects or organisms. Develop a classification key to help people identify the objects or organisms.

Reading in Science

VOCABULARY
genus p. 91
species p. 91

SCIENCE CONCEPTS
▶ how organisms are grouped into levels
▶ what information is provided by a two-part scientific name
▶ how a dichotomous key works

READING FOCUS SKILL
MAIN IDEA AND DETAILS Look for details about how living things are classified.

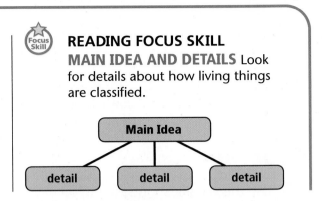

Grouping and Naming Organisms

Suppose you need some nonfiction books for a report. In your school library, you will find that the books are arranged in the same way they are arranged in your town's public library. Most public and school libraries classify books in the same way. They use a system that classifies nonfiction books by topic into ten major categories. Each major category is divided into nine smaller groups, or subcategories. Each subcategory is broken down into nine even smaller groups of specialized topics. By using the same system of classification, libraries make it easier for people to locate books in any library.

In the past, scientists in different parts of the world had trouble communicating about the organisms they were studying. They called the organisms by different names in their different languages. This made it difficult for them to work together.

Scientists use the Latin name *Giraffa camelopardalis* for the giraffe. The genus name is *Giraffa*, and the species name is *camelopardalis*.

Animal Phyla

Number of Species in Some Phyla of the Animal Kingdom		
Number	**Phylum**	**Includes**
1,000,000	Arthropoda	insects, spiders, crabs
50,000	Mollusca	oysters, snails, squid
43,000	Chordata	fish, mammals, birds
9000	Annelida	earthworms, leeches
6000	Echinodermata	starfish, sea urchins

The classification system von Linné designed took care of this problem. He grouped all organisms into several levels, to which he gave Latin names. Latin is a language that all scientists understand. Scientists now use a total of seven levels to classify animals. A group on one level is made up of smaller, related groups on the level below it. The highest level is *kingdom*. The two lowest levels are *genus* and *species*. A **genus** is a group of organisms that share major characteristics and, therefore, are closely related. A **species** is a single kind of organism, defined by the fact that it can reproduce among its own kind.

Species is the most precise classification category. The way an organism is classified determines its scientific name. The first part of an organism's name tells its genus. For example, cats that purr are part of the genus *Felis*, which is Latin for "cat." A genus name begins with a capital letter and is either underlined or written in italics.

The second part of an organism's name tells its species. The house cat is *Felis domesticus*, and the mountain lion is *Felis concolor*. A species name begins with a lowercase letter and is underlined or written in italics.

When scientists use two-part scientific names, they can be sure that they are referring to the same organism when they talk or write about it. The names also provide information about how organisms are related to one another.

 MAIN IDEA AND DETAILS What does an organism's scientific name tell about it?

Seven Levels of Classification

Using the Linnaean System

Living things are classified into seven levels. At each level, all organisms share particular characteristics. The table on these pages shows the classification of *Felis domesticus,* the common house cat. As you can see from the table, members of a group at a lower level of classification resemble each other in more ways than members of a group at a higher level do.

Members of a species share at least one characteristic that no other animals have. For example, *Felis domesticus,* the house cat, is different from *Felis pardalis*, the ocelot, because it is smaller and can't run as fast. All members of the house cat species can mate with one another and have live offspring of the same species. There are estimated to be about 100 million house cats in the Western

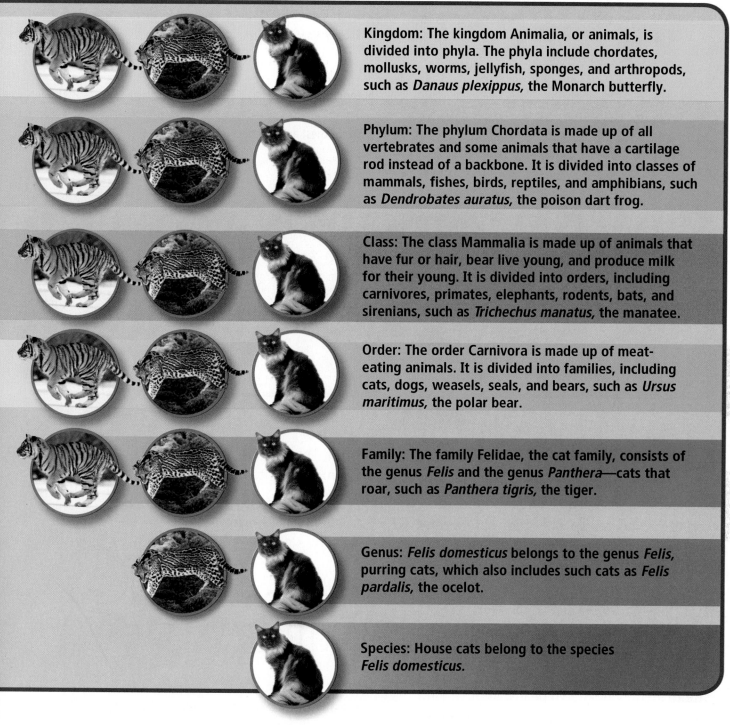

Kingdom: The kingdom Animalia, or animals, is divided into phyla. The phyla include chordates, mollusks, worms, jellyfish, sponges, and arthropods, such as *Danaus plexippus,* the Monarch butterfly.

Phylum: The phylum Chordata is made up of all vertebrates and some animals that have a cartilage rod instead of a backbone. It is divided into classes of mammals, fishes, birds, reptiles, and amphibians, such as *Dendrobates auratus,* the poison dart frog.

Class: The class Mammalia is made up of animals that have fur or hair, bear live young, and produce milk for their young. It is divided into orders, including carnivores, primates, elephants, rodents, bats, and sirenians, such as *Trichechus manatus,* the manatee.

Order: The order Carnivora is made up of meat-eating animals. It is divided into families, including cats, dogs, weasels, seals, and bears, such as *Ursus maritimus,* the polar bear.

Family: The family Felidae, the cat family, consists of the genus *Felis* and the genus *Panthera*—cats that roar, such as *Panthera tigris,* the tiger.

Genus: *Felis domesticus* belongs to the genus *Felis,* purring cats, which also includes such cats as *Felis pardalis,* the ocelot.

Species: House cats belong to the species *Felis domesticus.*

world and over a hundred recognized breeds of domesticated cats.

The way an organism is classified gives a lot of information. The group it belongs to at each level tells some of the characteristics of the organism. For example, the house cat belongs to the class Mammalia, so you know that it has fur, bears live young, and feeds its young with milk. It belongs to the order Carnivora, so you know that it eats meat. The fact that the house cat is a member of the family Felidae tells you that it shares some characteristics with the tiger and the ocelot.

 MAIN IDEA AND DETAILS Are all mammals carnivores? How do you know?

1a. Long yellow legs . . . . Go to **2**

1b. Short yellow legs . . . . Green heron,
Butorides virescens

2a. Long, pointed bill . . . . Go to **3**

2b. Long thick bill . . . . Great blue heron,
Ardea herodias

3a. White chest and rust neck . . Tricolor heron,
Egretta tricolor

Using a Key

Have you ever walked along the beach and discovered the shell of an animal you did not recognize? Even people who study nature can't identify every living thing they find. When people go hiking or camping, they often carry guides that help them identify species of living things they may come across. One type of guide is a field guide—a book with pictures or photographs of local animals or plants.

In the Investigate, you used a key you had made to identify unknown beans. Another kind of key is called a *dichotomous key. Dichotomous* means "divided into two parts." A dichotomous key is made up of choices that guide you to the correct name of the item or organism you want to identify. Each step of the key provides a pair of phrases that describe two possible sets of characteristics. Only one of the phrases applies to the object or organism you are identifying. That choice directs you to another pair of

phrases. The process continues until you reach the name of the item or organism.

MAIN IDEA AND DETAILS How do dichotomous keys work?

Use a Key

Look at the dichotomous key at the top of the page. It will help you to identify the photos of the three herons. Choose one of the birds. Look at the first set of characteristics, and follow the directions that apply to the bird you are identifying. Continue the process until you reach the name of the heron you are trying to identify. Repeat the process with the others.

1. MAIN IDEA AND DETAILS Draw and complete this graphic organizer.

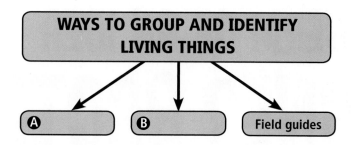

WAYS TO GROUP AND IDENTIFY LIVING THINGS

Ⓐ   Ⓑ   Field guides

2. SUMMARIZE Use the graphic organizer to describe how organisms can be identified.

3. DRAW CONCLUSIONS Why do scientists use scientific names for organisms?

4. VOCABULARY Write your own definition for each vocabulary term.

Test Prep

5. Critical Thinking What does the classification of the cat tell you about how it meets its energy needs?

6. Which is the correct way to write the scientific name for a gray wolf?

A. Canis lupus   **C.** *Canis lupus*

B. *canis lupus*   **D.** *canis Lupus*

Links

Writing

Expressive Writing

Write a **poem** you can use as a mnemonic to help you remember the order of the seven levels of classification of living things. Your poem can be a nonsense sentence, but each line should begin with the initial letter of the level.

Math

Use a Calculator

Some scientists estimate that 137 species become extinct every day. At this rate, how many species become extinct in 1 year?

Social Studies

Discover Species Habitats

A species name often indicates where an organism lives. Use library or Internet sources to learn some species names of this type. List the scientific names you find and the habitats of the organisms.

 For more links and activities, go to **www.hspscience.com**

GERM OF AN IDEA
DESIGNER BACTERIA

How cool would it be to never wash your smelly gym socks again? Imagine never having to throw out your favorite sneakers or clean your favorite shirt.

A professor at a university in Massachusetts says he is close to producing the first fabric that never has to be cleaned. The material is called a "bio-active fabric."

Filled with Bacteria

Alex Fowler and other scientists are developing the bio-active fabric by infusing it with dirt-eating bacteria, tiny one-celled living things. Fowler says he is using *Escherichia coli,* a common bacterium that already exists in the human intestines.

Fowler is experimenting with ways of injecting the bacteria into cotton and milkweed fibers. Those fibers can then be woven into clothing. The bacteria will eat any stains or dirt that land on the fabric.

Fowler says that bio-active fabric can fight dirt up to a certain point. If a bio-active fabric fell in a puddle of mud, for example, the bacteria wouldn't magically clean off the mud. However, the material would fight small food stains and sweat stains and odors effectively, says Fowler. For a person who wears business suits all the time, that might result in a significant drop in dry-cleaning bills.

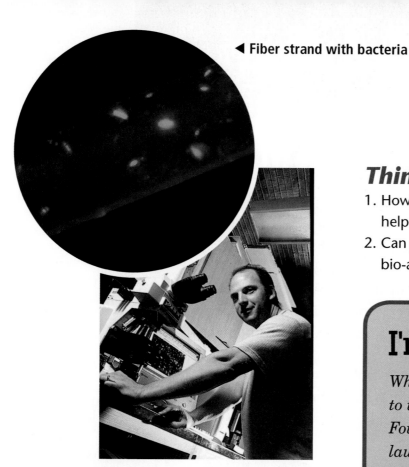

◀ Fiber strand with bacteria

▲ Scientist observing fiber strand

Many Uses

Fowler anticipates that the development of such a fabric might mean the formation of the first self-cleaning fashion line. "A sneaker that actually is guaranteed odor-free for a lifetime would be a hugely marketable thing," Fowler said.

In addition to self-cleaning clothes, Fowler's research might lead to other types of fabric. In medicine, doctors might someday apply bandages that administer life-saving drugs to wounds. And in the military, soldiers could soon be wearing uniforms that contain substances that can detect deadly chemical weapons. Although bio-active fabrics may not be ready for the market just yet, shoe and textile companies are interested in developing the technology.

Think About It

1. How might self-cleaning clothes help protect the environment?
2. Can you think of other uses for bio-active materials?

I'm Glad You Asked

What happens when a person has to wash a bio-active garment? Fowler says a special kind of laundry detergent would be needed. One company has already expressed interest in producing such a detergent. Not only would the detergent clean the fabric, but it would also feed the bacteria living in the fabric.

Find out more! Log on to **www.hspscience.com**

Professor Longlegs

Gonzalo Giribet gets excited over daddy longlegs, but not the garden variety kind. This biologist searches the world for daddy longlegs that are barely visible.

Giribet has collected more than 160 species, or types, of the creepy-crawly creatures. Giribet wants to identify more species of daddy longlegs from the group of spiders called Cyphophthalmi (sy•FOH•thal•mee).

Giribet, 32, and an assistant recently went on a six-week trip to New Zealand and Australia. He expects his research to increase the number of known species to about 240.

Career   Zoologist

Imagine hiking through the woods near your house. Suddenly you see a weird-looking worm that glows. You can tell it's a worm, but what kind of worm? To help you figure that out you might call a zoologist. Zoologists are biologists who specialize in the study of animals. They study the origin, behavior, diseases, life processes, and interactions of animals. There are many branches of zoology.

Quick and Easy Project

Materials
- 5 or 6 kinds of uncooked pasta

Identifying Pasta

Procedure

1. Begin a key by writing these statements:
   - 1a. The pasta is tube-shaped.   Go to 2.
   - 1b. The pasta is not tube-shaped.   Go to 3.
2. Sort your pasta into two piles—one for tube-shaped and one for not tube-shaped.
3. Add this pair of statements to your key:
   - 2a. The tube is straight.
   - 2b. The tube is not straight.
4. Continue to divide the pasta into pairs of groups to complete your key.

Draw Conclusions

Why do the statements in a pair of choices need to be opposites? How do the choices help you identify unknown pieces of pasta?

Design Your Own Investigation

Dichotomous Key

Dichotomous keys help people identify items based on the physical characteristics of the items. Choose another type of object, such as marbles or rocks, and make up another dichotomous key. Divide your objects into pairs of groups. Ask a classmate or family member to test your key and suggest improvements. Revise your key, if needed.

Review and Test Preparation

Vocabulary Review

Use the terms below to complete the sentences. The page numbers tell you where to look in the chapter if you need help.

classification p. 76   **protist** p. 85
adaptation p. 82   **genus** p. 91
fungus p. 84   **species** p. 91

1. The first part of an organism's scientific name is the _____ .

2. A microscopic organism that can be animal-like, plantlike, or funguslike is a _____ .

3. The smallest category in the classification of living things is _____ .

4. The arrangement of things into groups of similar items is called _____ .

5. A mushroom is an example of a _____ .

6. A feature that helps an organism survive in its surroundings is an _____ .

Check Understanding

Write the letter of the best choice.

7. **MAIN IDEA AND DETAILS** Which of the following is a protist?
   A. amoeba
   B. daffodil
   C. mushroom
   D. zebra

8. **COMPARE AND CONTRAST** How is a fungus different from a plant?
   F. A fungus may make people ill.
   G. A fungus may have many cells.
   H. A fungus does not make its own food.
   J. A fungus does not have cell walls.

9. How would the organism shown below be classifed?
   A. animal
   B. bacteria
   C. fungus
   D. protist

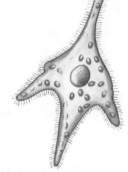

10. Which is the correct way to write the scientific name for the red fox?
    F. Vulpes vulpes
    G. *vulpes vulpes*
    H. *Vulpes vulpes*
    J. *vulpes Vulpes*

11. Which structures do bacteria lack?
    A. cell walls
    B. cell membranes
    C. DNA
    D. nuclei

12. Wolves and dogs belong to the same genus. Which other levels do they share?
    F. kingdom, phylum, class, order, family
    G. phylum, class, order, family, species
    H. family and species
    J. species only

13. Why do scientists use scientific names to refer to specific organisms?
    A. to describe physical characteristics
    B. to identify them easily
    C. to use a dichotomous key
    D. to describe their adaptations

14. How are organisms in a species different from others in their genus?

F. Organisms in a genus and species do not share the same family.

G. Organisms in the species have the same traits as the organisms in the genus.

H. Organisms in the species are less like one another than organisms in the genus.

J. Organisms in a species have characteristics that differ from those of other organisms in their genus.

15. What is an organism's scientific name made up of?

A. genus and species

B. kingdom and phylum

C. kingdom and species

D. order and class

16. Which is the highest level of classification?

F. genus

G. kingdom

H. phylum

J. species

Inquiry Skills

17. Use the dichotomous key to classify the beans shown.

Dichotomous Key

❶ a. Bean is round . . . . Garbanzo beans
b. Bean is kidney-shaped or oval . . . . go to 2

❷ a. Bean is white . . . . White Northern
b. Bean is dark-colored . . . . go to 3

❸ a. Bean is spotted . . . . Pinto beans
b. Bean is evenly colored . . . . go to 4

❹ a. Bean is black . . . . Black beans
b. Bean is reddish brown . . . . Kidney beans

18. Common names of organisms often vary with location. For example, a particular kind of bird is called a buzzard in one part of the United States and a vulture in another part. Hypothesize about what might happen if scientists used only common names of organisms when sharing information.

Critical Thinking

19. How do you use classification in your everyday life?

20. The two smallest levels in the system that is used to classify organisms are genus and species.

PART A Can two species be members of the same family but not of the same genus? Explain.

PART B Can two species be members of the same genus but not of the same family? Explain.

Chapter 3

Plants and Plant Growth

Lesson 1 How Do Plants Meet Their Needs?

Lesson 2 How Do Plants Respond to Their Environment?

Lesson 3 What Are Some Types of Plants?

Lesson 4 How Do Angiosperms Reproduce?

Vocabulary

vascular plant
xylem
phloem
nonvascular plant
tropism
phototropism
gravitropism
moss
asexual reproduction
spore
fern
gymnosperm
conifer
angiosperm
pollination
fruit

What do YOU wonder?

This orchid belongs to the largest family in the plant kingdom. There are more than 20,000 species of orchids. Prized for their beauty, these flowers also can have good-tasting parts! Vanilla flavoring comes from pods of the orchid *Vanillae planifolia*. Where do you think orchids grow? What conditions does an orchid need in order to grow?

How Do Plants Meet Their Needs?

Fast Fact

Sprouting Seeds Like most plants, cacti grow from seeds. Cactus seeds have adaptations that allow them to grow in harsh desert climates. During hot, dry periods, the seeds are dormant, or inactive. When it rains, a protein in the seed attracts water, improving the chance that the seed will grow into a new plant. In the Investigate, you will observe how seeds of other plants germinate.

Germinating Seeds

Materials
- **5 clear plastic cups**
- **water**
- **masking tape**
- **permanent marker**
- **20 bean seeds**
- **shoe box with lid**
- **paper towels**
- **measuring cup**

Procedure

1 Line each cup with a folded paper towel. Then fill the cups with crumpled paper towels.

2 Between the paper lining and the side of each cup, place four bean seeds.

3 Use masking tape and a marker to label the cups A, B, C, D, and E. For each cup, follow the directions next to its letter.

> **A.** Drip water into the cup until the towels are moist. Place the cup in the shoe box. Close the lid. Add water daily as needed to keep the towels moist.
>
> **B.** Fill the cup with water.
>
> **C.** Add *no* water.
>
> **D.** Moisten the towels as for A. Keep them moist.
>
> **E.** Moisten the towels as for A. Keep them moist.

4 Place cups A, B, C, and D in a warm place (not in direct sunlight). Place cup E in a refrigerator. Observe the cups daily. Record your observations.

Draw Conclusions

1. In which cups did you observe the seeds sprouting? In which were they sprouting the best?

2. **Inquiry Skills** From your observations, draw conclusions about what seeds need in order to germinate, or begin to grow.

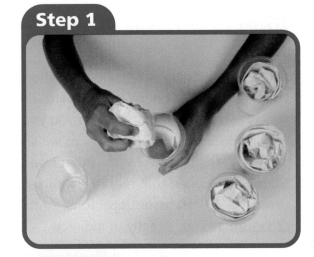

Step 1

Step 3

Investigate Further

You controlled a number of variables in this investigation. What variables did you test? Choose one variable, and design a simple investigation to test it.

Reading in Science

VOCABULARY
vascular plant p. 108
xylem p. 108
phloem p. 108
nonvascular plant p. 110

SCIENCE CONCEPTS
▶ what the needs of plants are
▶ how plants make and store food

READING FOCUS SKILL
MAIN IDEA AND DETAILS Look for ways plants meet their needs.

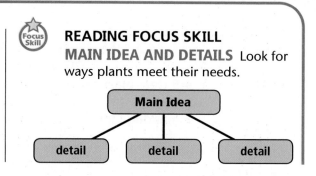

How Plants Meet Their Needs

Look around you. You see plants wherever you look—in your house, in your yard, on the way to school, in so many places. Do you realize that life on Earth could not exist as we know it if there were no plants? Why is that true? Plants supply the oxygen that most organisms need to stay alive. They also supply food for many organisms, either directly or indirectly.

Plants grow almost everywhere on Earth, from arid deserts to the marshy Everglades to the Arctic Circle. In the Investigate, you found that seeds need certain conditions in order to germinate. How, then, do seeds in harsh climates sprout and their seedlings grow? The answer is that they are *adapted* to get what they need from their surroundings. To be adapted means that the species has changed over time to be suited to where it lives.

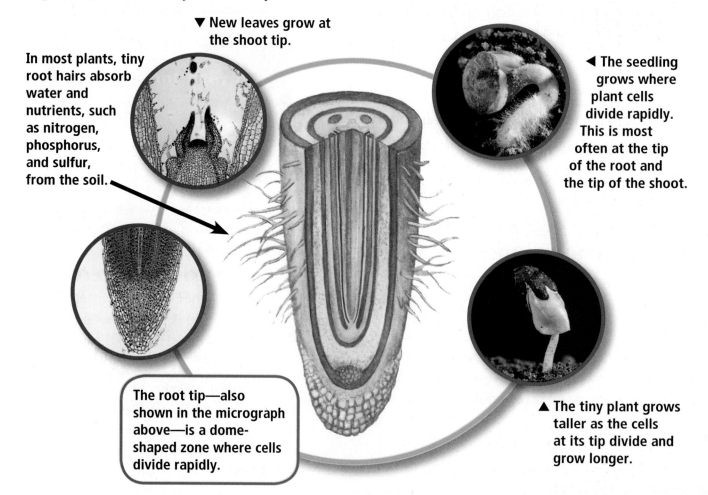

▼ New leaves grow at the shoot tip.

In most plants, tiny root hairs absorb water and nutrients, such as nitrogen, phosphorus, and sulfur, from the soil.

◀ The seedling grows where plant cells divide rapidly. This is most often at the tip of the root and the tip of the shoot.

The root tip—also shown in the micrograph above—is a dome-shaped zone where cells divide rapidly.

▲ The tiny plant grows taller as the cells at its tip divide and grow longer.

Photosynthesis

Plant cells contain chloroplasts. These structures are green because they contain the pigment chlorophyll.

Chlorophyll captures the sun's energy, which is used to combine carbon dioxide and water to make sugar. Plant cells use sugar for energy to carry out their life processes.

Photosynthesis Formula

carbon dioxide + water	sunlight + chlorophyll	sugar + oxygen

$$6CO_2 + 6H_2O \longrightarrow C_6H_{12}O_6 + 6O_2$$

Gases, such as carbon dioxide and oxygen, can enter and leave the leaf through pores called *stomata*. During a process called *transpiration*, water, too, is released through the stomata.

Seeds need water and air to germinate. When the conditions are right, the seed absorbs water. The seed coat swells and splits open, and the tiny seedling inside emerges. A little root begins to grow downward, and a shoot begins to grow upward. This growth takes place at the tips of the root and shoot. In some plants, branches may grow from side buds as well. As with the roots and shoots, the tips of the side branches grow. The branches produce leaves and more side buds, from which new branches grow.

The new plant needs five things to stay healthy—water, light, carbon dioxide, oxygen, and nutrients. These materials are used to carry out all the life processes that take place in the plant's cells.

Plants are among the living things that make their own food by photosynthesis. This process requires water, carbon dioxide, and sunlight.

Water is absorbed from the soil by the roots. Carbon dioxide enters the plant through tiny openings, or pores, in the leaves. Sunlight is also taken in by the leaves. The green pigment *chlorophyll,* found in the leaves' chloroplasts, captures the sun's energy. This energy is then used to change carbon dioxide and water to sugar and oxygen. The sugar (glucose) is stored in the plant, and oxygen is released into the air.

Once the sugar is made, plants can use some of the oxygen to release the chemical energy that is stored in the sugar. In a process called *respiration,* oxygen combines with the sugar to produce energy, carbon dioxide, and water. The energy is used to carry out life processes within the plant cells.

MAIN IDEA AND DETAILS How do plants get the materials they need?

Vascular Plants

All of the cells in a plant have the same basic needs. They need water, nutrients, and food. The water and nutrients absorbed by a plant's roots are carried throughout the plant. The food, in the form of sugar, made in the plant's leaves is delivered to each cell, too. In many plants, these materials are transported by specialized tissues. Plants that have transport tissues for carrying water, nutrients, and sugar to plant cells are called **vascular plants.** The tree shown on these pages is a vascular plant.

Because they have transport tissues, many vascular plants can become very large. The transport tissues form a system of tubes that extends from the roots to all parts of the plant. These tubes are made up of two kinds of tissue.

Xylem tissue carries water and nutrients from the roots to the leaves. **Phloem** tissue carries sugar from the leaves to other cells of the plants. Sugar that is not immediately needed for energy is stored in different parts of the plant.

What causes water to move through xylem tissue? You can model the process of water and nutrient transport by sipping water through a straw. The straw represents the xylem. The movement of water into your mouth represents the loss of water from the plant by transpiration.

In a vascular plant, transpiration causes negative pressure—or suction—that draws water upward through xylem. Put very simply, transpiration pulls water and minerals upward through the plant.

Xylem tissue forms continuous, hollow tubes. These tubes reach from the roots all the way up the trunk and through the branches to the leaves.

Some plants, like the trees shown here, have woody stems that grow thicker each year as new xylem and phloem form. The rings of xylem at the center are the oldest. These tubes no longer carry water, but their strong walls continue to support the tree.

How does sugar move through phloem? Positive pressure is responsible for the flow of materials in phloem. When a solution is more concentrated in one area, water flows into the area and dilutes it. The sugar solution in phloem is concentrated. It draws water from neighboring xylem into the phloem. The added water increases pressure, causing the sugar in the phloem to move through adjoining cells toward areas where it is needed.

Some of the sugar is stored. Much of the sugar moves through the phloem to the root tips and stem buds. There it provides the energy for cell division and growth.

 MAIN IDEA AND DETAILS What causes the movement of materials through xylem and phloem?

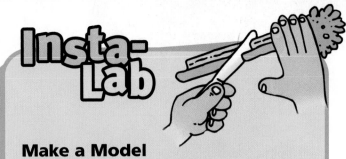

Insta-Lab

Make a Model
Use a plastic knife to trim the end from a stalk of celery. Examine the cut ends of the celery. Use a hand lens to identify the xylem and phloem. Draw a diagram to show the vascular tissues. Label the parts of the diagram and the materials they transport.

From the roots, water and nutrients move upward through the xylem. ▶

◀ Phloem carries sugar made in the leaves to all parts of the plant. Some of the sugar is converted to the energy needed for life processes. The rest is stored.

109

Some moss plants can grow by vegetative, or asexual, reproduction. When a leaf is broken off, a whole new plant can grow from it.

If you carefully observe this plant, you can see parts that look like capsules on stalks. These form after male cells fertilize female cells. When conditions are right, the capsules open and a fine dust of spores is released.

Nonvascular Plants

Some plants, such as mosses, liverworts, and hornworts do not have xylem and phloem tissues. Plants that lack tissues that transport water, nutrients, and sugar are called **nonvascular plants**.

Nonvascular plants are different from vascular plants in several ways. Because they do not have tissues to carry the materials that cells need to stay healthy, they don't grow very large. These plants don't have true roots to absorb water. Instead, each cell absorbs the water and nutrients it needs directly from the soil or air. Because they live very close together, the cells of these plants may also get materials they need from neighboring plant cells.

Nonvascular plants are anchored in the soil by long cells that look like roots. These structures are called rhizoids.

Many nonvascular plants thrive in moist, shady places such as forests and swamps. There, they can get enough water to meet their needs. These plants require water for sexual reproduction. The male sex cells must swim through water to get to the female sex cell to fertilize it.

Nonvascular plants have structures that function like leaves, stems, and roots, but they are less complex than those in vascular plants. Like vascular plants, the leaflike parts of mosses and liverworts contain chlorophyll and produce food for the plant.

 MAIN IDEA AND DETAILS Why do nonvascular plants remain small?

110

1. MAIN IDEA AND DETAILS Draw and complete this graphic organizer.

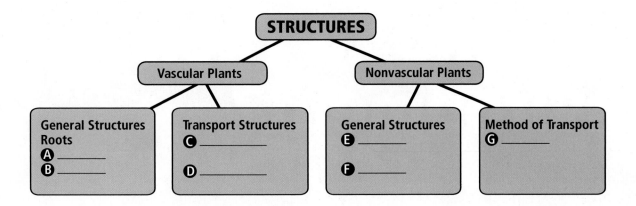

STRUCTURES

Vascular Plants

Nonvascular Plants

General Structures Roots
Ⓐ _____
Ⓑ _____

Transport Structures
Ⓒ _____
Ⓓ _____

General Structures
Ⓔ _____
Ⓕ _____

Method of Transport
Ⓖ _____

2. SUMMARIZE Use the information in the graphic organizer to describe the differences between vascular plants and nonvascular plants.

3. DRAW CONCLUSIONS Why is photosynthesis important to animals?

4. VOCABULARY Write a short paragraph that uses each of the vocabulary words in this lesson.

Test Prep

5. Critical Thinking Compare the steps in photosynthesis with the steps that take place when plants use sugar for energy.

6. Which part of a tree makes food for the whole plant?

   A. leaves   **C.** roots

   B. phloem   **D.** xylem

Links

Writing

Descriptive Writing

A *travelogue* is a description of a person's travels. Write a **fantasy travelogue** to describe the travels of sugar through phloem. Be creative! Describe the places the sugar visits and what it sees and does in each place.

Math

Calculate Percentages

Germination rate tells the percent of seeds that sprout. If 75 out of 100 seeds sprout, the germination rate is 75 percent. Calculate the following rates as percents: 10 out of 25; 28 out of 50; 36 out of 50; and 64 out of 100.

Social Studies

Research

Peat moss is an important energy source in many parts of the world. Use Internet resources to learn about peat moss and its importance in nineteenth-century Scotland. Share your findings with the class.

 For more links and activities, go to www.hspscience.com

How Do Plants Respond to Their Environment?

Fast Fact

Climbing High These wisteria vines have tendrils that wrap around a support, allowing them to climb. Among wisteria plants, one group of them twines from right to left, and another group twines from left to right. In this Investigate, you will explore another growth response in plants.

Do All Roots Grow Downward?

Materials
- **paper towels**
- **sprouted bean seed**
- **clear plastic cup**
- **water**

Procedure

1. Fold a paper towel so that its width is the same as the height of the cup. Line the cup with the towel. Fill the cup with crumpled paper towels.

2. Drip water onto the towels until they are just moist. For the rest of the investigation, check the towels daily, and keep them moist.

3. Carefully place the sprouted bean seed between the paper towel liner and the side of the cup. The root should be pointing down.

4. Put the cup in a place that is dark all the time.

5. After two days, observe the seedling's root. Record your observations. Then turn the cup on its side. Hypothesize how this change might affect the growth of the root. Observe the seedling again after another two days.

Step 3

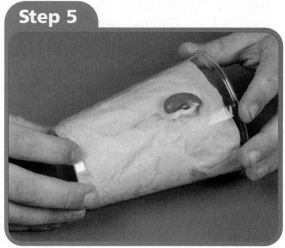

Step 5

Draw Conclusions

1. What happened to the seedling's root after you turned the cup on its side?

2. What was your hypothesis in Step 5? Did the growth of the root support or disprove your hypothesis?

3. **Inquiry Skills** Based on your observations, what can you conclude about the direction of root growth?

Investigate Further

What might happen to the direction of growth of the shoot and root if you put the seedling in the cup in a different position? Form a hypothesis for this question, and then test it.

Reading in Science

VOCABULARY
tropism p. 114
phototropism p. 114
gravitropism p. 114

SCIENCE CONCEPTS
▶ how plants respond to certain conditions
▶ how plant responses help them meet their needs

 READING FOCUS SKILL
CAUSE AND EFFECT Look for what causes plants to respond to certain conditions the way they do.

cause ──▶ effect

How Plants Respond to the Environment

Have you ever seen a field of sunflowers with all their "faces" turned toward the sun? If you were to watch the sunflowers all day, you would see their flowerheads move as the direction of the sunlight striking them moved. You would observe that the flowers always face the sun, no matter where it is in the sky.

A growth response of a plant toward or away from anything in its environment is called a **tropism**. The word *tropism* comes from a Greek word that means "to turn."

The directional growth response of plants to light is called **phototropism**. In 1880, Charles Darwin and his son Francis were the first to show that the tip of a plant shoot senses light. The tip produces chemicals that cause cells on the "dark" side to grow faster. This causes the plant to bend toward the light. This is called *positive phototropism.* In the Investigate, you observed another type of tropism. You saw **gravitropism**, the response of a plant to gravity. The roots of your tiny bean plant showed *positive gravitropism.* They grew in the direction of the pull of gravity. In nature, this tropism guides plant roots to grow down into the soil, where they can absorb water and nutrients. The shoot of the seedling showed *negative gravitropism,* growing away from the pull of gravity. This tropism guides plant shoots to grow up through the soil to where they can get sunlight.

Some plants respond to touch. For example, peas, pumpkins, and morning glories have sensitive, threadlike tendrils. The tendrils grow toward the side of the plant that is touched. The tendrils help support the plant by growing around objects that touch them.

Plant Responses

The stem of this plant is bending toward the sun. Sunflowers exhibit solar tracking. They follow the sun.

A plant's growth response to touch is called *thigmotropism*.

Roots respond to touch, too, but their response is negative. They grow *away* from things that touch them.

Tropisms help plants get what they need from the environment. In the Arctic region, the flowers of some plant species "track" the sun, as sunflowers do. This is called *solar tracking*. In many of these species, facing the sun increases the amount of energy the plants can absorb. It also keeps the flowers warm so that insects, attracted by heat, pollinate them.

 CAUSE AND EFFECT What causes tropisms in plants?

Touchy Plants

Line a clear cup with a moist paper towel. Place four morning glory seeds between the cup and the towel. Put the cup in a warm, well-lighted place, and keep the towel moist. After the seeds sprout (in two to three weeks), tape four pencils to the outside of the cup. How do the plants respond? What causes this response?

On Earth, roots grow down in response to the pull of gravity, and shoots grow upward, away from the pull of gravity.

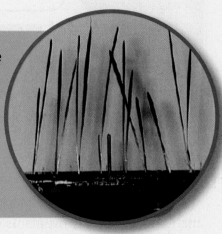

In space, the force of gravity is much less than it is on Earth.

The mimosa is a tree with delicate green leaves and pink flowers.

When touched, the leaves of the mimosa immediately fold together. Because of its response to touch, it is often called the "sensitive plant."

115

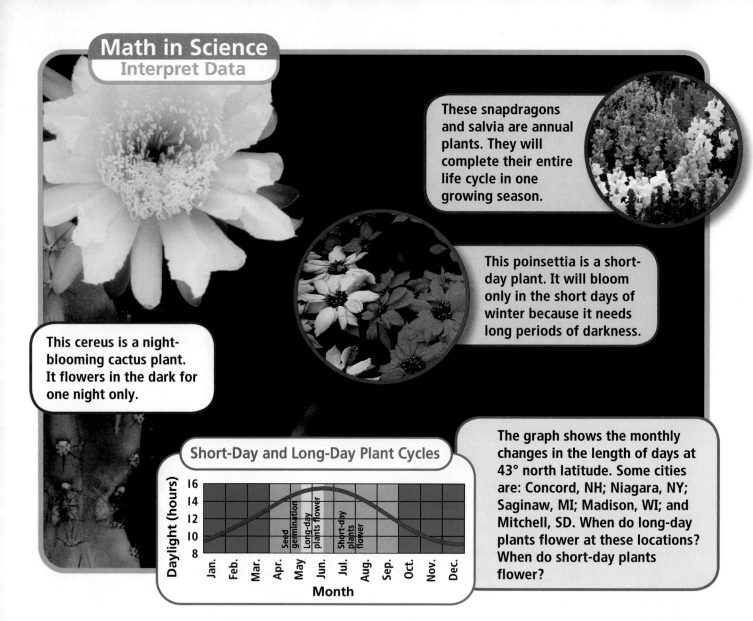

These snapdragons and salvia are annual plants. They will complete their entire life cycle in one growing season.

This poinsettia is a short-day plant. It will bloom only in the short days of winter because it needs long periods of darkness.

This cereus is a night-blooming cactus plant. It flowers in the dark for one night only.

Short-Day and Long-Day Plant Cycles

The graph shows the monthly changes in the length of days at 43° north latitude. Some cities are: Concord, NH; Niagara, NY; Saginaw, MI; Madison, WI; and Mitchell, SD. When do long-day plants flower at these locations? When do short-day plants flower?

Plant Rhythms

To survive, plants must adapt to the changing seasons. Most plants grow when it is warm and die or become inactive—*dormant*—when it is cold. To do this, plants must respond to changes in temperature. Many plants respond to changes in the length of the day.

Long-day plants flower when there are more than a certain number of daylight hours. Even though they are called long-*day* plants, it is really the amount of darkness that determines when the plants bloom. Long-day plants are really *short-night* plants!

Sunflowers, snapdragons, and begonias are long-day plants—they bloom in late spring or early summer, when nights are shortest.

Short-day plants flower when there are fewer than a certain number of daylight hours. They need long periods of darkness in order to bloom. Therefore, they are really long-night plants. Poinsettias, strawberries, and ragweed are short-day plants.

Some plants germinate, flower, make seeds, and die within one growing season. These plants, called *annual plants,* include impatiens, begonias, and marigolds.

Other plants return year after year. They are called *perennial plants*. They include Florida paintbrush, honeysuckle, and other woody plants. Trees, of course, live for many years.

 CAUSE AND EFFECT What causes plants to be either short-day or long-day bloomers?

1. CAUSE AND EFFECT Draw and complete this graphic organizer.

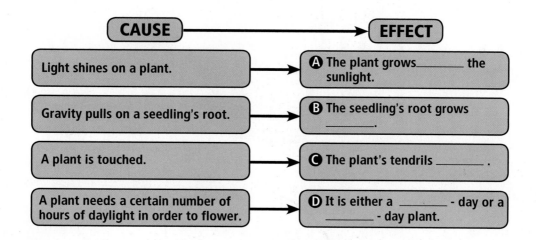

CAUSE → **EFFECT**

CAUSE	EFFECT
Light shines on a plant.	**A** The plant grows_____ the sunlight.
Gravity pulls on a seedling's root.	**B** The seedling's root grows _____.
A plant is touched.	**C** The plant's tendrils _____.
A plant needs a certain number of hours of daylight in order to flower.	**D** It is either a _____ - day or a _____ - day plant.

2. SUMMARIZE Use the graphic organizer to summarize the ways plants respond to their environment.

3. DRAW CONCLUSIONS In Darwin's experiments, uncovered shoots grew toward light, while covered shoots did not. What can you conclude from this?

4. VOCABULARY Define each of the vocabulary words.

Test Prep

5. Critical Thinking In a phototropism experiment, which **variable(s)** would you **control**? Which would you test?

6. If roots grow toward leaking underground pipes, what might the plant be showing a tropism toward?

A. light **C.** touch

B. minerals **D.** water

Links

Writing

Expository Writing
Write and illustrate a **pamphlet** to explain what plant tropisms are. Your audience is third-grade students. Include the tropisms in this lesson plus others you find in research sources.

Math

Day:Night Ratio
A cocklebur plant flowers when there are at least 16 hours of daylight. What is the ratio of day to night, expressed in the simplest form, that the cocklebur needs to bloom?

Art

My Garden
Use library or Internet resources to research the types of plants that grow well in your area. Plan a garden that will flower from early spring to late fall. Use the information about tropisms and plant behaviors to guide you. Make a layout diagram.

 For more links and activities, go to **www.hspscience.com**

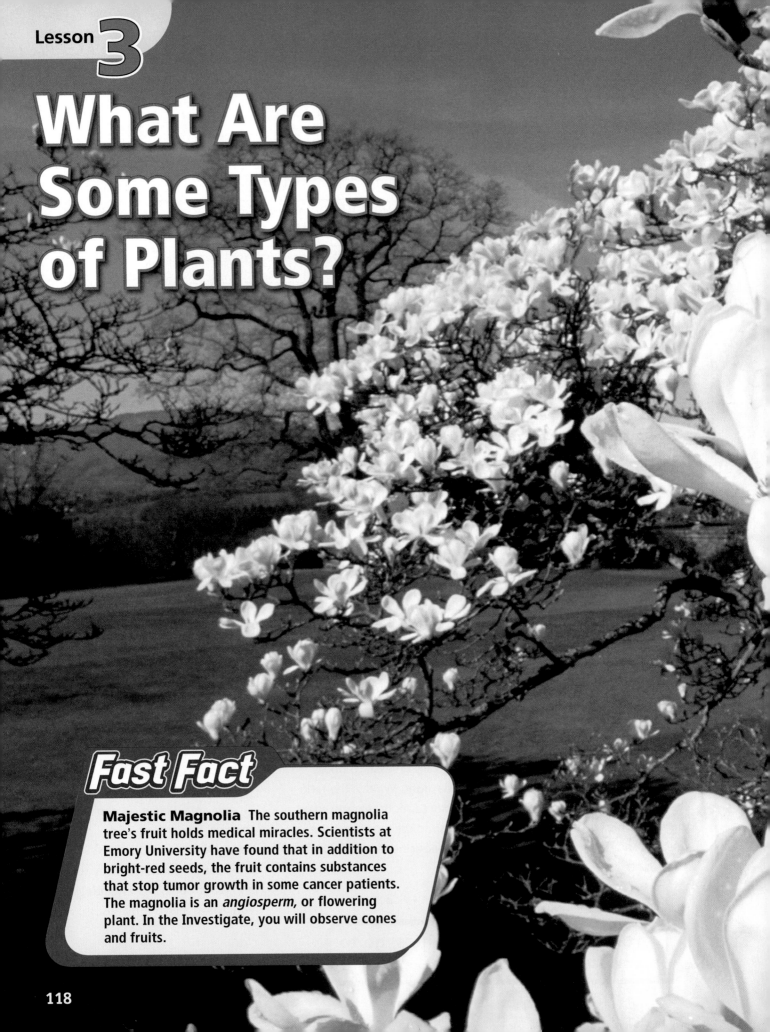

What Are Some Types of Plants?

Fast Fact

Majestic Magnolia The southern magnolia tree's fruit holds medical miracles. Scientists at Emory University have found that in addition to bright-red seeds, the fruit contains substances that stop tumor growth in some cancer patients. The magnolia is an *angiosperm,* or flowering plant. In the Investigate, you will observe cones and fruits.

Comparing Cones and Fruits

Materials
- lemon leaves
- lemon fruit half
- conifer needles
- conifer cone
- hand lens
- safety goggles

Procedure

1. Observe the lemon leaves and conifer needles. Both are leaves with adaptations that help the plants survive.

2. Use a hand lens to observe the leaves. Compare the leaves, and record your observations by drawing the leaves. Write a description of what you observe.

3. Observe the lemon half. Record your observations.

4. CAUTION: Put on safety goggles. Carefully break open the cone, and observe the inside. Record your observations.

Draw Conclusions

1. Are lemon trees vascular plants? Are conifers? How can you tell?

2. Lemon trees grow fairly quickly. Conifers can survive periods when there is little water. Infer how the leaf adaptations you observed help these different plants survive.

3. **Inquiry Skill** Compare the lemon half and the conifer cone. What similarities do you observe? What can you infer about the function of these structures in the plants' life cycles?

Step 2

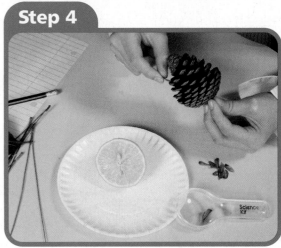

Step 4

Investigate Further

The seeds of conifers are adapted so that they can travel. Formulate a hypothesis about ways a seed could be adapted to travel. Design an experiment to test your hypothesis.

119

Reading in Science

SCIENCE CONCEPTS

▶ how plants can be classified

▶ how the structures of plants make it possible for them to survive

READING FOCUS SKILL

COMPARE AND CONTRAST Look for ways to compare vascular plants with nonvascular plants and compare angiosperms with gymnosperms.

alike ————— different

Mosses, Liverworts, and Hornworts

Have you ever taken a walk along a stream and noticed "furry" green growth on stones? Or have you hiked in a forest and observed a velvety green covering on the ground or on the side of a tree? If so, you've seen mosses in nature. Mosses grow best in moist, shady places. They often can be found on a shady forest floor or beside a pond or stream.

A **moss** is a very small plant. Mosses do not have vascular tissues, so they do not have true roots, stems, or leaves. Mosses have structures that look like simple roots, stems, and leaves. Like the roots of vascular plants, the rootlike structures of mosses anchor the plants in the soil. However, they do not absorb much water or many nutrients. The stemlike structures of

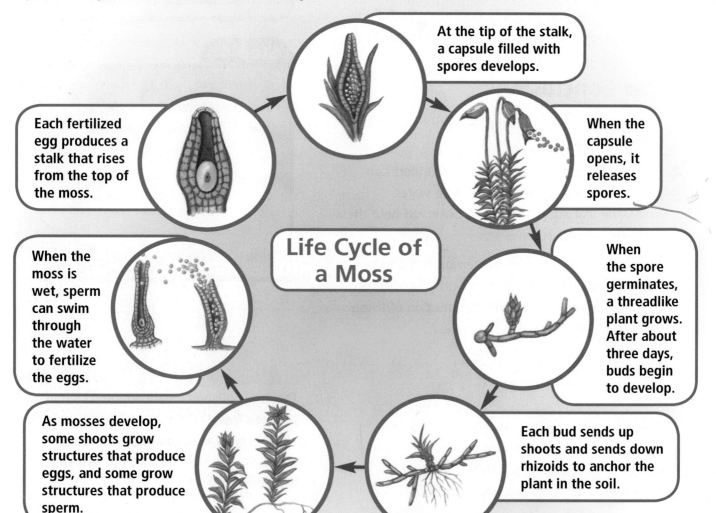

Life Cycle of a Moss

At the tip of the stalk, a capsule filled with spores develops.

When the capsule opens, it releases spores.

When the spore germinates, a threadlike plant grows. After about three days, buds begin to develop.

Each bud sends up shoots and sends down rhizoids to anchor the plant in the soil.

As mosses develop, some shoots grow structures that produce eggs, and some grow structures that produce sperm.

When the moss is wet, sperm can swim through the water to fertilize the eggs.

Each fertilized egg produces a stalk that rises from the top of the moss.

Although these mosses are all different, each has structures that act like roots, stems, and leaves.

The hornlike structures of this hornwort can continue producing spores over a long period of time.

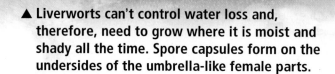

▲ Liverworts can't control water loss and, therefore, need to grow where it is moist and shady all the time. Spore capsules form on the undersides of the umbrella-like female parts.

mosses have cells for carrying water. Cells that move food surround these cells. Unlike xylem and phloem, these cells do not form tubes. They move materials through the plant from cell to cell. The leaflike structures in mosses are green and carry out photosynthesis. They don't have veins and are flat—only one or two cells thick.

Mosses have a life cycle with two very different stages, or generations. One stage is *sexual reproduction,* in which egg and sperm cells join to form a new moss plant.

In the other stage, **asexual reproduction**, a new plant is formed without the joining of an egg cell and a sperm cell. A capsule on the stalk produces **spores**, or structures that contain cells that can grow into new plants without joining with other cells.

Mosses are not the only nonvascular plants. Others are liverworts and hornworts. These plants thrive in the same type of environment as mosses. Like mosses, liverworts and hornworts have life cycles of two different generations.

Although they have many things in common with mosses, liverworts and hornworts differ from mosses in many ways. Both liverworts and hornworts are smaller than mosses. Liverworts do not have leaflike structures all around the stems, as mosses do. Instead, they have flat, scaly leaves. Hornworts, as their name suggests, have spore-producing structures that look like an animal's horns. They have no stemlike structures and no flat leaflike parts.

COMPARE AND CONTRAST Compare the structure of mosses to that of vascular plants.

The cells in the center of a club moss carry water. The cells on the outside carry food. What vascular plant structures do these two groups of cells resemble?

121

Ferns

Ferns are vascular plants. They appeared on Earth more than 350 million years ago and were the first plants with roots. By 100 million years later, there were more ferns than any other plants on Earth, growing from pole to pole. The climate during the Age of Ferns was tropical, and the ferns grew to be very large. As the climate has changed, ferns have decreased in number. Today there are about 12,000 species of ferns. Most live in tropical rain forests, where their broad fronds capture enough sunlight for them to make food even in the dim light of the forest floor. Some ferns are able to live in the cooler, drier temperate forests.

One rather unusual tropical fern is the staghorn fern. It doesn't look like a typical fern with lacy fronds. A lower frond of the staghorn fern acts like a suction cup to hold the fern to a tree's bark. The plant got its name from the shape of the rest of the fronds, which look like the horns of a stag, or male deer. This fern grows high in the branches of rain-forest trees. The fern is an epiphyte, or air plant, and takes its nutrients from water and the air. The trees are not harmed by the ferns. Because the ferns live high in the trees, they receive the light they need to carry out photosynthesis.

Like other ancient plants, ferns reproduce without seeds. The life cycle of the fern, like that of mosses, includes two different generations. The asexual generation reproduces

▼ Tree ferns have trunklike structures that lift the fronds above ground level. They grow best in warm, humid rain forests. The lacy tree fern shown here, is native to Australia.

◄ This heart-shaped plant is the sexual generation of ferns. A fiddlehead is growing from it.

Under the heart-shaped plant parts are small structures that produce egg cells and sperm cells during the sexual generation of the ferns' life cycle.

The asexual generation reproduces by spores that grow on the undersides of the ferns' leaflets, or pinnae.

This is the sexual generation of a fern with a fiddlehead just starting to grow.

The spots on the underside of fern leaflets are called sori. Spores form in the sori.

When fern fronds push up through the soil, they are tightly coiled. They look like the curl at the top of a violin—which is why these frond tops are called fiddleheads. As they grow, they uncoil and spread out into leafy fronds. The fronds have many leaflets.

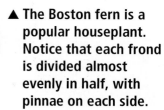

▲ The Boston fern is a popular houseplant. Notice that each frond is divided almost evenly in half, with pinnae on each side.

by spores that grow on the undersides of the leaflets that make up the whole frond. Spores form in brownish structures called *sori* on the undersides of the leaflets. When the spores in the sori are mature, they are released.

When a spore falls to the ground, it doesn't grow fronds. Instead, a tiny, flat, heart-shaped structure grows. Egg and sperm cells are produced. After a sperm cell joins with an egg cell, a new fern plant with fronds begins to develop. This is the beginning of the asexual generation of the fern's life cycle.

 COMPARE AND CONTRAST Compare fern reproduction with that of mosses.

Insta-Lab

Observe
Examine a fern frond. **Infer** how it is adapted to enabling the plant to live in shady places. Use a hand lens to **observe** the undersides of the frond leaflets. Draw and describe what you see. What do you **infer** about the structures that you see?

Gymnosperms

As you now know, both vascular and nonvascular plants may produce spores. However, you are probably more familiar with plants that produce seeds. Most plants on Earth are of these types.

Seeds can be thought of as "survival kits" for new plants. Inside a seed is a tiny plant—an *embryo*—and a supply of food for the embryo. The food and embryo are surrounded by a tough, protective outer coat.

Being able to produce seeds gives plants a survival advantage. The tiny embryo inside a seed is protected until conditions are right for germination. When the seed sprouts, the embryo plant uses the supply of food to start its growth.

There are two groups of plants that make seeds. In a **gymnosperm**, the seeds are not surrounded by a fruit. The word *gymnosperm* comes from ancient Greek words meaning "naked" and "seed." Can you infer why the name was chosen? Because gymnosperms do not produce flowers or fruits, they are called *nonflowering plants.*

You are probably familiar with one kind of gymnosperm. Cone-bearing gymnosperms, called **conifers**, include pine, juniper, cedar, and cypress trees. Most trees with narrow, needlelike leaves that stay green all year long are conifers.

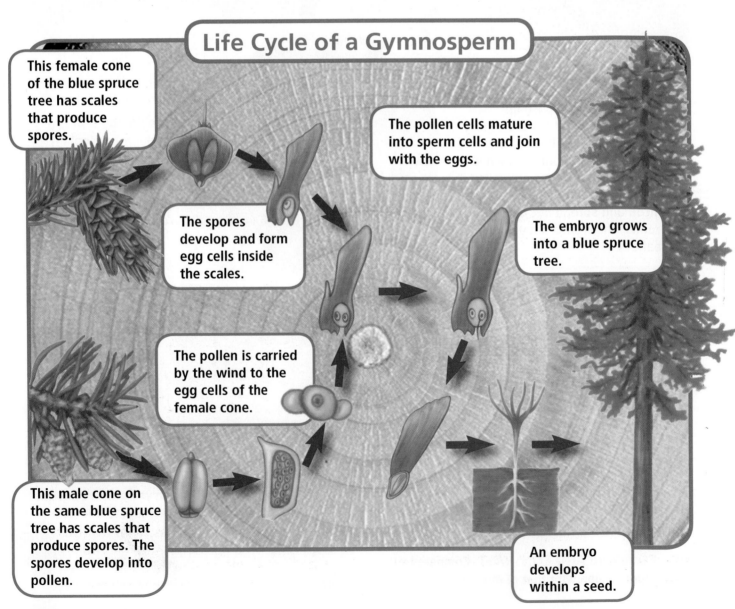

Life Cycle of a Gymnosperm

This female cone of the blue spruce tree has scales that produce spores.

The spores develop and form egg cells inside the scales.

The pollen is carried by the wind to the egg cells of the female cone.

This male cone on the same blue spruce tree has scales that produce spores. The spores develop into pollen.

The pollen cells mature into sperm cells and join with the eggs.

The embryo grows into a blue spruce tree.

An embryo develops within a seed.

The ginkgo is often called a living fossil because it is very similar to trees that lived millions of years ago. A ginkgo's leaves grow on the ends of shoots, are fan-shaped, and have parallel veins.

Cycads look like palms, but they belong to a different group of plants. Like ginkgoes, cycads are ancient plants. Their seeds form in cones at the top of the stem.

▲ The welwitschia (wel•WIT•chee•uh) grows in the deserts of southwestern Africa. This plant produces only two leaves, which split as they grow, making the plant appear to have many more.

Recall the Investigate. Seeds of conifers develop inside cones like the one you observed. Conifers have two types of cones, and both kinds usually grow on the same tree. The smaller male cones produce *pollen,* which can be carried by the wind. The female cones produce egg cells. The egg cells remain inside the female cones.

When the egg cells in a female cone are mature, the cone makes a sticky liquid. Grains of pollen, carried by the wind, are trapped in this liquid. The pollen grains join with egg cells.

The fertilized eggs in the female cone form embryos inside seeds. When the seeds are mature, the female cone opens and releases them. The seeds of many conifers have wings that help them travel on the wind. When conditions are right, the seeds germinate and new plants begin to grow.

Conifers are the largest of four groups of gymnosperms. The other groups are pictured on this page.

 COMPARE AND CONTRAST How do the two kinds of cones of a conifer differ?

Another ancient conifer, the yew, makes seeds in red, berrylike structures. The yew does not produce true flowers, and the berries are not true fruits. Substances made by the yew are used to make medicines that fight cancer.

125

Angiosperms

The two groups of plants that form seeds are gymnosperms and angiosperms. Most plants are angiosperms. Grasses in yards, flowers in gardens, most trees in parks, and crops in farm fields are all angiosperms. An **angiosperm** is a flowering vascular plant whose seeds are surrounded by a fruit. The term *angiosperm* means "covered seed." How is this different from the gymnosperms? The angiosperms shown on this page appear to have little in common, but all angiosperms share one important trait. Fruits form from flowers, which are the plants' reproductive organs.

Angiosperms can be divided into two groups, based on how many seed leaves a plant's seed has. The seed leaves store food for the embryo—the tiny, undeveloped plant. One group of angiosperms has one seed leaf, and the other group has two seed leaves. The bean you observed in Lesson 1 had two seed leaves. You will learn more about angiosperms in Lesson 4.

COMPARE AND CONTRAST Compare and contrast angiosperms and gymnosperms.

Oak trees, Kentucky bluegrass, peonies, and cherry trees are all angiosperms.

1. **COMPARE AND CONTRAST** Draw and complete this graphic organizer.

PATTERNS OF REPRODUCTION			
Mosses	Ferns	Gymnosperms	Angiosperms
Two generations: sexual and asexual	Ⓐ	Ⓑ	Ⓒ

2. **SUMMARIZE** Use the graphic organizer to summarize the differences in plant reproduction.

3. **DRAW CONCLUSIONS** Why don't conifers need water to reproduce?

4. **VOCABULARY** Write a clue for each of the vocabulary words. Construct a word-search puzzle. Hide the vocabulary words in a grid of letters. Trade with a classmate.

Test Prep

5. **Critical Thinking** If a tree has needlelike leaves, what kind of plant would you **hypothesize** it is? What other characteristics would you look for to support your hypothesis?

6. Which are nonvascular plants?
  A. bacteria
  B. ferns
  C. gymnosperms
  D. hornworts

Links

Writing

Persuasive Writing

Because they are sensitive to pollution, mosses can help show the "health" of an area. Suppose that you live beside a factory where mosses are dying nearby. Write a **letter** to the Environmental Protection Agency explaining your concerns about pollution from the factory.

Math

Write a Ratio

A liverwort may reach a height of 2 cm. A redwood tree may reach a height of 100 m. What is the ratio of the height of the liverwort to the height of the redwood tree?

Health

Moss as Medicine

During the Civil War and World War I, sphagnum moss was used to bandage wounds. Use library or Internet resources to discover what properties made the moss useful. Share your findings with the class.

 For more links and activities, go to **www.hspscience.com**

How Do Angiosperms Reproduce?

Fast Fact

The Land of Flowers More than 500 years ago, Spanish explorer Ponce de León landed in what is now Florida. He named it *La Florida*—the Land of Flowers. Since then, many of Florida's natural habitats have been harmed. However, Florida has begun programs to restore and protect native wildflowers. In the Investigate, you will examine the parts of a flower.

The Parts of a Flower

Materials   ● flower   ● paper towel   ● hand lens

Procedure

① Place the flower on a paper towel.

② Handle the flower gently as you observe its parts. Be sure to look at the center between the petals.

③ Use the hand lens to examine the parts of the flower. Make drawings to record what you observe.

④ The flower includes at least three different kinds of structures. If there are not at least three different parts in your drawing, observe the flower again and revise your drawing.

Draw Conclusions

1. Describe the structures you observed in the flower. Infer the function of each structure.

2. **Inquiry Skill** Scientists communicate in many ways. They use drawings, diagrams, words, and measurements. Compare these methods. Choose one of the flower structures you drew. Which method or combination of methods do you think would be the most helpful for communicating information about the structure? Explain.

Step 2

Step 3

Investigate Further

Use your observations to hypothesize which structures you would find in any flower. Design an experiment to test your hypothesis.

VOCABULARY
pollination p. 132
fruit p. 134

SCIENCE CONCEPTS

▶ what adaptations flowering plants have that help them reproduce

▶ how fruits are classified

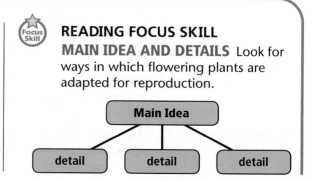

READING FOCUS SKILL
MAIN IDEA AND DETAILS Look for ways in which flowering plants are adapted for reproduction.

Flower Parts

As you have learned, angiosperms are vascular plants that produce flowers. Angiosperms produce fruits from their flowers, which are the reproductive organs. Many angiosperms, such as grasses and grains, have flowers so small that you might not notice them. Others, such as oak trees, have flowers that hardly look like flowers at all. Still others have large, showy flowers and small fruits that are not easily seen.

In the Investigate, you observed some of the parts of a flower. The largest and most noticeable parts of a flower are its *petals.* The petals help protect the other parts of the flower. Often brightly colored and sweetly scented, petals also help attract insects and other animals that are important to the plant's reproduction. Below the petals are the *sepals.* Sepals are usually smaller than petals and may look like green leaves. Before a flower blooms, the sepals cover the bud, protecting it as it develops. After the flower blooms, the sepals spread apart.

Clustered within the center of a flower are several stemlike structures. These structures, called *stamens,* are the flower's male reproductive organs. A stamen has two parts. The *anther* produces pollen grains. The *filament* is a stalk that connects the anther to the plant.

At the center of the flower is a structure called the *pistil.* This is the female reproductive organ. It is made up of three parts. At its top

is the *stigma.* This sticky structure captures pollen grains that fall on it. In the middle is the stemlike part called the *style.* The style connects the stigma to the *ovary* at the base of the pistil. Inside the ovary are *ovules* that contain egg cells. The egg cells can develop into seeds if they are fertilized.

 MAIN IDEA AND DETAILS What are the functions of a flower's pistil and stamens?

The reproductive organs of a daffodil are easy to see. This large flower has six petals.

Angiosperms vary in the number, shape, and color of their reproductive parts. The petals of different flowers give each a unique appearance. Although they share many of the same characteristics, the calla lily, black-eyed susan, and gardenia all have their own shapes and colors.

131

▲ Butterflies, bees, hummingbirds and other animals help transfer pollen to the stigmas of flowers.

Flowers and Pollination

Have you ever watched a bee buzzing from flower to flower or a hummingbird sipping nectar? These animals were helping plants reproduce.

Pollination is the first step in angiosperm reproduction, and it occurs when pollen from an anther lands on the stigma of a flower of the same kind. *Self-pollination* occurs by transfer of pollen within the same flower or between different flowers of the same plant. *Cross-pollination* occurs by transfer of pollen from the anther of one plant's flower to the stigma of a flower of the same kind of plant.

A tube grows down from each pollen grain through the style to the ovary. There, sperm cells from the pollen grains enter the ovules and join with the egg cells. This is known as *fertilization.* The fertilized egg cells then develop into seeds. As this happens, the ovary forms a fruit that surrounds and protects the seeds. You can see how fruits form in the illustration on page 133.

In order for a species to survive, its members must reproduce. To improve their chance of success, many flowering plants have adaptations that promote pollination.

Flowers often have brightly colored petals and strong scents. Many produce a sweet liquid called *nectar* that some animals use as food. The colors and scents of the flowers are signs to these animals that the flowers have nectar.

Plants that are pollinated by animals have flowers that produce heavy, sticky pollen. The pollen sticks to a passing animal's body. When the animal brushes against the pistil of another flower, the pollen rubs off on the stigma. Insects, birds, bats, and other animals may carry pollen from one flower to another. In some cases, one species of animal pollinates only one species of plant. The plant and the animal depend on each other. The animal gets something—such as nectar or protection—and the plant gets help with pollination. For example, yucca plants are pollinated only by the female yucca moth. The moth that does this lays her eggs in the plant's ovary. As the plant's seeds develop, so do the moth's eggs. When the moth larvae hatch, they eat some of the seeds. The rest of the seeds are released by the yucca to grow into new plants.

Plants that are not pollinated by animals often rely on the wind to carry pollen from flower to flower. These plants produce large amounts of powdery pollen. The wind carries this pollen from the anther of one flower to the stigma of another flower of the same kind. Many trees, including oaks, birches, and maples are pollinated in this way. Corn and other grasses are also pollinated by the wind. The flowers of these plants are small and unscented. They do not need to attract animals, and they do not produce nectar.

 MAIN IDEA AND DETAILS
How do wind-pollinated flowers differ from animal-pollinated flowers?

Once a flowering plant has been pollinated, pollen tubes grow down the style from the stigma to the ovary.

When the egg cells in the ovules have been fertilized, the ovary begins the process of becoming a fruit. The petals, which are no longer needed, fall off the plant.

As the seeds develop, the ovary forms a fruit around them.

Fruits and Seeds

Angiosperms can be divided into two groups based on their seed structure. Monocotyledons—monocots—have one seed leaf (cotyledon). Dicotyledons—dicots—have two. Seed leaves store food for the embryo plant inside the seed. There are several other differences between monocots and dicots. Study the table on the next page. In what other ways do the two groups of angiosperms differ?

The outsides of seeds differ, too. To increase the seedlings' chances of survival, plants have adaptations for scattering their seeds. Some seeds, such as those of cockleburs, have a rough covering. These seeds catch on the fur of passing animals, who then rub or scratch them off in other places. Other seeds, such as those of dandelions, are carried on the wind. Still others are thrown through the air by seed cases that burst open.

 MAIN IDEA AND DETAILS Why isn't a strawberry a true berry?

Science Up Close

Types of Fruit

Although they have different adaptations, all angiosperm seeds are surrounded by fruits. A fruit is the ripened ovary of a flowering plant. Dry fruits include nuts and the pods that contain seeds, such as peas and beans. Fleshy fruits include apples, cucumbers, and other fruits with pulp. The fruits on this page develop from different plant structures.

◀ A *berry* has seeds throughout the flesh of a single enlarged ovary. That's why a watermelon is classified as a berry, as are blueberries and tomatoes.

◀ Strawberries are *aggregate fruits* made up of many fruitlets. Each fruitlet develops from one pistil of a flower with many pistils.

The seeds of a pear are in its core. It's called a *pome.* The core forms from a single flower's ovary. The flesh forms from flower parts that surround the ovary. Apples are also pomes. ▼

◀ A *drupe*, such as this plum, has a single seed with a hard covering. The seed develops from a single pistil and the flesh forms from a single ovary. Cherries and peaches are drupes.

Angiosperm Groups

monocots

one cotyledon

flower parts in threes

parallel leaf veins

scattered stem vascular tissue

fibrous (spread-out) roots

dicots

two cotyledons

flower parts in fours or fives

netlike leaf veins

stem vascular tissue in a ring

taproots

◄ The hooks of cocklebur seeds catch in animals' fur or on people's clothing. The seed may be carried far away before being rubbed or scratched off.

◄ The seeds of the dandelion have fluffy "parachutes." They are light enough to be carried by the wind.

Black raspberries are groups of tiny fruitlets that form from a single flower. They are not berries but are classified as an aggregate fruit. Each fruitlet develops from one pistil of a flower with many pistils. ▼

◄ A pineapple is classified as a *multiple fruit*. It is made up of fruitlets that develop from the pistils of several flowers on the same plant. Figs are also multiple fruits.

For more links and activities, go to www.hspscience.com

◀ Spider plants produce long runners. New plants grow from buds on the runners and send roots into the soil.

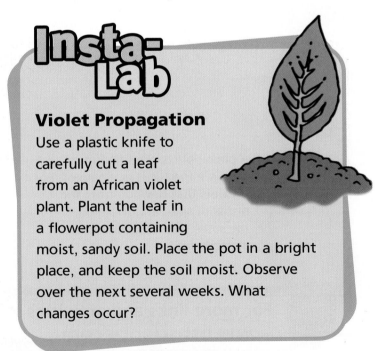

Here, parts of two plants are being joined to make one plant in the process known as *grafting*.

Asexual Reproduction

Some plants reproduce without using seeds. Asexual reproduction can produce new plants that are identical to the parent plants. Often, plants that have been bred with very desirable traits will be reproduced asexually so these traits can be passed on more reliably.

Many plants can grow from leaf cuttings. Leaves from the parent plant that are placed in water or soil can develop into new plants.

Some plants, such as strawberries and spider plants, reproduce by runners. Runners are long, slender stems that grow close to the ground and put out roots and shoots. The new plants can grow with or without the parent plant. Some other plants, such as tulips, produce underground stems called bulbs that divide. Each section grows into a new plant.

Some plants have underground stems, called *tubers*, that swell to store food. Potatoes are tubers. Their "eyes" are buds that can sprout and grow into new plants.

Plant nurseries grow certain plants, such as roses and citrus trees, by a form of asexual reproduction called *grafting.* They join parts of two plants to develop a single plant that has characteristics of both parents.

 MAIN IDEA AND DETAILS What are three kinds of asexual reproduction?

Insta-Lab

Violet Propagation

Use a plastic knife to carefully cut a leaf from an African violet plant. Plant the leaf in a flowerpot containing moist, sandy soil. Place the pot in a bright place, and keep the soil moist. Observe over the next several weeks. What changes occur?

1. MAIN IDEA AND DETAILS Draw and complete this graphic organizer.

Angiosperms	
Water distribution	**Ⓐ**
Plant size	**Ⓑ**
Ⓒ	Usually, sexual
Ⓓ	Animals, wind
How seeds are scattered	**Ⓔ**

2. SUMMARIZE Use the graphic organizer to write a short paragraph describing angiosperms.

3. DRAW CONCLUSIONS How does scattering seeds increase the chance that some new plants will grow?

4. VOCABULARY Write sentences that use and define each vocabulary word.

Test Prep

5. Critical Thinking Suppose a gardener has developed a variety of rose bush that bears huge red blooms. Which method of reproduction would be best to use to produce more of the same rose bushes?

6. Which of the following is **NOT** a fruit?
- **A.** apple
- **B.** potato
- **C.** raspberry
- **D.** tomato

Links

Writing

Descriptive Writing

Suppose you are a pollen grain. Write a detailed **description** of the path you follow from your plant's male reproductive parts until you pollinate a flower on another plant.

Math

Find Multiples

Suppose you find a flower that has 18 petals. Is the flower a monocot or a dicot? Explain your answer.

Health

Five a Day

Use library or Internet resources to learn more about various kinds of fruits. Plan a garden in which you plant a variety of fruits. Include one of each kind of fruit you learned about on pages 134–135.

For more links and activities, go to www.hspscience.com

THE Burning Amazon

Think of a mysterious place where beetles are as big as teacups, a place where hairy spiders have 18-cm (7-in.) legs and frogs are too poisonous for humans to touch. This is an exotic place where trees are so tall that they blot out the sun.

Welcome to the Amazon rain forest. The forest covers nearly 2 million square miles and spreads across nine South American countries. It was once an unspoiled region of dense jungle. In recent years, however, the forest has come under attack.

Shrinking Rain Forest

The largest area of rain forest is in Brazil. The sky above the forest there is often thick with smoke. That smoke is caused by ranchers and farmers illegally torching acres of forest. Biologists have been studying the Amazon's deforestation, or the removal of trees and other plant life. The scientists estimate that about 15 percent of Brazil's rain forest has been destroyed over the past 30 years.

Diverse Jungle

Why is the rain forest important? For one thing, about one fourth of all medicines come from rain forest plants. More than 1400 varieties of

The capybara is the world's largest rodent. It can weigh as much as 45 kg (100 lb). Now *that's* a big guinea pig!

plants in the rain forest are thought to be potential cures for cancer.

The tropical rain forest is also the Earth's most diverse ecosystem. An ecosystem is a community of plants and wildlife.

Making Progress

South American governments are making efforts to protect the region. In some areas, ranchers and farmers who clear more than 20 percent of their land face heavy fines or jail sentences. In northern Brazil, the government recently turned 9.6 million acres of forest into the world's largest tropical national park.

In other parts of the Amazon rain forest, however, the fires continue to burn—and rare plant and animal species face an uncertain future.

Think About It

1. What other steps could governments take to prevent deforestation of the Amazon?
2. How would making parts of the forest into a national park help to protect the forest?

Natural Numbers

In the Amazon region, there are more than 1600 species of birds and 1200 species of butterflies. There are more than 1 million species of insects.

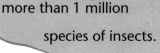

Find out more! Log on to www.hspscience.com

A RARE COLLECTOR

When Ynes Enriquetta Julietta Mexia was 55 years old she started a new collection. Mexia didn't collect buttons, signs, or dolls. She collected plants.

Over the course of 13 years, Mexia collected about 145,000 different species of plants and identified about 500 new plants. Those plants had never before been seen by botanists, scientists who study plants. As a result of her work, Mexia has about 50 kinds of plants named after her.

In 1929, when she was 59 years old, Mexia went on a two-year trip to South America. During that time she was trapped with a group of people for three months in a gorge that was 600 m (1968 ft) deep. The group had to finally build a raft to float down a dangerous river out of the gorge. Mexia collected rare plants during the entire three-month period.

Career   Botanist

Imagine that a fungus has been killing the pine trees in your town. But town leaders don't want to cut all the trees down. To figure out what's wrong, a botanist might be called. Botanists study plants and how they live. Some study the causes and cures of plant diseases. Other botanists work to discover new plants.

You Can Do It!

Materials

- fern with brown spores
- pot of potting soil mixed with peat moss
- water in sprinkling can
- plastic wrap
- saucer of water
- rubber band

Quick and Easy Project

Growing Plants from Spores

Procedure

1. Sprinkle the spores over the soil. Gently sprinkle water over the top of the soil but don't soak it.

2. Cover the pot with plastic wrap. Hold the wrap in place with a rubber band.

3. Move the pot to a light, but not sunny, location. Place the pot in the saucer.

4. Keep water in the saucer.

5. When the ferns are 2.5-4 cm tall, move clumps of them to their own pots.

Draw Conclusions

How does fern reproduction differ from reproduction in other plants? In what ways do you think spores have helped ferns survive for so many millions of years?

Design Your Own Investigation

Growing Plants from Seeds

Design an experiment to observe how plants grow from seeds. Set up the experiment. Observe **the growth over several weeks.** Compare **the results with those you obtained when growing plants from spores. How are the growth processes alike? How do they differ? Is one growth process better than the other? Why or why not?**

Vocabulary Review

Use the terms below to complete the sentences. The page numbers tell you where to look in the chapter if you need help.

vascular plant p. 108
xylem p. 108
tropism p. 114
phototropism p. 114
moss p. 120
spore p. 121
angiosperm p. 126
pollination p. 132

1. The growth response of plants to light is called _____ .

2. Tissue in vascular plants used to transport water and nutrients is _____ .

3. A structure that contains cells that can grow into a new plant without joining with other cells is called a _____ .

4. A plant that has tissues to transport water, nutrients, and food is a _____ .

5. A growth response of a plant to something in its environment is a _____ .

6. The first step in angiosperm reproduction is _____ .

7. A plant whose seeds are inside a fruit is an _____ .

8. An example of a very small, green nonvascular plant is a _____ .

Check Understanding

Write the letter of the best choice.

9. In which plant group would the plant whose part is shown be classified?

    A. angiosperm
    B. fern
    C. gymnosperm
    D. moss

10. Which tissue is used to carry water from the roots to the leaves of a plant?

    F. fruit
    G. ovary
    H. phloem
    J. xylem

11. A plant seedling grows toward the window. Its roots reach into the soil. Which of the following does the seedling show?

    A. positive phototropism and positive gravitropism
    B. positive phototropism and negative gravitropism
    C. negative phototropism and positive gravitropism
    D. negative phototropism and negative gravitropism

12. Which plants make seeds that are not inside a "container"?

    F. angiosperms
    G. gymnosperms
    H. nonvascular plants
    J. vascular plants

13. Which is a vascular plant?

   A. fern   **C.** liverwort

   B. hornwort   **D.** moss

14. Which are plants that flower when there are fewer than a certain number of daytime hours?

   F. annuals

   G. long-day plants

   H. perennials

   J. short-day plants

15. **COMPARE AND CONTRAST** Both xylem and phloem carry materials in a plant. How are they different?

   A. Xylem carries food, while phloem carries water and nutrients.

   B. Phloem carries food, while xylem carries water and nutrients.

   C. Xylem carries food, water, and nutrients, while phloem removes waste.

   D. Xylem carries water and nutrients, while phloem makes food for the plant.

16. **MAIN IDEA AND DETAILS** A white carnation is placed in water colored red with food coloring. Why do its petals turn red?

   F. The colored water travels through phloem up the stem to the petals.

   G. The colored water travels through the root hairs to the petals.

   H. The colored water travels through xylem up the stem to the petals.

   J. The colored water travels through the leaves to the petals.

Inquiry Skills

17. Suppose you have a packet of seeds and want to know whether they are seeds of a monocot plant or dicot plant. Design an experiment to identify the seeds as coming from a monocot or a dicot.

18. Observe the fruit shown below. Infer its classification, based on its structures. Communicate how it formed from flower parts.

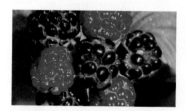

Critical Thinking

19. Why do fruit farmers often keep beehives in their orchards?

20. Look at the picture. This tree has certain characteristics. Answer the questions, based on the picture.

   Part A What kind of plant would you hypothesize this is? Why?

   Part B What other characteristics would you look for to support your hypothesis?

Interactions in Ecosystems

Eagle Watch Weekend

TO: dena@hspscience.com

FROM: nathan@hspscience.com

RE: Winona, Minnesota

Dear Dena,

I'm glad to hear that you and your family will be able to visit us over Eagle Watch Weekend. The landing area that we'll watch the eagles from is located where the Chippewa River flows into the Mississippi River. The eagles feed on fish there and perch along the banks of the river. They choose this spot because there isn't ice to get in their way as they stop along their migration route. In the past we have seen as many as seventy-five eagles at one time. It really is an incredible sight.

See you soon!

Nathan

TO: jay@hspscience.com

FROM: ashton@hspscience.com

RE: Alaska

Dear Jay,

My family went on a trip to Alaska. The part I liked best was kayaking in a place called Rudyerd Bay in Misty Fiords National Monument. The fiords are spectacular, with high, rocky cliffs and lush plant life. I am putting together a photo essay of the many and varied plants to use for a school project. I'll e-mail a copy to you when I'm finished.

We went fishing for salmon and I caught the biggest one. We saw a brown bear, wolves, mountain goats, and several bald eagles. I never thought a "science vacation" would be so much fun. Pretty amazing!

Write back soon,

Ashton

Experiment!

Air Pollution Nobody wants to live in an environment that contains a lot of trash or pollution. Is there a difference in the air quality at some of the locations where you spend your day? Plan and conduct an experiment to find out.

Chapter

4 Ecosystems

Lesson 1 What Are Ecosystems?

Lesson 2 How Do Organisms Get Energy?

Lesson 3 How Do Organisms Interact?

Lesson 4 What Are Biomes?

Vocabulary

ecosystem
population
community
habitat
niche
diversity
producer
food chain
consumer
food web
energy pyramid
competition
symbiosis
parasite
host
biome

There are many types of environments, each with its own kinds of plants and animals. What features can you observe in this environment? What plants and animals might live in an area like the one you see here?

What Are Ecosystems?

Fast Fact

Full of Life Tropical rain forests, such as this one in Puerto Rico, cover between 6 and 8 percent of Earth's land area. Surprisingly, between 50 and 90 percent of Earth's land-based species live in them! In the Investigate, you will compare your local climate with that of a rain forest.

Comparing Climates

Materials
- local weather information
- graphs on this page
- graph paper
- colored pencils

Procedure

1. Find out the average monthly rainfall for each month in your area. Record the data.

2. Find out the average monthly temperature for each month in your area. Record the data.

3. On a sheet of graph paper, draw a double-bar graph to compare monthly rainfall where you live with monthly rainfall in a rain forest. Use the data in the first graph to make the bars for the rain forest. Use a different color to add the bars for your area.

4. Repeat Step 3 to make a double-bar graph to compare temperatures in the two areas. Use the data in the second graph for the rain forest.

Draw Conclusions

1. How does the monthly rainfall in the rain forest compare with rainfall in your area?

2. How do the monthly temperatures in the rain forest compare with temperatures in your area?

3. Draw conclusions about whether you would find more kinds of organisms in your area or in the rain forest. Would the same kinds of plants and animals live in both places? Explain your answer.

4. **Inquiry Skill** Scientists often interpret data from graphs to compare the characteristics of regions. How did the graphs help you compare climates in the two regions?

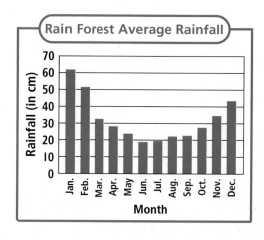

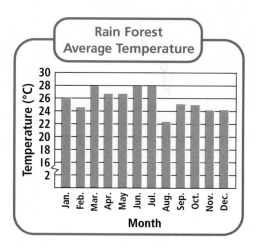

Investigate Further

Plan and conduct an investigation to test a hypothesis about how the climate of another area, such as a desert, might differ from the two areas you compared in this Investigate.

Reading in Science

VOCABULARY
ecosystem p. 151
population p. 152
community p. 152
habitat p. 153
niche p. 153
diversity p. 154

SCIENCE CONCEPTS
▶ what an ecosystem is and how organisms interact in ecosystems
▶ what factors affect diversity

READING FOCUS SKILL
MAIN IDEA AND DETAILS Look for details about ecosystems.

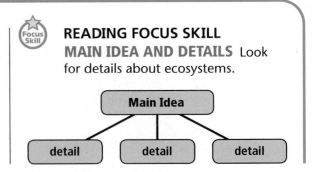

Ecosystems

It's a warm, sunny day at the park. You've brought your lunch, which includes some plump red strawberries. You bite into one, and it's sweet and juicy. Attracted by the fruit, bees begin buzzing around you. As you duck away from them, you think, "I wish all bees would disappear!"

What might happen if you actually got your wish? Bees pollinate many plants, enabling the plants to produce fruits, such as strawberries. Without bees, you might not have that delicious fruit. The problem with removing any organism—no matter how annoying—from an area is that other organisms depend on it. Each organism interacts with other organisms

A Forest Ecosystem

1 **White-tailed deer are plentiful. They eat lower branches and shoots of young trees, causing more light to reach the forest floor.**

2 **Trillium grows in shady, damp areas on the forest floor. Ants gather trillium seeds for their oil, and this helps spread the plant throughout the forest.**

3 **Wood beetles bore into tree trunks and fallen logs.**

4 **In autumn, a deep layer of fallen leaves covers the forest floor. They decompose and mix with the soil, making it richer.**

in one or more ecosystems. An **ecosystem** (ᴇᴇ•koh•sis•tuhm) is an area where organisms interact with one another as well as with the nonliving parts of the environment. It can be as large as a lake or a forest. It can also be as small as a puddle of water or a rotting log. Whatever its size, an ecosystem has both biotic (by•ᴀʜᴛ•ik) and abiotic (ay•by•ᴀʜᴛ•ik) parts. The *biotic* parts are the living parts of an ecosystem. They include everything from the tiniest bacteria to the tallest trees. The *abiotic* parts of an ecosystem are its nonliving parts, such as its climate, water, soil nutrients, light, and air.

The biotic parts of ecosystems help shape the environment. Plant roots anchor soil. They help split rock and break it down into new soil. Burrowing animals, such as moles and prairie dogs, change the shape of the ground. Tiny animals, such as earthworms, loosen and mix the soil as they tunnel through it.

An ecosystem's biotic parts also interact with one another. Bees pollinate flowers. Larger animals eat plants and other animals. Fungi decompose dead organisms. Squirrels nest in oak trees and help scatter acorns.

An ecosystem's abiotic parts help determine what lives in it. Think about the climate differences you found in the Investigate. You learned that climate varies from place to place. As a result, the organisms that live in an ecosystem vary, too. Most organisms can live only within a certain range of temperatures and moisture levels.

MAIN IDEA AND DETAILS What are the biotic and abiotic parts of an ecosystem?

5 Skunks roam the forest at night, looking for insects and rodents.

6 The male cardinal's red color makes it easy to see him in the dark green forest. The females are not as brightly colored. Cardinals eat seeds, fruit, and insects.

7 Wild blueberries are common in northern forests. Their growing season runs from April through October. They are one of the few fruits that are native to North America.

A Place to Live

When you look around an ecosystem, you see different types of plants and animals. In a forest, you might see a group of squirrels nesting in a tree, a hive of honeybees, or a grove of oak trees. These are populations. A **population** is a group of organisms of the same species living together in an ecosystem.

All of the populations living in an ecosystem make up a **community**. The populations of a community interact, using one another for food and shelter. They change the environment in ways that enable other organisms to live in it.

Cacti have connections with many animals of the desert ecosystem. Roadrunners seek the shade of cacti during the hottest part of the day. Woodpeckers build nests in holes they drill

1. Coyotes hunt and eat other desert animals. They also eat parts of desert plants, such as cactus fruits and mesquite beans.

2. Scorpions hide in burrows or in cracks in rocks during the heat of day. They hunt for food at night.

3. To store body heat before the cold desert nights, roadrunners ruffle their feathers and let the sun warm the skin on their backs. Because their skin is black, it absorbs and holds heat well.

4. Tarantulas are large "hairy" spiders. They come out of their burrows at night to look for insects. Sometimes they eat other foods, such as small rodents.

5. For protection, cactus wrens build nests within the arms of the saguaro (suh•GWAR•oh) cactus.

6. Gila monsters are venomous lizards. During the hottest part of the year, they can live underground for weeks or months without eating.

in cacti. Insects, bats, and birds pollinate cactus flowers as they drink nectar. Many small animals eat ripe cactus fruits that drop to the ground.

You may live in a town with many families. Within that town, your family has its own home or apartment. It's the same with organisms in an ecosystem. Each has a certain habitat. An organism's **habitat** (HAB•ih•tat) is the part of the ecosystem in which it lives. The habitat supplies everything the organism needs—heat, light, water, food, and shelter.

Two populations with similar needs can share a habitat. For example, hawks and owls may live in the same area of a forest. Two populations can't, however, share the same niche. An organism's **niche** (NIHCH) is its role in an ecosystem. The niche includes everything the organism needs and everything it does, such as how it gets food and where it finds shelter. It includes how it interacts with all of the biotic and abiotic parts of the ecosystem.

The hawk and the owl can share a habitat because their niches are slightly different. They eat the same type of foods, but the hawk hunts in the daytime, and the owl hunts at night.

Organisms can have broad niches or narrow ones. Organisms with broad niches are able to live in a variety of places and eat many different foods. Flies, raccoons, mice, and people have broad niches.

Organisms with narrow niches usually live in one particular habitat. They eat only one food or a few foods and can live in only a small range of conditions. The giant pandas of China have a narrow niche. Bamboo is just about the only food they eat. How do you think a narrow niche relates to a species becoming endangered?

What would happen if two populations in a habitat had the same niche? They would have to compete for food, shelter, sunlight, and other resources. For both to stay in the same habitat, they would have to develop slightly different niches. If they did not, one would use the resources better and force the other out of the habitat.

 MAIN IDEA AND DETAILS How are a population and a community related in an ecosystem?

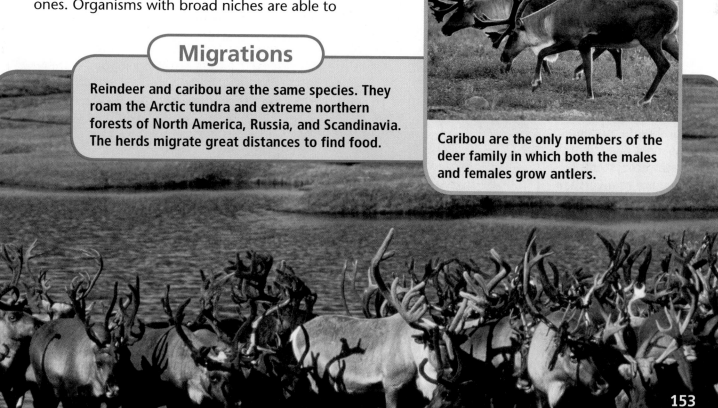

Migrations

Reindeer and caribou are the same species. They roam the Arctic tundra and extreme northern forests of North America, Russia, and Scandinavia. The herds migrate great distances to find food.

Caribou are the only members of the deer family in which both the males and females grow antlers.

153

Diversity

Hummingbirds drink nectar from flowers, so they need flowers for food. They also need other organisms for other purposes. Hummingbirds feed small spring flies to their young. They line their nests with the downy leaves of the mullein (MUHL•luhn) plant. Therefore, an ecosystem that includes hummingbirds must also have mullein plants, spring flies, and New Jersey tea plants, which attract the spring flies. Without all of these species, there will be no hummingbirds in an ecosystem.

Hummingbirds depend on the diversity within an ecosystem. **Diversity** refers to the variety of species in an ecosystem. Some ecosystems are very diverse, while others have just a few species.

Why are some ecosystems more diverse than others? Climate and location are two of the most important factors. In general, ecosystems closer to the equator have more species and so are more diverse. Ecosystems closer to Earth's poles have fewer species and so are less diverse. The wet, hot forests of the tropics have the most species. In 1 hectare (HEK•ter) (2.5 acres) of tropical forest, there might be 100 kinds of trees.

The actions of people are making ecosystems less diverse. People cut forests, plow grasslands, and drain swamps to build roads, houses, and shopping centers. This destroys habitats and food sources. If one population is harmed or destroyed, the entire ecosystem suffers.

 MAIN IDEA AND DETAILS Why are climate and location the two most important factors in determining ecosystem diversity?

Marble Diversity

Your teacher will pass around a jar of marbles. Reach into the jar, and pull out a handful of marbles. Sort the marbles by type. How many types do you have? Compare your results with those of classmates. Who has the most diverse handful of marbles?

Coral reefs are among the most diverse of all water ecosystems. They are as diverse in the ocean as rain forests are on land.

1. MAIN IDEA AND DETAILS Draw and complete this graphic organizer.

MAIN IDEA:
ECOSYSTEMS HAVE BOTH ABIOTIC AND BIOTIC PARTS.

Abiotic parts include

A

Temperature

B

C

D

Biotic parts include

Plants

E

F

2. SUMMARIZE Write a paragraph that summarizes this lesson.

3. DRAW CONCLUSIONS Two forest bird species nest in the same type of tree. They eat insects and seeds. They both hunt at night. One bird migrates south in winter. The other does not. Do these birds share a habitat or a niche? Explain your answer.

4. VOCABULARY Explain ecosystem diversity.

Test Prep

5. Critical Thinking Two ecosystems are thousands of kilometers apart, but they have very similar plants and animals. What might explain this?

6. Which of the following is **NOT** a population?
   A. a grove of maple trees
   B. a herd of bison
   C. a pile of clamshells
   D. a patch of fungi

Links

Writing

Expository Writing

Explore a nearby ecosystem, and choose a plant or an animal to research. Write a brief **report** that describes the community in which it lives, its habitat, and its niche.

Math

Make a Graph

In the Investigate, you found monthly rainfall data for your area for one year. Find annual rainfall data for the past ten years. Make a bar graph that shows the data. Describe the pattern that you observe.

Art

Take Photographs

Take photographs of a nearby ecosystem, and write a caption for each one. Draw a map of the area you photographed. Then set up a classroom gallery to display your photographs, captions, and map.

 For more links and activities, go to www.hspscience.com

155

Lesson 2

How Do Organisms Get Energy?

Fast Fact

Keen Sight All animals that hunt for food use senses that are adapted to helping them find their prey. This snowy owl can spot its prey on the ground from up to 0.8 km (0.5 mi) away! In the Investigate, you will find out more about owls and what they eat to get energy.

156

The Diet of Owls

Materials
- safety goggles
- toothpicks
- owl pellet
- index card
- paper towel
- bone chart

Procedure

① **CAUTION: First, put on safety goggles.** Your teacher will give you and your partner an owl pellet. Put it on the paper towel.

② Use toothpicks to pick apart the pellet.

③ Separate the bones in the owl pellet from the other material. Your teacher will tell you where to dispose of the other material.

④ Put the bones on the index card. Using the bone chart, classify the bones into groups. All the bones in one group should be from one kind of animal.

Draw Conclusions

1. Based on what you found in the owl pellet, infer whether owls eat plants, other animals, or both. Explain your answer.

2. An owl usually produces one pellet each day. Based on your observations, draw a conclusion about how many organisms the owl ate to produce the pellet you studied.

3. **Inquiry Skill** Scientists gather data and use it to infer facts. How could you use the results of this investigation to infer whether owls hunt during the day or at night? What other information would you need?

Step 2

Step 4

Investigate Further

Combine everyone's data to find out how many kinds of organisms the owls ate. To interpret data, make a bar graph to compare numbers. How might results differ in another part of the country?

Reading in Science

VOCABULARY
producer p. 158
food chain p. 159
consumer p. 159
food web p. 160
energy pyramid p. 162

SCIENCE CONCEPTS
► what the source of energy is in an ecosystem
► how energy moves through an ecosystem

 READING FOCUS SKILL
SEQUENCE Look for the sequence of organisms, from producers to decomposers, in a food chain.

Getting Energy

Everything you do requires energy—from digesting your lunch to dunking a basketball. All living things need energy to move, eat, grow, and reproduce. Where does all that energy come from? It starts with the sun.

The sun is the source of energy in almost all ecosystems and, therefore, is the first step in most food chains. The process of getting energy from the sun starts with green plants. They are the producers in most ecosystems. A **producer** is an organism that makes its own food.

When the sun shines on green plants, a process called *photosynthesis* takes place. In this process, plants use energy from the sun to turn carbon dioxide from the air and water and nutrients from the soil into glucose, a kind of sugar. Plants store the food in their leaves,

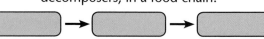

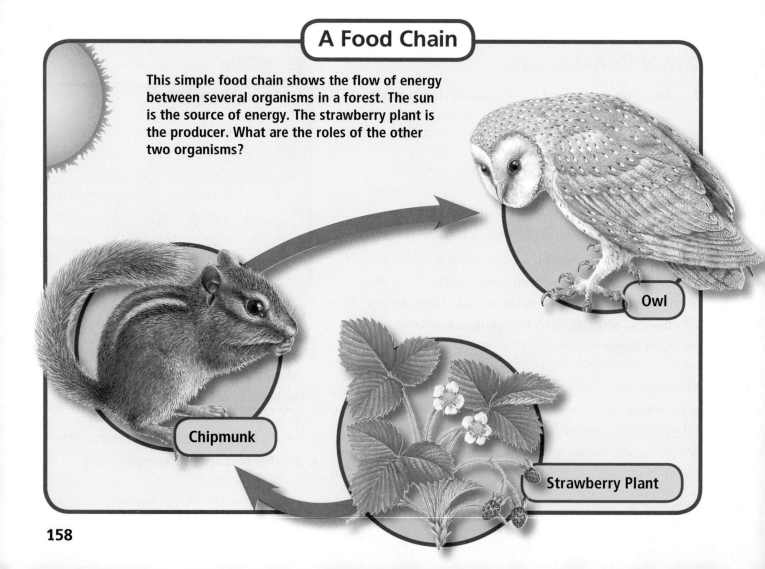

This simple food chain shows the flow of energy between several organisms in a forest. The sun is the source of energy. The strawberry plant is the producer. What are the roles of the other two organisms?

Owl

Chipmunk

Strawberry Plant

An Aquatic Food Chain

In an aquatic, or water, food chain, algae are often the producers. This simple food chain could occur in a pond or lake ecosystem.

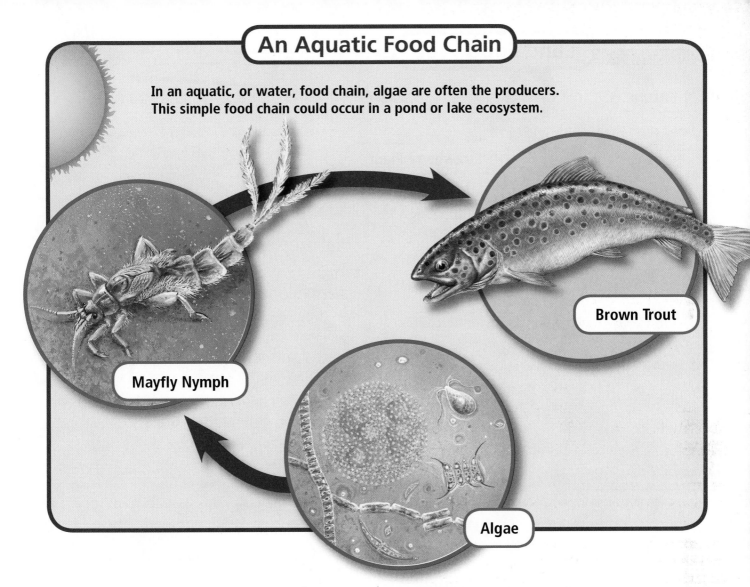

Mayfly Nymph

Algae

Brown Trout

stems, and roots as chemical energy. When another organism eats the plant, some of the stored energy passes to that organism.

A **food chain** is a sequence of connected producers and consumers. A diagram of a food chain shows how energy flows through an ecosystem. The second step in passing this energy along happens when consumers eat plants. A **consumer** is an organism that eats other organisms. You are a consumer. So are other animals. A primary consumer is a *herbivore* (HER•buh•vawr), or an animal that eats only plants. Rabbits are herbivores, so they are primary consumers. Secondary consumers eat primary consumers. A secondary consumer is a *carnivore*, or a meat-eating animal. A weasel that eats a rabbit is a carnivore, so it is a secondary consumer. There are consumers that

are both plant-eating and meat-eating. These consumers are *omnivores*. You are probably an omnivore. Omnivores get energy from producers and also from primary and secondary consumers. Because omnivores are higher-level consumers, there are fewer of them.

Ecosystems also have decomposers and scavengers. *Scavengers,* such as vultures, eat the remains of dead animals. *Decomposers* are consumers, usually bacteria and fungi, that break down plant and animal wastes and return the nutrients in them to the soil. This completes the energy cycle. Plants then take up the nutrients from the soil and use them in the process of photosynthesis.

 SEQUENCE At what point do producers appear in a food chain?

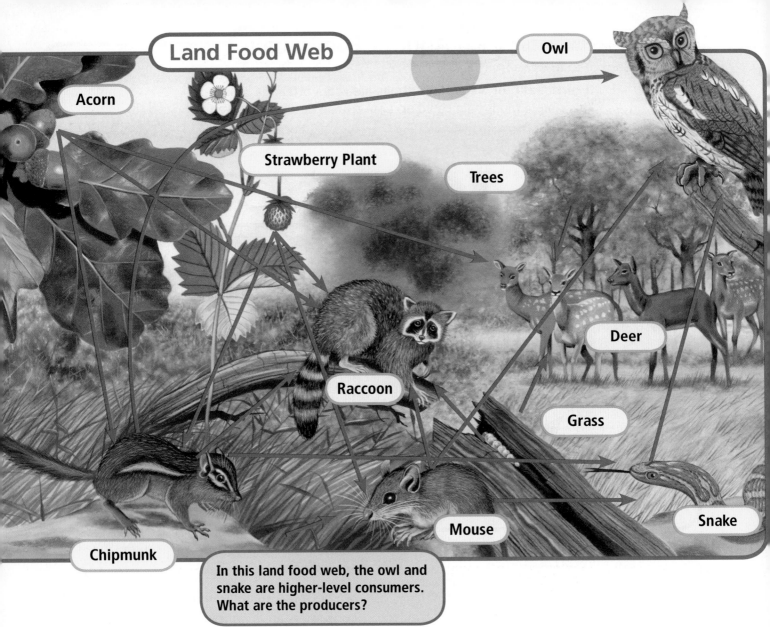

Land Food Web

Owl

Acorn

Strawberry Plant

Trees

Deer

Raccoon

Grass

Mouse

Snake

Chipmunk

In this land food web, the owl and snake are higher-level consumers. What are the producers?

Food Webs

A food chain shows feeding relationships in ecosystems. However, most feeding relationships are not that simple. Because organisms are often part of more than one food chain, a food web is a better way to show feeding relationships. A **food web** is a group of connected food chains in an ecosystem.

Most organisms eat more than one type of food. Primary consumers usually eat more than one type of producer. In the land food web above, the mouse eats a strawberry plant and grass. Secondary consumers eat more than one type of food, too. The owl eats the chipmunk and also the mouse. In the aquatic food web on

the next page, the raccoon eats the trout and the bluegill.

Each food web contains several food chains. One food chain in the land food web is the sun-strawberry-chipmunk-owl food chain. Identify all the food chains in these two food webs.

The land and aquatic food webs shown on these pages aren't separate. If you look closely, you'll see that they overlap. For example, the raccoon is in both of them.

You have read that a change in one population in an ecosystem can affect other populations. You can see this clearly by looking at a food web. What would happen in the land food web if the mouse population decreased or disappeared? The animals that feed on the mouse would have less food. As a result, their populations would decrease, too.

Suppose the trees and other plants were cleared from an area of this forest. Producers would be gone. They are the base of the food web. Consumers that eat only plants would have to go somewhere else to find food, or they would die. As a result, the number of primary consumers would decrease. With fewer primary consumers, secondary consumers would also be affected.

 SEQUENCE What is the first step in the production of energy in a food chain?

Make Connections

Brainstorm a list of organisms in your area. Write the name of one on a large index card. Use string to attach the card with your organism's name to other students' cards with the names of organisms that eat yours or are eaten by it. What have you and the other students made? Display your results on a bulletin board.

This aquatic food web shows organisms that live in water, and their connection with organisms that live on land. What are the producers in this ecosystem? What organisms are primary consumers?

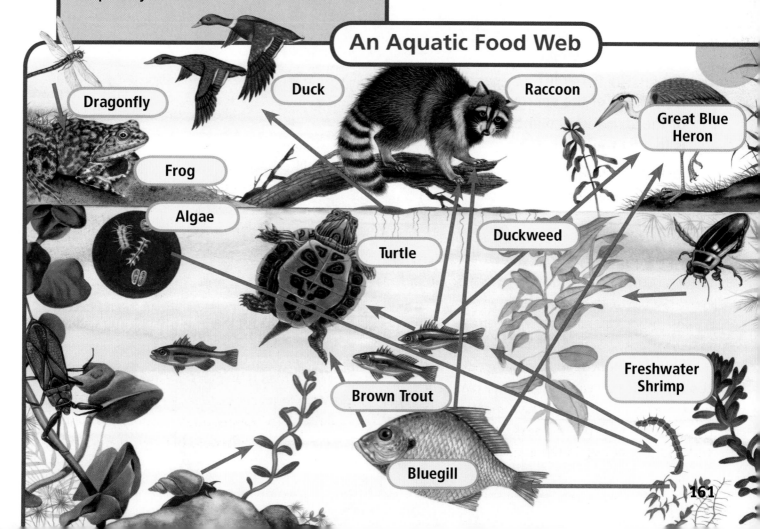

An Aquatic Food Web

Dragonfly

Duck

Raccoon

Great Blue Heron

Frog

Algae

Duckweed

Turtle

Freshwater Shrimp

Brown Trout

Bluegill

161

The Energy Pyramid

Think again of the land food web. When a chipmunk eats a strawberry, the chipmunk gets the energy that was stored as food in the plant. The chipmunk then uses some of the energy to move and grow. Some of the energy in the strawberry can't be used by the chipmunk. It is lost from the food chain as waste heat. This heat is the result of bodily and chemical processes. The rest of the energy is stored in the chipmunk's body.

When an owl eats the chipmunk, the same thing happens. The owl uses some of the energy from the chipmunk, loses some as heat, and stores the rest. How much of the energy from the strawberry reaches the owl? Not very much.

Energy is lost each time it passes from one organism to another. Scientists have found that 90 percent of an organism's energy is lost at each step of the food chain. This means that the chipmunk gets only 10 percent of the energy stored in the strawberry. When the owl eats the chipmunk, it gets just 10 percent of the energy stored in the chipmunk.

An **energy pyramid** shows that energy is lost at each level of the food chain. Because of this energy loss, the number of organisms decreases from one level to the next. For example, you can see that there are fewer hawks than strawberry plants, chipmunks, and snakes in this energy pyramid.

 SEQUENCE Why are there fewer organisms higher on the energy pyramid?

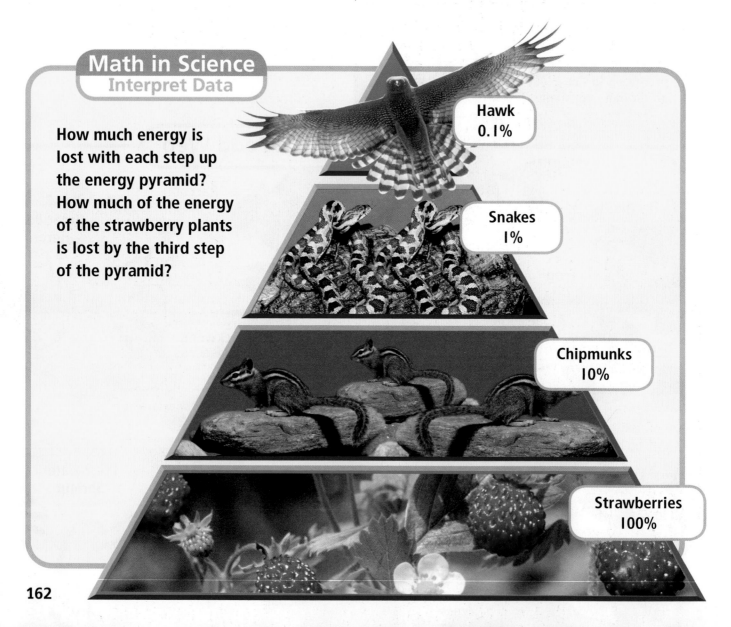

Math in Science
Interpret Data

How much energy is lost with each step up the energy pyramid? How much of the energy of the strawberry plants is lost by the third step of the pyramid?

Hawk
0.1%

Snakes
1%

Chipmunks
10%

Strawberries
100%

1. SEQUENCE Draw and complete this graphic organizer.

THE SEQUENCE OF ORGANISMS IN A FOOD CHAIN IS:

Ⓐ _____ → Ⓑ _____ → Secondary consumers → Ⓒ _____ → Decomposers

2. SUMMARIZE Use the lesson vocabulary to write a summary of this lesson.

3. DRAW CONCLUSIONS In terms of energy, why might it be a good idea to eat foods that are as low as possible on the energy pyramid?

4. VOCABULARY Make up a crossword puzzle that uses all the lesson vocabulary terms. You may also use Lesson 1 terms.

Test Prep

5. Critical Thinking How could you use a food web to explain why the protection of a threatened species is important?

6. Which is the primary source of energy in almost all ecosystems?
  A. decomposers
  B. primary consumers
  C. secondary consumers
  D. the sun

Links

Writing

Expository Writing

Draw an energy pyramid that has at least three levels. Write a **report** about how your energy pyramid can be used to explain how energy in ecosystems is passed through the inhabitants.

Math

Use Percents

Only 10 percent of the energy at one level of an energy pyramid is passed on to the next level. In a pyramid with four levels, what percent of the energy from the bottom level reaches the top level? Convert the percent to a decimal and a fraction.

Art

Food Chain

Draw a food chain that includes you and some of the foods you have eaten today. Compare your food chain with those of some classmates.

 For more links and activities, go to www.hspscience.com

How Do Organisms Interact?

Fast Fact

Slow Motion The sea anemone's tentacles have cells that sting other animals. The hermit crab places sea anemones on its shell to protect itself from predators. In this relationship, both animals benefit. The hermit crab is protected, and the sea anemone is moved around the sea floor and finds food. In the Investigate, you will observe another relationship in a water organism—a hydra.

Observing Hydras

Materials
- **MicroSlide Viewer**
- **microslides of a hydra and of a hydra and *Daphnia***
- **sheet of white paper**
- **colored pencils**

Procedure

1 Set up your MicroSlide Viewer, and place the microslide of the hydra on the viewer platform.

2 Carefully observe the hydra. Draw a picture of what you see. Include all the important details, such as color and body parts.

3 Look for details inside the hydra's body. Draw what you see.

4 Now observe the microslide of the hydra and *Daphnia*. Draw a picture of their interaction.

Draw Conclusions

1. What can you infer about the interaction between the hydra and *Daphnia*? Does the hydra make its own food, or does it eat other organisms?

2. Describe the body of the hydra. Can you see different body parts? Describe them.

3. The green objects you saw when you looked at the hydra are green algae. Where in the hydra did you observe the algae? What is the algae's habitat?

4. **Inquiry Skill** What conclusions can you draw about what a hydra might get from the algae? What might the algae get from the hydra? What can you infer about the habitat of the hydra?

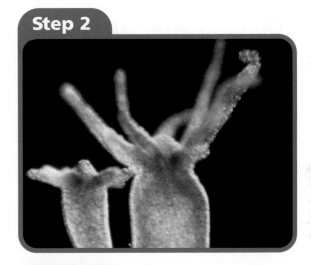

Step 2

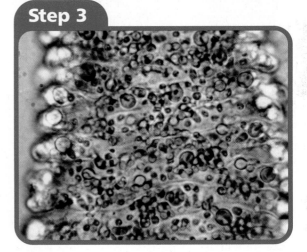

Step 3

Investigate Further

Find hydras and *Daphnia* in pond water samples. Observe what happens when hydras come into contact with *Daphnia*. How would you show the relationship of these organisms in a food chain?

165

Reading in Science

VOCABULARY
competition p. 166
symbiosis p. 168
parasite p. 168
host p. 168

SCIENCE CONCEPTS
▶ how organisms compete within an ecosystem
▶ what symbiotic relationships are

 READING FOCUS SKILL
CAUSE AND EFFECT Look for causes and effects of competition in ecosystems.

Limiting Factors—Competition for Resources

Suppose your family wants to have a cookout at a park. There are only a few good spots with a picnic table and shade. On a summer day, many families go to the park. Each tries to get one of these good spots. Some families succeed. Others settle for less-desirable spots or leave the park.

In the park, your family competes with other families for resources—space on the grass, picnic tables, and shade. In an ecosystem, organisms compete for space, light, food,

water, air, and nutrients. **Competition** is the struggle among organisms for limited resources in an area. Every ecosystem has limited resources, so all species must compete to stay alive.

There are several types of competition in an ecosystem. In one type, one species might prevent another from using an important resource. Some plants in deserts and grasslands release into the soil certain chemicals that keep other plants from growing.

When organisms use the same resources, they usually have different niches. For example, five species of a bird called a warbler live in

Urban Wildlife

The movement of people into areas that have been the habitats of animals has caused some problems. When their habitats are destroyed the animals often try to find a way to live within the urban environment. Raccoons, skunks, and even bears have moved into communities.

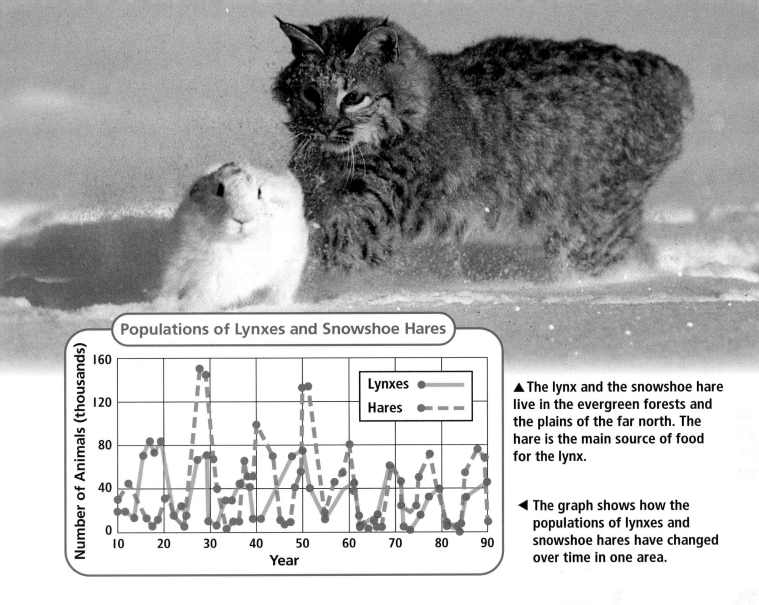

Populations of Lynxes and Snowshoe Hares

Number of Animals (thousands)

Legend:
- Lynxes ●———●
- Hares ●----●

Year: 10, 20, 30, 40, 50, 60, 70, 80, 90

▲ The lynx and the snowshoe hare live in the evergreen forests and the plains of the far north. The hare is the main source of food for the lynx.

◀ The graph shows how the populations of lynxes and snowshoe hares have changed over time in one area.

Maine's spruce forests. They all eat insects and nest in spruce trees. To reduce competition, the birds have different niches. Each species eats a different kind of insect and nests in a different part of the trees.

The predator-prey relationship also affects competition for resources in an ecosystem. A *predator* is an animal that feeds on other living animals. *Prey* is an animal that predators eat.

The graph shows the cycle of the rise and fall in the populations of one kind of predator (the lynx) and its prey (the snowshoe hare). This cycle has two main causes.

The first cause is that the primary food supply affects the hare population. When the hares have more plants to eat, their population increases. In time, there are too many hares

for the amount of food there is, and some die. As the hare population decreases, more plants begin to grow. With more food, the hare population increases. The cycle begins again.

The second cause is that the supply of prey affects the predator population. If the number of hares decreases, the lynxes have less to eat. This causes the number of lynxes to decrease. With fewer lynxes and more plants, the number of hares goes up. The increased supply of hares allows the lynx population to increase. In time, the large number of lynxes causes a decrease in the hare population, and the cycle begins again.

 CAUSE AND EFFECT Why does an increase in the number of prey affect the number of predators?

167

Organisms Interact to Meet Their Needs

Not all organisms in an ecosystem compete. Some organisms live together in a relationship called symbiosis (sim•by•OH•sis). **Symbiosis** is a close relationship between organisms of different species in which one or both of the organisms benefit. There are three types of symbiosis.

In *parasitism* (PAIR•uh•syt•iz•uhm), one species benefits while the other is harmed. A **parasite** (PAIR•uh•syt) is an organism that lives in or on another organism. The organism that a parasite lives in or on is called the **host**. Parasites are usually smaller than their hosts. Although they can weaken their hosts, parasites usually don't kill them.

Some parasites live on the outside of their hosts. Ticks and fleas live on a host animal's skin. They bite the animal and suck its blood. Other parasites, such as the dog heartworm, live inside their hosts. Adult heartworms produce tiny larvae that live in a host dog's blood.

Plants as well as animals can be hosts for parasites. Red spider mites are ticklike

▲ The honey badger and the honeyguide bird have a unique relationship. The bird eats beeswax and bee larvae. When it spots a hive, the honeyguide finds a badger and chatters to get the badger to follow. The badger breaks open the hive, and both organisms benefit.

animals. They live on houseplants, sucking sap from them.

A second type of symbiosis is *mutualism* (MYOO•choo•uhl•iz•uhm). In this relationship, both organisms benefit. You already know about one example of mutualism. Flowers provide bees with nectar for food. As bees feed, they pollinate the flowers, helping the plants reproduce.

In one photograph on this page, you see the honey badger and the honeyguide bird. The honey badger eats honey, but it has poor eyesight and can't easily find beehives. The honeyguide bird eats beeswax and bee larvae. It can find beehives easily, but it can't break them open. The two animals meet their needs by working together.

Another example of mutualism is shown in the lesson opener

The heartworm twists through the heart and lungs of dogs and other animals. The worms can grow to be 41 cm (16 in.) long.

photograph. There, you see a hermit crab carrying a sea anemone (uh•NEM•uh•nee). Normally, it would be dangerous for another animal to be so close to a sea anemone. The anemone uses its tentacles to sting prey before eating it. The anemone and the crab, however, live together peacefully. The crab gets protection among the tentacles. The anemone benefits by being taken to different areas where it feeds. Both organisms benefit.

The cleaner wrasse (RASS) removes parasites and dead skin from fish that pass by. Wrasses move in and out of the mouths of fish that would normally eat such small animals. But the fish don't eat the wrasse. The wrasses get food—the parasites—and the fish have harmful parasites removed. The same kind of relationship exists between fish and cleaner shrimp.

 CAUSE AND EFFECT What effect does mutualism have on organisms?

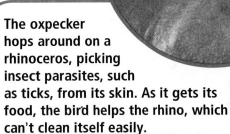

The oxpecker hops around on a rhinoceros, picking insect parasites, such as ticks, from its skin. As it gets its food, the bird helps the rhino, which can't clean itself easily.

169

These orchids are growing on a tree instead of in the soil. Unless the number of orchids on its surface becomes too great, the tree will not be harmed.

Neither Help nor Harm

The third type of symbiosis is *commensalism* (kuh•MEN•suhl•iz•uhm). In this relationship, one organism benefits and the other organism is neither helped nor harmed. This is the definition of commensalism. However, as scientists study the relationships between many of these organisms, there is some question whether either one is completely unaffected.

The barnacle and mussel are an example of commensalism. Barnacles are shelled animals. They produce a cement that helps them stick to objects such as piers and rocks. They also stick to hard surfaces of other organisms. Each barnacle in the photo has attached itself to a mussel. From there it can easily feed on tiny organisms it filters from the water. The mussel isn't helped or harmed, but the barnacle benefits.

Remoras are sucker-fish. They live near sharks or other large fish. The dorsal (back) fin of the remora forms a sucker. This allows the remora to attach itself to a shark. The small remora doesn't harm the shark, but it is protected by the shark and gets its food from the scraps the shark leaves.

Commensalism can also be seen among plants. Orchids have such a relationship with certain trees in tropical forests. Orchids are epiphytes, or air plants. They usually don't grow in soil but grow on the trunks or branches of trees. This lets the orchids live high in the forest canopy, where they can get more sunlight, moisture, and nutrients. The trees get no benefit, but they usually are not harmed.

Commensalism also happens on your body. Millions of bacteria live on your skin. They feed on dead skin cells. This doesn't help or harm you, but the bacteria benefit.

These barnacles will remain stuck to these mussels throughout their lives.

 CAUSE AND EFFECT How are the effects of commensalism and parasitism different?

1. CAUSE AND EFFECT Draw and complete this graphic organizer.

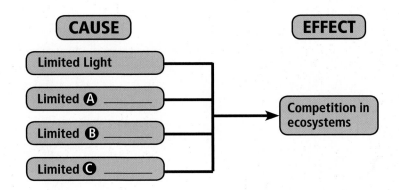

CAUSE   **EFFECT**

Limited Light

Limited Ⓐ _____

Limited Ⓑ _____

Limited Ⓒ _____

→ Competition in ecosystems

2. SUMMARIZE Write a summary of this lesson. Start with the sentence "Organisms in ecosystems interact in many ways."

3. DRAW CONCLUSIONS Do a pet and its owner have a "symbiotic relationship"? If so, which type of symbiosis is the relationship? Explain.

4. VOCABULARY Write a brief paragraph that compares the three types of symbiosis.

Test Prep

5. Critical Thinking Do you have a predator-prey relationship with any other organisms? Explain your answer.

6. Which relationship exists between organisms in commensalism?

  A. Both organisms benefit.

  B. Neither organism benefits.

  C. One organism benefits, and the other is harmed.

  D. One organism benefits, and the other is neither helped nor harmed.

Links

Writing

Persuasive Writing

In many areas, new roads and buildings are expanding into what once were forests, grasslands, and wetlands. Should this development be limited? Write an **essay** that expresses your opinion.

Math

Display Data

In the line graph on page 167, you saw how the hare and lynx populations rise and fall. Find something else in nature that changes in regular cycles. Construct a line graph to show the cycles of change.

Music

Write a Song

Compose song lyrics about the ways organisms in an ecosystem interact. Set the lyrics to the tune of any well-known song. Perform the song live, or record it on audiotape and play it for the class.

 For more links and activities, go to **www.hspscience.com**

What Are Biomes?

Fast Fact

You're Getting Colder In general, as a mountain's altitude increases, the temperature drops about 6°C for every 1000 m (11°F for every 3300 ft). If you travel into the mountains, even during the summer months, you are likely to find cooler temperatures. You will also notice differences in the kinds of plants that grow there. In the Investigate, you will find out about climates in different parts of Earth.

World Biomes

Materials
- world map of biomes on pages 174 and 175
- paper
- pencil

Procedure

1. Look at the world map on pages 174 and 175. Use the key to identify the different climate areas, or biomes.

2. Copy and complete Table A, using the information from the map. Look for the biomes found at each latitude. To get started, run your finger along latitude line 75°N. For each biome at that latitude, mark an X in the correct box in the table. Do the same for all the other latitude lines on the map.

3. Copy Table B on a different sheet of paper. Look for the biomes found at each longitude. Run your finger along longitude line 0°. For each biome at that longitude, mark an X in the correct box of the table. Repeat for all lines of longitude listed in the table.

Draw Conclusions

1. From the data you recorded, infer whether latitude or longitude is more important in determining the location of a biome. Explain.

2. Observe the area between latitudes 30°N and 45°N in North America. What is the order of biomes from west to east in the area?

3. **Inquiry Skill** How did interpreting the data in your tables help you determine whether latitude or longitude has a greater effect on the location of biomes?

Table A

Biomes	tundra	taiga	deciduous forest	grasslands	desert	tropical rain forest
75°N						
60°N						
45°N						
30°N						
15°N						
0°						
15°S						
30°S						
45°S						
60°S						
75°S						

°Latitude

Table B

Biomes	tundra	taiga	deciduous forest	grasslands	desert	tropical rain forest
0°						
30°E						
60°E						
90°E						
120°E						
150°E						
180°						
150°W						
120°W						
90°W						
60°W						
30°W						

°Longitude

Investigate Further

Formulate a hypothesis to explain why there is no taiga and very little deciduous forest in the Southern Hemisphere. Then **plan and conduct a simple investigation** to test your hypothesis.

Reading in Science

VOCABULARY
biome p. 174

SCIENCE CONCEPTS
▶ what a biome is
▶ how plants and animals are adapted to live in different biomes

READING FOCUS SKILL
COMPARE AND CONTRAST
Look for ways biomes are alike and different.

| alike | different |

Biomes

Have you ever taken a long trip? If so, the place you visited may not have looked or felt like home. You probably saw different types of plants and animals. The temperature may have felt much warmer or colder than what you're used to. When you go to an area with different plants, animals, and climate, you're probably passing from one biome to another.

A **biome** (BY•ohm) is a region of the world defined by its climate and by the types of plants and animals that live there. Some biomes, such as tropical rain forests, are hot and humid. Others are cold and snowy and have very few animals. There are wet biomes and dry biomes.

Science Up Close

World Biomes

Grassland

Grassland covers a large area in South America. The grassland's dry climate doesn't provide enough water for the growth of large trees.

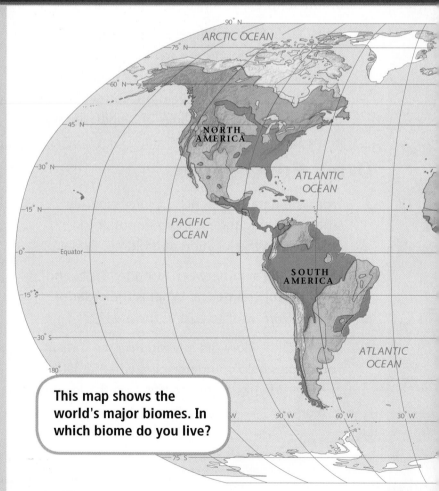

This map shows the world's major biomes. In which biome do you live?

174

Some biomes have wide, grassy plains. Others have high meadows surrounded by tall mountains.

What determines the locations of biomes? The most important factor is climate—yearly patterns of temperature and precipitation. The plants and animals in each biome are adapted to its climate. For example, many desert plants have small, thick leaves with a waxy coating that helps prevent water loss. In the cold Arctic plains, polar bears have thick fur and extra layers of fat that help them stay warm.

A biome's climate is affected by its latitude. The climate near the equator generally is warm and wet. These conditions are perfect for lush tropical forests and the animals that live in them. Closer to the poles, climates are colder and drier. Forests change from deciduous to evergreen, and the numbers of plant and animal species decrease. At the highest latitudes, no trees can grow. The climate is so harsh that very few species can live there.

Altitude also helps determine a biome's climate. Temperature drops as altitude increases. Some mountain peaks have snow on them all year, even in summer. At lower altitudes, where temperatures are warmer, green meadows can be found.

 COMPARE AND CONTRAST How does climate at low latitudes compare with climate at higher latitudes?

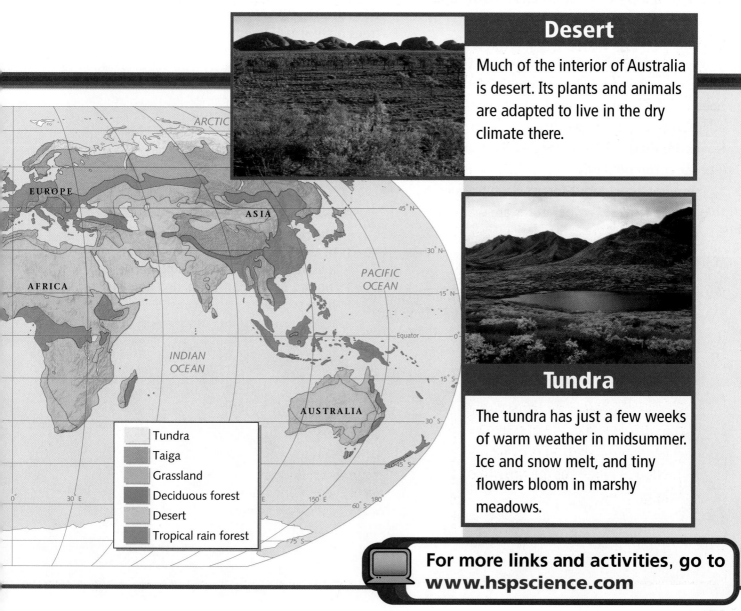

Desert

Much of the interior of Australia is desert. Its plants and animals are adapted to live in the dry climate there.

Tundra

The tundra has just a few weeks of warm weather in midsummer. Ice and snow melt, and tiny flowers bloom in marshy meadows.

Tundra
Taiga
Grassland
Deciduous forest
Desert
Tropical rain forest

For more links and activities, go to www.hspscience.com

Forest Biomes

All forests have some things in common. They form in areas with enough rainfall and warmth for trees to grow, and trees are the main vegetation in each. However, the types of trees and other plants in forests differ, depending on climate and landforms.

In tropical forests, towering trees grow close together to form a dense layer of leaves. The leaves provide shade for the forest floor. Tropical rain forests grow where temperatures are always warm and there is a lot of rainfall—often more than 254 cm (100 in.) each year.

The vegetation of the rain forest grows in layers. Plants that need the most sun grow in or near the canopy, or topmost layer. Plants that need shade grow below. Diversity is greater in tropical rain forests than in any other biome.

Many rain-forest animals are adapted to live in the forest canopy. They can meet all their needs in the treetops. Rain-forest plants are adapted to a hot climate with daily rain. Many leaves are long, with narrow tips. This shape lets water run off easily.

Temperate deciduous forests have trees with thin, broad leaves. Temperatures are warm in summer, but winters are cold and often snowy. Precipitation is plentiful, but these forests get about half the rain that tropical forests get.

In fall, leaves in the temperate deciduous forests turn brilliant shades of orange, gold, and red and then fall off the trees. This happens because temperatures are colder and there are fewer hours of sunlight during the day. The trees remain leafless until spring, when they form new leaves and the growth cycle starts again.

The forest biome that is farthest north is the taiga (TY•guh). Summers there are short and mild. Winters are long and cold. The taiga gets less precipitation than other forest biomes, and most of what it gets falls as snow. Most trees in the taiga are conifers. Because these trees have small, needlelike leaves with a waxy

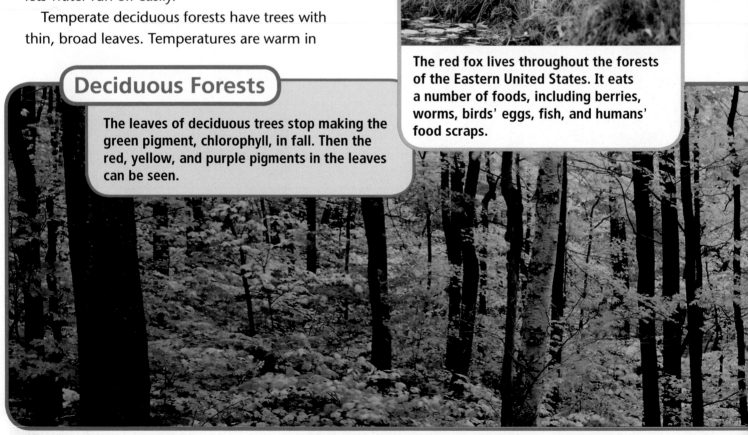

The red fox lives throughout the forests of the Eastern United States. It eats a number of foods, including berries, worms, birds' eggs, fish, and humans' food scraps.

Deciduous Forests

The leaves of deciduous trees stop making the green pigment, chlorophyll, in fall. Then the red, yellow, and purple pigments in the leaves can be seen.

Conifer Forests

Conifers are the main vegetation of the taiga. Because of the harsh climate, trees can't grow north of this biome.

Marmots are plant eaters of the taiga. They fatten up in fall and then hibernate through the winter in burrows.

surface, they can stand very cold, dry winters.

Large areas of Earth's forests have been cut down to make room for farms and expanding towns. Some people are especially concerned about the loss of tropical rain forests. About 45 percent of prescription drugs contain ingredients that originally came from plants found in tropical rain forests. Many rain-forest

species have not been studied yet. Scientists fear that many useful plants are being lost with the loss of the tropical rain forests. How do the needs of people for living space conflict with needs for further scientific discovery?

 COMPARE AND CONTRAST What differences are there between plants in a rain forest and those in a temperate deciduous forest?

Like many rain-forest animals, this toucan lives in the forest canopy. Many animals never leave the treetops.

Tropical Rain Forests

Tropical rain forests stay green and wet all the time. Although the treetops are thick with leaves, vines, and flowers, the forest floor is very open.

The Gobi is a large area of northern China and southern Mongolia. *Gobi* means "desert" in Mongolian. The Gobi has mountains, grasses, sand, and sand dunes.

The Bactrian camel of central Asia has long fur that helps it stay warm during cold winters. It can eat almost any type of desert vegetation and can live for weeks without water.

Desert and Tundra Biomes

When you think of a desert, you probably think of a hot, dry place. If so, you're only partly right. Deserts are dry. In general, they get less than 25 cm (10 in.) of rain each year. However, they're not always hot. Some deserts get cold at night. Some have daytime temperatures below freezing in winter.

Hot deserts are often found in areas between latitudes 20° and 30° north or south. In those areas, masses of dry air sink toward Earth's surface, preventing the formation of rain clouds. Deserts in higher latitudes are usually toward the middle of a continent and far from the ocean. They are also behind mountain ranges that block the wet air masses that blow off the ocean. These are rainshadow deserts.

In order to survive, desert animals must find and conserve water and avoid overheating.

Many desert plants have leaves with a waxy coating to hold in moisture. Some plants, such as the mesquite (meh•SKEET), have deep root systems that seek out water. The saguaro cactus has a shallow root system that collects scarce rainfall before the water soaks into the ground.

Many animals in hot deserts adapt to the climate by staying inactive in burrows and in cracks in the rocks during the heat of the day. At night, when it's cooler, they move around and hunt. Insects and reptiles have thick body coverings to prevent moisture loss.

The tundra is a treeless region next to the polar ice caps and high on some mountains. Its climate is bitterly cold in winter, and it gets very little precipitation. Snow covers the ground most of the year.

It is too cold and dry for trees to grow in the tundra. Because of strong winds, lack of moisture, and a short growing season, plants are small and grow close to the ground. Like some desert plants, tundra plants have small, tough leaves with waxy coatings. This coating keeps the leaves from losing moisture.

Many tundra animals, such as the caribou, migrate south during the coldest part of the year. Animals that stay on the tundra through the winter have adaptations that help them survive the cold. The arctic fox, arctic wolf, and musk ox have thick fur. The snowy owl has thick feathers. Animals such as the arctic ground squirrel hibernate underground, conserving energy. Lemmings spend the winter in tunnels in the snow, eating grass.

 COMPARE AND CONTRAST Compare the adaptations of desert and tundra leaves, and explain how they help plants survive.

Canadian Tundra

The Canadian tundra is a harsh environment just south of the ice fields of the Arctic.

Caribou move north to the tundra in spring. They graze during the warmer months and have their young. As temperatures drop, they head south again.

Grasslands

The Russian steppe is a dry grassland in the heart of Asia. The steppe is cut off from moisture by mountains and by its distance from large bodies of water.

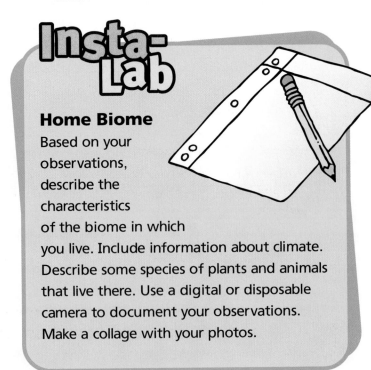

The gray wolf is a common predator on the steppe. It can live in many different environments with a wide range of temperatures.

Grassland Biomes

Grasslands are biomes in which the main plants are grasses. There are vast grasslands in the middle of several continents.

Rainfall varies, but in general, grasslands do not receive enough precipitation for many trees to grow. There are two types of grasslands—temperate and tropical. Temperate grasslands, such as those in North America, have hot, dry summers and very cold winters. Grasses go dormant during dry or cold periods, but the roots remain active. The plants sprout new leaves when conditions become favorable. Tropical grasslands are warm all year, with a wet season and a dry season. Tropical grasslands are often called savannas (suh•VAN•uhz). Grazing animals, such as antelope, are common in grasslands.

Unlike the broad leaves of the trees in deciduous forests, leaves of grassland plants are long and narrow to prevent water loss. Grasses also have large, fibrous root systems that quickly soak up much of the scarce rain that falls.

 COMPARE AND CONTRAST How do the climates of temperate and tropical grasslands differ?

Insta-Lab

Home Biome

Based on your observations, describe the characteristics of the biome in which you live. Include information about climate. Describe some species of plants and animals that live there. Use a digital or disposable camera to document your observations. Make a collage with your photos.

1. **COMPARE AND CONTRAST** Draw and complete this graphic organizer.

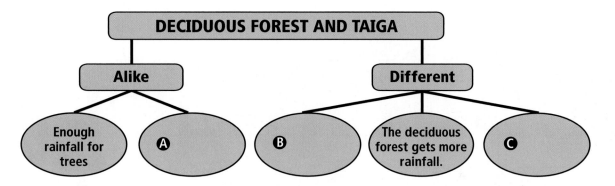

DECIDUOUS FOREST AND TAIGA

Alike
- Enough rainfall for trees
- Ⓐ

Different
- Ⓑ
- The deciduous forest gets more rainfall.
- Ⓒ

2. **SUMMARIZE** Write a paragraph that summarizes the most important information in this lesson.

3. **DRAW CONCLUSIONS** A certain type of leaf is green in color, flat, thin, and broad. To which biome might this leaf be adapted? Explain your answer.

4. **VOCABULARY** Write your own definition of the term *biome*. How is an ecosystem different from a biome?

Test Prep

5. **Critical Thinking** Places very high in the mountains have cold temperatures, snow, a short growing season, and a lack of trees. Which biome is found in these high places?

6. Which of these is a characteristic of the tundra biome?
   A. wet all year   **C.** hot, dry summers
   B. scarce rainfall   **D.** warm even in winter

Links

Writing

Expressive Writing

Think about a biome that you haven't visited but would like to see someday. Write a **personal letter** to a friend, describing the biome and telling why you'd like to go there.

Math

Collect and Display Data

Make a table that compares the climate characteristics of the biomes. Include data on annual temperatures and precipitation. List other characteristics as well. Display your table in the classroom.

Social Studies

Changing Environment

How have people changed the natural characteristics of the biome in which you live during the last 200 years? With a partner, do research to find out. Use photographs and illustrations as you give a brief oral report to the class.

 For more links and activities, go to www.hspscience.com

UNDERWATER KILLING FIELDS

Roger Mak enjoys eating shark fin soup. He pays $40 a bowl twice a month for the delicacy. "I love this stuff," he raves as he scoops up a second helping at a noisy Hong Kong restaurant.

Mak doesn't know that the fishermen who caught the shark are turning coral reefs into aquatic graveyards. Coral reefs are formed by millions of tiny sea animals called corals. When they die, they leave limestone "skeletons" that form coral reefs. New corals grow on top of the skeletons.

When fishing near coral reefs, fishermen use sodium cyanide, a poison, to temporarily stun fish. Scientists say that this chemical is slowly killing the coral reefs. Other fishermen use dynamite to stun and catch the fish, destroying huge chunks of coral in the process.

Such techniques are some of the main causes of the destruction of 27 percent of the world's coral reefs. Air and water pollution from factories, cities, and farms contribute to their ruin.

Many countries have already taken steps to combat the causes of the rising ocean temperatures, but scientists say more needs to be done. Although destructive fishing techniques are already illegal, many countries find policing such activities very difficult.

Think About It

1. What role do you think coral reefs play in the ocean's ecosystem?
2. How can satellites help scientists protect coral reefs?

Ecological Disaster

An estimated 35,000 to 60,000 marine species live in and around coral reefs. Those organisms are part of a unique ecosystem. Members of an ecosystem depend on one another for food and shelter. If one species of the ecosystem dies, the other members are in danger.

Another threat to coral reefs is bleaching. Bleaching occurs when rising sea temperatures put a lot of stress on corals. The corals then expel the microscopic plants in their systems that provide them with food and color.

Some scientists say the rising temperature is caused by the buildup of greenhouse gases in the atmosphere. Greenhouse gases trap heat from the sun, preventing it from escaping into space.

A VIEW FROM ABOVE

Scientists study coral reefs by visiting specific sites or by studying detailed images taken by satellites, such as Landsat 7. The images show where the reefs are found. Over time they can also show changes in reefs.

Using images, observations and data, scientists hypothesize that the planet's coral reefs might be destroyed in less than 20 years. "Like rain forests, reefs harbor much of the planet's wealth of species and are being rapidly degraded by humans," said Dirk Bryant, a scientist at the World Resources Institute.

Find out more! Log on to **www.hspscience.com**

Elephant Talk

Joyce Poole is not exactly Dr. Dolittle, but she swears that elephants can talk. She said the animals' squeals, screams, snorts, rumbles, and groans have special meanings—just like the words humans use.

Poole lives among about 1000 African savanna elephants in Kenya's Amboseli National Park. The park is on Kenya's border with Tanzania and near Mount Kilimanjaro, Africa's highest peak.

Poole, a wildlife biologist, has discovered that elephants use more than 70 vocal sounds to communicate with other elephants. The sounds range from soft whispers to ear-splitting roars.

According to Poole, elephants use their "voices" to warn others of danger, to form packs, to defend themselves, and to tell other elephants what they want.

Poole and other biologists have studied much more than how elephants "talk." They have found that the pachyderms also use 160 different types of touch, sight, and even chemical signals to interact with one another.

Career Ecologist

To help protect the ecosystem of an endangered animal, conservationists might turn to an ecologist. Ecologists study the relationships among organisms. They also study the relationship between the organisms and their environments. Ecologists look at such things as the impact of population size, pollutants, and rainfall.

You Can Do It!

Materials
- 3 paper towels
- bowl with water
- large cookie sheet
- wax paper
- paper clips

Quick and Easy Project

Desert Leaves

Procedure

1. Wet each paper towel. Squeeze out some of the water so that it's not dripping.
2. Place one towel flat on the cookie sheet.
3. Roll up the second towel, and place it next to the flat towel.
4. Roll up the third towel. Roll the wax paper around it, and paper-clip it in place. Place this roll next to the other roll.
5. Place the cookie sheet in a sunny place. Wait 24 hours.
6. Unroll the towels. Feel each towel to see if it is still damp.

Draw Conclusions

Which towel kept the most water? Which kept the least? Why? Use your results to explain how the structure of leaves of desert plants helps them conserve the desert's limited water.

Design Your Own Investigation

Do People Affect Ecosystems?

What effects do people have on ecosystems? Observe a part of an ecosystem where you live. What are the human effects? Are any parts of the natural ecosystem still there? If not, what has replaced them? Design an investigation that will help you determine how to make observations and collect data to identify changes in an ecosystem. Compare your results with those of other students in your class.

Vocabulary Review

Use the terms below to complete the sentences. The page numbers tell you where to look in the chapter if you need help.

ecosystem p. 151   **community** p. 152
habitat p. 153   **niche** p. 153
producer p. 158   **consumer** p. 159
symbiosis p. 168   **biome** p. 174

1. An organism's role in an ecosystem is its _____ .

2. All the populations living in an ecosystem make up a _____ .

3. A close relationship between organisms of different species that benefits one or both of the organisms is _____ .

4. The part of an ecosystem in which an organism lives is its _____ .

5. A region of the world defined by its climate and by the kinds of plants and animals that live there is a _____ .

6. All the living and nonliving things that interact with one another in an area make up an _____ .

7. An organism that makes its own food is a _____ .

8. An organism that eats other organisms is a _____ .

Check Understanding

Write the letter of the best choice.

9. **COMPARE AND CONTRAST** Which of these is **NOT** an abiotic part of an ecosystem?
   A. bacteria
   B. humidity
   C. soil
   D. sunlight

10. **CAUSE AND EFFECT** Which would happen if all the rabbits in this ecosystem died from a disease?

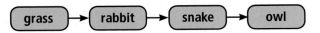

grass → rabbit → snake → owl

   F. Snakes would eat grass instead of rabbits.
   G. No energy would flow through the ecosystem.
   H. Producers would not make food.
   J. The population of snakes would decrease.

11. Which of the following ecosystems would be likely to have the greatest diversity?
    A. a high mountain meadow
    B. a desert valley
    C. a temperate deciduous forest
    D. a lake in the taiga

12. Which is the source of energy in an ecosystem?
    F. decomposers
    G. nutrients in the soil
    H. sunlight
    J. water

13. Which of these is an example of commensalism?
    A. You catch a fish and eat it.
    B. A mosquito bites you.
    C. You pick and eat a peach from a tree.
    D. A virus gives you the flu.

14. Why do organisms compete within ecosystems?
    F. There are limited resources.
    G. They occupy different niches.
    H. They want to increase diversity.
    J. Humans cause them to compete.

15. Which of these is **NOT** a forest biome?
    A. the taiga
    B. the tundra
    C. an area in which most of the plants are deciduous trees
    D. an area in which most of the plants are conifers

16. Which of these would be a useful adaptation for living in a desert biome?
    F. thick leaves with a waxy coating
    G. trees that lose their leaves in the fall
    H. broad, thin leaves
    J. fur that repels water

Inquiry Skills

17. To compare the climates of two different biomes, why is it more useful to interpret data from graphs and tables than to take notes from direct observation?

18. From your observations of owl pellets, what can you infer about the foods owls eat?

Critical Thinking

19. A company wants to build a new shopping center. To do so, it must drain a swamp and cut down several hectares of a forest. The company promises to replant trees as part of a new park when the shopping center is finished. How will these plans affect the swamp and forest ecosystems? Will the new park provide a solution? Explain your answer.

20. As you learned, the chief way to analyze biomes is by looking at temperature and precipitation data from a region.
    Part A Summarize the temperature and precipitation data shown in the graphs.
    Part B In which biome is it most likely that these temperature and precipitation readings were taken? Explain your answer.

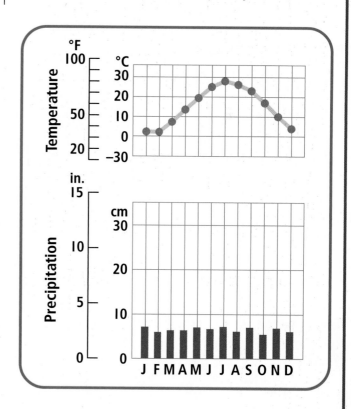

Chapter 5

Resources in Ecosystems

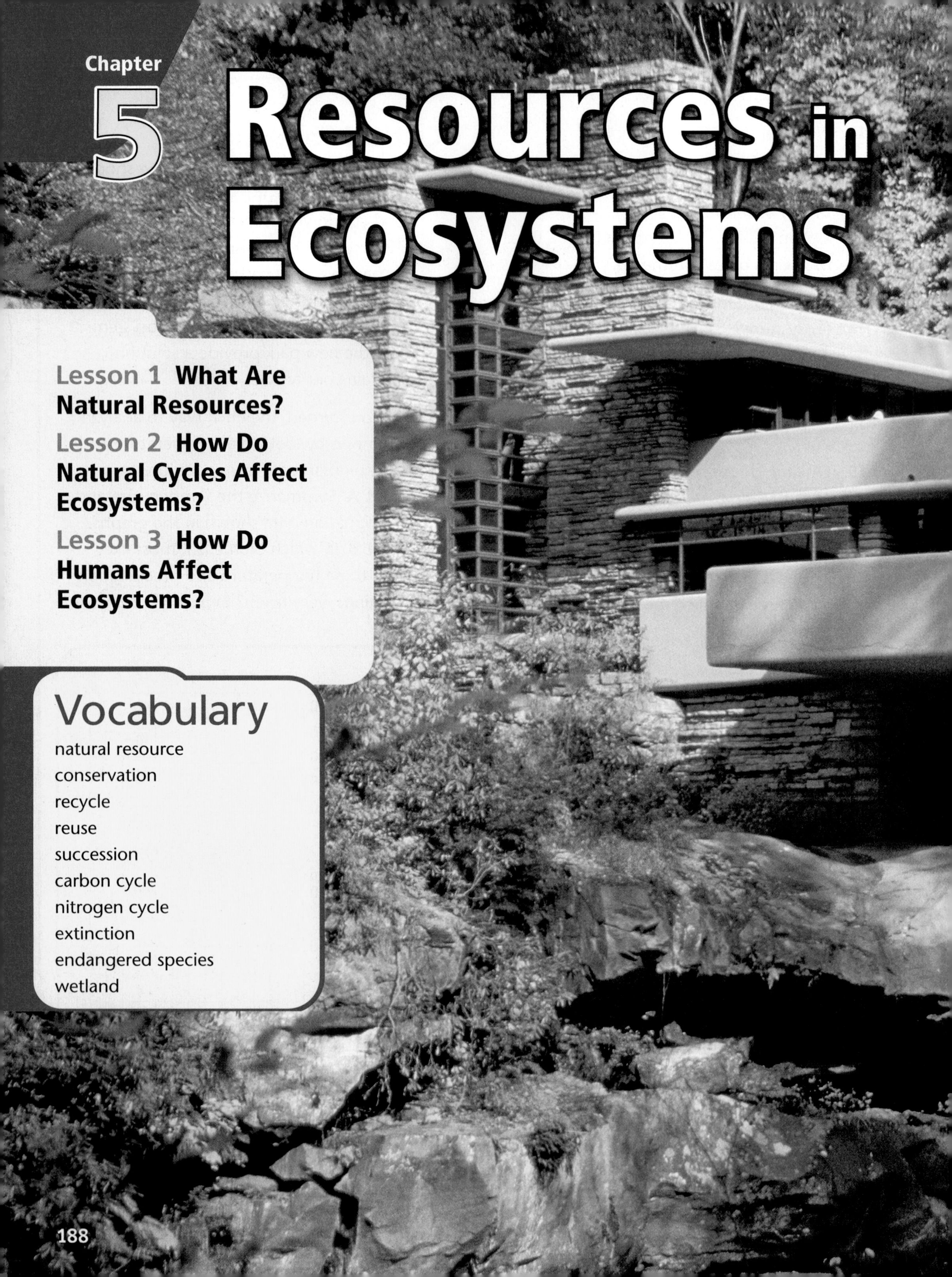

Lesson 1 **What Are Natural Resources?**

Lesson 2 **How Do Natural Cycles Affect Ecosystems?**

Lesson 3 **How Do Humans Affect Ecosystems?**

Vocabulary

natural resource
conservation
recycle
reuse
succession
carbon cycle
nitrogen cycle
extinction
endangered species
wetland

What do YOU wonder?

The structures people build can change ecosystems or blend into them. Frank Lloyd Wright designed this house, which he named Fallingwater. How did Wright blend the house into the forest? How might a house that doesn't blend in as well change this ecosystem?

What Are Natural Resources?

Fast Fact

Tall Trees California redwood trees can grow as tall as 122 m (367 ft)—the height of a 35-story building. Trees are an important natural resource. They can be used to construct buildings and to make furniture and paper. They also provide shade and produce oxygen. In the Investigate, you will make your own recycled paper.

New Paper from Old Paper

Materials
- safety goggles
- water
- piece of wire
- window screen with taped edges
- scrap paper
- laundry starch
- eggbeater
- metric ruler
- measuring cup
- 2 pages of newspaper
- basin
- thick dowel

Procedure

1. Tear the scrap paper into strips no longer than 2 cm. Put the strips in the basin.

2. Add water. Keep track of the number of milliliters you add.

3. For each 240 mL of water, add 16 mL of starch.

4. **CAUTION: Put on safety goggles.** Beat the mixture with the eggbeater until it forms a watery pulp.

5. Dip the screen into the mixture, coating one side with a thin layer of pulp. Put the screen between the sheets of newspaper.

6. Roll the thick dowel over the newspaper to remove as much water as possible from the pulp. Let the pulp air-dry. Then carefully peel your new sheet of paper off the screen.

Step 1

Step 4

Draw Conclusions

1. Compare the paper you made with paper you use in school.

2. Some of the paper you use has been recycled from old paper. Draw conclusions about why people might choose to make paper from waste materials instead of from trees.

3. **Inquiry Skill** Like scientists, you used a model to see how something might work on a larger scale. Using what you learned, suggest ways recycled paper can be made in a large factory.

Investigate Further

Use scraps from other types of paper to make a different type of recycled paper. What differences do you observe?

Reading in Science

VOCABULARY

natural resource p. 192
conservation p. 196
recycle p. 196
reuse p. 197

SCIENCE CONCEPTS

▶ what things are natural resources

▶ how we use and conserve natural resources

READING FOCUS SKILL

MAIN IDEA AND DETAILS Look for details about how to conserve resources.

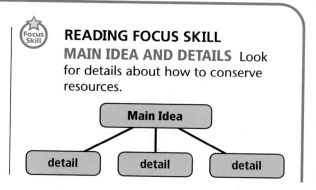

Natural Resources in Our Community

Right now, you're probably inside a school building made of wood, stone, or bricks. Maybe you walked across an asphalt street or parking lot to get there. There's a good chance that electric lights are on in your classroom. You may have used metal coins to buy your lunch in the cafeteria. The foods in your lunch may have been brought to your school from far away by diesel-fueled trucks or trains.

As you can see, you've used a lot of natural resources since you got out of bed this morning. A **natural resource** is a material that is found

Math in Science
Interpret Data

In the United States, we not only use a lot of resources, but we also throw a lot away. The circle graph shows the percent of resources we dispose of each year. Use the information in the graph to make a list of waste from greatest to least. Mark the list to show what materials are recyclable. What percent of total waste would be saved if we recycled four of those materials?

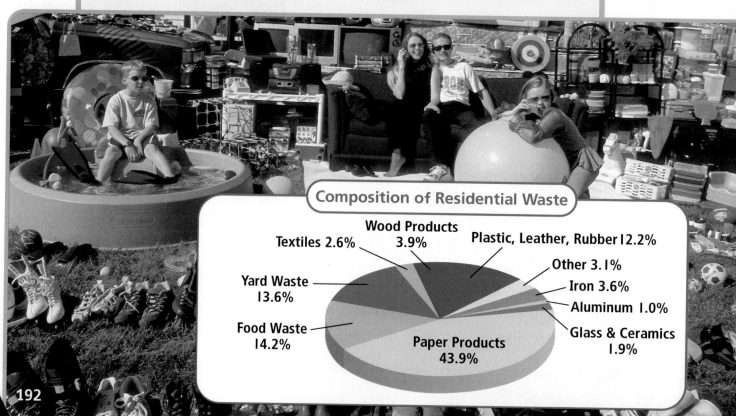

Composition of Residential Waste

- Textiles 2.6%
- Wood Products 3.9%
- Plastic, Leather, Rubber 12.2%
- Other 3.1%
- Yard Waste 13.6%
- Iron 3.6%
- Aluminum 1.0%
- Food Waste 14.2%
- Glass & Ceramics 1.9%
- Paper Products 43.9%

Construction of a House

Construction of a house requires many natural resources—wood, copper, and stone.

Construction of a Road

Most roads are paved with asphalt, a thick substance made from crude oil—petroleum taken directly from underground wells.

in nature that is essential or useful to people. Natural resources include the trees from which this page was made and the wood, the stone, or the clay for the bricks of your school building. They include the oil used to produce your school's electricity and to fuel the vehicles that transport your food. They include the air you breathe and the water you drink.

How much of each resource does your community need? Each year, miners remove from the land about 8000 kg (17,600 lb) of gravel, stone, and sand for each American. These materials are used to pave roads, make cement, and build houses.

The United States uses about 3500 kg (7700 lb) of oil per person per year. The oil heats homes and generates electricity. It fuels cars, trucks,

and planes. It also makes materials such as asphalt, plastic, and paint.

Your community uses metals for everything from bridges, appliances, and factory machines to pots, soft drink cans, and paper clips. Each person in the United States uses about 25 kg (55 lb) of aluminum per year. For iron and steel, we use more than 20 times as much.

 MAIN IDEA AND DETAILS What does oil provide to your community?

Every one of these items can be recycled. How many of them does your community recycle?

Resources from the Environment

Many natural resources come from Earth. They grow in soil. They are dug or pumped from the ground. They flow on Earth's surface. They cycle between Earth's land, atmosphere, and oceans.

There are about 500,000 mines in the United States. Some of our most important resources, including coal, gravel, and metals such as iron, copper, nickel, and gold, come from them. In places where resources are deep below the surface, miners tunnel underground to uncover them. In places where resources are close to the surface, miners can simply scrape them out from beneath the vegetation and soil.

Crude oil is found, usually with natural gas, in pockets in the rock layers beneath Earth's surface. Millions of years ago, small sea organisms died and were buried under thick layers of sediment. Over time, under the intense pressure of the rock above them, their remains formed crude oil. To get the oil, people drill through the layers of rock. Wells on land and offshore pump the crude oil to the surface. Pipes, trucks, and oil tankers then take the oil to refineries. There the crude oil is made into the many products we use.

Forests provide lumber and paper products. Most lumber still comes from natural forest ecosystems, but an increasing amount now comes from forest plantations. These are farms that grow certain species of trees as crops. When the trees mature, loggers cut them down. Then the tree farmers plant a new crop.

Water use in the United States is higher per person than in any other country. People in cities use 150–400 L (50–100 gal) of water each

◄ People use forests for hiking, camping, and other recreational activities. Forests are home to many plants and animals. The trees help prevent soil erosion. Cutting forests impacts the environment. New trees need to be replanted soon after trees are harvested.

Millions of trees are cut each year for lumber and paper. In selective logging, loggers cut some trees in each area, reducing the impact on the forest ecosystem.

day. Drinking water comes from surface sources, such as rivers and lakes, and from water that collects underground. Water can also be an energy resource. The energy of water rushing through hydroelectric (hy•droh•ee•LEK•trik) dams is used to generate electricity.

Soil is another important resource. Think back to the food chains you learned about in Chapter 4. Plants are the foundation of food chains on land. In most cases, plants need the nutrients and water they get from soil to grow.

Animals are important food resources. Beef and dairy cattle produce meat and milk. People all over the world eat fish and other water-dwelling organisms. Animals are also used to produce clothing. For example, leather is made from animal skins.

The sea provides important energy resources. You have read about the crude oil that is pumped from beneath the sea floor. Several

Cranberries can be harvested using the "dry" method or the "wet" method. The method of harvesting determines the ways the berries will be used. Good soil is needed to grow the best cranberries.

power plants also produce electricity from the energy of tides and ocean waves.

 MAIN IDEA AND DETAILS What are two sources of drinking water?

In some places, resources such as coal and metals are dug from huge pits in surface mines.

The aluminum in cans is made from bauxite ore. Bauxite is refined to produce a white powder called alumina. Passing a strong electric current through alumina turns it into liquid aluminum metal.

Recycled cans are made from used cans instead of from new aluminum. The cans are melted down and pressed into new sheets of metal. These are then formed into new cans.

Managing Resources

Suppose you have seven peaches. They are all the peaches you will get for a week. You might like them so much that you eat them all in just two days. Or you might make them last by eating just one each day.

Conserve In the second case above, you are practicing conservation. **Conservation** is the careful use of resources so that they will last as long as possible. You are practicing conservation if you eat only one peach a day. Conservation of some resources is important because their supplies are limited. They are nonrenewable. A *nonrenewable resource* is one that can't be replaced within a human lifetime. Coal, oil, natural gas, and metals are nonrenewable resources.

There are also renewable resources. A *renewable resource* is one that can be replaced within a human lifetime. Animals and plants are renewable resources. Young animals and plants quickly replace those that die.

Trees are renewable resources. However, the ecosystems in which they grow are not. Once trees are cut down, the ecosystem may never recover, especially if the area is used for a housing development or a shopping center.

Soil is forming all the time, but it is still considered a nonrenewable resource. It can take a thousand years for a thin layer of new soil to form.

Recycle When you finish a soft drink, what can you do with the can? You can recycle it. To **recycle** is to process used products into new products by using the materials again.

Why recycle? It saves resources and energy. Making new aluminum cans from recycled ones saves bauxite ore, the rocks from which we can

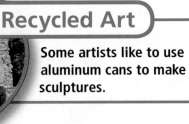

Some artists like to use aluminum cans to make sculptures.

196

get aluminum. It uses 95 percent less energy and results in less pollution.

Reduce Using less of a resource helps conserve it. This is especially important for fuels. The United States has about 5 percent of the world's people, but it uses about 25 percent of the world's energy resources. Americans can conserve fuel by driving less and walking or biking more. They could drive smaller cars that go farther on a gallon of gas. They could save electricity by turning off lights and computers when they are not using them. If people used less electricity, power plants would use less fuel and produce less pollution.

Reuse Another way to conserve resources is to reuse things. To **reuse** items is to use them again after their original use. For example, you can reuse a cardboard shoe box to keep things in. You can make a planter or a bird feeder out of a used milk container. What other ways can you think of to reuse things?

 MAIN IDEA AND DETAILS Why is it important to recycle?

When you take a reusable tote bag to the grocery store, you save the resources that are used to make paper and plastic bags.

Reduce

Insta-Lab

Finding Ways to Reuse Things

Look at objects around your house. Design a way to reuse one of them. Bring the object to class, and explain how you plan to reuse it. Then use the object for that purpose at home or at school. Did your idea work? Why or why not?

Reuse

Rubber plants produce the rubber that is made into some types of tires. Unlike aluminum, rubber can't be melted down and recycled. When tires wore out, millions of them were dumped into landfills each year.

Today, many old tires are shredded into rubber crumbs, which can be made into safe playground surfaces.

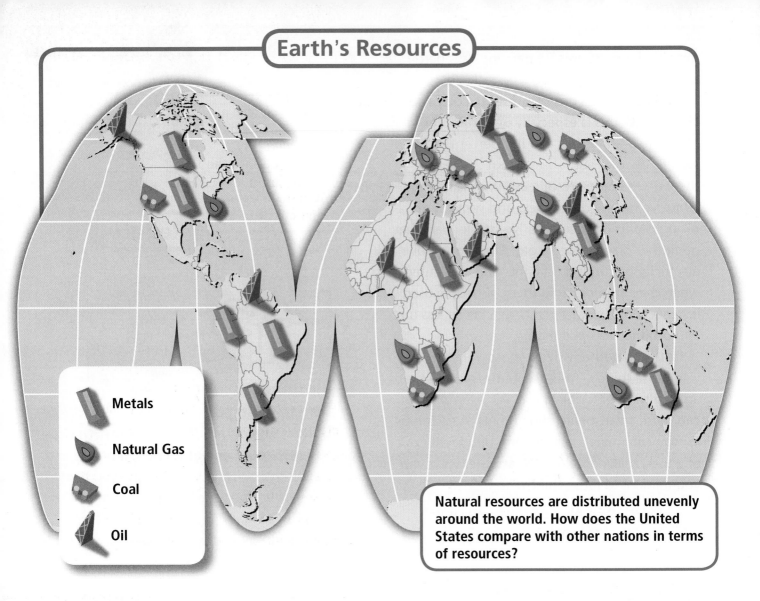

Metals

Natural Gas

Coal

Oil

Natural resources are distributed unevenly around the world. How does the United States compare with other nations in terms of resources?

Where Resources May Be Found

Americans use a lot of energy resources. Most of these are nonrenewable resources such as coal, oil, and natural gas. The United States has just 3 percent of the world's crude oil, but it uses about 25 percent of the oil the world produces. It imports more than half of the oil it uses from places such as Saudi Arabia, Mexico, Nigeria, and Venezuela.

The United States has large supplies of coal and natural gas, so it does not have to import large amounts of these resources. Look at the map. What parts of the United States have supplies of coal and natural gas?

Forests cover about one-third of Earth's land surface. Forests provide wood as well as food and wildlife resources. What parts of the United States have the most forests?

Your community has its own resources. You may live in an area where there are coal mines or oil wells. There may be forests nearby where loggers cut trees. Perhaps your area has stone quarries where stone that is used by artists is quarried. Maybe you live near a hot spring. Every community has soil, water, and air that people need and use. What other natural resources are found where you live?

 MAIN IDEA AND DETAILS Why does the United States import more than half of the oil it uses?

1. **MAIN IDEA AND DETAILS** Copy and complete the graphic organizer.

WAYS TO MANAGE RESOURCES

Ⓐ   Ⓑ   Ⓒ   Ⓓ

2. **SUMMARIZE** Write three or four sentences that summarize this lesson.

3. **DRAW CONCLUSIONS** According to the definition of *natural resource* on page 192, is air a natural resource? Explain.

4. **VOCABULARY** Make a word search puzzle that uses all the lesson vocabulary words.

Test Prep

5. **Critical Thinking** The United States depends mostly on nonrenewable resources for energy. Can this continue forever? Explain.

6. Which of the following resources does the United States import from other countries?

   A. coal   **C.** oil

   B. natural gas   **D.** water

Links

Writing

Persuasive Writing

Imagine that you run an electric generating plant. Write a **business letter** to your customers, explaining why they should use less electricity and how doing so will help your community.

Math

Calculate Using Percent

The United States has about 5 percent of the world's people, but uses about 25 percent of the world's energy resources. If the United States has about 300 million people, what is the world's population?

Social Studies

Check Out Resources

Choose a natural resource. Draw a map showing where it is found. Write a caption explaining how the resource is used, and whether and how it could be conserved. Attach an index card to your map with this information.

 For more links and activities, go to www.hspscience.com

How Do Natural Cycles Affect Ecosystems?

Fast Fact

Autumn Color Warm, sunny days, followed by nights with temperatures that drop below 7°C (about 45°F), bring out vivid autumn colors. Chlorophyll production stops, so the green fades, and yellow and orange pigments become visible. With the fading of the green, photosynthesis also stops. In the Investigate, you will explore the process of photosynthesis.

Observing Elodea

Materials
- scissors
- water
- 3 elodea stems
- plastic funnel
- large glass jar
- glass test tube

Procedure

1. Use the scissors to clip the ends off the elodea stems.

2. Fill the jar nearly to the top with water.

3. Put the elodea stems into the funnel, with their cut ends pointing down. Turn the funnel over, keeping the plants inside, and place it upside down in the jar of water.

4. Hold the test tube under water in the jar to fill it. Without removing the test tube from the water, push it over the bottom stem of the funnel.

5. Put the jar in a bright, sunny window. Leave it there for several hours.

6. Observe the test tube. What do you see inside?

Draw Conclusions

1. Infer what has collected inside the test tube. Explain how you arrived at your answer.

2. Inquiry Skill Scientists often use data from one investigation to predict the outcome of another investigation that has slightly different variables. Predict what the results would be if you left a setup like this one in the dark instead of in sunlight.

Step 3

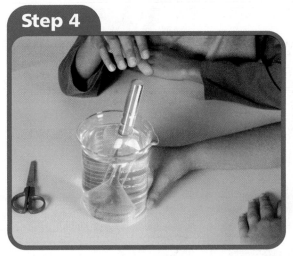

Step 4

Investigate Further

Plan and conduct a simple investigation **to test your** prediction **on the outcome of the investigation with different variables from those used here. Write a** hypothesis **first.**

Reading in Science

VOCABULARY
succession p. 202
carbon cycle p. 204
nitrogen cycle p. 206

SCIENCE CONCEPTS
▶ what natural cycles affect ecosystems
▶ how people can affect natural cycles

READING FOCUS SKILL
SEQUENCE Look for the steps in the carbon cycle.

The Importance of Natural Cycles

You already recognize some cycles. The change from darkness to daylight and back to darkness is the cycle of night and day. In some places, the change in the color of leaves is part of the cycle of seasonal changes. If you're on the coast, you might see the cycle of daily tides—high tide to low tide and back again.

Earth has several other cycles. They may not be as easy to see as some cycles, but they are all necessary for ecosystems to function and for life to exist on Earth.

One of the most important cycles is the water cycle. The sun's energy causes water to evaporate from Earth's surface and form clouds. Then gravity causes precipitation to fall to Earth and the cycle begins again.

Ecosystems go through cycles called succession. **Succession** is the gradual long-term change of species in an ecosystem. In succession, certain plant species establish themselves. As conditions change, those species die out and others take their places. These changes continue until the ecosystem becomes somewhat stable, although changes are always occurring.

There are two major types of succession—primary and secondary. Primary succession occurs when plants first take root in an area that has no plants. This could happen after a volcanic eruption covers an area with lava.

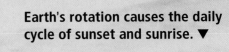

Earth's rotation causes the daily cycle of sunset and sunrise. ▼

Rain falls from clouds to Earth's surface in the water cycle. The amount of precipitation that falls stays in balance with the amount of water that evaporates to form clouds. ▶

An oak-hickory forest contains many species of trees and other plants, but oaks and hickories are the dominant species.

After the lava cools, the first plants that grow on the barren lava begin the process of primary succession.

Secondary succession is more common. It takes place when most, but not all, vegetation in an area has been removed. A farmer might cut down trees to plant a cornfield, or a fire might burn a grassland. In secondary succession, there is some leftover vegetation and some soil on which new plants can grow.

How would succession happen in an oak-hickory forest? Suppose an area of a forest was cut down. Grasses and weeds would be the first plants to return. Next, shrubs would grow. As time passed, trees would appear in the field of grass and shrubs. Pine trees would grow first. Then, oak and hickory trees would replace the pines. The process might take as long as 150 years. If people cut down the forest again, the cycle of succession would begin once more.

Some animal populations rise and fall in cycles. Populations of lemmings increase and decrease in a cycle of 3 to 4 years. As you learned in Chapter 4, the populations of lynxes and snowshoe hares rise and fall in a cycle of about 10 years.

There are important elements and compounds that cycle between the air, oceans, and land. You breathe in oxygen from the air. Plants use nitrogen from the soil to make food. These are limited resources, but they don't get used up. This is because they move constantly between the living and nonliving parts of ecosystems in chemical cycles. Next, you'll learn about two of Earth's most important chemical cycles—the carbon cycle and the nitrogen cycle.

 SEQUENCE What are the steps in secondary succession that end in an oak-hickory forest?

These boats are marooned on sand banks at low tide in a river in the country of Wales.

Carbon Is Elemental

You would not exist without the element carbon. Carbon is a part of every organism on Earth. Many compounds, such as carbohydrates, fats, and proteins, contain carbon. So does your DNA. Compounds that contain carbon are called *organic compounds*.

There is a limited supply of carbon on Earth. But carbon never runs out, because it is constantly recycled in the carbon cycle. The **carbon cycle** is the movement through Earth's ecosystems of carbon as solids, liquids, or gases.

To understand the carbon cycle, it's a good idea to start with living organisms. Carbon enters the biotic parts of ecosystems through producers. Plants undergo the process of photosynthesis, which makes the sugars that are their food. Photosynthesis in land plants uses carbon dioxide (CO_2) from the air, water from the soil, and energy from the sun. Photosynthesis makes sugars from, among other materials, the carbon from carbon dioxide. The food can be used right away by the plant, or it can be stored as starch. As a result of photosynthesis, oxygen is released into the air.

The same process goes on in aquatic environments. Aquatic producers, such as phytoplankton, float on the water's surface. These producers use the water, along with CO_2 and sunlight, to make food. Then oxygen is released into the air. Phytoplankton produce most of the oxygen in the atmosphere—more than all the trees on Earth!

Respiration, the process of using food, cycles the carbon from living things back into the air and water. This process can start when animal consumers eat plants, including the food that plants store as starch. The digestive systems of animals break down the plant tissue to get the starch stored in it. Sugars and other nutrients from plant starch move to the

animals' cells. In the cells, oxygen that animals take in releases the energy in the food. As this occurs, CO_2 is produced and released into the air.

Plants make their own food. But, like animals, plants need the energy stored in the food to

Science Up Close

The Carbon Cycle

The sun produces energy for photosynthesis, which moves carbon dioxide and oxygen through ecosystems.

During photosynthesis, plants take in carbon dioxide and release oxygen.

For more links and activities, go to www.hspscience.com

add new cells and to carry on their cellular processes. At certain times, plants take in oxygen from the air to release energy from the food. They then return CO_2 to the air.

Decomposers, such as fungi and bacteria, also play a part in the carbon cycle. They break down dead organisms and wastes to get food. Like animals, most decomposers take in oxygen to release the energy from their food, and then they give off CO_2.

 SEQUENCE What does an organism do after it gets energy from food?

Without human interference, the balance of gases in the atmosphere remains fairly constant. Air is about 0.03 percent carbon dioxide and about 21 percent oxygen.

The burning of coal and other fossil fuels releases additional carbon into the atmosphere.

During respiration, insects and other consumers take in oxygen and release carbon dioxide.

As they use waste and dead organisms for food, decomposers such as fungi take in oxygen and release carbon dioxide.

205

The Nitrogen Cycle

Like carbon, nitrogen cycles through the living and nonliving parts of ecosystems. The movement of nitrogen in different forms from living organisms to the nonliving part of the environment and back is the **nitrogen cycle**.

An important role of nitrogen is to make proteins. Proteins make up a large part of every cell. They help build and maintain cells. Antibodies are animal proteins that help the body fight off diseases. Another protein is hemoglobin, which carries oxygen throughout the blood to the body's tissues. Animals get much of their protein from plants or from animals that have eaten plants. Some proteins come only from plants—animals can't make them at all. But to make proteins, plants need nitrogen.

Nitrogen isn't very hard to find. About 78 percent of the gas in Earth's atmosphere is nitrogen. However, most organisms can't use nitrogen gas straight from the air. So an important part of the nitrogen cycle is the changing of nitrogen into a form that plants can use. This is called *nitrogen fixation*. Nitrogen can be "fixed" by bacteria in plants and soil or as the result of lightning strikes.

Legumes (LEG•yoomz) are plants such as soybeans, peas, peanuts, all kinds of beans, and clover. These plants help make nitrogen available for other living organisms. Their roots have small growths, or nodules, that contain a certain type of bacteria. These bacteria fix nitrogen from nitrogen gas to form ammonia and nitrates. These are nitrogen compounds that plants can absorb. Other decomposers in the soil also fix nitrogen into these compounds.

Plants take in the nitrogen compounds from the soil to make amino acids, the building blocks of proteins. When animals eat these plants, they get nitrogen from the proteins in the plants. When animals eat other animals that have eaten plants, they, too, get proteins and nitrogen.

Nitrogen gas in the atmosphere is in molecular form, which most living things can't use directly. One molecule of nitrogen gas is made up of two nitrogen atoms.

Bacteria in the roots of some plants fix nitrogen from gas in nitrogen compounds that the plants can absorb.

Lightning also converts nitrogen in the air into forms that living things can use. As lightning streaks through the sky, it fixes nitrogen from the air into nitrogen compounds. Rain or snow then carries these compounds

The Nitrogen Cycle

Animals get some proteins from the foods they eat, but they need nitrogen to make other proteins.

Lightning fixes small amounts of nitrogen from nitrogen gas into nitrogen compounds that plants can absorb.

Living things, such as plant leaves, contain nitrogen compounds. When the living things decay, these compounds return to the soil.

Nitrogen gas and other materials are converted to compounds, such as nitrates and ammonia.

Some bacteria in soil break down nitrogen compounds, releasing nitrogen gas back into the air.

from the air to the ground. The compounds seep into the soil, where plants can absorb them.

When plants and animals die, decomposers begin to break down the nitrogen-containing compounds in the decaying organisms. The decomposers release nitrogen gas back into the air, and the nitrogen cycle begins again.

 SEQUENCE What must happen to nitrogen before plants can absorb it?

How Humans Affect Cycles

Many human activities can change Earth's chemical cycles. For example, when forests burn, more CO_2 enters the air faster and in greater amounts than is natural. The same thing happens when fossil fuels are burned. Power plants and motor vehicles burn a lot of fuel very quickly. This causes CO_2 to enter the air at high rates.

Human activities can change the nitrogen cycle. Nitrogen is a main ingredient in soil fertilizer. Rain washes nitrogen off fields and into lakes, rivers, and bays. Nitrogen compounds increase the growth of algae in the water. When the algae die, decomposers move in to feed, removing oxygen from the water. This upsets water ecosystems by killing fish and other living things that need oxygen.

 SEQUENCE What happens after rain washes nitrogen from fertilizer into a body of water?

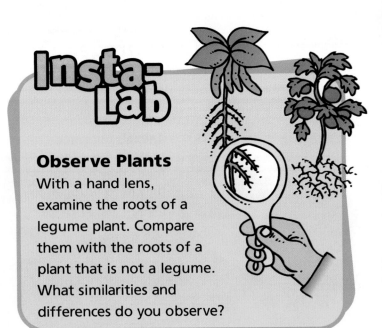

In some places, people cut and burn large forests to make new farmland. Deforestation destroys forest ecosystems. The burning of the trees adds carbon dioxide to the atmosphere.

1. SEQUENCE Copy and complete the graphic organizer to describe the steps of the carbon cycle.

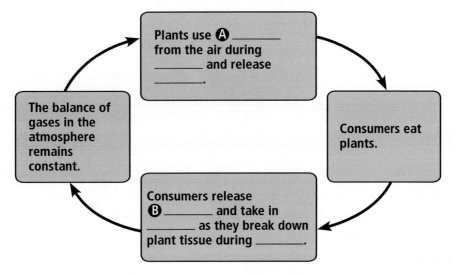

Plants use **A** _____ from the air during _____ and release _____.

Consumers eat plants.

Consumers release **B** _____ and take in _____ as they break down plant tissue during _____.

The balance of gases in the atmosphere remains constant.

2. SUMMARIZE Write a summary of the lesson. Start with this sentence: *The Earth has many important natural cycles.*

3. DRAW CONCLUSIONS How might cutting down forests increase the amount of carbon dioxide in the air, even if the trees are not burned?

4. VOCABULARY Use each of the lesson vocabulary words in an original sentence.

Test Prep

5. Critical Thinking What part do you play in the carbon cycle?

6. What do plants and animals need nitrogen to make?
- **A.** ammonia
- **B.** carbon
- **C.** oxygen
- **D.** protein

Writing

Narrative Writing

Choose one of Earth's natural cycles. Write a **story** about how that cycle has affected life in a community like yours—or how the community has affected the cycle.

Math

Make a Circle Graph

Make a circle graph that shows the percents of different gases in the atmosphere. Nitrogen is 78 percent; oxygen is 21 percent; carbon dioxide and the remaining gases make up about 1 percent.

Social Studies

Looking at Succession

Research a type of succession in the biome in which you live. Illustrate its steps. Write a caption to explain each step. Display your illustration in the classroom, and be ready to explain it to the class.

 For more links and activities, go to www.hspscience.com

How Do Humans Affect Ecosystems?

Fast Fact

Disappearing Wetlands In a wetland, water covers the soil or is present at or near the surface of the soil. Wetlands have been called "nature's kidneys" because they effectively filter pollutants from water runoff. The human-made wetland shown here filters sewage from waste water before it is released into a nearby river. In the Investigate, you will explore ways to clean dirty water.

Filtering Polluted Water

Materials
- beaker of dirty water
- piece of wire screen
- coffee filters
- large gravel
- 2 small graduates
- funnel
- potting soil
- large jar
- sand
- small pebbles

Procedure

1. Get a beaker of dirty water from your teacher.

2. Pour some dirty water from the beaker into a graduate.

3. Decide on the way you will clean the dirty water left in the beaker. Plan and design the steps you will take and the materials you will need. You may use any of the materials listed above.

4. Conduct the investigation, using the design and materials you decided on in Step 3.

5. Pour into another graduate some of the water you have cleaned.

6. Observe and compare the water in the two graduates. Write down what you observe.

Draw Conclusions

1. Which graduate appears to have clearer water?

2. What happened to the dirt and pollution that were removed from the original sample of dirty water?

3. **Inquiry Skill** Scientists design and conduct experiments to find data or determine the solution to a problem. How did the design of your experiment help you solve the problem of cleaning the dirty water?

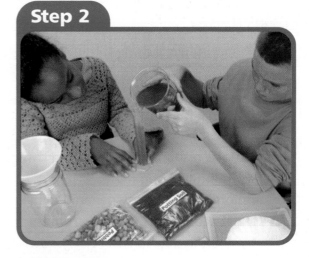

Step 2

Step 6

Investigate Further

Scientists often design experiments several times before they get the best results. Can you redesign your setup to get cleaner water? Try it. Compare the water from your first and second attempts. Explain the differences.

VOCABULARY
extinction p. 213
endangered species p. 213
wetland p. 215

SCIENCE CONCEPTS
▶ how people change ecosystems
▶ how people can help ecosystems

Focus Skill
READING FOCUS SKILL
CAUSE AND EFFECT Look for causes of change in ecosystems.

cause ⟶ effect

Humans Change Ecosystems

People change ecosystems all the time, sometimes in harmful ways. Mining, farming, and logging provide resources people need, but these activities can harm land, water, and air. When people burn fossil fuels, the pollution can harm living things. Dumping the wastes that are made as resources are harvested can harm the environment even more.

Burning coal in energy-generating plants can affect ecosystems far away from the plants. Burning coal releases the gas sulfur dioxide, which can travel on the wind for many kilometers. It can mix with water vapor in the air to form sulfuric acid. This acid travels through the air and falls in precipitation on forests and farmlands far from the original source. The acid can damage the leaves and stems of trees and other plants. It can damage tree roots, making it harder for trees to get nutrients. The trees weaken and are more likely to die. Acid in precipitation has not only damaged forests. It has also harmed water ecosystems, killing fish in some lakes.

Burning oil, another fossil fuel, doesn't release as many gases as coal does. However, many people depend on oil shipped from faraway places, and sometimes there are spills from tankers, pipelines, and offshore wells. Those spills harm ecosystems, too. Chemicals in the oil can kill aquatic life. Lumps of oil often wash up on

Kudzu is a plant that is not native to North America. It can grow up to 0.3 m (about 1 ft) per day! The plant covers everything and chokes the life out of native trees

As factories make the products we use, harmful pollution is sent into the air. Air pollution has been linked to heart disease, asthma, cancer, and many other health problems.

shore and spoil beaches.

People change ecosystems by introducing exotic plants and animals. An *exotic* organism is one that is not native to the ecosystem. These species are often harmful because they have no natural enemies in the new area. As a result, their numbers rise, and they crowd out native species.

Most exotic species arrive by accident, but some are introduced on purpose. This was the case with kudzu, a plant that is native to Japan. It was planted in the United States to stop soil erosion, but then it spread out of control in many parts of the country. Many competing native plants have died because of kudzu.

Acts of people have caused the extinction of many species. **Extinction** is the loss of an entire species. Extinction does occur naturally, but the actions of people have increased extinction rates by 100 to 1,000 times the natural rate. The greatest cause of extinction today is habitat loss. Pollution, hunting, and competition from exotic species also cause extinction.

The government keeps track of the numbers of many species

Oil is shipped thousands of miles across oceans and bays in huge tankers. When tankers spill oil, it coats the water, beaches, and wildlife. To save this bird, people must scrub the oily material from its feathers.

of plants and animals. It lists those that are threatened or endangered. An **endangered species** is one with so few individuals that it could die out. Some species are decreasing in number but are not yet endangered. These species are listed as *threatened*. Many species in danger are not well known, but others are. The black rhinoceros, the African elephant, and the blue whale are among the endangered species.

 CAUSE AND EFFECT What harmful effect can exotic species have on ecosystems? Explain.

Lemurs survive only on several islands off the east coast of Africa, including Madagascar. Because of the destruction of the lemurs' forest habitat, many species of lemur are endangered.

Ecosystems in Danger

The Marina District is a beautiful neighborhood in San Francisco. The area sits right next to San Francisco Bay. In fact, many years ago, it was part of the bay. Filling in part of the bay with soil enabled people to build homes in this section of the city. However, it changed the bay ecosystem and caused habitat destruction.

People constantly change Earth's surface to meet their needs. They drain wetlands and cut down forests to make room for homes, roads, and shopping centers. They turn natural grasslands into farms, and they fill in bays to add more dry land to cities. But while these changes might be useful for some people, they harm or destroy ecosystems.

Tropical forest ecosystems are the most diverse ecosystems on Earth. They are also very much in danger. People in tropical areas need farmland, so they clear the forest land, and they cut trees to get fuel for heating and cooking. Tropical wood is also popular for use as lumber for homes and furniture. As a result, some scientists say that about 20 percent of the world's tropical forests were cut or burned between 1960 and 1999.

Grasslands are among the most-disrupted ecosystems. Many important crops—such as wheat, corn, and oats—are grasses, so they grow as well in these areas as natural grasses do. Grasslands often have fertile soil. For these reasons, people have plowed the grasslands and turned them into farmland. Much of the interior of North America was once grassland, but very little of this natural ecosystem is left. In fact, 99 percent of the tallgrass prairie is gone. Many species that depend on the natural grasses in grasslands have decreased in numbers or disappeared entirely.

Tallgrass prairie once covered more than 56 million hectares (138 million acres) in the United States. Only about one percent of it is left.

An estuary is an area where fresh water and salt water meet and mix. Some estuaries form bays that teem with fish, crabs, and lobsters. Pollution from nearby farms and factories often threatens the bays' water quality. Overfishing can cause some fish and crab populations to decline.

214

The wetlands of the Everglades contain different ecosystems, including this area of marsh.

Higher areas of the Everglades often remain dry. Their ecosystems are dominated by trees such as live oaks and royal palms.

More than half of the original wetlands of the United States are gone. A **wetland** is an area of land that is covered by water all or much of the time. Swamps and marshes are wetlands. Years ago, most people thought of wetlands as useless, soggy places full of mud, insects, and dangerous animals. So, people drained and filled many wetlands to make dry land for farms and homes. They destroyed so much wetland that many wetland species are now endangered.

The Everglades was once a huge wetland that covered much of the southern tip of Florida. Over the past century, people have drained and filled some of the Everglades. Today, people control the water that used to flow freely through it. As a result, many of the ecosystems of the Everglades are in danger of being destroyed.

 CAUSE AND EFFECT Why have many wetlands been destroyed?

Insta-Lab

Observing Change

Look around your community for ways people have changed the natural environment. Sketch or photograph some places that have been changed. What were the effects on local plants and animals? Go to the local library to look for photographs of the area as it was 50 or 100 years ago. Write about the changes that have taken place. Do you think the changes have been helpful? Why or why not?

215

Humans Can Help Ecosystems

People can destroy ecosystems, but people can also preserve them and help restore damaged ones.

In the United States, laws have been passed to protect ecosystems. Some laws have cut back on the amount of pollution that is allowed. Many ecosystems are protected because they have become part of national parks. There is a law that protects wetlands. It says that most wetlands can't be drained or filled. If people do destroy a wetland, they must develop or restore an equal area of wetland in another place.

The United States government recognizes the value of the grasslands that once covered much of the country's interior. It has decided to preserve some of this area. In 1996, the Tallgrass Prairie National Preserve was designated in the Flint Hills region of Kansas. It contains one of the few remaining areas of natural prairie grassland.

The roots and stems of sea oats and other dune plants hold sand dunes in place. Vegetation has been replanted on some dunes where people have destroyed it. ▼

Many people are trying to help the sea turtles that nest on eastern beaches. There are eight species of these turtles, and they are all endangered. The females lay their eggs in nests on the shore. People guard the nests as the eggs mature and then protect the newly hatched turtles as they cross the beach on their way from the nests to the sea. Fishing boats use nets that are designed to catch fish but allow the sea turtles to escape.

More than thirty years ago, the United States government passed the Endangered Species Act (ESA) to protect the habitats of endangered and threatened species. Because of the ESA, several species have been saved from extinction.

Focus Skill **CAUSE AND EFFECT** What has been the effect of the Endangered Species Act?

Sea turtles make nests on some beaches along the Atlantic and Gulf Coasts of the United States.

DO NOT REMOVE
SEA TURTLE NEST
VIOLATORS SUBJECT TO FINES AND IMPRISONMENT

Sea turtles hatch in nests near the dunes. Then the newly hatched turtles crawl across the beach to the ocean.

1. CAUSE AND EFFECT Copy and complete the graphic organizer. Tell the effect of each cause.

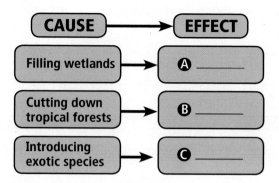

2. SUMMARIZE Write one paragraph that summarizes the most important information in this lesson.

3. DRAW CONCLUSIONS How have people worked to preserve ecosystems that are damaged or endangered?

4. VOCABULARY Write a definition in your own words of the term *endangered species*.

Test Prep

5. Critical Thinking Suppose you're in a national park. You see an unusual flower, but signs say not to pick the flowers. You think, "It's just one flower. What harm would picking it do?" What should you do, and why?

6. Which of these was thought to be a good idea but turned out badly?

    A. deforestation   **C.** habitat loss

    B. draining wetlands   **D.** pollution

Links

Writing

Expository Writing

The Everglades is a unique environment that is in danger of being destroyed. Write an **explanation** of one of the main problems the area faces. Then explain how people are trying to solve that problem.

Math

Make a Bar Graph

Choose an animal species that is endangered. Find out how its population has changed over the last 10 years. Draw a line graph that shows the change. Write a paragraph that explains reasons for the change.

Social Studies

The EPA

Research the United States Environmental Protection Agency. What is its mission? How does it help protect ecosystems? Write a brief report about your findings.

 For more links and activities, go to www.hspscience.com

LOSING GROUND

As Willie Smits, a Dutch scientist, walked through a busy outdoor market in Balikpapan, Indonesia, in 1989, he came across a sickly baby orangutan for sale as a pet. Smits decided he had to save the tiny ape. "She was gasping for breath," Smits recalled. "They thought she was going to die, so they just threw her away."

Smits took the infant ape to the Wanariset Forest Research Station, where he lived and worked. He nursed the animal back to life and later released her back into the wild. In 1991, Smits founded a center on the grounds of the forest station to help other orangutans return to the wild.

Center's Work

Despite the center's good work, there is still a lot of work to do to protect orangutans. Orangutans once ranged throughout Southeast Asia. Today the animals are endangered and found only in parts of Indonesia and Malaysia.

The center works mainly to rescue orangutans and return them to the wild. To see how orangutans cope with being released, a team of fieldworkers follows the animals from dawn to dusk. The team keeps a record of what the orangutans eat, how they behave, and where they go. The monitoring process is crucial to the success of the re-introduction process since scientists must know if the orangutans are doing well or not.

Outlook Is Grim

Still, experts say the outlook for the animals is grim. Scientists estimate that in the last 10 years, the number of wild orangutans on the planet has decreased by about 50 percent, to approximately 13,000 animals.

The illegal market in orangutans is not the only threat to the animals. Most experts agree that loss of habitat is the orangutan's worst enemy.

Extensive logging in Indonesia has destroyed much of the orangutan's living area. Scientists say humans have destroyed at least 80 percent of the orangutan's habitat in the rain forest.

As a result of surveys of orangutan populations and the loss of forest, scientists estimate that orangutans could be extinct in the wild within the next 10 to 20 years. "Without immediate action, the orangutans are doomed," Smits said.

Il-log-ical

Although most logging is banned in Indonesia, illegal logging is responsible for the cutting of huge areas of forest. The timber is then sold overseas, where it is turned into picture frames, window blinds, pool cues, and other products.

Most loggers cut down the trees to buy food. "The forests belong to the people. That's how we survive," said a man who lives in the Indonesian village of Pelindung.

Agriculture also plays a large part in the orangutan's habitat destruction. Farmers clear large tracts of land for palm oil and rubber tree plantations. Forest fires make the problem worse. According to Smits, thousands of orangutans died during massive forest fires in 1997 and 1998 that destroyed huge amounts of Indonesian rain forest.

THINK ABOUT IT

1. What might be some other ways of saving the orangutan from extinction?

2. How is the loss of rain forest affecting orangutan populations?

Find out more! Log on to **www.hspscience.com**

DANGEROUS WATERS

Tom Pitchford studies manatees, an endangered marine mammal. Manatees enjoy grazing on beds of sea grass in the warm, shallow water along Florida's coast. Scientists say the biggest enemy of the manatees is powerboats.

Pitchford has attached devices to several dozen manatees that allow him to use satellites to track their every move. Those devices show where manatees swim and where they might encounter boats. Pitchford and his team will study the information to see how they can help protect the manatees.

Career Marine Biologist

Coastal areas, such as those in Florida, are under increasing environmental pressure as more people move to shoreline communities. The increased population has put coastal marine life at risk. Marine biologists study these risks and try to protect the plants and animals that live in those waters.

Quick and Easy Project

Do Plants Make Carbon Dioxide?

Materials

- bowl with small pieces of red cabbage
- hot distilled water
- 3 large glass jars and 1 lid
- branch of elodea plant
- drinking straw

Procedure

1. Pour the hot water into the bowl of cabbage. Let the water stand until it cools.
2. Remove the cabbage and throw it away. Pour equal amounts of the cabbage water into the three jars.
3. Put the plant in one jar. Put the lid on, and put the jar in the sun.
4. Blow through the straw into the water in the second jar. Be careful not to inhale.
5. Leave the third jar as it is.

Draw Conclusions

What happened to the water that you blew into? Why do you think this happened? Did the water containing the plant change? Why or why not? Explain what happened in the third jar. Look at the title of the project. Judging by the appearance of the water that contains the plant, what is the answer to the question? Look at the jar you blew into. What can you infer happened in this jar? In a later chapter you will learn about what took place in this activity.

Design Your Own Investigation

How Can You Save Resources?

Make a list of as many resources as you can think of that you use in one day and how much you use of each. Choose one thing you do regularly, and plan an alternative that would use fewer resources. Design a process that will allow you to test whether you have decreased the amount of resources you use. Carry out your plan. Compare your results with those of others in your class.

Review and Test Preparation

Vocabulary Review

Use the terms below to complete the sentences. The page numbers tell you where to look in the chapter if you need help.

natural resource p. 192
recycle p. 196
reuse p. 197
succession p. 202
carbon cycle p. 204
nitrogen cycle p. 206
extinction p. 213
wetland p. 215

1. To use items again after their original use is to _____ .

2. The gradual long-term change of species in an ecosystem is _____ .

3. The movement of nitrogen in different forms from living organisms to the nonliving part of the environment and back is the _____ .

4. A material found on Earth that occurs in nature and is essential or useful to people is a _____ .

5. An area of land that is covered by water all or most of the time is a _____ .

6. The loss of a species is _____ .

7. To process used products into new products by using the materials again is to _____ .

8. The movement through Earth's ecosystems of carbon as a solid, liquid, or gas is the _____ .

Check Understanding

Write the letter of the best choice.

9. **CAUSE AND EFFECT** Which is an effect of conserving oil?
   A. The supply of oil will never run out.
   B. The supply of oil increases.
   C. The supply of oil will last longer.
   D. The supply of oil becomes renewable.

10. **SEQUENCE** Which will most likely occur next if an endangered species is not protected?
    F. The species will become extinct.
    G. The species will reproduce more.
    H. The species will move to a new area.
    J. The species will destroy its ecosystem.

11. Which of these is a natural resource?
    A.

    B.

    C.

    D.

12. Which of the following is a way to conserve resources?

    F. driving instead of walking

    G. using cloth bags at the grocery store

    H. throwing away recyclable cans

    J. leaving the computer on when you leave the room

13. Which of these is **NOT** a part of the nitrogen cycle?

    A. Some plant roots fix nitrogen gas in compounds that other organisms can use.

    B. Animals use oxygen to get energy from food stored in plants.

    C. Plants take in nitrates and ammonia from soil.

    D. Decomposers break down nitrogen-containing compounds in the soil.

14. Which human activity affects the carbon cycle?

    F. burning oil and forests

    G. using fertilizers on farm fields

    H. eating greater amounts of legumes

    J. mining copper in deep pit mines

15. Which of these is **NOT** a way people change forest ecosytems?

    A. cutting forests

    B. picking a few berries in forests

    C. burning forest trees

    D. introducing exotic trees to forests

16. Which law did the United States pass to help save endangered species?

    F. the AAA

    G. the EPA

    H. the ESA

    J. the FBI

Inquiry Skills

17. When you **compare** the values of a variable at the beginning and end of an experiment, what can you learn?

18. What can you **infer** about a species that is threatened?

Critical Thinking

19. A town has grown and needs more water. It can get a lot of what it needs by diverting water from a nearby wetland. There are other ways to get the water, but they are much more expensive. How would you handle the situation? Explain your answer.

20. Study the diagram shown. Then answer the questions below.

carbon dioxide + water	sunlight + chlorophyll →	sugar + oxygen
$6CO_2 + 6H_2O$	⟶	$C_6H_{12}O_6 + 6O_2$

Part A Describe what happens in the process shown in the diagram.

Part B How is this process for acquiring food different from the process used by people?

UNIT C

Exploring Earth

EARTH SCIENCE

Petroglyph National Monument

TO: ariana@hspscience.com

FROM: patty@hspscience.com

RE: New Mexico

Dear Ariana,

You and I exchange several e-mails a day without blinking an eye. It takes only a minute or two of our time. Can you imagine having to carve our messages into stone? I can tell you that my letters would be few! At Petroglyph National Monument, the rocks have been carved with 25,000 pictures made by native people and early Spanish settlers. Some of these images are easy to recognize, while others are very hard to distinguish as they are more complex. One thing is certain, they tell the story of 12,000 years of human life. Imagine putting that in an e-mail!

Keep on writing!

Patty

TO: desiree@hspscience.com

FROM: jermaine@hspscience.com

RE: Chicago, Illinois

Dear Desiree,

Could you imagine coming face-to-face with one of the largest beasts ever to roam the planet? Well, as you explore the Chicago Field Museum, you might want to take care not to accidentally run into this creature. A mere walk around an animal that has bird-like feet, huge legs, and a dainty tail causes some concern. Oh yes, and let's not forget to mention the razor-sharp teeth and strong jaws. But who is "Sue"? No one knows for sure if it is male or female, but whatever it is, Sue is the most complete *T. rex* fossil ever discovered. Sue is not exactly pretty, but she is certainly the real thing. This is no replica!

Write back soon.

Jermaine

Experiment!

Shifting Sand When a heavy rain falls on the land, some of the soil is carried away. Does the size of a particle determine how far it will be carried by running water? Plan and conduct an experiment to find out.

Chapter

6

Changes to Earth's Surface

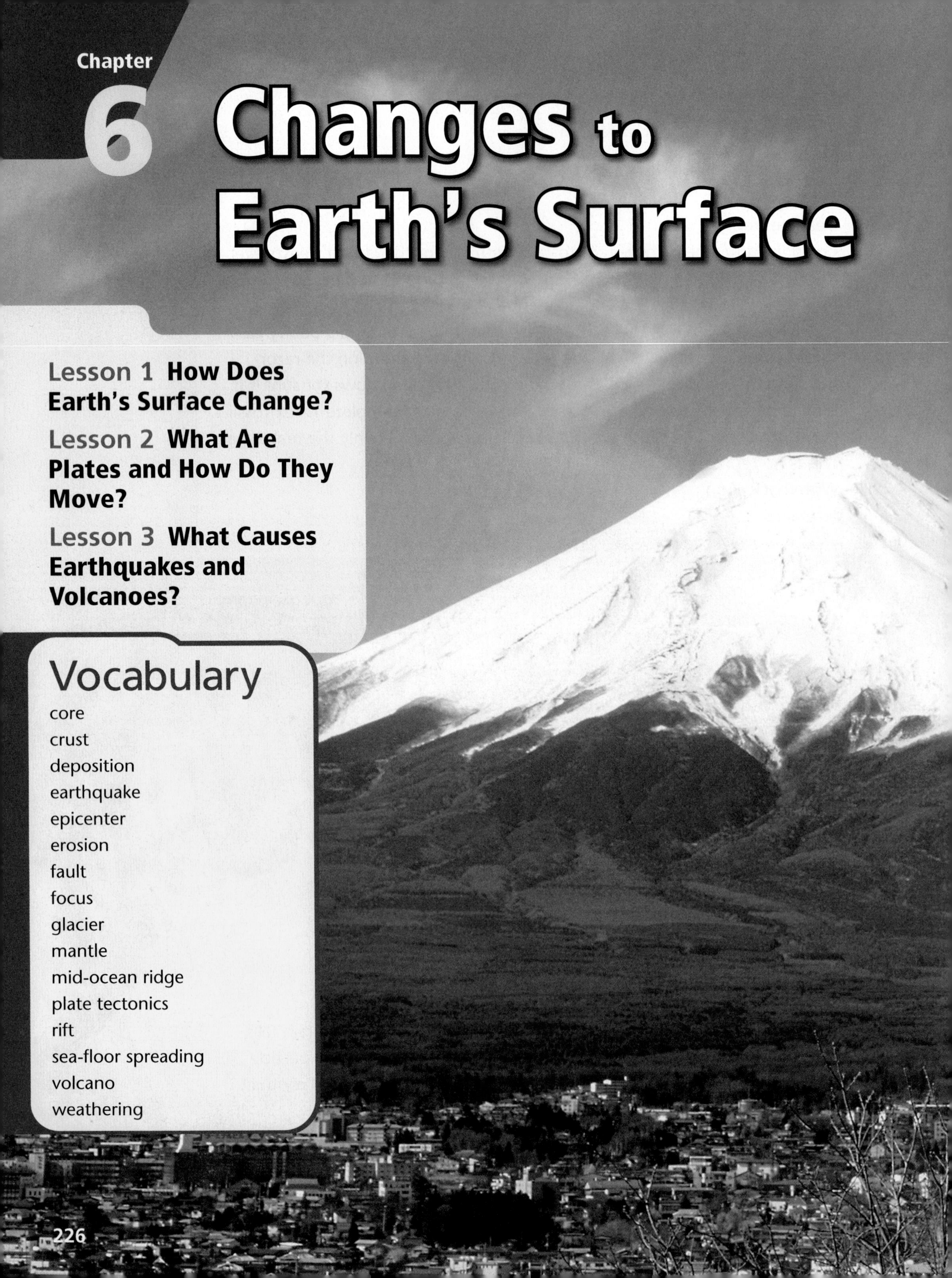

Vocabulary

core
crust
deposition
earthquake
epicenter
erosion
fault
focus
glacier
mantle
mid-ocean ridge
plate tectonics
rift
sea-floor spreading
volcano
weathering

What do YOU wonder?

Mount Fuji is the tallest mountain in Japan. Its summit is more than 3.7 km (2.3 mi) above sea level! Look at the shape of Mt. Fuji. Does it look like most other mountains you have seen? How do you think Mt. Fuji was formed?

How Does Earth's Surface Change?

Fast Fact

Disappearing Act Ship Rock, in New Mexico, resulted from a volcanic eruption about 30 million years ago. At that time Ship Rock was covered by more than 800 m (2600 ft) of other rock! All that rock later eroded away, leaving Ship Rock exposed. In the Investigate, you'll learn about even larger layers that make up Earth.

Earth's Layers

Materials
- newspaper
- metric ruler
- modeling clay—yellow, brown, red
- clear plastic straw
- white paper (1 sheet)

Procedure

① Copy the table.

② You will make a model of Earth's layers. Use the scale 1 cm = 1000 km. Write your scale measurements in the table.

③ Before you make your model, cover your work area with newspaper. From the inside out, Earth's layers are in this order: inner core, outer core, mantle, and crust. Use the yellow clay for the inner core, brown clay for the outer core, red clay for the mantle, and the white paper for the crust.

④ Use the plastic straw to take a sample of your model. Push the straw through the layers. Then pull it out. Draw a picture of the layers in the straw.

Earth's Layers		
Layer	Approximate Thickness	Model
Crust	8 km	
Mantle	3000 km	
Outer core	2500 km	
Inner core	1000 km	

Step 4

Draw Conclusions

1. From your model, what can you infer about the thickness of the crust compared with the thickness of each of the other layers?

2. The core and the mantle are too far below the surface for scientists to sample. But scientists can take samples of the layers in the crust in the same way that you used the straw to take a sample of your model. What does your sample show?

3. **Inquiry Skill** Scientists use models to study the parts of Earth that they can't observe directly. Using your model, what can you infer about Earth's layers?

Investigate Further

Which of Earth's layers has the greatest volume? Which has the least volume? Experiment to find a way to use your model to compare the volumes of Earth's layers.

Reading in Science

VOCABULARY
crust p. 230
mantle p. 231
core p. 231
weathering p. 232
erosion p. 232
deposition p. 233
glacier p. 234

SCIENCE CONCEPTS
▶ how Earth is structured
▶ ways that Earth's surface changes

READING FOCUS SKILL
MAIN IDEA AND DETAILS Look for details about how Earth's surface changes.

```
        Main Idea
   ┌────────┼────────┐
 detail   detail   detail
```

Earth's Layers

Have you ever cut an onion? The outside is a thin, dry skin. But when you slice into the onion, you realize that there are many layers hidden under the skin. Just like an onion, Earth has many layers underneath its thin outer skin, or its **crust**. The crust includes both dry land and the ocean floor. No organism lives beneath the Earth's crust. In fact, the crust is the only layer of Earth that people have actually seen.

Scientists have had to learn about the layers beneath the crust through indirect evidence. For example, energy moves through objects of different densities at different speeds. Scientists have measured how fast energy waves move through Earth to calculate the densities and

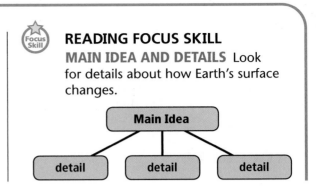

Science Up Close

Earth's Layers

Within Earth's main layers lie several other layers that differ in their physical properties. The layers differ in temperature, pressure, and composition.

Outer Core (2200 km thick)
The outer core is made of very hot liquid iron and nickel. The movement of the outer core produces Earth's magnetic field.

Inner Core (1250 km thick)
The inner core is very hot, but it's been pressed into a solid metal ball by pressure from the layers around it.

Mantle (2900 km thick)
The upper part of the mantle consists of two layers. The upper layer is part of the lithosphere, with the asthenosphere lying below it. The lower mantle is made up of iron and magnesium silicate minerals.

The crust is much thicker under continents than under the ocean floor. The crust is thickest under tall mountain ranges, such as the Alps and Himalayas.

thicknesses of all of Earth's layers. Through their calculations, scientists have learned that the crust is the thinnest and least dense layer.

Underneath Earth's thin crust is a very thick layer of Earth called the **mantle**. Some of the upper mantle is partially melted, and the rest is solid.

Beneath the mantle is the last major layer of Earth, called the **core**. There are two parts to the core—a liquid outer core and a solid inner core. The core extends from the bottom of the mantle to Earth's center. Scientists think the core is made mostly of iron and nickel because of the core's density. Earth's iron-rich core also acts as a magnet, producing Earth's magnetic field. Like a magnet, Earth has a magnetic north pole and a magnetic south pole. This is why a compass works. The compass needle aligns itself with Earth's magnetic field and points toward the magnetic north pole.

MAIN IDEA AND DETAILS What are the three main layers of Earth?

Crust (0–100 km thick)

Earth's crust is the thinnest of Earth's layers. It is thinner under the oceans than under the continents.

Lithosphere (averages 1.6–130 km thick)

The *lithosphere* (LITH•uh•sfir) is the crust and the upper, solid part of the mantle.

Asthenosphere (72–250 km thick)

The *asthenosphere* (as•THEN•uh•sfir) is the upper part of the mantle below the lithosphere. The rock is molten and taffy-like.

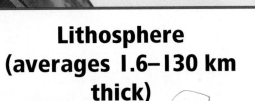

For more links and activities, go to www.hspscience.com

Wind, Water, and Gravity Change Earth's Surface

Earth's crust is constantly changing. Some of these changes are caused by the movements of the asthenosphere. Other changes are caused by conditions on Earth's surface. For example, suppose a large boulder is sitting in a meadow. On a windy day, wind carrying small bits of sand blows against the boulder. The sand hits the boulder at high speeds and breaks off tiny bits of rock. The boulder is undergoing **weathering**, or the process of being broken down into smaller pieces.

Of course, wind is not the only force that can weather Earth's surface. Water is another powerful weathering agent. Suppose it rains on the same boulder in the meadow. In a process known as **erosion**, or the removal and transportation of weathered material, the pieces of rock are carried away.

Gravity is a very powerful agent of erosion. Think how a large boulder could have ended up in a meadow in the first place. If there's a nearby hill or mountain, you have your answer. Gravity probably caused the boulder to roll down the mountain. Gravity also carries away bits of rock by causing rock slides and mudflows. As rocks move downward during a rock slide, they collide with one another. This causes the rocks to break into smaller pieces, leading to further weathering and erosion.

The amount of weathering and erosion that takes place depends on many factors. A soft rock erodes much faster than a hard rock. And stronger forces cause more weathering and erosion than weaker forces. For example, suppose that the

This sea cave was formed as ocean waves crashed against a rock cliff. Over time, the waves produced a pocket in the rock, forming a cave.

These sand dunes have been formed by wind deposition. When the wind hits an obstacle, the wind slows down. Heavy material, such as sand, carried by the wind then falls to the ground and builds up.

The Cuckmere River in Sussex, England, has meanders, or bends. They form when eroded material from one meander is deposited on the inside of the next meander as the speed of the water decreases.

boulder in the meadow were in a fast-moving river. The water in the river would quickly weather and erode the surface of the boulder. Instead of having jagged edges, the boulder would become rounded and smooth.

What happens to the small pieces of rock that are weathered and eroded? These small pieces, called *sediment,* are carried by wind and water. Eventually, the wind and water lose energy and slow down. When this happens, the sediment drops out of the air or water, and deposition occurs. **Deposition** is the dropping or settling of eroded material.

Deposition can occur very close to where the sediment was originally produced. This happens often when gravity is the weathering agent. For example, if gravity causes a rock slide or a mudflow, the materials usually don't move very far before settling. However, sediment from weathering can sometimes travel very far. For example, sediment that is picked up at the beginning of the Nile River, in Africa, may travel more than 6600 km (4100 mi) before being deposited at the river's mouth!

 MAIN IDEA AND DETAILS How do wind, water, and gravity change Earth's surface?

Ice Changes Earth's Surface

You've already learned that liquid water changes Earth's surface. Frozen water does this, too. In some areas of the world, the environment is cold enough for huge sheets of ice to form and stay frozen year-round. These immense ice sheets are called **glaciers**. They do not stand still but flow as slow-moving rivers of ice. Glaciers vary in size. A small one might be found in a mountain valley and be about the size of a football field. Several large glaciers cover the whole continent of Antarctica. This ice sheet is more than 4000 m (13,000 ft) thick and spreads over an area of 13 million sq km (5 million sq mi)! That's about one and a half times the size of the United States.

Now just imagine what might happen to the land underneath a glacier as the huge, heavy sheet of ice moves. The glacier carries rocks, debris, and sediment along with it as it flows forward. This smoothes out the landscape as the glacier erodes small hills and other sharp features. When the glacier stops moving forward or retreats by melting, it leaves behind mounds of sediment. Whole islands, including Long Island, New York, were formed from glacial deposits.

"Hanging" valleys leading into larger ones in Yosemite National Park were formed a million years ago by small glaciers.

Sometimes a glacier is so heavy that it pushes down the land it flows over. When the glacier retreats, the land rises back up in a process called *uplift*. In fact, the retreat of the same group of large glaciers that formed Long Island also caused uplift along much of the northeast coast of the United States. This produced many of the sea cliffs that are found in that region today.

 MAIN IDEA AND DETAILS What are three ways that glaciers can change the landscape?

Insta-Lab

Modeling Glaciers

Half-fill two paper cups with water. Pour 2 tablespoons of sand into one cup. Put both cups in a freezer overnight. The next day, take the two pieces of ice out of the cups and rub each piece across a sheet of aluminum foil, representing Earth's surface. Describe what happens to the foil when you rub it with each piece of ice. Let the ice with sand in it melt over the foil. Describe what happens.

Valley Formation: During

As a glacier advances down a mountain valley, it erodes the sides of the valley.

Valley Formation: After

When the glacier retreats, it reveals a U-shaped valley. A broad valley like this is called a *glacial trough*.

Impacts Change Earth's Surface

Have you ever seen pictures of the surface of the moon? It is pockmarked with hundreds of craters. The craters formed when rocks from space, known as **meteorites**, collided with the moon. Meteorites have also struck Earth. However, Earth has experienced fewer meteorite impacts than the moon because Earth's atmosphere is much thicker. The atmosphere causes many of the falling objects to burn up before they reach Earth's surface.

If an object is large enough to survive entry through Earth's atmosphere, it may form a crater when it hits the surface. Many craters have been found around the world, including in the United States.

 MAIN IDEA AND DETAILS What causes craters to form?

Meteor Crater, in Arizona, was formed by a meteorite that hit Earth about 20,000 years ago. The meteorite made a hole about 1.2 km (0.7 mi) across. ▶

This map shows the locations of Meteor Crater and Chicxulub Crater.

▼ About 65 million years ago, a huge meteorite made Mexico's Chicxulub Crater, 290 km (180 mi) wide. It was land area at that time. On this image it is the blue-colored area that is under the land. Some scientists hypothesize that this blocked sunlight and killed off the dinosaurs.

1. MAIN IDEA AND DETAILS Draw and complete the graphic organizer.

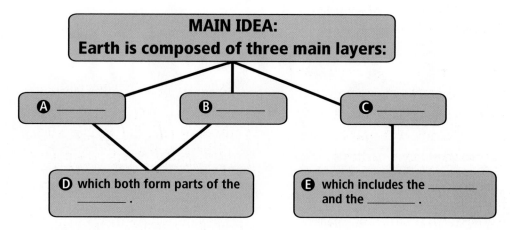

MAIN IDEA:
Earth is composed of three main layers:

Ⓐ _____ Ⓑ _____ Ⓒ _____

Ⓓ **which both form parts of the** _____ .

Ⓔ **which includes the** _____ **and the** _____ .

2. SUMMARIZE Make a table that shows different agents of weathering and how each agent can change Earth's surface.

3. DRAW CONCLUSIONS Describe how you think a river canyon, such as the Grand Canyon, may have formed.

4. VOCABULARY Draw a picture illustrating the following terms: *core, crust, lithosphere,* and *mantle.*

Test Prep

5. Critical Thinking Suppose you're hiking through the mountains and come across a valley that is V-shaped at one end and U-shaped at the other. What most likely caused this landform?

6. Which of the following events would most likely change Earth's surface the fastest?

A. glacial uplift   **C.** water erosion

B. a rock slide   **D.** wind erosion

Links

Writing

Expository Writing

Choose a nearby place such as a field, mountain, riverbank, or beach. Write a **description** of how Earth's surface in that place might have changed over time.

Math

Compare Numbers

The distance from Earth's surface to its center is about 6400 km. The deepest anyone has ever gone is 5 km below the surface. How many times that depth is the distance to Earth's center?

Social Studies

Ice Ages

Earth has had many Ice Ages, in which glaciers covered large parts of several continents. Research one of the Ice Ages. Then draw a map showing where the glaciers were on one of the continents.

For more links and activities, go to www.hspscience.com

What Are Plates and How Do They Move?

Fast Fact

Rising Rocks If you could examine rocks from the top of the Alps, you'd find that they contain fossils of animals from the sea! Surprisingly, the rocks at the top of these mountains were once part of an ancient ocean floor. As you'll learn in the Investigate, movements of Earth's crust cause major changes to Earth's surface.

How Earth's Plates Move

Materials
- shoe box
- paper
- metric ruler
- modeling clay
- scissors

Procedure

1. Turn the shoe box upside down, and cut a 1-cm by 10-cm slit across the bottom. Then, at the center of one of the box's long sides, cut out a hole large enough for your hand.

2. Cut two 8-cm by 25-cm strips of paper. Run each strip through the slit in the box. Leave about 10 cm sticking out through the slit. Fold the strips back on opposite sides of the slit.

3. Use the clay to make models of North and South America. Press your models onto the left strip of paper. Make models of Europe and Africa, and press them onto the right strip.

4. Slowly push the strips up through the slit. Observe what happens to the clay models.

Step 2

Draw Conclusions

1. The rising paper in your model represents molten rock that is moving out of a crack between plates of Earth's crust. Use your models to infer what happens to the continents as the plates they are part of move apart.

2. Plates can also move toward or slide past each other. Use your model to demonstrate these other two kinds of plate movements. Describe what happens to the continents.

3. **Inquiry Skill** By observing and by using models, scientists infer how the continents move. Based on your model, what can you infer about the positions of these four continents millions of years ago?

Step 4

Investigate Further

Develop a hypothesis about how mountains form. Use two flattened pieces of modeling clay to test your hypothesis.

Reading in Science

VOCABULARY
plate tectonics p. 241
mid-ocean ridge p. 242
rift p. 242
sea-floor spreading p. 242

SCIENCE CONCEPTS
▶ how plates move
▶ what happens when plates move

READING FOCUS SKILL
COMPARE AND CONTRAST Look for different ways plates can move.

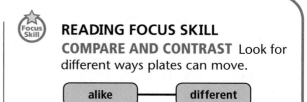

alike ——————— different

Earth's Plates

In Lesson 1, you learned that the crust and the rigid upper part of the mantle form the part of Earth called the lithosphere. The lithosphere is not one continuous sheet of rock. Instead, it's made up of many plates of rock. Some of the plates, such as the Pacific plate, span tens of thousands of kilometers and are capped mostly by thin, oceanic crust. Other plates, such as the Cocos plate, are quite a bit smaller. And some plates, such as the Eurasian plate, are capped mostly by the thicker continental crust.

Look at the globes on these pages. As you can see, the lithosphere's plates fit against each other like pieces of a huge jigsaw puzzle. But unlike puzzle pieces, the plates are constantly on the move. At first glance, this may seem impossible. After all, the continents aren't moving, are they? Actually, they are!

Remember that Earth's lithosphere sits on top of the asthenosphere. The asthenosphere is part of the mantle. The rock of the asthenosphere

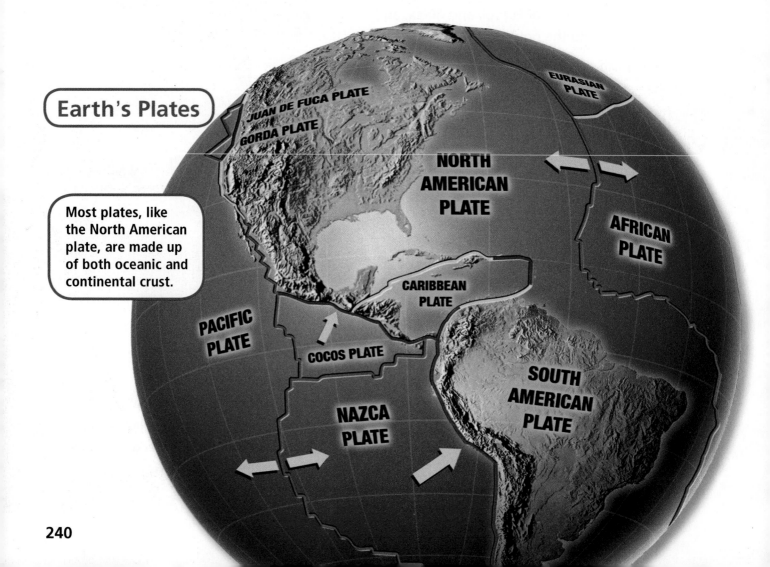

Earth's Plates

Most plates, like the North American plate, are made up of both oceanic and continental crust.

JUAN DE FUCA PLATE
GORDA PLATE
EURASIAN PLATE
NORTH AMERICAN PLATE
AFRICAN PLATE
PACIFIC PLATE
COCOS PLATE
CARIBBEAN PLATE
NAZCA PLATE
SOUTH AMERICAN PLATE

240

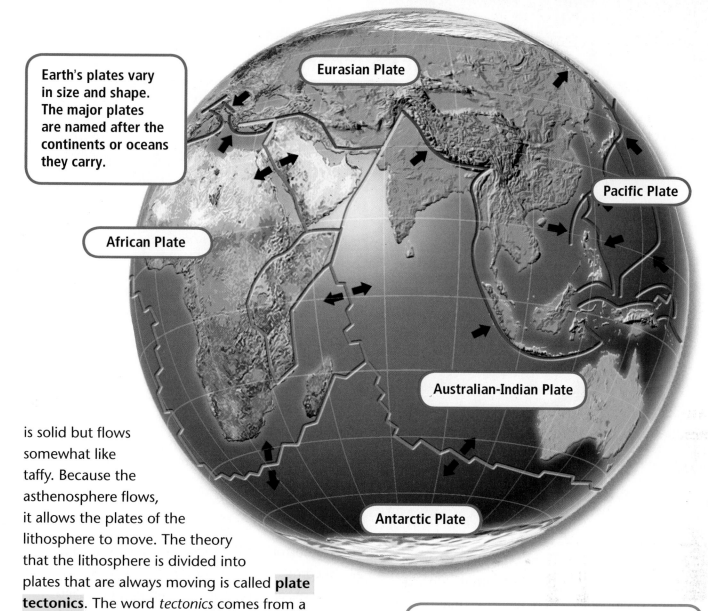

Earth's plates vary in size and shape. The major plates are named after the continents or oceans they carry.

Eurasian Plate

Pacific Plate

African Plate

Australian-Indian Plate

Antarctic Plate

is solid but flows somewhat like taffy. Because the asthenosphere flows, it allows the plates of the lithosphere to move. The theory that the lithosphere is divided into plates that are always moving is called **plate tectonics**. The word *tectonics* comes from a Greek word meaning "to build," because plate movements build Earth's largest landforms.

The lithosphere does not move quickly. In fact, most plates move only a few centimeters a year. But over many years, this movement can cause major changes in the plates. Some plates may break apart. Others may move together and become one. Some plates may shrink as their edges are pushed down, heated up, and recycled into the mantle. New plates can grow as hot rock from the mantle moves up and part of it melts. The melted rock cools and forms thin, new oceanic crust.

 COMPARE AND CONTRAST Look at the map on page 240. Compare the North American plate with the Pacific plate.

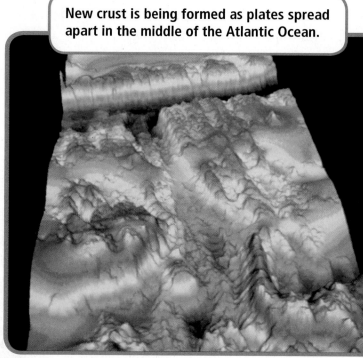

New crust is being formed as plates spread apart in the middle of the Atlantic Ocean.

At a divergent boundary, plates move apart. As hot mantle oozes upward, it partially melts, forming new crust.

◄ This divergent boundary in Tanzania is on land. As the plates spread apart, the land grows.

Plate Boundaries

Tectonic plates meet each other along plate boundaries. There are three main types: divergent boundaries, convergent boundaries, and transform fault boundaries.

A divergent boundary is a place where two or more plates are moving away from each other. Most divergent boundaries are found along the **mid-ocean ridge**, a chain of mountains that runs about 67,000 km (41,600 mi) through the world's oceans. Along the highest part of the mid-ocean ridge is a deep valley, or **rift**, where plates move apart. As the plates separate, hot rock from the mantle moves up. The melted rock cools and freezes, forming new crust. The crust and mantle near the bottom of the ocean are able to cool and become rigid, forming new lithosphere. This process along the mid-ocean ridge is called **sea-floor spreading**.

At a transform fault boundary, two plates move past each other. Crust is neither formed nor destroyed there. Instead, the plates along the boundary grind past each other as they move in opposite directions. This movement

Transform Fault Boundary

often causes earthquakes. A famous transform fault boundary is the San Andreas fault in California.

Where two tectonic plates push into each other, a convergent boundary forms. There are three kinds of convergent boundaries. The first kind occurs where a continental plate collides with another continental plate. The colliding plates fold and bend, forming mountain ranges. The second kind occurs where a continental plate collides with a denser oceanic plate. Where this happens, the oceanic plate sinks under the continental plate. Mountains and volcanoes form along this boundary. The third kind of convergent boundary occurs where two oceanic plates collide. One of the two plates will sink under the other. This causes a deep-ocean trench to form and causes melting in the asthenosphere, leading to an arc of volcanic islands.

 COMPARE AND CONTRAST Compare and contrast the different kinds of convergent boundaries.

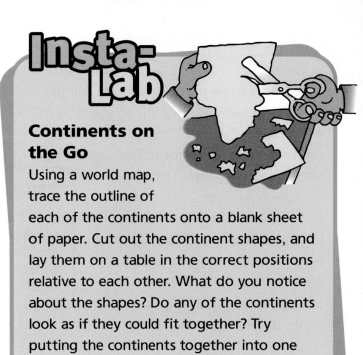

Many volcanoes form along convergent boundaries. Melted rock is slowly pushed upward and then erupts at the surface, forming mountains. ▼

Convergent Boundary

At a convergent boundary, plates move together.

243

Plate Movements Change Earth's Surface

You now know that plates move. But in which directions do they move, and where were they in the past? Scientists have used several kinds of evidence to find out where plates were long ago. The shapes of some continents, such as South America and Africa, seem able to fit together. Also, rock types along the edges of some continents are the same. Furthermore, the same kinds of plant and animal fossils show up on different continents that are now separated by oceans.

By examining traces of Earth's magnetic field in rocks, by matching rock types and fossils, and by studying how plates move, scientists have concluded that all the continents once formed a single supercontinent. Scientists call it *Pangea* (pan•JEE•uh), and it existed about 220 million years ago. Pangea may not have been the first supercontinent. Scientists hypothesize that at several times in Earth's history, the continents joined to form a supercontinent and then pulled apart.

Today, the Atlantic Ocean is growing and the Pacific Ocean is shrinking. This is causing North and South America to move farther away from Europe and Africa and closer to Asia. In addition, Africa is shifting north toward Europe. If these changes continue, the Earth's surface will look very different in another 200 million years.

COMPARE AND CONTRAST Contrast the movements of the continents in the past with how they are moving now.

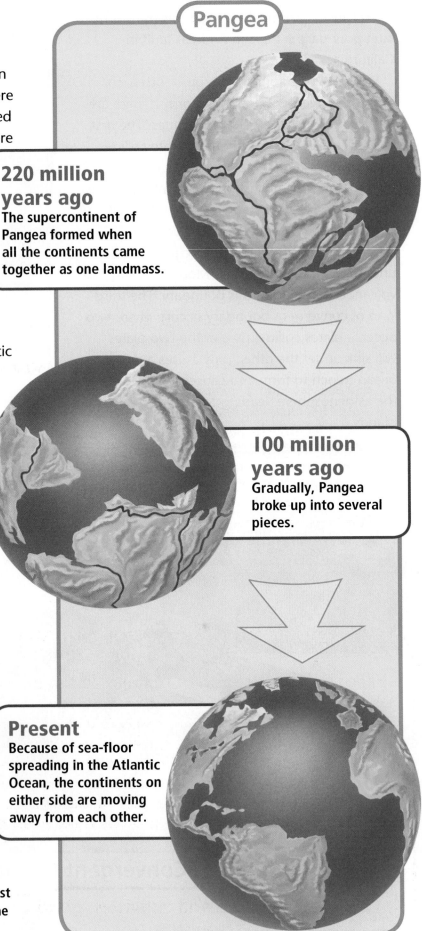

Pangea

220 million years ago
The supercontinent of Pangea formed when all the continents came together as one landmass.

100 million years ago
Gradually, Pangea broke up into several pieces.

Present
Because of sea-floor spreading in the Atlantic Ocean, the continents on either side are moving away from each other.

1. **COMPARE AND CONTRAST** Draw and complete the graphic organizers.

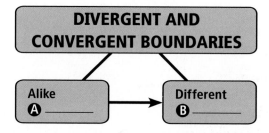

DIVERGENT AND CONVERGENT BOUNDARIES

Alike **A** _____ → Different **B** _____

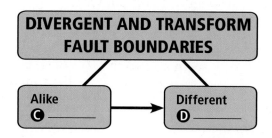

DIVERGENT AND TRANSFORM FAULT BOUNDARIES

Alike **C** _____ → Different **D** _____

2. **SUMMARIZE** Write a summary of this lesson by comparing and contrasting Earth and a jigsaw puzzle.

3. **DRAW CONCLUSIONS** The Himalayas are mountains between India and the rest of Asia. They grow several centimeters each year. What do you think causes this?

4. **VOCABULARY** Use all of this lesson's vocabulary terms to explain why the Atlantic Ocean is growing wider.

Test Prep

5. **Critical Thinking** How does weathering compare with plate tectonics?

6. At which of the following types of plate boundaries do plates grind past each other?

   A. convergent   **C.** tectonic

   B. divergent   **D.** transform fault

Links

 Writing

Expository Writing

Find out about Alfred Wegener, the scientist who first supported the "continental drift" hypothesis, the idea that the continents move. Write a brief **report** about Wegener, his background, and his scientific discoveries, and tell whether he was interested in any other field of science.

 Math

Extend Patterns

New York is about 5,800 km from Paris. The two cities are on different plates that move away from each other at an average speed of 2.5 cm/year. At this speed, how long will it take the cities to be 11,600 km apart?

Art

Future World Map

Find out in which directions all the major plates are moving. Then draw a map of what you think the world may look like 200 million years from now. Assume that each plate moves as much as about 5000 km (3100 mi).

 For more links and activities, go to www.hspscience.com

What Causes Earthquakes and Volcanoes?

Fast Fact

A Disruptive Volcano The island of Montserrat, West Indies, is the site of the Soufriere Hills volcano. When the volcano erupts, rapidly moving avalanches of hot rocks, ash, and gas flow downward at speeds of 100–150 km/hr (62–93 mi/hr). In the Investigate, you'll find out about other Earth processes that can be disruptive and destructive.

Locating an Earthquake

Materials • map of the central United States • drawing compass

Procedure

1 Copy the table.

2 An earthquake produces different kinds of waves that travel at different speeds. The table shows the differences in arrival times between two types of waves. You can tell how far away an earthquake is by using these differences. For each 100 km that the waves traveled, there is an 8-sec time difference.

3 Calculate the distance from the source of the earthquake to each city. First, divide each time by 8 sec. Then, multiply the result by 100 km. Record this data in the table.

4 Use the map scale to set the radius of your compass to match the distance from the earthquake to one of the cities.

5 Center your compass on the city you selected. Draw a circle to show all the points that are the calculated distance from that city.

6 Repeat Steps 4 and 5 for the other cities in the table. You should draw three circles that all intersect at or near one city. This is where the earthquake occurred.

Draw Conclusions

1. Where did the earthquake occur?

2. **Inquiry Skill** Scientists interpret data and use numbers to study earthquakes. Based on this Investigate, what are some of the ways scientists use the data they get from earthquake waves?

Earthquake Wave Data		
City Where Waves Were Recorded	Time Difference	Distance from Earthquake
Lexington, Kentucky	38.4 sec.	
Memphis, Tennessee	12.8 sec.	
St. Louis, Missouri	18.4 sec.	

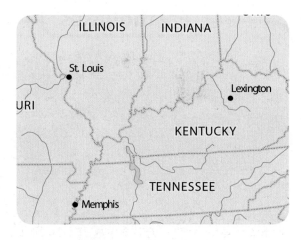

Investigate Further

Research other information that scientists can get from earthquake waves. **Communicate** your findings to the class in a multimedia report.

Reading in Science

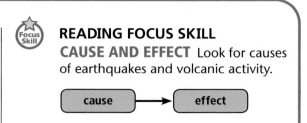

VOCABULARY
fault p. 248
earthquake p. 248
focus p. 249
epicenter p. 249
volcano p. 252

SCIENCE CONCEPTS
▶ how plate movements cause earthquakes and volcanic activity
▶ what the different types of volcanoes are

READING FOCUS SKILL
CAUSE AND EFFECT Look for causes of earthquakes and volcanic activity.

cause ⟶ effect

Earthquakes

Suppose you're holding a wooden ruler at both ends. If you put pressure on both ends at the same time, the ruler will bend slightly. If you press very hard, the ruler will snap in two.

Earth's plates behave in a similar way. Under pressure, they bend. When the pressure is great, the rocks that make up a plate break. When the rocks break, a fault is formed. A **fault** is a break in Earth's crust where rocks can slide past each other. Most faults form along plate boundaries because the pressure there is great. However, faults can also form within a plate, far from the edges.

As Earth's plates move, pressure builds up along the plates' faults. The rocks along the faults bend or stretch, almost like rubber bands. And again like rubber bands, if the rocks stretch too far, they will snap and energy will be released as they suddenly slide past each other. The snap and slide of rocks as energy is released in Earth's crust is known as an **earthquake**.

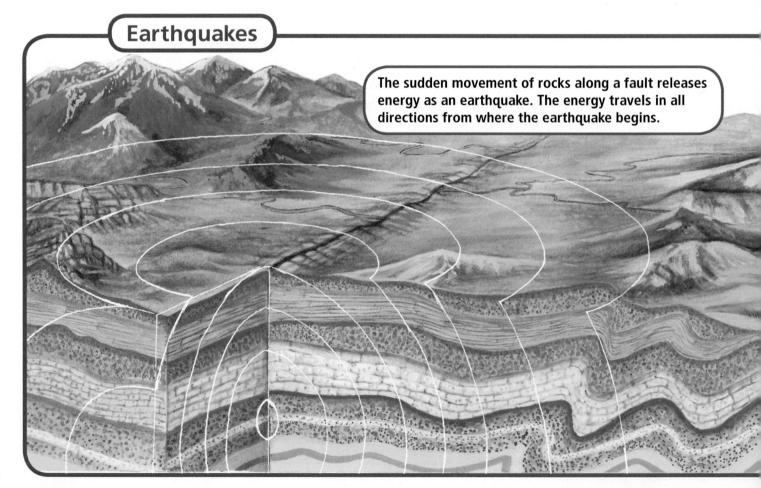

Earthquakes

The sudden movement of rocks along a fault releases energy as an earthquake. The energy travels in all directions from where the earthquake begins.

Earthquakes can occur close to Earth's surface or very deep inside the crust or mantle. The point inside Earth where an earthquake begins is called the **focus**. The point on Earth's surface directly above the focus of an earthquake is the **epicenter**.

When an earthquake begins, the released energy travels away from the focus in waves. The fastest waves caused by earthquakes are primary waves, or *P waves.* These are the first waves to be detected. P waves compress and expand the ground as they travel. Their movement is similar to an accordion's movement. The second-fastest waves caused by an earthquake are secondary waves, or *S waves.* S waves move across the direction in which the P waves are traveling. They can move up and down or side to side.

Both P waves and S waves travel through the Earth's interior. In addition, a third type of wave called a *surface wave* travels along Earth's surface. Some surface waves shake the ground from side to side. Other surface waves roll across the land like ocean waves. Both of these types of surface waves cause most of the damage that is done to buildings during an earthquake.

 CAUSE AND EFFECT What causes an earthquake?

Making Waves

Hook one end of a spring toy to the knob of a closed door. Hold the other end of the spring toy in your hand, and walk backward until the spring doesn't sag much. Quickly jerk your hand toward the door and back toward you. What type of wave did you just model? Now jerk your hand up and down once. What type of wave did you model with this movement?

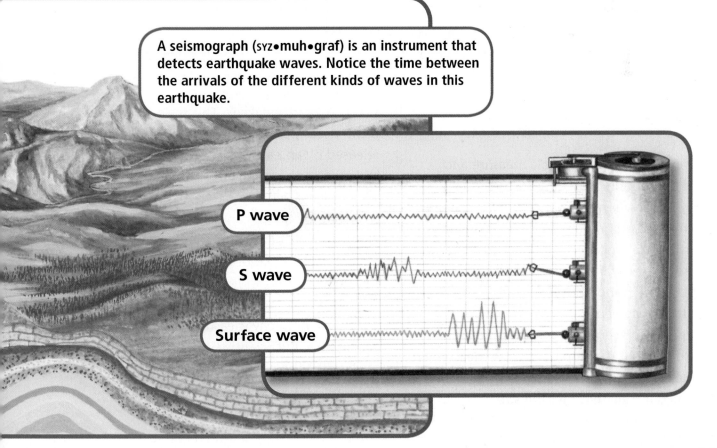

A seismograph (SYZ•muh•graf) is an instrument that detects earthquake waves. Notice the time between the arrivals of the different kinds of waves in this earthquake.

P wave

S wave

Surface wave

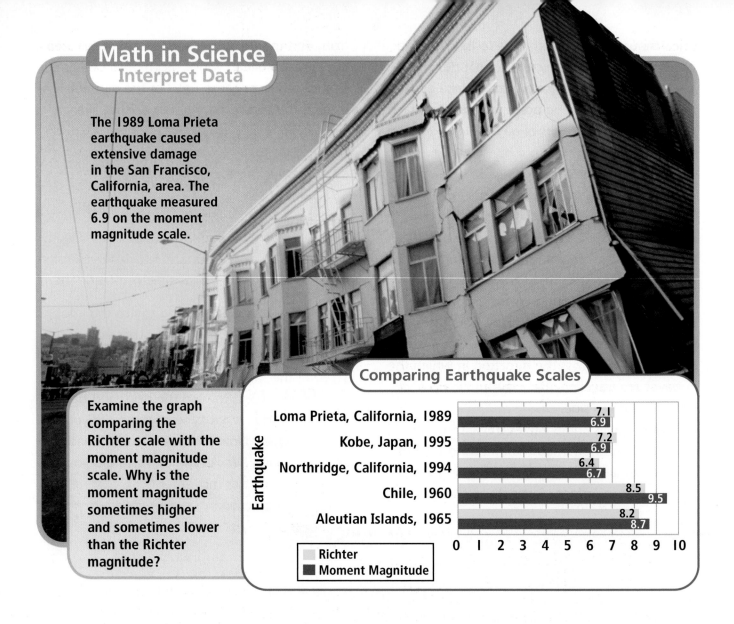

Math in Science
Interpret Data

The 1989 Loma Prieta earthquake caused extensive damage in the San Francisco, California, area. The earthquake measured 6.9 on the moment magnitude scale.

Examine the graph comparing the Richter scale with the moment magnitude scale. Why is the moment magnitude sometimes higher and sometimes lower than the Richter magnitude?

Comparing Earthquake Scales

Earthquake

Loma Prieta, California, 1989 — Richter 7.1, Moment Magnitude 6.9
Kobe, Japan, 1995 — Richter 7.2, Moment Magnitude 6.9
Northridge, California, 1994 — Richter 6.4, Moment Magnitude 6.7
Chile, 1960 — Richter 8.5, Moment Magnitude 9.5
Aleutian Islands, 1965 — Richter 8.2, Moment Magnitude 8.7

Richter
Moment Magnitude

Measuring Earthquake Strength and Damage

Seismographs electronically measure and record the motion caused by an earthquake's energy waves. As you saw in the Investigate, data from seismographs can be used to find an earthquake's location. The time that elapses between the arrival of P waves and S waves at different seismographs is recorded. The more time that elapses, the farther away is the earthquake's epicenter.

Seismographs can also be used to measure an earthquake's strength. In 1935, Charles Richter developed a scale that uses the size of waves recorded on a seismograph to determine how strong an earthquake is. This scale, called the Richter scale, estimates the amount of energy released by an earthquake. On the Richter scale, an earthquake with a magnitude of 2.0 is considered very minor. An earthquake with a magnitude of 4.0 can be felt, but it causes only minor damage. And an earthquake with a magnitude of 6.0 or greater can cause major damage.

Based on seismograph records, the Richter scale only indirectly measures the strength of an earthquake. But scientists have developed a new scale called the *moment magnitude scale* that is not based on seismograph readings. Instead, the energy released during an earthquake is

250

calculated from measurements of the distance that the rock moved along the fault. The numbers for an earthquake's magnitude on the moment magnitude scale are very similar to the numbers on the Richter scale. However, the moment magnitude scale is considered much more accurate.

Both the Richter scale and the moment magnitude scale measure an earthquake's strength, not the amount of damage it caused. A scale that does measure an earthquake according to the damage is the Mercalli intensity scale. This scale uses Roman numerals. A rating of I to III indicates very minor damage. A rating of IV to VI indicates slight damage. Ratings higher than this indicate that buildings in the area had moderate to heavy damage. A rating of XII indicates that most buildings in the area were completely destroyed.

An earthquake can cause damage to an area even if its epicenter is not nearby. If a powerful earthquake occurs beneath the ocean, it will cause the ocean floor to rise and fall. The effect will be movement of the water above the floor. This may lead to the formation of a large wave called a *tsunami* (tsoo•NAH•mee).

A tsunami can travel great distances. As it approaches land, it may be more than 30 m (100 ft) high. The giant wall of water then slams into the coast. Large tsunamis have been known to carry water hundreds of meters inland. The force of the water is strong enough to cause massive damage to buildings near the shore. It also causes erosion and can even strip the sand from a beach completely.

 CAUSE AND EFFECT **What are the effects of a tsunami?**

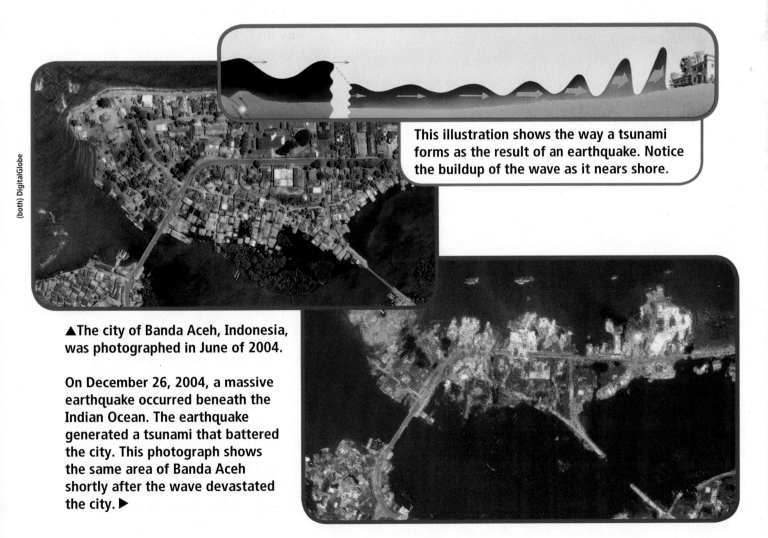

This illustration shows the way a tsunami forms as the result of an earthquake. Notice the buildup of the wave as it nears shore.

▲The city of Banda Aceh, Indonesia, was photographed in June of 2004.

On December 26, 2004, a massive earthquake occurred beneath the Indian Ocean. The earthquake generated a tsunami that battered the city. This photograph shows the same area of Banda Aceh shortly after the wave devastated the city. ▶

Volcanoes

You've learned that mountains form when rocks at convergent boundaries are deformed and lifted. But some mountains form in another way. Mountains called **volcanoes** form when molten rock, or *magma,* is pushed to the surface and builds up.

Most volcanoes are along the boundaries of Earth's plates. Some volcanoes form at divergent boundaries, where two plates are pulling apart. As the plates separate, magma is generated and can rise to the surface. Other volcanoes form at convergent boundaries where oceanic crust is pushed down.

Mantle rock is very hot and dry. The melting temperature of dry rock is much higher than the melting temperature of wet rock. When a slab of crust sinks, it releases water and other chemicals. The overlying rock absorbs the water and the surrounding temperature is hot enough to cause part of it to melt and form magma. The magma is lighter than the solid rock in the crust, so it moves upward. If there is an opening to the surface, or a vent, the magma can erupt and form a volcano.

There are many kinds of volcanoes formed from many kinds of materials. However, volcanoes fall into three basic categories: shield volcanoes, cinder cone volcanoes, and composite volcanoes. The type of volcano depends on the type of volcanic eruption that formed it.

How Volcanoes Are Formed

Volcanoes are often formed as oceanic crust moves down and under continental crust. The sinking of oceanic crust causes the plate over it to melt and form magma. The magma is less dense than the mantle, so it moves up to the surface.

Shield Volcano

Shield volcanoes are broad, slightly dome-shaped volcanoes. They may erupt many times in a period of more than a million years.

Volcanoes can erupt explosively, with materials being thrown violently out of the vent. Volcanoes can also erupt nonexplosively. The lava, or magma that reaches Earth's surface, flows slowly out of the vent almost the way honey flows out of a jar.

Nonexplosive eruptions form shield volcanoes as layer after layer of lava slowly builds up. Explosive eruptions form cinder cone volcanoes composed of ash and rock thrown out of the vent. Cinder cone volcanoes often erode quickly because their ash and rock are not cemented together by lava. The third type of volcano, the composite volcano, is formed by a mixture of explosive and nonexplosive eruptions.

Focus Skill **CAUSE AND EFFECT** What causes a volcano to form?

Composite Volcano

This is a composite volcano. Like shield volcanoes, these may erupt on and off for as long as a million years.

Cinder Cone Volcano

Cinder cone volcanoes have steep sides. They erupt for a short period of time, so most are not taller than about 300 m (1000 ft).

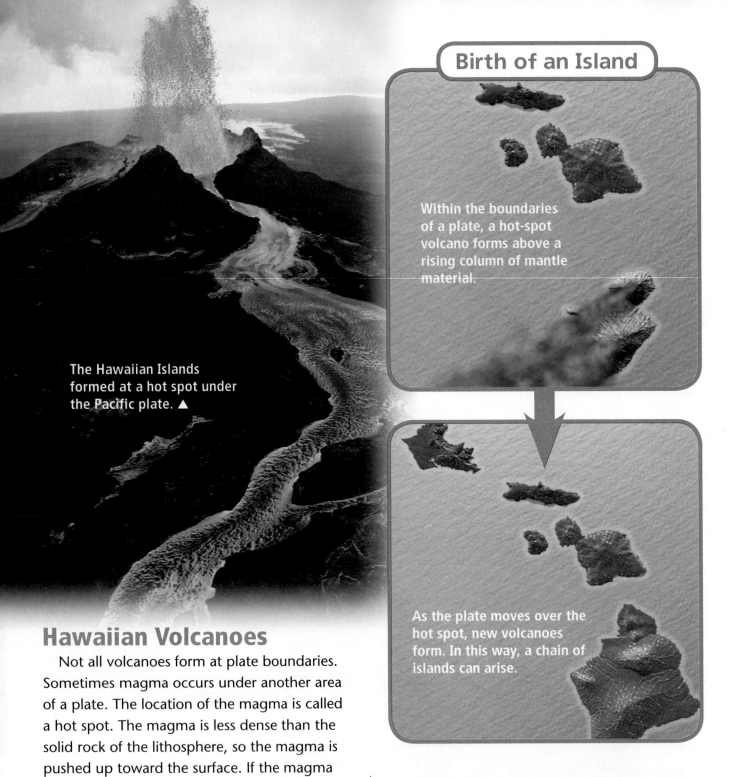

The Hawaiian Islands formed at a hot spot under the Pacific plate. ▲

Birth of an Island

Within the boundaries of a plate, a hot-spot volcano forms above a rising column of mantle material.

As the plate moves over the hot spot, new volcanoes form. In this way, a chain of islands can arise.

Hawaiian Volcanoes

Not all volcanoes form at plate boundaries. Sometimes magma occurs under another area of a plate. The location of the magma is called a hot spot. The magma is less dense than the solid rock of the lithosphere, so the magma is pushed up toward the surface. If the magma erupts above the surface, it can form a volcano.

As the plate moves over the hot spot, the volcano that was formed stops erupting and a series of new volcanoes may form. If the hot spot lies under oceanic crust, the series of volcanoes may become a chain of islands.

That's how the Hawaiian Islands formed. The Pacific plate moved over a hot spot, and island after island rose up out of the water as magma

flowed from inside Earth and hardened. If you look at a map, you can see that the Hawaiian Islands are in line with the northwest movement of the Pacific plate. The youngest island, Hawai'i, currently has three active volcanoes. One of these has been erupting continuously since 1983!

 CAUSE AND EFFECT What caused the Hawaiian Islands to form?

Focus Skill

1. **CAUSE AND EFFECT** Draw and complete the graphic organizer.

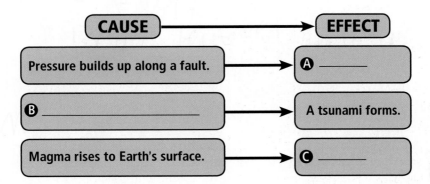

| CAUSE | → | EFFECT |

Pressure builds up along a fault. → **Ⓐ** _____

Ⓑ _____ → **A tsunami forms.**

Magma rises to Earth's surface. → **Ⓒ** _____

2. **SUMMARIZE** Explain how the movement of plates leads to earthquakes and volcanic activity.

3. **DRAW CONCLUSIONS** Is a volcanic eruption likely to occur on the east coast of the United States? Explain.

4. **VOCABULARY** Write an imaginary news report about an earthquake that just occurred. Use the terms *earthquake, epicenter, fault,* and *focus.*

Test Prep

5. **Critical Thinking** Suppose you're at an extinct volcano with steep sides. The ground is composed mostly of ash and small rock. What type of volcano is this?

6. Which is the most accurate scale for measuring the amount of energy released during an earthquake?

   A. Mercalli intensity scale
   B. moment magnitude scale
   C. Richter scale
   D. seismograph scale

Links

Writing

Narrative Writing
Find out about an explosive volcanic eruption that occurred in the past. Then write a personal **story** that might have happened to someone who was there during the eruption.

Math

Use Numeric Patterns
On the Richter scale, an increase of 1 point means 32 times as much energy. How many times as much energy is released by a 7.2 earthquake as compared with a 4.2 earthquake?

Art

Views of Mount Fuji
Katsushika Hokusai (1760–1849) was an artist known for his many pictures of Mount Fuji, a volcano in Japan. Go to the library and find examples of his work. Then draw your own picture of Mount Fuji or another volcano.

 For more links and activities, go to www.hspscience.com

A Volcano Awakens

Like a sleeping giant that had been rudely awakened, Mount St. Helens in Washington State recently erupted. As scientists and observers watched, giant clouds of smoke, ash, and steam belched from the top of the volcano. During this activity, there were no injuries or damage caused by the volcano.

That has not always been the case with Mount St. Helens, which, in 1980, erupted in a massive display of power and destruction.

A Violent Past

The recent eruption was a lot less violent and destructive than the previous eruption. In 1980, the upper part of Mount St. Helens blew off as gigantic clouds of ash and steam hurtled skyward. According to scientists, the cloud of ash from the volcano reached an altitude of about 24,000 m (80,000 ft) in just 15 minutes and circled the planet in only 15 days.

On the ground, the volcano killed 57 people and caused massive damage. According to geologists, the blast from the volcano traveled at about 500 km (300 mi) per hour and reached temperatures as high as 350°C (660°F). As a result, about 1 billion cubic meters of trees were blown down. That's enough to build 300,000 homes!

What Is a Volcano?

According to the U.S. Geological Survey, volcanoes are mountains. But they are different from most mountains in that they are formed by the piling up of lava, ash, and dust. At or near the top of a volcano is a vent that is connected to a *reservoir*, or pool, of molten rock below the surface of the Earth.

Observers and scientists are keeping a close eye on Mount St. Helens as it periodically belches clouds of smoke and ash into the sky. Since 1980, scientists have monitored the volcano with telescopes and sensors, such as seismographs. Seismographs sense movement within Earth (earthquakes), which may signal increased volcanic activity.

For now, scientists say that the volcano will probably go back to sleep, but that could change quickly, and violently.

Think About It

1. What do earthquakes tell scientists studying volcanoes?
2. Why is it important for scientists to study volcanoes?

Find out more! Log on to
www.hspscience.com

SEEING EARTH'S WATER SHOW

Earth's surface is constantly changing. Recently, Isabelle Anderson got an up-close and personal look at one of those changes.

When visiting Yellowstone National Park, Isabelle saw one of the most famous geysers in the world, Old Faithful. Geysers are caused when water, leaking through cracks in Earth's crust, comes in contact with heat from a volcanic source, called a hot spot or a plume. When the water becomes hot enough to boil, it shoots upward above the surface.

Every 30 to 90 minutes, Old Faithful sends plumes of water and steam high up into the air. According to park officials, the geyser sends about 38,000 to 45,000 liters (about 10,000 to 12,000 gallons) of water skyward at each eruption. The water shoots about 30 to 54 meters (100 to 180 feet) into the air.

Isabelle had never seen anything like it. She's planning to study how these geysers occur. She's also interested in how people might be able to use resources like this to meet energy needs.

SCIENCE Projects
for Home or School

You Can Do It!

Materials
- large bowl
- clean glass jar
- water
- food coloring

Quick and Easy Project

Using S Waves to Study Earth's Core

Procedure

1. Fill the jar and the bowl half-full of water. Add food coloring to the water in the jar.
2. Place the jar in the center of the bowl.
3. Use your finger to tap the water surface several times near the side of the bowl, creating ripples.
4. Observe how the ripples react when they reach the jar.

Draw Conclusions

What do the ripples represent? What does the jar represent? How do the ripples react when they reach the jar? S waves can move through solids but not through liquids, such as the liquids in Earth's core. The ripples in this experiment also can't move through "Earth's core." What can scientists learn by studying the reflections of S waves?

Design Your Own Investigation

Earthquake-Resistant Buildings

In many earthquake-prone areas of the world, architects have experimented with different building materials and designs in order to construct buildings that can withstand earthquakes. What materials do you think should be used in an earthquake-resistant building? Build models to show how different building materials and structures are affected by earthquakes. If there is time, hold a contest with your classmates to see who can produce the most earthquake-resistant model.

Review and Test Preparation

Vocabulary Review

Use the terms below to complete the sentences. The page numbers tell you where to look in the chapter if you need help.

crust p. 230   **plate tectonics** p. 241
mantle p. 231   **rift** p. 242
core p. 231   **fault** p. 248
erosion p. 232   **focus** p. 249
deposition p. 233 **epicenter** p. 249

1. The theory that the plates of the lithosphere are always moving is called _____ .

2. The point inside Earth where an earthquake begins is the _____ .

3. The removal and transportation of weathered material is _____ .

4. The deep valley along the mid-ocean ridge is a _____ .

5. The asthenosphere is part of Earth's _____ .

6. The process by which eroded material drops or settles is _____ .

7. A break in Earth's crust where rocks can slide past each other is a _____ .

8. Earth's center is called its _____ .

9. The point on Earth's surface directly above an earthquake's focus is the _____ .

10. Earth's outermost layer is the _____ .

Check Understanding

Write the letter of the best choice.

11. Look at the picture below. Which layer is responsible for Earth's magnetic field?

   A. crust
   B. inner core
   C. mantle
   D. outer core

12. Which process is responsible for forming a sea cave?
   F. deposition
   G. earthquake
   H. erosion
   J. volcanic activity

13. What are Earth's plates composed of?
   A. the crust alone
   B. the crust and the asthenosphere
   C. the crust and upper part of the mantle
   D. the inner and outer core

14. **COMPARE AND CONTRAST** How do the positions of the continents today compare with their positions 220 million years ago?

F. The continents are now closer together.

G. The continents are now farther apart.

H. The continents are now farther north.

J. The continents are now farther south.

15. An earthquake occurs. Which type of waves will be detected first?

A. P waves

B. S waves

C. surface waves

D. tsunamis

16. **CAUSE AND EFFECT** Which caused the Hawaiian Islands to form?

F. a convergent boundary

G. a divergent boundary

H. a hot spot

J. an earthquake

Inquiry Skills

17. The Appalachians are a mountain range that runs through the eastern United States and Canada. Mountains of about the same age and structure are found across the Atlantic Ocean in the British Isles and Scandinavia. From this evidence, what can you infer about the positions of the continents of North America and Europe long ago? Explain your answer.

18. How do scientists interpret data from seismographs to determine the location of an earthquake?

Critical Thinking

19. An earthquake that measures 7.0 on the moment magnitude scale affects two cities. In one city, the damage on the Mercalli intensity scale is IX (9). In the other city, the damage on the Mercalli intensity scale is V (5). Describe the difference between the moment magnitude scale and the Mercalli intensity scale. What might explain the difference in damage done to the two cities?

20. Look at the diagram below of the volcano. Use the diagram to answer Parts A and B.

Part A What type of volcano is shown? Explain your answer.

Part B Suppose the vent becomes plugged by hardened lava. What do you think may happen to this volcano?

Chapter 7

Earth's Rocks

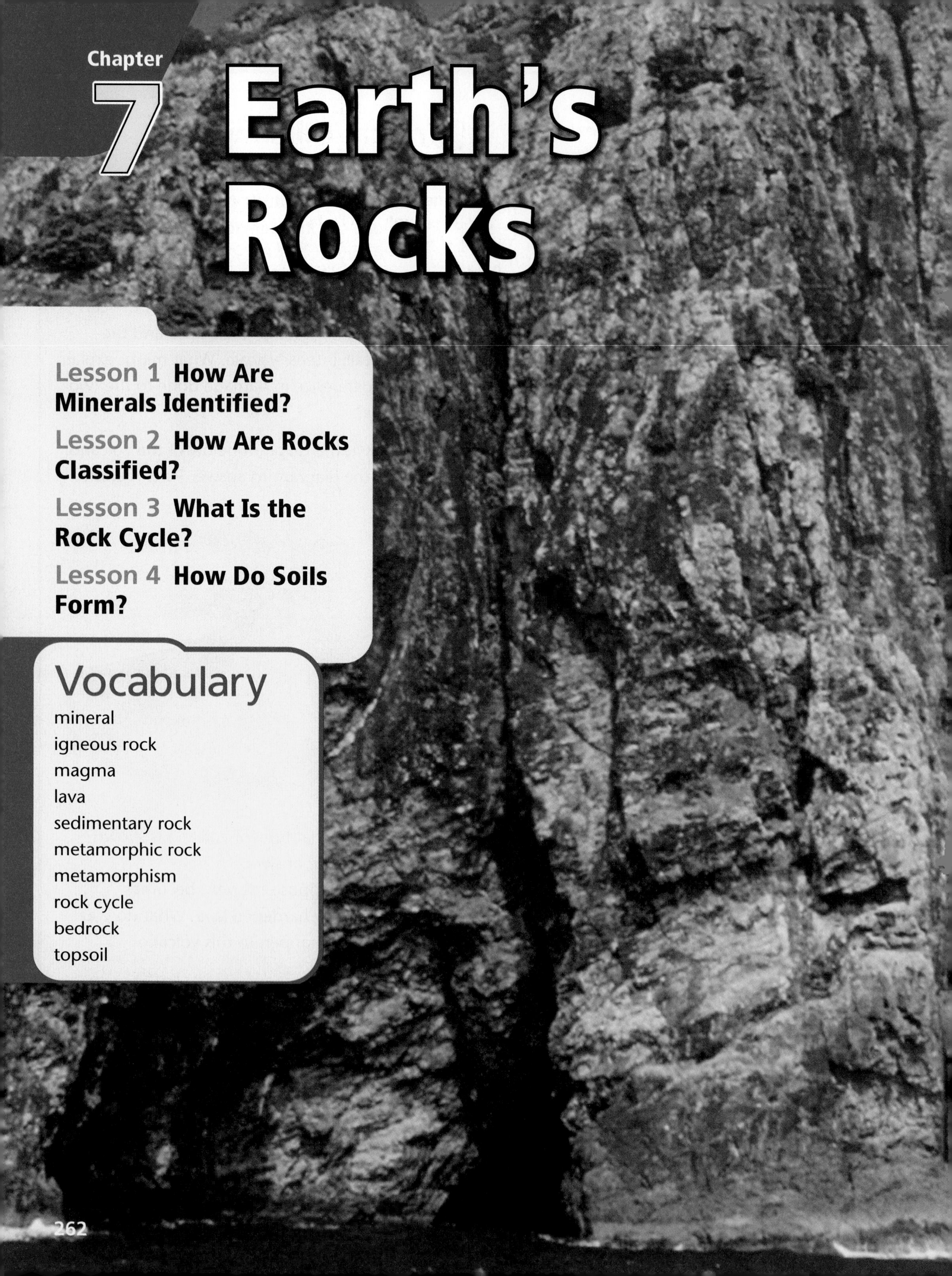

Vocabulary

mineral
igneous rock
magma
lava
sedimentary rock
metamorphic rock
metamorphism
rock cycle
bedrock
topsoil

When the tide is high enough, powerboats can speed through the Hole in the Rock off Cape Brett, in New Zealand. How do you think the hole in this rock formed? How might it change over time?

How Are Minerals Identified?

Fast Fact

Cave Crystals Minerals grow as crystals. The crystals in this photo are of the mineral selenite, and they're growing in a cave. If there's enough space, crystals like these can grow to be as large as 1 m (3 ft) in diameter and about 15 m (50 ft) long. Crystal shape is one property of minerals. In the Investigate, you'll find out about other properties that are used to identify minerals.

Properties of Minerals

Materials
- safety goggles
- hand lens
- magnet
- 6 labeled mineral samples
- copper penny
- steel nail
- streak plate

Procedure

1 Copy the data table.

2 Use the hand lens to observe each mineral. In the table, record your description of each mineral's color.

3 CAUTION: **Put on your safety goggles.** Draw a line across the streak plate by using each mineral. In the table, record the color of each streak.

4 CAUTION: **The nail may be sharp**, **so be careful.** Test the hardness of the minerals by trying to scratch each one with your fingernail, the steel nail, the penny, and the other samples. Record your observations in the table.

5 Test each mineral with the magnet to see if it is magnetic. Record your observations.

6 How can you classify the minerals according to their hardness and their magnetic properties? Make a table for organizing your results from Steps 4 and 5.

Draw Conclusions

1. Which properties are most useful for identifying a mineral?

2. Which mineral that you tested is the hardest? Which is the softest? Explain how you know.

3. Inquiry Skill Scientists observe and compare minerals so they can organize and study them. What are some ways, other than the ones above, that scientists might use to compare minerals?

Comparing Minerals				
Sample	Color	Streak	Hardness	Magnetic?
A				
B				
C				
D				
E				
F				

Step 2

Investigate Further

Use a field guide to minerals to identify the samples you observed. Compare your observations to the descriptions and illustrations in the field guide.

Reading in Science

Properties of Minerals

Imagine a diamond sparkling in a ring and the dark "lead" in a pencil. What do these have in common? They're both minerals and they're both made of carbon. A **mineral** is a natural, solid substance that has a definite chemical composition and physical structure. Every mineral can form as a crystal with a regular geometric shape.

Scientists identify minerals by using many different properties. Among these are streak, fluorescence, crystal structure, cleavage, and hardness.

Streak is the color of the powder left behind when a mineral is rubbed on a piece of unglazed tile. The unglazed tile is called a streak plate. Usually the streak color is the same as the mineral color, but sometimes they're different. For example, the mineral chalcopyrite is gold in color but has a black streak. Pyrite has a gold color but makes a greenish-black or brownish-black streak.

A mineral that glows under ultraviolet light is said to show fluorescence. The property can be used to classify and identify some minerals. Calcite, fluorite, and some other minerals can show fluorescence.

Crystal shape is another property of minerals. A mineral is always a solid, with its atoms arranged in a certain repeating pattern. The

> Cleavage in the mineral halite is cubic. If you break a large piece of halite, the smaller pieces will be cubes.

> The streak of silver hematite is rust-colored, which is different from the mineral's appearance.

crystal shape is the result of this pattern. A scientist can use the pattern to identify a crystal. The box on the next page has more information on six types of crystal shapes found in minerals.

However, using crystal shape to identify minerals does not always work. Most minerals are not formed in the best conditions. There is usually not enough space for crystals to form perfectly, so the minerals grow to fill the available space, and the true crystal shape will not be visible. However, minerals that grow

266

in caves often have enough space and time to form perfectly. Because of this, spectacular crystals often grow there.

Cleavage can also be used to identify minerals. Minerals tend to break along a plane, or cleave, along flat surfaces parallel to the crystal faces. The mineral mica, for example, breaks very easily and always in the same direction. A scientist who wants to identify a mineral easily can tell from its cleavage if the mineral is mica.

 COMPARE AND CONTRAST How does the streak of a mineral compare with its color? Are they alike or different? Give an example.

The mineral fluorite may glow under ultraviolet light.

Crystal Shapes

There are six basic groups of crystal shapes. Each of these crystals has a different crystal shape.

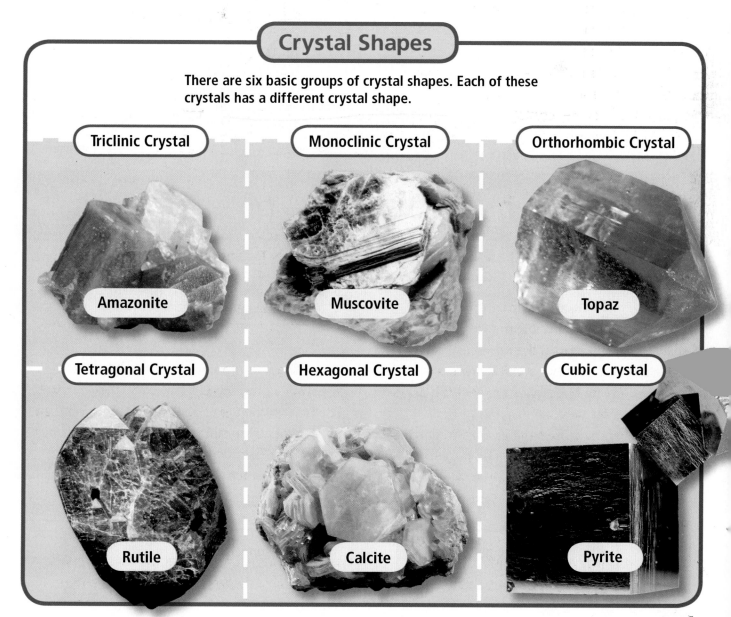

Triclinic Crystal	Monoclinic Crystal	Orthorhombic Crystal
Amazonite	Muscovite	Topaz

Tetragonal Crystal	Hexagonal Crystal	Cubic Crystal
Rutile	Calcite	Pyrite

Mineral Hardness and Uses

Another property scientists use to compare and identify minerals is hardness. Hardness is a measure of the ability of a mineral to resist being scratched. Scientists use the Mohs (MOHZ) hardness scale, which rates minerals from 1 (softest) to 10 (hardest). A mineral with a higher number can scratch a mineral with a lower number. Diamonds are a 10 on the Mohs scale. You can tell if a mineral is a diamond because no other mineral can scratch it.

Because their hardness is known, common objects like your fingernail, a steel nail, and glass can be used to see where an unknown mineral fits on the Mohs scale. You can also identify and compare minerals by testing them against each other.

Minerals have many everyday uses. As you might expect from its hardness, the diamond has important uses besides that of jewelry. Because of its hardness, diamond is used to cut rocks and other very hard materials. Sandpaper is made from a mineral called corundum (kuh•RUHN•duhm), which has a hardness of 9 and so can scratch most other materials. This property makes it useful for smoothing the rough edges of wood.

Minerals are also useful in many other ways. Because graphite is very soft and easily makes a streak, it is used in pencils. Quartz is used

Math in Science
Interpret Data

Mohs Hardness Scale
An unknown mineral scratches fluorite and a steel knife blade. It can't scratch feldspar. What is its approximate hardness?

1 Talc
2 Gypsum
3 Calcite
4 Fluorite
5 Apatite

Fingernail: hardness of 2.5

Copper penny: hardness of 3

to make glass. Many minerals are important sources of metals. Copper, silver, and gold in their natural states are minerals. Other metals, such as lead, are found in minerals such as galena.

Copper is needed for making many of the parts in computers. Iron is used to make steel, which is an important material. It's used in paper clips, cars, ships, and buildings, among other things. The mineral halite, or rock salt, makes your food tasty. These are just a few examples of minerals that people use every day.

 COMPARE AND CONTRAST Suppose you know where a mineral falls on the Mohs hardness scale. How can you use that information to compare the mineral with another mineral?

Insta-Lab

The Scratch Test
Use a steel nail, a copper penny, and your fingernail to test four mineral samples. Use your observations to infer where each mineral falls on the Mohs scale. Record your analysis. How can the scratch test help identify minerals?

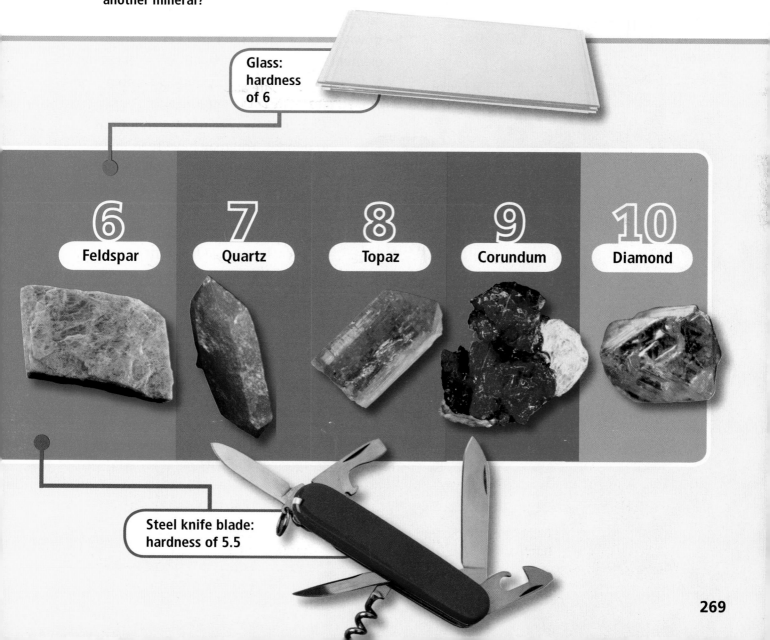

Glass: hardness of 6

6	7	8	9	10
Feldspar	Quartz	Topaz	Corundum	Diamond

Steel knife blade: hardness of 5.5

How Minerals Form

Minerals form in places such as seawater, Earth's crust, and even animals' shells. In all, there are more than 3000 different minerals on Earth. While minerals form only in nature, they all form from materials that were never alive. Some minerals form from a single element. For example, diamonds and graphite form from carbon. Most other minerals, though, are compounds made of several elements.

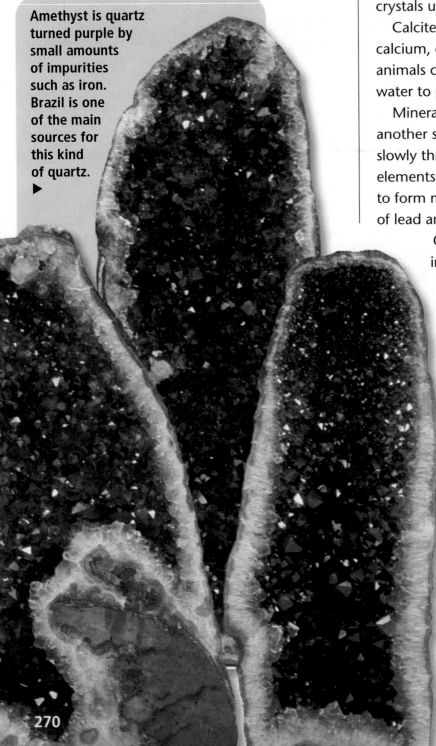

Amethyst is quartz turned purple by small amounts of impurities such as iron. Brazil is one of the main sources for this kind of quartz. ▶

Minerals may form deep within Earth. Diamonds form in Earth's mantle, where enormous pressure and heat turn black carbon into hard, glistening, sometimes colorless diamond crystals. Closer to the surface, other minerals—such as calcite—form in Earth's crust.

Another place minerals form is in caves. Calcite can form as water evaporates in limestone caves. As the water evaporates, white, colorless, or gray crystals form on the sides of the cave. Miners have found calcite crystals up to 7 m (23 ft) long.

Calcite crystals also form in seawater, when calcium, oxygen, and carbon combine. Ocean animals can also take these elements from water to produce protective calcite shells.

Mineral-rich hot water from Earth's crust is another source of minerals. As the water moves slowly through cracks in Earth's crust, the elements in the water mix with other elements to form minerals such as galena, a combination of lead and sulfur.

One other way minerals can form is in geodes. You may have seen these beautiful rocks. Often dull and round on the outside, geodes can be split open to reveal an inside surface covered with crystals. A geode may begin as a fossil shell buried in sediment. As time passes, the interior of the fossil shell becomes filled with water. When the water evaporates, the minerals in the water are left as dazzling crystals on the shell walls.

 COMPARE AND CONTRAST How are the three ways calcite is formed alike? How are they different?

270

1. COMPARE AND CONTRAST Copy the table. For each entry at the left, choose the correct term from the column heading. Make a check in the box under that term.

HOW TO COMPARE MINERALS						
	Cleavage	Powder	Hardness	Shape	Streak	Fluorescence
Rub the mineral on a _____ plate to see what color the _____ is.						
Crystal _____ is not always helpful in identifying a mineral.						
A mineral with _____ glows under ultraviolet light.						
A mineral has a unique way of breaking, or _____.						
Use _____ to find out where the mineral falls on the Mohs scale.						

2. SUMMARIZE Write a short paragraph that summarizes how people use four properties of minerals to identify them.

3. DRAW CONCLUSIONS Identifying minerals is sometimes described as a process of elimination. Explain why.

4. VOCABULARY Write a definition for the word *mineral,* and use the word in a sentence.

Test Prep

5. Critical Thinking Tim cracks open a geode. "It's just like a cave," he says. Explain what Tim means.

6. Which of these describes cleavage?

   A. how a mineral breaks

   B. a mineral's crystal shape

   C. how fast a mineral grows

   D. a mineral's softness

Links

Writing

Expository Writing

Research a cave that tourists visit to see mineral crystals and formations. Write a **brochure** describing the cave, what the crystals look like, and how they formed.

Math

Make a Table

Use a balance to find the mass of six mineral samples that are about the same size. Record the mass of each sample in a table. Why does the mass for similar-size mineral samples differ?

Health

Mineral or Mineral?

Research minerals to find out how the kinds discussed in this lesson are different from the kinds the human body needs. Make a table that lists the minerals the body needs, the sources of each one, and their uses in the body.

 For more links and activities, go to **www.hspscience.com**

How Are Rocks Classified?

Fast Fact

Layers on Layers The Grand Canyon, in
Arizona, at its deepest point, is about 1800 m
(6000 ft) from rim to river. That dramatic drop
provides a cutaway view of a stunning variety
of rocks. In the Investigate, you'll observe
differences in several rock samples.

Classifying Rocks

Materials
- safety goggles
- 5 rocks
- hand lens
- paper plate
- dropper
- vinegar

Procedure

1 Copy the data table.

2 Use the hand lens to observe each rock. In the table, record the color or colors of each one.

3 As you observe the rocks, use the Texture column in the table to record the answer to each of the following questions. Do grains make up the rock? Are the grains small or large? Do they have smooth edges or sharp edges? Do the grains fit together like puzzle pieces, or do they seem to float near each other? In the Picture column of the table, draw a picture of each rock.

4 **CAUTION:** **Put on the safety goggles.** Vinegar bubbles when it comes in contact with the mineral calcite. Place one rock sample at a time on the paper plate. Use the dropper to put a few drops of vinegar on the rock. Observe and record what happens.

5 Classify the rock samples into groups, based on the ways the rocks are similar.

Draw Conclusions

1. On what basis did you classify the rock samples?

2. How do your classifications compare with those of two classmates?

3. Inquiry Skill Scientists use observations to draw conclusions. What conclusions can you draw, based on what you observed?

Data Table

Rock Sample	Color	Texture	Picture	Bubbles When Vinegar Added
A				
B				
C				
D				
E				

Step 4

Investigate Further

Choose another characteristic that you could use to classify the rock samples. Analyze the samples by including the new characteristic, and then decide if you want to change your original groupings.

Reading in Science

VOCABULARY
igneous rock p. 274
magma p. 274
lava p. 275
sedimentary rock p. 276
metamorphic rock p. 278
metamorphism p. 278

SCIENCE CONCEPTS
► what a rock is
► what igneous, sedimentary, and metamorphic rocks are and how they form

 READING FOCUS SKILL
COMPARE AND CONTRAST Notice words such as *either* and *unlike*.

alike	different

Igneous Rock

Look toward a mountain range and you see rock. Rock rises in the jagged beauty of mountain peaks, and rock sits in piles of rubble in the valleys. Rock makes up landforms everywhere on Earth. A rock is made up of one or more minerals.

One type of rock, formed when melted rock hardens, is called **igneous rock**. This type of rock develops when melted rock within Earth, called **magma**, is pushed up from the mantle to the crust, which is cooler. The cooler temperatures cause the magma to harden into rock. The process is also called crystallization.

Depending on where the magma cools, the igneous rock will be either *intrusive* or *extrusive*.

Pumice

Extrusive

When extrusive igneous rocks form, lava cools quickly, producing fine crystals that are hard to see or, sometimes, no crystals at all.

Obsidian

Rhyolite

Intrusive igneous rock cools underground, deep within Earth's crust. Extrusive igneous rock cools on Earth's surface.

All intrusive rocks have a similar texture. This is because they cool slowly, over thousands or tens of thousands of years. As a result, large crystals form. This gives intrusive igneous rocks a coarse texture. Granite is an example of an intrusive igneous rock.

Extrusive rock is different from intrusive rock in that it cools on Earth's surface, not below it. Magma may explode from volcanoes or ooze from cracks in Earth's surface.

Once magma is exposed at Earth's surface, it is called **lava**. Temperatures on the surface are much cooler than within Earth's crust, so lava cools much more quickly than magma. As a result, extrusive rock is more finely grained than intrusive rock. Sometimes, lava cools so quickly that there is no time for crystals to develop. Extrusive rocks that form this way, such as obsidian, have a glassy appearance.

 COMPARE AND CONTRAST How is extrusive igneous rock different from intrusive igneous rock?

Insta-Lab

Forming Crystals

Cut a circle of black paper to fit the inside of a large jar lid. Stir 2 tablespoons of Epsom salts into 50 mL of water, and pour a thin layer into the lid. Allow the lid to sit undisturbed for a day or two. After the water evaporates, observe the appearance of the lid. What do you think would happen if the water evaporated more quickly?

Intrusive

When intrusive igneous rocks form, magma cools slowly, producing large crystals that are easy to see.

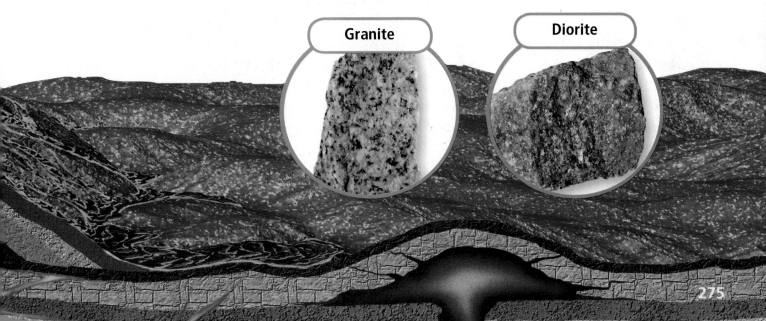

Granite

Diorite

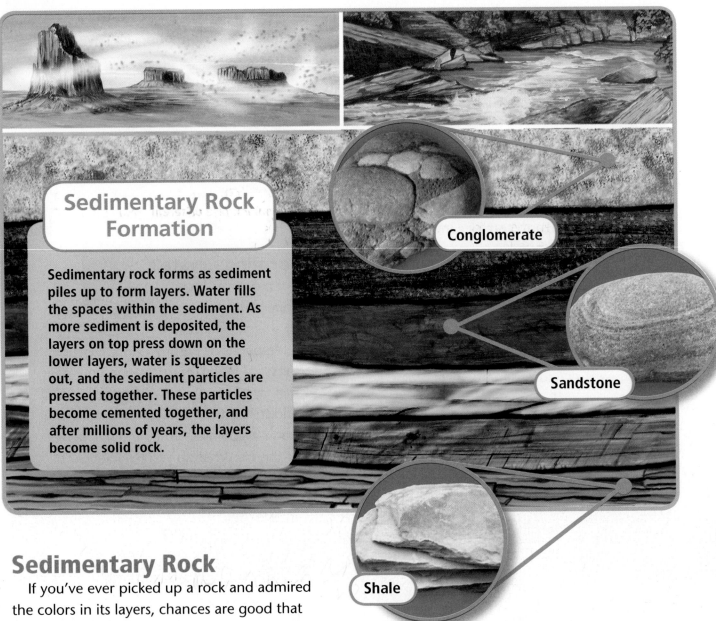

Sedimentary Rock Formation

Sedimentary rock forms as sediment piles up to form layers. Water fills the spaces within the sediment. As more sediment is deposited, the layers on top press down on the lower layers, water is squeezed out, and the sediment particles are pressed together. These particles become cemented together, and after millions of years, the layers become solid rock.

Conglomerate

Sandstone

Shale

Sedimentary Rock

If you've ever picked up a rock and admired the colors in its layers, chances are good that you were holding a sedimentary rock. The conditions that form sedimentary rocks are much more likely to exist at Earth's surface than deep underground. As a result, these rocks are common near Earth's surface and rare deep within the crust.

The best clue to how a sedimentary rock forms is in the name itself. **Sedimentary rock** forms when layers of sediment—bits of rock carved by wind, water, or ice—settle over time and bind together. Sedimentary rocks are divided into two main groups—clastic and chemical—depending on how they formed.

The word *clastic* comes from a Greek word meaning "broken." Clastic rocks begin to form when rock is broken into smaller pieces through weathering. This is the result of natural processes such as wind and rain wearing away rock, forming sediment. Next, wind and water move the sediment to new places. Layers of sediment build up, a process that can take a very long time. Water deposits minerals such as calcite in the spaces between the particles. These minerals bind the layers together. Finally, the layers are pressed and cemented, or glued, together to form rock.

Clastic rocks are classified by the size of the particles that form them. Fine particles form rocks such as shale. Medium-size particles form sandstone. Coarse, pebble-size particles with smooth, round edges form conglomerates.

Unlike clastic sedimentary rocks, chemical sedimentary rocks form when chemicals in water come out of the water and form solids. This happens when water that contains a large amount of a solid compound evaporates and leaves the solid behind. In a similar way, you may have let salt water evaporate in a dish. You couldn't see the salt when it was dissolved in the water, but when the water evaporated, you could see the salt crystals.

Limestone, one of the most common chemical sedimentary rocks, forms in a different way. When animal shells or skeletons pile up

at the bottom of an ocean or lake, they can become cemented together and form rock. Sometimes you see shells in the rock, but not always. If the shells have been destroyed, the limestone may look like a fine-grained shale. You can often distinguish limestone from shale by applying vinegar, which will bubble if the rock is limestone.

 COMPARE AND CONTRAST How is a conglomerate different from limestone?

Limestone often contains fossils, as you can see here.

The formations in or near hot springs are the result of dissolved minerals that leave deposits of limestone and other rocks.

277

Metamorphic Rock

The word *metamorphic* (met•uh•MAWR•fik) comes from the word root *meta*, which means "change." **Metamorphic rock** is made from igneous or sedimentary rock that has been changed by pressure, high temperature, very hot water, or a combination of these factors.

Pressure causes metamorphic rock to form in two ways. Deep within Earth, rock layers constantly press down on the layers below them. Also, pressure from collisions between plates can squeeze and bend rocks.

High temperature is the most important cause of **metamorphism**, the process by which metamorphic rock is formed. When rock from the surface is pushed deep into Earth, the extreme temperature there breaks the chemical bonds in the rock. Its minerals crystallize into new minerals. This can also happen when lava flows over the surface and "bakes" rock below. It may also happen when magma is pushed up into Earth's crust and heats the rock around it.

Metamorphic rock may be formed by extremely hot, mineral-rich water, which is usually found near magma. The water heats the rock around it, causing minerals in the rock to change. Sometimes, the heated water adds new materials to the rock, forming new minerals.

Metamorphic rock can form both in small pockets and in huge areas. Metamorphism that takes place over a large area, or *regional metamorphism,* happens when rocks in a region are changed by extreme pressure and high temperature. Regional metamorphism is common during mountain building. Most metamorphic rock is the result of regional metamorphism.

Another kind of metamorphism is *contact metamorphism.* This happens in a smaller area when magma or lava that touches rock changes only the rock that it contacts.

 COMPARE AND CONTRAST Contrast the ways pressure, high temperature, and hot water form metamorphic rock.

Metamorphic Rock Formation

With enough pressure and high temperature, both sedimentary and igneous rock can be changed into metamorphic rock. Even metamorphic rock can be changed into other kinds of metamorphic rock.

Slate

Slate can form from shale, an easily broken sedimentary rock. When shale undergoes a low level of pressure and a small increase in temperature in regional metamorphism, it becomes slate. Slate is also easily split. However, it's harder than shale and it's often used as building material.

278

Schist

When the temperature and pressure that formed slate increase, the slate can become schist. Schist is a flaky, hard rock. This usually occurs in regional metamorphism.

Gneiss

When the temperature and pressure that formed schist increase, it forms gneiss (NYS). When you look at a piece of gneiss, you can see bands of rock. Sometimes pressure folds the rock into bands.

Marble

When the temperature and pressure on limestone are great enough, it becomes marble, a rock often used for statues and buildings. The pure calcite of the limestone forms new minerals. They grow closely together, removing any of the spaces that might have been in the limestone.

For more links and activities, go to www.hspscience.com

Uses of Rock

Rocks are all around you in one form or another. Many buildings are made of granite, and walkways are often made of stone. Even the windows in buildings are made of glass that comes from sand and sandstone.

Igneous rocks are used in everything from construction materials to jewelry. Granite is an igneous rock that builders use because it lasts a long time. Some of New York City's Empire State Building is made of granite. Obsidian was once used for blades in tools because of the sharp edges it has when broken. Obsidian's shiny black surface also makes it a favorite of jewelry makers. Pumice is an igneous rock that can be ground into powder and used in cleaning products. At one time, people used pumice to clean their teeth. They don't anymore because it also filed the teeth down!

A marble rolling pin's beauty and heaviness make it a prized item for a cook.

Sedimentary rocks have a wide variety of uses. Shale and mudstone are used in construction. Energy resources such as petroleum and natural gas are found in sedimentary rock.

Metamorphic rock is a popular building material. Marble is prized for its unique look and is used in many public buildings and artistic sculptures. Years ago, slate was a common material for chalkboards and shingle roofs. Today, builders often use it for floors.

COMPARE AND CONTRAST How are the uses of igneous, sedimentary, and metamorphic rocks alike and different?

The Great Wall of China, which stretches thousands of miles, is made of rock and brick.

1. COMPARE AND CONTRAST Copy and fill in the graphic organizer. Write the different ways igneous, sedimentary, and metamorphic rocks are formed. Then write how all rocks are alike.

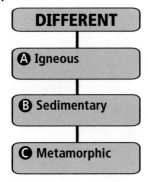

DIFFERENT

A Igneous

B Sedimentary

C Metamorphic

ALIKE

D

2. SUMMARIZE Write a paragraph that identifies how scientists classify rocks. Include characteristics of each type of rock.

3. DRAW CONCLUSIONS Why are fossils not found in igneous rock?

4. VOCABULARY Compare and contrast magma and lava. Write about their characteristics, where they are formed, and the role they play in rock formation.

Test Prep

5. Critical Thinking Explain the role of temperature in the formation of different types of rock.

6. What are the two main types of sedimentary rock?

   A. intrusive and extrusive

   B. magma and lava

   C. chemical and clastic

   D. slow-cooling and fast-cooling

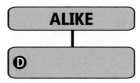

Links

Writing

Expository Writing

Write a **paragraph** that describes intrusive and extrusive igneous rock and tells younger students how to identify each type. Add pictures that will help them identify some kinds of intrusive and extrusive rocks.

Math

Display Data

A sample of granite contains these minerals: feldspar, 64 percent; quartz, 22 percent; mica, 8 percent; amphibole, 6 percent. Show this information in a circle graph.

Social Studies

Rocks and History

Research what kinds of rock were used for buildings and sculptures in one of the great civilizations of the past. Describe one of these kinds of rock, where it was found, and how it was used. Tell how the rock was moved and how it was shaped.

For more links and activities, go to www.hspscience.com

What Is the Rock Cycle?

Fast Fact

Carved by Water These rocks are part of the Great Falls National Park, 24 km (15 mi) from Washington, D.C. Over thousands of years, erosion of rocks by the Potomac River has caused Great Falls to move 14 km (9 mi) upstream. In the Investigate, you'll make a model to show other kinds of changes in rocks.

Modeling Changes in Rock

Materials
- clay of 3 different colors
- 2 sheets of wax paper
- metric ruler
- plastic foam pellets
- dowel
- 2 blocks of wood

Procedure

1. Use clay of one color to make a model of a layer of sediment about 12 cm square and 2 cm thick. Place the clay on a sheet of wax paper.

2. Use clay of another color to make 5 to 10 clay pellets, each about 2 cm in diameter. Place the clay pellets and the plastic foam pellets on top of the sediment model.

3. Use the third color of clay to make a second layer of sediment. Place it over the pellet layer.

4. Place a sheet of wax paper on top of the model, and press gently to form a model of sedimentary rock.

5. Use the dowel as a rolling pin to apply pressure to the top of the sedimentary rock model. Next, place the wooden blocks at the sides of the model, and press the rock model into a new shape. The model now represents a different type of rock.

6. Now use the model to show how rock can change again from one type into another. Make a series of drawings to illustrate the results you observed, starting with Step 4.

Step 2

Step 5

Draw Conclusions

1. What new type of rock did the model represent in Step 5? In Step 6?

2. **Inquiry Skill** How might using models help scientists understand the ways rocks are formed?

Investigate Further

Design and use a model that can help you observe how the process of weathering occurs. Would the materials differ from those you just used? If so, why?

Reading in Science

VOCABULARY
rock cycle p. 285

SCIENCE CONCEPTS
▶ how a rock can change into any other kind of rock through the rock cycle

READING FOCUS SKILL
CAUSE AND EFFECT Look for words and phrases such as *because* and *as a result*.

cause	→	effect

The Rock Cycle

When you travel by car, you look out at the landscape you are passing through. You see trees, buildings, animals, fields planted with crops, and rocks and stones. Depending on where you're traveling, you may see sand dunes, beaches, ocean water, ships, and pleasure boats. Or you may see tall mountains covered with rocks. The landscape you see is constantly changing. This is also true of the rocks you see. The changes in rocks may take thousands or millions of years, but any rock can

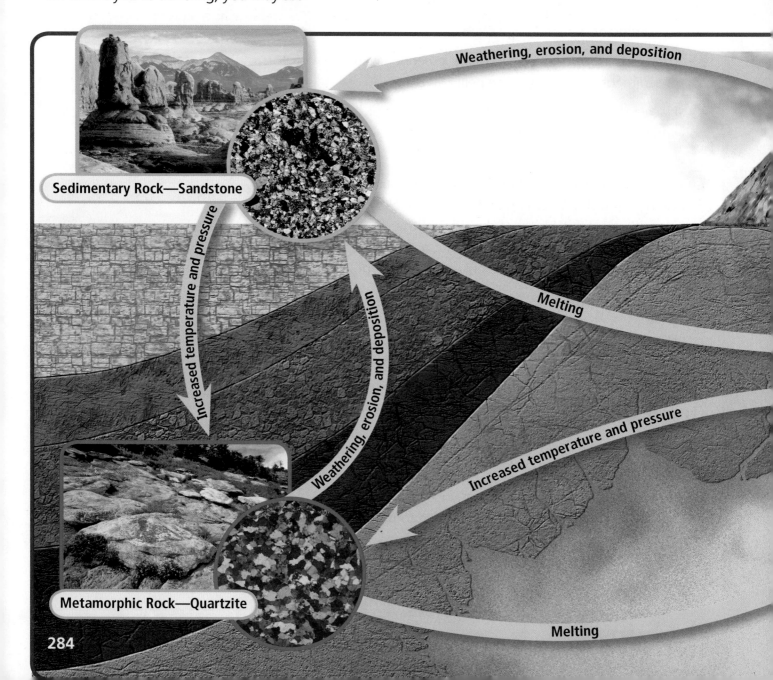

Weathering, erosion, and deposition

Sedimentary Rock—Sandstone

Increased temperature and pressure

Weathering, erosion, and deposition

Melting

Increased temperature and pressure

Metamorphic Rock—Quartzite

Melting

become any other kind of rock. Together, all of the processes that change rock from one kind to another are called the **rock cycle**.

Any rock can change into a sedimentary rock. The forces of wind and water can eventually weather even the hardest rock. Weathering causes rock to break into bits of sediment. Wind and water can carry away those bits and can deposit them in other places. Over time, layers of sediment build up. After still more time, pressure and chemicals can cement the bits of sediment together to form sedimentary rock.

Any rock can be changed into an igneous rock. If rock is exposed to a high enough temperature, it will melt into magma or lava. Usually, in order for rock to melt, it must be deep below Earth's surface. The process of melting, like all parts of the rock cycle, may take a long time. Once the magma or lava cools, igneous rock is formed.

Any rock can become a metamorphic rock. This happens when rock in Earth's crust is exposed to an elevated temperature and pressure but does not melt completely. One of the most common ways for metamorphic rock to form is during the process of mountain building. As rock is pressed together, huge amounts of pressure and high temperature can change igneous or sedimentary rock into metamorphic rock.

As you can see, the rock cycle is constantly changing Earth's surface and the rocks that make up that surface.

 CAUSE AND EFFECT How do pressure and chemicals cause sedimentary rock to form?

Igneous Rock—Granite

Insta-Lab

Instant Weathering
Break a piece of chalk into several pieces. Place the chalk in water in a jar. Close the lid tightly, and shake the jar for about five minutes. Then pour the water and chalk through a strainer. How does this activity show the processes of weathering and erosion?

The Rock Cycle and Plate Boundaries

The surface of Earth is not a single slab of rock. Instead, the surface is a group of plates made of crust and upper mantle rock. Even though these plates are enormous and heavy, they float on the soft rock underneath. At the boundaries where land and ocean plates meet and sometimes collide, all three types of rock can form.

Sedimentary rock can form at these boundaries through the buildup of sediment. Rivers on the land carry sediment. They deposit most of it where the rivers end at the ocean's edge. Over a long time, the sediment builds up, eventually forming sedimentary rock.

Metamorphic rock forms at these plate boundaries, too. Ocean plates are made of dense igneous rock. Land plates are made mostly of less-dense rock. At the places where the plates collide, the dense igneous rock sinks, dragging down some sedimentary rock with it. All this rock can change into metamorphic rock from the pressure and temperature happening as the rock slips.

Igneous rock can form at plate boundaries when existing rocks melt and become magma. This can happen in two ways. One way is when metamorphic and sedimentary rocks from the surface are dragged down into the high temperature of Earth's interior. Another way is when plates move apart and hot rock moves upward causing melting.

 CAUSE AND EFFECT What causes metamorphic rock to form at plate boundaries?

Formation of Rocks

This diagram shows how all three types of rock can be formed at the boundaries where ocean and land plates meet.

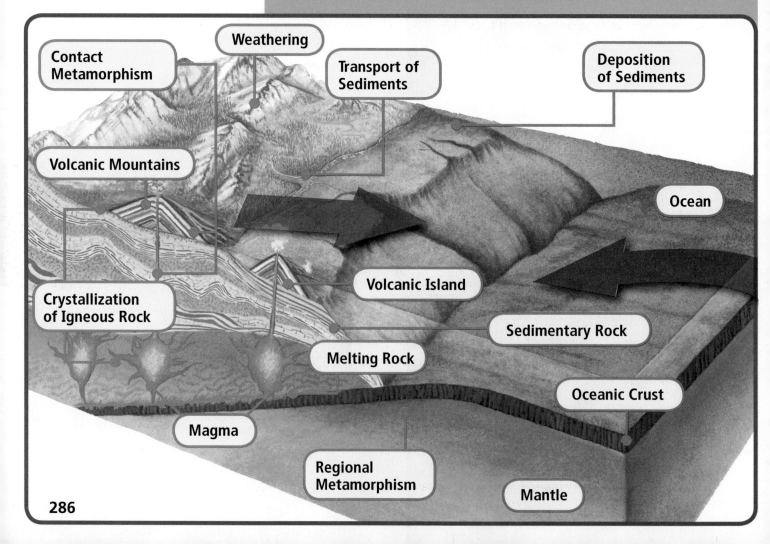

Contact Metamorphism

Weathering

Transport of Sediments

Deposition of Sediments

Volcanic Mountains

Ocean

Crystallization of Igneous Rock

Volcanic Island

Sedimentary Rock

Melting Rock

Oceanic Crust

Magma

Regional Metamorphism

Mantle

1. **CAUSE AND EFFECT** Write what causes each type of rock to form as part of the rock cycle.

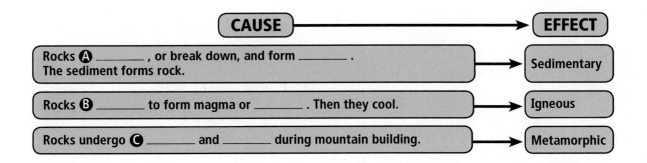

CAUSE	EFFECT
Rocks **A** _____ , or break down, and form _____ . The sediment forms rock.	Sedimentary
Rocks **B** _____ to form magma or _____ . Then they cool.	Igneous
Rocks undergo **C** _____ and _____ during mountain building.	Metamorphic

2. **SUMMARIZE** Write two sentences that tell the most important information in this lesson.

3. **DRAW CONCLUSIONS** Why is a plate boundary an active place for rock formation?

4. **VOCABULARY** Use the term *rock cycle* in a sentence about mountains.

Test Prep

5. **Critical Thinking** If you found sedimentary rock deep underground, what could you conclude, and why?

6. Which is an example of a sedimentary rock becoming a metamorphic rock?

  A. sandstone to quartzite

  B. quartzite to granite

  C. granite to quartzite

  D. granite to sandstone

Links

Writing

Expository Writing

Choose an unlabeled rock sample. Suppose you're a geologist who has just found that rock. Classify the rock, and write a **report** about it, based on what you know about rocks.

Math

Make a Bar Graph

Rock forms at different temperatures. Make a bar graph showing that shale begins to form at 100°C, slate begins to form at 150°C, schist at 250°C, gneiss at 600°C, and granite at 700°C.

Art

Mosaics

Mosaics are an ancient art form. Gather pebbles and other bits of rock, glass, and clay to make a mosaic. Try to determine how the rocks you use would be classified.

For more links and activities, go to **www.hspscience.com**

How Do Soils Form?

Fast Fact

Ancient Secrets In the 1400s, the Inca civilization of the Andes Mountains used terraces to grow 20 varieties of corn and more than 240 varieties of potato. The terraces prevented rain from eroding what little good soil there was in the high mountains. In the Investigate, you'll make a model to discover how to decrease soil erosion.

Stopping Erosion

Materials
- newspaper
- three 9-in. × 9-in. pans
- garden soil
- metric ruler
- watering can
- water
- measuring cup
- craft sticks
- sand
- gravel

Procedure

1. Cover your work area with newspaper. Form the soil into a mound 10 cm high in the center of one pan. Remove any loose soil from the rest of the pan.

2. Use the watering can to sprinkle 250 mL of water over the mound of soil. Wait for the water and eroded soil to collect at the bottom of the pan. Remove the mound, and place it in another pan. Pour the water/soil mixture from the first pan into the measuring cup, and let the soil settle. Record the amount of eroded soil.

3. Experiment with the materials you have, to keep the water from eroding the soil. Make sure the mound remains at a height of 10 cm.

4. Repeat Step 2, keeping the watering can at the same height and pouring at the same rate. Record the amount of eroded soil. Is it more than or less than the amount in the first trial?

5. Repeat the experiment one more time. Use different materials and a different method to reduce the erosion. Pour the water/soil mixture into the measuring cup, and record the results.

Step 2

Step 3

Draw Conclusions

1. Compare the effectiveness of the second and third trials in reducing erosion. Which materials and methods seemed to work better?

2. **Inquiry Skill** In an experiment, you must control variables. What variables did you control in these experiments? What did you change?

Investigate Further

Design an experiment in which methods for controlling soil erosion are tested in a garden. Does working outside change the effectiveness of the models? Why or why not?

Reading in Science

VOCABULARY
bedrock p. 291
topsoil p. 291

SCIENCE CONCEPTS
▶ what the composition of soil is and how soil forms
▶ what methods can be used for conserving soil

 READING FOCUS SKILL
CAUSE AND EFFECT Watch for words such as *because* and *then*.

How Soil Forms

You probably give little thought to the soil you see every day. But soil is important in supporting the lives of everyone and nearly everything on Earth. Farmers need soil to grow the food that humans and other animals depend on.

Weathering is the process by which rocks are broken down into smaller and smaller pieces.

Weathering is the most important factor in the process of soil formation. There are two types of weathering—physical weathering and chemical weathering.

Physical weathering is caused by wind, water, plants, and ice. *Chemical weathering* occurs when chemicals break up rocks—often in water—by dissolving parts of them, such as the cement that holds pieces together.

Composition of Soil

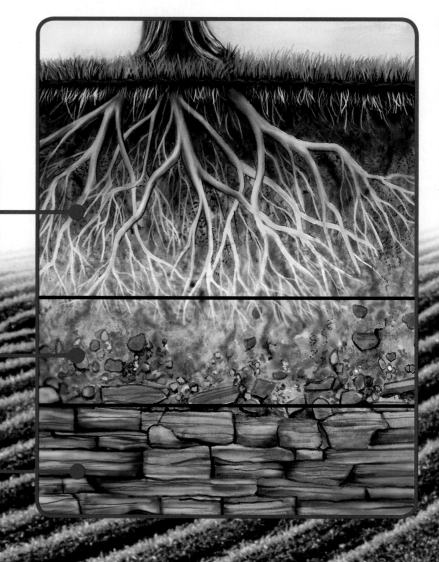

The top layer of soil, topsoil, is composed of minerals, living organisms, and decaying plant and animal matter.

The second layer is the subsoil. It is made up of small rocks and little if any organic matter.

The last layer is bedrock, from which the soil above it is formed.

If you could look underneath the soil, what you would see would tell a lot about the history of the area's soil. The very bottom layer of soil is called **bedrock**, which is largely solid rock. The minerals in bedrock help determine the type of soil that forms, since much of the soil in the upper layers is made from bedrock. The next layer up is subsoil. This is made mostly of small rocks. Temperature changes help break up these rocks. Tree roots that force their way through the rocks also help break them up. The upper part of the subsoil is clay-rich. It also contains minerals that were dissolved and filtered down from the top of the ground.

The top layer is **topsoil**, which is made in part from broken pieces of the lower layers of rock. Topsoil is a much more crumbly and varied mixture than the lower layers.

Topsoil contains bits of rock, air, water, and humus, which is decayed plant and animal matter. This rich mixture of ingredients is good for growing plants, which need the phosphorus and nitrogen found in humus to grow well.

Soils around the world vary greatly. They can vary in color, in the minerals they contain, and in texture. The color of a soil is often a clue to the kinds of minerals and the amount of humus it contains. Red soils may contain a lot of iron. Dark soil is often rich in humus. Gray soil may be a sign of poor soil that has little iron or oxygen.

Soils can be classified by the size of their particles. Soils may be sandy, silty, or mostly clay. Sandy soil is coarse and has large bits of rock. It feels gritty between the fingers. Water runs quickly through sandy soil. This may cause problems for farmers, both because plants need water and because the water can carry away valuable minerals and nutrients. Farmers who work with sandy soil may add material such as humus to help hold the water.

Silty soil is made of smaller bits of rock. When rubbed between the fingers, silty soil feels like flour. Clay soils have the smallest particles. You can't see these particles with the unaided eye. Clay soils are often sticky and muddy when they're wet. Too much water is bad for plant growth. Farmers may add humus to break up the soil, or they may use machines to add air and volume to the soil.

 CAUSE AND EFFECT How does weathering help form soil?

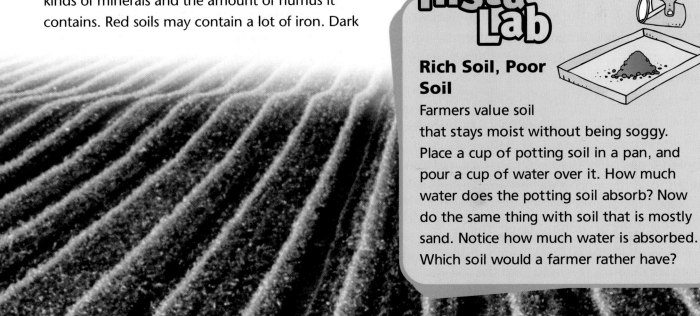

Insta-Lab

Rich Soil, Poor Soil

Farmers value soil that stays moist without being soggy. Place a cup of potting soil in a pan, and pour a cup of water over it. How much water does the potting soil absorb? Now do the same thing with soil that is mostly sand. Notice how much water is absorbed. Which soil would a farmer rather have?

During the dust storms of the 1930s, the sky from Oklahoma to New York sometimes turned almost black with blowing soil.

◀ Today, methods such as contour plowing help protect soil from erosion.

Conserving Soil

On April 14, 1935, the daytime sky over the central United States was dark. The cause of the darkness was soil—tons of it—blowing away from farms. That day's dust storm was the worst of many in the 1930s. Because there were so many severe dust storms in that area during the 1930s, the area came to be known as the Dust Bowl. When the dust storms finally stopped, many farmers could no longer farm—no soil was left.

How did the Dust Bowl form? For many years before, farmers had plowed deep-rooted grasses into the soil and had planted shallow-rooted crops such as wheat. Livestock had also overgrazed the land. Ranchers and farmers at that time knew little about soil conservation. So when years of drought came, there were not enough plants to hold the soil in place. Then windstorms followed, and the soil was blown away.

Today, farmers know much more about saving, or conserving, soil. They plant in strips so that crops with shallow roots are next to crops with deep roots—roots that can hold down the soil. They use methods such as contour plowing and terracing to stop water from running straight down a hill and carrying away precious soil. Contour plowing is plowing across slopes to prevent water and soil from flowing downhill. Farmers also plant windbreaks, lines of trees that stop the wind from blowing away the soil.

Soil forms over many years. Forces of nature such as wind and ice constantly break up rock from which soil forms. Living things such as bacteria further break up the rock, and then they die, forming humus. However, nature takes a long time to produce just a few inches of topsoil. It takes many thousands of years for a few inches of topsoil to be formed, so it makes sense that we should use and conserve our soil carefully. Modern farming practices that protect the soil will ensure that there is soil for future generations.

 CAUSE AND EFFECT What caused the severe dust storms of the 1930s to blow away all the topsoil?

1. CAUSE AND EFFECT Describe three things that cause soil to form and be enriched.

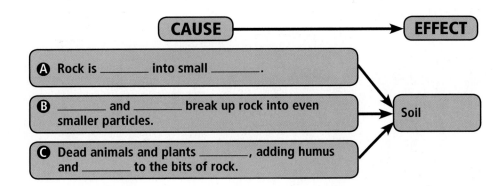

CAUSE ⟶ EFFECT

A Rock is _____ into small _____.

B _____ and _____ break up rock into even smaller particles.

C Dead animals and plants _____, adding humus and _____ to the bits of rock.

Soil

2. SUMMARIZE Write two sentences that tell how soil forms and how to conserve it.

3. DRAW CONCLUSIONS How is soil formation an extension of the rock cycle?

4. VOCABULARY. Define the words *topsoil* and *bedrock*. Describe these soil layers by where they are located and the materials they contain.

Test Prep

5. Critical Thinking If you saw a dark brown field next to a gray field, what could you conclude about the soil in the fields and how well crops would grow there?

6. Which kind of soil can hold more water than the others?

A. clay   **C.** sandy

B. humus   **D.** silt

Links

Writing

Narrative Writing

Imagine that you are a child who lived through the dust storm of April 14, 1935. Write a **story** about what happens to your family and your farm on and after that day.

Math

Estimation

Find examples of clay, silt, and sandy soil. Put the same amount of each soil into a strainer. Pour a cup of water through each sample, and make an estimate of the percent of the water that each type of soil absorbs.

Literature

Living in the Dust Bowl

Read a book about the Dust Bowl. Keep track of the pictures and descriptions that have the most impact on you. Share your findings with one other person.

 For more links and activities, go to www.hspscience.com

Volcano Alert!

Wafula, a volcano expert, lives in the Democratic Republic of the Congo. On January 8, 2002, Wafula sent an urgent message to local officials warning them of a buildup of lava inside Mount Nyiragongo (nee-rah-GONG-goh), an active volcano 12 miles north of the city of Goma. "We can expect an eruption in the very near future," Wafula wrote. "This mountain is dangerous." He also alerted volcano experts in other countries.

However, the local authorities ignored Wafula's warning. Much to everyone's surprise the 11,400-foot-tall mountain erupted nine days later.

Volcano Didn't Wait

The volcano destroyed about one-third of Goma, leaving thousands of people homeless. If Wafula's warnings had been listened to, the people in and around Goma might have had time to move their families and belongings to safety in an orderly way. Instead, people ran for their lives as burning lava blanketed entire neighborhoods. Many children became separated from their families.

Volcanologists, people who study volcanoes, want to avoid a repeat of such scenes by forecasting eruptions with greater accuracy.

"We know when a volcano is restless—it almost always gives warning," said Chris Newhall, a University of Washington geologist.

Newhall has studied volcanoes around the world for more than 30 years. "Volcanoes erupt when molten rock and gases dissolved in the molten rock break onto the surface of the Earth," Newhall said. As this hot material, called magma, moves up through the Earth's crust, it causes mild earthquakes. Scientists measure those tremors with an instrument called a seismograph.

Advance Warning

Newhall and other volcanologists take additional measurements and observe active volcanoes over time. For example, the scientists note any swelling on the surface caused by the magma underneath. "Think of a balloon inflating and its surface starting to bulge," Newhall said.

If sulfur gases leak out of the ground at a fast rate, the volcanologists usually warn officials of a possible eruption. "Our track record is getting better. Very few eruptions occur now when we didn't know they were coming," Newhall said.

Life Savers

Volcanologists saved an estimated 5000 lives by accurately predicting the 1991 eruption of Mount Pinatubo in the Philippines days in advance.

Think About It

1. Why might volcanoes be a good source of information about Earth's interior for geologists?
2. What might small earthquakes near a volcano signify?

Find out more! Log on to
www.hspscience.com

Studying Rocks in the Field

Miguel Velez says there are few things better than spending the day looking for rocks for his collection. Pieces of quartz, granite, and shale are all part of his collection.

Recently, Miguel and his family traveled to a site they heard had many unique rocks. Miguel and his family climbed rocks and walked along a stream where they found many interesting smaller rocks. They were able to see how the larger rocks had broken down.

Miguel noticed the soil was a different color than other parts of the area. He carefully studied the erosion that had taken place along the stream and found one of the most unusual rocks he had ever found. Miguel said this was the best vacation ever!

You Can Do It!

Materials
- sand
- sandstone rock
- white glue
- 2 paper cups
- craft stick
- scoop

Quick and Easy Project

Sandstone Rock

Procedure

1. Half-fill one paper cup with sand. Add some white glue.
2. Use the craft stick to mix the sand and glue. Add enough glue to make the mixture sticky.
3. Use the second cup to press down on the mixture. Remove the second cup, and let the mixture dry overnight.
4. Remove the first paper cup from around the mixture. Compare your "sandstone" with the sandstone rock.

Draw Conclusions

Which of the three rock types did you model? How is your "rock" similar to and different from the sandstone rock? How does the way you made it model one way this type of rock is formed in nature?

Design Your Own Investigation

What's Your Soil Like?

Examine a sample of soil from a location near your home. Think about what you have learned about soil, how it's made, what's in it, and what its properties are. Design some tests to help you learn more about the soil in your sample. Then test the soil and report the results.

Review and Test Preparation

Vocabulary Review

Use the terms below to complete the sentences. The page numbers tell you where to look in the chapter if you need help.

mineral p. 266

igneous rock p. 274

magma p. 274

lava p. 275

sedimentary rock p. 276

metamorphic rock p. 278

rock cycle p. 285

topsoil p. 291

1. A natural, solid substance that has a definite chemical composition and physical structure is a _____ .

2. Melted rock that reaches Earth's surface is _____ .

3. A soil layer made of small bits of rock, humus, air, and water is _____ .

4. Rock formed when magma or lava cools is _____ .

5. The processes by which rocks are formed from other rocks make up the _____ .

6. Rock formed by layers of material stuck together is _____ .

7. Melted rock within Earth is _____ .

8. Rock formed by high temperature, pressure, or very hot water is _____ .

Check Understanding

Write the letter of the best choice.

9. **CAUSE AND EFFECT** Which effect do high temperature and pressure have on igneous rock?

   A. They turn igneous rock into soil.

   B. They have no effect.

   C. They change igneous rock to sedimentary rock.

   D. They change igneous rock to metamorphic rock.

10. **COMPARE AND CONTRAST** A mineral can scratch a steel knife. If a second mineral can scratch the first, how do the two minerals compare?

    F. The first mineral is harder than the second.

    G. The second mineral is harder than the first.

    H. Both minerals have the same hardness.

    J. Both minerals are softer than steel.

11. Which characteristic of soil might be most important to farmers?

    A. the kind of rock from which it formed

    B. the types of leaves that have decayed in it

    C. the amount of water it can retain

    D. the temperature at which it will become rock

12. Which best explains the glassy look of obsidian?

    F. It cooled very slowly.

    G. Its crystals are large.

    H. It cooled very quickly.

    J. It formed as one large crystal.

13. Which is a way that layers of sedimentary rocks bind together?

A. by melting

B. by pressure

C. by weathering

D. by decay of organic materials

14. Which is a cause of regional metamorphism?

F. a volcano

G. a field of lava

H. mountain building

J. a cave of crystals

15. Which letter in this diagram shows where igneous rocks are likely to form?

A. A	**C.** C
B. B	**D.** D

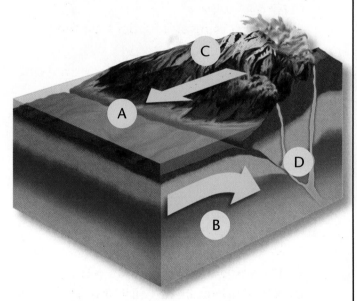

16. Which of the following is **NOT** true of the rock cycle?

F. Soil never becomes rock.

G. Igneous rock can become sedimentary rock.

H. Any rock can become any other kind of rock.

J. Metamorphic rock forms by exposure to heat and pressure.

Inquiry Skills

17. How does an intrusive rock **compare** with an extrusive rock?

18. Describe an **experiment** in which you measure how much water two different types of soil absorb.

Critical Thinking

19. You want to identify a mineral you have found. Write four tests you could use to identify the mineral, and tell how you could do each test.

20. **Part A** Make a drawing to show how the rock cycle works. Label the types of rock and the steps that show the stages of the cycle.

Part B For each stage of the rock cycle, write the name of a rock that belongs in that stage. Then, for each rock, explain how it can become another type of rock.

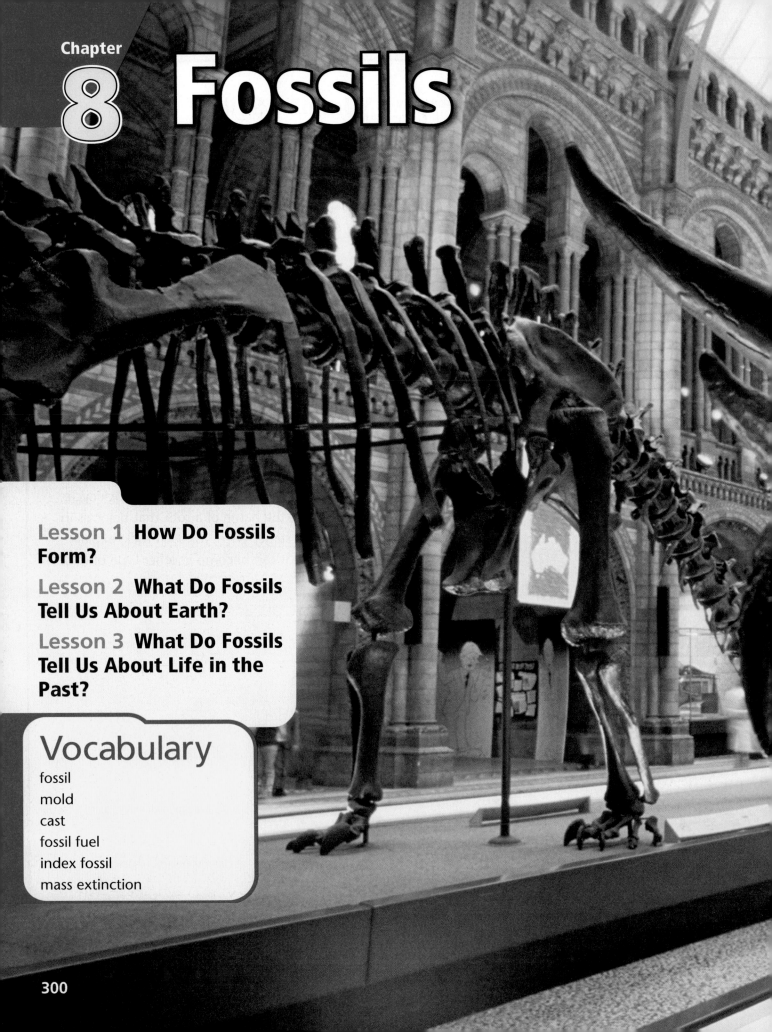

Lesson 1 How Do Fossils Form?

Lesson 2 What Do Fossils Tell Us About Earth?

Lesson 3 What Do Fossils Tell Us About Life in the Past?

Vocabulary

fossil
mold
cast
fossil fuel
index fossil
mass extinction

What do YOU wonder?

Millions of years ago, dinosaurs lived on Earth. No one has ever seen a living dinosaur, but scientists have a good idea about what they were like because of fossils. How might the fossils you see here give scientists insight into the lives of dinosaurs?

How Do Fossils Form?

Fast Fact

Protection by Coiling This coiled fossil was the shell of a kind of squid-like animal. The coils may have made it difficult for predators to remove the animal to eat it. In the Investigate, you will model one way a fossil formed.

Make a Fossil

Materials • modeling clay • paper plate • various objects, such as a shell, a leaf, and a plastic toy animal

Procedure

1. Press a thick layer of modeling clay onto the paper plate. Make the surface of the clay flat and smooth.

2. Press one of the objects into the clay, and then carefully remove it. Repeat with other objects. You have just formed a model of the kind of fossil that is an impression of an organism.

3. Observe and compare your impressions. Decide what type of object makes the best impression.

4. Trade plates with another student. Try to identify the object that made each of the impressions on the other student's plate.

Draw Conclusions

1. What type of object makes the best impression?

2. You modeled the way one kind of fossil forms in nature. Infer the conditions that would need to exist for a real fossil to form in this way.

3. **Inquiry Skill** Scientists use fossils to draw conclusions about organisms that lived in the past. What could be inferred from a fossil of an organism's footprints?

Step 1

Step 2

Investigate Further

Another kind of fossil is formed when sediment fills in an impression and then hardens to become rock. Experiment with different ways to make models of these filled-in fossils.

Reading in Science

VOCABULARY
fossil p. 304
mold p. 305
cast p. 305
fossil fuel p. 308

SCIENCE CONCEPTS
▶ what fossils are and how they form
▶ how fossil fuels form and where they are found

 READING FOCUS SKILL
SEQUENCE Look for the order of the steps by which fossils and fossil fuels form.

How Fossils Form

Suppose you are playing with a friend on the beach near a lake. Every time you take a step, you leave a footprint. What will happen to the footprints? The wind and the waves will probably wash them away. Sometimes, however, footprints get filled in by sediments and are preserved as fossils.

A **fossil** is any naturally preserved evidence of life. Most people think of shells and bones when they think of fossils. In fact, a fossil can be a footprint, an impression of a leaf, an animal's burrow, or even an organism's waste!

Fossils form in different ways. Sometimes an organism's whole body becomes fossilized. This may happen if the body dries out, gets trapped in a bog, or is frozen. For example, the remains of woolly mammoths have been found in glaciers. Mammoths were large, elephantlike animals that became extinct around 10,000 years ago.

Small animals, such as insects, may become trapped in a flow of tree sap. Then the sap hardens, and the insect is preserved within it.

Most of the time, a whole organism is not preserved. For example, when a small animal

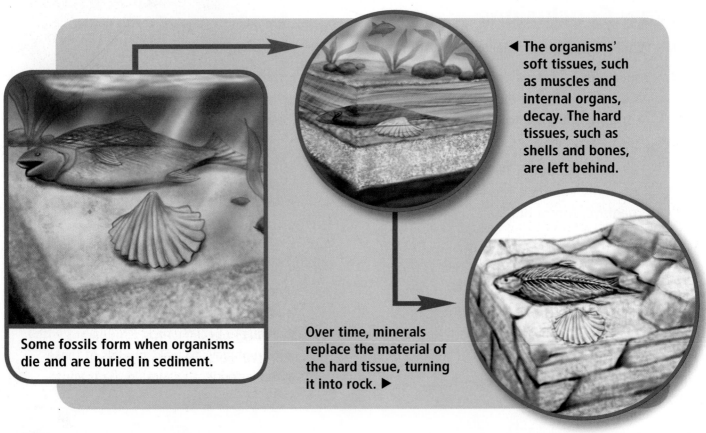

Some fossils form when organisms die and are buried in sediment.

◀ The organisms' soft tissues, such as muscles and internal organs, decay. The hard tissues, such as shells and bones, are left behind.

Over time, minerals replace the material of the hard tissue, turning it into rock. ▶

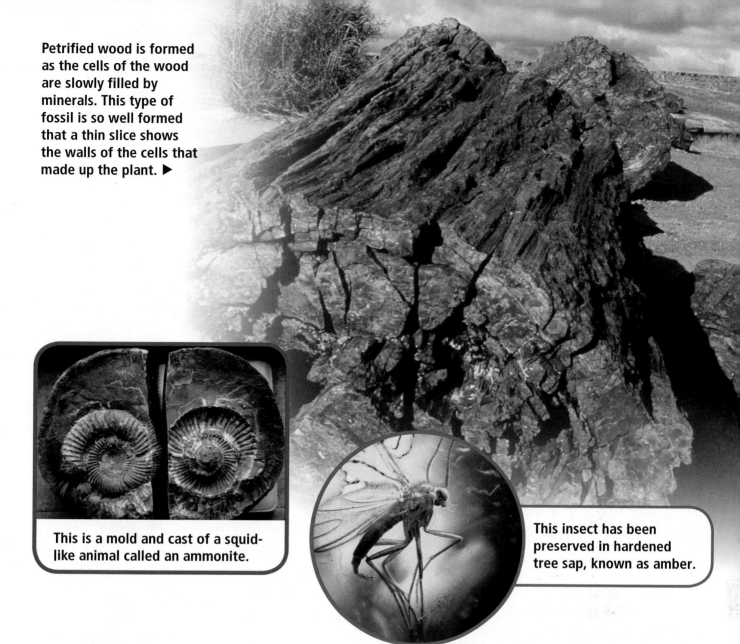

Petrified wood is formed as the cells of the wood are slowly filled by minerals. This type of fossil is so well formed that a thin slice shows the walls of the cells that made up the plant. ▶

This is a mold and cast of a squid-like animal called an ammonite.

This insect has been preserved in hardened tree sap, known as amber.

dies, decomposers quickly consume the soft tissue. If the hard skeleton is buried in sediment, it may slowly be changed into rock.

Some fossils are not parts of organisms but only impressions of the organism's body. For example, suppose a clam is buried in sediment. Over time, the sediment around the clam's body may harden, while the clam itself decays and its shell dissolves. The hardened sediment around the clam forms a **mold** of the clam's shape. If sediment fills the mold and hardens, a **cast**, or model, of the original organism forms.

 SEQUENCE What are the steps necessary for a fossil cast to form?

The shell of this ammonite became fossilized as minerals replaced the original material of the shell.

305

Types of Fossils

Think about the kinds of living things in the world today. Birds, fish, insects, garden slugs—which of these could become fossils? In fact, any organism, whether it is a bacterium, a plant, or an animal, can become a fossil. However, some organisms are much more likely than others to be fossilized. Organisms with hard tissues, such as skeletons and shells, are more likely to be fossilized than organisms with only soft tissues. Also, organisms that live in water have a better chance of being fossilized than organisms that live on land. It is less likely that an organism would be buried by sediment on land. When an organism is not buried, scavengers easily can find its body and feed on it. What is left of the body undergoes weathering.

A third factor that determines whether an organism becomes fossilized is the amount of energy in the environment. For example, organisms in a calm lake are more likely to fossilize than organisms in a fast-moving stream. Fast-moving water breaks up the remains of an organism. Also, less sediment is deposited in fast-moving water than in slow-moving water.

Hard-tissue fossils are very common, but in some conditions, soft-tissue fossils can also form. In fact, some of the oldest fossils ever found are of bacteria that lived 3.5 billion years ago. Fossils of larger soft-tissue organisms, such as plants, jellyfish, and worms, have been found in shale that is much younger. The soft tissues of the organisms can be preserved as a thin carbon film between the layers of the shale. Very fine details, such as the veins in a plant's leaf, can still be seen in this kind of fossil.

 SEQUENCE What is a possible sequence of events that might take place when a land organism dies?

Science Up Close

Fossils

Fossils are found all over the world. They vary by type of fossil, species preserved, and material the fossil is made of. What do all of the fossils on these pages have in common?

Fish

Fossils of bony fish skeletons began to appear very early in the history of life on Earth. There are many kinds of fish fossils. A fossil hunter can find everything from fish scales to sharks' teeth, depending on where he or she is searching.

Coral

Corals are a simple type of animal. Because they live in fairly calm water, their strong external skeletons are easily fossilized. Coral fossils are found throughout the midwestern states, where a shallow sea once covered the land.

For more links and activities, go to **www.hspscience.com**

Snail

This is a fossil of a snail that was very common along the coast of Maryland around 15 million years ago. It had a very thick shell that could stand up to heavy waves and still be fossilized. It is the state fossil of Maryland.

Brachiopods

Brachiopods (BRAK•ee•oh•pahdz) look much like clams, but these two animals are not related. Fossils of brachiopods are very common throughout the midwestern states. The organisms shown in this photograph were about the size of a nickel. These fossils are molds of the inside of the brachiopod shell.

Trilobite

Trilobites (TRY•luh•bytz) were animals that lived in the oceans long ago. Horseshoe crabs living today are related to the ancient trilobites.

Diatoms

Diatoms (DY•uh•tahmz) are tiny protists that still live in ocean water today. Their thin, glasslike shells are often preserved as fossils. Scientists use these fossils to help them identify and match rock layers.

Crinoid

Crinoids (KRY•noydz) are relatives of starfish. They have long stalks made up of hard pieces that look much like the bones of a human spine. At one time, these animals were so common that their remains make up a large percentage of some kinds of rock. Crinoids are still found in oceans around the world today.

How Fossil Fuels Form

Have you ever been in a race? You run as fast as you can. Your muscles begin to burn, but somehow you still find the energy to keep going. Where does this energy come from? Like all living things, you have energy stored in your cells. That energy came from the sun. It was captured by plants and converted to food. When you ate plants, or animals that had eaten plants, you got energy that originally came from the sun.

When an organism dies, much of its stored energy remains in the cells of its body. In fact, most of the energy people use to run machines and to produce electricity comes from the energy stored by organisms that lived millions of years ago. After the organisms died, they were covered by sediment. Over millions of years, the temperature and pressure caused by the layers above them changed the dead organisms into fossil fuels. **Fossil fuels** are energy-rich resources that form from the buried remains of once-living organisms. The three kinds of fossil fuels are coal, natural gas, and petroleum.

Petroleum and natural gas formed

How Petroleum Forms

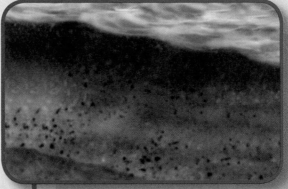

Protists that lived in the ocean captured the energy of the sun and converted it to stored chemical energy. When they died, they fell to the ocean floor and were buried by sediment.

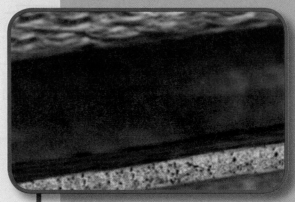

As more sediment covered the buried protists, temperature and pressure built up. Over time, their remains were changed into petroleum and natural gas.

The petroleum and natural gas collected in pockets between layers of rock. People drill oil wells to recover these resources from under the ground.

◄ This offshore oil rig pumps to the surface the petroleum that lies beneath the ocean floor.

How Coal Forms

Swamp plants died and sank to the bottom of the swamp, where they decayed.

The decayed matter was buried under sediment. As the sediment built up, pressure on the decayed plant matter increased.

Over time, most of the moisture and oxygen were pressed out, leaving a high carbon concentration known as coal.

Bacteria, plants, and fungi all played an important role in the formation of coal.

mainly from the remains of organisms that once lived in the sea. Study the diagrams on page 308 to see how these energy resources formed.

Coal formed not from ocean organisms but from decayed swamp plants. When a swamp plant died, it sank to the bottom of the swamp. There, bacteria and fungi decomposed the plant. More layers of dead plants piled on top of the decayed plant material. Over time, their weight and the weight of layers of sediment and rock pressed the layers into coal.

 SEQUENCE Explain the sequence of steps by which coal formed.

Insta-Lab

Take a Closer Look
Use a hand lens to examine a piece of coal. What features do you see? Break the coal open, and examine the inside. Record your observations. If possible, use a microscope to examine a small section of the coal. What evidence do you see that it was formed from the remains of dead plants?

Where Fossil Fuels Are Found

Once you know how fossil fuels form, you can figure out where they can be found. Since petroleum and natural gas form mainly from protists that lived in the oceans, these resources are found where oceans existed millions of years ago. For example, the oil-rich areas of Texas were once a sea floor. The fossil fuels beneath today's oceans are brought to the surface by deep-sea oil rigs, such as those operating in the Gulf of Mexico and the North Sea.

On land, the country of Saudi Arabia has the largest known reserves of petroleum. Russia has the largest known reserves of natural gas.

Coal deposits are found under the sites of ancient swamps. The United States has the largest coal deposits in the world. Coal was once the most widely used fossil fuel. However, the burning of coal produces more air pollution than the burning of other fossil fuels. Much less coal is burned today. Natural gas, which burns more cleanly, is often used in place of coal.

 SEQUENCE Use the map to rank the countries that have petroleum from largest to smallest reserves.

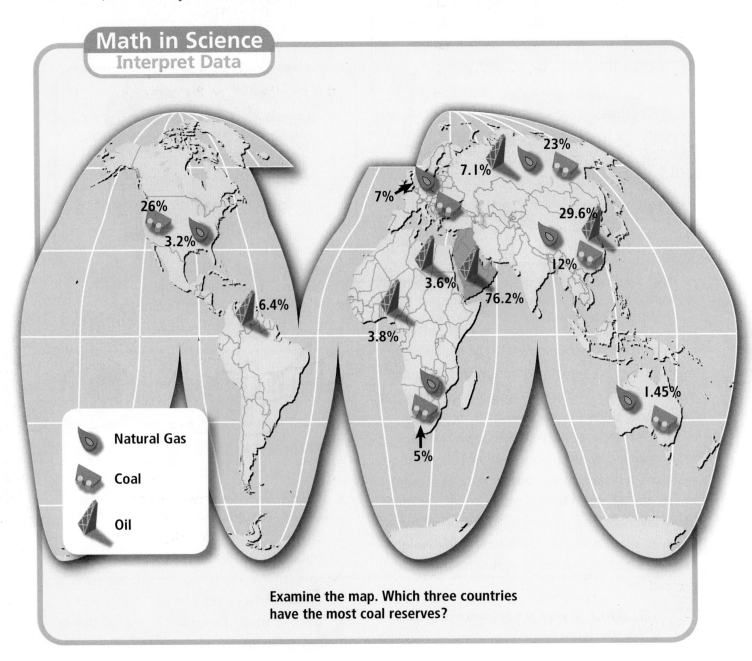

Examine the map. Which three countries have the most coal reserves?

1. SEQUENCE Draw and complete this graphic organizer on the formation of fossil fuels.

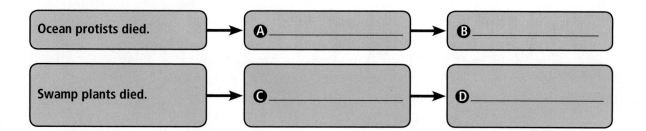

| Ocean protists died. | → | **A** _____ | → | **B** _____ |

| Swamp plants died. | → | **C** _____ | → | **D** _____ |

2. SUMMARIZE Write a short paragraph relating the sequence of fossil formation to the sequence of fossil fuel formation.

3. DRAW CONCLUSIONS Fossil fuels are considered nonrenewable resources. Explain the reason for this thinking.

4. VOCABULARY How would a cast fossil and a mold fossil of a clam be different from the actual organism?

Test Prep

5. Critical Thinking The state of Pennsylvania is rich in coal deposits. What can you conclude about the prehistory of the area that is now Pennsylvania?

6. Which of the following is a fossil fuel that is more plentiful in the United States than anywhere else?

   A. coal   **C.** natural gas

   B. crude oil   **D.** petroleum

Links

Writing

Expository Writing
Find out about a fossil that is common in your state. Write a **report** about the fossil, including information about where it is or was found and what the organism was like when it was alive.

Math

Display Data
Do research to find out which countries consume the most fossil fuels per person. Use the information to make a graph. Compare your graph with the map on page 310, which shows fossil fuel reserves.

Art

Fossil Model
Choose an organism that lives today. Make a model fossil of a part of that organism or of other evidence of the organism (such as a footprint). Use modeling clay or other art materials to make the model.

For more links and activities, go to www.hspscience.com

What Do Fossils Tell Us About Earth?

Fast Fact

Disappearing Act Diatoms are protists that make their own food. Their shells are very delicate and made of quartz. Scientists can use the abundance of certain kinds of diatoms to determine the temperatures of ancient oceans. In the Investigate, you'll see another way fossils can be used to tell about rock layers.

Using Fossils to Date Rocks

Materials • **8 note cards** • **marker**

Procedure

1. Write one of these letter sets on each note card.
   YD   HOR   CAY   RN
   GC   NLG   LG   EH

2. Each card represents a layer of rock. Each letter on it represents a type of fossil that is found in that layer. You will use the ages of the "fossils" to put the "rock layers" in the correct order. Spread the cards out on the table in front of you.

3. The oldest fossils are *E* and *H.* Put the card representing the rock layer with the oldest fossils at the bottom.

4. Look for another card that has one of these oldest fossils. Put this card on top of the first card. It represents the second-oldest rock layer.

5. Order the rest of the cards in the same way until you have completed a stack of cards that represents a sequence of rock layers.

Draw Conclusions

1. Use your card stack to write down the sequence of letters from the youngest layer to the oldest layer. Use each letter only once.

2. Is fossil *A* younger or older than fossil *D*?

3. **Inquiry Skill** Scientists use time/space relationships to compare rock layers around the world. Hypothesize the age of fossil *G* if you know that fossil *C* is 25 to 50 million years old and fossil *R* is 75 to 110 million years old.

Step 1

Step 4

Investigate Further

Use clay and small objects to formulate a model of rock layers that contain different fossils. Cut the model in half vertically, and arrange the halves to model a fault. How could scientists examining such a cross-section determine that a fault has formed?

Reading in Science

VOCABULARY
index fossil p. 315

SCIENCE CONCEPTS
▶ how fossils are used to date a rock layer
▶ what fossils can tell us about Earth's history

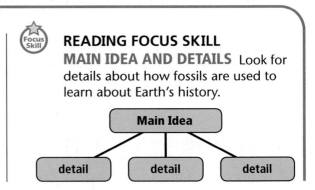

READING FOCUS SKILL
MAIN IDEA AND DETAILS Look for details about how fossils are used to learn about Earth's history.

Fossils and Earth's History

Earth is about 4.6 billion years old. Rocks are constantly being formed and destroyed, so no rocks on Earth's surface are as old as Earth itself. Some, however, come very close. The oldest rock found so far is about 3.8 billion years old! Do you wonder how scientists can know a rock's age? They can tell how old some rocks are by measuring the amounts of radioactive atoms in them.

Sedimentary rocks often form layers. In a group of undisturbed rock layers, the oldest layer will be on the bottom because it was deposited first, and the youngest layer will be on the top. Scientists use this fact to help them determine the relative age of each layer. Because sedimentary rocks form from older rocks, it is difficult to date them by using the radioactive atom method. Instead, scientists often use the fossils found in these rocks as an indication of their age.

Earth's History

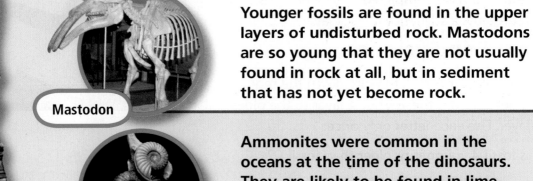

Mastodon

Younger fossils are found in the upper layers of undisturbed rock. Mastodons are so young that they are not usually found in rock at all, but in sediment that has not yet become rock.

Ammonite

Ammonites were common in the oceans at the time of the dinosaurs. They are likely to be found in limestone and chalk. In rock layers that represented the whole history of life on Earth, ammonites would be close to the middle.

Trilobite

Trilobites lived before the first dinosaurs walked the Earth. In a stack of rocks representing all life on Earth, they would be found near the bottom.

This fossilized fish was found in the Green River Formation. Note that the fish is swallowing a juvenile of the same species.

These fossils were found at the Ulrich Fossil Quarry in the Green River Formation of Wyoming.

Index fossils are fossils of organisms that lived during a relatively short time span. Fossils that are common and are found in many places on Earth make the best index fossils. A fossil that is rare or is found in only one place is not useful as an index. Knowing when an index fossil organism lived tells scientists the age of the rock in which it is found. For one part of Earth's history, trilobites are important index fossils. The many types of trilobites are easy for an expert to identify.

Fossils tell more about Earth's history than the age of certain rock layers. They also provide clues about how Earth's surface has changed over time. For example, fossils of sea animals have been found on mountaintops. This shows that the land there was once at or below sea level. Fossils of temperate plants and animals have been found in Antarctica. This shows that Antarctica was once much warmer than it is today.

 MAIN IDEA AND DETAILS What can fossils reveal about Earth's history?

Insta-Lab

Disturbing Events
Using colored modeling clay, model layers of sedimentary rock. Use various small objects, such as paper clips, buttons, and glitter to add "fossils" to at least one of the layers. Deform the layers to model a mountain range. Then use a plastic knife to carefully cut through the layers vertically to show a cross section of the mountains. Where did the fossils end up? How could index fossils help scientists date disturbed rock layers, such as those found in mountains?

Continental Movement

The same fossils found on different continents provide evidence that the continents were once joined in one giant landmass.

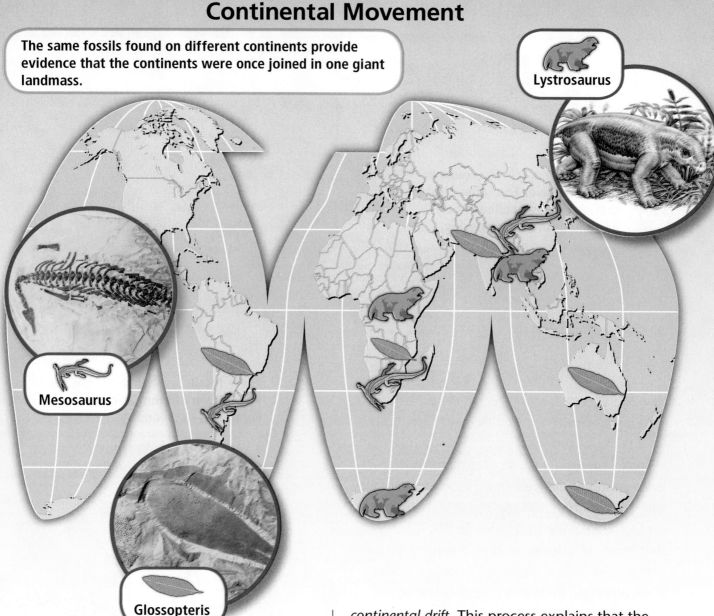

Lystrosaurus

Mesosaurus

Glossopteris

Fossils and Continental Drift

Fossils of *Glossopteris* plants and *Lystrosaurus* reptiles have been found in Antarctica. Neither of these organisms could have lived in the cold climate that Antarctica has today. Does this mean that Earth's South Pole was once a much warmer place?

On the map, you can see that places on Earth that are very far apart have fossils of these same two organisms. Since these organisms could not have crossed large bodies of water, how could they be found in Africa and India?

This mystery is explained by the process of *continental drift.* This process explains that the continents are slowly moving. The South Pole's climate has always been too cold and too dark in winter for *Glossopteris* and *Lystrosaurus* to live there. What has changed is the position of Antarctica. More than 200 million years ago, it was not at the South Pole. It was closer to the equator and was connected with the pieces of land that are now Africa, India, and Australia. Other fossil evidence shows that South America and Africa were also joined. This is revealed by the presence on each continent of fossils of *Glossopteris* plants and *Mesosaurus,* a reptile.

 MAIN IDEA AND DETAILS How does fossil evidence show that Antarctica was once farther north?

1. **MAIN IDEA AND DETAILS** Draw and complete this graphic organizer.

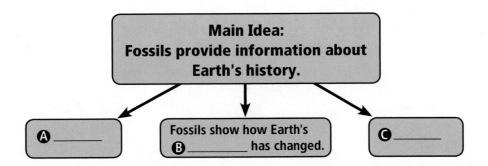

Main Idea:
Fossils provide information about Earth's history.

A _____

Fossils show how Earth's
B _____ has changed.

C _____

2. **SUMMARIZE** Use the graphic organizer to write a lesson summary.

3. **DRAW CONCLUSIONS** In what situations would rock layers not be found in their original order?

4. **VOCABULARY** In a set of rock layers, you see that every layer has the same type of fossilized snail. Would the snail fossil be a good index fossil? Explain.

Test Prep

5. **Critical Thinking** Suppose that on a hike through the mountains, you find a rock wall with a layer containing fossilized fish bones. What can you conclude?

6. What does fossil evidence indicate?
   A. Africa was once at the South Pole.
   B. Antarctica has moved.
   C. Landforms do not change.
   D. Earth does not change over time.

Links

Writing

Persuasive Writing

Suppose that your local museum is about to open an exhibit of fossils from around the world. Write a radio **advertisement** encouraging people to visit the museum's exhibit.

Math

Find Lines of Symmetry

Fossils of shells are often identified based on whether they are symmetrical or asymmetrical. Find pictures of symmetrical fossilized shells. Make copies of the pictures, and draw lines of symmetry on them.

Physical Education

Fossil Walk

Do research to find parks in your area where fossils may be seen. Go on a hike there with an adult family member. Sketch the fossils you find, and try to identify them.

 For more links and activities, go to www.hspscience.com

What Do Fossils Tell Us About Life in the Past?

Fast Fact

Warriors of the Water *Dunkleosteus* (duhng•kuhl•AHS•tee•uhs), a powerful predator fish, ruled the ancient seas. Its body was about 7 m (24 ft) long and was armored with bone. Its razor-sharp teeth and strong jaws made a quick meal out of whatever crossed its path. In the Investigate, you'll study fossils of its distant cousin, the shark.

Fossil and Modern Organisms

Materials
- shell
- cast of a fossil shell
- hand lens
- shark tooth
- fossilized shark tooth
- fern leaf
- cast of a fossil leaf

Procedure

1. Copy the table. Add names of specimens as you observe them.

2. Your teacher will provide you with specimens of modern and fossilized parts of organisms. Classify the specimens into groups according to their similarities. Each group should contain at least one modern specimen and one fossil.

3. Use the hand lens to observe each specimen closely. Compare the modern specimens with the fossil specimens. Look at different features such as shape, size, and texture.

4. Record the observations you made when comparing the specimens.

Specimens	Alike	Different
Fern leaves		
Shark tooth		

Draw Conclusions

1. How are the fossil specimens similar to the modern ones?

2. How are the fossil specimens different from the modern ones?

3. **Inquiry Skill** Scientists compare fossils they find with modern organisms in order to infer the behavior and appearance of organisms that are now extinct. Compare the fossilized shark tooth and the modern shark tooth. What can you infer about how sharks eat? What can you infer about how sharks have changed over time?

Step 3

Investigate Further

Choose a type of organism to research. Predict what you will learn about how it has changed over time. Then examine fossils of the organism to check your predictions.

Reading in Science

VOCABULARY
mass extinction p. 323

SCIENCE CONCEPTS
▶ how fossils can be used to learn about past environments
▶ how fossils can be used to learn about the history of life on Earth

READING FOCUS SKILL
MAIN IDEA AND DETAILS Look for details about how fossils tell us what life on Earth was like in the past.

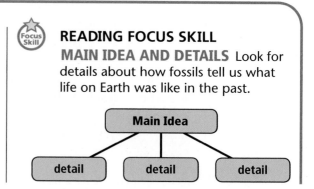

Ecosystems of the Past

Look around you. Even in the classroom, you are living in an ecosystem. Like the ecosystems of the past, it will change over time. What do you think it might look like in 100 years? In 1000 years? In 1,000,000 years?

The ecosystem in your area has undergone major changes throughout Earth's history. You have already learned how ecosystems in Antarctica changed because of continental drift.

Ecosystems can change for other reasons as well. For example, changes in climate brought about by the Ice Ages caused ecosystems around the world to change.

How can you find out what kinds of ecosystems existed in your state in the past? You can examine fossils. Fossils are evidence of the kinds of organisms that lived in a place during a certain period of time. Consider the states of Indiana and Kentucky. Today, both have deciduous forests and cold winters. Long ago, the environment in this part of the country was very different. If you went back about 390 million years, you would find not a forest, but a warm, tropical sea. Proof of this can be seen

Coral from Falls of the Ohio State Park

When the fossilized coral reef at Falls of the Ohio State Park was forming, the region that is now Indiana was about 2000 km (1200 mi) south of the equator!

Fossils from
231 species of
vertebrates,
234 species of
invertebrates, and
159 species of
plants have been
discovered in the
La Brea Tar Pits.

▲ Organisms of today
still get trapped
in the bubbling La
Brea Tar Pits!

at Falls of the Ohio State Park in Indiana. There, the rushing waters of the Ohio River have carried away layers of sediment, exposing more than 220 acres of fossilized coral reef.

You learned in Lesson 1 that organisms living in water have a better chance of being fossilized than organisms living on land. Because of this, scientists know more about ancient saltwater and freshwater ecosystems than about ancient land ecosystems. In certain locations, however, large numbers of organisms from a land ecosystem have been fossilized. One of these

places is the La Brea Tar Pits in Los Angeles, California. For the last 40,000 years, mammals, birds, seeds, and insects moving over the sticky tar have become trapped. The organisms that could not escape sank into the tar, where their bodies were preserved. Today, scientists remove fossils from the tar pits to study them. From this evidence they have learned that only a few thousand years ago, southern California's climate was cooler and wetter than it is today.

 MAIN IDEA AND DETAILS How can fossils give information about past ecosystems?

Fossils and Life in the Past

Among the fossils removed from the La Brea Tar Pits in California, scientists have found evidence of many kinds of organisms that are extinct. This means that there are no living specimens. Extinct animals found in the La Brea Tar Pits include saber-toothed cats, mammoths, and several bird species. These animals became extinct 10,000 to 4000 years ago. The only way for scientists to learn about these species now is through the fossil record.

By studying the fossil record, scientists have found that the kinds of organisms that have lived on Earth have changed greatly over time. For large periods of time, one type of organism would be much more common than others. For example, early in the history of life on Earth, many kinds of armored fish, lungfish, sharks, and other marine animals roamed the oceans. There was very little land life. As a

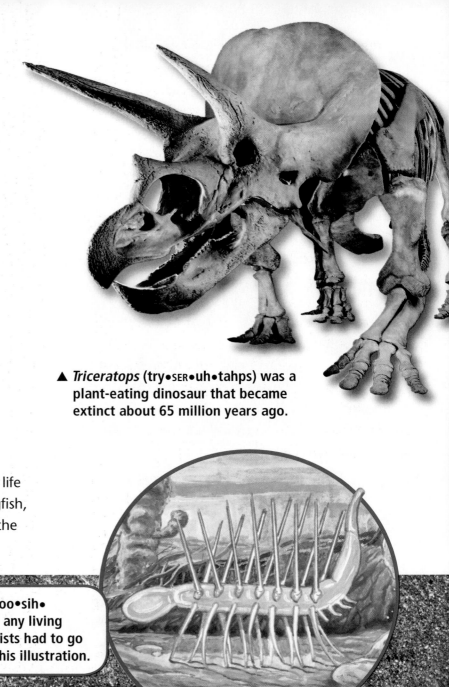

▲ *Triceratops* (try•SER•uh•tahps) was a plant-eating dinosaur that became extinct about 65 million years ago.

Hallucigenia (huh•loo•sih•JEN•ee•uh) is unlike any living organism, so scientists had to go by fossils to draw this illustration.

This *Hallucigenia* fossil was discovered in Canada.

result, this period of time is often called the Age of Fish. Later, a mass extinction of ocean animals occurred. A **mass extinction** is a period in which a large number of species become extinct. Scientists are not certain what causes this to happen, but most hypothesize that any event that greatly changes the environment can lead to a mass extinction. For example, a mass extinction could be caused by the impact of a large asteroid, a decrease in the food supply, a loss of habitat, a climate change, or all of these.

There have been many mass extinctions throughout Earth's history. From the fossil record, scientists have learned that there was a mass extinction of both ocean and land animals around 250 million years ago. After this mass extinction, dinosaurs dominated the land for a period known as the Age of Reptiles. The Age of Reptiles came to an end when the dinosaurs, in turn, suffered a mass extinction.

 MAIN IDEA AND DETAILS What kinds of events could cause a mass extinction?

Following the Footprints

Scientists learn a lot about extinct animals by analyzing their footprints. What can they learn about an animal and its activities from its footprints? Set up an area in which to study your own footprints. This could be a patch of damp sand or mud or even a just-vacuumed carpet. Walk across the area. Next to those tracks, run across the area. Have a second person do the same. How do the footprints compare?

Eurypterids (yoo•RIP•ter•idz) are often called sea scorpions. At one time, these huge, lobsterlike organisms dominated the seas.

Eurypterid fossils can be found on every continent.

Fossils and Changes Through Time

While some species that lived in the past became extinct, others survived by adapting to changes in their environments. The fossil record provides evidence about how organisms have slowly changed over time. Fossils found in younger layers of Earth are more like modern organisms than fossils found in older layers of Earth. The fossil record shows that some organisms, such as birds, have changed a great deal, while other organisms, such as sharks, have changed very little.

 MAIN IDEA AND DETAILS Why do organisms change over time?

Mammoths were elephantlike animals that lived from about 1.6 million years ago. They became extinct only 10,000 years ago.

Rudists were ancient marine animals. They looked like some ancient corals but were actually clams that built reefs. They became extinct at about the same time as the dinosaurs.

Cycads (SY•kadz) are ancient palmlike plants. They were once abundant, but today only a few kinds still exist.

Archaeopteryx (ar•kee•AHP•ter•iks) was an early type of bird that had some characteristics of dinosaurs. For example, it had teeth. Almost no modern birds have teeth.

Dimetrodon is often wrongly called a dinosaur. It actually belonged to the branch of reptiles that gave rise to mammals.

Lepidodendrons were primitive tree-size plants that grew to more than 30 m (98 ft) tall. Their modern cousins, club mosses, reach only a few cm (less than 1 ft) in height.

Trilobites were early members of the group that today includes insects, spiders, crabs, and horseshoe crabs.

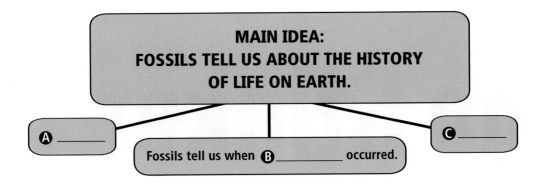

1. MAIN IDEA AND DETAILS Draw and complete this graphic organizer.

MAIN IDEA:
FOSSILS TELL US ABOUT THE HISTORY OF LIFE ON EARTH.

A _____

Fossils tell us when **B** _____ occurred.

C _____

2. SUMMARIZE Write a summary of this lesson that explains what fossils tell us about life in the past.

3. DRAW CONCLUSIONS Fossil evidence shows that sharks have changed very little over time. What might explain this?

4. VOCABULARY Define *mass extinction* and give an example.

Test Prep

5. Critical Thinking How might scientists use fossils to study ancient ecosystems?

6. The first animals lived in the ocean. Some of these animals adapted to living on land. Which class of modern animals most closely resembles the first land-dwelling organisms?

   A. amphibians   **C.** mammals

   B. birds   **D.** reptiles

Links

Writing

Expository Writing
Find out more about the *Archaeopteryx* fossil. Then write a **report** that explains why *Archaeopteryx* is considered an especially important fossil.

Math

Find Median and Mode
A scientist finds 21 snail fossils in *Layer A* of a rock formation, 108 in *Layer B*, 35 in *Layer C*, 48 in *Layer D,* and 35 in *Layer E*. What are the median and mode of the numbers of snail fossils found in all the layers?

Social Studies

Geologic Time Scale
Research the geologic time scale. Make an illustrated time line of the geologic time scale. Include information about when certain organisms lived.

 For more links and activities, go to www.hspscience.com

Dino Stinker

It has sharp teeth like a *T. rex.* It roars like a *T. rex.* It moves like a *T. rex.* But, ph-ew! What is that smell? That would be the *Tyrannosaurus rex* model unveiled at the Natural History Museum in London recently.

Museum officials wanted the 7-meter (23-foot) long, 4-meter (13-foot) high robotic *T. rex* to be as lifelike as possible. So in addition to moving limbs and textured skin, officials made sure the model even had a dinosaur smell. The scent gives viewers a whiff of what the real dinosaur might have smelled like.

Ah! The Stink of Dead Flesh

Museum officials originally wanted to duplicate the smell of a *Tyrannosaurus rex,* which is Latin for "tyrant lizard king." But scientists say that the exact odor of rotting flesh between the dinosaur's 15-centimeter (6-inch) long teeth and infected wounds on its skin would have been too foul for visitors to the museum.

Instead, the museum hired a British company called Dale Air Deodorizing, which specializes in brewing aromas for museums and zoos. The company went to work mixing up an earthy, smoky, swamp-water smell that would be disgusting but not too nasty.

Oil, Garbage, and Fish

The result of all that work is called Maastrichtian Miasma. (*Miasma* is another word for mist.) "It took us about a month to do the dinosaur smell," said the company's owner. To get just the right scent, workers used a concoction of machine oil, garbage, smoked fish, and other odd scents to give the Cretaceous creature its horrible smell.

"Whenever *T. rex* opened its huge mouth, a strong aroma of rotten flesh would certainly have filled the air," said Angela Milner, the museum's dinosaur expert. "Its breath would have smelled of the remains of decaying meat trapped between its huge teeth."

Think About It

1. Why would it be important to give museum visitors an idea of what the *T. rex* might have smelled like?
2. How might scientists determine that *T. rex* was a meateater?

Per-phew-m

Museum goers can purchase a bottle of the stinky scent in the museum shop. Hmmm! There's nothing quite like the smell of a *T. rex* in the morning.

Find out more! Log on to www.hspscience.com

A CLOSE LOOK AT THE PAST

When you think about fossils, you probably think of a huge *Tyrannosaurus rex,* towering over museum visitors. Lisa White isn't interested in those big old bones, however. She studies fossils that are so small that she needs a microscope to see them. The name for this type of scientist is *micropaleontologist.*

White studies fossilized diatoms, tiny one-celled organisms with shells. They aren't from the bottom of the Pacific Ocean if they are found in present-day soils. These ancient organisms can be found in soil and dirt near Earth's surface. By studying the fossils, White learns about the environment and the conditions in which diatoms lived.

As part of her work, White is trying to educate tomorrow's scientists. She coordinates a program in which she tells students about her work and how exciting it is to be a scientist.

Career   Museum Curator

A big part of being a museum curator involves keeping the past alive. The job of a curator is to preserve valuable items for permanent storage or display. Curators usually work for museums and are experts in preserving and keeping track of artifacts. For example, a curator might catalog and carefully file away dinosaur bones, ancient sea shells, and other fossils.

You Can Do It!

Materials
- piece of granite
- piece of limestone
- piece of sandstone
- paper towel
- dropper
- water

Quick and Easy Project

How Can Petroleum Move Through Rock?

Procedure

1. Place the pieces of granite, limestone, and sandstone on a paper towel.
2. Fill the dropper with water.
3. Drop several drops of water onto the granite. Observe what happens. Record your results.
4. Repeat Step 3 with the two other rocks.

Draw Conclusions
Compare the ways the drops of water behaved when they hit the surfaces of the three types of rock. What happened to most of the water? Was some of the water able to enter the rocks? How do you think petroleum might enter and move through rock?

Design Your Own Investigation

Re-create an Ancient Ecosystem

Choose an ancient ecosystem represented in the fossil record. You may want to choose an ecosystem that existed in your state. Research the different forms of organisms that lived in your chosen ecosystem. Design a diorama that illustrates the ecosystem. How did the organisms represented in your diorama interact? What happened to the ecosystem in time? Include note cards with your diorama that answer these questions.

Review and Test Preparation

Vocabulary Review

Use the terms below to complete the sentences. The page numbers tell you where to look in the chapter if you need help.

fossil p. 304
mold p. 305
cast p. 305
fossil fuel p. 308
index fossil p. 315
mass extinction p. 323

1. An energy-rich resource that formed from the buried remains of once-living organisms is a _____.

2. A period in which a great number of species becomes extinct is a _____.

3. A fossil that is an impression left by a plant or animal is a _____.

4. Any naturally preserved evidence of life is a _____.

5. A fossil of an organism that lived widely during a relatively short time period is an _____.

6. A fossil formed when sediment fills a mold is a _____.

Check Understanding

Write the letter of the best choice.

7. Which part of an organism is the most likely to be fossilized?
   A. the feet
   B. the hard tissues
   C. the head
   D. the soft tissues

8. Which of the following is **NOT** a kind of fossil?
   F. amber
   G. cast
   H. footprint
   J. sediment

9. Which fossil represents an ancient land environment?
   A. clam
   B. coal
   C. natural gas
   D. petroleum

10. If a stack of sedimentary rock layers were turned upside down, where would you expect to find the oldest fossils?
    F. in the top layer of rock
    G. in the bottom layer of rock
    H. in the middle layer of rock
    J. in both the top and the bottom layers

11. Which idea does the process of continental drift suggest?
    A. that continents float on water
    B. that continents get smaller
    C. that continents bump into one another
    D. that continents move slowly

12. **SEQUENCE** Examine the sequence of undisturbed rock layers shown below. Which layer is the youngest?

    F. Layer 1

    G. Layer 2

    H. Layer 3

    J. Layer 4

13. **MAIN IDEA AND DETAILS** Which can scientists learn from clam fossils?

    A. the age of Earth

    B. the shapes of ancient continents

    C. the temperatures of ancient landforms

    D. the environments of ancient times

14. In which place would someone be most likely to find the largest reserves of petroleum?

    F. inside mountains

    G. under the oceans

    H. under the United States

    J. on an oil tanker

15. During the process of coal formation, which thing occurs first after swamp plants die and sink to the bottom of the swamp?

    A. Bacteria and fungi decompose the plants.

    B. Petroleum and natural gas are removed from the plants.

    C. The plants become fossils.

    D. Water is pressed out of the plants.

16. Which type of fossil makes the best index fossil?

    F. a fossil of an animal that has no hard tissue

    G. a fossil that is found over a wide geographic area

    H. a fossil that is very large

    J. a fossil that is very rare

Inquiry Skills

17. Woolly mammoth fossils have been found with human-made arrowheads embedded in them. Using this evidence, infer what could have helped lead to the mammoth's extinction.

18. Most fossils are found in sedimentary rock, but some have been found in metamorphic rock. Using what you know about how rocks form, draw a conclusion about how organisms could become fossilized inside both kinds of rock.

Critical Thinking

19. The state of Indiana has cold winters and deciduous forests. However, the waters of the Ohio River have uncovered more than 220 acres of fossilized coral reef. What does this find imply about the climate and the organisms that inhabited this area long ago?

20. Study the picture. Then answer Parts A and B.

Part A What kind of fossil is this? How did it form? Explain your answer.

Part B Is there original material in this fossil? Explain why or why not.

UNIT D

Cycles on Earth and in Space

EARTH SCIENCE

○○○ **Hoover Dam**

TO: joey@hspscience.com

FROM: christina@hspscience.com

RE: Boulder City, Nevada

Dear Joey,
I liked your story about riding the rapids of the Colorado River. Our class just took a field trip to Hoover Dam. It was made to "harness the mighty Colorado." It now looms 726 feet above the raging water. Thousands of workers risked their lives to build this structure. Four tunnels, each 50 feet in diameter, were drilled into solid rock to divert the river. Hoover Dam not only tamed the waters, but also brought electricity to places in need. Even today, Hoover Dam helps to light the state of California.
Christina

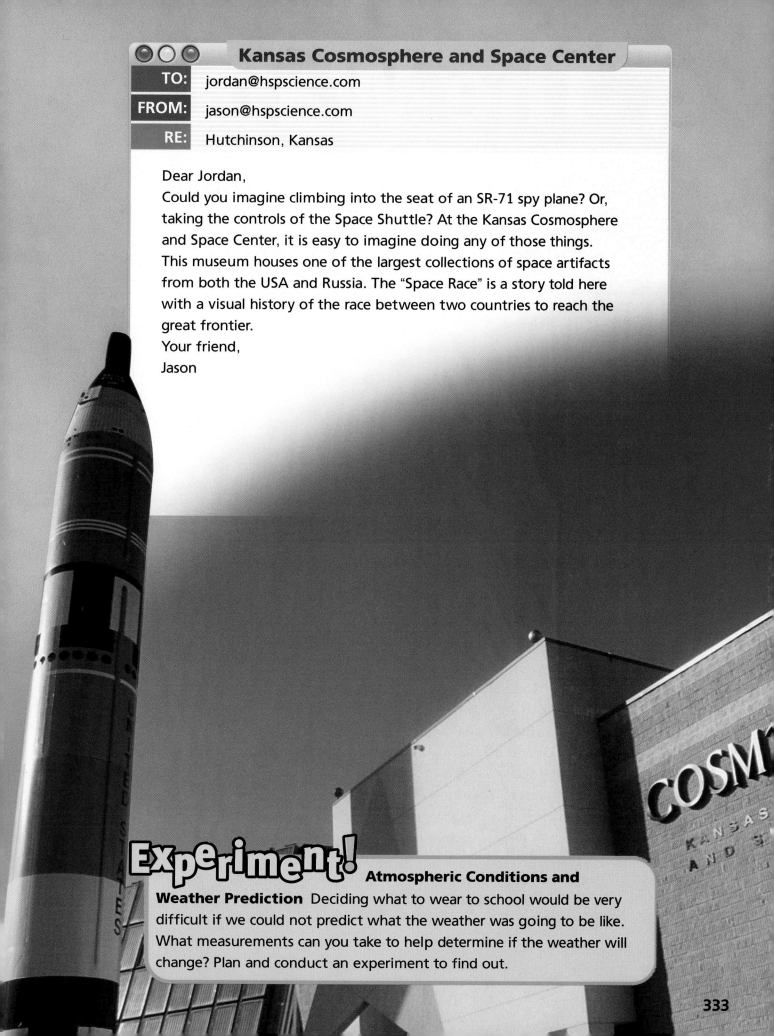

Kansas Cosmosphere and Space Center

TO: jordan@hspscience.com

FROM: jason@hspscience.com

RE: Hutchinson, Kansas

Dear Jordan,

Could you imagine climbing into the seat of an SR-71 spy plane? Or, taking the controls of the Space Shuttle? At the Kansas Cosmosphere and Space Center, it is easy to imagine doing any of those things. This museum houses one of the largest collections of space artifacts from both the USA and Russia. The "Space Race" is a story told here with a visual history of the race between two countries to reach the great frontier.

Your friend,

Jason

Experiment!

Atmospheric Conditions and Weather Prediction Deciding what to wear to school would be very difficult if we could not predict what the weather was going to be like. What measurements can you take to help determine if the weather will change? Plan and conduct an experiment to find out.

Vocabulary

water cycle
evaporation
condensation
precipitation
groundwater
continental shelf
continental slope
abyssal plain
currents
intertidal zone
near-shore zone
open-ocean zone
coral reefs

What do **YOU** wonder?

As this waterfall cascades down this cliff on the coast of a Hawaiian Island, thousands of gallons of water return to the Pacific Ocean. But where did the water in the waterfall come from? And when the water reaches the ocean, where will it go next?

What Is the Water Cycle?

Fast Fact

Waterworks Hot water helps bring the colors to these rocks at Mammoth Hot Springs, in Yellowstone National Park. Pockets of groundwater are superheated by magma beneath Earth's surface. The water rises to the surface through holes in the limestone. As the water evaporates, colorful dissolved minerals are left behind. In the Investigate, you will find out more about groundwater.

Exploring Groundwater

Materials
- clay soil
- watering can
- book
- clear plastic box
- water
- potting soil
- gravel
- food coloring
- sand
- spoon

Procedure

1. Place a layer of clay soil in the plastic box, and pack it down firmly. On top of the clay soil, place a layer of gravel. Cover the gravel with a layer of sand. Then add a layer of potting soil.

2. Add food coloring to water in the watering can. Make the water "rain" over the soil by sprinkling it over the box. Sprinkle enough water to soak the soil. Observe the water moving through the soil layers by looking through the side of the box.

3. Model a pond at one end of the box. Spoon some soil from the top layer to make a dip in the ground. Tilt the box by placing the book beneath the end of the box opposite the dip. Sprinkle water gently over the raised end of the box. Watch the water movement through the side of the box. Stop the rain when a pond forms in the dip.

Draw Conclusions

1. Describe how the "rain" soaked into the soil layers. Which layers did it move through? Which layer did the water **not** move through?

2. Most ponds and lakes form in places where dips in the ground fill with water. How did the water in your investigation reach the pond?

3. Inquiry Skill Scientists use models to learn about natural processes. What did you learn about water by using the model in the activity?

Step 1

Step 2

Investigate Further

Use what you learned in the investigation to hypothesize how local soils and physical features might affect your area's supply of water. Test your hypothesis.

Reading in Science

VOCABULARY
water cycle p. 338
evaporation p. 338
condensation p. 338
precipitation p. 339
groundwater p. 339

SCIENCE CONCEPTS
▶ how water is cycled through the environment
▶ why freshwater resources are important to preserve

READING FOCUS SKILL
SEQUENCE Look for details about the order in which the water cycle occurs.

The Water Cycle

Earth is often called the water planet because about 70 percent of its surface is covered with water. Water flows over the land. Water rains down from the sky. Water even runs underneath the ground. So where does all this water come from? And where is it going? In this lesson, you will learn that Earth's water is continuously being recycled. Water moves above, across, and through Earth's crust and ecosystems in a process known as the **water cycle**. The water cycle is driven by energy from the sun.

Most of Earth's water can be found in the oceans. As the sun heats the surface of the ocean, it causes water to evaporate. **Evaporation** is the process of liquid water changing into water vapor. Water vapor joins the other gases in the atmosphere. As it rises high into the air, the water vapor cools. If water vapor cools enough, it will condense. **Condensation** is the process in which water vapor changes into liquid water.

When water vapor condenses in the atmosphere, clouds form. Drops of condensed

Sun

When water vapor condenses on dust particles in the air, clouds form.

Each day, hundreds of trillions of liters of water evaporate into the air. Most of this water soon falls back to Earth's surface as precipitation.

Some precipitation soaks into the ground. Some water flows underground until it reaches the ocean or another body of water.

Energy from the sun causes water in lakes, ponds, rivers, and oceans to evaporate.

water in the clouds collide, and the drops grow larger. When drops are too heavy to remain suspended in the clouds by air currents, they fall as precipitation. **Precipitation** is solid or liquid water that falls from the air to Earth. Rain, snow, sleet, and hail are forms of precipitation.

Most precipitation falls back into the oceans. Precipitation that lands on the ground can run off the surface into rivers and lakes, or it can soak into the ground. Some of this water quickly recycles back to the atmosphere through evaporation or *transpiration*. This is the process by which plants release water vapor into the air through their leaves. The rest of the water in the soil slowly trickles down through gaps and

pores in rock. **Groundwater** is water located within the gaps and pores in rocks below Earth's surface. It can collect in large underground "lakes" called *aquifers*.

 SEQUENCE What happens to precipitation after it reaches Earth?

Some precipitation flows as runoff along the surface of the land. In time, the runoff in this river will mix with seawater near Loutre, Louisiana.

Rain falling on this mountain will run downward due to gravity.

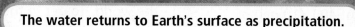

The water returns to Earth's surface as precipitation.

Plants lose water to the air during transpiration.

A little over 97 percent of all water on Earth is unusable to humans.

◀ This glacier contains frozen fresh water.

◀ Most of Earth's water is found in oceans and seas. It is salt water and is undrinkable.

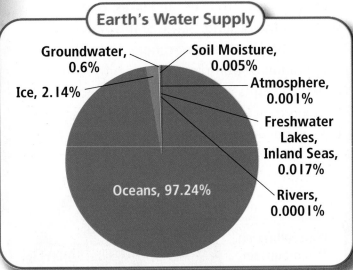

Earth's Water Supply

Groundwater, 0.6%

Soil Moisture, 0.005%

Ice, 2.14%

Atmosphere, 0.001%

Freshwater Lakes, Inland Seas, 0.017%

Oceans, 97.24%

Rivers, 0.0001%

Sources of Fresh Water

Did you know that the human body is made up of 60 to 75 percent water? That means you probably have about 40 L (10 gal) of water flowing around inside you! Water is vital to human health. Water is also necessary for growing many kinds of plants that people rely on for food. People wouldn't be able to survive without water. But not just any water will do. People, as well as many other organisms, need fresh water. Fresh water is water with a very low salt content. It may seem as if Earth is just swimming in water. But only about 3 percent of all the water on Earth is fresh water. The other 97 percent of Earth's water is salt water.

So, where can fresh water be found on Earth? Of all of the fresh water on Earth, over three-fourths of it is almost impossible for people to use. That's because it is frozen in ice caps and glaciers near Earth's poles. These places are far from where large populations of people live. Almost all of the rest of Earth's fresh water is groundwater. In fact, groundwater is the only source of fresh water for many people around the world. To get to the groundwater, people must dig wells and pump the water up to the surface. The rest of the fresh water includes the water in the air, soil, rivers, and freshwater

Many people get their drinking water by pumping up groundwater.

Lake Como, along the border of Italy and Switzerland, is a freshwater lake that formed from a melting glacier. Only about 0.009 percent of all of the water on Earth is found in freshwater lakes. ▶

lakes. This makes up only 0.5 percent of all of the fresh water on Earth.

You may wonder how fresh water stays fresh. The water cycle constantly moves ocean water to the land and back. Remember that salt water is a solution of pure water and different kinds of minerals. The minerals are what make salt water salty. When water evaporates from the ocean, the minerals are left behind. The water vapor that joins the other gases in the air is made of individual molecules of fresh water. As the water vapor condenses again, drops of fresh water form. These drops of fresh water then fall to Earth. Large volumes of fresh water are trapped in lakes and rivers. The water that seeps into the ground is also fresh water. The fresh water in the rivers then flows downstream until it eventually reaches the sea. There, the fresh water mixes with minerals and becomes salt water again.

 SEQUENCE Describe the sequence of events that take place as water cycles from being salt water to fresh water and back to salt water again.

Insta-Lab

How Much Water?

Fill a 1-L container with water. This represents all of the water on Earth. Add 4 drops of food coloring. Measure 28 mL of the water into a small, clear container. This represents all of the fresh water on Earth. From the small container, measure 7 mL of water into another small, clear container. This is all of the nonfrozen fresh water on Earth. Observe how much water is in each container. How important do you think it is to protect our freshwater resources?

341

Preserving Our Water Resources

Water is one of our most important natural resources. People use fresh water for growing crops and for cooking, cleaning, drinking, and much more. Many people also use saltwater organisms, such as fish, as food sources. Both fresh water and salt water are important for human health and to the world's economy. For these reasons, it is crucial to protect our water. Groundwater is our richest source of fresh water. If people do not take the time to dispose of chemicals correctly, groundwater sources may be harmed or destroyed. For example, pouring oil, paint, and other toxins on the ground can pollute groundwater.

Much of Earth's water is already polluted with oil, pesticides, plastics, and other things. For these reasons, most water must be treated before people can use it. In most places today, fresh water goes through water treatment plants before entering the public water system. In a water treatment plant, water from a lake or river is put in a holding tank. Sticky chemicals that attract dirt particles are added. As the dirt sticks to the chemicals, the particles grow heavy. They sink out of the water. Next, the clear water flows through a filter, which removes even smaller particles. Then a small amount of chlorine is added to the water. The chlorine kills any microorganisms that may be in the water. Finally, the disinfected water enters the water system for a community.

 SEQUENCE What steps take place at a water treatment plant?

Fresh water used by humans can be partially purified and reclaimed in water treatment plants. However, this is expensive and does not leave the water as clean as it was originally.

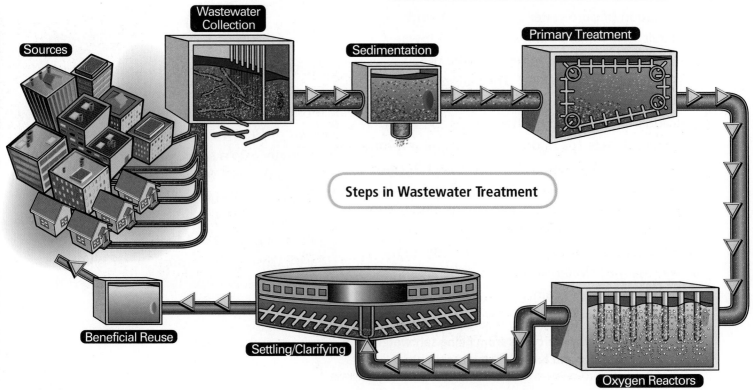

Steps in Wastewater Treatment

Sources · Wastewater Collection · Sedimentation · Primary Treatment · Oxygen Reactors · Settling/Clarifying · Beneficial Reuse

1. SEQUENCE Draw and complete the graphic organizer.

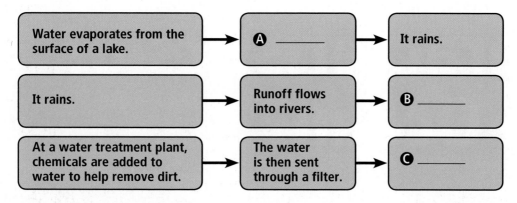

| Water evaporates from the surface of a lake. | → | **A** _____ | → | It rains. |

| It rains. | → | Runoff flows into rivers. | → | **B** _____ |

| At a water treatment plant, chemicals are added to water to help remove dirt. | → | The water is then sent through a filter. | → | **C** _____ |

2. SUMMARIZE Write a paragraph summarizing the journey of a water drop through the water cycle.

3. DRAW CONCLUSIONS Explain how the sun affects various steps in the water cycle on Earth.

4. VOCABULARY Draw an illustration of the water cycle, and label it with the vocabulary terms from this lesson.

Test Prep

5. Critical Thinking Explain how groundwater can become polluted and why it is important to keep groundwater supplies clean.

6. Which of the following processes carries water vapor from plant leaves back into the atmosphere?

   A. condensation   **C.** perspiration

   B. evaporation   **D.** transpiration

Links

Writing

Expository Writing
Find out more about new ways to treat oil spills. Write several **how-to paragraphs** explaining how to remove pollution from water that is polluted by oil. Illustrate your paragraphs, and share your work with the class.

Math

Use Scientific Notation
In the United States, we use about 150,000,000,000,000 gallons of fresh water every year. Write this number in scientific notation.

Social Studies

Water Resources and Urban Geography
Choose a country, and examine a map of the country. Write an essay explaining how the location of water resources may have influenced the locations and economies of the major cities.

 For more links and activities, go to www.hspscience.com

What Are the Characteristics of the Ocean?

Fast Fact

Shallow and Deep Waters Light blue water around this island indicates that the water is shallow. As the water gets deeper, it looks darker because less and less sunlight reflects back from the bottom. In the deepest parts of the ocean, the bottom is nearly 11,000 m (36,000 ft) down! In the Investigate, you'll model some features of the ocean floor.

Mapping the Ocean Floor

Materials
- scissors
- tape
- cm graph paper
- poster board
- chopstick
- shoe box with lid
- metric ruler

Procedure

1. Cut a strip of poster board about 1½ times as long as the shoe box but just wide enough to fit into it. Fold the strip to make a model of an ocean floor. It can show mountains, plains, slopes, and canyons. Trim your model so that it fits into the shoe box. Tape the ends in place.

2. Cut a slit about 0.5 cm wide along the center length of the lid. Then tape the lid to the box.

3. Trade models with another group. Do not open the lid on the model you get.

4. Plan a way to use the chopstick and the ruler to measure the depth of the ocean floor at different places in the model. Collect the data you need to make a cross-section drawing. On the graph paper, draw a cross section that shows the shape of the ocean floor as it would look from the side.

5. Now open the lid of the box, and compare your drawing with the actual model.

Draw Conclusions

1. How did you use the materials to measure the depth of the ocean floor in the model?

2. What measurements did you need in order to model the ocean floor in the box?

3. **Inquiry Skill** How did you interpret the data to draw the side view of the ocean floor?

Step 1

Step 4

Investigate Further

Suppose you want to map the bottom of a lake. Plan an investigation to do this that uses simple equipment and a small boat. What steps would you take?

Reading in Science

VOCABULARY
continental shelf p. 346
continental slope p. 346
abyssal plain p. 347
currents p. 348

SCIENCE CONCEPTS
▶ what the features of the ocean floor are like
▶ how the ocean affects climate

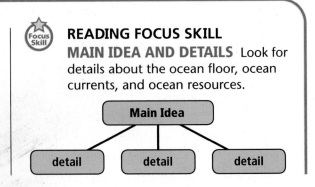

READING FOCUS SKILL
MAIN IDEA AND DETAILS Look for details about the ocean floor, ocean currents, and ocean resources.

The Ocean Floor

As you walk from the beach into the ocean, the water gradually gets deeper and deeper. You may think that the ocean floor continues to gradually slope downward until its surface is smooth and flat. But this is only partly true. In reality, the ocean floor is just as varied as the land above water. There are towering mountains, deep valleys, wide plains, and other features. However, even with all of this variety, all ocean floors across the world can be divided into three major regions.

The first region is the **continental shelf**. The continental shelf is a gradually sloping portion of the ocean floor that is made of continental crust. When you wade into the ocean at the beach, you are walking along the continental shelf. In some places, the continental shelf extends into the ocean as little as 30 km (19 mi) from the coast. The continental shelf comes to an end at the edge of the continental slope. The **continental slope** is found at the border between continental crust and oceanic crust. Parts of the "slope" are actually more like

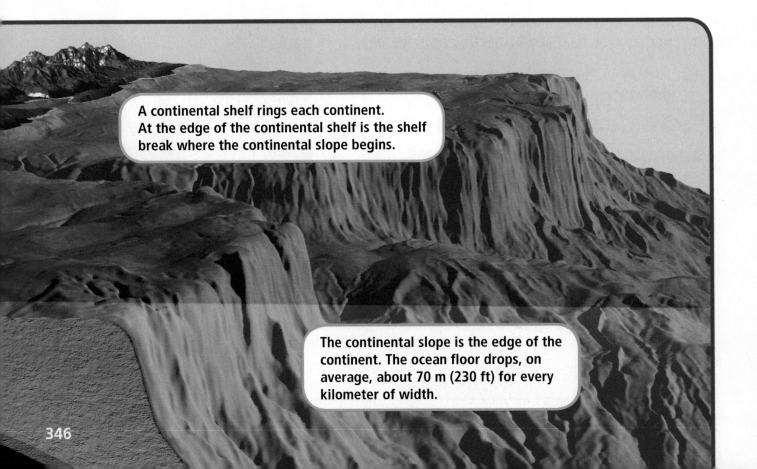

A continental shelf rings each continent. At the edge of the continental shelf is the shelf break where the continental slope begins.

The continental slope is the edge of the continent. The ocean floor drops, on average, about 70 m (230 ft) for every kilometer of width.

cliffs as it plunges down steeply to the deep-ocean floor. The average depth of the ocean is 3720 m (12,200 ft). However, there are some areas that are much deeper.

At the end of the continental slope, the ocean floor gradually flattens out into the abyssal (uh•BIS•uhl) plain. The **abyssal plain** is the vast floor of the deep ocean. This part of the ocean covers almost half of Earth's surface. A layer of thick sediment covers the abyssal plain. This makes it the flattest place on Earth. But this flat plain is not without features. That's because the abyssal plain is broken up by deep trenches, ridges, and mountains. In fact, some of the world's highest mountains and deepest canyons lie beneath the ocean's surface. Many of these landforms are found along the *mid-ocean ridges*. Here, the tectonic plates of Earth's crust are being split apart. As the plates are pulled apart, molten rock pushes up from below. It forms new ocean floor and a vast mountain range. Where two oceanic plates run into each other, the dense ocean crust sinks down into Earth's mantle, rolling under like a conveyer belt, to

form a deep-ocean *trench.* Such trenches are the deepest parts of the ocean. Some of them plunge more than 10,000 m (33,000 ft) below the surface. The Mariana Trench in the Western Pacific is 11,033 m (36,198 ft) deep.

 MAIN IDEA AND DETAILS What are the three main regions of the ocean floor?

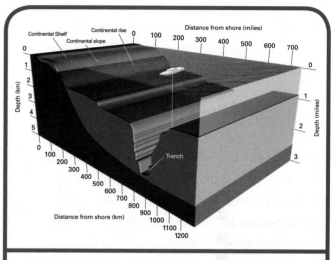

This diagram shows the continental shelf and slope off the edge of the East Coast of the United States.

This shelf break off the coast of California marks the border between the North American continental shelf and the continental slope.

High ridges and deep trenches form where the rocky plates of Earth's crust meet.

How Oceans Affect Climate

Oceans cover nearly three-fourths of Earth's surface. Because of this, oceans have important effects on Earth's climate. In fact, without oceans, Earth's climate would be too harsh to support life. This is because water takes much longer to heat up and cool down than land does. Because water takes longer to heat up, it helps keep land cooler during the summer. And because water takes longer to cool down, it helps keep land warmer during the winter. This is why seasons are more extreme in the middle of continents.

The differences in water and land temperatures also cause winds to form. During the day, land temperatures rise faster than water temperatures. As the air warms, it becomes less dense. The denser, cooler air over the ocean moves toward the land and the warm air moves upward. This is how a sea breeze forms. The air on land stays cooler during the day because of the sea breeze. The opposite situation occurs at night. The land cools down more quickly than the ocean water. The warmer air over the ocean moves upward and the cooler air over land moves in to take its place. This movement of air is called a land breeze.

Earth's oceans also affect climate in another way. Suppose you placed a beach ball in the middle of the ocean. Even if there was no wind, would the ball stay in that same spot? Probably not. That's because ocean water flows in steady, streamlike movements known as **currents**. Currents are caused by many factors, including wind, gravity, heating from the sun, and Earth's rotation.

Surface currents, or currents near the surface of the ocean, are produced by global winds. Global winds move in fairly regular patterns, so surface currents also move in regular patterns. The movements of surface

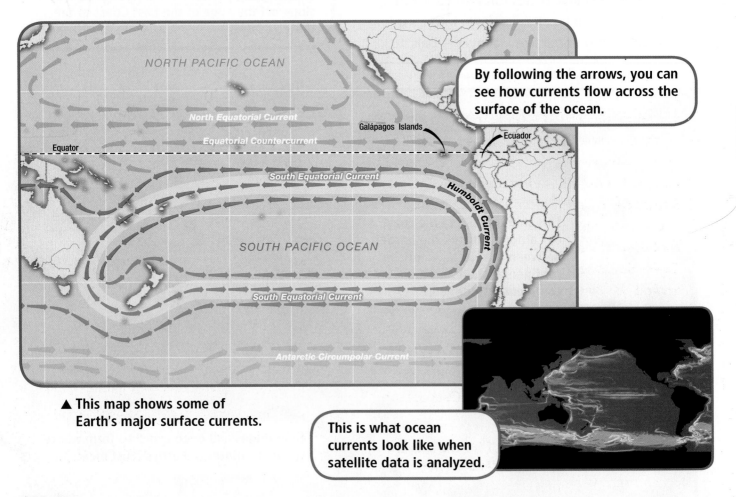

By following the arrows, you can see how currents flow across the surface of the ocean.

▲ This map shows some of Earth's major surface currents.

This is what ocean currents look like when satellite data is analyzed.

This California surfer must wear a wet suit to stay warm because the California Current carries cool water down the West Coast of the United States.

currents are predictable. The temperatures of surface currents are also predictable. Warm-water currents, such as the Gulf Stream, begin in tropical regions. The Gulf Stream flows northeast from the Caribbean Sea. It carries warm water across the North Atlantic toward Europe. During the winter, the warm Gulf Stream helps keep Europe's climate mild.

Currents can also cause warm climates to cool down. Cool-water currents, such as the California Current, form near the poles and flow toward the equator. This current then flows southward down the West Coast of the United States. The current helps keep summers along the West Coast cool. The current also keeps the ocean water on the West Coast much cooler than the ocean water on the East Coast of the United States.

 MAIN IDEA AND DETAILS How does the ocean help keep Earth's climate mild?

Heating Things Up
Fill a paper cup with water. Leave a second cup empty. Place a thermometer in each cup. Record the temperatures in both cups. Set both cups under a lamp with a 100-W bulb. Turn the lamp on. Record the temperatures in both cups every 5 minutes for 15 minutes. Turn the lamp off. After 5 minutes, record the temperatures of both cups. Graph your data to show how the temperatures in the two cups changed over time. Which heated up and cooled down faster—air or water?

◄ Ships use the oceans as "highways" to transport goods around the world.

Ocean Resources

You have learned that people rely on freshwater resources for drinking water, irrigation, bathing, recreation, and many other uses. Although people do not drink salt water, they use many saltwater resources. People in some places, such as deserts and small islands, don't have large supplies of fresh water. They turn to the ocean for their freshwater supply. To do this, they must remove the salt and other minerals from the water. This happens in desalination plants.

Saltwater organisms such as fish, shrimp, seaweed, squid, and lobster are very important to many people's diets. All of these organisms must be gathered from the ocean.

Marine organisms are also gathered for nonfood products. For example, oysters are valued for the pearls that sometimes form in their bodies. This happens when a piece of sand or other foreign matter gets trapped in the oyster's shell. The gland in the oyster that secretes mother-of-pearl for the shell secretes it around the sand piece to reduce the irritation it feels. It takes about a year for a pearl to form. Oysters can be harvested for their pearls, but some pearls are expelled from oysters and are found on the ocean floor. About 100 years ago, a Japanese man developed a way to put bits of foreign matter into oysters. Pearls formed in this way are called *cultured pearls.*

This commercial shrimping boat is gathering a catch that will be sold in port.

Salt water is also a source of sea salt. Sea salt is used for cooking, in agriculture, as an important nutrient for farm animals, in refining metals, for making bath salts, for preserving meat, and for many other uses.

The oceans can be "mined" for other resources as well. For example, in many places, petroleum is pumped up from beneath the ocean floor by the use of offshore rigs. Even sand from the ocean floor is mined in some areas. It is used to make concrete.

 MAIN IDEA AND DETAILS What are five products that can be made from or are found in the ocean?

This offshore oil rig is pumping petroleum that formed from the remains of marine microorganisms.

1. **MAIN IDEA AND DETAILS** Draw and complete the graphic organizer.

MAIN IDEA:
THE OCEAN HAS MANY CHARACTERISTICS.

The ocean floor has three regions, which include

Ⓐ _____   **Ⓑ** _____   **Ⓒ** _____

The oceans affect the world's **Ⓓ** _____ .
The ocean has many resources, including

Ⓔ _____   **Ⓕ** _____   **Ⓖ** _____

2. **SUMMARIZE** Write a short paragraph summarizing various ways people use the ocean.

3. **DRAW CONCLUSIONS** Ships often use currents to cut their travel time from one place to another. Where might ships travel to by using the Gulf Stream?

4. **VOCABULARY** Write a short paragraph using vocabulary terms from this lesson to describe what the ocean floor is like.

Test Prep

5. **Critical Thinking** At the beach, you notice a strong breeze blowing in from the water. Explain how this breeze is formed.

6. If Earth had no oceans, how would the temperatures on Earth change?

  A. They would be higher.

  B. They would be lower.

  C. They would be milder.

  D. They would be more extreme.

Links

Writing

Expository Writing
Oceanographers use sonar to map the ocean floor. Write an **essay** explaining what sonar is and how it is used to map the ocean floor.

Math

Solve Problems
Sound travels through seawater at about 1500 m/sec (4921 ft/sec). A ship sends out a sonar pulse that takes 4 sec to travel to the ocean floor and back. How deep is the ocean at that point? How deep would it be if the pulse took only 1 sec?

Literature

Books Set at Sea
Many great pieces of literature, such as *Moby Dick* and *20,000 Leagues Under the Sea*, are set at sea. Read a book, short story, or poem in which the story takes place at sea. Write a report about the story, giving special attention to the story's setting.

For more links and activities, go to
www.hspscience.com

What Lives in the Ocean?

Fast Fact

Going to School This photo shows part of an aquatic ecosystem—a school of fish. Almost 80 percent of all fish species school, or swim in groups, at some point during their life cycles. Some schools can be small, with only 10 to 20 members. Other schools can have millions of members and cover an area as large as a small city! In the Investigate, you will make and observe an aquatic ecosystem.

Ecosystem in a Jar

Materials
- glass jar with lid
- pond water
- masking tape
- gravel
- pond snails
- marker
- 500-mL beaker
- aquatic plants (duckweed or elodea)
- tap water
- duct tape

Procedure

1. Label a clean glass jar with your name and the date. Cover the bottom of the jar with gravel or small rocks. Half-fill the jar with room-temperature tap water.

2. Measure 200 mL of pond water. Add this water to the jar. Put some aquatic plants into the jar. Use the gravel at the bottom of the jar to anchor the plants.

3. Add 1 or 2 pond snails. Add more room-temperature tap water to the jar until the water level is within 2.5 cm of the top.

4. Put the lid on the jar, and seal the lid closed with duct tape.

5. Place the jar in a bright area, but do not put it in direct sunlight. Observe the jar for several days.

Draw Conclusions

1. Describe some observations you made of your mini-ecosystem.

2. How do you think temperature, light, and moisture affected the organisms in your ecosystem?

3. **Inquiry Skill** Scientists use models to infer things about how organisms interact with their environment. What can you infer about aquatic ecosystems by examining your model of a freshwater ecosystem?

Step 1

Step 3

Investigate Further

Many aquatic organisms are microscopic. Predict what organisms may be living in the pond water. Put a drop of pond water on a microscope slide to test your predictions.

Reading in Science

VOCABULARY
intertidal zone p. 354
near-shore zone p. 356
open-ocean zone p. 356
coral reefs p. 358

SCIENCE CONCEPTS
▶ what kinds of ecosystems can be found in the ocean
▶ what environmental conditions help define each ocean ecosystem

READING FOCUS SKILL
COMPARE AND CONTRAST Look for the ways different ocean ecosystems are alike and different.

| alike | — | different |

Intertidal Zones

Earth's oceans contain the world's largest animals as well as countless microscopic organisms. With all of this biological diversity, it should be no surprise that the oceans have many different types of ecosystems. Recall that an *ecosystem* is a community of organisms and their nonliving environment. Each of the ecosystems in the ocean exists in a major ocean zone. Each ocean zone is a layer of the ocean that has unique types of plant and animal communities.

Ocean zones are determined by the depth of the water. As depth increases, there is less light. The shallowest and brightest ocean zone is the intertidal zone. The **intertidal zone** is the area of the ocean between the levels of high tide and low tide. The environment of the intertidal zone is always changing. At low tide, organisms in this zone may have to find shelter from the hot sun. As the tide comes in, they must survive the

▼ Intertidal Zone

Math in Science
Interpret Data

The amount of sunlight determines which organisms can live at which depth in the ocean. Do you think more organisms live closer to the surface or closer to the bottom of the ocean? Explain.

Sunlight Zone	Twilight Zone	Midnight Zone	Abyssal Zone	Hadal Zone
0 m to 200 m	200 m to 1000 m	1000 m to 4000 m	4000 m to 6000 m	6000 m to 11,000 m

This squid lives deep beneath the surface of the ocean.

Dolphins and other marine mammals must live close to the ocean's surface so they can come up for air to breathe.

▲ The intertidal zone is an important feeding ground for birds and other animals.

When the tide goes out, tide pools still hold water. Tide pools are home to many different organisms.

rough water of incoming waves. They may spend hours in an undersea world until the tide goes out again.

Intertidal organisms handle the changes in their surroundings in different ways. Many of them bury themselves in the mud during low tide. This keeps them moist and protected. Crabs hide under rocks and in other sheltered, moist spots when the tide goes out.

Mussels and barnacles close their shells tightly during low tide, trapping water inside. During high tide, they open up to feed on *plankton* (PLANGK•tuhn) and other organic matter. Plankton is made up of microscopic organisms that live near the ocean's surface. A single gallon

of seawater may contain more than a million plankton organisms! Many use sunlight to produce food by photosynthesis. Because many marine organisms feed on plankton, they are the base of most marine food chains. This means that most marine organisms, just like land organisms, acquire their energy directly or indirectly from sunlight.

 COMPARE AND CONTRAST How does the environment of the intertidal zone differ during high tide and low tide?

Near-Shore and Open-Ocean Zones

Moving seaward from the intertidal zone, you enter the near-shore zone. The **near-shore zone** includes most of the ocean over the continental shelf, where the water gets no deeper than about 200 m (650 ft). The near-shore zone is relatively shallow and receives a great deal of sunlight. It is a much more stable ecosystem than the intertidal zone. This is why it is teeming with life. Many different kinds of marine organisms inhabit the near-shore zone. These include fish, jellyfish, krill (a small shrimp-like animal), seaweed, shrimp, and plankton. The plentiful supply of fish attracts sea birds. It also attracts larger marine animals. Dolphins, porpoises, sharks, and whales often feed on fish and krill in the near-shore zone.

Some types of whales, even the huge baleen whales, feed almost entirely on krill, small fish, other small crustaceans, and plankton! Baleen whales eat by sucking seawater in through their mouths. Comb-like structures in their mouths capture the food.

Farther out to sea, past the continental shelf, you enter the open-ocean zone. The **open-ocean zone** includes most of the water over the continental slope and abyssal plain. Most of the animals in the open-ocean zone live near the surface. Dolphins, krill, seals, swordfish, tuna, whales, and plankton live in the open-ocean zone.

Because of the depth of the open-ocean zone, food is limited to water near the surface. In this zone, many organisms are active swimmers. They must be able to swim long distances to obtain food.

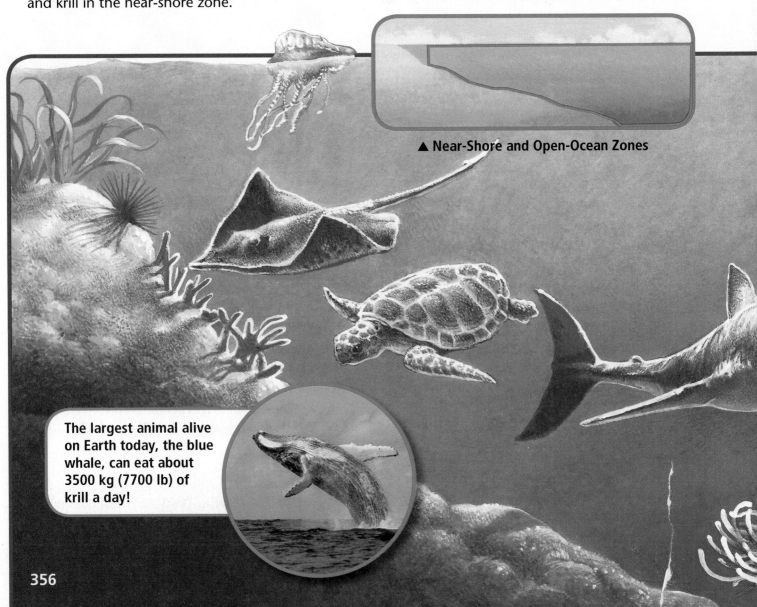

▲ Near-Shore and Open-Ocean Zones

The largest animal alive on Earth today, the blue whale, can eat about 3500 kg (7700 lb) of krill a day!

Food becomes even scarcer as the ocean becomes deeper. At about 1000 m (3200 ft) below the surface of the ocean, there is little or no light. The extreme darkness means that no producer organisms that rely on sunlight can live there. Those that can be found have sunk down from the surface. Life is also difficult at these depths because of enormous pressure from the water above. At this depth, most organisms with lungs would be crushed! However, sperm whales can dive to 3000 m (9600 ft) where they feed on giant squid. This deep region of the ocean, which makes up about 90 percent of all the oceans, is like the barest of deserts on land. Much of this zone is cold, deep, and dark.

 COMPARE AND CONTRAST What are some differences between the near-shore zone and the open-ocean zone?

Squid live in both the near-shore zone and the open-ocean zone. They eat fish, shrimp, and other squid.

The organisms found in a particular ocean zone depend on the depth and on the amount of light the zone receives.

Coral Reefs

Small animals called corals, which live in shallow, sunlit, near-shore ocean waters, form **coral reefs**, some of the largest structures on Earth built by living organisms. Despite their large size, coral reefs are very delicate and easily damaged.

The corals that make up reefs use minerals dissolved in ocean water to form hard outer skeletons. The living corals attach themselves

Coral reefs take up a little less than 1 percent of the ocean floor, but about 25 percent of different marine species live in or around coral reefs! Sea urchins, corals, sponges, surgeonfish, and many other organisms are found around coral reefs.

Coral Reef Habitat

This type of coral is not like the others. It is called an octocoral and can often be found in and near reefs.

Most corals are polyps that form groups. A polyp (PAHL•ip) has a body that is shaped like a cylinder. Its mouth, which is surrounded by stinging tentacles, is located at the end of its body.

 For more links and activities, go to www.hspscience.com

358

to the skeletons of dead corals. Very slowly a reef forms. Many kinds of algae and some kinds of plants live on reefs. The reefs provide underwater surfaces that sunlight can reach easily. They also provide shelter for many kinds of animals, as well as a large variety of producers. Producers in coral-reef food webs include seaweed and plankton that live within the corals.

 COMPARE AND CONTRAST Contrast a coral reef with the deep ocean.

Many of the animals, including the coral animals themselves, rely on plankton for their food source. Some types of fish eat the coral. Parrotfish eat the algae on the corals. They often bite chunks off the reef and grind up the coral skeletons with teeth in their throats.

These are soft corals. These animals are like corals, but they do not form a hard skeleton.

Deep-Ocean Vents

Until recently, scientists hypothesized that all of Earth's ecosystems used sunlight as their energy source. However, researchers have discovered a new kind of ecosystem in the deep oceans. These ecosystems, which lie more than 1000 m (3200 ft) beneath the surface, seem to get energy from chemical reactions.

On some parts of the ocean floor such as the abyssal zone and along mid-ocean ridges, volcanic vents spew water heated to around 350°C (662°F). The water contains dissolved sulfur- and iron-based chemicals. Certain bacteria use these chemicals, rather than sunlight, to produce and store energy. These bacteria are the primary producers in deep-ocean vent ecosystems. All other members of the ecosystem depend on the energy the bacteria store. In fact, some animals in these ecosystems have no stomachs or mouths. Instead, they live with these bacteria in their bodies. They take nutrients from the bacteria directly into their blood. Many species living near deep-ocean vents were unknown before these ecosystems were discovered.

 COMPARE AND CONTRAST How do deep-ocean vent ecosystems differ from all other known ecosystems?

This meter-long (39-in.-long) tube worm is one of the many unusual organisms that live near deep-ocean vents.

Deep-ocean vent ecosystems have been found in the Atlantic, Pacific, and Indian Oceans. ▼

A certain kind of bacterium is the primary producer in deep-ocean vent ecosystems.

1. COMPARE AND CONTRAST Draw and complete the graphic organizer to tell how intertidal zones, near-shore zones, and deep-ocean vents are alike and different.

OCEAN LAYER	LOCATION	DEPTH	ORGANISMS
Intertidal zone	Along the coastline	Ⓐ	Ⓑ
Near-shore zone	Ⓒ	Ⓓ	Ⓔ
Deep-ocean vent	Ⓕ	Ⓖ	Ⓗ

2. SUMMARIZE Draw a cross section of the ocean floor that shows all of the ocean zones. Include labels that describe each zone.

3. DRAW CONCLUSIONS What would most likely happen to the ocean ecosystems discussed if the species that make up plankton suddenly became extinct?

4. VOCABULARY Use the lesson vocabulary to explain the various ecosystems found in the oceans.

Test Prep

5. Critical Thinking Why might coral reefs be considered to be the "tropical rain forests" of the ocean?

6. Which of the following organisms would most likely be found in the open-ocean zone?

 A. bacteria
 B. barnacles
 C. corals
 D. whales

Links

Writing

Narrative Writing
Suppose you have built an exploratory submarine that can take you from the surface of the ocean all the way to the bottom of the abyssal plain. Write a **story** about a trip you make in the sub. Describe what you see.

Math

Calculate Pressure
Air pressure at sea level is about 14.7 pounds per square inch (psi). Near the bottom of the Mariana Trench, the water pressure is 16,883 psi. About how many times as great as the pressure at sea level is this?

Art

Coral Reefs
Coral reefs are some of the most colorful places on Earth. Find some pictures of coral reefs. Use them as inspiration to paint a picture or make a sculpture of some coral reef organisms.

 For more links and activities, go to www.hspscience.com

Mysteries Beneath the Sea

Archaeologists, scientists who study the remains of past civilizations, often make their discoveries in remote places such as mountaintops or deserts. Recently, however, several discoveries have taken place under the surface of the Mediterranean Sea that shed new light on ancient cultures.

Perhaps the most exciting discovery is that of Herakleion (her-AK-lee-on), an ancient Egyptian city. Herakleion's ancient temples were discovered 9 meters (30 feet) below the surface of the Mediterranean Sea, about 4 miles west of the modern city of Alexandria.

Ancient Treasures

Scientists used large cranes aboard barges to carefully hoist their discoveries from the

water. The pieces included 6-meter (20-foot) tall pink granite statues of a pharaoh and a queen. Scientists also found a 10-ton black granite stone inscribed with the Egyptian name for Herakleion, "Rahinet."

What Happened?

Once a thriving seaport, Herakleion fell off the map about 1,200 years ago. A major earthquake and tidal wave had doomed the city to a watery grave. "We found an intact city frozen in time," said Franck Goddio, head of the recovery team.

To learn more about what happened to the city, scientists took core samples from the seafloor near the relics. A core sample is a long, narrow piece of sediment pulled out of the ground by a special drill. The cores may provide additional clues about what occurred to cause the city to sink under water.

Think About It

1. What difficulties did the scientists face when they discovered Herakleion?
2. Why will scientists return the statues to the water in the harbor?

Cleopatra's Palace

Before Herakleion, Goddio discovered the undersea remains of the Royal Quarter of Alexandria.

More than 1600 years ago, an earthquake shook Alexandria, the most important city in ancient Egypt. The Royal Quarter, where royalty lived, crumbled into the harbor. Today, scuba divers can explore the ruins of the Royal Quarter.

The Egyptian government has allowed the short-term removal of some of the Royal Quarter's statues so researchers can make plastic molds for study. To preserve the statues, scientists will return the artifacts to the depths of the harbor.

Find out more! Log on to
www.hspscience.com

Swimming with Dolphins

You don't need to look far beyond Jessica Browne's room to know she loves dolphins. Her walls and bookshelves are filled with pictures, decorations, and books all about dolphins.

Jessica remembers being interested in dolphins since she was a little girl and saw a television program about them. Since then, Jessica has studied dolphins and visited aquariums and oceanographic centers whenever she could. She enjoys learning where dolphins live, what they eat, and how they raise their young. One of Jessica's fondest memories comes from when she visited dolphins in the ocean. After a presentation by a scientist, Jessica was able to get into the water and actually touch a dolphin. When she grows up, Jessica hopes to study dolphins and help protect them.

You Can Do It!

Materials
- two plastic cups
- water
- blue food coloring
- medium-size rock
- transparent tape

Quick and Easy Project

Model the Water Cycle

Procedure

1. Pour about 5 cm of water in a plastic cup. Add 2 or 3 drops of food coloring. The water represents ocean water.

2. Place the rock in the center of the cup. Some of the rock should stick up above the water. The rock represents a continent.

3. Turn the second cup over, and place it on top of the first cup. Tape the cups together, using the transparent tape.

4. Place your model in a sunny window, and observe it for several days.

Draw Conclusions

What did you observe occurring inside your model? What was causing the water to evaporate? Did you observe condensation occurring in a certain place in the cups? What color was the condensation? What happened to the food coloring? How is the food coloring similar to the salt in the oceans?

Design Your Own Investigation

Diagram an Aquatic Food Web

Choose a marine ecosystem, and research some of the organisms that live in that ecosystem. Find out what the organisms rely on for their food source. Which are the producers? Which are the consumers? Are there scavengers and decomposers in the community? Use the information you learn to diagram the transfer of energy in the aquatic web. Write a description of the food web, and describe the predator/prey relationships in the community.

Review and Test Preparation

Vocabulary Review

Use the terms below to complete the sentences. The page numbers tell you where to look in the chapter if you need help.

water cycle p. 338

evaporation p. 338

condensation p. 338

precipitation p. 339

groundwater p. 339

continental shelf p. 346

continental slope p. 346

abyssal plain p. 347

currents p. 348

intertidal zone p. 354

1. The process of liquid water changing into water vapor is called _____ .

2. Ocean water flows in streamlike movements known as _____ .

3. The area of the ocean between the levels of high tide and low tide is the _____ .

4. Water moves above, across, and through Earth's crust and ecosystems in a process known as the _____ .

5. Water located within rocks below Earth's surface is _____ .

6. A gradually sloping portion of the ocean floor that is made of continental crust is called the _____ .

7. Solid or liquid water that falls from clouds to Earth is _____ .

8. The process in which water vapor changes into liquid water is _____ .

9. The vast floor of the deep ocean is called the _____ .

10. The portion of the ocean floor that is found at the border between continental crust and oceanic crust is called the _____ .

Check Understanding

Write the letter of the best choice.

11. **SEQUENCE** In the water cycle, water evaporates from the ocean. Which will most likely occur next?

    A. The water will become salty.

    B. The water will condense in a cloud.

    C. The water will transpire from a plant.

    D. The water will form groundwater.

12. In which region would a cool-water current be most likely to originate?

    F. Arctic Ocean

    G. Caribbean Sea

    H. Indian Ocean

    J. Mediterranean Sea

13. Examine the graph below. What percent of Earth's water can be found in lakes and rivers?

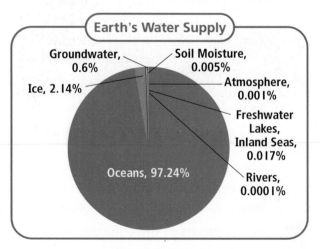

Earth's Water Supply

Groundwater, 0.6%
Soil Moisture, 0.005%
Ice, 2.14%
Atmosphere, 0.001%
Freshwater Lakes, Inland Seas, 0.017%
Oceans, 97.24%
Rivers, 0.0001%

  A. < 0.05%   **C.** about 1%

  B. 0.1%   **D.** > 1%

14. MAIN IDEA AND DETAILS Which part of the ocean floor contains mid-ocean ridges?

   F. abyssal plain

   G. deep-ocean trenches

   H. continental shelf

   J. continental slope

15. In which of the following ocean zones would you be most likely to find coral?

   A. deep-ocean vents

   B. intertidal zone

   C. near-shore zone

   D. open-ocean zone

16. Examine the illustration of an ocean zone below. Which ocean zone is being shown?

   F. abyssal zone

   G. intertidal zone

   H. near-shore zone

   J. open-ocean zone

Inquiry Skills

17. Using your observations of the water cycle, explain how groundwater is formed.

18. You want to compare two ocean ecosystems. What features should you look at?

Critical Thinking

19. Examine the photograph below. What would happen to this ecosystem if there were a rapid increase in global ocean levels? Explain your answer.

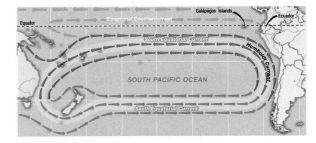

20. Below is an illustration of the Humboldt Current, which moves up the coast of western South America. Use the illustration to answer Parts A and B.

Part A Is the Humboldt Current a cool-water current or a warm-water current? How do you know?

Part B How do you think the Humboldt Current affects the climate of the Galápagos Islands? Explain your answer.

Chapter 10

Earth's Weather Patterns

Vocabulary

atmosphere
air pressure
relative humidity
front
climate
thunderstorm
tornado
hurricane
blizzard

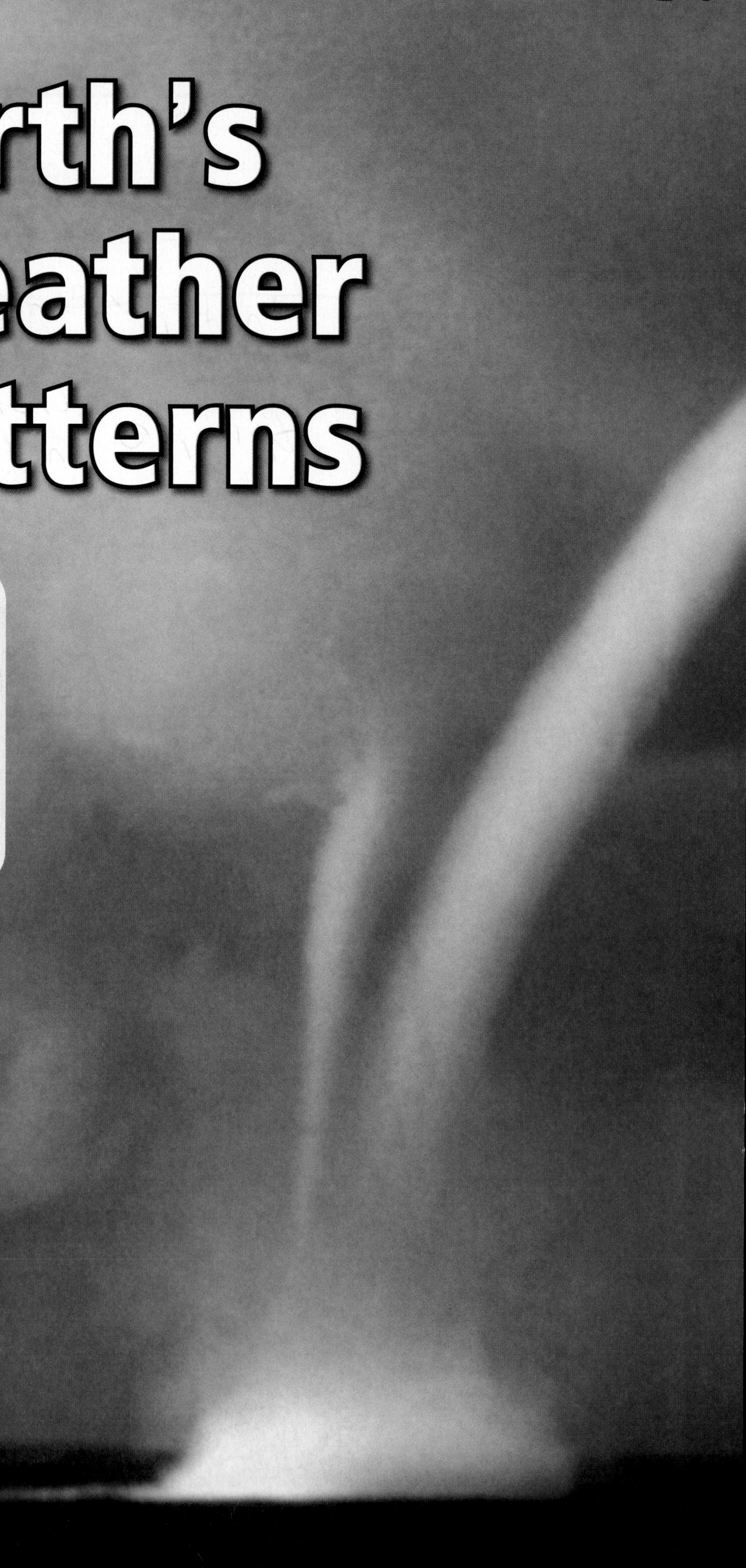

What do YOU wonder?

This picture shows a waterspout, a kind of tornado over water. Waterspouts usually don't do much damage, but tornadoes on land can cause great destruction. What causes tornadoes?

What Makes Up the Atmosphere?

Too Cold for Comfort The layers of gases that surround Earth are about 560 km (350 mi) thick. The temperature of the layer we live in is a cold –60°C (–76°F) at its top—only 10 km (6 mi) above Earth. What are the other layers like? The Investigate will help answer this question.

Layers of the Atmosphere

Materials ● graph paper ● metric ruler

Procedure

① The data table shows average temperatures in Earth's atmosphere. Use the numbers in the table to plot temperature points on a sheet of graph paper. Let the *y*-axis show the height above sea level. Let the *x*-axis show the average temperature. Use the grid at the right to set up your graph. Notice that the heights above sea level are not all at equal intervals, so be careful when plotting the points on your graph.

② Connect the points on your graph.

③ Interpret the data you plotted. Observe points at which the temperature changes as height increases and points at which the temperature stays the same. Look for three boundaries where the temperature levels off. Draw a horizontal straight line to mark each boundary.

④ Label the layers from the bottom up on the graph. The first layer is the *troposphere*. The second is the *stratosphere*. The third is the *mesosphere*. The fourth is the *thermosphere*.

Draw Conclusions

1. What happens to the temperature as you go through the stratosphere toward space?

2. What can you infer as a basis for dividing Earth's atmosphere into four layers?

3. **Inquiry Skill** Scientists often use numbers to help them interpret data. Would a bar graph be more helpful in interpreting your data? Explain.

Average Temperatures in Earth's Atmosphere	
Height Above Sea Level (km)	Average Temperature (°C)
0	12
5	−30
10	−60
15	−60
20	−60
25	−55
30	−50
35	−30
40	0
45	0
50	0
60	−30
70	−60
80	−90
85	−90
90	−85
100	−60
500	−30
600	0

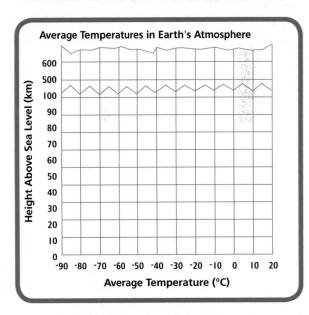

Average Temperatures in Earth's Atmosphere

Investigate Further

Investigate the causes for the temperature changes in the different layers.

Communicate your findings in an unusual way so that others will be interested in your results.

Reading in Science

VOCABULARY
atmosphere p. 372

SCIENCE CONCEPTS
▶ what makes up the atmosphere
▶ how the sun affects the atmosphere

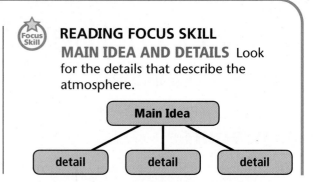

READING FOCUS SKILL
MAIN IDEA AND DETAILS Look for the details that describe the atmosphere.

The Atmosphere

What gas are you taking in when you breathe? You probably said "oxygen," but the air contains other gases, too. All these gases make up the **atmosphere**, the layers of air that surround Earth.

The graph below shows the amounts of the different gases that make up the atmosphere. *Water vapor*, water in the form of a gas, is also found in the atmosphere. It ranges from 0 percent to 7 percent of the air.

Another important gas is *ozone*, a form of oxygen that absorbs ultraviolet (UV) radiation from the sun. Ozone in the atmosphere helps protect life at Earth's surface from the harmful effects of UV radiation. However, ozone at Earth's surface is harmful. This is found in smog that hangs over some cities as pollution.

The atmosphere also contains solids, such as dust. Dust particles provide surfaces on which water vapor condenses into water droplets or ice crystals.

The atmosphere is composed of five layers, which fade from one into another. The *troposphere* (TROH•puh•sfir) is the layer closest to Earth's surface. Nearly all life on Earth exists

Math in Science
Interpret Data

Air contains many gases. Nitrogen and oxygen make up most of the volume of dry air. Living things need both of these gases. Carbon dioxide, which plants use in photosynthesis, is another gas necessary for life. How much of the atmosphere do oxygen and nitrogen make up? What percent of the atmosphere is carbon dioxide?

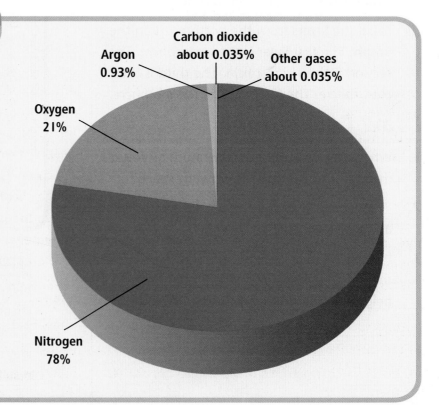

Carbon dioxide about 0.035%

Argon 0.93%

Other gases about 0.035%

Oxygen 21%

Nitrogen 78%

The topmost layer is the exosphere. It begins about 600 km (370 mi) from Earth and extends into space. Most of the molecules in this layer are hydrogen and they are very far apart. Some artificial satellites orbit in this layer.

The thermosphere extends out to about 600 km (370 mi) from Earth, where space begins. The international space station orbits in this layer.

The mesosphere starts at that point and ends at about 85 km (53 mi) from Earth.

The stratosphere extends from there to about 50 km (31 mi) above Earth's surface.

The troposphere begins at Earth's surface and ends at about 8 to 14.5 km (5 to 9 mi) above sea level.

in this layer. Almost all weather occurs here, too. The air is densest in this layer, which makes up about 75 percent of the total mass of the atmosphere. The greater the distance from Earth's surface, the thinner and colder the air is. Mount Everest's top is near the upper limit of the troposphere. Climbers on Mount Everest carry oxygen to help them breathe.

The *stratosphere* (STRAT•uh•sfir) is the next layer of the atmosphere. The air in this layer is thinner and drier than that of the troposphere. The stratosphere makes up about 24 percent of the total mass of the atmosphere. Like the troposphere, the stratosphere contains ozone. As the distance from Earth increases, the air becomes thinner, but the temperature becomes warmer.

Above the stratosphere is the *mesosphere* (MES•oh•sfir), the coldest layer of the atmosphere. Though the air here is very thin, it still produces enough friction to cause *meteoroids* to burn up. These are chunks of rock moving through space at very high speeds. You see them as *meteors*, or shooting stars.

The *thermosphere* (THER•muh•sfir) is the layer above the mesosphere. Temperatures here are extremely high—up to 1200°C (2200°F).

The *exosphere* (EKS•oh•sfir) is the outermost layer of the atmosphere. There is no exact boundary between the exosphere and space. The air simply becomes thinner and thinner as its atoms and molecules escape into space.

 MAIN IDEA AND DETAILS What are the five layers of the atmosphere?

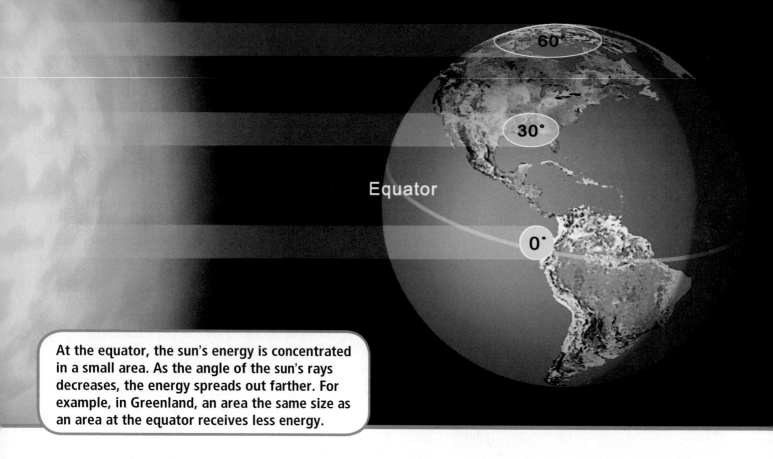

At the equator, the sun's energy is concentrated in a small area. As the angle of the sun's rays decreases, the energy spreads out farther. For example, in Greenland, an area the same size as an area at the equator receives less energy.

How the Sun Affects the Atmosphere

You may have noticed that when night falls, the outdoor air temperature usually becomes cooler. This is because the sun heats Earth's atmosphere just as it does the surface. However, some parts of Earth are warmer or colder than other parts. What causes these differences?

The sun does not heat Earth evenly. Because Earth is round, sunlight strikes Earth at different angles. It strikes the equator from almost directly overhead, at a 90° angle to the surface. This concentrates the energy over a small area and results in warm temperatures. At the equator, the air is warmed more than the air to the north or the south.

The sun's rays strike the poles indirectly, at a lower angle to the surface. This spreads out the energy over a larger area and results in lower temperatures. The level of energy hitting the equator and the poles is the same, but the energy is more spread out at the poles.

The uneven heating of Earth causes the movement of large bodies of air called air masses. The air masses over Canada are usually colder and drier than the air masses over the Gulf of Mexico. The movements of air masses cause changes in the weather.

 MAIN IDEA AND DETAILS Why is the equator warmer than the North Pole?

Let It Shine!
On a large sheet of black paper, tape down two thermometers, one in the middle and one at the upper edge. Shine a lamp a few centimeters from the middle thermometer, at a direct angle. After three minutes, read the temperatures. How does this activity model the heating of Earth by the sun?

1. MAIN IDEA AND DETAILS Draw and complete this graphic organizer.

THE ATMOSPHERE

Layers
- Ⓐ _____
- Ⓑ _____
- Ⓒ _____
- Ⓓ _____
- Ⓔ _____

Effects of the Sun
causes Ⓕ _____ heating of Earth's surface; causes movement of Ⓖ _____ , which causes changes in weather

2. SUMMARIZE Write two sentences that tell what this lesson is mainly about.

3. DRAW CONCLUSIONS Why do people who visit high mountains on vacation sometimes feel short of breath?

4. VOCABULARY Describe the structure of the atmosphere, and tell what it is composed of.

Test Prep

5. Critical Thinking Why is the dust in the atmosphere important to life on Earth?

6. How must the sun hit an area for it to receive the most concentrated energy?

- **A.** at more than a 90° angle
- **B.** at a 90° angle
- **C.** in an uneven way
- **D.** at less than a 90° angle

Links

Writing

Persuasive Writing

The ozone layer that protects Earth from harmful ultraviolet rays has been damaged by chemicals called CFCs. Find out about CFCs. Then write a **letter to the editor** of a newspaper, offering your opinion about what to do about this problem.

Math

Compare Numbers

The depth of Earth's atmosphere is about 560 km. The distance from Earth to the moon is about 385,000 km. About how many atmospheres could fit between Earth and the moon?

Social Studies

Up, Up, and Away

The first explorations of the atmosphere took place in hot-air balloons. Research the voyages of some of the early explorers. What information did they discover? Write a short story based on your findings.

 For more links and activities, go to www.hspscience.com

What Is Weather?

Fast Fact

Frightening Lightning There is enough energy in a typical lightning bolt to light one million 100-watt bulbs for a week! On average, the world receives 8,640,000 lightning bolts per day. Lightning usually occurs in connection with thunderstorms. In the Investigate, you will take a close look at some of the effects of air pressure.

Air Pressure

Materials ● hot water ● bucket ● 0.5-L plastic bottle ● cold water

Procedure

Step 1

① **CAUTION:** **Be careful around hot water.** Carefully run hot tap water into the bucket until it is about three-fourths full. Remove the cap from the bottle. Hold the bottle in the hot water so that the water comes up to its neck. Keep the bottle there for two minutes.

② Before you remove the bottle from the hot water, screw the cap on tightly.

③ Remove the bottle from the water. Pour the hot water out of the bucket, and replace it with very cold water. Without removing the cap, hold the bottle in the water. Observe what happens.

④ Remove the bottle from the water. Hold the neck of the bottle near your ear as you slowly twist off the cap. What do you hear?

Step 3

Draw Conclusions

1. When air is warmed, it expands, causing it to put pressure on its container. Was the air inside the bottle more or less dense than the air outside the bottle when you put on the cap?

2. Did cooling the air in the bottle increase or decrease the pressure inside the bottle?

3. How do you explain what you observed when you cooled the bottle?

4. **Inquiry Skill** Scientists often make inferences about things they cannot see directly. What do you infer caused the sound you heard when you opened the bottle?

Investigate Further

Use a weather map to find areas of high and low pressure. Hypothesize what the winds would be like with each type of pressure. Design and conduct a simple experiment to test your hypothesis.

VOCABULARY
air pressure p. 378
relative humidity p. 379
front p. 380
climate p. 384

SCIENCE CONCEPTS
▶ how air masses affect weather
▶ what factors affect climate

 READING FOCUS SKILL
CAUSE AND EFFECT Look for causes of weather changes.

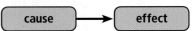

Air Masses

Recall that air masses are large bodies of air. Their temperature and humidity are affected by the areas over which they form. *Humidity* is the amount of water vapor in the air. For example, the Gulf of Mexico is a warm sea. An air mass that forms over this area is warm and wet. Air masses can cover huge areas.

Air masses affect the weather of an area. *Weather* is the condition of the atmosphere at a particular time and place. Maritime air masses are humid because they form over the ocean. Continental air masses are dry because they form over land. Tropical air masses are warm because they form over the tropics. Polar air masses are cold because they form over Arctic areas. Air masses are named according to their temperature and humidity. An air mass that forms over the Gulf of Mexico is a tropical maritime air mass.

Gravity pulls the gases in the atmosphere toward Earth, causing the air to push down on Earth's surface. **Air pressure** is the force of the weight of air pressing down on a unit of area.

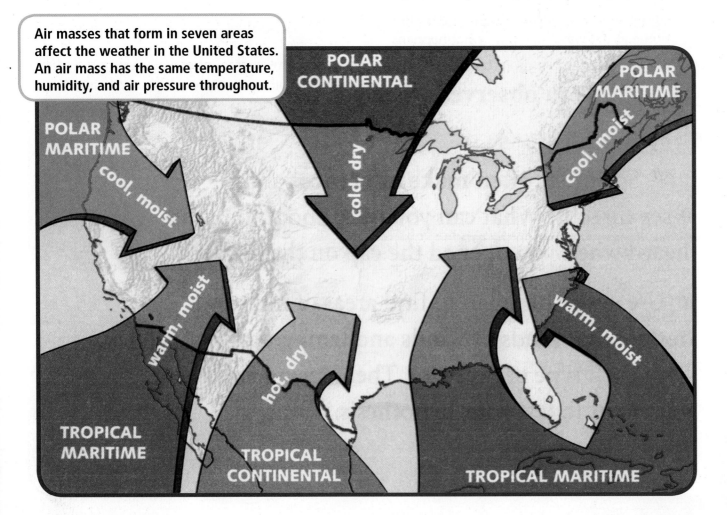

Air masses that form in seven areas affect the weather in the United States. An air mass has the same temperature, humidity, and air pressure throughout.

POLAR CONTINENTAL

POLAR MARITIME

POLAR MARITIME — cool, moist

cold, dry

cool, moist

warm, moist

hot, dry

warm, moist

TROPICAL MARITIME

TROPICAL CONTINENTAL

TROPICAL MARITIME

Fog is actually a stratus cloud that rests on or near the ground.

An instrument called a *hygrometer* measures the amount of water vapor in the air.

Differences in air pressure at Earth's surface are caused by the unequal heating of Earth. Warm air masses have fewer air molecules than cold air masses with the same volume. This means that warm air masses are less dense. They have a lower air pressure than cold air masses. A change in air pressure is a sign that a different air mass is moving into an area. The result is a change in weather.

Some air masses bring rain or snow. When air masses hold as much water vapor as possible, the water vapor condenses to form clouds. The water droplets in clouds grow larger and heavier until they fall.

Air that is saturated, or is holding as much water vapor as possible, has a relative humidity of 100 percent. **Relative humidity** is a comparison of the actual amount of water vapor in the air to the amount of water vapor that would be in the air if it were saturated. Relative humidity is expressed as a percent.

Relative humidity depends on two factors—the temperature and the amount of water vapor available. If the amount of water vapor stays the same, reducing the temperature will raise the relative humidity. Increasing the temperature will lower it.

 CAUSE AND EFFECT What causes differences in air pressure at Earth's surface?

Insta-Lab

Air Action

Attach an empty balloon to the end of an empty thread spool. Blow up another balloon, and twist the neck to keep the air in. Attach the opening to the other end of the spool, and then untwist the neck. What happens to each balloon? Why?

Weather Fronts

As air masses move across the surface of the Earth, they may collide. These collisions usually happen halfway between one of the poles and the equator. Most of the United States lies in one of those regions. The two air masses do not mix much when they collide. Each keeps its own temperature, humidity, and air pressure. As a result, a boundary forms. The boundary between two air masses that collide is called a **front**. The air masses are usually moving at different speeds. The faster air mass pushes against the slower one. No matter which air mass pushes, the warmer, less-dense air will always be pushed up over the cooler, denser air. The result is that the weather changes.

Scientists classify fronts by the characteristics and movements of the two air masses. When a warm air mass moves into an area of cooler air, the boundary between the air masses is called a *warm front*. The warmer, less-dense air slides up over the cooler, denser air in a wide, gentle slope. As the warm air cools, its relative humidity increases, and the water vapor condenses into clouds. A warm front usually brings a steady rain.

When a cold air mass moves into an area of warmer air, the boundary between the air masses is called a *cold front*. The colder, denser air slides under the warmer, less-dense air. As a result, the warmer air is pushed up. As it cools, the water vapor condenses and forms clouds that bring precipitation.

Cold air masses can move rapidly. When they do, they push warm air up so quickly that heavy clouds form. Water vapor condenses in the clouds, and thunderstorms often result.

The boundary between two air masses that are not moving against each other is called a *stationary front*. Some of the warmer air mixes with the cooler air, causing clouds to form. As the clouds are pushed upward, they cool and produce light rain or snow. Because the front is not moving, the precipitation can last for a long time.

 CAUSE AND EFFECT What causes thunderstorms?

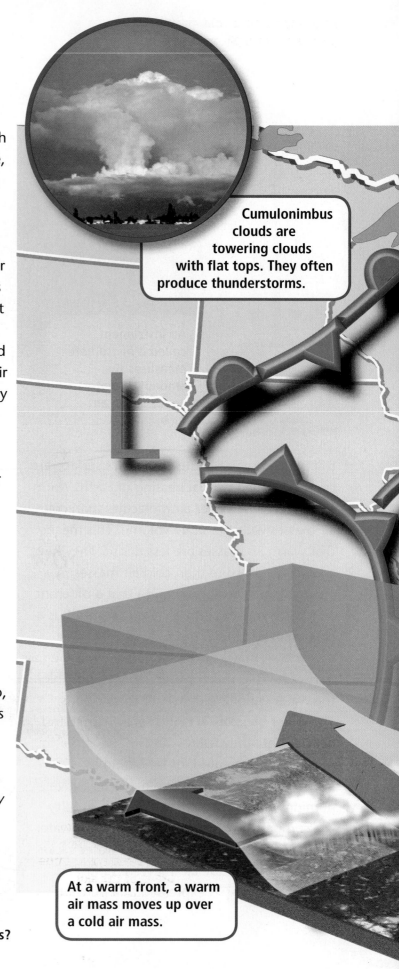

Cumulonimbus clouds are towering clouds with flat tops. They often produce thunderstorms.

At a warm front, a warm air mass moves up over a cold air mass.

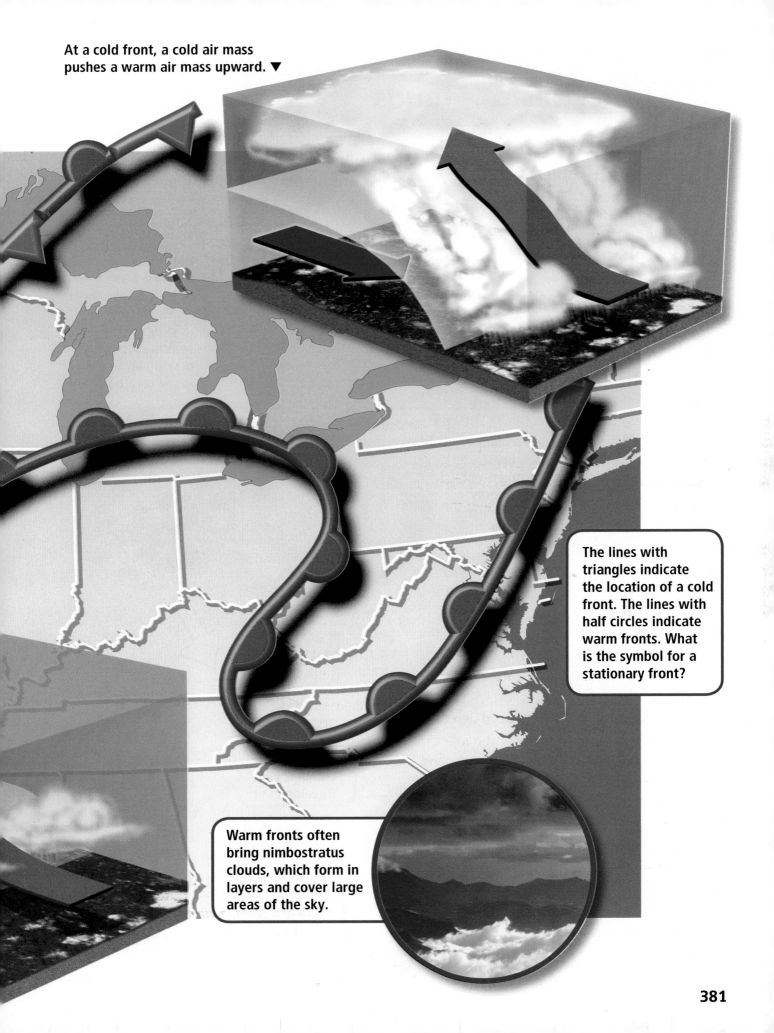

At a cold front, a cold air mass pushes a warm air mass upward. ▼

The lines with triangles indicate the location of a cold front. The lines with half circles indicate warm fronts. What is the symbol for a stationary front?

Warm fronts often bring nimbostratus clouds, which form in layers and cover large areas of the sky.

381

Types of Clouds

A cloud is a mass of tiny water droplets or ice crystals visible in the atmosphere. Clouds form when water vapor condenses on the surfaces of tiny particles in the air. Clouds are classified by their appearance and their height above sea level.

Cirrus

Cirrocumulus

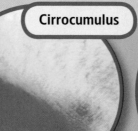

Cirrostratus

High clouds are made mostly of ice crystals. Cirrus clouds are usually seen in fair weather, but they may signal a change in the weather.

Mid-level clouds are made up of water droplets and are white to gray. They may produce light snow or drizzling rain.

Altostratus

Altocumulus

Stratus

Low clouds are made up of water droplets. Stratus clouds produce gray days. If there is rain, the cloud is a nimbostratus.

As cumulus clouds develop upward, they form cumulonimbus (kyoo•myoo•loh•NIM•buhs) clouds. These towering clouds bring thunderstorms. They may also produce hail.

Cumulus

Cumulus with Development

Cumulonimbus

For more links and activities, go to
www.hspscience.com

Polar Easterlies
These winds move cold air from both poles toward the equator.

Prevailing Westerlies
These winds blow toward the poles, in a direction opposite to that of the trade winds. They affect most of the weather in the United States.

Trade Winds
Warm air from the equator moves at high altitudes over the Atlantic Ocean and other oceans to about the 30° north and south latitudes. There it cools, descends, and begins to flow back toward the equator. These air movements are known as the trade winds. When the winds meet near the equator, they form a relatively calm area over the ocean called the *doldrums,* which are caused by the rising movement of air rather than by the horizontal movement.

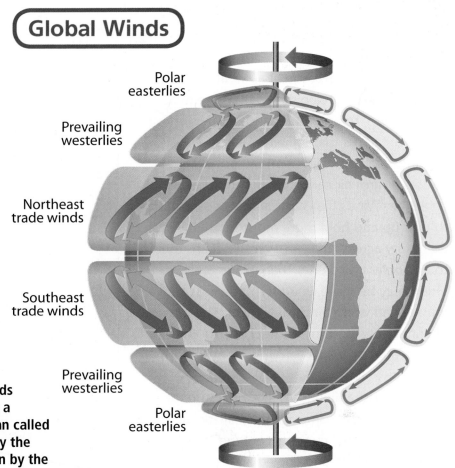

Global Winds

Polar easterlies

Prevailing westerlies

Northeast trade winds

Southeast trade winds

Prevailing westerlies

Polar easterlies

Global Wind Patterns

Wind is the movement of air from an area of higher pressure to an area of lower pressure. Recall that these differences in air pressure are caused by the uneven heating of the Earth. As air cools, air pressure increases. As air warms, air pressure decreases.

Global winds are winds that blow across long distances in predictable patterns. These winds carry air masses from one region to another. Each of these winds always blows in the same direction. Global winds do not follow a straight path as they blow from the poles toward the equator or from the equator toward the poles. They curve clockwise in the Northern Hemisphere and counterclockwise in the Southern Hemisphere because of Earth's rotation on its axis. This curving of the winds is called the *Coriolis effect*.

A *jet stream* is a band of very strong wind that blows from east to west high in the atmosphere, usually above 6000 m (20,000 ft). Jet streams form along the upper boundaries of large air masses when warm air from the tropics meets cold air from the poles. The sudden temperature change causes a huge difference in air pressure. This results in wind speeds of up to 498 km/hr (310 mi/hr).

Global winds and jet streams can affect local weather. For example, the prevailing westerlies move from the Pacific Ocean to the Pacific Coast of the United States. They bring moist, mild weather. The westerlies bring most of the weather changes across the country from west to east. During the winter, a jet stream often dips south into the United States, bringing cold weather from Canada.

 CAUSE AND EFFECT What causes wind?

383

Factors That Influence Climate

Climate is the average of all weather conditions in an area over a period of time. Precipitation, temperature, and ocean currents are three factors that influence climate.

Winds affect precipitation by moving air masses. Warm air carries more moisture than cooler air. Winds that blow across oceans tend to pick up and hold more moisture than winds that blow across land. Areas near oceans tend to be cooler and wetter than inland areas. There may be more cloud formations as cool air masses and warm air masses meet. The interiors of continents tend to be drier because they are not affected by winds carrying moisture from the oceans.

Oceans also influence the temperature of an area. Warm ocean currents heat the air above them. Cool currents cool the air. Winds blow the warmed and cooled air onshore, affecting the climate along coastal areas. The warm Gulf Stream begins in the warm waters south of Florida. It carries warm air masses near the United Kingdom and northern Europe. Therefore, the winter temperatures onshore are somewhat mild. They are able to cultivate plants that require mild temperatures such as azaleas.

A unique weather event takes place in the central and eastern Pacific Ocean every three to seven years. This event, known as *El Niño,* results from unusual warming of surface water in that area. The warmer water pushes energy and moisture into the atmosphere, changing global wind and rainfall patterns. In the past, El Niño years have brought tornadoes to Florida, mudslides to California, smog to Indonesia, and forest fires to Brazil.

Other events—some as sudden as volcanic eruptions and asteroid impacts and others as gradual as glacier formation—also influence climate. Even humans have caused climate changes by building large cities and by polluting the air and water.

CAUSE AND EFFECT What effects have El Niño events had on South America?

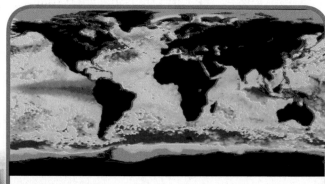

A thermograph continuously records temperatures. It can help scientists predict and track weather disturbances such as an El Niño.

The changes in weather patterns that an El Niño brings can spell disaster for some parts of the world. While South America suffered flooding in 1982–1983, Australia and Indonesia experienced severe drought.

1. CAUSE AND EFFECT Copy and complete this graphic organizer.

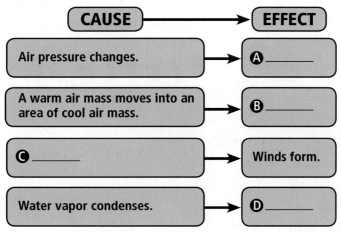

CAUSE → **EFFECT**

- Air pressure changes. → Ⓐ _____
- A warm air mass moves into an area of cool air mass. → Ⓑ _____
- Ⓒ _____ → Winds form.
- Water vapor condenses. → Ⓓ _____

2. SUMMARIZE Summarize this lesson in a short paragraph. Begin the first sentence with *Weather is caused by . . .*

3. DRAW CONCLUSIONS Why should a farmer in New Zealand be concerned that an El Niño event is predicted in Peru?

4. VOCABULARY Write a sentence that explains what a front is.

Test Prep

5. Critical Thinking You see cumulonimbus clouds forming. What can you conclude has caused them?

6. Which term describes an air mass that forms over land?
- **A.** continental
- **B.** maritime
- **C.** polar
- **D.** tropical

Links

Writing

Expressive Writing

A haiku is a poem with three lines. The first and third lines each have five syllables, and the second has seven syllables. Write a **haiku** about the weather. It should have a seasonal word as part of the poem.

Math

Solve a Problem

Warm air cools 15°C (27°F) for every 305 m (1000 feet) it is pushed up over a cold air mass. If air with a temperature of 27°C (80°F) is forced up 1525 m (5000 feet), what is the new temperature? Show the steps you used to find the solution.

Art

Cloudy Impressions

Use cloth, cotton, and other materials to make a display showing the different types of clouds. Use library resources to find the names of other clouds not in your text. To go with the display, write a report in which you identify the weather the clouds would bring.

 For more links and activities, go to www.hspscience.com

How Can You Track Severe Storms?

Fast Fact

The Big Ones In 2004, four hurricanes came ashore in Florida in less than six weeks. They resulted in deaths, injuries, and property damage. Meteorologists track hurricanes and predict their paths so they can warn people to evacuate or to prepare for these powerful storms. In the Investigate, you will use data to plot the track of a hurricane.

Tracking Hurricanes

Materials
- hurricane tracking map
- forecast/advisory for Hurricane Chase
- history table for Hurricane Chase
- 3 colored pencils

Procedure

1. On the hurricane tracking map, plot the path of Hurricane Chase, using the data from the history table and the forecast/advisory. Use a regular pencil to draw a small circle on the map for each location listed in the history table.

2. Your first circles should show Chase as a tropical depression. Fill in the tropical depression circles with one color. When winds become stronger than 39 mi/hr, a tropical depression is classified as a tropical storm and is given a name. Write *Tropical Storm Chase* under the place where the tropical depression becomes a tropical storm. Fill in the tropical storm circles with another color.

3. When winds become greater than 74 mi/hr, a tropical storm becomes a hurricane. Write *Hurricane Chase* under the place where Chase reaches hurricane strength. Use your third color to fill in the hurricane circles.

Draw Conclusions

1. **Observe** the track of the storm on the map. What is the general pattern of the storm's direction and wind speed?

2. **Inquiry Skill** When and where do you predict the storm will hit land? Use the tracking map and the latest data.

History of Hurricane Chase			
Date and Time	**Latitude**	**Longitude**	**Maximum Wind Speed**
08/11 2:00 UT*	22.0°N	66.0°W	35 mi/hr
08/11 7:00 UT	22.5°N	67.0°W	35 mi/hr
08/11 14:00 UT	24.5°N	67.5°W	40 mi/hr
08/11 22:00 UT	25.0°N	68.0°W	45 mi/hr
08/12 1:00 UT	26.5°N	68.5°W	50 mi/hr
08/12 7:00 UT	28.5°N	70.5°W	60 mi/hr
08/12 13:00 UT	30.0°N	73.5°W	70 mi/hr
08/12 19:00 UT	31.0°N	75.0°W	75 mi/hr
08/13 1:00 UT	31.0°N	76.0°W	85 mi/hr

Forecast/Advisory
BULLETIN

HURRICANE CHASE FORECAST/ADVISORY NUMBER 12

NATIONAL WEATHER SERVICE MIAMI FL 13:00 UT

HURRICANE CENTER LOCATED NEAR 32°N, 78°W AT 13:00 UT AT 8/13 PRESENT MOVEMENT TOWARD THE NORTHWEST AT 20 MI PER HR

*UT means Universal Time and is the same as Greenwich Mean Time. In this 24-hour system, the time one hour after 12:00 noon is 13:00.

Investigate Further

Find out what happens when hurricanes cross islands in the Caribbean. Draw a conclusion as to whether they will continue as hurricanes.

Reading in Science

VOCABULARY
thunderstorm p. 390
tornado p. 391
hurricane p. 392
blizzard p. 394

SCIENCE CONCEPTS
▶ how meteorologists study weather conditions
▶ how severe storms form

READING FOCUS SKILL
MAIN IDEA AND DETAILS Look for the details that describe each severe storm.

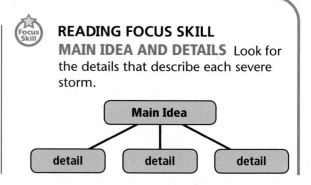

Weather Forecasts

Weather forecasts help people decide what to wear and how the weather will affect their plans. A *forecast* is a prediction about the weather. Forecasts are accurate up to about three to five days into the future.

Meteorologists are scientists who study weather conditions to provide forecasts.

Meteorologists use instruments developed to measure conditions in the atmosphere. You already know that a thermometer measures temperatures. Meteorologists use barometers to measure air pressure. They use anemometers to measure wind speed.

Meteorologists also use more complex equipment. Advances in technology have increased the accuracy of forecasts. Weather

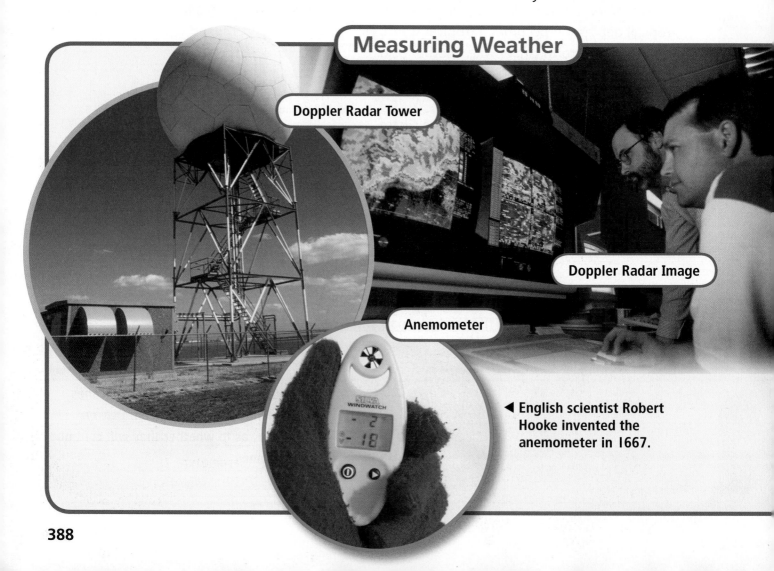

Measuring Weather

Doppler Radar Tower

Doppler Radar Image

Anemometer

◀ English scientist Robert Hooke invented the anemometer in 1667.

balloons and weather satellites collect data high up in the troposphere. They provide information on weather patterns and storms that can't be obtained at ground level.

Weather balloons and weather satellites carry instruments that record air pressure, temperature, and humidity. Satellite images show how an area's weather is changing. The images, which show clouds and storms, are sent to meteorological centers around the world. Doppler radar uses radio waves to detect wind and the movements of rain, snow, and ice. It tracks the movement of severe storms, such as tornadoes and hurricanes. The collected data is analyzed by weather professionals, and updates are sent to local weather stations.

Meteorologists use weather data to make maps. A *weather map* is a map that shows recent weather conditions across a large area. Symbols on the map indicate storms, regions of high and low pressure, fronts, and other weather conditions. Meteorologists use weather maps to make forecasts.

MAIN IDEA AND DETAILS What equipment is used to collect weather data beyond the troposphere?

Insta-Lab

What's the Weather?

Find a copy of yesterday's weather map in a local newspaper. Interpret the map. Compare the three-day forecast with the weather that actually occurs in your area. Was the weather forecast accurate? Why or why not?

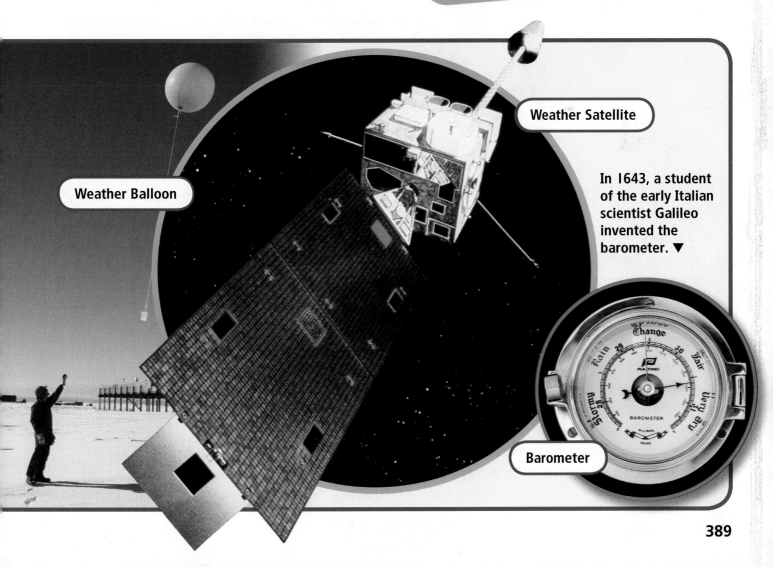

Weather Satellite

Weather Balloon

In 1643, a student of the early Italian scientist Galileo invented the barometer. ▼

Barometer

A large mass of warm air moves up rapidly. Large amounts of water vapor condense to form thick cumulonimbus clouds. Heavy rain falls, causing a downward movement of air.

A Doppler radar image shows the size and location of a thunderstorm.

Thunderstorms and Tornadoes

At any time, about 2000 thunderstorms are occurring on Earth. A **thunderstorm** is a strong storm with rain, lightning, and thunder.

A thunderstorm begins to form when warm, humid air moves upward rapidly. The sun heats a place on Earth's surface, which, in turn, warms the air mass above it. Then a cold front may push under the warm air mass, or wind may force it upward. The higher surrounding air is colder than the rising air mass.

As the warm air cools, the water vapor in it condenses into water droplets, which form a cumulonimbus cloud. Soon the water droplets

become heavy enough to fall as rain. The falling rain pulls in cool air with it. Winds blow both upward and downward in the cloud.

Negative electric charges build up in the bottom of the cloud. The charges travel through the air in a lightning discharge. The air along the path of a lightning bolt is extremely hot. The intense heat makes the air expand so fast that sound waves are produced. You hear the sound as thunder. Most of the lightning occurs at the beginning and at the end of a thunderstorm.

Most thunderstorms are over within an hour. The rain and cool air moving downward through the clouds prevent more warm air from moving up into the cloud. Sometimes, however, the cool air rushing down to Earth's surface pushes more warm air up, causing another cumulonimbus cloud to form.

Whenever forecasters detect a strong thunderstorm, they look for another severe weather event. A **tornado** is a violently rotating column of air that extends downward from thunderclouds and touches the ground. Tornadoes form in fewer than one percent of thunderstorms. A tornado may also form from the severe thunderstorms spun off by a hurricane.

A tornado starts when winds spin a column of air that bulges from the bottom of a cumulonimbus cloud. Strong updrafts, or rising air, are already present inside this bulge. Next, warm, humid air is pulled into the often funnel-shaped column. The air spins so fast that an area of very low pressure forms in the center. The swirling funnel starts to descend. Because of the low pressure, nearby air on the ground rushes into the funnel. The air in the funnel rotates upward around the center, joining the storm above.

The wind speed in a tornado can reach 400 km/hr (250 mi/hr) or more. The force of the tornado's winds destroys houses, cars, and anything else in its path. The greatest danger is flying debris, or wreckage.

These violent storms can last from a few minutes to a few hours. Their storm path is usually quite narrow. They are more difficult to predict than other storms. However, meteorologists can usually issue warnings that give people enough time to take cover.

 MAIN IDEA AND DETAILS Why do most thunderstorms stop?

Compare the Doppler radar image of this tornado with the Doppler radar image of a thunderstorm.

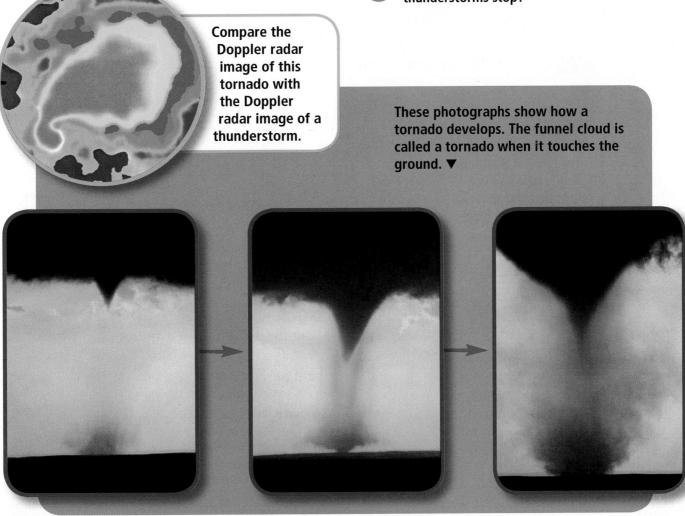

These photographs show how a tornado develops. The funnel cloud is called a tornado when it touches the ground. ▼

Hurricanes

If you have seen pictures of hurricanes bending tall palm trees, then you have an idea of the power of a hurricane. A **hurricane** is a large, rotating tropical storm system with wind speeds of at least 119 km/hr (74 mi/hr).

A hurricane might start as a low-pressure area over the Atlantic Ocean off the coast of Africa. The storm is first called a tropical depression, because the air pressure is low, or depressed. As winds blow into the low-pressure area, Earth's rotation causes them to rotate, or spiral, around that area.

If the winds reach a constant speed of 63 km/hr (39 mi/hr), the tropical depression is called a tropical storm and given a name. About half of the tropical storms that form each year develop into hurricanes.

The eye of a hurricane is a calm center. It is caused by dry, cool air pulled down from above. Around the eye is the eye wall, the most intense part of the storm. The warm, wet air that rushes to the center of a hurricane is pulled upward in the eye wall. As the air travels upward, it causes low pressure at the surface. This pulls in more air. The water vapor that is being pulled upward condenses into rain, releasing heat that strengthens the storm. Heat and moisture from below increase the energy of both the upward-moving and the downward-moving air.

Pushed ahead of the storm, the ocean's surface can rise up to 10 m (33 ft) high. These rises are called *storm surges*. They can be as wide as 80 to 161 km (50 to 100 mi). Storm surges can smash into the coast, causing great

Warm, wet air is pulled into the base and the sides of a hurricane.

The spiral is made up of cumulus clouds that can tower 12 km (7 mi) into the atmosphere.

In the hurricane's center, known as the eye, the winds are quiet and no rain falls.

The hurricane is pushed by winds at 15 to 40 km/hr (9 to 25 mi/hr).

The hurricane's fastest winds rotate around the eye in the eye wall.

harm to people and property. Other hurricane dangers include high winds, flooding, and tornadoes.

Large amounts of warm, humid air keep hurricanes in motion. A typical hurricane may be as large as 483 km (300 mi) across. It can travel for thousands of kilometers and last for more than a week. In time it will reach cooler seas or move across land. Because the air is cooler and less humid there, the hurricane will at last die out.

Hurricane is the name given to a tropical cyclone in the North Atlantic Ocean, the North Pacific Ocean (east of the international date line), and the South Pacific Ocean (east of 160° E). In the Northwest Pacific Ocean (west of the date line), a tropical cyclone is called a *typhoon*. When you hear or read

about a typhoon hitting Japan or Bangladesh, you will know that it is the same kind of storm we call a hurricane in the United States.

Because meteorologists can track hurricanes from the time they form, people who may be in the storm's path can be given plenty of warning. People living near the coasts may have to evacuate their homes until the hurricane danger has passed. People must leave mobile homes and manufactured housing, which can be severely damaged. Hurricane shelters are opened for those who have no safe place in which to wait out the storm.

Focus Skill **MAIN IDEA AND DETAILS** What are three ways hurricanes cause damage?

Compare this Doppler radar image of a hurricane to the images of the thunderstorm and the tornado.

This satellite photograph taken above the Gulf Coast shows how large a hurricane can become.

North Atlantic Hurricanes August to October, 1950–2001

Legend: La Niña, El Niño, Neutral

Y-axis: Number of Hurricanes (0 to 12)
X-axis: Year (1950 to 2000)

The blizzard record for amount of snow is held by Mount Shasta, California. In 1959 a blizzard dropped more than 480 cm (189 in.) of snow there.

Severe blizzards have winds of at least 72 km/hr (45 mi/hr). They also have temperatures of less than −12°C (10°F).

Blizzards

A winter storm with strong winds and large amounts of heavy, blowing snow is a **blizzard**. The wind blows for at least three hours at 56 km/hr (35 mi/hr). Visibility, or the ability to see, is very low—usually less than ¼ mile and often nearly zero.

Blizzards, like other storms, develop because of differences in air pressure. Strong winds blow the falling snow and also pick up snow that has fallen to the ground. Traveling by car during a blizzard can be dangerous because of possible "whiteout" conditions. When a driver can see nothing but white snow, it is impossible to tell where the road is and where other drivers are. It's easy to become lost or to run into a ditch or other cars.

People who live in the northern parts of the United States know the risks of this severe weather. They know that if they must go out on the roads in a blizzard, they need to take blankets, extra clothing, food, water, flashlights and batteries, and flares that they can use to signal rescuers. If they leave their vehicles to seek help, they risk frostbite and hypothermia. *Frostbite* is injury to the skin from freezing. *Hypothermia* is a condition in which the body temperature falls dangerously low. Both of these conditions require the care of a doctor to prevent permanent damage or death.

 MAIN IDEA AND DETAILS What are the dangers of blizzards to people?

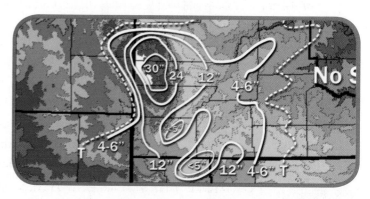

▲ This Doppler radar image shows a blizzard in progress.

1. MAIN IDEA AND DETAILS Copy and complete this graphic organizer.

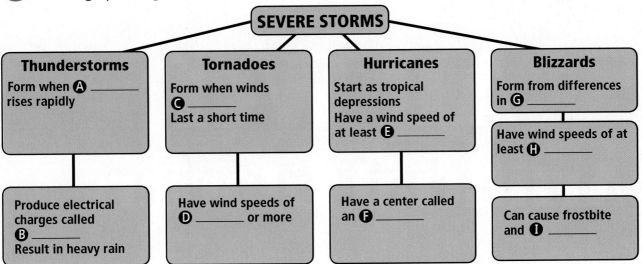

SEVERE STORMS

Thunderstorms
Form when **A** _____ rises rapidly

Tornadoes
Form when winds **C** _____
Last a short time

Hurricanes
Start as tropical depressions
Have a wind speed of at least **E** _____

Blizzards
Form from differences in **G** _____
Have wind speeds of at least **H** _____

Produce electrical charges called B _____
Result in heavy rain

Have wind speeds of D _____ or more

Have a center called an F _____

Can cause frostbite and I _____

2. SUMMARIZE Use the graphic organizer to write a summary that describes severe storms.

3. DRAW CONCLUSIONS Why is a mobile home an unsafe place to be during a tornado?

4. VOCABULARY Use *forecast* and *weather map* in a sentence that explains both.

Test Prep

5. Critical Thinking How have Doppler radar and satellites increased the accuracy of weather forecasts?

6. Where do hurricanes form?
  A. on shore   **C.** over oceans
  B. over land   **D.** in the stratosphere

Links

Writing

Expository Writing
Find out about waterspouts. Write and illustrate a short **magazine article** about them. Explain what waterspouts are, tell how they form, and describe their effects.

Math

Use Decimals
Sound travels more slowly than light. If you see lightning and hear the thunder 5 seconds later, the flash was about 1.6 km away. If you see a lightning flash and hear thunder 12 seconds later, how far away is the storm? Show the formula you used to answer.

Health

Storm Safety Steps
Research steps people can take to protect themselves in severe storms. Make a pamphlet of tips for each type of storm, illustrate it, and share it with your family.

For more links and activities, go to www.hspscience.com

All Wet
with
Artificial Glaciers

Less than an inch of rain falls each year in India's Ladakh region, in the northwest part of the nation. As a result of such arid conditions, farmers there have a tough time finding reliable sources of water to raise crops.

The one source of water farmers can rely on is meltwater from nearby glaciers. Glaciers are large masses of compacted ice and snow. But meltwater is only available in the late summer when temperatures warm up enough to melt the ice and snow. To use the water, farmers had to store it in special buildings far from their fields.

Now, however, retired engineer Chewang Norphel has brought the glacier meltwater closer and made access to it easier for farmers.

A Long Thin Glacier

To help farmers water their crops, Norphel invented an artificial glacier. Norphel began by diverting water from streams into a low-lying area. That area is in the shadow of a nearby mountain.

The engineer then placed half-inch-wide iron pipes connecting the stream to the low-lying area. Water from the stream would collect in the pipes during the day and then freeze at night. As more water seeps in, it pushes out the frozen blocks. This keeps happening in a continuous cycle, and the frozen blocks form layers upon layers of ice, just as a glacier would.

Irrigation Water

In March and April, the "glaciers" begin to melt and farmers can then draw water from the glaciers to irrigate their crops. The longest artificial glacier was about 304 meters (1000 feet) long and 45 meters (150 feet) wide, with an average depth of about 1.2 meters (4 feet). Norphel said a glacier that size could supply water to a village of 700 thirsty people during dry periods.

Throughout the region, Norphel has constructed several artificial glaciers.

Some people think the technique might one day bring relief to other water-starved regions in other areas of Asia or in Africa.

Water Works

"I saw a lot of water just running off and getting wasted," Norphel said. "Then it occurred to me. Why not try [to] make artificial glaciers in the vicinity of the villages so that local farmers [can] get...water when they most need it."

Think About It

1. Why could farmers in the Ladakh region use water from glaciers only during the summer?
2. Why is it important that the artificial glacier sit in a low-lying area in the shadow of a hill or mountain?

Find out more! Log on to
www.hspscience.com

It's All About Weather

For Marshall Shepherd, it all started with a bee sting. When he was young, Shepherd was convinced he was going to be an *entomologist*, a scientist who studies insects. While conducting a study on bees, however, Shepherd was stung. He quickly learned that he is highly allergic to bee stings. Just as quickly, his interest in science turned elsewhere. After completing a sixth-grade science project about predicting the weather, his career path was set.

Shepherd went on to become the first African American to receive a Ph.D. in meteorology from Florida State University. Today, Shepherd is a *meteorologist*, a scientist who studies weather conditions. Shepherd works for the National Aeronautics and Space Administration (NASA) and uses computers and satellites to study rainfall, clouds, and hurricanes.

Career Meteorologist

Meteorologists are not just people you watch on television to find out if you should take an umbrella to school. The weather experts are scientists who use complex computer models and historical data to study weather patterns over many years. By gathering all this information, meteorologists can predict the weather for tomorrow or for next year.

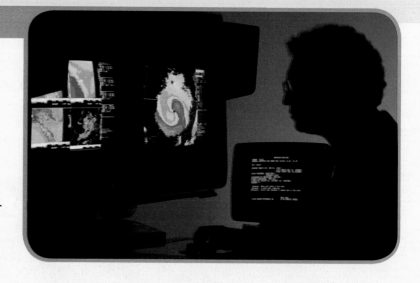

You Can Do It!

Quick and Easy Project

Bottle Tornado

Materials
- 2 clear plastic 2-L bottles
- water
- duct tape
- scissors
- pencil

Procedure

1. Fill one bottle with water.
2. Tightly cover the opening of the filled bottle with a square of duct tape. Use the pencil to poke a hole in the tape.
3. Turn the second bottle upside down over the neck of the taped bottle. Tape the two openings of the bottles together with duct tape.
4. Turn the bottles upside down so that the filled bottle is on top. Observe what happens.

Draw Conclusions

How is the action you watched in the bottles like the action of a tornado? How do you think changing the size of the hole in the duct tape would affect what happens in the bottle?

Design Your Own Investigation

Design a Weather Station

Meteorologists set up weather stations with instruments that will help them measure and observe the weather. Think about the conditions of the weather that meteorologists measure. Then design and make instruments for your own weather station. Decide how many times a day you will observe and record the weather. Use your weather station for two weeks, and report the results.

Vocabulary Review

Match the words to the correct definitions below. The page numbers tell you where to look in the chapter if you need help.

atmosphere p. 372   **climate** p. 384
air pressure p. 378   **tornado** p. 391
front p. 380   **hurricane** p. 392

1. A large, rotating tropical storm is a _____.

2. The boundary between two air masses that collide is a _____ .

3. The layers of air that surround Earth make up the _____ .

4. The weight of air pressing down on an area is _____ .

5. A violently rotating column of air that touches the ground is a _____ .

6. The usual weather conditions a place has over time make up its _____ .

Check Understanding

Write the letter of the best choice.

7. Which is the most common gas in the atmosphere?
   A. carbon dioxide
   B. hydrogen
   C. nitrogen
   D. oxygen

8. How many layers are in the atmosphere?
   F. 3   **H.** 5
   G. 4   **J.** 7

9. Which happens as you go up into the atmosphere?
   A. Air pressure increases.
   B. Air pressure decreases.

C. Air pressure first increases and then decreases.
D. Air pressure first decreases and then increases.

10. Which is the primary cause of air masses?
    F. high relative humidity over the poles
    G. low pressure near the equator
    H. uneven heating of Earth's surface
    J. the formation of large tropical storms

11. **MAIN IDEA AND DETAILS** Which statement is **true** about air pressure?
    A. It is the same throughout an air mass.
    B. It is the same everywhere on Earth.
    C. It is lower in cold air than in warm air.
    D. It increases with height above Earth.

12. **CAUSE AND EFFECT** Which is an effect of warm air from the tropics meeting cold air from the poles high in the atmosphere?
    F. stationary front   **H.** jet stream
    G. air mass   **J.** air pressure

13. Which does the illustration below show?

    A. unequal heating of Earth
    B. a cold front
    C. a tornado
    D. global winds

14. Which kind of cloud would you **most** likely see in fair weather?
     F. altocumulus
     G. cirrus
     H. cumulonimbus
     J. nimbostratus

15. Why is dust an important part of the atmosphere?
     A. It keeps ozone in the atmosphere.
     B. It protects the Earth from ultraviolet rays.
     C. It provides a surface on which water vapor can condense.
     D. It keeps the temperature of the troposphere low.

16. Which labeled layer of the atmosphere is the **highest** layer that will sustain life?

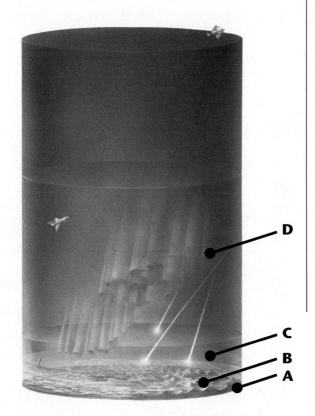

     F. A   H. C
     G. B   J. D

Inquiry Skills

17. Infer why most thunderstorms occur in the afternoon.

18. A hurricane is moving from over the ocean to over land. Predict what will happen next.

Critical Thinking

19. Hot-air balloons that carry people travel at fairly low altitudes. What are two reasons for this?

20. Weather never stays the same for very long. Several factors affect weather changes.
     Part A Explain what causes air pressure in an area to change.
     Part B It is a hot summer day, and a cold air mass is moving quickly into the Great Plains. Explain what you think will happen, step by step, once the cold air mass reaches the warm air above the Great Plains.

Vocabulary

rotation
axis
revolution
eclipse
tide
new moon
first quarter
full moon
third quarter
asteroid
satellite
meteor
comet
galaxy

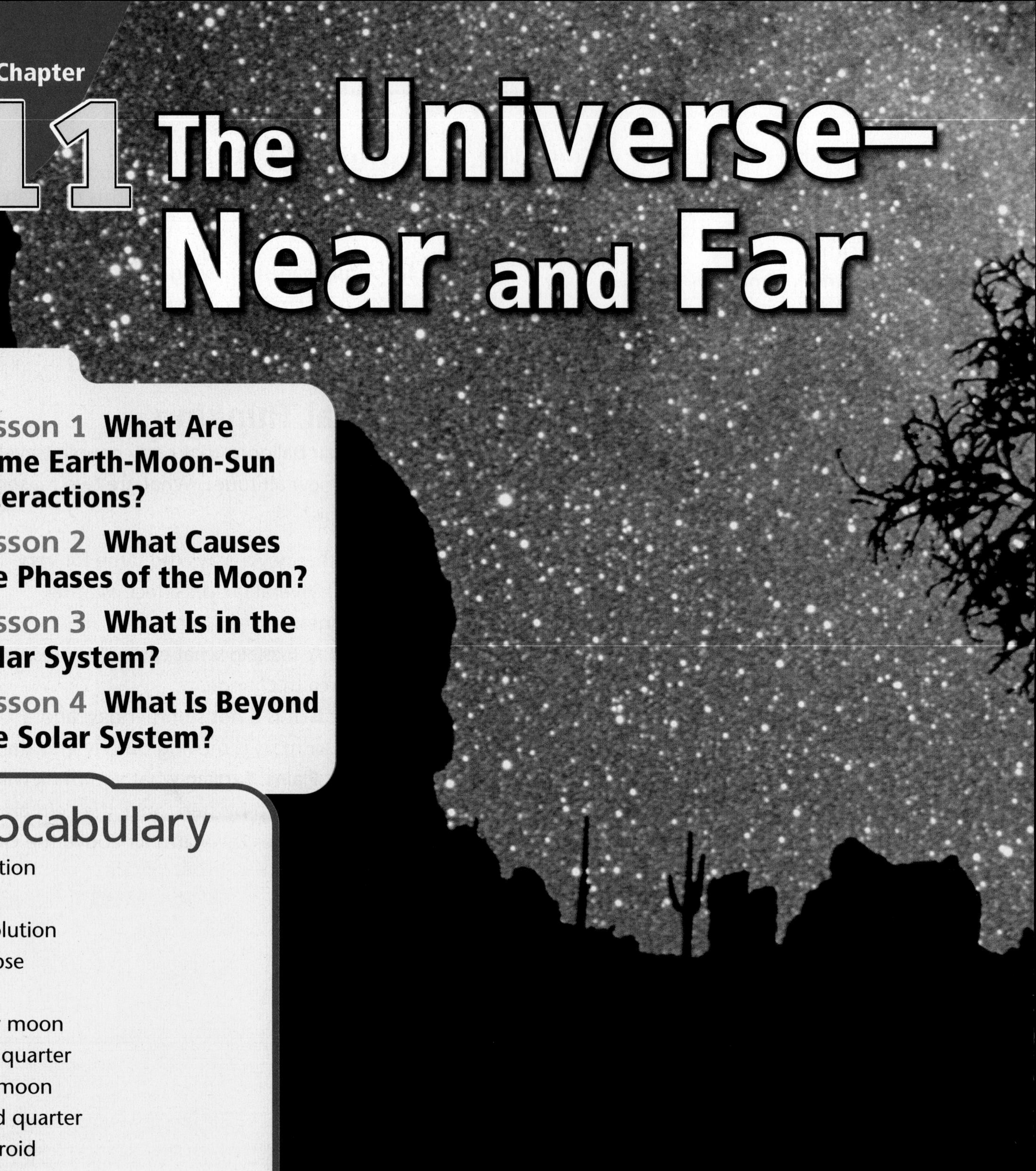

What do YOU wonder?

In some parts of the country you can see the Milky Way galaxy on a clear night. Until telescopes were invented about 300 years ago, no one realized that the Milky Way was made of stars. Why do you think that you can't see the Milky Way galaxy from a city at night? How many stars could you count without using a telescope?

What Are Some Earth-Moon-Sun Interactions?

Fast Fact

Ancient Astronomy The builders of Stonehenge, in southern England, were aware of the ways Earth's moon and the sun appear to move. They brought huge stones hundreds of miles to build Stonehenge at a carefully chosen point on Earth's surface. There, the positions of the moon and the sun in relation to the stones may have helped farmers know when to plant and harvest crops. In the Investigate, you will model the orbit of a planet around the sun.

Sunrise at Stonehenge on the first day of summer

Modeling a Planetary Orbit

Materials
- I sheet of light-colored construction paper
- thick section of newspaper
- pencil
- metric ruler
- 2 pushpins
- string (35–40 cm)
- coin

Procedure

1. Use the newspaper to make a thick, flat surface on a table. Put the construction paper on top.

2. On the construction paper, make two dots that measure 10 cm apart. Stick a pushpin into each dot.

3. Tie the ends of the string together to make a loop. Place the loop around the pushpins. The loop should be loose.

4. Put the point of the pencil inside the loop, and pull until the string is tight. You may need a partner to hold the pushpins down as you pull the string into a triangular shape. Move the point all the way around the pushpins, keeping the string tight as you draw a line. You are making a model of an ellipse (an oval) with a focus, or fixed point, at each pushpin. An ellipse has two foci (FOH•sy).

5. Place the coin with its center on the ellipse. Trace the coin to represent a planet. Draw the sun at one focus of the ellipse.

Step 3

Step 4

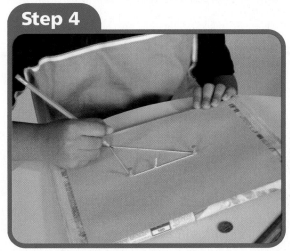

Draw Conclusions

1. How is an elliptical orbit different from a circular one? How many foci would a circular orbit have?

2. **Inquiry Skill** In this activity, you made a model by drawing the elliptical orbit of a planet around the sun. Why might a scientist make models of planetary orbits instead of studying them directly?

Investigate Further

Use the same tools to make three more models. Make a wider elliptical orbit, a narrower elliptical orbit, and a circular orbit. What do you need to change each time?

Reading in Science

VOCABULARY
rotation p. 406
axis p. 406
revolution p. 406
eclipse p. 410
tide p. 412

SCIENCE CONCEPTS
▶ what causes days, years, and seasons
▶ what causes eclipses and tides

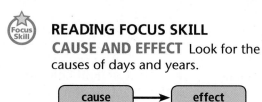

READING FOCUS SKILL
CAUSE AND EFFECT Look for the causes of days and years.

cause ⟶ effect

Days and Years

Can you feel Earth spinning? When you spin around in circles, you get dizzy, but you can't feel Earth spin. Still, the spinning of Earth controls the lengths of day and night. Without it, there would be no day and night as we know them.

This spin is called rotation. **Rotation** is the turning of an object on an axis. Earth's **axis** is an imaginary line running through the center of Earth from the North Pole to the South Pole. As Earth rotates on its axis, only part of its surface faces the sun at one time, so half of Earth is in sunlight while the other half is in darkness.

As Earth rotates, the part of it that is in sunlight moves into darkness, and the part that is in darkness moves into sunlight. In this way, Earth's rotation causes day and night, with one complete rotation every 24 hours.

All the planets rotate, but they do so at different speeds. For example, Jupiter rotates faster than Earth, so its day lasts only 9.8 Earth hours. Venus rotates much more slowly. Its day lasts 243 Earth days.

As each planet rotates on its axis, it also revolves around the sun. **Revolution** is the movement of one object in an orbit around another object. Each planet's orbit follows a slightly elliptical path around the sun.

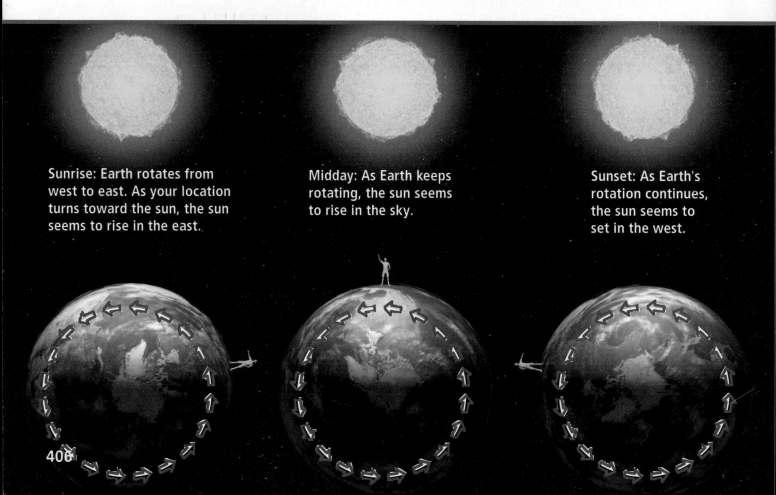

Sunrise: Earth rotates from west to east. As your location turns toward the sun, the sun seems to rise in the east.

Midday: As Earth keeps rotating, the sun seems to rise in the sky.

Sunset: As Earth's rotation continues, the sun seems to set in the west.

Jupiter
Day: 9.8 hours
Year: 12 Earth years

Mars
Day: 25 hours
Year: 687 Earth days

Earth
Day: 24 hours
Year: 365 days

Venus
Day: 243 Earth days
Year: 225 Earth days

Uranus
Day: 18 hours
Year: 84 Earth years

Mercury
Day: 59 Earth days
Year: 88 Earth days

Saturn
Day: 10 hours
Year: 29.5 Earth years

Pluto
Day: 6 Earth days
Year: 248 Earth years

Neptune
Day: 19 hours
Year: 165 Earth years

The length of each planet's year depends on its distance from the sun.

The time it takes a planet to orbit the sun is one year. But just as the length of a day differs from planet to planet, the length of a year differs, too. For Mercury, a year is 88 Earth days long. For Pluto, a year is 248 Earth years long.

Study each planet in the diagram on this page. Compare the length of its year with its distance from the sun. Do you see a pattern? Johannes Kepler did.

In the sixteenth century, Kepler discovered that a planet's orbital speed decreases as its distance from the sun increases. This means that the planets farthest from the sun move the slowest. Since they also travel the greatest distances, for them, one revolution around the sun—one year—lasts a long time.

On the other hand, the planets closest to the sun have less distance to travel and move faster, so their years are much shorter.

 CAUSE AND EFFECT If Earth began to rotate more slowly, what would change?

407

Seasons

Does the weather change much from season to season where you live? Why do seasons change from winter to spring to summer to fall?

The temperature changes that take place from season to season are caused by a change in the way the sun's rays hit Earth's surface. When the rays hit a spot on Earth's surface directly, the surface absorbs a lot of energy. This heats the air above the surface, causing air temperatures to rise. As Earth revolves, the sun's rays begin to hit the same spot at an angle. When this happens, the surface absorbs less energy and temperatures drop. What changes the way the rays hit Earth's surface? It's the tilt of Earth's axis. As Earth revolves around the sun, this tilt is always the same—23.5 degrees. As a result, the Northern Hemisphere is sometimes tilted toward the sun or away from the sun. There are times during an orbit when both the Northern Hemisphere and the Southern Hemisphere receive light at nearly the same angle.

When the Northern Hemisphere is tilted toward the sun, the rays hit this part of Earth's surface more directly. As a result, there are more hours of daylight, and the surface absorbs more heat. This heat, in turn, warms the atmosphere, resulting in summer.

On around December 22, the Northern Hemisphere is tilted away from the sun. It has its day with the fewest hours of daylight, the first day of winter. The Southern Hemisphere has its day with the most hours of daylight, the first day of summer. ▶

On around March 21, the Northern Hemisphere is not tilted either toward or away from the sun. In both hemispheres, days and nights are of nearly equal length. Spring begins in the Northern Hemisphere, and fall begins in the Southern Hemisphere. ▶

As Earth continues its revolution around the sun, it reaches a point at which its hemispheres are not tilted either toward or away from the sun. Now days and nights are nearly of equal length. The sun's rays begin to hit the Northern Hemisphere at more of an angle, causing temperatures to start dropping and the season of fall to begin.

As Earth keeps moving through its orbit, the Northern Hemisphere is tilted farther away from the sun. The sun's indirect rays provide less energy than when the sun shines more directly on an area, resulting in winter's low temperatures. The Northern Hemisphere receives fewer hours of sunlight each day, resulting in more hours of darkness. The sun appears to be lower in the sky.

The year goes on, and Earth continues in its orbit, again reaching a point at which its hemispheres are not tilted either toward or away from the sun. Now the days and nights are of nearly equal lengths again. The sun's rays begin to hit the Northern Hemisphere more directly, warming the air, and spring begins. As Earth keeps following its orbit, the Northern Hemisphere has more hours of sunlight, and spring turns into summer. During all this time, the Southern Hemisphere experiences the opposite seasons.

CAUSE AND EFFECT How would the seasons be different if Earth's axis were not tilted?

◀ On or about September 23, the Northern Hemisphere is not tilted either toward or away from the sun. Everywhere on Earth, days and nights are of nearly equal length. Fall begins in the Northern Hemisphere, and spring begins in the Southern Hemisphere.

◀ On about June 21, the Northern Hemisphere is tilted toward the sun. It has its day with the most hours of daylight—the first day of summer. The Southern Hemisphere has its day with the fewest hours of daylight, the first day of winter.

Eclipses

If you have ever seen the moon slowly begin to darken and turn reddish in color, you may have observed an eclipse. An **eclipse** (ih•KLIPS) occurs when one object passes into the shadow of another object. An eclipse can be either lunar (of the moon) or solar (of the sun).

The moon's revolution around Earth causes both kinds of eclipses by causing Earth, moon, and sun to line up in two different ways. When the order is sun-Earth-moon, Earth blocks sunlight from reaching the moon, resulting in a lunar eclipse. When the order is sun-moon-Earth, the moon blocks sunlight from reaching a small part of Earth, resulting in a solar eclipse.

Let's look at a lunar eclipse first. The moon shines only because its surface reflects light from the sun. Look at the diagram below. When the moon moves into Earth's darker shadow, no sunlight can reach it, so the moon is totally dark. This is a total lunar eclipse. When only part of the moon is in this dark shadow, some sunlight shines through the lighter shadow. This light then reflects off the moon. During this partial lunar eclipse, you can see Earth's curved shadow on the moon.

A solar eclipse occurs when the moon comes directly between the sun and Earth, casting a shadow on Earth. The small moon cannot block all the sun's rays, so what you see during a solar eclipse depends on where you are on Earth.

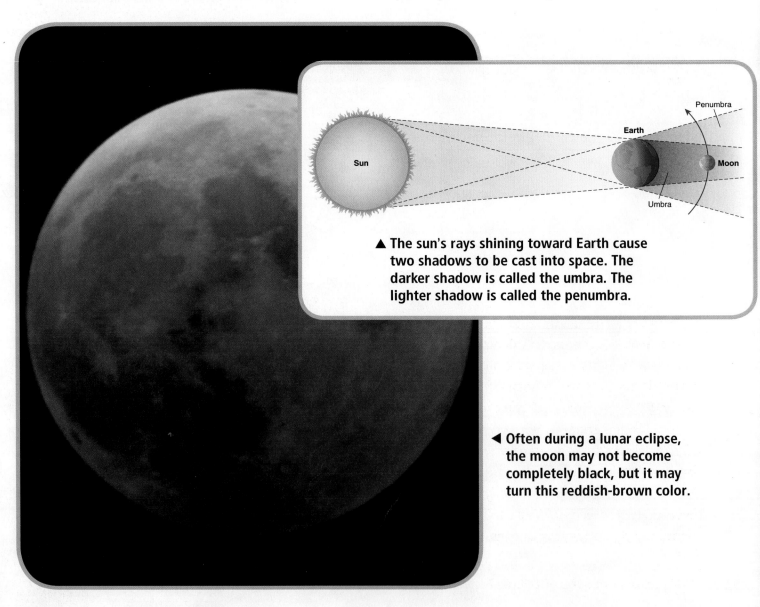

▲ The sun's rays shining toward Earth cause two shadows to be cast into space. The darker shadow is called the umbra. The lighter shadow is called the penumbra.

◄ Often during a lunar eclipse, the moon may not become completely black, but it may turn this reddish-brown color.

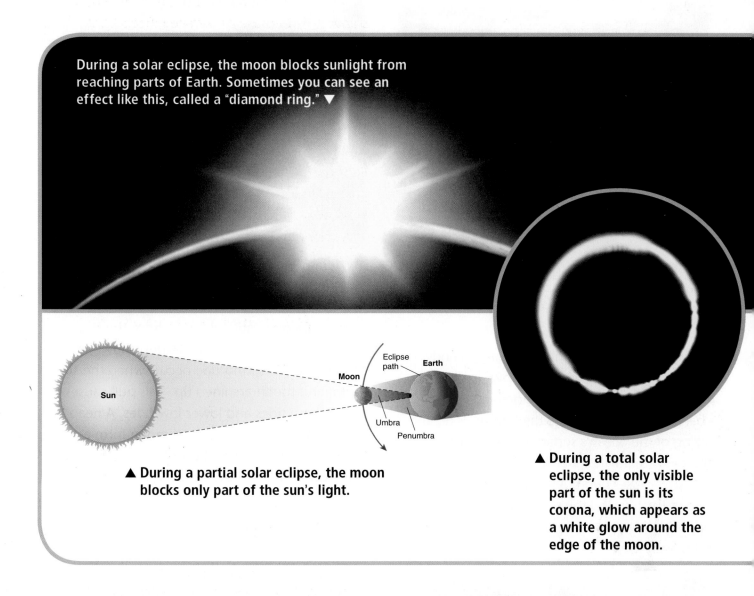

During a solar eclipse, the moon blocks sunlight from reaching parts of Earth. Sometimes you can see an effect like this, called a "diamond ring." ▼

Sun

Eclipse path

Moon

Earth

Umbra

Penumbra

▲ During a partial solar eclipse, the moon blocks only part of the sun's light.

▲ During a total solar eclipse, the only visible part of the sun is its corona, which appears as a white glow around the edge of the moon.

Like Earth, the moon casts two shadows. If you are within the moon's darker shadow, you will see a total solar eclipse. Only a white glow from the sun, called the solar corona, will show around the dark moon. If you are within the moon's lighter shadow, you will see a partial solar eclipse. Only part of the sun will be blocked by the moon.

You must **NEVER** look directly at the sun, even during an eclipse. The sun's rays can permanently damage your eyes.

 CAUSE AND EFFECT How does the moon cause both types of eclipses?

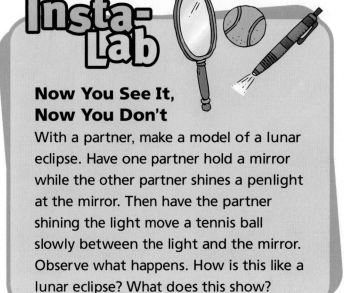

Insta-Lab

Now You See It, Now You Don't

With a partner, make a model of a lunar eclipse. Have one partner hold a mirror while the other partner shines a penlight at the mirror. Then have the partner shining the light move a tennis ball slowly between the light and the mirror. Observe what happens. How is this like a lunar eclipse? What does this show?

The Bay of Fundy, in Canada, is very narrow, making its tides very low and very high.

Tides

These photographs show the Bay of Fundy, between New Brunswick and Nova Scotia, Canada, where one of Earth's greatest tide changes occurs. **Tides** are the regular rising and falling of the ocean's surface caused mostly by the moon's gravitational "pull" on Earth's oceans. This pull causes two bulges of water—one on the side of Earth facing the moon and one on the opposite side. Some shorelines have two high tides every day.

An extra gravitational "pull" from the sun causes spring tides and neap tides, shown in the diagram. A spring tide occurs when the sun, Earth, and moon are lined up. This pull causes higher high tides and lower low tides. A neap tide occurs when the sun and moon form a right angle with Earth. This pull makes the high tides lower and the low tides higher.

CAUSE AND EFFECT What happens at the Bay of Fundy during a spring tide?

During a spring tide, the sun and moon line up with Earth.

During a neap tide, the sun and moon form a right angle with Earth.

1. **CAUSE AND EFFECT** Draw and complete this graphic organizer.

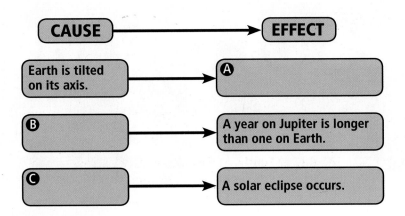

CAUSE	EFFECT
Earth is tilted on its axis.	Ⓐ
Ⓑ	A year on Jupiter is longer than one on Earth.
Ⓒ	A solar eclipse occurs.

2. **SUMMARIZE** Write a summary of this lesson, beginning with this sentence: *Many things on Earth are caused by our planet's movement through space.*

3. **DRAW CONCLUSIONS** Why does the sun seem to be higher in the sky during warmer months?

4. **VOCABULARY** Write a sentence that defines each vocabulary word in this lesson.

Test Prep

5. **Critical Thinking** Near the equator, why is it harder to notice seasonal weather changes?

6. Which object's motion causes eclipses of the sun?
   - **A.** the axis
   - **B.** Earth
   - **C.** the moon
   - **D.** the sun

Links

Writing

Narrative Writing
Suppose that it is possible to travel to and live on the planet Jupiter. Write a **short story.** Tell how the main character adjusts to the differences in the lengths of Jupiter's day and year from Earth's.

Math

Measure Angles
Find out the tilt of each planet's axis. Make an illustration that compares these tilts. Use a ruler and a protractor to measure the angles accurately.

Social Studies

Ancient Explanations
Use library references to locate myths that explain the ways the sun and moon seem to move. Share the myths with your classmates.

 For more links and activities, go to www.hspscience.com

What Causes the Phases of the Moon?

Fast Fact

The Moving Moon A billion years ago, the moon orbited Earth in 20 days. Every year, the moon moves 3.8 cm (1.5 in.) farther from Earth. At its current distance, the moon takes 29.5 days to go from new moon to new moon. In the Investigate, you'll explore how the moon's orbit around Earth changes our view of the moon.

Displaying the Moon's Cycle

Materials
- construction paper
- ruler
- information about phases of the moon, from a current newspaper

Procedure

1. Look in a newspaper for current information about the phases of the moon. You might find it on the page with the weather forecast.

2. Use the ruler and construction paper to make a calendar with seven columns. Write the days at the tops of the columns, and add the numbers for the days of the current month. To show all the moon's phases, you may need to make a calendar for next month, too.

3. Draw a new moon, a first quarter, a full moon, a third quarter, and another new moon on your calendar. Use the newspaper information to draw the symbols on the correct dates.

4. How will the moon gradually change from one phase to the next? Draw your predictions in the spaces between the symbols you have drawn.

Step 2

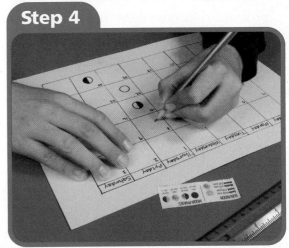

Step 4

Draw Conclusions

1. How long is the complete lunar cycle—from one new moon to the next?

2. What pattern did you see in the moon phases? Do you think this pattern is always the same? Explain.

3. **Inquiry Skill** How does your calendar communicate changes in the phases of the moon over time?

Investigate Further

For one complete lunar cycle, observe and draw the moon and its phases as you see them from your home. Compare these drawings to the drawings on your calendar. How accurate were your predictions?

Reading in Science

VOCABULARY
new moon p. 416
first quarter p. 416
full moon p. 416
third quarter p. 417

SCIENCE CONCEPTS
▶ what the phases of the moon are and how to describe them
▶ why phases of the moon occur in the way they do

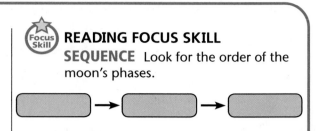

READING FOCUS SKILL
SEQUENCE Look for the order of the moon's phases.

Phases of the Moon

You've seen the moon when it is bright and round. Perhaps you remember seeing it as a thin sliver of light. And think about the dark nights when the moon seems to have completely disappeared from the sky. Have you ever noticed a pattern to these changes? The changes are very predictable as the moon moves in a cycle from one *phase* to the next. The moon's phases are the different shapes that the moon seems to have when you view it from Earth.

What causes these phases? Instead of producing its own light, the moon reflects light

If the moon produced its own light, it would always look like this.

from the sun. The side of the moon facing the sun is always lighted by the sun, just as one side of Earth is always lighted by the sun. As the moon revolves around Earth, you may see all, part, or none of the moon's lighted side. The part of the moon you see from Earth is the moon's phase.

Just as Earth rotates on its axis, the moon rotates on its own axis. The moon rotates once in about the same time it takes it to make one revolution around Earth. This means that the same side of the moon always faces Earth. No matter what phase the moon is in, the same side is always facing Earth. Unless you're an astronaut in space, you'll never see the other side of the moon!

During its orbit, the moon is sometimes between Earth and the sun. When that happens, the lighted part of the moon can't be seen from Earth. With little light reflected from the moon toward Earth, you see only a dim outline of its shape, or the **new moon**.

As the moon continues through its orbit, you see more and more of its lighted side. When you can see half of this side, the moon is in its **first quarter**, one-quarter of the way through its orbit.

When the moon reaches the side of Earth opposite the sun, you see all of the moon's lighted side, a bright, round phase called a **full moon**.

416

As the full moon moves through the last half of its orbit, you see less and less of its lighted side. When you can see only about half of the lighted side, the moon is in its **third quarter**, three-quarters of the way through its orbit.

Finally, after 29½ days, the moon is again between Earth and the sun, so its dark side faces Earth again. The moon has completed one lunar cycle.

 SEQUENCE Which phase occurs when the moon is on the opposite side of Earth from the sun?

Science Up Close

Moon Phases

When you can see more than one-half of the moon's lighted side, it's called a *gibbous* (GIB•uhs) moon. Gibbous comes from a Latin word that means "humpbacked." ▼

 ◄ First Quarter

After a new moon, you see more of the moon each night. The phases are said to be waxing. ▼

 Sun ►

▲ During a full moon, some people claim to see "the man in the moon," a face formed by the moon's craters.

The new moon rises and sets at about the same time as the sun, which is another reason a new moon is hard to see.

▲ After a full moon, you see less of the moon each night. The phases are said to be waning (WAYN•ing).

◄ Third Quarter

▲ When you can see less than one-quarter of the moon's lighted side, it's called a crescent moon.

 For more links and activities, go to www.hspscience.com

▲ During its full phase, Venus is moving to the far side of the sun in relation to Earth.

▲ You can see part of Venus in its first quarter, one-quarter through its 225-day orbit around the sun.

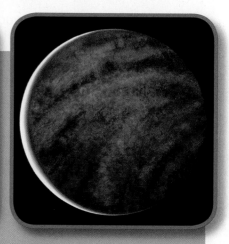

▲ When Venus is close to Earth, it is seen in its crescent phase. Because of its closeness to Earth, the planet appears much larger than during its full phase.

Other Phases in the Solar System

Earth's moon is not the only body in the solar system that has phases. If you could travel to and stand on the surface of other planets, you could observe the phases of the dozens of moons orbiting those planets.

In 1609, Galileo proved that planets themselves also show phases. He was the first to observe and record the phases of Venus. At the time, many people still thought that Earth was the center of the universe, but Galileo's observations helped prove that Earth, Venus, and the other planets orbit the sun.

Venus is actually visible from Earth three hours before sunrise or three hours after sunset. The time of day depends on where Venus is in its orbit. This bright planet is visible when most stars are not. In fact, some people call it the "morning star" when they see it at sunrise and the "evening star" at sunset.

Galileo could not have seen the complete full phase of Venus because this occurs when Venus is behind the sun. Its full lighted side faces Earth, but the sun blocks it from view on Earth.

Space probes, though, have been able to photograph the full phase. They have also sent back pictures of the phases of Mars and Jupiter. In time, probes may show phases of other planets, too.

 SEQUENCE What happens after you see nearly full Venus?

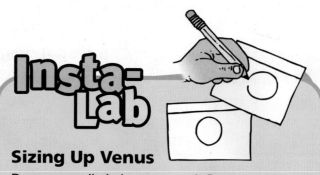

Insta-Lab

Sizing Up Venus

Draw a small circle on a card. Draw an identical circle on another card and blacken all but a thin crescent on it. Hold the full circle at arm's length. Hold the crescent near your face. Why does Venus look smaller in its full phase and larger as a crescent?

1. SEQUENCE Draw and complete this graphic organizer.

WHAT IS THE SEQUENCE OF MOON PHASES?

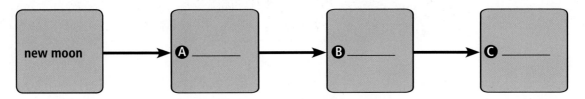

new moon → **A** _____ → **B** _____ → **C** _____

2. SUMMARIZE Use the completed graphic organizer to write a lesson summary.

3. DRAW CONCLUSIONS Does Earth have phases? Explain your answer.

4. VOCABULARY Make up a quiz that requires matching this lesson's vocabulary terms with information about them.

Test Prep

5. Critical Thinking Does the sun have phases? Explain your answer.

6. During which phase of the moon is it easiest to study the moon's structures?

A. first quarter   **C.** new moon

B. full moon   **D.** third quarter

Links

Writing

Expository Writing

Find out the next time Venus will cross the surface of the sun, as seen from a point on Earth. Write a **report** about this event, called the transit of Venus.

Math

Extend a Pattern

The second full moon in a month is called a "blue moon." Find out the current phase of the moon, and use a calendar to predict when the next blue moon will occur.

Art

Compare Styles

Find three artistic representations of the moon, and compare them. For example, how realistic is each one? What is the mood of each one? Which one appeals to you the most? Why?

 For more links and activities, go to www.hspscience.com

What Is in the Solar System?

Fast Fact

Hot! Hot! Hot! Temperatures on the sun range from about 5500°C (10,000°F) at the surface to 15,000,000°C (27,000,000°F) at the center. In the Investigate, you will make a model of the solar system, which is named for its most important component—the sun.

Modeling the Solar System

Materials
- 10 balloons
- tape
- 10 straws
- marker
- meterstick

Procedure

1. Choose a safe area outside your school for your model of the solar system. (Or ask permission to construct your model in a school hallway.)

2. Study the table. Use numbers to decide on a scale for the distances in your model. For example, you might have 1 cm equal 1 million km. That would place Mercury 58 cm from the sun in your model.

3. Figure out the distances you will use in your model. Write them on a sheet of paper.

4. Blow up the 10 balloons, and tape each balloon to a straw.

5. Use the marker to label one balloon as the sun and the other nine as the planets.

6. Push the straw with the sun balloon into the ground at one end of your model. Use the meterstick to measure the distance from the sun to each planet. Push each "planet's" straw into the ground at the correct position.

Draw Conclusions

1. In your model, which two planets are closest to each other? Is this true of these planets' orbits in the solar system? How do you know?

2. **Inquiry Skill** You used numbers to show relative distances. What was your most important consideration in choosing a scale for your model?

Planetary Information		
Planet	**Diameter (km)**	**Distance from Sun (km)**
Mercury	4,878	58 million
Venus	12,100	108 million
Earth	12,756	150 million
Mars	6,786	228 million
Jupiter	142,984	778 million
Saturn	120,536	1,424 million
Uranus	51,108	2,867 million
Neptune	49,538	4,488 million
Pluto	2,350	5,909 million

Step 6

Investigate Further

You've made a model of distances in the solar system. Now use numbers to calculate a scale for a model of the diameters of the planets. Could you make a practical model by using the same scale for both distances and sizes of planets?

Reading in Science

VOCABULARY
asteroid p. 423
satellite p. 424
meteor p. 426
comet p. 428

SCIENCE CONCEPTS
▶ what the characteristics of the inner and outer planets are
▶ how scientists describe asteroids, meteors, and comets

READING FOCUS SKILL
MAIN IDEA AND DETAILS Look for details about each planet.

Main Idea

detail | detail | detail

The Inner Planets

Long ago, astronomers were fascinated by the planets. They tried to measure the planets' sizes and distances from Earth and to analyze their orbits. However, they had only the information they could gather with their own eyes. Space probes—even telescopes—would not be invented until far into the future.

The planets in our solar system are divided into two groups. These are the inner planets and the outer planets. The inner planets—Mercury, Venus, Earth, and Mars—are smaller and denser than most of the outer planets. The inner planets each have a core, a mantle, and a crust, but their thicknesses vary from planet to planet. Each inner planet has an atmosphere,

The Inner Planets

The innermost part of our solar system includes the inner planets and an asteroid belt.

◀ Mercury, the eighth-largest planet, has a surface much like that of our moon. It also has the widest temperature range in the solar system, from −183°C (−297°F) to 427°C (800°F). Most of the planet is probably an iron core covered by a thin, cratered crust. Solar winds that blow constantly result in a very thin atmosphere, which the high temperatures quickly burn off.

Venus, the sixth-largest planet, is the brightest object we can see in the sky, after the sun and our moon. Venus is nearly as wide as Earth and has 80 percent of Earth's mass. Its surface is mostly plains, much like those on Earth. However, its dense atmosphere of carbon dioxide results in a "super greenhouse effect." Temperatures range from 127°C (261°F) to more than 467°C (872°F), hot enough to melt lead. ▶

too. Its density ranges from very thin on Mercury (100 times thinner than Earth's) to very thick on Venus (90 times thicker than Earth's).

In the early 1500s, the Polish astronomer Nicolaus Copernicus (koh•PER•nih•kuhs) showed that the sun, not Earth, was the center of our system of planets. By the early 1600s, the German astronomer Johannes Kepler had figured out that the planets' orbits are elliptical, not circular.

Now scientists gather information about the inner and outer planets from powerful telescopes both on Earth and in space. Space probes send data back to Earth,—an action early astronomers never dreamed possible.

MAIN IDEA AND DETAILS What is one important characteristic of each inner planet?

Math in Science
Interpret Data

Charting Asteroids

An **asteroid** is a piece of rock and metal that orbits the sun. This table shows some asteroids in order of size. Revise the table to show them in the order in which they were discovered. What can you learn by comparing their sizes and their discovery years?

Asteroid	Diameter	Discovery
Aten	1 km	1976
Apollo	1.4 km	1932
Gaspra	16 km	1916
Juno	246 km	1804
Eunomia	272 km	1851
Ceres	932 km	1801

Earth, the fifth-largest planet, is the densest major body in the solar system. It may be the only planet with distinct inner and outer cores and the only one with solid plates floating on top of a hot mantle. It is the only planet with liquid water on its surface. This water and our weather constantly change and renew Earth's surface, keeping it very "young" compared with the surfaces of the other planets. ▶

The inner planets are separated from the outer planets by the asteroid belt. It lies between Mars and Jupiter. ▶

The surface of Mars, the seventh-largest planet, is much like that of Earth. It has mountains, canyons, hills, plains, and ice caps. Mars has a very thin atmosphere with surface temperatures ranging from −133°C (−207°F) to 27°C (80°F). Scientists disagree about whether life ever existed on Mars. But evidence of erosion and water frozen into the ice caps at its poles indicate that this planet once may have had liquid water. ▶

The Outer Planets

Beyond the asteroid belt are the outer planets—Jupiter, Saturn, Uranus (YOOR•uh•nuhs), Neptune, Pluto, and perhaps a tenth planet, named Sedna. The first four of these planets, which are very similar, are called gas giants because they have no solid surface. Their small, solid cores are surrounded by a thick, slushy layer of methane and ammonia ice and huge amounts of gas, mostly hydrogen and helium.

As the solar system formed, the strong pull of gravity to these outer planets drew in gases, ice, rock, metals, and other materials, making the planets even larger. Jupiter, for example, is more massive than everything else in our solar system combined, except for the sun.

Jupiter, Saturn, Uranus, and Neptune also give off enormous amounts of heat. But they are too small to be stars.

The five known outer planets all have satellites. A **satellite** is a body in space that orbits a larger body. We usually call planetary satellites moons. Jupiter has at least 63 moons, and Saturn has at least 33. Some of these are larger than the planets Mercury or Pluto. Even tiny Pluto has a moon, named Charon, which is half the size of Pluto.

In contrast to Jupiter and Saturn, Earth has only one moon and Mars has only two. The other two inner planets have no moons at all.

 MAIN IDEA AND DETAILS What is one important characteristic of each outer planet?

The Outer Planets

Jupiter, by far the largest planet, is 318 times bigger than Earth. Its core alone has 10 to 15 times Earth's mass. This core may be as hot as 30,000°C (54,000°F)—so hot that Jupiter sends more heat into space than it receives from the sun. Jupiter's atmosphere crackles with lightning and swirls with high winds that blow in opposite directions. The Great Red Spot is a huge storm that began before the astronomer Galileo was born, in 1564. ▶

Asteroid Belt

Saturn, the second-largest planet, is the least dense. If there were a tub of water large enough to hold this planet, Saturn would float! Similar to Jupiter in structure, it also radiates more heat than it receives from the sun. Its rings are 250,000 km (155,000 mi) wide, but less than 1 km (0.6 mi) thick. They contain just a small amount of material spread over a vast distance. ▶

The outermost part of the solar system includes the outer planets—Jupiter, Saturn, Uranus, Neptune, Pluto—and a possible tenth planet, Sedna.

▲ Uranus, the third-largest planet, has a core like those of Jupiter and Saturn. But the core of Uranus is not surrounded by such enormous clouds of hydrogen. A collision billions of years ago with an object the size of Earth may have knocked Uranus on its side. Now it rolls around in its orbit. Uranus has at least 27 moons and 11 known rings made of particles that range from 10 m (33 ft) wide to fine dust.

Neptune, the fourth-largest planet, is similar to Uranus and has a core about the size of Earth. Neptune sends out twice as much energy as it gets from the sun. Like Jupiter, Neptune has many huge storms. Its winds are the fastest on any planet, reaching about 1000 to 2000 km/hr (600 to 1200 mi/hr). Neptune has several thin rings and at least eight moons. ▼

▲ Pluto is smaller than the other planets and smaller than seven of their moons. It is made of mostly rock and water in the form of ice. Some astronomers consider it to be an asteroid, not a planet. Pluto orbits with its moon, Charon, and their orbits are sometimes inside the orbit of Neptune. Because of this orbit, Pluto can be either the eighth or ninth planet from the sun.

A Possible Planet

In 2004, some scientists identified a possible tenth planet. They named it Sedna after an Inuit goddess said to live in the Arctic Ocean. The warmest temperatures on Sedna are probably −240°C (−400°F). This possible planet is about three-fourths the size of Pluto. It is three times as far from the sun as Pluto and takes about 10,500 Earth years to orbit the sun once.

The craters that dot the moon's surface resulted from meteorite collisions that took place billions of years ago. ▼

Asteroids are rocky chunks that move in their own orbits, mostly between Mars and Jupiter.

Meteor Crater in Arizona is more than 1 km (0.6 mi) across. The impact crater was formed more than 30,000 years ago.

Asteroids and Meteors

You read earlier that an asteroid is a piece of rock and metal that orbits the sun. Most asteroids are in an area between Mars and Jupiter called the *asteroid belt*.

So what is a meteor? A **meteor** is a piece of rock, smaller than an asteroid, that enters Earth's atmosphere and burns up. As the meteor falls in the atmosphere, friction heats it and the air around it. This produces a trail of light. A meteor with a mass less than 1g (0.04 oz) can produce a spectacular trail of light.

You might have seen such a meteor and called it a "shooting star." Fortunately, a meteor is not a star entering our atmosphere—or coming anywhere near Earth. If it were, Earth would have been destroyed long ago!

Most meteors burn up completely before they reach Earth's surface. A chunk of rock that survives this fall to Earth or to another body is called a *meteorite*. Some meteorites are large enough to leave huge craters, as you can see in the photos.

Sometimes a loose group of meteors hits Earth's atmosphere and falls together like a

426

▲ Because so many meteorite collisions have left craters on Mercury, it looks very similar to the moon.

◄ The largest meteorite found in the United States is a huge chunk of nickel-iron, found in Oregon's Willamette River valley in 1902. It has a mass of more than 13,600 kg (15 tons).

shower. A meteor shower can last several hours or several days.

Most meteors are formed as the result of collisions between asteroids. Some come from the debris of comets. However, some meteors travel to Earth from the moon or Mars. Every day, up to 4 billion meteors reach Earth's atmosphere, but most of them are very tiny and fall unnoticed.

 MAIN IDEA AND DETAILS What are two details about meteors?

Incoming!

Fill a bowl with flour or confectioners' sugar. Level the surface. Then hold a marble or ball bearing about 15 cm above the bowl and drop it. You have made a model of a crater that was formed by a meteorite as it hit Earth's surface. What factors do you think determine the size of a crater that a meteorite leaves? Try dropping the object from different heights.

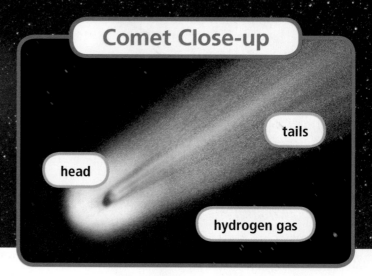

A comet can have two or more visible tails. They are made of different materials. One of them always points away from the sun.

Comet Close-up

tails

head

hydrogen gas

Comets

A **comet** is a ball of ice, rock, and frozen gases that orbits the sun. It may pass close to the sun and then swing out past the orbit of Pluto, to the edge of the solar system. Each time a comet approaches the sun, however, it changes. As some of its ice melts, the heat releases a cloud of dust from the comet. Wind blowing off the sun causes the cloud to form a tail, which always points away from the sun.

After a comet passes the sun many times, it has little ice left. Then the comet tends to break into small pieces that are spread throughout its former orbit. Some of these pieces may enter Earth's atmosphere as meteors.

Many comets have been named, and people watch for them as they approach Earth. One is Halley's (HAL•eez) comet, which was last seen from Earth in 1986. It will appear again in 2061–2062 as part of its 76-year orbit around the sun. During each pass near the sun, Halley loses about 6 m (20 ft) of ice and rock. In 1986, it was barely visible without a telescope. However, in 1066, Halley was so bright that it frightened millions of Europeans. Now bits of Halley are part of meteor showers.

 MAIN IDEA AND DETAILS What is a comet made of?

1. MAIN IDEA AND DETAILS Draw and complete this graphic organizer.

MAIN IDEA: THE SOLAR SYSTEM CONSISTS OF MANY BODIES.

Inner Planets | Outer Planets | Other Bodies

A   E   H   K
B   F   I   L
C   G   J   M
D

2. SUMMARIZE Write a sentence that tells the most important information in this lesson.

3. DRAW CONCLUSIONS If someone described a planet without naming it, how could you identify that planet?

4. VOCABULARY Explain how the four kinds of objects named in the vocabulary list are similar and different.

Test Prep

5. Critical Thinking Will we ever find a new inner planet? Explain your answer.

6. Which of these planets does not produce its own heat?
A. Mercury
B. Neptune
C. Saturn
D. Uranus

Links

Writing

Persuasive Writing
Choose a planet other than Earth, and write a **travel brochure** to persuade people to visit it. Describe what they might see there, and add interesting facts to encourage them to make the trip.

Math

Display Data
Mount Everest, Earth's tallest mountain, is about 8.9 km (5.5 mi) high. However, Olympus Mons on Mars is 27 km (17 mi) high. Make a bar graph that shows this difference in height.

Music

Planet Music
Listen to a recording of *The Planets* by Gustav Holst. Decide whether you think each part of the music fits its planet. Choose your favorite part, and write about why you like it.

 For more links and activities, go to **www.hspscience.com**

What Is Beyond the Solar System?

Fast Fact

Not-So-Nebulous Nebulae A nebula like the Dumbbell Nebula seems to be delicate and fragile. Yet, nebulae often contain stars that are hundreds of times more massive and millions of times more brilliant than our sun. In the Investigate, you'll explore why these stars look so pale in the sky.

Experimenting with Brightness

Materials ● **1 large flashlight** ● **2 penlights** ● **meterstick**

Procedure

1. Place the large flashlight and one penlight side by side. Turn them on and walk 2 m away. Compare their brightness and record your observations.

2. Now place the two penlights together, turn them on, and walk 2 m away. Again, compare their brightness and record your observations.

3. Think of a way to make one penlight look dimmer than the other one. Form a hypothesis and write it down. Then experiment to test your hypothesis, and record the results.

4. Think of a way to make a penlight seem to be just as bright as the large flashlight. Form another hypothesis and write it down. Then experiment to test your hypothesis, and record the results.

Draw Conclusions

1. In Step 3 of the procedure, what variable did you change? What happened when you changed it? How did the actual brightness of the flashlights change?

2. How did you make the large flashlight and one penlight appear equally bright?

3. **Inquiry Skill** Scientists experiment to find out whether their hypotheses are supported by their test results. Hypothesize how you could make one of the penlights look brighter than the large flashlight. Plan and conduct an experiment to test your hypothesis.

Step 1

Step 2

Investigate Further

Darken the room, and shine a flashlight on a wall. Holding the flashlight, walk toward the wall. What do you observe? How does the light on the wall change? How does it relate to the observed brightness of stars?

Reading in Science

VOCABULARY
galaxy p. 436

SCIENCE CONCEPTS

▶ what types of stars we can observe and what their life cycles are

▶ how scientists identify galaxies and explain the formation of the universe

READING FOCUS SKILL

MAIN IDEA AND DETAILS Look for details about stars.

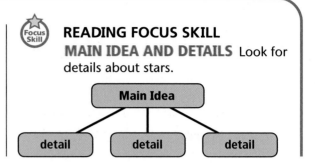

Types of Stars

The stars we see in the night sky may all seem to be the same, but they differ in many ways. A star is a huge ball of hot, glowing gases. It gets its heat and light from *fusion* (FYOO•zhuhn), a process that joins, or fuses, the nuclei of hydrogen atoms to form the nuclei of helium atoms. Fusion occurs at the core of a star, helped by the tremendous heat and pressure there.

Astronomers compare stars by color, actual brightness, and surface temperature. They use a diagram like the one shown below, called the Hertzsprung-Russell diagram. About 90 percent of stars fit into the long band that runs diagonally from the upper left corner to the lower right corner. This band is called the

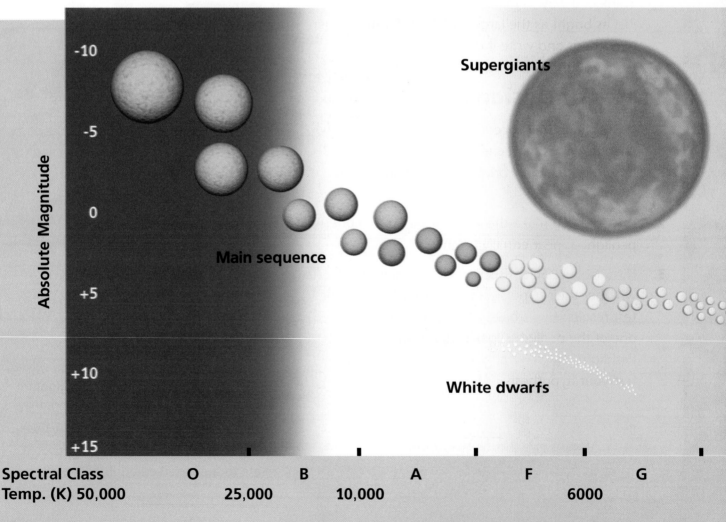

432

main sequence. Stars that lie on this band are called main-sequence stars. In the diagram, the brightest stars are at the top, with the dimmer ones toward the bottom. The hottest stars are on the left, and the coolest ones are on the right.

As you can see, the stars in the main sequence range from the bright, hot blue stars at the upper left to the dim, cool red stars at the lower right. The colors indicate a star's surface temperature. The diagram also shows that the hottest, brightest stars have the greatest mass. The coolest, dimmest stars have the least mass. Our sun is medium in temperature, brightness, and mass.

Stars outside the main sequence are different. Red giants and supergiants are cool red stars. They are bright because they are so large. White dwarfs are very hot, but they appear dim because they are very small. Scientists measure the light a star gives off, not how bright it seems to be. Many distant stars that look dim in our sky are actually much, much brighter than our sun, even though the sun looks brighter to us than any other star.

Where do stars come from? A star begins as part of a huge, cool, dark cloud of gas and dust called a *nebula*. Gravity pulls some of the particles in the cloud together. When the center of the group of particles has enough mass, pressure causes the temperature there to rise. Then fusion begins. One nebula might produce many stars over millions of years.

The mass of a star determines what kind of main-sequence star it is. A star can begin as a hot blue star, an average yellow star, or a cool red star. The more massive the star, the hotter it is.

 MAIN IDEA AND DETAILS What is a main-sequence star?

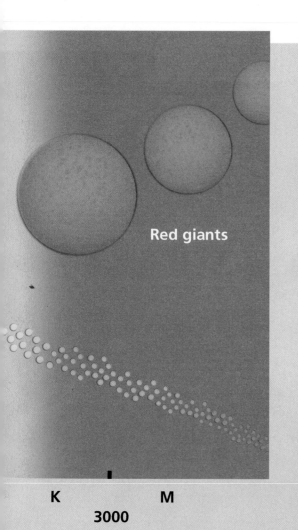

Red giants

K   M

3000

◄ **The Hertzsprung-Russell (H-R) diagram categorizes stars by their brightness and temperature. Ejnar Hertzsprung and Henry Norris Russell developed the diagram in the early 1900s.**

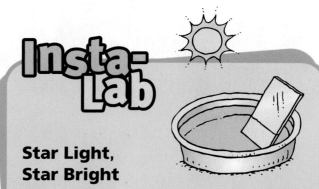

Insta-Lab

Star Light, Star Bright

Place a pan of water so that the sun shines into it. Slide a mirror partly into the water. Move the mirror until it reflects a rainbow of colors onto a wall, like a prism. What happens to the light? How might scientists use this or a similar technique to study a star?

From Red Giants to Black Holes

Nothing lasts forever, not even huge stars. The fusion in a star's core converts hydrogen nuclei into helium nuclei. When its hydrogen is gone, the star is no longer a main-sequence star.

The more massive the star, the faster it uses up its hydrogen. As a result, the biggest stars have the shortest "lives." A massive, very hot star might last a million years. However, a small, cool star may shine—dimly—for 30 billion years!

Stars come to an end in different ways, depending on their mass. A high-mass star quickly uses up its hydrogen and swells into a supergiant. Then the supergiant explodes as a supernova. The core of a supernova might form a small, dense *neutron star*. The biggest supernovas collapse as extremely dense *black holes*. It was once thought that nothing escaped from a black hole. But, new information about black holes is coming from space telescopes and satellites.

The Eagle Nebula is known as a "nursery of stars." The vivid colors are evidence of the many young stars there.

A high-mass star eventually swells into a red supergiant. Then it becomes a supernova, followed by either a neutron star or a black hole.

High-Mass Star

434

Low-Mass Star

A low-mass star becomes a red giant, then a white dwarf that's first surrounded by a planetary nebula, and finally a black dwarf.

▲ A nebula is a mass of gas and dust particles in space. The Crab Nebula is the result of a star that exploded in 1054.

A medium-mass star takes longer to use up its hydrogen. Then it swells into a red giant. Instead of exploding, a red giant collapses. It throws off gases and shrinks into a small, dense white dwarf. A low-mass star takes the longest of all stars to use up its hydrogen. Then it moves to the white dwarf stage.

 MAIN IDEA AND DETAILS What happens during the life cycle of a medium-mass star?

▲ Nebulae exist in all galaxies, including our own Milky Way Galaxy. They can be dark or bright. The most famous dark nebula is the Horsehead Nebula.

You are here

This drawing shows how the Milky Way Galaxy would probably appear if we were able to view it from above—as a spiral. It contains 100 billion to 200 billion stars and is about 100,000 light-years across. (A light-year is the distance light travels through space in one year—about 9 trillion km, or 6 trillion mi.)

Types of Galaxies

A **galaxy** is a huge system of stars bound together by gravity. We live in the Milky Way Galaxy, one of billions of galaxies. It's hard to appreciate how immense our galaxy is because only the closest stars are visible.

Galaxies are classified by shape: spiral, barred spiral, elliptical, and irregular.

The Milky Way and about 20 percent of all galaxies are spirals. A spiral galaxy has huge, curved arms formed by stars and gases. The center of the spiral is reddish because of the many red giants there, which are reaching the end of their lives. The spiral's arms are bluish because they contain many bright, young blue stars.

About 10 percent of galaxies are barred spirals. They have two bar-shaped clusters of stars that stretch out from the center.

Most galaxies—60 percent—are elliptical. Most of these are flat and small and do not form new stars. Some elliptical galaxies rotate.

The remaining 10 percent of galaxies are irregular. These are loose collections of stars in no distinct pattern or arrangement. Two irregular galaxies, the Large and Small Magellanic Clouds, orbit the Milky Way Galaxy. They were identified by Magellan in 1519, during his famous voyage around the world. He had time, it appears, to explore the skies, too.

 MAIN IDEA AND DETAILS **Name the four types of galaxies.**

A spiral galaxy seen face-on shows large curved arms of stars.

An edge-on spiral galaxy looks like a flattened disk. It contains both old and young stars.

Barred spiral galaxies have bar-shaped features in their center.

In edge-on barred spiral galaxies, you can see the bar structure even in a side view.

Elliptical galaxies have an overall lack of form and are made up mostly of old stars.

Irregular galaxies consist mostly of young stars.

How Did the Universe Form?

No one is sure exactly how the universe formed, but astronomers have several theories. According to one well-accepted model, the universe began 10 to 20 billion years ago with a huge explosion called the *Big Bang*. Instantly, the universe changed from a tiny, dense dot to an enormous mass of rapidly expanding matter. From this matter, stars, galaxies, and planets have formed.

This theory supports the idea that matter has been expanding and that everything in the universe has been moving, since the Big Bang first occurred. In fact, astronomers have found that galaxies are all moving away from each other at great speeds. They have also detected background radiation from the first great explosion—the glow left over from the Big Bang.

What is the future of the universe? One hypothesis is based on the average density of all matter in the universe. If this density is three hydrogen atoms for every cubic meter of space, the universe is in a balanced state. Everything will stay as it is now, and gravity will keep the universe from expanding farther.

However, if the average density is below this, the universe will continue to expand. If the density is greater than three hydrogen atoms per cubic meter of space, gravity will take over, expansion will stop, and the universe will collapse on itself. According to this hypothesis, called the Big Crunch, another Big Bang would then take place, and the cycle would begin again.

Scientists keep finding new clues about the Big Bang and other theories. Perhaps someday, we will understand more of the details about how the universe began.

 MAIN IDEA AND DETAILS What are two details that support the Big Bang Theory?

The Future?

According to scientists, the universe has been expanding since it began billions of years ago. What will happen to the universe? Several models predict possible outcomes.

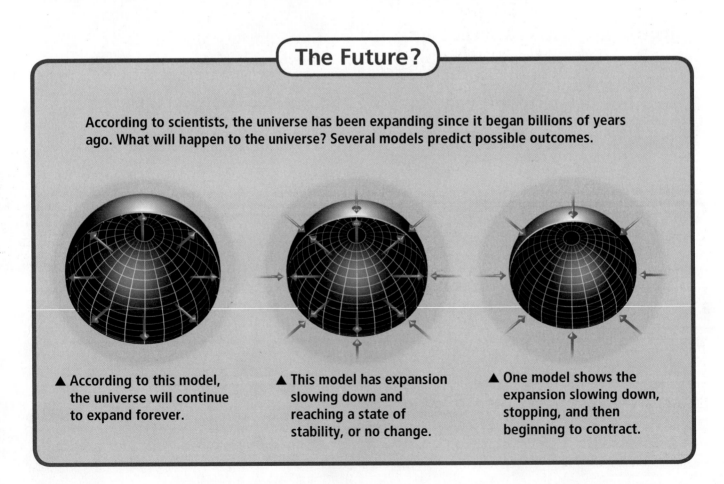

▲ According to this model, the universe will continue to expand forever.

▲ This model has expansion slowing down and reaching a state of stability, or no change.

▲ One model shows the expansion slowing down, stopping, and then beginning to contract.

1. MAIN IDEA AND DETAILS Draw and complete this graphic organizer.

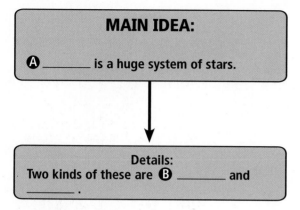

MAIN IDEA:

A _____ is a huge system of stars.

Details:
Two kinds of these are **B** _____ and _____ .

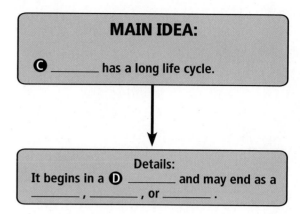

MAIN IDEA:

C _____ has a long life cycle.

Details:
It begins in a **D** _____ and may end as a _____ , _____ , or _____ .

2. SUMMARIZE Use the completed graphic organizer to write a lesson summary. Add other details, as necessary.

3. DRAW CONCLUSIONS Why does the caption on page 436 refer to how the Milky Way "probably" looks?

4. VOCABULARY Write a sentence that explains this lesson's vocabulary word.

Test Prep

5. Critical Thinking Will our sun eventually become a black hole? Explain your answer.

6. Which type of galaxy is **NOT** the birthplace of stars?
A. barred spiral   **C.** irregular
B. elliptical   **D.** spiral

Links

Writing

Narrative Writing

Write a **script** about this situation: You're a television reporter on a spacecraft, watching a supernova. As you tell your viewers how a huge blue star reached this stage, you're suddenly pulled into . . . oh, no!

Math

Make a Table

The apparent magnitude of a star can be measured. The lower the number, the brighter the star. Put these stars in order from least bright to brightest: Antares (1.00), Arcturus (–0.05), Sirius B (–1.45), Vega (0.03).

Language Arts

Name Origins

Research the names of stars, galaxies, and nebulae. For example, what is the Ghost of Jupiter? Why was a star named Antares? Find one or more interesting names to explain to the class.

 For more links and activities, go to www.hspscience.com

Catching Some Rays

For most people, "catching some rays" means slapping on some sunscreen and getting a tan. To a group of NASA scientists, catching some rays meant sending a robot spacecraft named *Genesis* around the sun to collect and bring home tiny bits of solar dust. Scientists hope that by studying those dust particles, they'll be able to find out more about how our solar system formed.

An Unfortunate Ending
The *Genesis* mission, however, did not go entirely as planned. The spacecraft, which was launched August 8, 2001, returned to Earth's atmosphere on September 8, 2004.

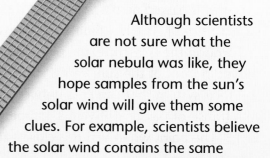

Upon arrival, the spacecraft was to deploy parachutes that would allow it to slowly descend. At the same time, helicopters were in position to snatch the craft before it landed. Unfortunately, the parachutes did not deploy, and the craft slammed into the ground in Utah.

Although the craft was badly damaged, scientists were able to retrieve many of the samples collected during the three-year mission. They are confident they will learn something from the materials collected.

A Dusty Wind

The *solar wind* that *Genesis* passed through is a high-speed stream of tiny particles given off by the sun. Those particles rush through the solar system at about 1.6 million km (1 million mi) per hour. Astronomers hypothesize that everything in the solar system, including the sun, planets, moons, comets, and asteroids, formed about 4.5 billion years ago from a large, swirling cloud of gas and dust called the *solar nebula*.

Although scientists are not sure what the solar nebula was like, they hope samples from the sun's solar wind will give them some clues. For example, scientists believe the solar wind contains the same kinds of elements as the solar nebula. By capturing the elements from the solar wind, scientists hope to learn how those elements came together to form the canyons on Mars, the oceans on Earth, and the moons of Jupiter.

Like a Flytrap

How did the craft collect its samples? When *Genesis* was passing through the solar wind, about 1.6 million km (1 million mi) from Earth, scientists signaled the probe to flip its lid. Once the probe's top was open, five collector plates—the size of bicycle tires—swung out and acted like giant flytraps, collecting stray bits of solar dust. Once through the solar wind, the traps were lowered.

Think About It

1. Why is it important for scientists to study the origins of the solar system?
2. From which materials do scientists think the solar system was created?

Find out more! Log on to
www.hspscience.com

Once in a Lifetime

Some events are very rare in the solar system. Recently, Jordan Friend got a chance to see one of them. Jordan was able to witness the planet Venus as it passed across the face of the sun. When this happens it's called a *transit.* The last time it happened was in 1882!

Through the telescope, the planet looks like a small black spot as it moves in front of the sun. Venus and Mercury are the only planets in the solar system that can pass between Earth and the sun.

A transit or passage of Venus, happens rarely. The next time will be in 2012. The point when Venus is closest to the sun's center is called the greatest transit.

Jordan had to be very careful. Scientists recommend that people who look at the sun use special filtering glasses to screen out harmful rays.

You Can Do It!

Materials
- 25-cm cardboard circle
- scissors
- string, 1-m piece
- 4 large paper clips

Quick and Easy Project

Spinning Planets

Procedure

1. Carefully use the scissors to make a hole in the center of the cardboard circle. Push one end of the string through the hole, and knot the string so it will not pull out.

2. Evenly space the four paper clips around the edge of the circle.

3. Hold the end of the string, and swing the circle back and forth. Observe what happens.

4. Now give the circle a quick spin toward you, and swing it again. Observe what happens.

Draw Conclusions

The circle represents a planet. What happened the first time you swung it? What happened after you spun it? What does the spinning represent? How does spinning affect a planet's movement in its orbit?

Design Your Own Investigation

Getting an Angle on the Sun

You've read that the sun's rays heat a surface more when they hit it directly than when they hit it at an angle. Using this as a hypothesis, think of a way you can experiment to see if the hypothesis is correct. For example, you might use a desk lamp to represent the sun and measure temperatures with thermometers. Decide on a way to set up your experiment and record your results. Then carry out your plan. Write a paragraph explaining how your experiment helps explain Earth's seasons.

Vocabulary Review

Use the terms below to complete the sentences. The page numbers tell you where to look in the chapter if you need help.

axis p. 406

revolution p. 406

eclipses p. 410

first quarter p. 416

third quarter p. 417

comet p. 428

1. The length of our year depends on Earth's _____ .

2. Certain alignments of Earth, the moon, and the sun cause _____ .

3. The imaginary line around which Earth rotates is its _____ .

4. After a new moon, the moon enters its _____ .

5. After a full moon, the moon enters its _____ .

6. A ball of ice and rock orbiting the sun is a _____ .

Check Understanding

Write the letter of the best choice.

7. **SEQUENCE** Which phase occurs when the moon is on the opposite side of Earth from the sun?
   A. first quarter
   B. full moon
   C. new moon
   D. third quarter

8. **CAUSE AND EFFECT** Which are caused by the pull of the moon and the sun on Earth?
   F. eclipses
   G. night and day
   H. seasons
   J. tides

9. Which of these is a main-sequence star?
   A. blue star
   B. neutron star
   C. red giant
   D. supernova

10. Which is another name for a moon?
    F. comet
    G. meteor
    H. nebula
    J. satellite

11. Which of these is composed of stars?
    A. asteroid belt
    B. black hole
    C. galaxy
    D. solar system

12. Which is shown in the diagram below?

    F. day-night cycle
    G. lunar eclipse
    H. solar eclipse
    J. summer season

13. Which phase occurs when the moon is on the same side of Earth as the sun?

A. first quarter

B. full moon

C. new moon

D. third quarter

14. Which is the final stage of a yellow star?

F. black hole

G. neutron star

H. red giant

J. white dwarf

15. Which occurs when the Northern Hemisphere is in the position illustrated below?

A. daytime

B. nighttime

C. summer

D. winter

16. Which is a major cause of temperature changes on Earth?

F. the pull of the moon

G. the tides

H. the angle of the sun's rays

J. lunar and solar eclipses

Inquiry Skills

17. To **make a model** of a solar eclipse, what materials could you use?

18. What are three ways you could **use numbers** to describe a planet?

Critical Thinking

19. What might the positions of different kinds of stars in a spiral galaxy tell about the movement of those stars within the galaxy?

20. Jacob uses a powerful telescope to look at a red main-sequence star in the night sky.

Part A How does he know that this star is part of the Milky Way Galaxy?

Part B How long can he expect this star to last, compared with the yellow and blue stars he sees near it?

Matter and Energy

PHYSICAL SCIENCE

○○○ **Thomas A. Edison Memorial Tower and Museum**

TO: john@hspscience.com

FROM: keith@hspscience.com

RE: Edison, New Jersey

Dear John,

I know we have been working really hard on our science fair project and have had some disappointing setbacks in our experiments. Let me offer a ray of hope to our cause. I visited the Edison Memorial Tower and Museum. It was encouraging to see that Edison himself had major setbacks when inventing the incandescent light. After much trial and error, his team tried using a filament thread inside a bulb. It burned thirteen and one-half hours. Imagine the thrill of that victory.

We can do it!

Keith

Blenko Glass Visitor Center and Factory Outlet

TO: kelly@hspscience.com

FROM: ivana@hspscience.com

RE: Huntington, West Virginia

Dear Kelly,

One of the industries that West Virginia is renowned for is glass blowing. Artisans use large amounts of silica sand, stone, and other chemical compounds. Visitors to the Blenko Glass Company can watch the steps taken to handcraft glass. The sand is placed in a furnace and combined with other materials. It is fused together with intense heat. The glass is then taken to a blower, who shapes the glass. The piece is reheated and sent to a finisher, who adds the finishing touches. Seeing this makes a person even more disappointed to accidentally break an object made of handblown glass!

Ivana

Experiment!

Chemical Reactions Making glass from sand and other materials is a chemical reaction that requires thermal energy. What kinds of changes occur during chemical reactions? Plan and conduct an experiment to find out.

Chapter 12 Atoms and Elements

Lesson 1 What Is Matter Composed Of?

Lesson 2 What Are Elements and Compounds?

Lesson 3 What Are the States of Matter?

Vocabulary

atom
proton
nucleus
neutron
electron
atomic number
element
metal
nonmetal
periodic table
compound
melting point
boiling point
plasma

What do YOU wonder?

Matter from the sun interacts with gas particles in Earth's upper atmosphere. Earth's magnetic field directs the charged gas particles toward the poles. When this happens you can see glowing, dancing streaks of color in the sky at night. These lights are known as auroras. Have you ever seen the lights of the auroras? Do you think they occur more often at certain times of the year?

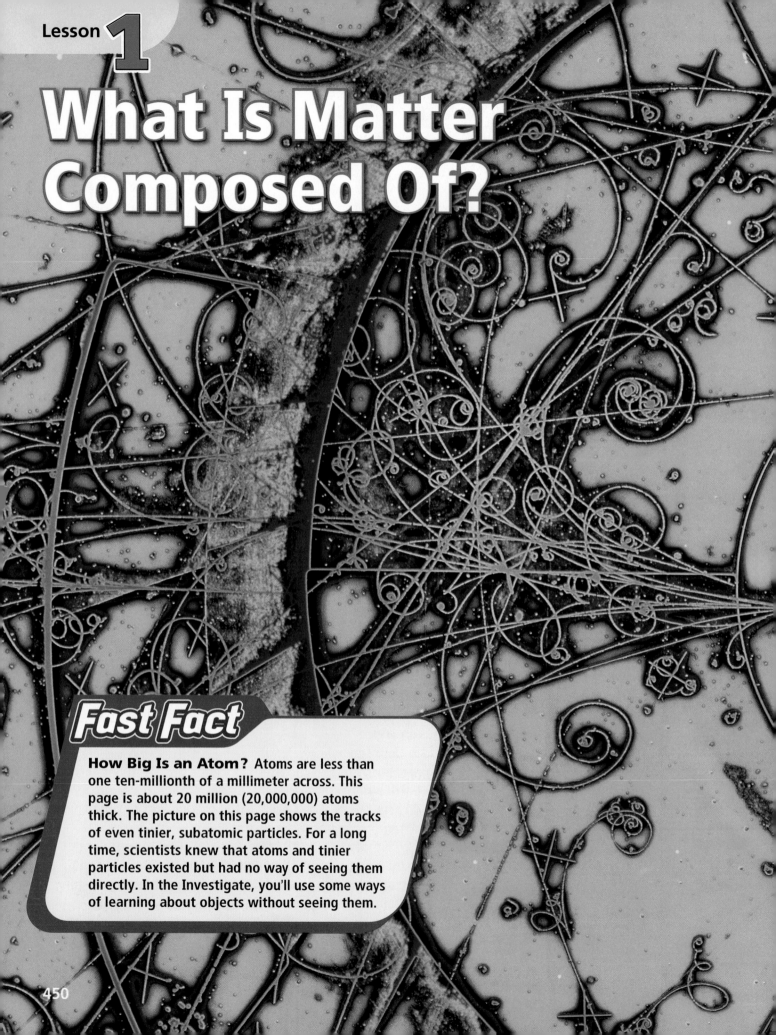

What Is Matter Composed Of?

Fast Fact

How Big Is an Atom? Atoms are less than one ten-millionth of a millimeter across. This page is about 20 million (20,000,000) atoms thick. The picture on this page shows the tracks of even tinier, subatomic particles. For a long time, scientists knew that atoms and tinier particles existed but had no way of seeing them directly. In the Investigate, you'll use some ways of learning about objects without seeing them.

Observing What You Can't See

Materials
- 8 wooden blocks
- large piece of cardboard
- mystery object
- marble

Procedure

1 Work on the floor. Put two blocks under each corner of the piece of cardboard.

2 Have a partner hide a mystery object under the cardboard when you aren't looking. No peeking!

3 Roll the marble under the cardboard. On paper, make a sketch of what you observe. Use an arrow to show where the marble goes in. Use another arrow to show where it comes out.

4 Record other observations. What do you hear?

5 Repeat Steps 3 and 4 at least 20 times. Roll the marble from a different side or at a different angle each time.

Draw Conclusions

1. How could you tell whether the marble hit the object?

2. What does your data tell you about where the object is?

3. How big is the object? Why do you think so?

4. What is the object made of? How can you tell?

5. **Inquiry Skill** From your observations, can you infer what the mystery object is? Use the data you recorded to communicate your idea.

Step 2

Step 3

Investigate Further

Try to gather information about objects sealed inside a shoe box. Without opening the box, use as many clues as possible to gather data and infer what's inside.

Reading in Science

VOCABULARY
atom p. 452
proton p. 453
nucleus p. 453
neutron p. 453
electron p. 453
atomic number p. 453

SCIENCE CONCEPTS
▶ what atoms are made of
▶ how atoms differ

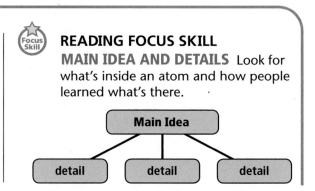

READING FOCUS SKILL
MAIN IDEA AND DETAILS Look for what's inside an atom and how people learned what's there.

Main Idea

detail   detail   detail

The Atom

Suppose you have an aluminum soft drink can. With tin snips, you cut it into smaller and smaller pieces. At what point will you have the smallest piece of aluminum that will still be aluminum? You probably can't answer that question, but you can guess that the piece would be too small to see. Centuries ago, philosophers wondered about the smallest unit that makes up matter. Although they didn't know how small the unit was, they gave it a name.

They called it an atom. An **atom** is the smallest unit of an element that still can be identified as that element. Elements are substances such as aluminum, gold, and helium.

Over many centuries, scientists worked as you did in the Investigate. They gathered indirect evidence and used it to infer things about the atom.

Today, we have a good idea about what an atom is and what is inside it. Experiments suggest that a single atom is made up of even smaller pieces, or *subatomic particles*.

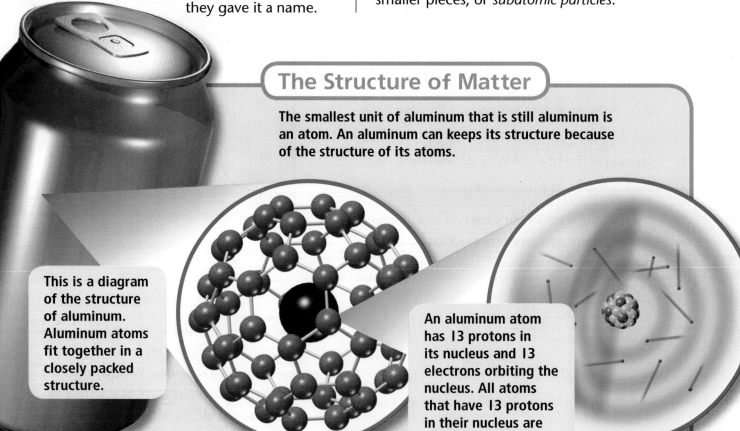

The Structure of Matter

The smallest unit of aluminum that is still aluminum is an atom. An aluminum can keeps its structure because of the structure of its atoms.

This is a diagram of the structure of aluminum. Aluminum atoms fit together in a closely packed structure.

An aluminum atom has 13 protons in its nucleus and 13 electrons orbiting the nucleus. All atoms that have 13 protons in their nucleus are aluminum atoms.

A **proton** is a subatomic particle that has a positive electric charge. The **nucleus** (NOO•klee•uhs), or center, of every atom contains at least one proton.

A **neutron** is a subatomic particle that has about the same mass as a proton but no electric charge. In most atoms, the nucleus contains one or more neutrons.

An **electron** is a subatomic particle that has a negative charge. It's much smaller and has much less mass than a proton or a neutron. Electrons aren't found in the nucleus. They orbit the nucleus at great speeds. Because an atom has equal numbers of protons and electrons, it has no overall charge.

Since all atoms contain the same subatomic particles, what makes elements different from one another? For example, you can see that aluminum is different from gold and that both are different from helium gas. Yet the atoms of all three are made up of the same subatomic

A powerful atomic-force microscope can take pictures of single atoms.

particles. How can that be?

Elements are different because they contain different *numbers* of subatomic particles. Most important is the number of protons. The number of protons in an atom is its **atomic number**. Different elements have different atomic numbers. They contain different numbers of protons, so their properties are different.

For example, each atom of aluminum contains 13 protons. Looking at it another way, any atom that contains 13 protons is an aluminum atom. Such an atom is different from an atom of gold, which contains 79 protons.

Both are different from an atom of helium, which has an atomic number of 2.

MAIN IDEA AND DETAILS What is an atom? What are its parts?

Helium

A helium atom has 2 protons in its nucleus. All atoms with an atomic number of 2 are helium atoms.

453

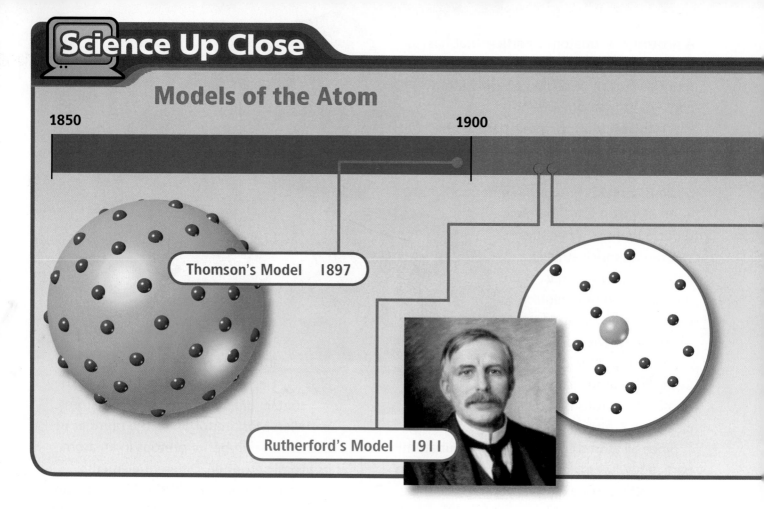

Models of the Atom

1850

1900

Thomson's Model 1897

Rutherford's Model 1911

Models of the Atom

People started talking about the atom more than 2400 years ago. At that time, the Greek philosopher Democritus first used the term. It wasn't until 1808 that the English scientist John Dalton published his atomic theory of matter. Dalton knew nothing about protons, neutrons, and electrons, but he realized that differences in substances' atoms made their properties different.

No one knew yet what was inside an atom. In 1897, while investigating electricity, the English scientist J. J. Thomson identified an electrically charged particle that he called an electron. It was a tiny particle, much smaller than the atom, and it had a negative electric charge.

The discovery of the electron raised an important question. It was known that atoms are not charged, yet Thomson had found that a part of the atom is charged. How could this

be? Thomson thought he had an answer. He suggested that electrons might be embedded in a sphere of positive charges like "raisins in a plum pudding." Thomson thought the positive charges of the "pudding" would cancel out the negative charges of the electrons. He reasoned that this would make the atom electrically neutral.

The New Zealand–born scientist Ernest Rutherford decided to test the plum-pudding model. He shot positively charged particles at gold foil as if they were bullets. He observed that most of them passed through, but a few bounced back.

From his observations, Rutherford concluded that the plum-pudding model was wrong. In 1911, he suggested that the atom was mostly empty space. That would explain why most of the particles in his experiment passed through. Those that bounced back were repelled by a strong positive charge. That charge must be

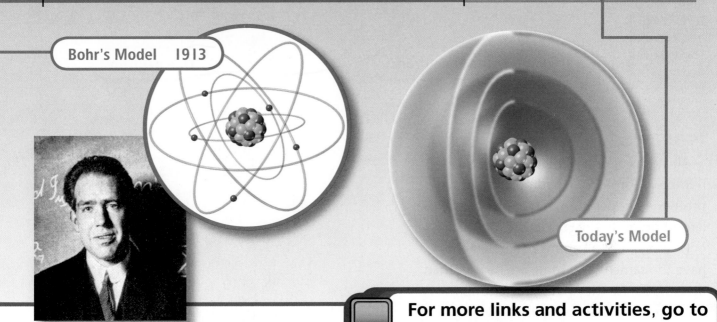

1950 2000

Bohr's Model   1913

Today's Model

For more links and activities, go to
www.hspscience.com

concentrated in one small part of the atom,
Rutherford thought. Electrons, he suggested,
must revolve around a positively charged
nucleus.

Rutherford's idea didn't explain why some
atoms give off heat or light. In 1913, Niels
Bohr suggested that electrons orbit at different
distances from the nucleus. When an electron
changes to a closer orbit, it gives off energy.
Today, electrons are usually shown in a "cloud"
around the nucleus. The cloud is the area in
which electrons are likely to be found.

Rutherford's model explained part of the
mass of an atom but not all of it. In 1920, he
predicted that neutrons accounted for the
rest of the mass. In 1932, James Chadwick
provided evidence to support this idea.

MAIN IDEA AND DETAILS How have
ideas about the atom changed in the last two
centuries?

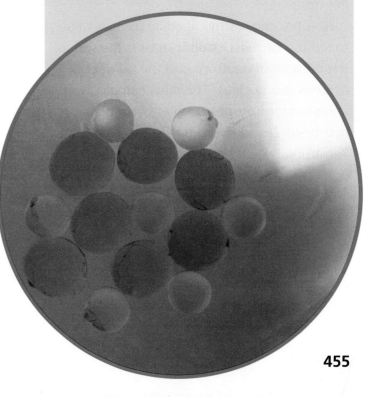

Rutherford's experiment, performed in 1911,
showed that the atom has a dense, positively
charged nucleus.

All hydrogen atoms have 1 proton. The atomic number of hydrogen is 1. Most hydrogen atoms have no neutrons, but some have 1 neutron and some have 2 neutrons.

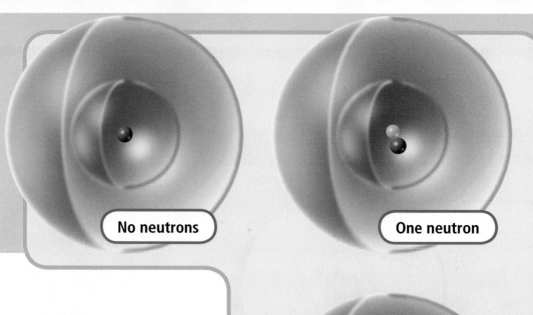

No neutrons

One neutron

Two neutrons

Isotopes

All atoms of one element have the same number of protons. A hydrogen atom has 1 proton. A copper atom has 29. Uranium, the largest atom that occurs in nature, has 92.

However, not all atoms of an element have the same mass. Some are heavier than others because they have different numbers of neutrons in their nuclei (NOO•klee•eye). Atoms that have the same number of protons but different numbers of neutrons are called *isotopes* (EYE•suh•tohps). For example, all hydrogen atoms have 1 proton, but hydrogen has three isotopes. One has no neutrons. Another has a single neutron. A third has 2 neutrons.

Isotopes can be identified by using a value called *atomic mass*. Atomic mass is the sum of the number of neutrons and the number of protons in a nucleus. The mass can be given in names for isotopes, such as hydrogen-1, hydrogen-2, and hydrogen-3.

Carbon, which has an atomic number of 6, has three isotopes: carbon-12, carbon-13, and carbon-14. How many protons are in the nucleus of each isotope? How many neutrons? What is the atomic mass of each of carbon's three isotopes?

 MAIN IDEA AND DETAILS What is an isotope? How are isotopes of an element different from one another?

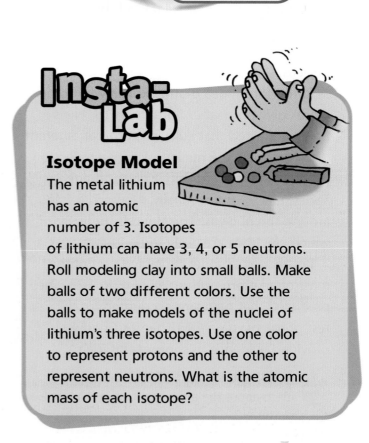

Insta-Lab

Isotope Model
The metal lithium has an atomic number of 3. Isotopes of lithium can have 3, 4, or 5 neutrons. Roll modeling clay into small balls. Make balls of two different colors. Use the balls to make models of the nuclei of lithium's three isotopes. Use one color to represent protons and the other to represent neutrons. What is the atomic mass of each isotope?

456

1. MAIN IDEA AND DETAILS Draw and complete this graphic organizer by listing details about the structure of atoms.

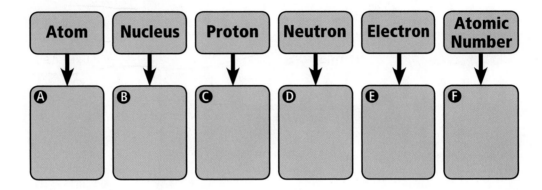

Atom	Nucleus	Proton	Neutron	Electron	Atomic Number
Ⓐ	Ⓑ	Ⓒ	Ⓓ	Ⓔ	Ⓕ

2. SUMMARIZE Use the completed graphic organizer to write a lesson summary.

3. DRAW CONCLUSIONS Explain how atoms of different elements are different from one another.

4. VOCABULARY Define *isotope* and give an example.

Test Prep

5. Critical Thinking Tell how Thomson, Rutherford, and Bohr helped figure out what is inside an atom.

6. What is the name of the particle of negative charge that orbits the nucleus of an atom?

    A. cyclotron   **C.** neutron

    B. electron   **D.** proton

Links

Writing

Expository Writing

Write a **paragraph** to compare and contrast different elements and different isotopes of the same element.

Math

Solve a Word Problem

The metal tantalum has an atomic number of 73. It has two natural isotopes with atomic masses of 180 and 181. How many neutrons are there in the atoms of tantalum's two isotopes?

Social Studies

The Nobel Prize

Many of the scientists who helped work out the structure of the atom won the Nobel Prize for their research. Find out who three of them are, what they contributed, and when they won their prizes. Write about one of them.

 For more links and activities, go to www.hspscience.com

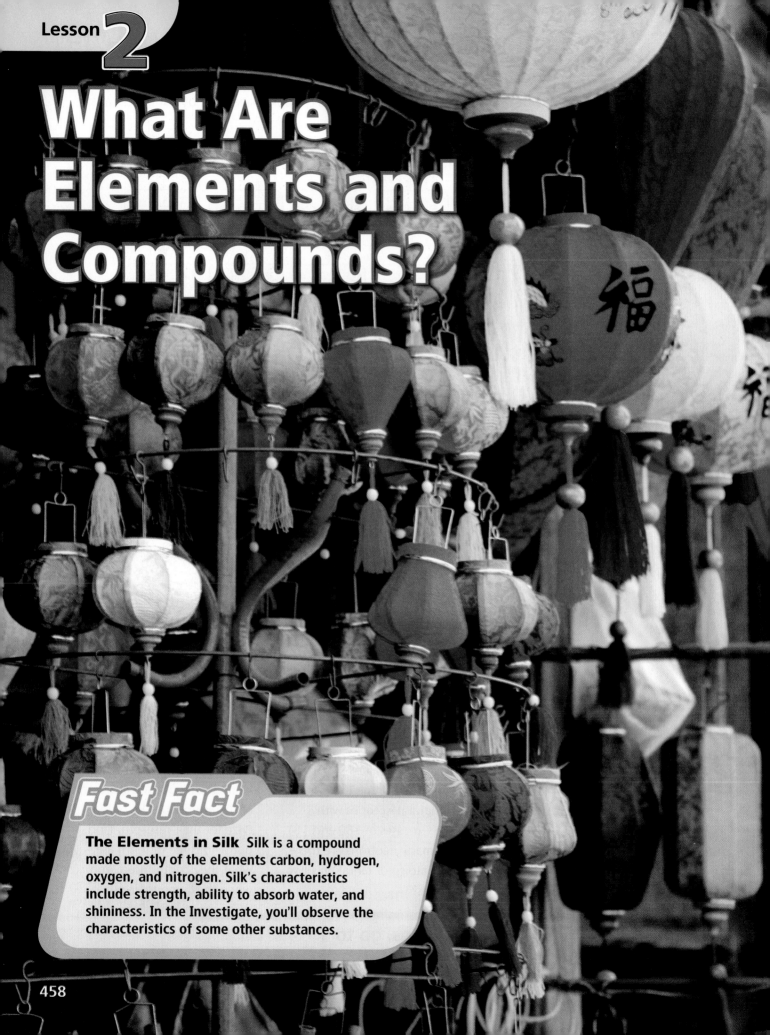

What Are Elements and Compounds?

Fast Fact

The Elements in Silk Silk is a compound made mostly of the elements carbon, hydrogen, oxygen, and nitrogen. Silk's characteristics include strength, ability to absorb water, and shininess. In the Investigate, you'll observe the characteristics of some other substances.

In Earth's crust, the most common element is oxygen, which is never found there in its free, pure state. Instead, it is combined with silicon, aluminum, and other metals in rocks and minerals. Sand is a combination of oxygen and silicon, the two most abundant elements in Earth's crust.

Elements can be classified according to their characteristics. About 75 percent of the elements are metals. **Metals** conduct heat and electricity well. Metals are malleable—they bend easily and can be rolled into sheets. Many but not all metals are shiny and have a silver-gray color. Gold is a yellow metal. Copper is reddish.

Elements that don't have these characteristics are nonmetals. A **nonmetal** doesn't conduct electricity and isn't shiny or malleable.

 COMPARE AND CONTRAST How do elements differ from one another?

◄ Silicon is abundant in Earth's crust, but not as a free element. It's combined with oxygen and other elements in sand and in many other minerals. Silicon's atomic number is 14.

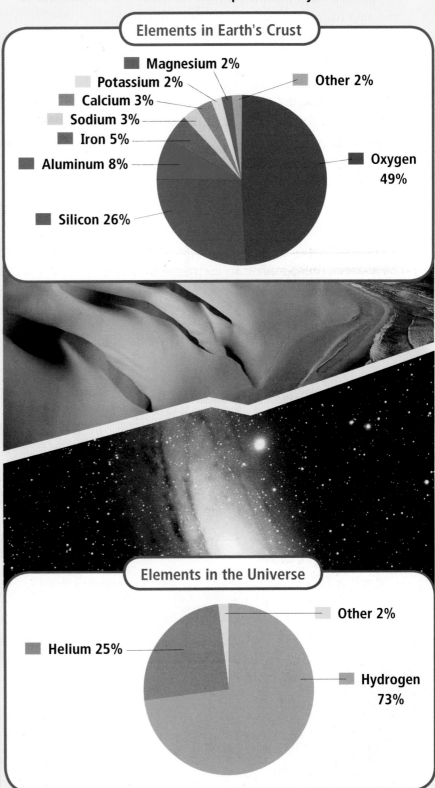

Math in Science
Interpret Data

Look at the graphs. For each graph, make a table that shows how abundant the elements are, in order from most to least. Compare the abundance of elements in Earth's crust with that of elements in the universe. What patterns do you notice?

Elements in Earth's Crust

- Magnesium 2%
- Potassium 2%
- Other 2%
- Calcium 3%
- Sodium 3%
- Iron 5%
- Oxygen 49%
- Aluminum 8%
- Silicon 26%

Elements in the Universe

- Other 2%
- Helium 25%
- Hydrogen 73%

Periodic Table

Distinguishing metals and nonmetals isn't the only way to classify elements. At room temperature, some elements are liquids. Others are gases or solids. Elements may also differ in color, in odor, and in other ways.

The first person to develop an organized system for classifying elements was the Russian chemist Dmitri Mendeleev (men•duh•LAY•uhv). In 1869, he organized the known elements in a table. He arranged them from lightest to heaviest, according to their atomic mass.

Today, we use the **periodic table**, a table arranged by atomic number. The table begins with atomic number 1, for the element hydrogen.

Each element has its place in the periodic table. The box for each element contains information about it, including its name, atomic number, and symbol. The symbol is one or more letters that stand for the element. Some symbols are easy to remember. For example, the symbol for carbon is C and the symbol for hydrogen is H. Some elements have symbols that come from their names in other languages. Gold's symbol is Au, from the Latin word

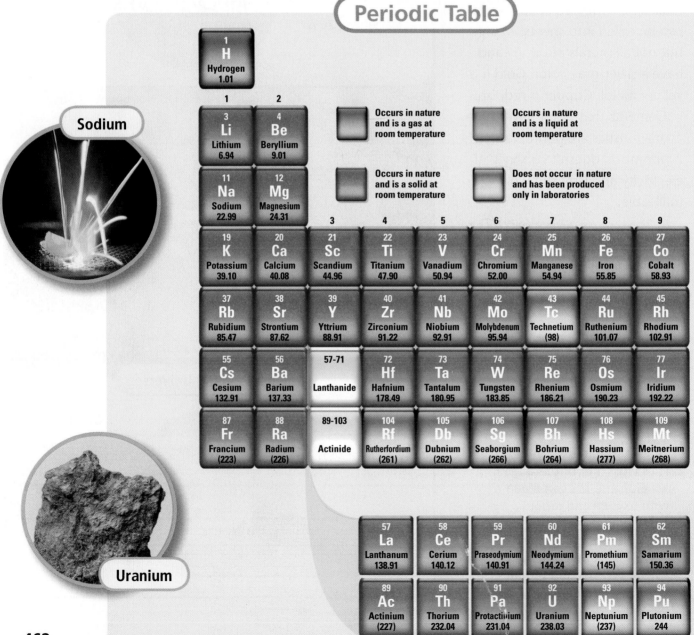

Sodium

Uranium

aurum. Silver's symbol is Ag, from *argentum.*

Each column of the periodic table shows a family. The elements in a family have similar properties. The rows of the table show periods. The elements in a period have similar arrangements of electrons.

Different colors in the table identify solids, liquids, and gases. Elements that don't occur in nature usually are shown in another color. Most of those elements have high atomic numbers.

 COMPARE AND CONTRAST How are elements in the same family alike? How are elements in the same period alike?

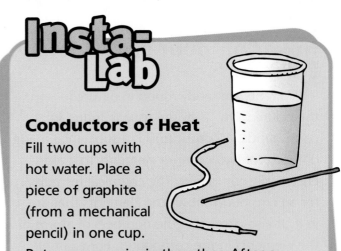

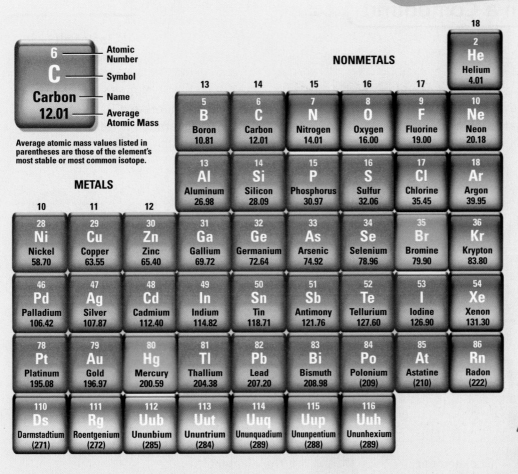

								18
				NONMETALS				2 **He** Helium 4.01
6 **C** Carbon 12.01 — Atomic Number, Symbol, Name, Average Atomic Mass		**13**	**14**	**15**	**16**	**17**		
		5 **B** Boron 10.81	6 **C** Carbon 12.01	7 **N** Nitrogen 14.01	8 **O** Oxygen 16.00	9 **F** Fluorine 19.00		10 **Ne** Neon 20.18

Average atomic mass values listed in parentheses are those of the element's most stable or most common isotope.

METALS

10	**11**	**12**	13 **Al** Aluminum 26.98	14 **Si** Silicon 28.09	15 **P** Phosphorus 30.97	16 **S** Sulfur 32.06	17 **Cl** Chlorine 35.45	18 **Ar** Argon 39.95
28 **Ni** Nickel 58.70	29 **Cu** Copper 63.55	30 **Zn** Zinc 65.40	31 **Ga** Gallium 69.72	32 **Ge** Germanium 72.64	33 **As** Arsenic 74.92	34 **Se** Selenium 78.96	35 **Br** Bromine 79.90	36 **Kr** Krypton 83.80
46 **Pd** Palladium 106.42	47 **Ag** Silver 107.87	48 **Cd** Cadmium 112.40	49 **In** Indium 114.82	50 **Sn** Tin 118.71	51 **Sb** Antimony 121.76	52 **Te** Tellurium 127.60	53 **I** Iodine 126.90	54 **Xe** Xenon 131.30
78 **Pt** Platinum 195.08	79 **Au** Gold 196.97	80 **Hg** Mercury 200.59	81 **Tl** Thallium 204.38	82 **Pb** Lead 207.20	83 **Bi** Bismuth 208.98	84 **Po** Polonium (209)	85 **At** Astatine (210)	86 **Rn** Radon (222)
110 **Ds** Darmstadtium (271)	111 **Rg** Roentgenium (272)	112 **Uub** Ununbium (285)	113 **Uut** Ununtrium (284)	114 **Uuq** Ununquadium (289)	115 **Uup** Ununpentium (288)	116 **Uuh** Ununhexium (289)		

Zinc

63 **Eu** Europium 151.96	64 **Gd** Gadolinium 157.25	65 **Tb** Terbium 158.93	66 **Dy** Dysprosium 162.50	67 **Ho** Holmium 164.93	68 **Er** Erbium 167.26	69 **Tm** Thulium 168.93	70 **Yb** Ytterbium 173.04	71 **Lu** Lutetium 174.97
95 **Am** Americium (243)	96 **Cm** Curium (247)	97 **Bk** Berkelium (247)	98 **Cf** Californium (251)	99 **Es** Einsteinium (252)	100 **Fm** Fermium (257)	101 **Md** Mendelevium (258)	102 **No** Nobelium (259)	103 **Lr** Lawrencium (262)

Neon

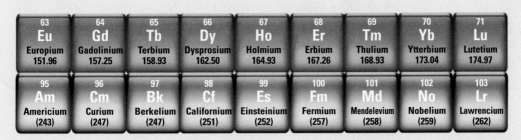

How Compounds Are Formed

Elements are rarely found in nature in their pure form. They are usually found in compounds. A **compound** is a substance made of atoms of two or more elements that are chemically combined. The chemical formula for a compound shows the elements that are in it. It also compares the numbers of atoms of the elements in the compound. For example, the chemical formula for the compound sand is SiO_2. This means that sand has 1 atom of silicon for every 2 atoms of oxygen.

Compounds don't have the same properties as the elements that form them. For example, ordinary table salt is a compound that has 1 atom of sodium for every 1 atom of chlorine. Its chemical formula is $NaCl$. Pure sodium is a soft,

Elements in a Compound

The mineral halite is a compound of sodium and chlorine. It's also known as rock salt. It's mined where ancient seas and salt lakes evaporated millions of years ago.

Table salt is a compound of 1 atom of sodium (Na) and 1 atom of chlorine (Cl). Its chemical formula is $NaCl$.

SODIUM

Chlorine

The element sodium is a metal.

The element chlorine is a gas.

bright, silvery metal that floats on water. Pure chlorine is a greenish-yellow gas. Does table salt give you any clue that it is made of sodium and chlorine?

Water is another familiar compound. In water, 2 hydrogen atoms combine with 1 oxygen atom. The chemical formula is H_2O. Both hydrogen and oxygen are gases at ordinary temperatures. When they combine, they give off so much energy that they explode. Would you have guessed that water can come from an explosion of gases?

Compounds hold together because atoms bond, or attach to one another. Some atoms of different elements bond by sharing electrons. In water, the atoms of hydrogen and oxygen have this kind of bond.

In other compounds, electrons have moved from the atoms of one element to the atoms of another. Table salt, NaCl, is this kind of compound. When it forms, electrons move from the sodium atoms to the chlorine atoms. Losing electrons leaves the sodium atoms with a positive charge. Gaining electrons gives the chlorine atoms a negative charge. The opposite charges attract and bind the atoms tightly together.

 COMPARE AND CONTRAST How do compounds differ from elements?

The stand the aquarium is on is made of a compound—steel. Steel has iron and carbon combined to give very different properties from either of the two elements separately. Water is also a compound with properties very different from the elements—oxygen and hydrogen—that make it up. What other compounds do you see in the photograph?

These fruits and vegetables contain organic compounds that we need in our diets for good nutrition.

Compounds in Nature and in Industry

Elements are occasionally found in their pure form. About 78 percent of the air, for example, is the element nitrogen, and about 21 percent is the element oxygen.

In general, though, our world is made up of compounds. To remove elements from compounds takes a lot of work. The ores mined from Earth's crust, for example, are usually compounds of metals, silicon, and oxygen. The ores must be crushed, heated, and treated with chemicals and electricity to get out the metals.

Compounds that contain carbon make up an important group. They are the organic compounds. They're called organic because they were originally obtained from living things or from the remains of living things. Today, many organic compounds are made in laboratories or in industries.

Organic compounds are atoms of carbon bonded with atoms of hydrogen, oxygen, nitrogen, sulfur, chlorine, or other elements. The elements bond by sharing electrons. Carbon atoms form many different compounds because they can link to each other in long chains. They bond by sharing 1, 2, 3, or 4 electrons.

 COMPARE AND CONTRAST How do organic compounds differ from other compounds?

1. COMPARE AND CONTRAST Draw and complete this graphic organizer.

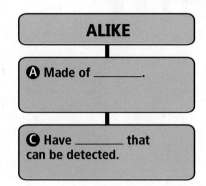
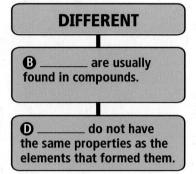

ELEMENTS AND COMPOUNDS

ALIKE	DIFFERENT
Ⓐ Made of _____.	**Ⓑ** _____ are usually found in compounds.
Ⓒ Have _____ that can be detected.	**Ⓓ** _____ do not have the same properties as the elements that formed them.

2. SUMMARIZE Use the completed graphic organizer to write a lesson summary.

3. DRAW CONCLUSIONS Could life exist without compounds? Explain.

4. VOCABULARY Write a sentence that explains the difference between an element and a compound.

Test Prep

5. Critical Thinking Explain what the periodic table is and how it is used.

6. How are elements arranged in the periodic table?

   A. by the compounds they form
   B. by their atomic mass
   C. by their atomic number
   D. by the number of neutrons

Links

Writing

Narrative Writing

Silicon is the main element in a class of meteorites called aerolites. Write a **story** from the point of view of a silicon atom in an aerolite. Tell how you, as the atom, became part of the meteorite and how you traveled through space before landing on Earth.

Math

Make a Circle Graph

Earth's atmosphere is a mixture of gases. Some are elements, and some are compounds. Find a table of percents of the gases in the air, and make a circle graph showing those percents.

Literature

Poetry for Scientists

Find and read poems about atoms, elements, or compounds. Then write a poem of your own about matter.

 For more links and activities, go to www.hspscience.com

What Are the States of Matter?

Fast Fact

Fascinating Glaciers Glaciers can be as large as a continent or as small as a valley between mountains. Glaciers are masses of snow, ice, rocks, water, and air. They include three states of matter. The snow and ice are solids. In and near a glacier is water in liquid form. And the air above a glacier contains water vapor, a gas. In the Investigate, you'll explore state changes.

Melting and Freezing

Materials
- 3 12-oz plastic cups
- piece of string, about 20 cm long
- masking tape and pen
- water
- measuring spoons
- 2 thermometers
- ice cubes
- salt
- stopwatch

Procedure

1 Nearly fill one cup with water. Float an ice cube in the water. Lay the string across the top of the ice cube. Lift the string. What happens?

2 Replace the string on the ice cube. Sprinkle ¼ teaspoon of salt on the string and the ice cube. Wait a few seconds. Lift again. What happens?

3 Use the masking tape to label one of the other cups *Salt* and the third cup *No Salt*.

4 Nearly fill these two cups with ice cubes. Add 3 teaspoons of salt to the cup labeled *Salt*. Add enough water to both cups to nearly fill them.

5 Put a thermometer in each cup. Stir gently. Read and record the temperature in each cup.

6 Start the stopwatch. Every 2 minutes, stir again and read the thermometers. Record the temperatures for both cups in a data table. Continue for 10 minutes or longer.

Draw Conclusions

1. Explain why you could lift the ice cube with the string after you added the salt, but not before.

2. **Inquiry Skill** Make a line graph of your time and temperature data. Draw one line for the *Salt* data and another line for the *No Salt* data. What can you conclude from your graph?

Step 2

Step 6

Investigate Further

Use the characteristics of salt to plan and conduct an investigation in which you make your own ice cream.

VOCABULARY
melting point p. 472
boiling point p. 472
plasma p. 474

SCIENCE CONCEPTS
▶ how solids, liquids, and gases differ
▶ what causes matter to change from one state to another

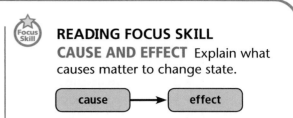

READING FOCUS SKILL
CAUSE AND EFFECT Explain what causes matter to change state.

cause ⟶ effect

States of Matter

If you walk by a large lake or river in winter, you'll likely see water in two of its three states. Like all matter, water can exist as a solid. A solid has a definite shape and volume. As a solid, water takes the form of ice or snow.

Water can also be a liquid. A liquid has a definite volume but no definite shape. A liquid takes the shape of the container that holds it. Rain is liquid water.

Matter can take a third form, as a gas. A gas has no definite shape or volume. It expands to fill whatever space is available. On a winter walk, you won't see the gaseous form of water, often called water vapor. It's in the air, and it's invisible. The mist you see rising off a pond or lake is not water vapor. Like the clouds in the sky, it is actually tiny droplets of liquid water.

As you know, water is a compound of two atoms of hydrogen bonded to one atom of oxygen. Atoms bonded in such a way are called *molecules*. Solids, liquids, and gases look and act

In ice, molecules of water are packed closely together. They move, or vibrate, back and forth, but not very much. The motion of the molecules is greater in liquid water and greater still in water vapor, a gas.

Solids have their own shape. Liquids take the shape of the container they are in, but they may not fill it. The molecules of gases move apart and fill whatever space is available, as they do in the balloon.

Solid

Liquid

Gas

differently because of the energy, or motion, of their atoms or molecules.

For example, solid ice, at a low temperature, has less energy than liquid water and water vapor. With so little energy, molecules in ice don't move around much. They are fixed in a regular pattern. The pattern is a crystal of ice. Ice crystals connect in icicles and hailstones. Solids are harder to compress than liquids or gases. Only great pressure can change the shape of a solid.

In the liquid state, water molecules have more energy. The molecules are close together, but they bounce around more than they do in ice. They can move around and slide over one another. That's why liquids flow and can be poured.

Liquids take the shape of the container they are in, but they may not fill it. Liquids can be compressed a little, but this is hard to do.

Like liquid water, water vapor can also flow. As a gas, water vapor takes the shape of the container it's in. But a gas will fill its container in all directions. Water vapor has a lot of energy. Its molecules bounce around freely. They move farther apart until something stops them. Because of the distance between molecules, gases are easy to compress.

The air always contains a certain amount of water vapor. Water vapor is part of the water cycle. Water evaporates from lakes, rivers, ponds, and oceans and transpires from the leaves of plants. This water vapor then condenses to form clouds, from which precipitation falls.

 CAUSE AND EFFECT What causes matter to exist in three different states?

Changes of State

Water provides a familiar example of three states of matter. It can be solid, liquid, or gas at ordinary temperatures.

The atoms and molecules of all elements and compounds can exist in each state. The temperatures at which their changes of state occur depend on the substance.

A **melting point** is the temperature at which a substance changes from a solid to a liquid. The melting point of ice, or solid water, is 0°C (32°F). The melting point of gold is 1064°C (1947°F). It takes much more heat to melt gold than to melt ice, but both substances can melt.

All substances can change from a liquid to a gas, too. The temperature at which a substance becomes a gas is its **boiling point**. The boiling point of water is 100°C (212°F). For gold, it is 2856°C (5172°F). It takes a lot of heat to turn liquid gold into a gas, but it can be done.

Adding or removing enough heat causes changes in state. Adding heat to things, or warming them, causes atoms and molecules to move faster. Removing heat causes atoms and molecules to move more slowly. Gases, when cooled below the boiling point,

At ordinary temperatures, gold is a solid. When heated in a forge, it becomes a liquid that can be poured into a mold.

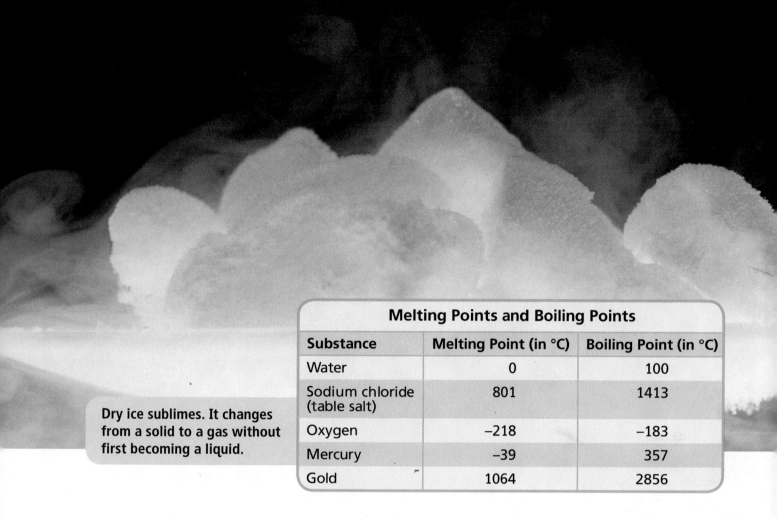

Melting Points and Boiling Points

Substance	Melting Point (in °C)	Boiling Point (in °C)
Water	0	100
Sodium chloride (table salt)	801	1413
Oxygen	−218	−183
Mercury	−39	357
Gold	1064	2856

Dry ice sublimes. It changes from a solid to a gas without first becoming a liquid.

become liquids. Liquids, when cooled below the melting point, become solids.

Adding and removing heat aren't the only ways to cause substances to change states. Pressure can do this, too. Under high pressure, gases form liquids because the pressure pushes their atoms and molecules together. Low pressure causes atoms or molecules to move apart. Liquids under low pressure become gases at temperatures lower than the usual boiling point.

Some substances can change from a solid directly to a gas without first becoming a liquid. This is called sublimation. Solid carbon dioxide, or dry ice, sublimes at room temperature. It becomes a gas without ever being a liquid. Water can sublime, too. Snowbanks can shrink on cold, windy winter days, the snow becoming water vapor without melting first. Ice cubes left

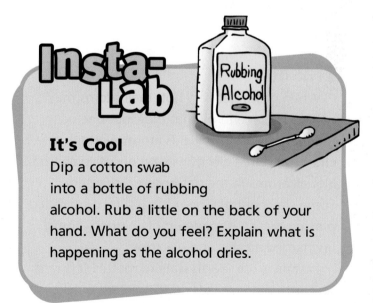

Insta-Lab

It's Cool
Dip a cotton swab into a bottle of rubbing alcohol. Rub a little on the back of your hand. What do you feel? Explain what is happening as the alcohol dries.

in trays in a freezer also sublime, shrinking more and more over a period of several weeks.

 CAUSE AND EFFECT What process causes changes of state?

473

The electrical energy of lightning causes plasma to form in the air.

Plasma

When gases get very hot, their atoms may gain so much energy that they lose one or more electrons. This yields atoms with positive charge and free electrons with negative charge. Not all atoms in the gas become charged. Some stay neutral. The result is a mixture called **plasma**, which is made up of charged atoms, uncharged atoms, and electrons.

Plasma is the fourth state of matter. It is rare on Earth, but it makes up 99 percent of all matter in the universe. Stars, interstellar clouds, and comets are mostly plasma. In Earth's magnetic field, plasma from the sun—the solar wind—produces the shimmering, colored lights of the auroras.

On Earth, we see plasma in the inner core of a flame. A bolt of lightning causes plasma to form in the air when oxygen and nitrogen atoms give up electrons.

Plasma has practical uses. When an electric current is passed through a fluorescent bulb, a neon sign, or a mercury-vapor street lamp, plasma forms in the gases inside. When the atoms of these gases recombine with electrons, they give off light. Plasma is also used to make computer chips and to weld steel.

In the sun, the nuclei of atoms in plasma unite, or fuse, releasing tremendous amounts of energy. If this process of nuclear fusion could be controlled here on Earth, it would provide a source of energy for generating electricity.

 CAUSE AND EFFECT What causes plasma to form?

1. **CAUSE AND EFFECT** Draw and complete this graphic organizer to show how adding heat affects each state of matter.

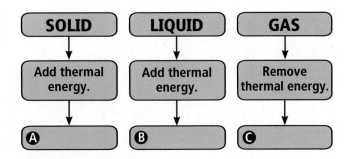

2. **SUMMARIZE** Write a summary of this lesson by using the words from the graphic organizer.

3. **DRAW CONCLUSIONS** Tell how and why it's possible for any element to exist in any of three states of matter.

4. **VOCABULARY** Use the terms *melting point* and *boiling point* to explain changes of state between solids and liquids and between liquids and gases.

Test Prep

5. **Critical Thinking** Which state of matter is the most common in the universe? How does it form?

6. Which of the following shows that some solids don't melt?

   A. Gases form at high temperatures.

   B. Dry ice sublimes into water vapor.

   C. Gases expand to fill any container.

   D. The mass of a gas can be measured.

Links

Writing

Expository Writing
Look out a window. Write a **paragraph** that describes what you see, classifying each object as an example of one of the four states of matter.

Math

Solve a Problem
Water's melting point is 0°C (32°F), and its boiling point is 100°C (212°F). For each increase of 1° on the Celsius scale (C), how much increase is there on the Fahrenheit scale (F)?

Art

Graphic Design
Think of a fusion-powered generating station of the future. At the station, plasma is used to generate electrical power. Design a logo for the station to represent what it does and how.

 For more links and activities, go to www.hspscience.com

A Honey of an Ad

As advertisements go, this one has created quite a buzz.

Each year a publisher in England produces a book listing amazing facts and records. Not long ago, the publishers of this record book wanted to advertise the fact that they were starting a new website.

But the company didn't want to do the same old newspaper or TV advertisement. They wanted to do something different to make a splash for their new site.

A Big Idea?

That's why, instead of buying a newspaper ad, the company got a bee in its bonnet to create the world's smallest ad and place it on the knee of a bee.

The ad is a little bit bigger than the diameter of a human hair but is so small that it shattered the record for the world's smallest ad. That record had been held by a tiny ad run in the world's smallest newspaper. "We knew we had to have something pretty extraordinary given the nature of our business," said one company spokesman.

Etched in Gold

To make the advertisement, scientists used a special laser. The laser etched the new Web address using evaporated or condensed gold onto film. The film was then attached to a band that was placed around the knee of a bee.

When it was done, the advertisement measured 100 by 100 microns. To give you an idea of how small that is, a human hair is

between 40 and 100 microns in diameter. But the question remains, why a bee and not an ant or a mosquito? According to the company officials, to be "the bee's knees" is another way of saying to be the best at something.

Think About It

1. Why do you think the company used gold and not some other metallic element?
2. Is the ad bigger or smaller than the diameter of a human hair?

Spin-In Find out more! Log on to **www.hspscience.com**

OVERCOMING OBSTACLES

Have you ever heard of Lise Meitner? Probably not, yet she is considered one of the great minds of science. Meitner was the first scientist to explain the process of nuclear fission.

Nuclear fission is the process through which atoms split apart and release tremendous amounts of energy. This release of energy has been used in nuclear power plants around the world. Fission is also important in nuclear weapons.

Meitner told the world about nuclear fission in 1939. However, her partner, Otto Hahn, received the Nobel Prize in 1944. Meitner's role in the explanation of fission was ignored until 1966, when her work was partly recognized. That year, Meitner, Hahn, and another scientist received the Enrico Fermi Award.

Career   Nuclear Engineer

When nuclear engineers go to work, they are using an energy source they can't see: the atom. Some nuclear engineers operate nuclear power plants, and others develop nuclear power sources for spacecraft. Many nuclear engineers find industrial and medical uses for radioactive materials, such as in equipment to diagnose and treat medical problems.

You Can Do It!

Quick and Easy Project

Magic Balloon

Materials
- freezer (optional)
- glass bottle
- balloon
- beaker, larger than the bottle
- hot water
- ice water

Procedure

1. This project works best if the bottle is cold. If a freezer is handy, put the bottle in it for 20 minutes.

2. Stretch the opening of the balloon over the mouth of the bottle. Make sure there are no leaks or tears in the balloon.

3. Set the bottle in a beaker of hot water. Observe and record what happens to the balloon.

4. After 15 minutes, discard the hot water in the beaker and replace it with ice water. Record your observations of the balloon.

Draw Conclusions

Describe the changes you observed. What caused them? What conclusion can you draw about the effect of temperature on a gas?

Design Your Own Investigation

Temperature and Volume

Design an experiment that will let you discover a relationship between the temperature of a gas and its volume. State the hypothesis you will test. Identify the variables you will control. What variable will you change on purpose? Plan to use a thermometer to measure temperature. Plan to observe gas volume by using a balloon and a tape measure. How will you measure the outcomes? Plan how you will record and display the data. Think ahead about how a graph can help you draw a conclusion.

12 Review and Test Preparation

Vocabulary Review

Use the terms below to complete the sentences. The page numbers tell you where to look in the chapter if you need help.

atom p. 452   **metal** p. 461
nucleus p. 453   **compound** p. 464
electron p. 453   **melting point** p. 472
atomic number p. 453   **boiling point** p. 472
element p. 460   **plasma** p. 474

1. In the periodic table, elements are arranged by _____ .

2. The temperature at which a liquid becomes a gas is a _____ .

3. A substance made of two or more elements is a _____ .

4. An element that is shiny, bends, and conducts heat and electricity is a _____ .

5. The temperature at which a solid becomes a liquid is a _____ .

6. A pure substance that contains atoms of only one kind is an _____ .

7. The dense center of an atom is the _____ .

8. A subatomic particle with a negative charge is an _____ .

9. Hot gas containing charged and uncharged atoms and free electrons is _____ .

10. The smallest unit of a pure substance that still has the identity of that substance is an _____ .

Check Understanding

Write the letter of the best choice.

11. **MAIN IDEA AND DETAILS** What is the model of the atom as we understand it today?
   A. the same as that proposed by John Dalton in 1808
   B. an idea first stated by the ancient Greeks 2400 years ago
   C. the model proposed by Ernest Rutherford in 1911
   D. a model that has changed many times as experiments yielded new evidence

12. **COMPARE AND CONTRAST** How are protons and neutrons alike?
   F. Both are found in the nucleus of the atom.
   G. Both are electrically charged.
   H. Both are used to arrange the rows of the periodic table.
   J. Both make up an electron.

13. Which is the major cause of changes in states of matter?
   A. change of speed of atoms or molecules
   B. cooling of matter to its evaporation point
   C. loss of electrons from atoms
   D. expansion of particles into available space

14. Which of the following is a true statement about subatomic particles in an atom?

    F. The number of electrons never changes.

    G. The numbers of neutrons and protons are equal.

    H. The number of subatomic particles is three.

    J. The number of neutrons determines the isotope.

15. What is a substance composed of 2 atoms of hydrogen, 1 atom of sulfur, and 4 atoms of oxygen?

    A. a compound

    B. an element

    C. an isotope

    D. plasma

16. How is the element with atomic number 82 in the periodic table different from the element with atomic number 81?

    F. It has one less electron.

    G. It has one more proton.

    H. It has an extra neutron in its nucleus.

    J. It has one more nucleus.

Inquiry Skills

17. What can you infer about two substances that have the same atomic number but different atomic masses? What term would you use to classify the two substances?

18. What can you infer about elements that are in the same column of the periodic table?

Critical Thinking

19. The water in a pot is brought to a boil. A student measures the temperature of the water in the pot every 5 minutes for 20 minutes as the water boils. How does the temperature change during the 20 minutes?

20. In places that get very cold, road crews put salt on icy roads.

    Part A What is the purpose of using salt on icy roads?

    Part B Explain the effect of the salt by using the concept of melting point.

Chapter
13 Matter and How It Changes

Vocabulary

physical property	chemical change
mass	chemical property
volume	reactivity
density	stability
physical change	acid
mixture	base
solution	indicator
suspension	pH scale
colloid	

What do YOU wonder?

Every part of this hotel is made of ice. People really rent rooms in the hotel and spend the night here. What conditions are needed for this hotel to exist? Why?

483

What Are the Physical Properties of Matter?

Fast Fact

This is the Keet Seel (Broken Pottery)
Ruin in the Navajo National Monument in Arizona. The Anasazi people built it in the sandstone cliffs during the last half of the 13th century. Sandstone has distinct properties that make it good for building. In the Investigate, you will examine a physical property of matter.

Push Up the Volume

Materials
- aluminum foil
- metric ruler
- wood block
- graduate
- pan balance
- water

Procedure

1. Observe the aluminum foil. Record as many of its properties as you can. Repeat for the block.

2. Use the balance to measure and record the mass of the foil and the mass of the block separately.

3. Find the volume of the block. The volume is equal to length × width × height. Measure each dimension in centimeters, and express the volume in cubic centimeters (cm³).

4. Fill the graduate about two-thirds full of water. Measure and record the volume of the water you added.

5. Roll the aluminum foil so it will fit lengthwise inside the graduate. There must be no trapped air inside the foil.

6. Place the foil in the graduate so that it's entirely beneath the water. Measure and record the new volume of the water. Calculate the volume of the foil.

Step 1

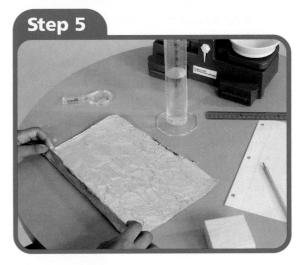

Step 5

Draw Conclusions

1. How did you calculate the volume of the aluminum foil?

2. Find the density of each object. The density is equal to the mass divided by the volume. The density will be in grams per cubic centimeter (g/cm³).

3. **Inquiry Skill** Compare the ways you calculated the volume of the foil and the volume of the block.

Investigate Further

Select several familiar objects from around the classroom. Conduct an investigation in which you compare the volumes and densities of these objects.

Reading in Science

VOCABULARY
physical property p. 487
mass p. 488
volume p. 488
density p. 488
physical change p. 490

SCIENCE CONCEPTS
▶ what defines a physical property
▶ what a physical change is and how to recognize it

READING FOCUS SKILL
MAIN IDEA AND DETAILS Look for the main physical properties of matter.

Main Idea
detail   detail   detail

Physical Properties

How would you define *matter*? It's not as easy as you might think. Almost everything you see, touch, and smell is matter. But how would you define it?

Words like *things* and *stuff* might come to mind. But those aren't very accurate definitions. You might try "anything you can see or feel." That sounds like a good definition. But what about air? Air is matter, even though you can't see it and might not be able to feel it.

Fortunately, scientists have had a very long time to work on this, and they've come up with a good definition: Matter is anything that has mass and takes up space. So, whether you're talking about air or water or a car or a grain of sand, they all have mass and take up space. They're all matter.

What is matter made of? At first, this might seem to be an odd question. Matter is made of . . . matter, right? Well, no. You can look into it more deeply than that.

Think of a sugar cube. What is it made of? It's made of sugar.

If you break the cube into smaller and smaller pieces, you eventually end up with a single grain of sugar.

Can you break a grain of sugar into smaller pieces? It turns out you can. But eventually you end up with a tiny particle of sugar. And if you break up that particle, it's not sugar anymore.

All matter is like this, not just sugar. All matter is made up of extremely tiny particles. You can end up with a small particle of oxygen or a particle of water or a particle of iron. And if you break up that particle, it won't be oxygen or water or iron anymore.

How can you describe matter—a specific piece of matter, that is? You could probably think of a hundred ways. You might come up with these descriptions: Water can be clear, cool, and wet. Air is invisible, and you breathe it. A car is big and heavy. A book has pages with words and pictures, and a cover. You read books because you enjoy them or need to know the information in them.

One way to describe something is to list its

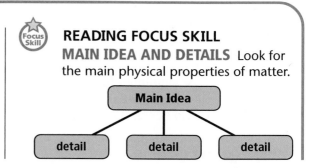

How can you tell that the air inside these balloons is matter?

486

physical properties. A **physical property** is something that describes a substance by itself and can be observed or measured without changing the identify of the substance.

Take a look back at some of the descriptions on the previous page.

- "Water can be clear, cool, and wet." Are those physical properties? Yes, all three of them are.
- "Air is invisible, and you breathe it." Being invisible is a physical property of air. But "you breathe it" doesn't describe air by itself. It describes what you do to air, so it's not a physical property of air.
- "A car is big and heavy." Those are two physical properties of a car.
- "A book has pages with words and pictures, and a cover." These are physical properties of a book.
- "You read books because you enjoy them or need to know the information in them." This fact helps describe how the book is used, but it's not a physical property of the book.

MAIN IDEA AND DETAILS What two physical properties are shared by all forms of matter?

One of the properties of the knobs at the end of these metal "sticks" is that they're magnetic.

Among the physical properties of this ice sculpture are that it's solid, clear, and cold. Which of these properties will still apply if the air becomes quite warm?

One of the physical properties of this lizard is its texture—rough and bumpy. What color is the lizard? Is this physical property of the lizard likely to change over time?

Mass, Volume, and Density

Any given substance will have any number of physical properties, but three physical properties apply to all substances.

Mass is the amount of matter something has. It can be measured in grams or in kilograms. Because mass is the amount of matter something has, it does not depend on where the thing is found. It could be on Earth's surface, on top of a mountain, or on planet Mars—its mass measurement would not change. **Volume** is the amount of space something takes up. It can be measured in liters or milliliters, or in cups, pints, gallons, or cubic centimeters.

Density is the amount of mass something has in relation to its volume. Density is equal to mass divided by volume and might be measured in grams per liter, grams per cubic centimeter, or similar units.

Any substance will float on a liquid that has a higher density than it does. For example, vinegar has a higher density than olive oil, so when salad dressing separates, the oil floats on top of the vinegar.

 MAIN IDEA AND DETAILS Name three physical properties that apply to all substances.

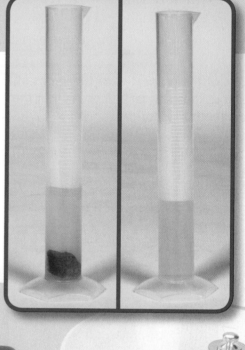

The cylinders are filled with water. The rock sinks because it's denser than water. Notice that the rock displaces water in the graduate. You can calculate the volume of the rock by using the amount of water that was displaced.

When the pans are balanced, you can add the masses in the right-hand pan to find the mass of the cube in the left pan.

Which is heavier—20 cm³ of lead or 20 cm³ of mercury?

Density of Some Common Substances

Substance	Density (g/cm³)
Helium	0.00018
Air	0.001
Wood (white pine)	0.5
Olive oil	0.9
Pure water	1.0
Diamond	3.5
Lead	11.3
Mercury	13.6

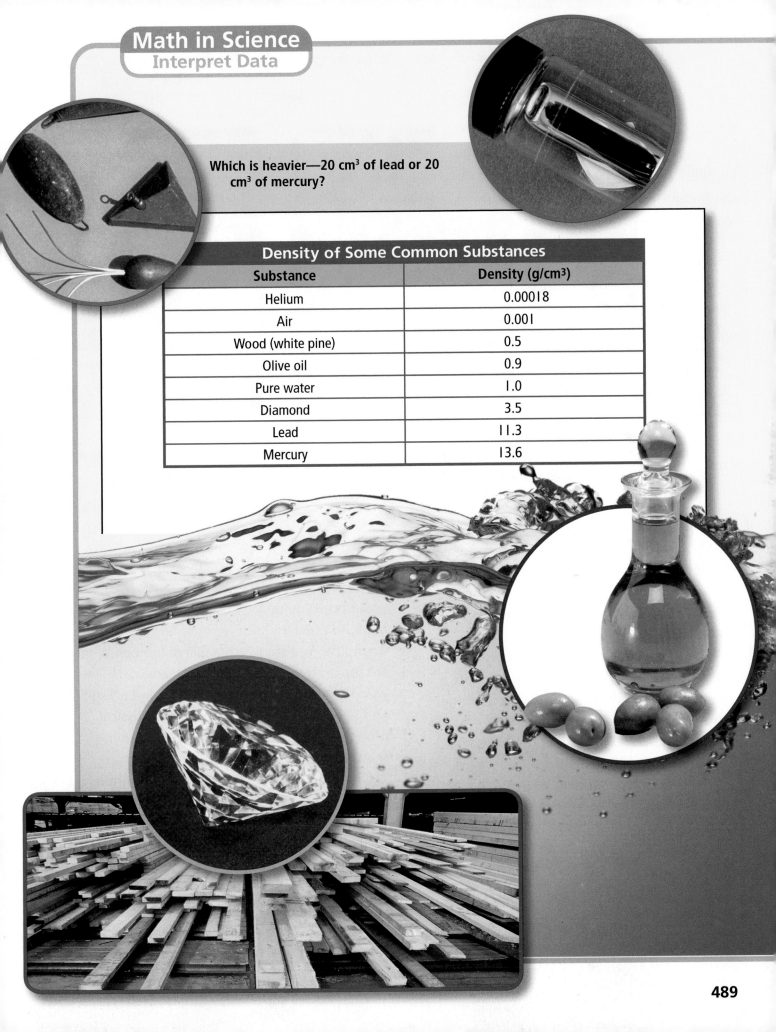

The clay goes through many changes on its way to becoming a pot. At first the clay is still soft and squishy, and it's easy to stretch and mold. What changes are shown in these pictures?

The finished pot is light brown, hard, and brittle. What kind of change does it go through when it hits the floor? ▶

Physical Changes

Think of all the things you can change. You can change your clothes, you can change your hairstyle, you can change your mind, and you can change the route you take to school.

With so many kinds of changes possible, it's useful to categorize them. One category is physical changes. When a substance undergoes a **physical change,** one or more of its physical properties change, but it does not become a different substance.

As an example, consider a mirror. What are the basic properties of a mirror? A mirror is flat, it's shiny, and it reflects images. Now suppose you smash the mirror. The size and shape of the mirror change as it shatters into smaller pieces. The mirror has undergone a physical change because some of its physical properties—size and shape—have changed. However, the pieces are still flat, shiny, and reflective. The mirror did not become a different kind of matter.

Suppose you're going to build a doghouse. You start with a pile of lumber. What are some physical properties of the wood? The wood is hard, it's light tan in color, and it's stiff and self-supporting. What are some physical properties of the nails? The nails are small, shiny, and sharp.

Once you've finished building the doghouse, is the wood still hard, light tan in color, stiff, and self-supporting? Yes. Are the nails still small, shiny, and sharp? Yes. What did change? Well, you turned some lumber and nails into a doghouse; that's definitely a change. To make the lumber fit, you cut it into smaller pieces; that's a change. But the materials did not change into new substances—the wood is still wood, and the nails are still nails. Building the doghouse was a physical change, but each part of the doghouse still has the basic physical properties it started with.

There's one important thing you need to know about physical changes. Think about that doghouse project again. You started with a large pile of nails and ended up with a small pile of unused nails. Did any of the nails disappear? No, of course not. The ones that aren't in the pile are in the doghouse.

You started with a large pile of wood and ended up with a doghouse and a small pile of unused wood. Did any of the wood disappear? No. If you added up the leftover wood, the wood in the doghouse, and the small amount of tiny wood particles on the ground (sawdust), you'd have exactly the same amount of wood you started with.

This doesn't apply just to doghouses. It's a fundamental rule of nature. When matter—any matter—goes through a physical change, its mass does not change. No matter appears, and no matter disappears. You always end up with the same amount of matter you started with.

 MAIN IDEA AND DETAILS What is a physical change?

Kirigami is a Japanese art that involves cutting paper. This kirigami is made up of one piece of cut paper. Did cutting the paper result in a physical change?

Insta-Lab

Making a Change
Put 200 mL of hot water in each of two cups. Pour 50 mL of sand into one cup and 50 mL of salt into the other. Stir both cups for one minute. Did a physical change take place in either cup? Explain.

Origami is a Japanese art that involves folding paper. These animals have each been folded from one sheet of paper.

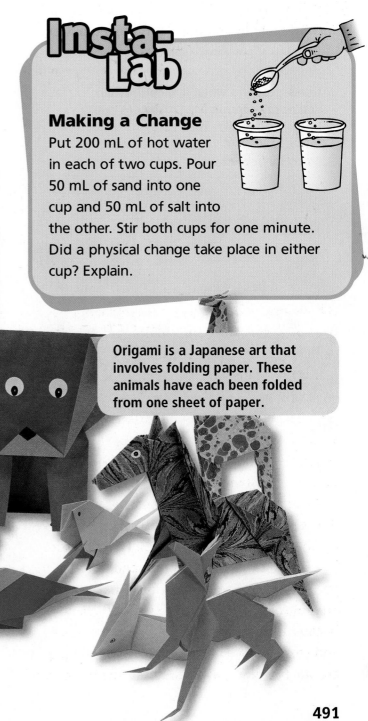

Dissolving, Melting, and Boiling

Have you ever stirred sugar into tea? When you were done, could you see the sugar? No, because it had dissolved. Even though you couldn't see it, you could still taste it.

The ability of a substance to dissolve is a physical property. The term for this property is *solubility* (sawl•yoo••BIL•uh•tee), a measure of how much of a substance will dissolve in a liquid.

You're already familiar with changes of state, such as melting and boiling. Is melted butter still butter? Is water vapor the same substance as water? Yes, because changes of state are a kind of physical change.

 MAIN IDEA AND DETAILS How can you tell that dissolving, melting, and boiling are all physical changes?

Glass is a solid when it is cold. When you apply enough heat it softens and becomes a liquid. Then it can be shaped into bottles and vases. When it cools it holds its new shape.

1. MAIN IDEA AND DETAILS Copy and complete the graphic organizer.

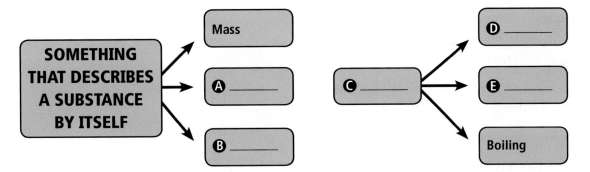

SOMETHING THAT DESCRIBES A SUBSTANCE BY ITSELF

Mass

Ⓐ _____

Ⓑ _____

Ⓒ _____

Ⓓ _____

Ⓔ _____

Boiling

2. SUMMARIZE Summarize this lesson by writing a paragraph that tells what the lesson is about.

3. DRAW CONCLUSIONS Pumice (PUH•mis) is a rock that floats on water. What does that tell you about one of the physical properties of pumice?

4. VOCABULARY Write a short newspaper article that contains all the vocabulary words from the lesson.

Test Prep

5. Critical Thinking Suppose you play chess with Darren. He has brown hair, blue eyes, he is tall, and he is funny. Are these all physical properties? Explain.

6. Which of the following is **not** a physical property?

  A. height   **C.** usefulness

  B. melting point   **D.** volume

Links

Writing

Expository Writing

Write a **friendly letter** to your cousin that tells what you learned in this lesson. Be sure to give examples that will help your cousin understand what you are writing about.

Math

Find Mean/Divide Decimals

A box contains 12 samples of the same mineral. The total mass of the samples is 413.88 g. What is the average mass of a sample?

Social Studies

History of Science

In the third century B.C., a Greek named Archimedes made an important discovery about buoyancy. Do some research into buoyancy, and then write a brief report about what Archimedes discovered. Share your report with classmates.

 For more links and activities, go to **www.hspscience.com**

What Are Mixtures?

Fast Fact

Color My World People in the United States use about 3 million gallons of paint every day. Once the paint in this picture is mixed, it can't be "unmixed," or separated into the original colors. Is that true for all mixtures? In the Investigate, you will discover whether it is possible to separate some mixtures.

Mix and "Unmix"

Materials
- cups
- sand
- magnet
- water
- iron filings
- paper towels
- salt
- gravel
- strainer
- spoons
- coffee filters

Procedure

1. Add a spoonful of salt to a cup of warm water. Stir and observe what happens.

2. Hypothesize how you could use the materials and tools you have to return the solid material in Step 1 to its original form.

3. Form a hypothesis for how you could return each solid material in Steps 4–6 to its original form. Test each hypothesis.

4. Add a spoonful of sand to a cup of warm water. Stir. Repeat Step 3.

5. Mix equal amounts of sand and iron filings in a cup. Stir. Repeat Step 3.

6. Mix equal amounts of salt, sand, iron filings, and gravel in a cup. Stir. Repeat Step 3.

Draw Conclusions

1. The first time you did the procedure, how did you test your hypothesis?

2. What was your hypothesis about separating the sand and water? Did you have to change or add to your hypothesis?

3. What actions did you include in Step 6 to test your hypothesis about how to separate the mixture of the four substances?

4. **Inquiry Skill** What can you infer about the salt when it was mixed with the water?

Step 1

Step 6

Investigate Further

Repeat Step 6 of the Investigate, but add 2 spoonfuls of water to the dry mixture. Plan and conduct a simple experiment to separate the water from the other substances.

Reading in Science

VOCABULARY
mixture p. 496
solution p. 498
suspension p. 500
colloid p. 500

SCIENCE CONCEPTS
▶ what characteristics a mixture has
▶ what a solution is

 READING FOCUS SKILL
COMPARE AND CONTRAST Notice the similarities and differences among the different kinds of mixtures you read about.

alike —— different

Mixtures

How often do you discuss breakfast cereals in science class? Probably not too often. But this section is about mixtures, and many cereals are good examples of mixtures.

A **mixture** is a combination of two or more substances that keep their original properties. A good example of a mixture is raisin bran. It's a mixture of raisins and bran flakes. Even though they're mixed together, the raisins still have all their properties—they're sweet, dark, and soft—and the flakes still have all their properties—they're brown, crisp, and brittle.

One important property of mixtures is that the proportions of the ingredients can change. One bowl of raisin bran might have 250 mL (8 oz) of flakes and 20 raisins, but another bowl could have 250 mL of flakes and 35 raisins.

Mixtures are all around you. Is there a box of nuts and bolts and screws in your garage? That's a mixture. You might find a pile of leaves and twigs under a tree. That's a mixture, too. Even a box of cake mix is a mixture.

 COMPARE AND CONTRAST Is a raisin in raisin bran cereal different from a raisin in oat bran cereal? Explain your answer.

Does each section of beach have the same number of shells? Even in nature you can find mixtures.

Would you like to eat this mixture? Think about the materials you could separate.

496

Mixtures can be separated in many ways. Here a large industrial magnet is separating some kinds of metals. The people are using a screen to separate diamonds from the rocks.

Separating Mixtures

If the materials in a mixture keep all their original properties, it should be possible to separate them from the mixture. In fact, in the Investigate at the beginning of this lesson, you separated several mixtures.

Why would someone want to separate a mixture? That depends on the person and the mixture. A small child might want to eat the raisins but not the bran flakes. Someone else might want to eat only the pineapple in a fruit salad. A shell collector wants to take home shells, not sand.

Some mixtures are easy to separate. You can pick raisins out of the bowl of cereal with your fingers. You can pick the pineapple pieces out of a fruit salad with your spoon. And you can separate the shells from the sand by simply picking the shells up and shaking off the sand.

Sometimes there are even easier ways to separate mixtures. Suppose you're sweeping the floor of a wood shop. You have a pile of sawdust, little bits of wood, and some steel nails. You want to save the nails and throw out the rest, but picking all the nails out one by one would take a lot of time. Is there another way?

Remember, things in a mixture keep their original properties. That means the nails will still be attracted to a magnet. Spread out the pile and move a strong magnet over it. You'll pick up the nails and leave the rest behind.

 COMPARE AND CONTRAST How is raisin bran like the paint mixture on the first page of the lesson? How is it different?

Solutions

Think about some of the mixtures you've read about. Are the raisins spread evenly throughout the cereal? Are the shells spread evenly across the beach? No, they're not.

That's because those mixtures aren't solutions. A **solution** is a mixture in which all the substances are evenly distributed. What happens if you stir a spoonful of salt into a glass of water? Is one part of the water saltier than another part? No, the salt is evenly distributed because salt water is a solution.

Earlier you read, "One important property of mixtures is that the proportions of the ingredients can change." Is that different from what you just read about solutions?

No, it isn't. One glass of salt water might have a spoonful of salt in 250 mL (8 oz) of water, while another has 3 spoonfuls of salt in 250 mL of water. But in each glass, the salt is spread evenly throughout the water.

A solution results when a solute (SAWL•yoot) dissolves in a solvent. In any solution, the substance that is dissolved is called the *solute*, and the substance it's dissolved in is called the *solvent*. With salt water, salt is the solute and water is the solvent.

The beaker contains a mixture of copper sulfate crystals and water. How is this different from a solution of salt and water?

Mixtures can be solids, liquids, or gases. Here an aerator is providing oxygen for the fish in the tank.

Alloys are mixtures of metals. The characteristics of an alloy are different from the individual metals that make it up.

Some Common Alloys		
Name	**Main Substances**	**Properties**
Brass	copper zinc	bright yellow, soft
Bronze	copper tin	resists corrosion, hard
Pewter	tin antimony copper	silver-colored, shiny
Steel	iron manganese carbon	much stronger than iron
Stainless Steel	steel chromium nickel	strong as steel, but will not corrode

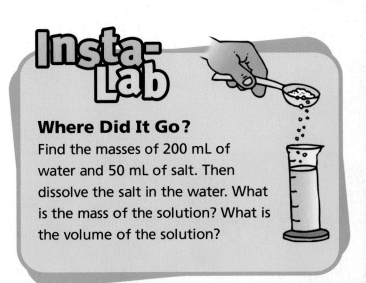

Many substances dissolve easily in water. Some don't dissolve at all in water but do dissolve in other liquids. Some dissolve completely, and some dissolve only a little. As you learned in the first lesson, solubility is the measure of how much of a substance will dissolve in a given solvent. It is also a physical property.

You're probably most familiar with solids that dissolve in liquids, but there are other kinds of solutions. For example, you can dissolve a gas in a liquid. Soda is carbon dioxide dissolved in water.

You can also dissolve a liquid in a liquid. Some small engines, like those in lawn mowers, run on a mixture of gasoline and motor oil. That mixture is a solution.

You can even dissolve a solid in a solid. You're probably familiar with several of these solid solutions already. Look at the table above, and see how many you recognize.

Solutions that involve two or more metals are called *alloys* (AL•oiz). As you might guess, it's hard to get a solid to dissolve in another solid. Often the two solids are melted, and then the two liquids are mixed together and allowed to solidify.

 COMPARE AND CONTRAST How is brass like salt water? How are they different?

Insta-Lab

Where Did It Go?
Find the masses of 200 mL of water and 50 mL of salt. Then dissolve the salt in the water. What is the mass of the solution? What is the volume of the solution?

Other Types of Mixtures

You have read about solutions and alloys. But there are still some other kinds of mixtures. What happens if you stir a spoonful of salt into one glass of water and a spoonful of potting soil into another glass? The salt forms a solution with the water, but the soil forms another kind of mixture, called a suspension.

A **suspension** is a uniform mixture that contains particles that are large enough to be seen. If you look at the glass, you'll see tiny specks of soil floating around in the water. An hour later, you won't see any soil floating around at all. You'll see a glass of clear water with some soil at the bottom. That's because suspensions don't stay mixed.

One kind of mixture that stays mixed is a colloid. A **colloid** (KAHL•oyd) is a mixture that contains particles that are too small to see. Except for the size of its particles, a colloid is exactly like a suspension. But because the particles are so small, they never settle to the bottom. Milk is a colloid. As long as it is refrigerated, it never separates into a glass of nearly clear water with white material on the bottom.

Another type of mixture is called an emulsion. An *emulsion* (ee•MUHL•shuhn) is a mixture of two liquids that don't dissolve. For example, mayonnaise is an emulsion of vegetable oil, egg yolks, and vinegar or lemon juice.

 COMPARE AND CONTRAST How are mayonnaise and the fuel in a lawn mower engine alike? How are they different?

This orange juice is a suspension within a solution. The liquid is a solution of several solids—such as ascorbic acid and citric acid—in water. In addition, bits of pulp are suspended in the liquid.

What you see here is a colloid of water droplets suspended in air. What is the common name for this colloid?

1. **COMPARE AND CONTRAST** Copy and complete the graphic organizer.

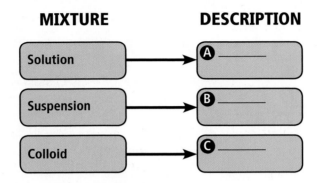

MIXTURE   **DESCRIPTION**

Solution → **A** _____

Suspension → **B** _____

Colloid → **C** _____

2. **SUMMARIZE** Write a summary of this lesson. Use the phrases "A mixture is . . ." and "Some kinds of mixtures are . . ."

3. **DRAW CONCLUSIONS** Some ingredients in salad dressings settle into layers. What kind of mixture are these dressings? How do you know?

4. **VOCABULARY** Use the lesson vocabulary words to construct a crossword puzzle.

Test Prep

5. **Critical Thinking** Seawater is a solution mostly of salt in water. Will every sample of seawater have the same proportion of salt to water? Explain.

6. If 3 g of salt and 50 g of water are mixed, what will the mass of the solution be?
A. 50 g   **C.** 53 g
B. less than 50 g   **D.** more than 53 g

Links

Writing

Narrative Writing
Think about two common mixtures, solutions, suspensions, or colloids. Imagine that each one is right in front of you. Write a detailed **description** of each one.

Math

Find Elapsed Time
A powder and a liquid were stirred together at 11:57 A.M. The two substances formed a suspension. By 12:39 P.M., all of the powder had settled to the bottom. How long did it take for the suspension to separate?

Health

Air Quality
Pollutants can form colloids with air, or they can form solutions with water droplets in the atmosphere. Research one common type of air pollution, and describe it in terms of a mixture.

For more links and activities, go to www.hspscience.com

What Are Chemical Properties of Matter?

Fast Fact

Rockets' Red Glare Fireworks have different colors because they contain different chemicals that react to form the colors and the sounds. You can use the same chemicals to make wood in a fireplace burn with different colors. In the Investigate, you will find out more about chemical reactions.

Different Kinds of Changes

Materials
- lab apron
- safety goggles
- dropper
- plastic knife
- baking soda
- water
- avocado
- plastic spoon
- vinegar
- paper towel
- 2 plastic cups
- marker

Procedure

1 CAUTION: **Put on a lab apron.** Use the plastic knife to cut the avocado in half. Place the halves, cut side up, on the paper towel. Check the cut halves several times during the activity, and note any changes.

2 CAUTION: **Put on safety goggles.** Put 1 spoonful of baking soda in each cup. Add a few drops of water to one cup. Label it Cup A. Observe and record any changes that take place.

3 Add a few drops of vinegar to the other cup. Label it Cup B. Observe and record any changes that take place.

Draw Conclusions

1. What change did you observe in the avocado halves? What do you infer caused the change? Do you think the change can be reversed?

2. Compare the results of adding the water to baking soda with the results of adding the vinegar to baking soda. What differences did you observe? Was anything new formed?

3. **Inquiry Skill** Interpret your data from this investigation to infer which of the changes you observed was a physical change and which was a different kind of change.

Step 1

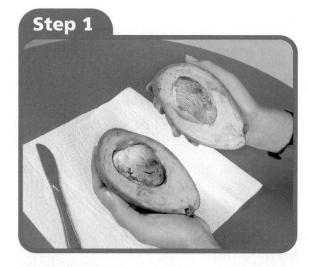

Step 2

Investigate Further

With a partner, make a list of changes that occur in nature. Compare lists with your classmates, and classify your changes as "physical changes" and "not physical changes."

Reading in Science

VOCABULARY
chemical change p. 504
chemical property p. 505
reactivity p. 505
stability p. 505

SCIENCE CONCEPTS
▶ how to identify the chemical properties of a substance
▶ what a chemical reaction is

 READING FOCUS SKILL
COMPARE AND CONTRAST Look for similarities and differences among the different kinds of chemical changes.

| alike | different |

Chemical Properties and Changes

When a substance goes through a physical change, the substance itself is not changed. You can tear a sheet of paper into tiny bits, but the bits are still paper. However, there are other kinds of changes besides physical changes. One kind is a chemical change.

Oxygen is necessary for burning. Hydrogen is an explosive gas. But the two combine to form water, which can be used to put out fires.

A **chemical change** is a change in which one or more new substances are formed.

One way to tell if a new substance has been formed is to look for new chemical properties. What are chemical properties? You read that a physical property is something that describes

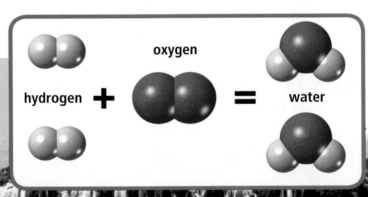

hydrogen + oxygen = water

A rainbow forms as the waters of the Zambezi River rush over Victoria Falls in Zimbabwe, Africa.

504

Double Replacement Reaction

Sodium chromate forms yellow crystals, and silver nitrate can be clear or white crystals. When combined, the two react to form sodium nitrate and silver chromate. Sodium nitrate is a white crystal like silver nitrate, but silver chromate is a bright reddish pink crystal.

sodium chromate + silver nitrate = sodium nitrate + silver chromate

Single Replacement Reaction

Silver reacts with hydrogen sulfide in the air to form silver sulfide. Most people know silver sulfide as tarnish. This is what happens to silverware and silver jewelry.

hydrogen sulfide + silver = silver sulfide + hydrogen

Synthesis Reaction

Sodium is a soft, silvery metal. Chlorine is a green gas. When a piece of sodium is placed in a container of chlorine gas, nothing happens. But when a small amount of water is added, the water reacts with the sodium and produces heat. The hot sodium then reacts with the chlorine, producing a bright yellow light, a lot of heat, and fumes of sodium chloride vapor, which cool into sodium chloride crystals.

sodium + chlorine = sodium chloride

Preventing Chemical Changes

In science class you find out how to make chemicals react. But sometimes it is just as important to prevent them from reacting.

When you turn on an electric light, the filament inside the bulb glows brightly. It also gets very hot. Heating things often causes a chemical reaction. In this case, the metal of the filament is prevented from reacting with anything else by the vacuum inside the bulb that surrounds it.

Heat can start or speed up a chemical reaction. In the same way, removing heat can slow or stop a reaction. The spoiling of food is a chemical reaction. Putting food in a refrigerator slows this reaction. Freezing the food slows the reaction even more. That's why food stays fresh longer in the refrigerator and even longer in the freezer.

In the Investigate, if you had brushed the avocado halves with lemon juice, you would have prevented them from turning brown. Many additives are used in foods to keep them fresh.

Electronic equipment has many metal parts. Metal rusts when it is in contact with water and air. If the inside of a stereo rusts, the stereo won't work anymore. That's why cartons of electronic equipment arrive with little packets of crystals inside. The material in the packets absorbs water. By keeping the water out of the air, it prevents rust from forming.

 COMPARE AND CONTRAST How is the way a refrigerator preserves food similar to the way a freezer does? How are they different?

The reactions food goes through when it spoils involve water. Dried fruit lasts longer than fresh fruit.

The outer walls of the Beinecke Rare Book and Manuscript Library at Yale University are made of translucent marble. They let visible light through but block ultraviolet light. Ultraviolet light starts a chemical reaction that turns paper brown and crumbly.

1. COMPARE AND CONTRAST Copy the graphic organizer that compares different chemical reactions. Fill in the empty boxes with the types of chemical reactions described.

Ⓐ _____ A + BC = B + AC

Ⓑ _____ AB = A + B

Ⓒ _____ A + B = AB

2. SUMMARIZE Write a sentence that tells the most important information in this lesson.

3. DRAW CONCLUSIONS A beaker contains a white, cloudy solid. You heat the beaker. After several minutes, the solid becomes a clear liquid. Can you tell whether a chemical reaction has occurred? Why or why not?

4. VOCABULARY Write a paragraph that contains all four lesson vocabulary terms.

Test Prep

5. Critical Thinking Cars rust more quickly on the coast than they do inland. How can you use what you know about chemical reactions to explain this?

6. Which of the following is a chemical change?
  A. burning candle
  B. clouds forming
  C. fruit freezing
  D. ice melting

Links

Writing

Expository Writing

Suppose you are preparing a guide for the students who will take this science class next year. Write a **how-to paragraph** describing how to tell if a change is physical or chemical.

Math

Round Decimals

Below is a list of the products of some chemical reactions. Round each mass to the nearest whole gram.

Substance A   42.092 g
Substance B   79.85 g
Substance C   867.399 g

Social Studies

Preserving History

Many of our nation's most important documents are kept at the National Archives in Washington, D.C. Research the National Archives, and then write a brief report describing how those documents are preserved.

For more links and activities, go to www.hspscience.com

What Are Acids and Bases?

Fast Fact

Underground Reactions Caves form over millions of years. There are four main ways that caves are formed. Caves like this one formed by acid in rainwater dissolving limestone rock to leave large underground spaces. In the Investigate, you will experiment with acids and bases.

Testing the Testers

Materials
- safety goggles
- red litmus paper
- household solutions (vinegar, ammonia, antacid liquid, lemon juice, milk, tea, liquid detergent, soda)
- lab apron
- blue litmus paper
- wide-range indicator papers
- paper towels
- droppers

Procedure

1. **CAUTION: Put on safety goggles and a lab apron. Avoid getting any of the solutions on your hands. Wash your hands after the Investigation.** Place a strip of red litmus paper and a strip of blue litmus paper on a clean paper towel. Using a clean dropper, place several drops of vinegar on each strip. Observe what happens, and record your observations.

2. Repeat Step 1, using each of the other solutions.

3. Repeat Steps 1 and 2, using wide-range indicator papers instead of litmus paper.

4. Using the directions that came with the wide-range indicator papers, find the pH value of each of the solutions you tested.

5. Using your results from Step 4, classify each solution you tested as an acid, a base, or neither.

Draw Conclusions

1. How did you use the wide-range indicator papers to classify the various substances?

2. **Inquiry Skill** What can you infer about the way acids and bases affect red and blue litmus paper?

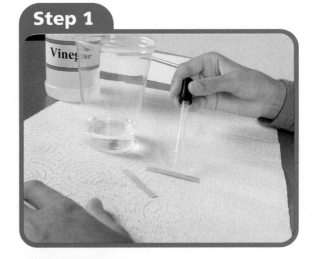
Step 1

Step 3

Investigate Further

What other substances can you test to find their pH values? Make a prediction about whether a substance is an acid or a base, and then ask your teacher if you may test it.

Reading in Science

VOCABULARY
acid p. 512
base p. 512
indicator p. 514
pH scale p. 514

SCIENCE CONCEPTS
▶ what an acid is and how to identify it
▶ what a base is and how to identify it

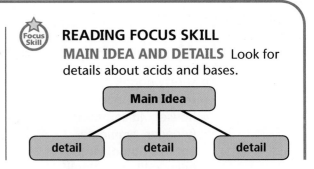

READING FOCUS SKILL

MAIN IDEA AND DETAILS Look for details about acids and bases.

Acids and Bases

You've probably heard the word *acid,* but do you know its definition? Maybe it's something that dissolves other substances or makes holes in other substances. Fortunately, not all acids are that strong. For example, orange juice is an acid, and it's safe to drink.

If you did the Investigate, you may be able to come up with a better definition. An **acid** is a substance that turns blue litmus paper red. The vinegar, the lemon juice, and anything else that turned the blue paper red are acids.

Most acids share certain physical properties. Weak acids, like lemon juice, taste sour.

However, NEVER taste a chemical in the lab to see if it's an acid—or for any other reason.

Acids are often talked about along with another group of substances called bases. A **base** is a substance that turns red litmus paper blue. The ammonia, the detergent, and anything else that turned the red paper blue are bases.

Common Acids

A car battery contains acid. So do vinegar and lime juice. What happens when lime juice is mixed with water?

512

Common Bases

Soap and baking soda are both bases. What happens when baking soda is dissolved in water? What happens when it is mixed with lime juice?

BAKING SODA

Like acids, most bases share certain physical properties. Many bases, such as soap and detergent, feel slippery to the touch.

You've probably noticed that many acids and bases are common items. Citrus fruits, such as oranges and lemons, contain citric acid. Vinegar is an acid, too. Are all acids foods? No. Aspirin is acetylsalicylic (uh•seet•uhl•sal•uh•SIL•ik) acid.

Household bases fall into two categories: cleaning products and upset-stomach remedies. In the first category are things like soap and ammonia. The second category includes items such as antacid tablets and baking soda.

Why do bases help relieve indigestion? Indigestion is often caused by too much acid in the stomach. Bases neutralize, or get rid of, acids. That's why some indigestion remedies are called antacids.

An important property of acids and bases is that they react together to form water and an additional substance. For example, this is the reaction between hydrochloric acid (hydrogen chloride) and lye (sodium hydroxide): hydrogen chloride + sodium hydroxide = water + sodium

chloride. You may remember from the previous lesson that this is a double replacement reaction.

 MAIN IDEA AND DETAILS Name one physical property of most acids and one physical property of most bases.

Insta-Lab

Neutralize Me

Drop a few antacid tablets into a container of vinegar. What happens? Keep adding tablets until they don't fizz anymore. What do you think is in the container now? Predict the pH of the liquid. Check with wide-range indicator paper.

Indicators

In the Investigate, you used something called a wide-range indicator. What is an indicator, and why is it used? Litmus paper and wide-range indicator papers are called **indicators** because they indicate whether a substance is an acid or a base.

You've probably noticed by now that some acids and bases are stronger than others. For example, vinegar and lemon juice are safe to use in food, but the acid in a car battery is very dangerous. You handle soap every day, but lye will burn your skin.

Is there a way to tell which acids and bases are strong and which are weak? Yes, there is. The **pH scale** is a measure of the strength or weakness of acids and bases.

The pH scale ranges from 0 to 14. Neutral is right in the middle, at 7. That means it is neither an acid nor a base.

The pH of acids ranges from 7 down to 0 or slightly below. The lower the pH value, or the closer it is to one end of the scale, the stronger the acid is.

The pH of bases ranges from 7 to 14 or slightly above. The higher the pH value, or the closer it is to the other end of the scale, the stronger the base is.

How can you measure the pH value of a substance? You already know about a general indicator. Blue litmus paper turns red when it's in contact with an acid. Red litmus paper turns

An indicator has been added to this flask of sodium hydroxide. Because sodium hydroxide is a base, the indicator turned pink. ▼

▲ Hydrochloric acid has been added to the flask. This caused the reaction you read about earlier. The products of this reaction are sodium chloride and water. Because both these products are neutral (pH 7), the indicator in the flask is clear.

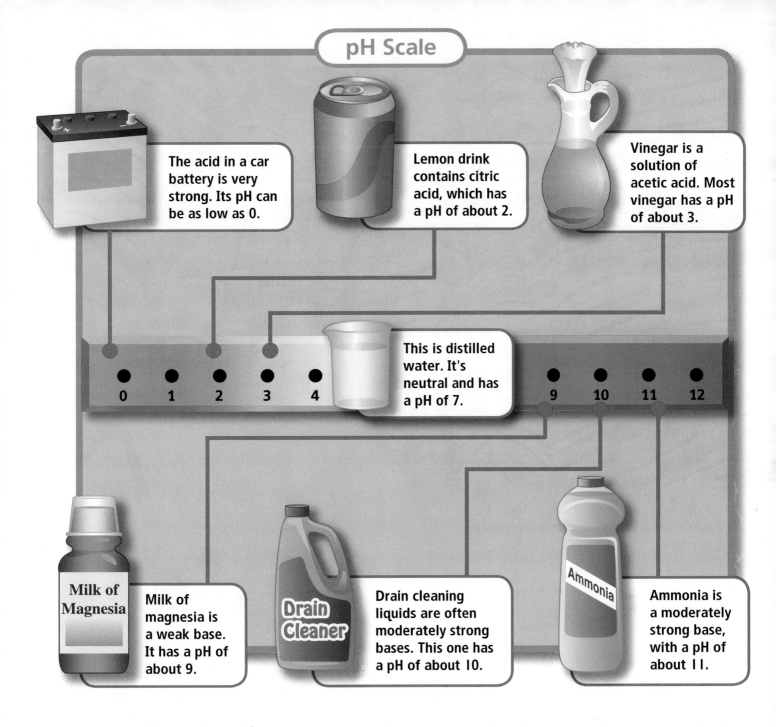

pH Scale

The acid in a car battery is very strong. Its pH can be as low as 0.

Lemon drink contains citric acid, which has a pH of about 2.

Vinegar is a solution of acetic acid. Most vinegar has a pH of about 3.

This is distilled water. It's neutral and has a pH of 7.

| 0 | 1 | 2 | 3 | 4 | | 9 | 10 | 11 | 12 |

Milk of Magnesia

Milk of magnesia is a weak base. It has a pH of about 9.

Drain Cleaner

Drain cleaning liquids are often moderately strong bases. This one has a pH of about 10.

Ammonia

Ammonia is a moderately strong base, with a pH of about 11.

blue in contact with a base. These indicators can show whether something is an acid or a base or neutral, but they can't give an exact pH value.

To get a more exact pH value, you need wide-range indicator papers like those you used in the Investigate. When these indicators are in contact with a substance, they might turn any color from red to purple. A diagram that comes with the papers tells you which pH value corresponds to the color of the paper. There are also electronic pH meters.

There are some natural indicators. You can boil some red cabbage. Red cabbage juice is red and has a pH of about 2, but it changes to greenish yellow at a pH of about 12. The flowers of many plants, such as geraniums, delphiniums, hydrangeas, and petunias, may bloom in colors ranging from red to purple, depending on the pH of the soil they're growing in.

 MAIN IDEA AND DETAILS What is an indicator used for?

Acids are used in the manufacture of dyes, while bases are often used in cleaning products.

How People Use Acids and Bases

You've already seen that many acids, such as vinegar and aspirin, and many bases, such as baking soda and soap, have everyday uses. But the usefulness of acids and bases goes well beyond those products.

As you read earlier in this lesson, you have acid in your stomach. In fact, it's hydrochloric acid, and it helps break down the food you eat. Hydrochloric acid has uses outside the body as well, for everything from cleaning metals to manufacturing artificial silk. Another acid, sulfuric acid, is used in industries such as chemical manufacturing and electronics.

You already know that most soaps and detergents contain one base or another. Bases are also used in the water purification industry, and they are found in most hair dyes. The next time you find yourself holding a flashlight or a personal stereo, take a look at the batteries. Do they say "alkaline" on them? If they do, they contain a base.

 MAIN IDEA AND DETAILS Name one way people use acids and one way they use bases.

1. MAIN IDEA AND DETAILS Copy and complete the graphic organizer.

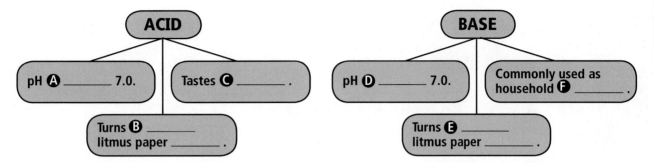

ACID

pH **A** _____ 7.0.

Tastes **C** _____ .

Turns **B** _____ litmus paper _____ .

BASE

pH **D** _____ 7.0.

Commonly used as household **F** _____ .

Turns **E** _____ litmus paper _____ .

2. SUMMARIZE Use the completed graphic organizer to write a lesson summary.

3. DRAW CONCLUSIONS Suppose you have cooked some beets, and now you must wash the pot. You run a little water in the pot, but when you squirt detergent in the pot, the water turns green. What should this tell you about beet juice?

4. VOCABULARY Write an original sentence for each lesson vocabulary term.

Test Prep

5. Critical Thinking You and your lab partner are given a beaker with a clear liquid in it. It doesn't seem to have an odor. Is the liquid safe to drink? Explain.

6. Which would be the pH value of a strong acid?

 A. 2   **C.** 9

 B. 7   **D.** 14

Links

Writing

Expository Writing

Imagine you are tutoring a fifth grader in science. Write a detailed **explanation** of what happens when acids and bases react. Give examples.

Math

Display Data

With a parent's permission, use wide-range indicator papers to test several household items to find their pH values. Make a display table like the one on page 515, using the items you tested. Did any of the results surprise you? Explain.

Health

Research an Acid

Your body needs ascorbic acid to stay healthy. Research ascorbic acid, and write a paragraph explaining what happens to someone who doesn't get enough ascorbic acid. Include information about how this was discovered.

For more links and activities, go to www.hspscience.com

Neon Nights

Some people look forward to winter because they enjoy the snow and holidays. Others like the colorful flashing lights. Those lights are not the kind that you see hanging all season long. They are *auroras*, colorful bands of light that shine in the night sky!

Auroras are nature's light shows. They usually occur around the North Pole and South Pole. People in Alaska and the northern parts of Canada, Europe, and Russia spot the bright displays every few years.

Auroras in the Northern Hemisphere are called aurora borealis (northern lights). Those in the Southern Hemisphere are called aurora australis (southern lights).

Solar Explosion

Winds from the sun cause auroras. The winds travel through space at a speed of a million miles an hour. They carry charged particles.

When these solar winds reach Earth, the electrically charged particles enter the upper atmosphere. The atmosphere is the layer of gases that surrounds our planet. Since the sun's particles are traveling at such a high speed, the collision is almost a mini explosion that produces light.

Auroras are not just pretty lights, however. When these light shows take place, they often disrupt radio and cellular phone signals. According to scientists, auroras may follow a particular cycle.

Night Lights

The auroras can be unpredictable, however. In one instance, scientists were surprised to see northern lights over Texas. In another occurrence, scientists noticed a surprising gap in the northern lights where they usually form a solid ring. Scientists observed the gap using the ultraviolet imager (UVI) camera aboard the Polar spacecraft, which is circling Earth above the poles. The camera takes pictures of auroras using special filters.

Auroras happen often but are rarely visible. They can be seen best on dark, clear nights between late fall and early spring. People watching an aurora never know what they might see. Sometimes the lights take on different shapes. They can look like ripples in the sky or form one long streak.

Think About It

1. What happens to the solar particles to cause auroras?
2. What is the layer of gas that surrounds Earth?

Find out more! Log on to
www.hspscience.com

Making Changes

Amber Knoll knows all about physical changes in matter. Unlike chemical changes, a physical change alters the appearance of matter without changing its chemical composition. There are many different types of physical changes. Tearing a sheet of paper in half, for example, is a physical change. So is crumpling a sheet of paper into a ball.

In school, Amber experimented with salt water to cause a physical change. Amber set up a container of salt water and allowed it to evaporate. Amber knew that during evaporation, liquid water changes into water vapor. The chemical composition of the water did not change, only the

physical state of the water changed. During her experiment, Amber discovered that the salt in the water was left behind because it did not evaporate with the water. This was just the first step of many that Amber took toward entering the school science fair.

SCIENCE Projects
for Home or School

You Can Do It!

Materials
- safety goggles
- hammer
- small clay flowerpot
- notebook paper
- egg
- bowl
- fork
- string
- newspaper

Quick and Easy Project

Procedure

1. **CAUTION: Put on safety goggles.** Use the hammer to carefully chip off a piece of the flowerpot's rim.
2. Crumple the paper into a ball.
3. Break the egg into the bowl, and mix it with the fork.
4. Tie a very tight knot in the string.
5. Now try to undo each of the physical changes you made in Steps 1–4.

Draw Conclusions
Which of the physical changes in Steps 1–4 are reversible?

Design Your Own Investigation

Are chemical changes reversible? Are only some of them reversible? Design an investigation that will help you answer these questions. Then gather the materials you need, and carry out your investigation.

Vocabulary Review

Use the terms below to complete the sentences. The page numbers tell you where to look in the chapter if you need help.

mass p. 488   **volume** p. 488

mixture p. 496   **solution** p. 498

suspension p. 500   **colloid** p. 500

chemical change p. 504 **stability** p. 505

base p. 512   **indicators** p. 514

1. Fog is an example of a _____ .

2. A substance that turns red litmus paper blue is called a _____ .

3. If you can see tiny particles floating in a liquid, you know you're looking at a _____ .

4. The amount of space an object takes up is referred to as its _____ .

5. One or more new substances are formed during a _____ .

6. The amount of matter an object contains is referred to as its _____ .

7. A combination of two or more substances that keep their original properties is a _____ .

8. The ability of a substance to resist entering into a chemical change is called its _____ .

9. A mixture in which all of the substances are evenly distributed is called a _____ .

10. Litmus paper and cabbage juice are _____ .

Check Understanding

Write the letter of the best choice.

11. **MAIN IDEA AND DETAILS** Which of the following is a chemical property?

   A. is attracted to magnets
   B. burns easily
   C. has a volume of 24 L
   D. has a smooth surface

12. **COMPARE AND CONTRAST** Which glass contains a suspension?

   F. Glass A
   G. Glass B
   H. Glass C
   J. Glass D

13. A board has a mass of 750 g. If you ground the whole board down to sawdust, what would be the mass of the pile of sawdust?
   A. much less than 750 g
   B. a little less than 750 g
   C. exactly 750 g
   D. more than 750 g

14. Which substance is the solvent in a glass of orange juice?
   F. vitamins
   G. the pulp
   H. water
   J. the glass

15. Which of the following is a physical property?
   A. burns easily
   B. does not react with other substances
   C. dissolves in vinegar
   D. combines with chlorine to form salt

16. Which would be the pH value of a strong base?
   F. 13
   G. 7
   H. 5
   J. 0

Inquiry Skills

17. In the lab, you put 500 mL of a liquid into a beaker. You use a magnet to pull pieces of gray crystal from a box. You stir 5 g of the crystals into the liquid. Your cell phone rings, and you talk for six minutes. When you look back at the lab bench, the beaker contains only a clear liquid. You hold a magnet just above the surface of the liquid, but nothing happens. What can you **infer** occurred inside the beaker? How do you know?

18. Below is a list of some common household items and their pH values. **Order** the items from strongest base to strongest acid.

Item	pH
apples	3
milk	6
lemon juice	2
milk of magnesia	9
drain cleaner	12
potatoes	5

Critical Thinking

19. You paint a reddish brown board yellow. Have any properties of the wood changed? Has a chemical reaction occurred? Explain.

20. Antacids, such as magnesium hydroxide (milk of magnesia), are used to relieve indigestion.
   Part A How does an antacid relieve acid indigestion?
   Part B If there were no antacids in the house, what might someone use instead? Why might doing so be dangerous?

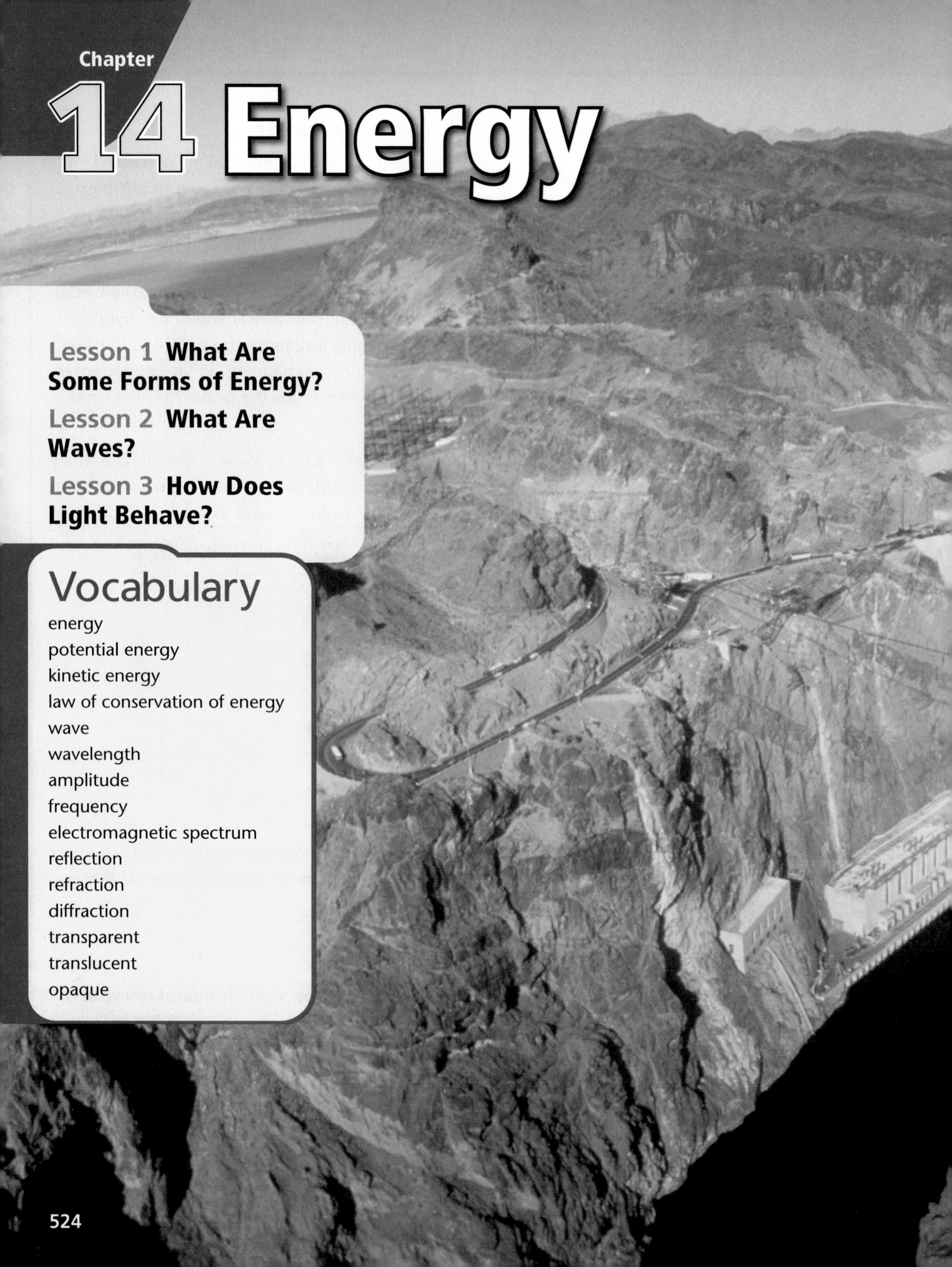

Chapter

14 Energy

Vocabulary

energy
potential energy
kinetic energy
law of conservation of energy
wave
wavelength
amplitude
frequency
electromagnetic spectrum
reflection
refraction
diffraction
transparent
translucent
opaque

What do YOU wonder?

Hoover Dam, on the Colorado River, stretches between Arizona and Nevada. At the base of the dam is a hydroelectric plant. Its turbines and generators can supply the electricity needed for a city of 750,000 people. Where does this energy come from? How does it get to where it's needed?

What Are Some Forms of Energy?

Fast Fact

A Balancing Rock This rock formation, an example of a pedestal rock or balancing rock, was formed as a result of erosion. A rock this big can have a mass of more than 1000 kilograms (more than 1 ton). This gives the top of a pedestal rock a lot of potential energy. In the Investigate, you will see how potential energy may be changed into kinetic energy.

Changing Energy

Materials
- board (about 1 m long)
- 5 books of about equal thickness
- metric ruler
- meterstick
- 4-wheeled cart

Procedure

1. Choose a smooth area of the floor with at least 2 m of clear space. Place the board on the floor, and put a book under one end of the board.

2. Lay the meterstick on the floor at the end of the board, beside the path the cart will take after it has rolled down the board. Copy the data table.

3. Measure and record the height from the floor to the top of the board.

4. Hold the cart so that its back wheels are at the top edge of the board. Let the cart go, but do not push it.

5. Measure and record the distance the cart travels along the floor from the lower edge of the board. Also record the speed of the cart (slow, medium, or fast).

6. Add another book to raise the high end of the board more. Repeat Steps 3 through 5. Continue adding books and repeating Steps 3 through 5 until you have used all five books.

Draw Conclusions

1. How did the height of the starting point affect the distance the cart traveled along the floor? How did it affect the speed of the cart?

2. **Inquiry Skill** Identify the variables you used in this experiment. Which variables did you control? Which variables did you change?

Comparing Height and Distance Traveled			
Number of Books	Height	Distance Traveled	Speed
1			
2			
3			
4			
5			

Step 4

Investigate Further

Does the mass of a cart affect how much energy it has? Design an experiment for observing how mass affects energy.

Reading in Science

VOCABULARY
energy p. 528
potential energy p. 528
kinetic energy p. 528
law of conservation of
energy p. 532

SCIENCE CONCEPTS
► what kinds of energy there are
► how energy changes from one form to another

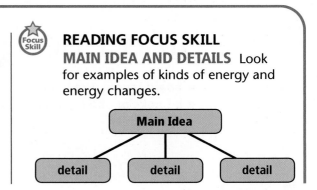

READING FOCUS SKILL
MAIN IDEA AND DETAILS Look for examples of kinds of energy and energy changes.

Potential and Kinetic Energy

Have you ever gone skiing? Imagine standing on your skis at the top of a ski slope. You take a deep breath and push off with your ski poles. At first you move slowly. Then you gain speed, gliding faster and faster over the snow. This motion takes energy, but you are not supplying it. Where does the energy come from?

Energy is the ability to cause change in matter. Energy moves you up the hill on the ski lift. Energy moves you down the hill on your skis.

As you move higher and higher up the hill, your potential energy becomes greater and greater. **Potential energy** is stored energy that is due to the position or condition of an object. You have a lot of potential energy when you are at the top of the hill. When you begin to ski down the hill, your potential energy changes into **kinetic energy**, the energy of motion. By the time you reach the bottom of the hill, almost all of your potential energy has changed into kinetic energy.

The amount of potential energy an object has depends on its position and its mass. A thick

At the top of the hill, the skier has a lot of stored or potential energy. As the skier skis down the hill, his potential energy changes to kinetic energy.

An avalanche devastated this village at the base of a mountain.

◀ In an avalanche, the potential energy of the mass of snow and ice becomes kinetic energy as the mass rushes down the mountain.

layer of snow at the top of a mountain has a huge amount of potential energy because it is so high. If that snow mass begins to slide down the mountain in an avalanche, its potential energy quickly changes into kinetic energy. The faster the snow moves downhill, the more kinetic energy it has. The moving snow has so much kinetic energy that it can destroy buildings and trees in its path.

Energy has different forms. You use many of them each day. For example, you use electrical energy when you turn on a lamp to produce light. You use thermal energy when you make toast. You produce sound energy when you play music.

Energy changes things. Think about things you use that run on electrical energy. You run on energy, too. The chemical energy in the food you eat keeps your body moving and working.

 MAIN IDEA AND DETAILS What are four forms of energy?

529

Energy Transformations

Fireworks light up the night sky. Red, blue, green, and gold sparks twinkle in the dark. The crowd gasps as a bright flash is followed by a loud bang.

When you watch a fireworks display, you're watching a series of energy transformations. One form of energy can be transformed into many other forms of energy. In fireworks, the energy transformations begin as stored chemical energy in a rocket. Different chemicals are packed into the rocket in layers so that their chemical energy will be used in sequence. First, a chemical reaction produces energy that pushes the rocket high into the sky—potential chemical energy is transformed into kinetic energy.

When the rocket is high in the sky, more chemical reactions cause the colored sparks.

Another reaction releases the bright flash that is followed by the bang as chemical energy is changed into light and sound energy. Some of the chemical energy also changes into thermal energy. You don't want to be close enough to feel this!

Chemical potential energy can be stored in a battery. When you turn on a flashlight, chemical potential energy is changed into electrical energy. The electrical energy is then changed into light energy, and the bulb shines.

Think about the energy changes that take place when food is cooked. In a toaster, electrical energy is changed into thermal energy, which is transferred as heat. The heat causes a change in the bread, making it warm, brown, and crisp. If you look into the toaster while it is turned on, you can see that the

Fireworks use a series of energy transformations to produce brilliant displays of light and color.

Chinese New Year in Sydney, Australia ▶

530

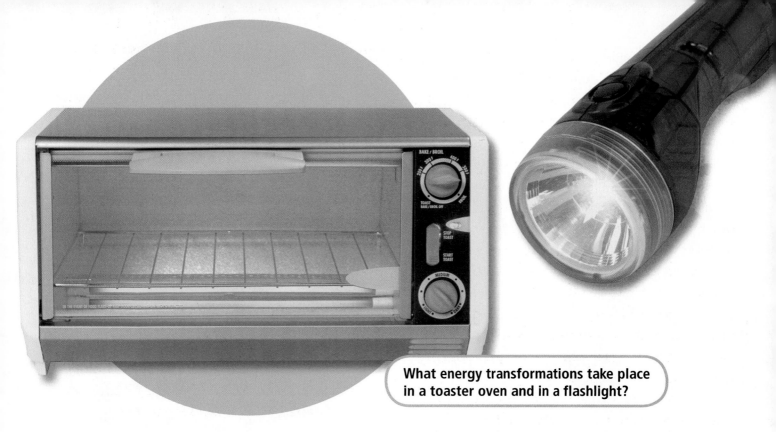

What energy transformations take place in a toaster oven and in a flashlight?

wires glow. This is because some of the electrical energy is changed into light energy.

Where does the electrical energy used by the toaster come from? Your home is connected to a system of electrical lines and cables that lead to a generating station. There, electrical energy is generated, or produced, from an energy source.

At some generating stations, electrical energy is produced by using the energy of moving water. Water held behind a dam has potential energy because of the height of the water. When the water flows down through the gates in the dam, its potential energy becomes kinetic energy.

At other generating stations, a fuel, such as oil, is burned. The chemical energy in the fuel is changed first into thermal energy, which changes liquid water into steam that turns large turbines, and finally into electrical energy. Some plants use nuclear energy to generate electrical energy. Nuclear energy is energy produced by nuclear reactions—the addition or emission of neutrons to or from the nucleus of an atom.

Solar energy, the energy of the sun, can also be transformed into electrical energy. You may have seen solar panels on water heaters, swimming pools, and even experimental cars. These panels absorb the sun's energy and change it into electrical energy.

 MAIN IDEA AND DETAILS What are three forms of energy that can be changed into electrical energy?

How Does Energy Change?
Turn on a personal CD or cassette tape player. Make a list of the forms of energy you observe as you do this. What energy transformations take place?

531

A lightning flash transfers energy between clouds or from clouds to Earth.

Law of Conservation of Energy

You see the flash of lightning, and you hear the rumble of thunder. If you're inside a building, you may notice the windows rattling. Many energy transformations happen during a thunderstorm.

Lightning is electrical energy moving between clouds or between a cloud and the ground. Some of this energy changes into light energy, which you see as the flash. Some changes into sound energy, which you hear as the thunder. The waves of sound energy change into kinetic energy when they meet an object, moving the tiny bones inside your ears or rattling the windows in their frames.

If lightning reaches Earth, some of its electrical energy changes into thermal energy. Heat from lightning can melt sand on a beach, split a tree in two, or set fire to a forest.

The many energy transformations that take place during a thunderstorm demonstrate the law of conservation of energy. The **law of conservation of energy** states that the total amount of energy in a system is always the same—energy cannot be created or destroyed. No energy is lost during a thunderstorm, and no new energy is produced. Energy just changes forms.

 MAIN IDEA AND DETAILS What is the most important idea of the law of conservation of energy?

1. MAIN IDEA AND DETAILS Draw and complete the graphic organizer.

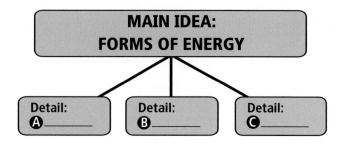

**MAIN IDEA:
FORMS OF ENERGY**

Detail:
A_____

Detail:
B_____

Detail:
C_____

2. SUMMARIZE Write three sentences that tell what this lesson is mainly about.

3. DRAW CONCLUSIONS In many generating stations, a fuel such as oil is burned as a source of energy. What energy transformation takes place in the process?

4. VOCABULARY How are potential energy and kinetic energy different?

Test Prep

5. Critical Thinking What energy transformations take place when you use an electric fan to cool a room?

6. Which kind of energy is stored in a battery?
- **A.** chemical
- **B.** heat
- **C.** kinetic
- **D.** light

Links

Writing

Descriptive Writing

Write a **description** of what it feels like to go back and forth and up and down on a swing. Describe how potential and kinetic energy change as you ride the swing.

Math

Write Equations

A liter of water that has a temperature of 45°C is mixed with a liter of water that has a temperature of 25°C. Which of the following equations shows the temperature of the mixture?

a. $45° + 25° = 70°$

b. $45° - 25° = 20°$

c. $(45° + 25°) \div 2 = 35°$

Art

Energy Collage

Look through magazines and newspapers to find pictures that represent ways you use energy every day. Use the pictures to make a collage on a small sheet of poster board.

 For more links and activities, go to www.hspscience.com

What Are Waves?

Fast Fact

An Energetic Wave The higher a wave is, the more energy it carries. This wave is about 5 times the height of the surfer, who is about 2 meters tall. This means that it has 25 times more energy than a wave the same height as the surfer. In the Investigate, you'll see how waves carry energy.

Making Waves

Materials   ● piece of brightly colored yarn   ● coiled spring toy   ● stopwatch

Procedure

① Tie the yarn around the wire of the spring toy to mark the center. With your partner holding one end, you pull the other end. Slowly stretch the spring along the floor to a length of about 4 m.

② While your partner holds one end of the spring toy so it can't move, jerk your wrist quickly to one side and back again. Observe the yarn and the wave movement of the spring. Use the stopwatch to measure and record the time it takes the wave to reach your partner.

③ Repeat Step 2, making a greater sideways movement in the wave. Measure and record the time it takes the wave to reach your partner.

④ Have your partner continue to hold still one end of the spring toy. In one quick motion, push the end of the spring toy forward and then pull it back to the original position. Observe the wave as it travels. Measure and record the time it takes the wave to reach your partner.

⑤ Repeat Step 4, but gather together 14 coils of the spring and then release them. Measure and record the time it takes the wave to reach your partner.

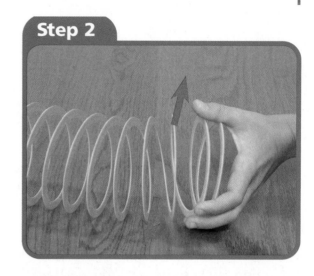

Step 2

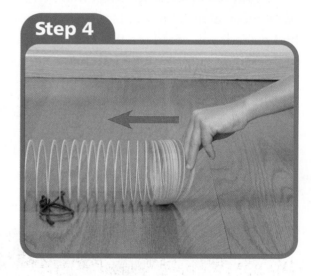

Step 4

Draw Conclusions

1. Compare the ways the piece of yarn moved when you made the two different kinds of waves.

2. **Inquiry Skill** Compare the measurements you made in this activity. Hypothesize about the speed of a wave in a spring toy.

Investigate Further

Try making more than one push/pull wave at a time. What do you observe about the distance between the waves as the number of waves increases?

Reading in Science

VOCABULARY

wave p. 536
wavelength p. 537
amplitude p. 537
frequency p. 539
electromagnetic
  spectrum p. 540

SCIENCE CONCEPTS

▶ what waves are
▶ how waves carry energy

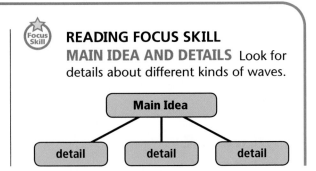 **READING FOCUS SKILL**
MAIN IDEA AND DETAILS Look for details about different kinds of waves.

Waves

Imagine sitting by a quiet pond. The water looks as smooth as glass until a frog jumps in. Ripples spread out from the point where the frog hit the water. The ripples are waves. A **wave** is a disturbance that carries energy through matter or space.

Think back to the waves you made in the Investigate. You started each wave by moving the spring toy in some way. You watched the wave move along the spring. But after the wave had passed, you could see that the spring was in the same place by observing the position of the yarn that was tied to it. Wave energy moved along the spring.

Waves spreading in water or moving along a spring are mechanical waves. A mechanical wave needs matter to travel from one place to another. Earthquake waves are also mechanical waves.

If you look carefully at a mechanical wave you can see that it has two parts. The first part of the wave is higher than the part behind it. The high part of a wave is called the *crest*. The low part is called the *trough*.

A complete wave is made up of one crest and

Wavelengths can vary greatly. Wavelengths of waves rolling onto a beach may be several meters in length, while those of ripples in a glass of water may be only millimeters.

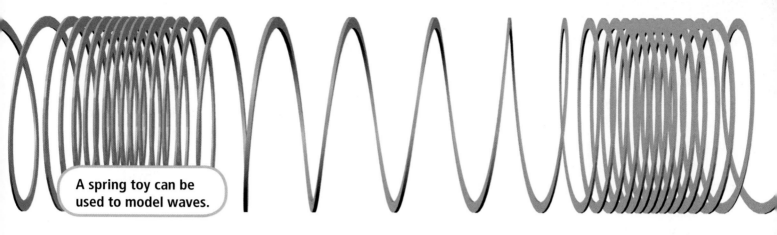

A spring toy can be used to model waves.

one trough. The distance from the middle of the crest of one wave to the middle of the next crest is called a **wavelength**.

When you made waves in the spring toy, you displaced—or moved—the spring from its resting position. The distance that the matter is displaced from its resting position is called amplitude. The **amplitude** is the distance from the resting position to either the top of the crest or the bottom of the trough.

 MAIN IDEA AND DETAILS What are two parts of a wave?

Water Waves
From a height of about 10 cm, release one drop of water from a dropper into a pan of still water. Observe the wave that forms. After the surface of the water has become still again, release three drops of water, one after the other. What do you see?

Wave Structure

Amplitude

Height

Crest

Trough

Wavelength

Sound Waves

Sound moves in waves as well. However, sound waves are a different type of wave than water waves. Have you ever played a guitar or watched someone else play one? Strumming a guitar string makes the string vibrate. The string pushes on the air molecules next to it. This push compresses, or squeezes together, molecules of the air, forming the compression part of a sound wave. The sound wave moves away from the string through the air.

You have seen that the crest of a water wave is followed by a trough. The compression part of a sound wave is followed by a *rarefaction* (rair•uh•FAK•shuhn). In this second part of a sound wave, the particles are far apart.

Think back to the Investigate activity. The second kind of wave you made on the spring toy was like a sound wave. After you compressed the spring, you pulled your hand back. Behind the compression, the spring was stretched. That stretched area was a rarefaction. A single sound wave is made up of one compression and one rarefaction.

Pitch Think about all the sounds you hear each day. Some sounds are high, like the wail of a siren. Some sounds are low, like the rumble of a truck engine. Some sounds are loud and others are soft. What makes these sounds different?

In the Insta-Lab, you saw that each drop of

compression   rarefaction   compression

538

water started another wave. When a guitar string vibrates, every vibration starts another sound wave. The number of times the string vibrates in a given amount of time is called **frequency**. If the guitar string vibrates five times in one second, the frequency is five vibrations per second. One wave per second equals what is called 1 hertz. Most people can hear sounds that have frequencies between 20 hertz and 20,000 hertz.

One way to describe sound is by its pitch. The *pitch* of a sound refers to how high or low it is. The higher the frequency of a wave, the higher the pitch. The frequency of a wave depends on the vibrating object that starts the wave. When you play a guitar, you can change the length of a string by pressing on it. That shortens the string and makes the frequency higher. The guitar produces a sound with a higher pitch.

Loudness Another way to describe sound is by its loudness. If you strum a guitar string gently, the vibration is small, so the amplitude of the wave is small and the sound is soft. If you strum the string with more force, the vibration has more energy. The amplitude of the wave is greater, and the sound is louder.

The loudness of sounds is measured in units called *decibels (db)*. This unit relates to the intensity of the sound wave. For every 10-decibel increase in loudness, the amplitude of the sound increases by a factor of 10. The sound of leaves rustling on a tree has a loudness of 10 decibels. A 20-decibel sound, such as a whisper, has an amplitude 10 times greater.

Loud sounds can cause pain, and sounds above 80 decibels can, over time, damage hearing. That's why people who work in noisy factories or around airplanes wear ear protection to block loud sounds.

 MAIN IDEA AND DETAILS What are two properties that can be used to describe a sound?

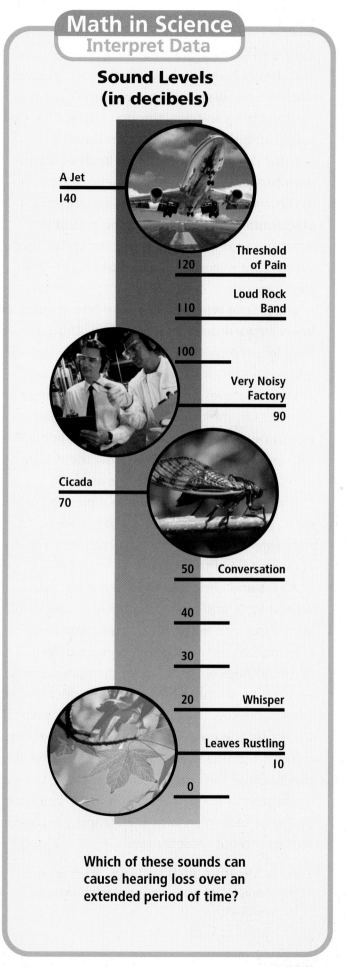

Sound Levels (in decibels)

A Jet
140

120 — Threshold of Pain

110 — Loud Rock Band

100

Very Noisy Factory
90

Cicada
70

50 — Conversation

40

30

20 — Whisper

Leaves Rustling
10

0

Which of these sounds can cause hearing loss over an extended period of time?

Light and Electromagnetic Waves

Light is a form of energy that travels in waves. Unlike sound waves, light waves don't need matter. They can travel through space. That's why you're able to see the light from the sun.

Light waves and some other kinds of waves are vibrating electric and magnetic fields that carry energy. These waves make up the **electromagnetic spectrum**. The part of the spectrum that you can see is called visible light. Visible light makes up only a small part of the electromagnetic spectrum.

Other light waves have longer wavelengths and lower frequencies than visible light. These waves have less energy than visible light. They include infrared waves, microwaves, and radio waves.

Infrared waves are heat waves. The warmer an object is, the more infrared waves it gives off. Some cameras can record infrared light. The pictures from these cameras show the hottest areas as white and coolest areas as black.

If you have made popcorn in a microwave oven, you have seen wave energy at work. The microwaves heat the moisture inside the kernels of corn, and burst them open.

X rays and ultraviolet light rays have shorter wavelengths and higher frequencies than visible light. Although humans can't see these rays, cameras can record them. X rays are used to record images of the inside of the human body. An X ray of a broken arm shows the doctor exactly where and how the bone is broken. This helps the doctor set the bone so that it will heal correctly.

You are probably very aware of ultraviolet (UV) rays because they cause sunburns. These rays can damage your skin and eyes. It is important that you wear sunscreen with SPF 30 and sunglasses that screen out most UV rays.

MAIN IDEA AND DETAILS What are four examples of waves in the electromagnetic spectrum?

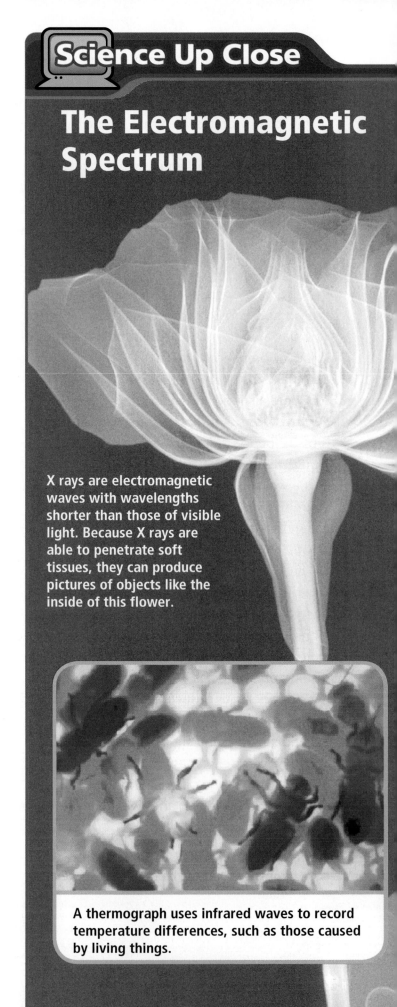

Science Up Close

The Electromagnetic Spectrum

X rays are electromagnetic waves with wavelengths shorter than those of visible light. Because X rays are able to penetrate soft tissues, they can produce pictures of objects like the inside of this flower.

A thermograph uses infrared waves to record temperature differences, such as those caused by living things.

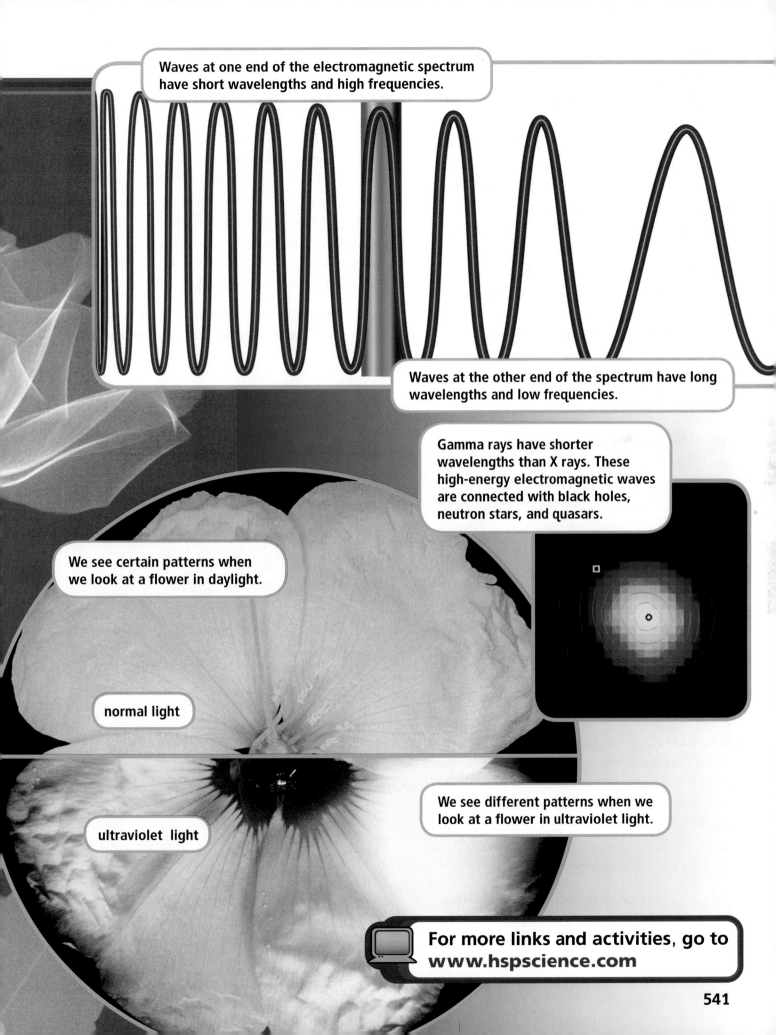

Waves at one end of the electromagnetic spectrum have short wavelengths and high frequencies.

Waves at the other end of the spectrum have long wavelengths and low frequencies.

Gamma rays have shorter wavelengths than X rays. These high-energy electromagnetic waves are connected with black holes, neutron stars, and quasars.

We see certain patterns when we look at a flower in daylight.

normal light

ultraviolet light

We see different patterns when we look at a flower in ultraviolet light.

For more links and activities, go to
www.hspscience.com

Light Energy from the Sun

Have you ever thought about how much you depend on the sun's energy? From the food you eat to the water you drink, the sun provides a continuous energy source for many critical processes and events on Earth.

If you stand outside on most sunny days, you can feel the warmth of sunlight. Just as energy from the sun warms you, it warms Earth's air, land, and water.

Different parts of Earth absorb different amounts of energy from the sun. This makes some areas warmer than others. These differences in warmth cause air to flow from place to place, causing the winds that move weather systems.

Energy from the sun causes water to evaporate from Earth's surface. This is one step in the all-important water cycle.

Energy from the sun is used to produce almost all the food on Earth. Plants absorb energy from the sun and use it, along with carbon dioxide and chlorophyll, to make their own food. Animals get this energy when they eat the plants. People eat food from plants and animals, so whether you eat a salad or a hamburger, the energy you get from your food originally came from the sun.

 MAIN IDEA AND DETAILS Name three things Earth gets from the sun's light energy.

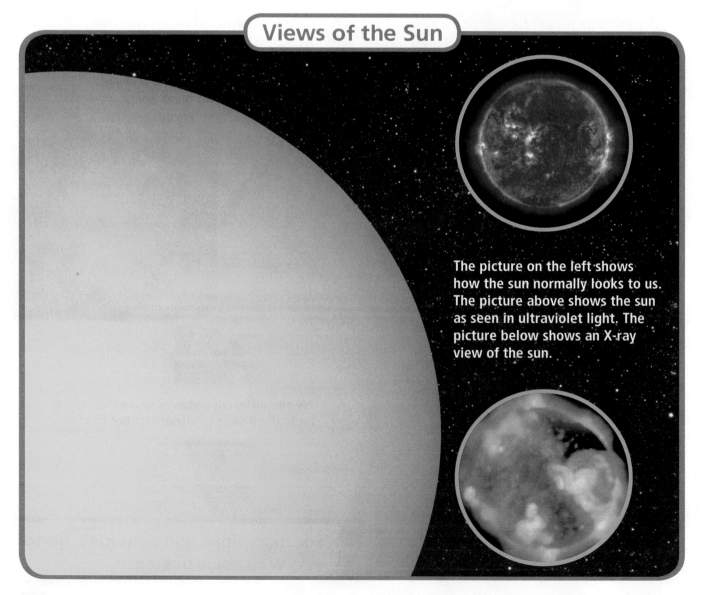

Views of the Sun

The picture on the left shows how the sun normally looks to us. The picture above shows the sun as seen in ultraviolet light. The picture below shows an X-ray view of the sun.

1. MAIN IDEA AND DETAILS Draw and complete the graphic organizer.

**MAIN IDEA:
THERE ARE DIFFERENT KINDS OF WAVES.**

Detail:
Sound waves are waves of vibrating **Ⓐ** _____ .

Detail:
Electromagnetic waves are waves of **Ⓑ** _____ .

Detail:
Electromagnetic waves that people can see are called **Ⓒ** _____ .

2. SUMMARIZE Use the graphic organizer to write a summary of the lesson.

3. DRAW CONCLUSIONS How would you describe the sound wave produced by gently strumming a shortened guitar string?

4. VOCABULARY How are the terms *loudness, amplitude, pitch,* and *frequency* related?

Test Prep

5. Critical Thinking You throw a small rock into a lake and notice the wave it causes. If you throw a larger rock into the lake, how will the wave be different? Explain your answer.

6. How do you measure one complete wavelength?
- **A.** amplitude to frequency
- **B.** crest to crest
- **C.** pitch to trough
- **D.** trough to crest

Links

Writing

Informative Writing
Most mechanical waves travel faster through solids and liquids than they do through gases, such as air. Research this fact and write a short **report** explaining it. Be sure to include examples.

Math

Make a Graph
Draw a graph that shows a wave with an amplitude of 1 cm and a wavelength of 2 cm. On the same graph, draw a wave with an amplitude of 1 cm and a wavelength of 1 cm. Start and end the waves at the same point. How do the frequencies of the waves compare?

Health

Noise Pollution
Research noise pollution. Find out about its causes and effects. Look for things that people can do to protect their hearing. Make a poster to present your findings to the class.

 For more links and activities, go to www.hspscience.com

How Does Light Behave?

Fast Fact

Diffractors in Motion Ctenophores (TEN•uh•fawrz), or comb jellies, are a group of ocean animals that move by using rows of tiny hairs called cilia (SIL•ee•uh). The rapidly beating cilia diffract, or scatter, light, producing a spectacular rippling-rainbow effect. In the Investigate, you will learn about another property of light—the way it is reflected in a mirror.

Locating an Image

Materials
- 15-cm x 15-cm piece of corrugated cardboard
- modeling clay
- small mirror
- metric ruler
- 3 pushpins

Procedure

1. Use a ruler to draw a straight line on the cardboard. Use clay to make the mirror stand up along the line. Mark a dot on the cardboard 5 cm from the middle of the mirror's edge. Push one of the pins into the cardboard at the dot.

2. Kneel so that the mirror is at eye level. Move to one side of the pin, and observe its reflection in the mirror. Push a second pin into the cardboard so that it blocks your view of the first pin's reflection. Push a third pin into the cardboard so that it blocks the reflections of the first and second pins. Mark the pinholes so that you can find them later.

3. Leave the first pin in position. Remove the other pins. Move to the other side of the first pin, and repeat Step 2.

4. Remove the pins and the mirror from the cardboard. Use a ruler to draw a straight line that includes the two pinholes you marked in Step 2 and extends past the mirror line. Do the same for the pinholes you marked in Step 3. Mark the point where the two lines intersect.

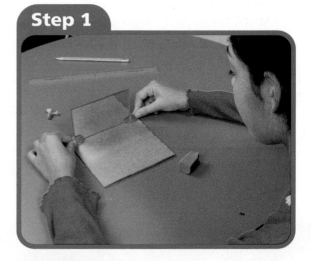

Step 1

Step 3

Draw Conclusions

1. How does the distance between the mirror and the first pin compare with the distance between the mirror and the intersection of the two lines?

2. **Inquiry Skill** What can you conclude about the position of a reflection compared with the position of the actual object being reflected?

Investigate Further

Images reflected in a plane mirror are the same size as the objects they reflect. Use the Investigate procedure to draw the image of a reflected triangle.

Reading in Science

VOCABULARY

reflection p. 546
refraction p. 548
diffraction p. 549
transparent p. 550
translucent p. 550
opaque p. 550

SCIENCE CONCEPTS

▶ ways light can change direction

▶ ways different materials affect light

READING FOCUS SKILL

CAUSE AND EFFECT Look for the effects different surfaces have on light waves.

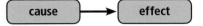

How Light Behaves

A strong beam of light shines from the lighthouse. If you look at the beam of light, you can see that it doesn't curve or bend. Light travels in a straight line.

A beam of light doesn't change direction unless it strikes something. When light strikes an object, some of the light bounces off the surface of the object. The bouncing of light off a surface is **reflection**.

You know that the sun produces light. The moon, however, does not produce light. You see the moon because it reflects sunlight. Astronauts on the moon were able to see Earth because Earth reflects sunlight, too.

A smooth surface, such as a mirror, reflects light well. When you stand in front of a mirror, you see yourself in the mirror. Your image appears to be as far behind the mirror as you are in front of it.

The light from the lighthouse warns ship captains about dangerous rocks or other obstacles. A lens (called a *Fresnel lens*) behind the light source in a lighthouse reflects the light out in one direction. The light source rotates so that its beam can light up a large area.

In fiber optics, light travels through fine optical fibers without being absorbed along the way. ▼

▲ A prism separates white light into the colors of the spectrum.

The amount of light an object reflects depends on the object's surface. A smooth surface, like that of a mirror, reflects nearly all of the light that strikes it. A rough surface, like that of soil, reflects much less of the light that strikes it. The rest of the light is absorbed.

You have seen that visible light is part of the electromagnetic spectrum. The light appears white. However, light is a mixture of different wavelengths of light. Each of these wavelengths is seen by the human eye as a different color. When white light passes through a prism, its path changes, and the white light is separated into the colors of the visible spectrum. These colors are red, orange, yellow, green, blue, and violet.

The color of an object depends on which wavelengths of light the object reflects. A cucumber looks green because it reflects green light and absorbs other wavelengths. A carrot looks orange because it reflects orange light and absorbs other wavelengths.

A white object, such as a blank sheet of paper, reflects all wavelengths of light. A black object absorbs all wavelengths of light and reflects very little light. Have you ever crossed a parking lot on a sunny day and felt the heat from the asphalt surface? The asphalt becomes hot because its black color absorbs so much light and thermal energy from the sun.

 CAUSE AND EFFECT What causes a blue marble to look blue?

We see a strawberry as red and its leaves as green because they reflect only those colors of light and absorb the rest.

Refraction and Diffraction

Have you ever looked at a clear glass vase of flowers from the side? Where the stems enter the water, they look as if they are broken. Why does this happen?

The stems aren't really broken. Your eye has been fooled by the way light reaches it. The speed of light is different through different materials. Light travels more slowly through dense materials. It travels faster through materials that are less dense. Light travels fastest through a vacuum where there is no matter at all (at about 299,792,458 m/s, or 186,282 mi/s).

Light travels faster through air than it does through water. When light leaves water and enters the air, it speeds up. The change in speed causes the light to bend. The bending of light as it passes from the surface of one material to another is called **refraction**.

Iceland spar is a transparent variety of the mineral calcite. When light strikes the mineral, it splits into two separate rays. This is known as double refraction.

The water refracts light, causing the stem to look bent.

The surface of a CD diffracts light, producing rainbow lines.

Light is diffracted by particles in the atmosphere during a sunset.

In the vase, light from the part of the stem that is above the water reaches your eye on one path. Light from the part of the stem that is under the water reaches your eye on a different path. As a result, you see the stem in two separate parts.

When an object blocks the path of light, the object casts a shadow. If you look closely at a shadow, you may notice that the edge of the shadow looks slightly blurry. When light passes the edge of an object, it bends slightly. The little bit of light that bends around the edge of the object blurs the edge of the shadow. This bending of light around the edge of an object is called **diffraction**.

Diffraction of sunlight causes colorful sunsets. Particles in the air block the path of light, causing diffraction. The longer wavelengths of visible light are affected more than the shorter wavelengths are, so you see more of the red

end of the spectrum. The effect is greater when light travels a greater distance through the atmosphere. This is why you see the red color at sunrise or sunset but not at midday.

CAUSE AND EFFECT What causes light to bend as it passes from one material to another?

Just Add Water
Place a penny in the bottom of a plastic foam cup. Move your head back until the penny just becomes invisible. Have your partner gently pour water into the cup. What do you see? Explain what happened.

Transparent, Translucent, and Opaque

When you look out a window, you get a clear view of what's outside. You can see through the glass clearly because almost all the light that strikes it passes through it. The glass is transparent. A **transparent** material allows most of the light to pass through it. Glass is transparent. Some kinds of plastic, such as plastic wrap, also are transparent.

Not all glass is transparent, however. Sometimes materials are added to glass to reduce the amount of light that can pass through the glass. You can't see clearly through this glass. A material that allows some light to pass through is **translucent**. Wax paper, tissue paper, and some plastics are translucent.

Things that don't allow any light to pass through them are **opaque**. Light that strikes opaque materials is reflected or absorbed. The light energy the materials absorb is transformed into heat, and the objects become warm. Wood is opaque. Metals are opaque, too. Most of your body is opaque. Plants, clay pots, soil, tree trunks, animals, bricks, houses, and even your best friend are all opaque!

 CAUSE AND EFFECT What causes you to be able to see through a transparent object?

A transparent glass vase allows all the light to pass through, so you can see the stems of the flowers clearly.

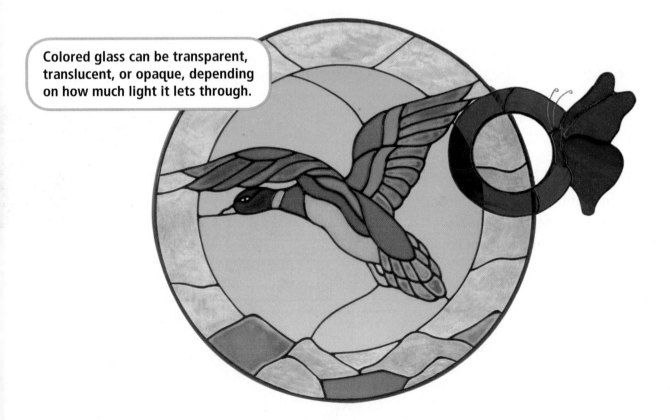

Colored glass can be transparent, translucent, or opaque, depending on how much light it lets through.

1. CAUSE AND EFFECT Draw and complete the graphic organizer.

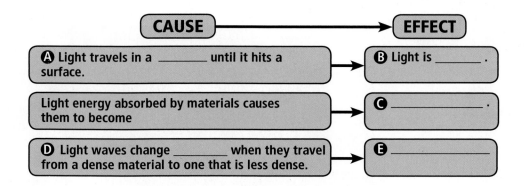

CAUSE → **EFFECT**

Ⓐ Light travels in a _____ until it hits a surface.

Ⓑ Light is _____ .

Light energy absorbed by materials causes them to become

Ⓒ _____ .

Ⓓ Light waves change _____ when they travel from a dense material to one that is less dense.

Ⓔ _____

2. SUMMARIZE Write two sentences that tell what this lesson is mainly about.

3. DRAW CONCLUSIONS Sometimes, condensation of water on glass makes a window look foggy. Is the fogged window transparent, translucent, or opaque? Explain your answer.

4. VOCABULARY Write one or more sentences to describe each of the ways light can change direction.

Test Prep

5. Critical Thinking A diamond is a very dense mineral. Would refraction of light by a diamond be different from refraction by glass, which is less dense? Explain your answer.

6. Which term is defined as "the bending of light around the edge of an object"?

A. absorption   **C.** reflection

B. diffraction   **D.** refraction

Links

Writing

Expressive Writing

The properties of light have been the subject of many poems. Write a short **poem** about reflection, refraction, or another effect of light. Illustrate it.

Math

Make a Bar Graph

The index of refraction is a number that tells how much a material bends light. Look up the index of refraction for four materials. Then make a bar graph that compares the refraction amounts of the materials.

Art

Design a Window

Draw a design for a stained-glass window that could be used as a decoration in a home. Choose different colors and textures of glass. Label the parts of your window as transparent, translucent, and opaque.

 For more links and activities, go to www.hspscience.com

Keeping Watch

Let's say you have spent all day with your friends at the mall. When you get home that night, your parents don't have to ask you where you have been. That's because they already know!

How do they know? They have been tracking and mapping you all day long using the Internet and that nifty watch on your wrist.

A Personal Locator

The watch, called a Personal Locator, sends a signal to a satellite in space. The satellite is part of the U.S. Department of Defense's multi-billion dollar Global Positioning System (GPS).

The GPS uses 24 different satellites that are about 20,200 km (12,550 mi) above Earth. Each satellite circles the Earth in 12 hours. A GPS satellite sends out radio signals as it circles Earth, where the signals are received by devices such as the Personal Locator.

Those devices can then calculate how far they are from

A personal locator watch helps to keep children secure, because they can be located at a moment's notice.

the satellite by measuring the time it takes for the signal to reach Earth from space. The receiver then takes similar measurements from at least three other satellites and uses these measurements to calculate its latitude and longitude. That way the GPS can tell a person's exact location.

The watch also features a built-in pager and a 911 panic button that alerts police in an emergency. It also tells parents when their children reach a pre-set destination, such as the mall, school, or library.

Tracking Kids

The Personal Locator is just one of a number of inventions different companies have recently developed to keep track of kids. Another device tracks a child by using a computer chip embedded in a sneaker. The chip sends out a radio signal that a receiver can track.

Some parents are buying the personal tracking devices so their children can be safe from kidnappers. Some people, however, say no tracking device can keep a child 100 percent safe.

That's why safety experts say that parents who buy personal tracking devices need to make sure they are also keeping their eyes and ears open for their kids' safety.

Think About It

1. What kind of signal does a GPS satellite send out?
2. How does a GPS device help to locate a person or thing?

Find out more! Log on to
www.hspscience.com

The Raman Effect

Imagine having a scientific discovery with your name on it! The Raman effect is named after the man who discovered it—Sir Chandrasekhara Venkata Raman. He was born in India in 1888 and was a physics professor at Calcutta University.

While there, Raman conducted studies about light. He learned that when a laser with a single-color wavelength of light is beamed through a material, the light waves become longer or shorter. The changes in the light waves depend upon the gas, solid, or liquid through which the light passes. Raman's discovery became known as the Raman effect. It has helped scientists analyze different chemicals and learn about the structure of molecules.

Raman's discovery earned him the Nobel Prize in Physics in 1930. He was the first scientist born and educated in India to receive the Nobel Prize in Physics.

Career Photographer

Photographs enable us to save images of the past. For a good picture, a photographer needs just the right amount of light. To get that light, a photographer may use a flash or strobe light, often "bouncing" the light off a wall or a ceiling to give just the right amount of light.

You Can Do It!

Materials
- colored markers
- sheet of white paper
- two rectangular mirrors

Quick and Easy Project

Kaleidoscope

Procedure

1. Use colored markers to make dots, stars, and other small shapes on a sheet of white paper. Your marks should be in an area about 3 cm square.

2. Stand one mirror on its short edge near your marks. Look down into the mirror so that you can see the reflection of your marks.

3. Stand a second mirror at an angle to the first one, and look at the reflections in the mirrors. Change the angle between the mirrors, and observe how the reflection changes.

Draw Conclusions

1. Describe the reflection you saw first with the two mirrors.

2. How did changing the angle between the mirrors affect the reflection?

Design Your Own Investigation

Vibrating Strings

Stringed instruments make sounds when the strings are plucked, bowed, or struck, causing them to vibrate. Use an empty tissue box and rubber bands of different sizes to make a stringed instrument. You will need two pencils to slip under the rubber bands, one on each side of the opening in the box. Use your stringed instrument to test variables that affect the kind of sound produced.

Vocabulary Review

Use the terms below to complete the sentences. The page numbers tell you where to look in the chapter if you need help.

potential energy p. 528
kinetic energy p. 528
wave p. 536
amplitude p. 537
electromagnetic spectrum p. 540
transparent p. 550
translucent p. 550
opaque p. 550

1. The energy of motion is _____ .

2. A material that allows some light to pass through it is _____ .

3. The distance from the resting position to the top of a crest or the bottom of a trough is a wave's _____ .

4. A material that allows almost all light to pass through it is _____ .

5. Light and other waves like it make up the _____ .

6. A disturbance that carries energy through matter or space is called a _____ .

7. Stored energy is called _____ .

8. A material that does not allow light to pass through it is _____ .

Check Understanding

9. Which energy transformation occurs as a boulder rolls down a hill?
   A. potential energy to chemical energy
   B. chemical energy to thermal energy
   C. kinetic energy to mechanical energy
   D. potential energy to kinetic energy

10. **CAUSE AND EFFECT** Mai was given the picture shown below. She must explain the flower stem's appearance.

Which explanation should she give?
   F. The water is absorbing the light.
   G. The water is refracting the light.
   H. The water is reflecting the light.
   J. The water is diffracting the light.

11. **MAIN IDEA AND DETAILS** Which form of energy is **not** produced when chemical energy stored in fireworks is transformed?
   A. electrical energy
   B. light energy
   C. sound energy
   D. thermal energy

12. Which wave has the greatest amplitude?

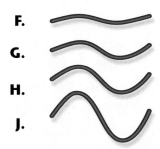

F.

G.

H.

J.

13. Which of these absorbs the smallest amount of light energy?

A. clay brick

B. metal

C. clear glass

D. wood

14. Which kind of wave is produced when air molecules vibrate?

F. light wave

G. infrared wave

H. microwave

J. sound wave

15. Which is the decibel level of the loudest sound a human can safely hear over time?

A. 1 db

B. 10 db

C. 80 db

D. 100 db

16. Tam can sing a higher note than anyone else in her class. What kind of sound quality do Tam's highest notes have?

F. low amplitude

G. low energy

H. high frequency

J. long wavelength

Inquiry Skills

17. **Compare** the ways an orange and a banana absorb and reflect light.

18. Why do you sometimes **observe** brilliant colors during a sunset or sunrise?

Critical Thinking

19. Sometimes, when you stand in front of a window, you can see outside and see yourself in the window at the same time. How does this happen?

20. Tom did an experiment to show his classmates how to make sounds by blowing across bottles filled with different amounts of water. One bottle was empty, one bottle was half full, and one bottle was three-fourths full.

Part A Which bottle made the sound with the lowest pitch?

Part B How could Tom explain his results to the class?

Lesson 1 **How Is Thermal Energy Transferred?**

Lesson 2 **What Is Electricity, and How Is It Produced?**

Lesson 3 **What Is a Circuit?**

Vocabulary

thermal energy
heat
conduction
convection
radiation
insulation
static electricity
current electricity
circuit
series circuit
parallel circuit
electromagnet

What do YOU wonder?

This is a thermographic image of a teapot pouring hot tea into a cup. The colors show the temperature differences in various parts of the liquid, the teapot, and cup. How was this photo taken? How is this technology used to aid engineers in their work?

How Is Thermal Energy Transferred?

Fast Fact

They Bubble and They Boil What makes these mud pots bubble? Thermal energy heats gases in the Earth. Steam rises to the surface and through mud puddles. In the Investigate, you will observe temperature differences in two materials.

Losing Heat

Materials
- 2 fishing sinkers, ¾ oz
- foam cup, 8 oz
- paper cup, 8 oz
- 2 large beakers
- hot and cold water
- graduate, 100 mL
- 2 thermometers
- stopwatch

Procedure

1. Put a fishing sinker or other weight in the bottom of each cup. The weight will hold the cup down.

2. Set each cup in a beaker.

3. Add cold water to each beaker, around the outside of the cup. Add water until its level rises nearly to the top of the cup.

4. **CAUTION:** **Use care when handling hot water.** Measure 100 mL of hot water. Add the water to the foam cup. Do the same for the paper cup.

5. Put a thermometer in each cup. Don't let the thermometers touch the sinkers. Measure and record both temperatures. Start the stopwatch.

6. After 1 minute, measure and record both temperatures again. Continue to measure and record temperatures for at least 10 minutes.

Step 4

Draw Conclusions

1. Make a line graph to display your temperature data. Use different-color lines to compare the temperatures in the cups.

2. Use numbers to explain what your graph shows.

3. **Inquiry Skill** A hypothesis is a possible explanation for something you observe. Hypothesize a possible reason for the temperature differences you measured.

Step 5

Investigate Further

Plan and conduct a simple investigation to discover other materials that help keep water temperatures from cooling rapidly.

Reading in Science

VOCABULARY
thermal energy p. 562
heat p. 564
conduction p. 564
convection p. 565
radiation p. 565
insulation p. 566

SCIENCE CONCEPTS
▶ how thermal energy relates to temperature
▶ how thermal energy is transferred
▶ how and why insulation works

 READING FOCUS SKILL
CAUSE AND EFFECT Find out what causes materials to get warmer.

Thermal Energy

Touch a table. Crumple a piece of paper. The materials are solid. They are made of billions of tiny particles too small to see. These particles are always moving. As you learned in Chapter 14, they have kinetic energy, or the energy of movement.

The kinetic energy of the moving particles of a substance or object is called **thermal energy**.

The more thermal energy an object or substance has, the warmer it is. It's often useful to know just how warm something is. To find this out, you can use a thermometer. A thermometer indicates the temperature of a material.

Temperature is a measure of the average kinetic energy of the particles in an object or a substance. The faster the particles move on average, the higher the temperature is.

The iceberg is a solid. Its particles move back and forth and it keeps its solid shape.

As thermal energy is added to the ice, the solid ice begins to thaw, and its particles begin to move back and forth more rapidly. They can move past and around each other, and the ice melts to become a liquid.

If the liquid water is exposed to the high temperatures of the flowing lava, the particles in the water begin to move very fast and farther away from one another. They enter the gas state—water vapor.

Which bowl of soup has more thermal energy at the same temperature—the large bowl or the small bowl?

When two things have the same temperature, the average kinetic energy of their particles is the same.

You may have seen temperatures given in two different scales. In the United States, the weather report usually gives the air temperature in degrees Fahrenheit (°F). On the Fahrenheit scale, water freezes at 32° and boils at 212°.

Nearly all other countries report the weather by using the Celsius (°C) scale. Scientists also use this scale. On the Celsius scale, water freezes at 0° and boils at 100°.

To understand how thermal energy moves, think about what happens to an ice cube in a glass on a hot day. The temperature of the ice is 0°C (32°F). The ice has some thermal energy, but not much. Its particles move slowly. The air in the room has more thermal energy. The air is much warmer than the ice, perhaps 27°C (81°F), and its particles are moving faster.

As time passes, some of the thermal energy of the air transfers to the ice. This causes the temperature of the ice to rise. Soon, the particles in the ice begin to move more. The temperature of the ice rises above 0°C (32°F). The ice melts and changes to water. As the temperature of the water continues to rise, the water particles continue to move faster. They have more thermal energy. If the water stays in the glass long enough, the temperature of the air and the water will be the same.

The amount of thermal energy in an object is related to its mass. If two objects at the same temperature are compared, the one with the greater mass has more thermal energy. Similarly, the object with the smaller mass has less thermal energy.

 CAUSE AND EFFECT How does a change in thermal energy cause ice to melt?

Insta-Lab

Ice Race

Add 10 mL of warm tap water to one cup and 100 mL of warm tap water to another cup. Get two ice cubes of the same size. Put one ice cube in each cup at the same time. Start the stopwatch. Observe the ice cubes carefully. Which one first melts completely? Why?

Thermal Energy Transfer

Convection

Explain how convection currents transfer thermal energy within this cloud.

In colonial times, blacksmiths used a hammer, anvil, and forge to make farm tools and iron rims for wheels. Today's blacksmiths use heat to shape metal into everything from horseshoes to works of art.

Heat—Thermal Energy on the Move

You use the word *heat* often. What exactly is heat? **Heat** is the transfer of thermal energy from warmer objects to cooler ones. Blacksmiths understand this principle well. They use very hot fires to heat iron and steel. The metal gets so hot that it becomes soft. The blacksmiths then shape it into useful and attractive objects before it cools and hardens again.

Three processes transfer thermal energy. One is conduction. **Conduction** is the transfer of thermal energy that results from the collision of particles. The particles of a cold solid don't have much thermal energy. When thermal energy is added, the object's particles move faster, and it gets warmer. When a warmer solid touches a cooler one, some of the warmer solid's thermal energy

transfers to the cooler solid through conduction.

Metal is a good conductor of thermal energy. Soup heated in a metal pot on the stove gets hot quickly because the metal easily conducts the thermal energy from the burner. You may have stirred a hot drink with a metal spoon and felt the spoon handle get warm. That's conduction at work.

It's important to remember that conduction transfers heat only from the warmer solid to the cooler solid. When you hold an ice cube, you may think that the cold moves from the ice into your hand, but that's not true. Instead, thermal energy is conducted from your hand into the ice cube. You feel the loss of heat as cold.

Have you watched someone pour cold milk into a cup of hot coffee without stirring it? The milk swirled in ribbons and clouds. Eventually, the

Conduction

Explain how conduction is transferring thermal energy in this picture.

Radiation

Discuss the process that transfers thermal energy to this baking bread. Are any other thermal energy transfers happening also?

For more links and activities, go to www.hspscience.com

thermal energy of the coffee and the milk became the same and the swirling stopped.

The process you watched in the coffee cup was **convection**, or the transfer of thermal energy through a fluid. That fluid may be a liquid or a gas. Convection happens because of temperature differences in different parts of the fluid. The volume of the warmer part of the fluid increases, which causes its density to decrease. Since the warmer fluid is now less dense than the cooler fluid around it, the warmer fluid moves upward in a current. The fluid starts to flow and mix. Cooler, denser material moves under the heated fluid and moves it up even more. The warmer fluid loses thermal energy to cooler regions as it moves through them.

The third process for transferring thermal energy doesn't require matter at all! It's **radiation**, or the transfer of thermal energy as waves. The most familiar source of radiant energy, or energy transferred by radiation, is the sun. Radiation transfers the sun's thermal energy and light through space to Earth. Radiation can also work over smaller distances. When you heat a cup of water in a microwave oven, you're transferring thermal energy through the process of radiation.

 CAUSE AND EFFECT How do conduction, convection, and radiation cause the transfer of thermal energy?

Insulation

When we heat water or soup, we want the transfer of thermal energy to occur quickly. But sometimes we prefer to slow down or stop that transfer. To do so, we use materials that don't conduct thermal energy well. **Insulation** is a substance that conducts thermal energy poorly.

People use insulation in many ways. Quilted or down-filled clothing acts as insulation for the human body. People wear such clothing when the weather is cold, to prevent loss of thermal energy from their bodies to the air.

When people build homes and other buildings, they put layers of insulation inside the walls and ceilings. The material, often fiberglass insulation, is a poor conductor of thermal energy. In winter, the thermal energy inside the building stays inside because it doesn't move out through the fiberglass.

Insulating buildings also helps them stay cool in summer. Thermal energy from the air outside doesn't travel through the insulation very well. A house with good insulation stays cooler in summer than a poorly insulated one.

Focus Skill **CAUSE AND EFFECT** How does insulation help keep the air inside buildings warm in winter and cool in summer?

Find the insulators in these pictures. Explain how they prevent the transfer of thermal energy.

566

1. **CAUSE AND EFFECT** Copy and complete this graphic organizer to show three ways thermal energy can be transferred.

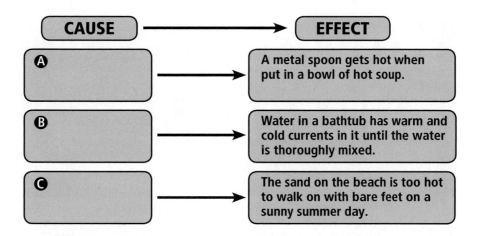

CAUSE	EFFECT
Ⓐ	A metal spoon gets hot when put in a bowl of hot soup.
Ⓑ	Water in a bathtub has warm and cold currents in it until the water is thoroughly mixed.
Ⓒ	The sand on the beach is too hot to walk on with bare feet on a sunny summer day.

2. **SUMMARIZE** Use the completed graphic organizer to write a lesson summary.

3. **DRAW CONCLUSIONS** How are insulators different from conductors of thermal energy?

4. **VOCABULARY** Write a sentence to explain how heat is related to thermal energy.

Test Prep

5. **Critical Thinking** "My hands get cold when I go outside on a cold day," says Kesha. Tell Kesha why that happens and why she should wear gloves.

6. What happens to the particles in any object when thermal energy is added?
   A. They move faster.   C. They melt.
   B. They split apart.   D. They spin into the air.

Links

Writing

Persuasive Writing
Suppose you are in the heating and cooling business. Write a **business letter** to a customer who is planning to build a new home. Explain what insulation is and why you recommend it.

Math

Make a Circle Graph
Use these percents to make a circle graph of places where thermal energy is lost from the average home: cracks, 38%; basement walls, 20%; walls, 17%; windows, 16%; other, 9%.

Social Studies

Geography
Research areas around the world that have bubbling mud pots. Mark the locations on a large map of the world. Add a label for each place. Write a guide to the areas, and explain reasons people should visit.

 For more links and activities, go to **www.hspscience.com**

What Is Electricity, and How Is It Produced?

Fast Fact

Lightning in a Room? Lightning is a buildup of static charge. The machine you see in this photo is a Wimhurst machine, a historical form of electrical generator for generating high voltages. Static charges build up and then are discharged between the balls of the machine. In the Investigate, you will experiment with static charges.

Experimenting with Charges

Materials
- 2 balloons
- 2 pieces of string, about 30 cm long
- masking tape
- piece of wool cloth

Procedure

1. Blow up two balloons to the same size. Tie them closed with the string.

2. Tape the string of one balloon to the edge of a table or desk. Let the balloon hang freely.

3. Hang the other balloon in the same way. The balloons should be about 10 cm apart.

4. Move the balloons toward each other, and then let them go. What do you observe? Record your observations.

5. Hold one balloon away from the other. With the wool, vigorously rub the side that faces the other balloon.

6. Move the rubbed balloon close to the other balloon. Let it go. Observe what happens. Record your observations.

7. Rub both balloons with the wool. Move them close to each other. Let them go. Observe what happens. Record your observations.

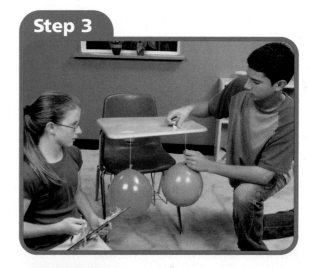

Step 3

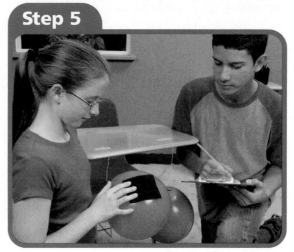

Step 5

Draw Conclusions

1. Why must you observe and record what happens to the balloons before you rub either one?

2. Describe the difference in what you observed after you rubbed one balloon and then after you rubbed two balloons. Identify the variable that accounts for the difference.

3. **Inquiry Skill** Use your data to hypothesize why the balloons behaved as they did after you rubbed one and after you rubbed both.

Investigate Further

Conduct a simple experiment, using a balloon, a piece of wool, and a damp sponge, to investigate how different surfaces affect static electricity.

Reading in Science

VOCABULARY
static electricity p. 570
current electricity p. 572

SCIENCE CONCEPTS
▶ how static electricity and current electricity behave
▶ what the sources of electricity are and how electricity is produced

 READING FOCUS SKILL
SEQUENCE Find out the steps that change different forms of energy into electrical energy.

Static Electricity

In the Investigate, you discovered that two balloons moved toward each other after you rubbed one with a piece of wool. They moved away from each other after you rubbed both of them. Recall what you learned about atoms in Chapter 12. An atom has positively charged protons in the nucleus and negatively charged electrons in an outer energy level. It's possible to remove some electrons from atoms, leaving them positively charged. The electrons can move to another object, making it negatively charged. Since unlike charges attract, the two objects come together. The electric charge that builds up on an object that has gained or lost electrons is **static electricity**.

When you rub a balloon with wool, the balloon gains some electrons from the wool and becomes negatively charged. When the balloon comes near a balloon that you haven't rubbed, it moves toward it. When the balloons come into contact some of the electrons of the unrubbed balloon are repelled by the rubbed balloon and the unrubbed surface becomes positively charged. Therefore, the two balloons stick to each other.

 SEQUENCE Describe the sequence of events that lead to a flash of lightning.

A charged object is attracted toward an object with the opposite charge. If the charges are the same, the objects move apart.

When pieces of clothing cling to each other or to the wearer, what can you infer about them?

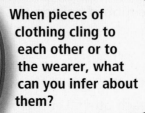

You may get a little shock as a result of static electricity, but it probably won't hurt much.

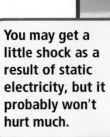

Lightning

Updrafts in a thunderstorm carry rain along. Friction rubs electrons off the drops giving the top of the cloud an all-over positive charge. The bottom of the thundercloud has extra electrons giving it a negative charge. The negative charge at the bottom of the cloud attracts positive charges on the ground. When the attraction is great enough, the cloud gives off its energy in a flash of lightning.

Downdraft in a thundercloud.

Updraft in a thunderhead. Electrons are being rubbed off the drops of rain in the winds.

Current Electricity

Static charges are temporary and somewhat unpredictable. Photocopiers and air cleaners are two devices that use static electricity. However, static electricity doesn't have many other uses, because it's hard to control. **Current electricity**, the flow of electric charge through a wire, is quite controllable and has many practical uses.

Before looking at some examples of current electricity, consider how charges flow. They move easily through conductors. Most materials that are good conductors of thermal energy also conduct electricity well. Metals, especially copper, are also good conductors of electricity. Charges flow easily through copper wires.

Materials that are poor conductors of thermal energy and electricity are insulators. Uncharged air is an insulator. Rubber and plastic insulate so well that they're used to wrap electric wires.

Look at the sequence of events that leads to making a light bulb glow. When a light switch is off, a gap of insulating air keeps charges from flowing between two copper wires. A flip of the switch closes the gap and brings the wires together. The wires touch, and charges flow.

The flow of charges can now move from the wall socket through the wires leading to the lamp. A metal plug attached to these wires makes contact with a metal receptacle (rih•SEP•tuh•kuhl) inside the wall socket. Where do the charges in the wall socket come from? You buy them from your local energy plant. They travel through wires from the plant to your home, through wires in the walls, and finally to the socket.

The charges flow through the plug along the wires into the lamp and then through a filament (FIL•uh•muhnt) inside the light bulb. The filament is a conductor. It glows as charges pass through it. The flow of charge continues in a complete circle—from the wall socket through the lamp and back to the wall. As long as the switch is on, the flow continues and the light glows. If the filament burns out, or if the wire breaks at any

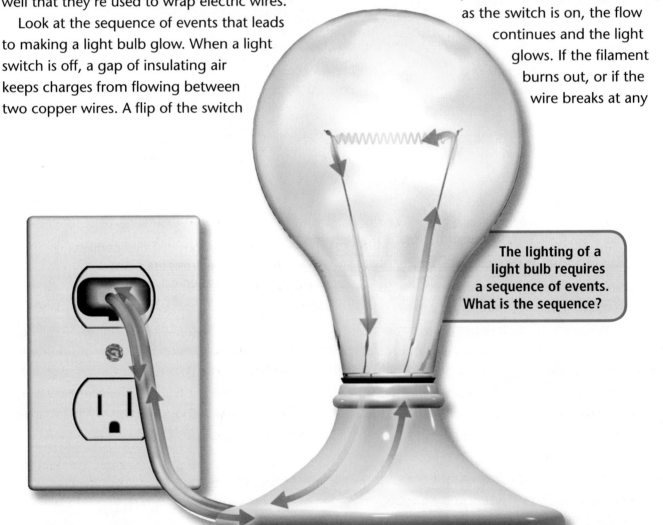

The lighting of a light bulb requires a sequence of events. What is the sequence?

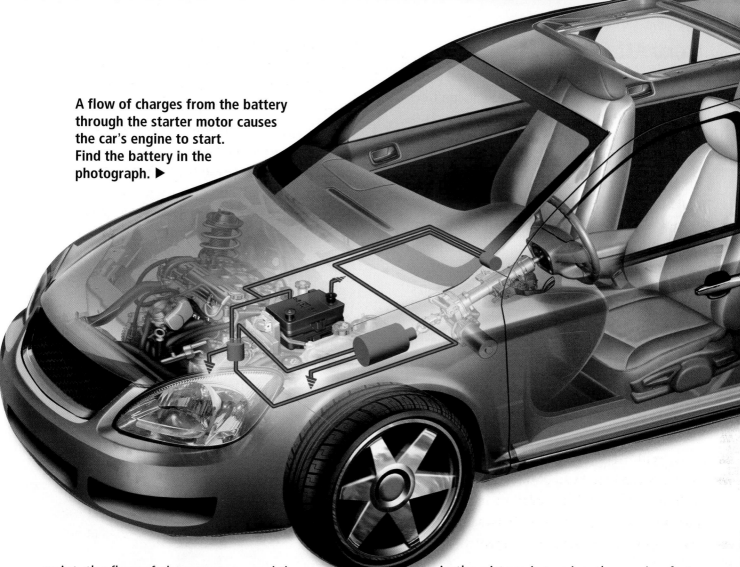

A flow of charges from the battery through the starter motor causes the car's engine to start. Find the battery in the photograph. ▶

point, the flow of charges stops and the bulb doesn't glow.

Turning the ignition (ig•NISH•uhn) key in a car starts a sequence of events similar to that started by flipping a light switch. However, the source of the energy is not a generating station. It is the car's battery. A battery stores electricity for future use. Turning the key closes the gap between two wires, allowing a small amount of current electricity to flow from the battery to a starter relay. The relay lets a large amount of current flow from the battery through the starter motor and back. The starter motor is a powerful electric motor with gears that make the engine turn. When this happens, the car's pistons draw in a mixture of gasoline and air. A spark from the car's ignition system makes the mixture explode. That's when you hear the car's engine start. As soon as the burning of the fuel

in the pistons is turning the engine fast enough, the starter motor shuts off.

Car batteries don't lose their charge, because they're recharged every time the car is driven. Inside a battery, two plates made of different metals hang in a liquid that conducts electricity. Chemical reactions between these plates and the liquid produce excess electrons. The battery gives up some of those electrons when the car starts or the radio plays. But while the car is moving, a device called an *alternator* (AWL•tuhr•nayt•uhr) sends current back to the battery. The current restores the original state of the two plates. They are ready to react again and provide electrons when needed.

 SEQUENCE Draw a flow chart and label the sequence and arrows showing the flow of electricity in a car battery.

How Electricity Is Produced

As useful as electricity is, it's only one form of energy. Like all forms of energy, it can't be made from nothing but must be produced from some other form of energy. In a car battery, electricity comes from chemical energy. An electric generating station can use any of several sources.

At a *hydroelectric* (hy•droh•ee•LEK•trik) plant, the energy comes from falling water. In some hydroelectric plants, a dam holds water as potential energy. In others, the plant relies on the natural flow of a river. In either case, the water moves over the blades of a turbine (TER•bin), making the turbine spin. A shaft connects the turbine to a generator. Inside the generator, a giant magnet surrounds a spinning coil of electric wire. The magnet has a *magnetic field*—a region of space, near a magnetized

Hydroelectric power is limited, because moving water is available only in certain places.

The current is carried by wires to locations where it is used.

The water behind the dam has potential energy.

When the gates of the dam are opened, the potential energy of the water changes to kinetic energy.

The rotation of the coils in the generator produces electric current.

The moving water turns a turbine that is connected by a shaft to a generator.

body, where magnetic forces can be detected. The spinning of the wire in the magnetic field produces an electric current in the wire.

Only about 6 percent of the electric energy used in the United States is generated from water power. About 70 percent is generated at electricity generating stations that use fossil fuels as their primary energy source. Such a station burns coal, oil, or natural gas in a giant furnace. The heat from the furnace causes water to boil and turn to steam. In a steam turbine, the pressure of the hot steam turns a shaft at high speeds. A generator is attached to the turbine. Inside the generator, large coils of copper wire spin in a magnetic field, producing electricity.

Another 21 percent of the electricity used in the United States comes from nuclear plants. In a nuclear plant, the process of turning turbines with steam and spinning generators is the same, but the source of the heat is different. The heat comes from splitting atoms. There is much disagreement about using nuclear reactions to produce electricity. Some people believe that the use of nuclear fuel is too risky. Others feel that the risk is outweighed by the benefits of having a relatively cheap way to produce electricity.

No matter what source generates electricity (you'll read about the other 3 percent on page 576), it's distributed in the same way. It moves from the generating station through high-voltage lines, which are large conducting wires, to local areas. There the current is changed from a high voltage to a lower-voltage current that can be used in homes, schools, and businesses.

In addition, no matter what the energy source, the generation of electricity depends on one thing. *Moving a coil of wire inside a magnetic field, or moving a magnet inside a coil of wire, produces an electric current in the wire.*

A car battery is a lead-acid battery. It stores electricity until it is needed to start the car or run the radio or lights. Then the electricity is used. It is replenished, however, as current flows back into it. It is in a constant state of discharging and charging.

The opposite is also true. *Moving electricity through a coil of wire produces a magnetic field.* That's how an electric motor works. The poles of magnets inside the motor attract and repel each other. The alternating push and pull causes the motor's shaft to spin.

SEQUENCE What are the steps in generating electric current in a generating station?

Insta-Lab

Attraction Action

Get a compass and a bar magnet. Keep the magnet away from the compass. Wrap a length of copper wire many times around a cardboard tube to make a coil of wire. Move a magnet back and forth inside the coil. Move the compass near the coil. What happens to the compass needle?

More Sources of Energy to Generate Electricity

Electricity is generated from other forms of energy. Today, people generate most electricity by burning fossil fuels, but fossil fuels will run out some day. Many people are working to develop other energy sources before the fossil fuels are gone.

One promising source is solar power, or the energy of the sun. Photovoltaic (foht•oh•vahl•TAY•ik) cells made of silicon generate electricity directly from sunlight. No generators are required.

Winds blow because some places on Earth are warmer than other places. On wind farms, wind turbines turn shafts in generators, which feed electricity into existing power lines.

In coastal communities, daily ocean tides can be used to generate electricity. Natural inlets can be dammed, or the natural rise and fall of the tides can turn shafts in generators.

Another energy source that's available in some places is geothermal energy, or the thermal energy within Earth. Geothermal energy plants turn shafts in generators by using steam that comes from supplies of hot water lying deep underground.

Focus Skill **SEQUENCE** Trace the steps in producing electricity from solar, wind, and geothermal sources.

The electricity generated by wind turbines goes into existing power lines, joins with electricity from other generating stations, and travels to customers.

The ocean's waves, its high and low tides, and temperature differences in its water can be used to generate electricity.

1. SEQUENCE Copy and complete this graphic organizer to show each sequence of steps.

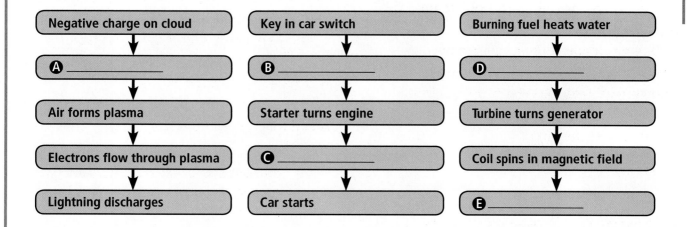

Negative charge on cloud	Key in car switch	Burning fuel heats water
Ⓐ _____	Ⓑ _____	Ⓓ _____
Air forms plasma	Starter turns engine	Turbine turns generator
Electrons flow through plasma	Ⓒ _____	Coil spins in magnetic field
Lightning discharges	Car starts	Ⓔ _____

2. SUMMARIZE Use the completed graphic organizer to write a lesson summary.

3. DRAW CONCLUSIONS Why is it important that we develop sources other than fossil fuels for generating electricity?

4. VOCABULARY Write a sentence to explain the difference between static electricity and current electricity.

Test Prep

5. Critical Thinking Explain how a car battery works.

6. What happens inside a generator?
   A. Steam turns a turbine shaft.
   B. Electrons discharge from pole to pole.
   C. A chemical reaction occurs.
   D. A coil of wire spins in a magnetic field.

Links

Writing

Expository Writing
Choose an energy source. Research the energy source in the library or on the Internet. Write a one-page **report** detailing the advantages and disadvantages of using the source (cost, availability, renewability).

Math

Use Scientific Notation
When lightning flashes, as many as a billion trillion electrons can travel to Earth in less than 0.001 sec. Write this number and time, using scientific notation.

Social Studies

Safety First!
Nuclear energy plants are equipped with safety systems designed to protect human health. Research the health risks associated with nuclear energy. Report to your class about nuclear plants' health and safety systems.

 For more links and activities, go to www.hspscience.com

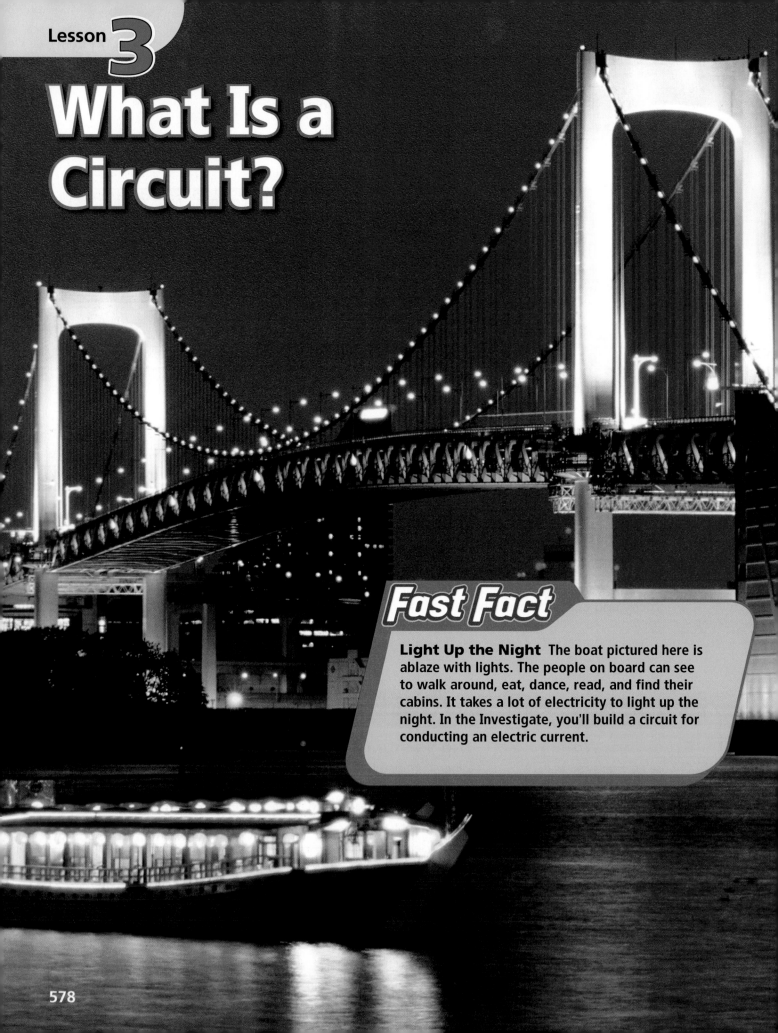

What Is a Circuit?

Fast Fact

Light Up the Night The boat pictured here is ablaze with lights. The people on board can see to walk around, eat, dance, read, and find their cabins. It takes a lot of electricity to light up the night. In the Investigate, you'll build a circuit for conducting an electric current.

Building a Circuit

Materials
- I battery (size D)
- I battery holder
- 2 light bulbs
- 2 light bulb holders
- 4 pieces of insulated electrical wire, 30 cm long, insulation stripped from ends

Procedure

1. Try different ways of hooking together one battery and one light bulb with wires. Keep working until you find a way that lights the bulb. Record your data by making a sketch of each way you try.

2. Unhook a wire at any one point. What happens? Record what you observe. Reattach the wire, and unhook a wire at another point. Record your observations.

3. Now, find a way to light two bulbs by using only one battery. Sketch a diagram. Repeat Step 2.

4. Find another way to light two bulbs with one battery. Make another sketch, and repeat Step 2.

Draw Conclusions

1. A circuit is a loop. Electric current travels in a circuit. Use your sketches and arrows to show the circuit in each of your setups.

2. What happens if the bulb is not screwed tightly into the holder? Why?

3. A circuit can be closed (a complete loop) or open (an incomplete loop). Which of your circuits were closed? What happened when you opened them?

4. **Inquiry Skill** We say that electricity is a flow of charges. Use that definition to infer why some of your setups worked and others didn't.

Step 1

Step 3

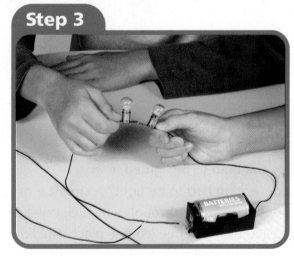

Investigate Further

Use a battery, a light bulb, and wire to build a model of an electric game that requires players to match answers to questions.

Reading in Science

VOCABULARY
circuit p. 580
series circuit p. 582
parallel circuit p. 582
electromagnet p. 584

SCIENCE CONCEPTS
▶ what a circuit is
▶ how different kinds of circuits work
▶ how an electromagnet works

READING FOCUS SKILL
MAIN IDEA AND DETAILS Learn how circuits work, and identify ways we use them.

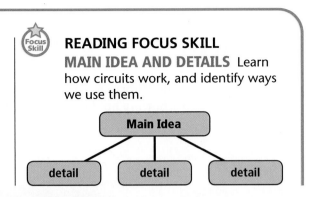

Trace the circuit in this picture. What happens if a wire comes loose?

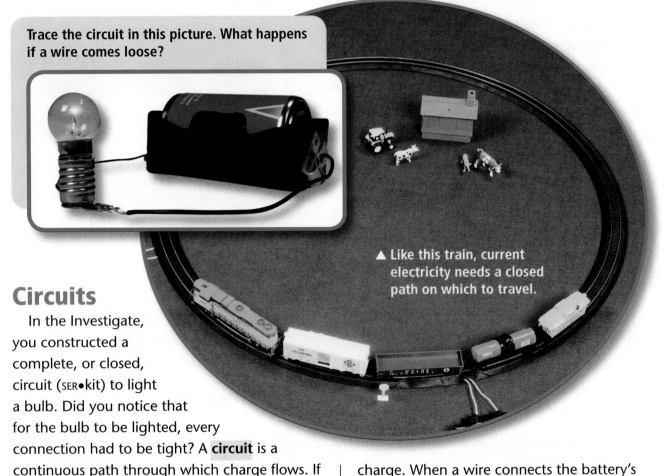

▲ Like this train, current electricity needs a closed path on which to travel.

Circuits

In the Investigate, you constructed a complete, or closed, circuit (SER•kit) to light a bulb. Did you notice that for the bulb to be lighted, every connection had to be tight? A **circuit** is a continuous path through which charge flows. If a circuit is open in even one place, the flow of electric charge stops.

You used a battery as your source of electric charge in the Investigate. Look closely at the battery. Its two ends have different shapes. One is marked (+), or positive. The other is marked (−), or negative. These are the *terminals* of the battery. Inside the battery, a chemical reaction separates charges. Electrons build up at one terminal, giving it a negative charge. The other terminal has fewer electrons, so it has a positive

charge. When a wire connects the battery's negative terminal to its positive terminal, charges flow from the negative terminal and through a wire. From the wire, they flow through the light bulb, through another wire, and back to the positive terminal of the battery. The wires conduct the electric charge. So does the filament inside the bulb. This makes a continuous path along which the charge flows.

In a home, school, or business, the source of electric current is not a battery. It's electric current from the generating plant, delivered

Electricity is measured in units called watts. A kilowatt is 1000 watts. A kilowatt-hour (kWh) is 1 kilowatt used for 1 hour.

On the first day of November, this electric meter read 73,256 kWh.

What was the reading on November 30? How many kWh of electricity did this business use in one month?

This table shows the cost of electricity in five cities. The rate is in cents per kWh.

City	Rate (cents/kWh)
Atlanta	7.3
Boston	14.3
Houston	9.5
Philadelphia	11.4
San Francisco	13.5

How much would this business pay for November's electric bill in each of these cities?

This electrician will install many switches in a home. Why?

through wires to a wall socket. Still, the idea of the circuit is the same. Lights and machines work only if the circuit is complete.

A switch controls a circuit. A switch in the off position opens the circuit, and charges don't move. A switch in the on position completes the circuit, and electric charge flows along the wires.

MAIN IDEA AND DETAILS What are circuits, and why are they important?

Series Circuits and Parallel Circuits

In the Investigate, you may have discovered more than one way to build a circuit. The simplest way is to construct a **series circuit**, in which there is only one path for the current to follow. Current can move through one, two, or more devices, but it must pass through one in order to get to the next. The devices in a circuit are called *resistors*. Resistors resist the flow of charges. The light bulbs in the circuits you built in the Investigate were resistors. So are bells, toasters, heaters, and other appliances that use electric current.

The light bulbs and battery in the photograph below are connected in a series circuit. Current flows in a continuous circuit from the battery, through the first bulb, through the second bulb, and back to the battery. Both bulbs glow as long as both are in place and undamaged. If one light bulb burns out, though, the remaining bulb doesn't light. If any part of a series circuit fails, the entire circuit fails.

Did you find a way around this problem in the Investigate? If you did, you built a parallel circuit. In a **parallel circuit**, devices are connected along separate paths, and current doesn't have to pass through one device to get to the next. If something stops electrons from moving along one path, they can take another path.

The photograph on the next page shows a parallel circuit with two light bulbs. The current still has a closed path to travel, but there are three ways it can go. It can travel through both bulbs, lighting them both. If one bulb is missing or damaged, the current can travel through the other, lighting it. The flow of charges doesn't stop when one connection is loose or when one device isn't working. When one part of a

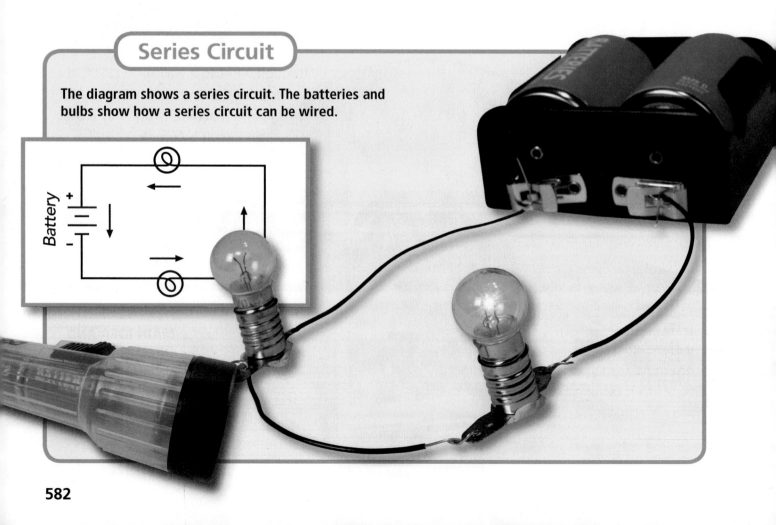

Series Circuit

The diagram shows a series circuit. The batteries and bulbs show how a series circuit can be wired.

Battery

Parallel Circuit

The diagram shows a parallel circuit. The batteries and bulbs show how a parallel circuit is constructed. If one bulb goes out, the other bulbs stay lighted. The photograph shows a real parallel circuit.

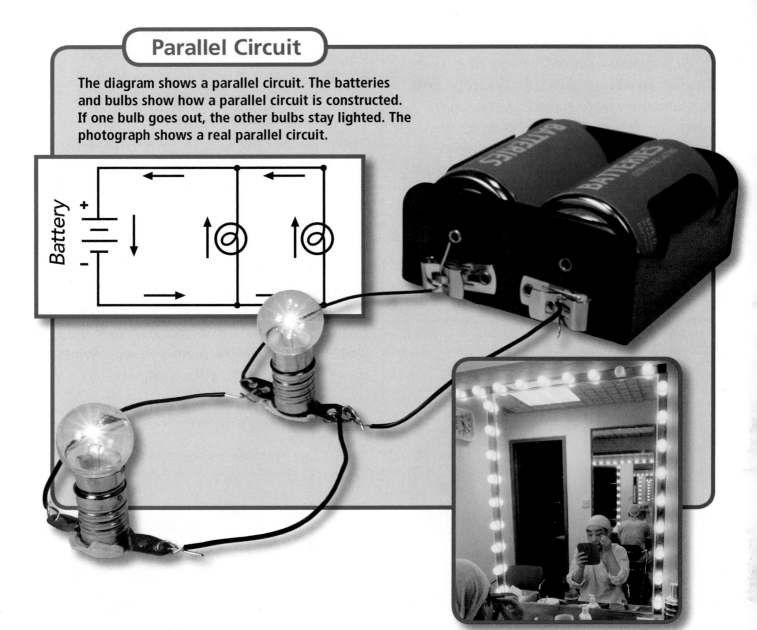

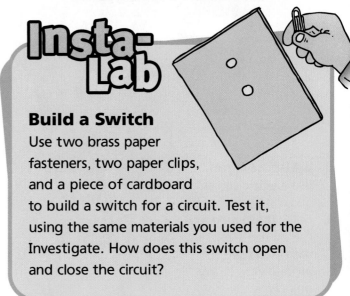

parallel circuit fails, other parts of the circuit continue to work.

This gives a parallel circuit some advantages over a series circuit. For one thing, it's easier to repair. If one device stops working, it's easy to know which one needs to be replaced. With a series circuit, all the devices must be tested to find a single damaged one. In addition, parallel circuits can have separate switches in them. Individual switches can turn off one device while other devices on the same circuit continue to work.

 MAIN IDEA AND DETAILS How do series and parallel circuits work?

Insta-Lab

Build a Switch

Use two brass paper fasteners, two paper clips, and a piece of cardboard to build a switch for a circuit. Test it, using the same materials you used for the Investigate. How does this switch open and close the circuit?

Using Electric Current

We use electric current in many ways. One use is in an electromagnet. An **electromagnet** is a temporary magnet made by passing an electric current through a coil of wire that surrounds an iron core. When the circuit is closed, the electromagnet attracts objects that contain iron, steel, or nickel.

An electromagnet works because current flowing through a coil produces a magnetic field. When current runs through a coil of wire, the magnetic field is strongest inside the coil. The field causes any iron-containing object inside the core to become temporarily magnetic.

Building an electromagnet is easy. All you need is a long wire, a nail, and a battery, put together as shown in the picture. The secret to making a strong electromagnet lies in wrapping the wire around the nail many times. The more loops there are in the coil, the stronger the magnetic field is. The stronger the field is, the stronger the magnet—in this case, the nail—is.

An electromagnet has an advantage over a permanent magnet—the electromagnet can be turned off when it's not needed. When the circuit is closed, the electromagnet is on. When the circuit is open, the electromagnet is off.

Focus Skill **MAIN IDEA AND DETAILS** What is an electromagnet, and how does it work?

▲ Electromagnets use electric current to generate a magnetic field. These magnets can be any size. They are often used to pick up very heavy objects.

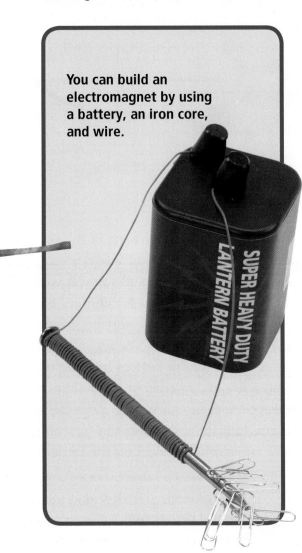

You can build an electromagnet by using a battery, an iron core, and wire.

SUPER HEAVY DUTY LANTERN BATTERY

1. MAIN IDEA AND DETAILS Copy and complete this graphic organizer. Write the correct term for each description.

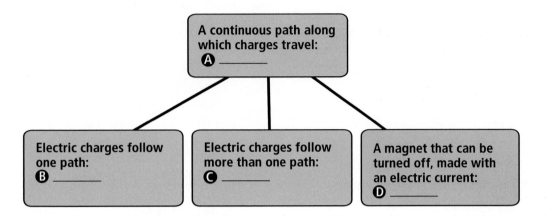

A continuous path along which charges travel:
Ⓐ _____

Electric charges follow one path:
Ⓑ _____

Electric charges follow more than one path:
Ⓒ _____

A magnet that can be turned off, made with an electric current:
Ⓓ _____

2. SUMMARIZE Use the completed graphic organizer to write a lesson summary.

3. DRAW CONCLUSIONS Which is better—a permanent magnet or an electromagnet? Why?

4. VOCABULARY Write a sentence to explain the difference between an open circuit and a closed circuit.

Test Prep

5. Critical Thinking Why is a parallel circuit easier to repair than a series circuit?

6. Which is a device that opens or closes a circuit?
   A. battery   **C.** switch
   B. bulb   **D.** wire

Links

Writing

Expository Writing
Write an **instruction manual** for a fourth-grade student. Give directions for building a quiz board. Suggest questions to use. Provide a list of needed materials and diagrams the student can use.

Math

Draw a Circuit Diagram
Hook up some batteries and bells in a circuit of your choice. Draw an accurate circuit diagram for your setup. Use the circuit diagrams on pages 582 and 583 as models.

Social Studies

History of Science
Michael Faraday is a famous name in the history of electricity. Find out what research he did, and make a poster to explain his experiments. Report to the class about his achievements.

For more links and activities, go to www.hspscience.com

Catch a Wave

Surfers aren't the only ones who can catch a wave. A Scottish company is making a splash with new technology that converts the energy from ocean waves into electricity.

The company, WaveGen, opened the world's first commercial ocean wave energy plant on the Scottish island of Islay. The plant can generate enough energy to supply electricity for more than 400 homes.

A Clean Energy

If harnessed correctly, the ocean could be an endless source of energy. Some energy experts believe that twice as much energy can be generated from wave power as is currently used to supply the entire world's electricity demand. But, unlike coal, oil, and gas, wave energy will not run out.

Also, energy generated by wave action does not pollute the environment the way burning fossil fuels does. Fossil fuels are those formed in the Earth, such as coal, natural gas, and oil.

But how does wave action work? Engineers built a 25-yard-wide concrete chamber on the island's shoreline. Seawater flows into the chamber and sloshes back and forth, setting up powerful air currents. The air currents turn the blades of a turbine. A turbine is a rotary engine usually made with a series of curved vanes on a rotating spindle. The turbine generates electricity.

WaveGen says that the wave generators can also act as artificial reefs. By placing the generators in

the open water, they can provide shelter for schools of fish and marine plants.

Future Issues

Many environmentalists support wave energy as long as companies do not build the new energy plants along fragile coastlines.

Critics say that generating energy from waves is three times as costly as using coal, gas, or oil. But some experts say that wave energy will be cheap to use in the future.

"They [scientists] will learn a lot from this system that will help them to make the next one more cheaply and more efficiently," said Tom Thorpe, an energy expert.

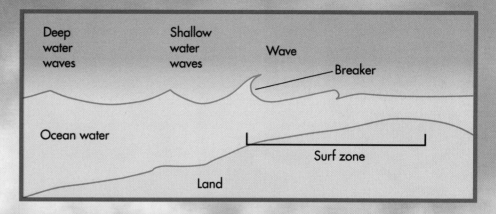

Deep water waves

Shallow water waves

Wave

Breaker

Ocean water

Surf zone

Land

Think About It

1. What are some other ways electricity is produced?
2. How might wave energy help protect the environment?

Spin-In
Find out more! Log on to
www.hspscience.com

Keeping Warm

What do astronauts and lunch boxes have in common? Matthew Geiger knows the answer to that after a recent trip to Space Camp in Alabama: insulation.

At Space Camp, Matthew learned that insulation is used to prevent the transfer of heat. Matthew learned that in space, insulation is important in preventing the sun's energy from being lost to cold space. Insulation also keeps the deep cold of space from changing warm matter. On Earth, insulation is used in many things from building construction to lunch boxes.

While at Space Camp, Matthew discovered another important use for insulation—keeping astronauts warm while in space. Matthew learned that space suits not only look cool, but are lined with special insulation. This insulation is designed to keep heat from an astronaut's body from escaping into the deep cold of space. In all, Matthew, who is interested in becoming an astronaut, learned a lot about how the study of space improves life on Earth.

You Can Do It!

Materials

- 3 batteries (size D) and battery holders
- 3 light bulbs and light bulb holders
- roll of insulated wire
- single-throw double-pole switch
- bell or buzzer

Quick and Easy Project

Switch It On or Off?

Procedure

1. Build a parallel circuit that will light three bulbs dimly.
2. Add extra batteries to the circuit so that one bulb will glow more brightly than the other two. Add a switch you can use to turn off and on one of the dimly lighted bulbs.
3. Add a bell or buzzer in place of one of the bulbs. Add a switch that causes the bell to ring at the same time that it turns *off* a light.

Draw Conclusions

How did you make one bulb glow more brightly? Where did you have to put the switch to control both the bell and the bulb at the same time? Why?

Design Your Own Investigation

The Travels of Electricity

You have learned about some of the ways electric current can be generated. However, getting the current from the generating plant to your TV set is a long process. Trace the path that the current travels from the time it is generated until it reaches your house. Diagram the process, and label the different stages the current goes through.

Review and Test Preparation

Vocabulary Review

Use the terms below to complete the sentences. The page numbers tell you where to look in the chapter if you need help.

heat p. 564

convection p. 565

insulation p. 566

static electricity p. 570

current electricity p. 572

series circuit p. 582

parallel circuit p. 582

electromagnet p. 584

1. The electric charge that builds up on an object that has gained or lost electrons is _____ .

2. A temporary magnet is an _____ .

3. A flow of electric charge through a wire is _____ .

4. The transfer of thermal energy through a current in a fluid is _____ .

5. The transfer of thermal energy is _____ .

6. A material that is a poor conductor of thermal energy and electric charge is _____ .

7. A single path for electric charge to follow is a _____ .

8. A set of separate paths for electric charge to follow is a _____ .

Check Understanding

Write the letter of the best choice.

9. **SEQUENCE** In an electrical circuit, which step follows the closing of a switch?

   A. The flow of electric charge reverses.

   B. The flow of electric charge slows.

   C. Electric current flows through wires.

   D. Electric current stops flowing.

10. **CAUSE AND EFFECT** Which of the following energy sources does not require a generator to produce electricity?

    F. geothermal

    G. hydroelectric

    H. solar

    J. tidal

11. How is sunlight transferred to Earth?

    A. by conduction

    B. by convection

    C. by magnetism

    D. by radiation

12. What can you infer from the circuit diagram?

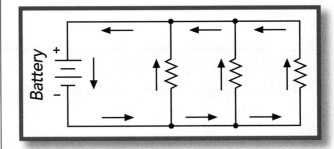

    F. The circuit is parallel.

    G. The source of electric current is a powerful switch.

    H. The circuit is open.

    J. A current is not being generated.

13. Tim is cooking pasta. When he drains the hot water, he uses potholders to hold the pot. Which pair of terms applies to this example?

A. convection; magnetism

B. conduction; insulation

C. convection; closed circuit

D. radiation; insulation

14. Lightning is seen as bright flashes in the sky that move from a cloud to the ground. What causes lightning?

F. Negative charges on the bottom of a cloud jump toward positive charges on the ground.

G. Air in the atmosphere is a good conductor, so lightning moves through it easily.

H. We need to have lightning so we can hear thunder.

J. Lightning reverses the charge on the atoms and molecules in air.

15. Why does a battery have a positive terminal and a negative terminal?

A. There's a right way and a wrong way to hook up the terminals.

B. No charges flow through the negative terminal.

C. One terminal conducts electricity and the other terminal doesn't.

D. More charges build up at one terminal than at the other terminal.

16. Why does a generator work?

F. A current traveling though a coil of wire produces a magnetic field.

G. Steam turns a turbine.

H. Convection transfers thermal energy.

J. Spinning a coil of wire in a magnetic field produces a current.

Inquiry Skills

17. Offer a hypothesis to explain why a down-filled sleeping bag keeps a sleeper warmer than a cotton-filled sleeping bag.

18. When Sally walks across the carpet and touches a doorknob, she feels a shock. When Sammy walks across the same carpet and touches the same doorknob, he doesn't feel a shock. Identify a variable that might explain the difference.

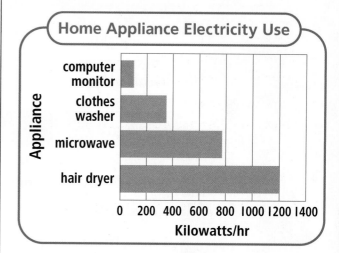

Critical Thinking

19. This graph shows the number of kilowatts of electricity four appliances use in one hour. If electricity costs 8.5 cents per kilowatt-hour, about how much will this family pay for running their clothes washer for 5 hours?

20. Use the graph above to answer these questions.

Part A Which of these appliances is the most economical for the family to use? Why?

Part B Over a week's time for a typical family, which appliance—the hair dryer or the clothes washer—is likely to use more electricity? Why?

591

PHYSICAL SCIENCE

Forces and Machines

⦿⦿⦿ Punkin Chunkin

TO: clarissa@hspscience.com

FROM: rudy@hspscience.com

RE: Lewes, Delaware

Dear Clarissa,

My town is famous for one thing only—that is, the "Punkin Chunkin"! I don't know about you, but I would be in trouble if I hurled a pumpkin a great distance. Believe it or not, this competition attracts people from all over the world. Adults and children alike make elaborate machines that will hurl a pumpkin as far as possible while thousands of spectators look on with admiration. Each year, the coveted trophy is handed down to that year's winner. You better start working on it now if you want to join the fun!

Rudy

Robot Hall of Fame, Carnegie Science Center

TO: tobi@hspscience.com

FROM: sia@hspscience.com

RE: Pittsburgh, Pennsylvania

Dear Tobi,

What do "Asimo" and "Astro Boy" have in common? They were both inducted into the Robot Hall of Fame at the Carnegie Science Center. I'm sure you'll be happy to hear that robots from science fiction are just as eligible as actual robots serving a useful function in life. Not only does the Mars Pathfinder Sojourner rover stand in this place of honor, but R2-D2 from Star Wars is also honored. After all, sometimes fiction leads to reality. You thought you'd heard it all!

Your friend,

Sia

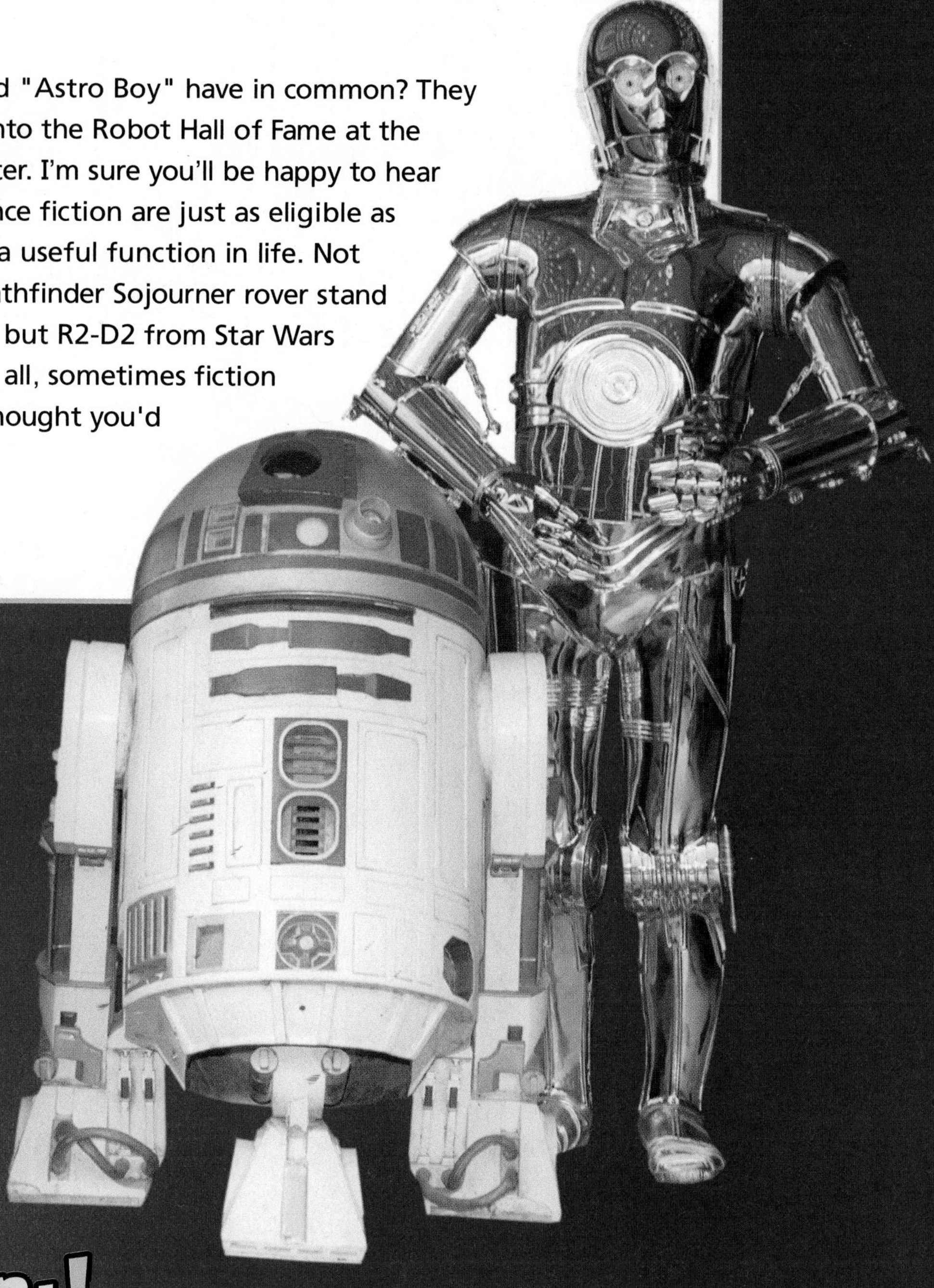

Experiment!

Protecting Eggs In the Punkin Chunkin contest, the pumpkin usually splatters when it hits the ground. Is there a way to protect an object when it strikes the ground? Plan and conduct an experiment to find out.

Chapter

16 Forces and Motion

Lesson 1 **How Do Forces Affect Us?**

Lesson 2 **How Do Forces Interact?**

Lesson 3 **What Is Gravitational Force?**

Vocabulary

velocity
force
acceleration
inertia
balanced forces
unbalanced forces
friction
gravitational force
weight

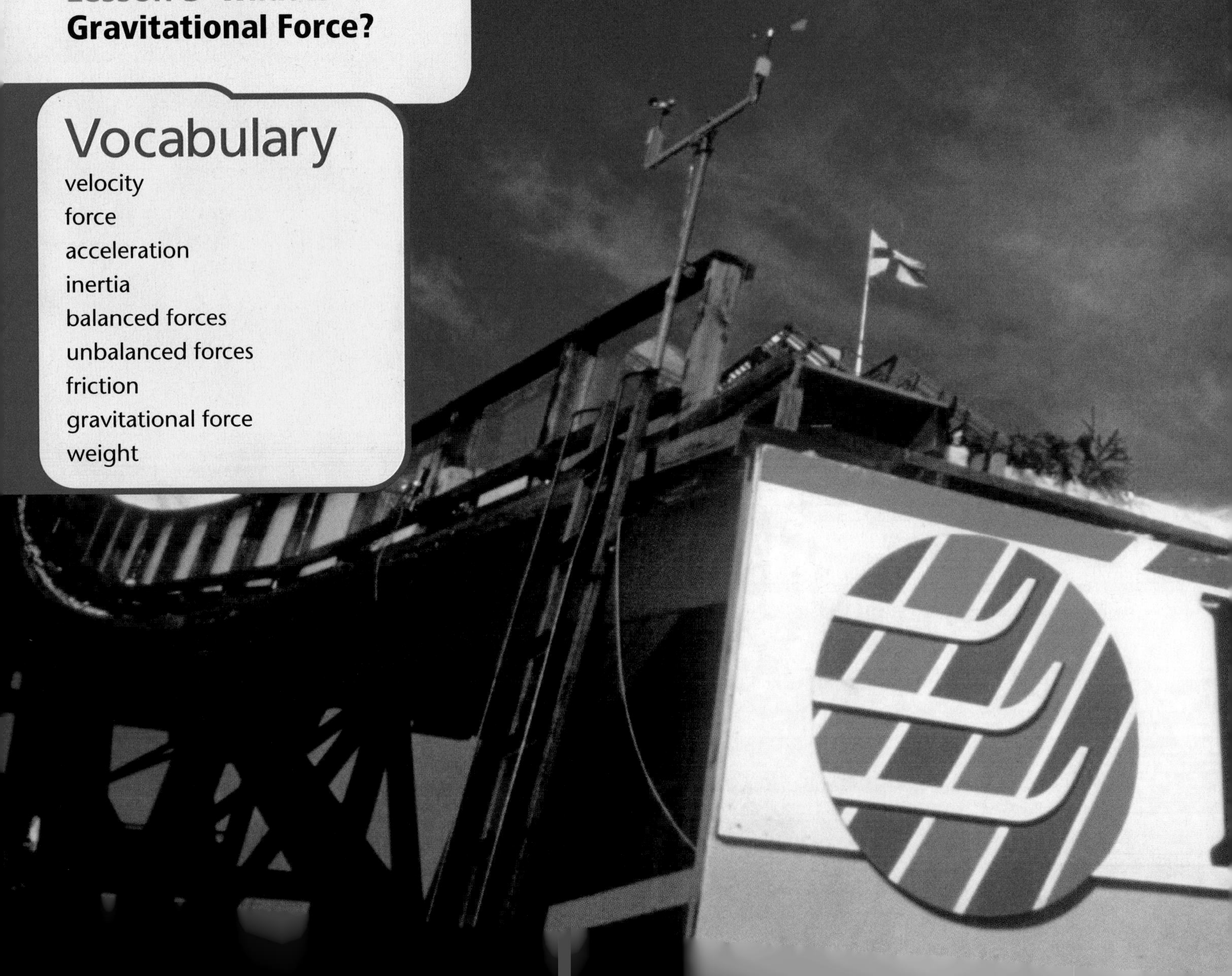

What do YOU wonder?

To ski, snowboard, or ride a sled safely, you need to control the way you apply the laws of force and motion. Many injuries are caused by going too fast. Why do you think it is difficult to control your speed on skis and snowboards? What can you do to control your speed?

How Do Forces Affect Us?

Fast Fact

Skateboard Scenes Skateboarding began in the 1960s in California and was called sidewalk surfing. Skaters began to experiment, and some built ramps and then more complicated structures. Street skating was joined by vert skating. Position, motion, speed, and velocity are important to skateboarders. In the Investigate, you will learn how to measure the speed and velocity of a moving object.

Measuring Speed

Materials
- ruler with a central groove
- marble
- compass
- books
- stopwatch
- meterstick
- pencil

Procedure

1. Copy Table A.

2. Make a ramp by putting one end of the ruler on enough books to total about 8 cm high.

3. Roll a marble down the ramp. Start timing the marble as soon as it leaves the bottom of the ramp. Measure the distance the marble travels in 5 sec.

4. Record your data in the table. Calculate the marble's average speed by dividing the distance it traveled by the time it took (5 sec).

5. Repeat Steps 3 and 4, but measure the distance the marble travels in 6 sec, 7 sec, and 8 sec. Start the marble at the same height and the same place each time.

6. Use the compass to find the direction in which the marble rolled after it left the ramp. (When you include the direction of an object with its speed measurement, you are measuring velocity.)

Draw Conclusions

1. Compare the average speeds of the marble for the 4 trials. Use numbers to interpret the data by identifying the pattern in the data.

2. At what point did the marble reach its greatest speed?

3. **Inquiry Skill** Draw a conclusion about the velocity of the marble. Did the velocity change? If so, in what way did it change?

Table A

	Measuring Average Speed		
Time (sec)	Distance (cm)	Average Speed (cm ÷ sec)	Velocity

Step 3

Investigate Further

How can you **use your data** to **predict** how far the marble will roll before it stops?

Reading in Science

VOCABULARY
velocity p. 599
force p. 600
acceleration p. 600
inertia p. 602

SCIENCE CONCEPTS
- ▶ how force affects objects of different masses
- ▶ how inertia relates to force

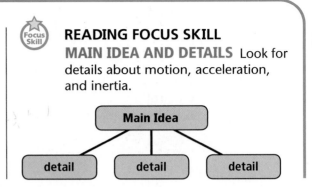

READING FOCUS SKILL
MAIN IDEA AND DETAILS Look for details about motion, acceleration, and inertia.

Describing Motion

Twisting, turning, creeping, leaping—there are many, many kinds of motion to observe every day. All motion, however, is the same in certain ways. All motion is change in position.

You can tell that something has moved if its position changes relative to something else. Suppose you are in a car stopped at a stoplight. A bus is next to you. You can tell that the bus is moving if it changes its position relative to you.

If you and the bus both move, how can you tell? You can compare your change of position and the bus's change of position to other objects that are stationary, or not moving. A stationary object or group of objects used to determine a position change is called a *frame of reference.*

A frame of reference is a point of view. It can change, depending on the viewer. For example, in the frame of reference of your classroom, you are sitting still at your desk. But an astronaut in space has a different frame of reference. From his or her point of view, you are moving. You, your desk, and your classroom are all spinning in space along with Earth.

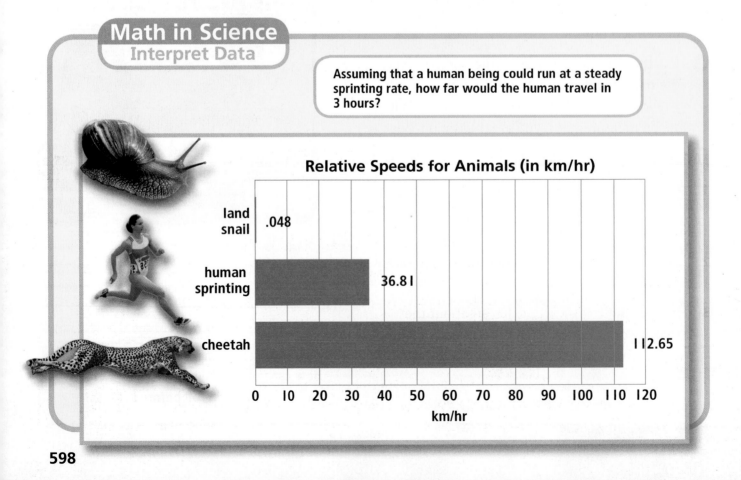

Math in Science
Interpret Data

Assuming that a human being could run at a steady sprinting rate, how far would the human travel in 3 hours?

Relative Speeds for Animals (in km/hr)

land snail: .048
human sprinting: 36.81
cheetah: 112.65

km/hr

One of the most important things to know about an object's motion is its speed. *Speed* is the distance something moves in a certain period of time. For example, suppose you ride 150 km (93 mi) to get to the state fair. If the trip takes 2 hr, what's your average speed? Simply divide the distance traveled by the time it takes. That's 150 km ÷ 2 hr (93 mi ÷ 2 hr), or 75 km/hr (46.5 mi/hr).

Speed tells how fast or slow an object's motion is, but it doesn't tell you the direction of motion. When you state the direction of a moving object as well as its speed, you're stating its **velocity**.

For example, if you say a truck is traveling at 50 km/hr (31 mi/hr), you're stating its speed. If you say the truck is heading northwest at 50 km/hr (31 mi/hr), you're describing its velocity.

The picture shows the velocities of birds flying, people swimming, and other things moving around a lake. Notice that in each case, the velocity given includes both speed and direction.

The birds are moving in a constant direction at a constant speed. Since their direction and speed do not change, the herons have constant velocity. If a bird flies in circles at a constant speed, is its velocity changing? Since the bird's direction is changing, the bird's velocity *is* changing. An object's velocity changes when there is a change in its speed, its direction, or both its speed and its direction.

Scientists sometimes use arrows to represent velocity. The length of a velocity arrow represents the speed measurement. The direction it points represents the direction measurement.

 MAIN IDEA AND DETAILS Why does your velocity constantly change when you move along a curve?

Velocity

The picture shows that direction is often expressed in terms of the compass. What other examples of velocity can you find in this picture?

Herons—moving east at 25 km/hr

Jet ski—moving west at 35 km/hr

The swimmer is moving west at a steady pace.

The rocket is moving upward from its firing pad.

What Forces Do

Gravity is a force. So is magnetism. There are other kinds of forces, too. Some may not be familiar to you. Familiar or not, a **force** is just a push or a pull. Pull a door and it opens. Push a door and it shuts. In both cases, the force comes from your muscles.

Forces act on objects. Forces slow things down, speed them up, stop them, start them, and turn them. Whenever you see any change of an object's velocity, you know that a force is at work.

Change of velocity is called acceleration. **Acceleration** (ak•sel•er•AY•shuhn) is an object's change in velocity divided by the time it takes for that change to occur.

To better understand acceleration, think about this example. A train sitting at a station and facing north has a velocity of 0 km/hr (0 mi/hr) north. As it leaves the station, it reaches a velocity of 75 km/hr (46.6 mi/hr) north in 30 sec. What is the train's acceleration?

The train's change in velocity is 75 km/hr (46.6 mi/hr) minus 0 km/hr (0 mi/hr) in a northerly direction. Divide this velocity change by the time taken, 30 sec. You'll find that the train's acceleration is 2.5 km/hr (1.6 mi/hr) per sec. What does this mean? The train's rate of acceleration, 2.5 km/hr per sec (1.6 mi/hr per sec), means that in each second, the train's speed increases by 2.5 km/hr (1.6 mi/hr).

When the train pulls into the next station, its speed decreases. The train's velocity is also changing—it's decreasing. Since acceleration is change in velocity over time, the train is accelerating.

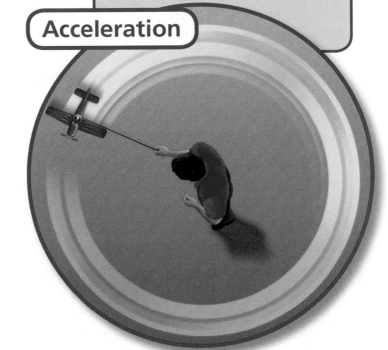

Acceleration

This plane's direction is changing, so its velocity is changing. In other words, the plane is accelerating.

Isaac Newton (1642–1727) is considered one of the greatest of all scientists. He is famous for many discoveries, including laws that describe gravity and other forces, and the ways objects in motion affect each other. One of those laws tells how force relates to mass and acceleration. This law states that the greater the force on an object, the greater its acceleration. You already have experience with this law. You know that if you lightly tap a door, it barely moves, but if you

Acceleration

Acceleration also takes place when speed decreases, such as when this car comes to a stop.

Force

The older girl can kick the soccer ball with more force than her little sister. Therefore the ball rolls farther. The big sister is taller and has more mass. She can kick the ball with more force.

give it a shove, it quickly swings wide open.

This law also says that if two objects are acted on by the same force, the object with less mass accelerates more than the object with more mass. You have experience with this, too. What happens when you use the same amount of force to push an empty shopping cart as you use to push a full one? For a push of the same strength, the cart with more mass accelerates less.

MAIN IDEA AND DETAILS How does the force necessary to move an object change when either the object's mass or acceleration changes?

Mass

When the same force acts on backpacks with different masses, the backpack with the greater mass accelerates less.

601

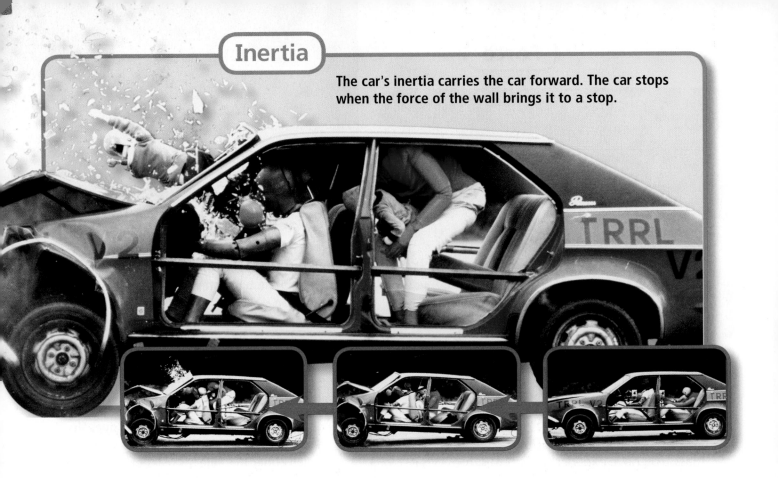

The car's inertia carries the car forward. The car stops when the force of the wall brings it to a stop.

Inertia

For hundreds of years, people thought that a moving object comes to a stop when the force that put it in motion is removed. This idea seems to make sense. For example, you may think that a marble rolling on the floor stops rolling because you stop pushing it.

However, Newton and other scientists have shown that this idea is wrong. It's not motion itself, but a *change* in motion, that requires a force. The force of friction brings the marble to a stop. If not for friction, it would keep going.

An object won't change its motion unless a force acts on it. It won't slow down, speed up, stop, start, or turn without an applied force. This tendency of matter to resist a change in its state of motion is called **inertia** (in•ER•shuh).

This law of motion is also called the *law of inertia.* This law states that an object at rest stays at rest, and an object in motion stays in motion at a constant velocity, unless the object is acted on by an outside force.

Another way to state this idea is that an object will not accelerate without a force acting on it.

MAIN IDEA AND DETAILS Why do all objects resist acceleration?

What Are Some Effects of Inertia?

Place an index card on top of a glass or plastic cup. Place a quarter in the center of the card. Flick the edge of the card hard and fast horizontally with your finger. (Don't hit the quarter!) Watch what happens to the quarter. How does its inertia affect its motion?

1. MAIN IDEA AND DETAILS Copy and complete this graphic organizer.

MAIN IDEA:
MOTION OCCURS WHEN AN OBJECT CHANGES POSITION.

A **Ⓐ** _____ is used to determine whether an object is moving.

An object's **Ⓑ** _____ is its speed and its direction.

The **Ⓒ** _____ of an object is its resistance to a change in motion.

2. SUMMARIZE Use the graphic organizer to write a lesson summary.

3. DRAW CONCLUSIONS A car moving in a straight line increases its speed every second. Its speed increases from 30 km/hr (18.6 mi/hr) to 35 km/hr (21.7 mi/hr) in the first second. In the next second, it goes from 35 km/hr (21.7 mi/hr) to 40 km/hr (24.8 mi/hr). What is its acceleration?

4. VOCABULARY In your own words, define each vocabulary term in this lesson.

Test Prep

5. Critical Thinking What law of motion states that an object in motion tends to stay in motion unless acted on by an outside force?

6. If the force acting on an object increases, what else increases?
 A. the object's acceleration
 B. the object's inertia
 C. the object's mass
 D. the object's frame of reference

Links

Writing

Narrative Writing
Take on the role of a sportscaster. Write a **script** describing a sport and the motion in that sport. Include the following concepts in your script: force, acceleration, velocity, inertia, and frame of reference.

Math

Calculate Average Speed
Look up the world record 100-m, 400-m, and marathon track times. Calculate the average speed of the runner in each case. Do you think the runner's speed at each instant varied much from the average speed in each case? Explain.

Social Studies

Biography
Aristotle, Galileo, and Newton all worked on theories of forces and motion. Use library and Internet resources to find out if scientists in other countries were researching these topics, too. Choose one scientist. Prepare a report about this scientist's work and about how one person's work built on the work of another.

For more links and activities, go to www.hspscience.com

How Do Forces Interact?

Fast Fact

Slip-Slidin' Water slides are a lot like roller coasters. On a water slide, your body takes the place of a roller coaster car. The water itself acts as a lubricant to keep you from sticking to the slide's surface. Gravity does the work of sending the riders down the slopes and around curves at high speeds. In the Investigate, you will observe what forces affect a rolling cart.

Making It Move

Materials • board (1 m or longer) • round pencils • wood cart • notebook paper

Procedure

1. Place a pencil crosswise under the center of the board. Put the cart at the center of the board. Plan and conduct an investigation to make the cart move without touching it. Record what happens.

2. Put the cart back at the center of the board. Plan and conduct an investigation to make the cart move, without touching it, from one end of the board to the other and back. Record what happens.

3. Now place the cart on a sheet of paper. Plan and conduct an investigation to remove the paper without touching the cart. The cart should roll very little. Record what happens.

4. Place the cart at the center of the board again. Slowly tip the board from one end. Estimate the angle at which the board must be tilted before the cart starts to roll. Hypothesize which force or forces prevent the cart from rolling until that angle is reached. Record your estimate and results.

Draw Conclusions

1. What force started the cart moving in Step 1? Tell how the force was transferred to the cart. Do the same for Step 2.

2. Look at your notes for Step 3. What property of the cart kept it from rolling?

3. **Inquiry Skill** Design an experiment to test your hypothesis in Step 4.

Step 1

Step 3

Investigate Further

Explore the motion of the cart on the board by planning and conducting a simple investigation that tests the motion of the cart using different surfaces.

Balanced and Unbalanced Forces

Have you ever played or seen a tug of war? What happens when one team and the opposing team start to pull on the rope with equal strength in opposite directions? Neither team wins.

Equal forces that act in opposite directions on an object are called **balanced forces**. Balanced forces cancel one another. Balanced forces have the same end result as no apparent force at all. Therefore, an object under the influence of balanced forces will not accelerate. It will not start, stop, speed up, slow down, or turn. It will continue at a constant velocity. An object will stay still if it was not moving before the balanced forces were applied to it. Or, if it was moving before the forces were applied, the object will keep moving in a straight line at a constant speed.

The total of all the forces acting on an object is called the *net force.* The net force is always zero when forces are balanced.

There are many examples in which the net force must be zero. Consider a bridge, for

The force of gravity pulls the vase downward, while the equal support force of the table pushes the vase upward.

In a tractor pull, the winning tractor is the one that can accelerate the load it is trying to pull. Forces on each object are balanced when their motion does not change.

There are several forces acting on the sleigh. The forces are unbalanced when its velocity changes.

The ballet dancers leap through the air, seeming to defy gravity. The forces on them are unbalanced.

example. Engineers must find ways to keep the net force on the bridge at zero. A bridge must be supported by strong girders. They push upward against the downward pull of gravity and the great weight of the cars using the bridge.

Usually there is more than one force acting on an object. Sometimes these forces do not cancel one another. Forces that do not cancel one another are called **unbalanced forces**. When unbalanced forces act on an object, the net force is not zero. An object with unbalanced forces acting on it will accelerate. Its velocity will change.

There are many times when unbalanced forces are needed. Unbalanced forces help you push your skateboard forward or throw a ball to a friend.

If you push a wheelbarrow to the right with a net force of 40 newtons (N), your unbalanced force on the wheelbarrow will move it to the right. But if your friend pushes the wheelbarrow

in the opposite direction with a 40-newton force, the net force on the wheelbarrow is now zero. It won't accelerate. Now suppose your friend decides to push in the same direction you are pushing, also with a 40-newton force. Now the net force on the wheelbarrow is 80 newtons. It accelerates to the right even more.

 COMPARE AND CONTRAST Give an example that describes the difference between balanced and unbalanced forces.

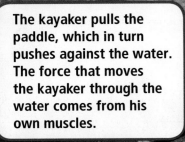

The kayaker pulls the paddle, which in turn pushes against the water. The force that moves the kayaker through the water comes from his own muscles.

Gravity pulls the parachutist downward. A force called air resistance pushes upward. The air resistance acts to slow the parachutist, and he floats to Earth at a constant velocity.

Forces in Our World

Think for a moment about how many times a day you apply a force to something. You push on the floor when you get up out of bed in the morning. You pull the covers over you when you go to sleep. In between, you use your muscles to apply forces in countless ways.

But there are many forces that do not come from human muscles. For example, look at the water strider in the picture. The insect is pulled downward by gravity, yet it does not accelerate. This is a clue that there must be a zero net force on the strider. What force cancels gravity, acting in the opposite direction with equal strength? The name of this force is *surface tension.*

Surface tension is a force that occurs at the surface of a liquid. Surface tension pulls the particles at a liquid's surface together into the smallest possible surface area. Surface tension is a little like a tight skin stretched over a liquid. Different liquids have different surface tensions. Water has two to four times the surface tension of gasoline or alcohol.

Have you ever wondered why some things can float on water? After all, gravity acts on things even when they are in water. Why doesn't everything just sink?

The answer is the *buoyant force.* The buoyant force

pushes upward on objects in a fluid—a liquid or a gas. It opposes gravity. When gravity and the buoyant force balance, an object floats. When gravity is greater, the object sinks.

Another interesting force is the *magnetic force.* It can pull or push. The magnetic force works between magnetic poles. On human-made magnets, these poles are sometimes labeled north-seeking and south-seeking. The

The balanced forces acting on the water strider are gravity and surface tension. ▼

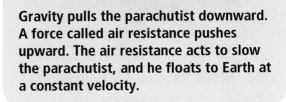

608

Electromagnetic Forces

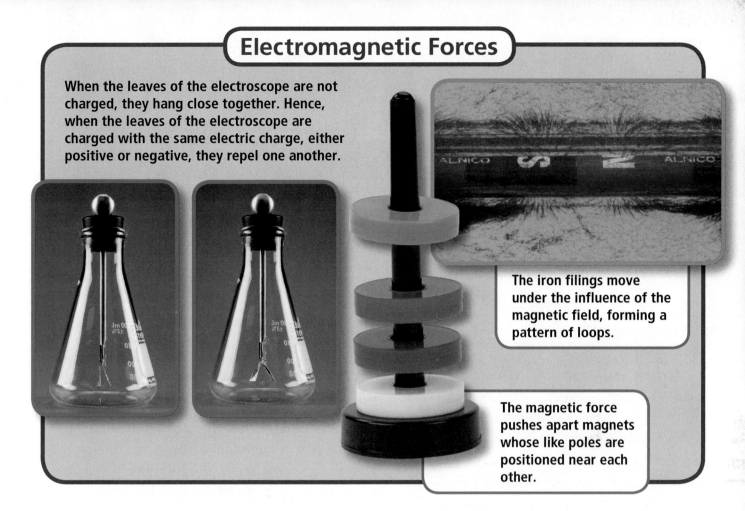

When the leaves of the electroscope are not charged, they hang close together. Hence, when the leaves of the electroscope are charged with the same electric charge, either positive or negative, they repel one another.

The iron filings move under the influence of the magnetic field, forming a pattern of loops.

The magnetic force pushes apart magnets whose like poles are positioned near each other.

magnetic force pulls opposite poles (N and S) together. This force pushes like poles (N and N or S and S) apart.

Forces even act inside the tiniest particles of matter. These forces are called *nuclear forces.* Nuclear forces keep atoms together, which is a good thing. After all, if atoms did not stay together, neither would you!

Another force at work in the world is the *electric force.* The electric force acts between objects that have an electric charge. The electric force can pull charged objects toward one another or push them apart.

There are two types of charges—positive and negative. Objects that have different charges attract one another. Objects with the same charge repel one another. This is like the magnetic force, in which "opposites attract." The difference is that the magnetic force acts between magnetic poles, while the electric force acts between charges.

Have you ever opened a box that was sent to you and had the foam packing pieces stick to your hands and clothes? The electric force draws the packing pieces and you together.

The electric force is very important in the particles making up matter. You can read about a device called the *electroscope* in the box on this page. It enables you to observe the push and pull that results from the electric force.

Objects can be pulled and pushed in many directions by a variety of forces acting upon them. Gravity, surface tension, the electric force, magnetic force, buoyant force, and others can all act at the same time. Even so, if all the forces balance, the net force on the object is zero. When this is so, the object maintains its state of motion—just as if no force is acting on it at all!

 COMPARE AND CONTRAST Describe how the buoyant force and gravity affect objects in your everyday environment.

The air hockey puck is actually not resting on the table surface. Instead, it rides on a thin layer of air. This reduces friction almost to zero, so the puck's motion is not slowed very much.

▲ The rough surface of the carpet produces a lot of friction. Does this make it harder or easier to push the furniture across it?

Friction Opposes Motion

Friction is a familiar part of everyday life. When you rub out a pencil mark with an eraser, you can feel the friction between the paper and eraser. Friction makes it hard to push the eraser. You can feel friction between your feet and the floor as you walk. If it weren't there, your feet would slide out from under you! **Friction** is a force that acts between any surfaces in contact with one another. It prevents motion or slows it down.

Sometimes people find ways to reduce friction to make things move more easily. There is more friction between rough surfaces than between smooth ones. This is why people sometimes put grease or oil on machine parts to lubricate them. The grease puts a layer

of lubricant between the parts so that they slide past one another easily. When friction is reduced in machines, the parts don't wear away as quickly and, therefore, they last longer.

Sometimes it's necessary to increase friction for safety reasons. Icy sidewalks are very slippery. Sand is put on them to give people more traction so they won't slip and fall. Rubber soles on shoes keep people from slipping on smooth floor surfaces.

Focus Skill **COMPARE AND CONTRAST** Is there more friction between a car and a road on a sunny day or on a rainy day? Why?

Feel the Friction
Rub your hands together.
How strong is the force of friction that you feel? Now put a small drop of hand lotion in the palms of your hands. Rub them together again. Do your hands now slide past one another more easily? Why?

1. COMPARE AND CONTRAST Complete the graphic organizer by stating the type of force that matches each description.

Ⓐ _____ : force between two surfaces that slows or stops motion

Ⓑ _____ : force between positive and negative charges

Ⓒ _____ : opposite poles attract, and like poles repel

Ⓓ _____ : a straight pin floats on water

2. SUMMARIZE Write a summary of this lesson. Begin with this sentence: *When unbalanced forces act on an object, the object accelerates.*

3. DRAW CONCLUSIONS Two dogs pull in opposite directions on a chew toy. The toy doesn't move. What is the net force on the toy?

4. VOCABULARY Use each of these terms in a sentence: *unbalanced force, balanced force, friction.*

Test Prep

5. Critical Thinking Why do people often use oil to lubricate the gears of a bicycle?

6. Which of the following is **not** a force?
 A. acceleration
 B. air resistance
 C. friction
 D. surface tension

Links

Writing

Narrative Writing
Picture a world with no friction. Write a fictional **short story** about a friction-free world. Describe what some of the effects would be and how life would be different.

Math

Write an Equation
Write an equation to describe this situation: A boy pushes a trunk with a force of 50 newtons. His friend pushes the trunk with a force of 60 newtons in the same direction.

Physical Education

Hands-On
Have an arm-wrestling contest with a classmate. Keep your elbows on a flat surface. Clasp hands, and push the hands against one another. After the contest, write about your results. Analyze the forces on you and your friend. Were they balanced? Unbalanced?

 For more links and activities, go to **www.hspscience.com**

What Is Gravitational Force?

Fast Fact

Which Thriller Thrills the Most? Looping roller coasters turn you upside down. Non-looping roller coasters take you up and down steep hills and valleys. Free-fall coasters have such steep drops that you drop nearly straight down! Can you tell by looking at this roller coaster what gravity would do to you? In the Investigate, you will explore measuring gravity by building your own spring scale.

Build a "Spring" Scale

Materials
- large hardcover book
- 2 large paper clips
- five 1-N masses
- sheet of paper
- large rubber band
- tape
- test objects with weights

Procedure

1. Assemble your scale as shown. Let it hang freely for a minute.

2. Calibrate your scale. To do this, make a mark on the sheet of paper at the spot the pointer reaches when your spring scale is hanging freely. Mark this spot 0 to begin your scale.

3. Hook a mass to your rubber band. Make a mark on the paper at the spot the pointer reaches. Next to your mark, write 1.0 N.

4. Hook another mass to the first one. Make a mark, and label this spot 2.0 N.

5. Continue to add masses and mark the spots the pointer reaches in 1.0-N units.

6. You can now use your spring scale to weigh objects in your classroom that are not too heavy. (Do not weigh more than 5 N.) One at a time, hook each of the test items to your scale. Find the weights. Record your results.

Draw Conclusions

1. What was the weight of each of your test objects?

2. **Inquiry Skill** An object's weight is a measurement of Earth's gravitational pull on it. Which object tested can you conclude is most strongly attracted toward Earth? The least attracted?

Step 1

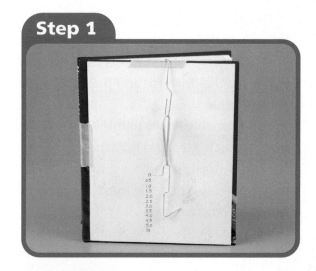

Step 6

Investigate Further

Use a kitchen scale or a postage scale to check the accuracy of your scale. Then analyze how your spring scale works.

Reading in Science

VOCABULARY
gravitational force p. 614
weight p. 618

SCIENCE CONCEPTS
▶ how gravitational force depends on mass and distance
▶ how gravity relates to weight

READING FOCUS SKILL
CAUSE AND EFFECT Find out how the gravitational force affects matter.

| cause | → | effect |

Gravitational Force

Gravitational force is a basic force of nature. It is present everywhere and acts all the time. The **gravitational force** acts between any two masses in the universe and pulls them toward each another.

You probably know that the force that pulls objects, such as falling parachutes, balls, and raindrops, toward Earth is gravitation. But you may not realize that the force of gravitation acts between *any* two masses.

All masses attract one another. You are pulled toward the bookshelf across the room, for example. You are even pulled toward the trees outside, to the planet Mars, and to the Statue of Liberty! The gravitational force is small in these cases. It is so small that you don't notice it. But it is still there. At the same time, all of these objects are pulled toward you.

This sled rider is pulled down the hill by gravity. The snow provides little friction for the sled.

The diver uses the force of her own muscles to propel herself from the platform. Gravity is the force that brings her straight down into the water in a perfect dive. ▶

614

▲ Why does the water fall downward? All objects near Earth's surface are pulled toward the center of Earth by gravity.

All masses are pulled toward one another through the gravitational force. Even this boy and his dog are pulled toward each other ever so slightly because of this force.

On Earth, the gravitational force we are most aware of is the pull of Earth on objects at Earth's surface. This force pulls us and everything around us toward the center of Earth. This force of gravitation is also called *gravity*.

Gravity does more than bring baseballs back to the ground and pull children downhill on roller skates. Gravity keeps the oceans on the surface of the planet. It keeps the surface of the water fairly level. It keeps our atmosphere from flying off into space. Gravity and gravitation are different from the forces people use to push and pull. When you use your muscles to apply a force to something, you have to touch it. To open a door, you need physical contact with

the door. There may be something between you and the door, such as a doorknob, that transfers the force from your muscles to the door. But in every case, mechanical forces, such as those people apply, require physical contact.

Gravitation is different. It is an "action-at-a-distance" force. Gravitation acts through empty space to pull objects toward one another. No intermediate objects are required to transmit the force.

 CAUSE AND EFFECT Raise a coin in the air and drop it. What happens? Why does this happen?

How Mass and Distance Affect Gravitation

As you learned earlier in this lesson, all masses attract one another through the gravitational force. You also learned that in some cases, this force is very weak. For example, the gravitational force between two tennis balls resting on a table is too weak to bring them together.

Why is the gravitational force sometimes strong and sometimes weak? The strength of the gravitational force depends on two things. It depends on the masses of the attracting objects and the distance between their centers. Earth's mass is huge. The more massive the attracting objects are, the stronger the gravitational force. Gravity is a strong force on objects near Earth's surface because the distance between the objects and Earth's center is relatively small compared with other distances in the solar system.

On the other hand, the attraction between two tennis balls on a table is weak because the masses of the balls are very small.

The sun also exerts a gravitational pull on you and other objects. However, the sun is so far away that the tug of Earth's gravity is the only force we notice.

Because the masses of planets and the sun are huge, gravitation is important in the solar system. All the planets attract one another. Yet because the sun has greater mass than any of the planets, its pull is greater than the pulls between all the other planets. This is why all the planets follow nearly circular paths, or orbits, around the sun.

Since the force of the sun's gravitation pulls each of the planets toward it, why don't the planets simply fall into the sun? What keeps them moving in

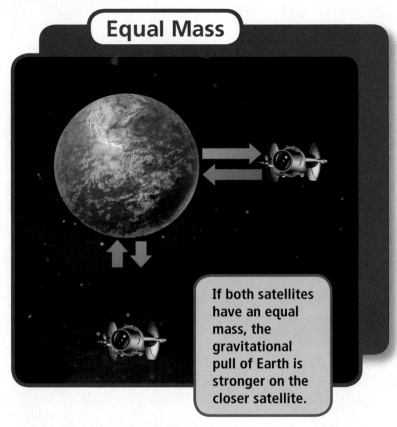

Equal Mass

If both satellites have an equal mass, the gravitational pull of Earth is stronger on the closer satellite.

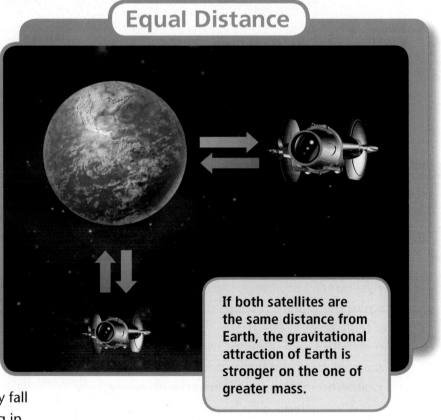

Equal Distance

If both satellites are the same distance from Earth, the gravitational attraction of Earth is stronger on the one of greater mass.

their orbits? The reason is that the motion of the planets around the sun is a result of two factors—gravitational force and inertia.

Recall that all masses have inertia, or a resistance to a change in motion. Because objects have inertia, they move in straight lines and at constant speeds unless they are acted on by net forces.

If no outside force acted upon it, a planet or an object such as a baseball would travel in a straight line forever. The baseball is slowed by air resistance and is pulled down by Earth's gravity. But a planet moves in outer space, where there is no air. A planet, such as Earth, would travel forever in a straight line if gravitational force did not change its motion.

The gravitational force between the sun and a planet combines with the planet's inertia to cause the planet to follow a curved path instead of a straight line. Both the planet and the sun pull on each other across space. The planet would tend to move in a straight line because of inertia. But the inward pull of the gravitational force constantly tugs on the planet. The result is the planet's curved orbit around the sun.

 CAUSE AND EFFECT Why do planets follow orbits around the sun?

Science Up Close

How Planets Move in Orbits

Earth's inertia causes the planet to tend to move at a steady speed in a straight line. However, the sun's gravitational force also acts on Earth. The sun's constant pull on Earth changes the direction in which Earth is moving from moment to moment. As a result, Earth "falls" in a continuously curved path around the sun.

For more links and activities, go to www.hspscience.com

Gravity and Weight

All objects on Earth's surface are about the same distance from Earth's center. This is why the force of gravity on any object on Earth depends only on the object's mass. The greater the mass, the greater the force of gravity. **Weight** is the measurement of the force of gravity on an object.

Weight is not the same thing as mass. Mass is the amount of matter an object contains. The mass of an object is not affected by changes in the gravitational force. The mass of an object on the moon is the same as its mass on Earth. An object's weight varies from place to place because gravitational forces vary.

Weight is measured by using a scale. Mass is measured by using a balance. The unit of weight is the same as the unit of any force—the newton. Mass, on the other hand, is measured in grams.

 CAUSE AND EFFECT How does gravity affect the weight of an object?

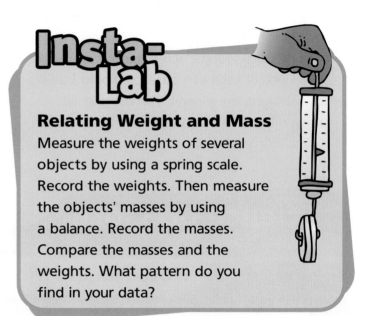

Insta-Lab

Relating Weight and Mass

Measure the weights of several objects by using a spring scale. Record the weights. Then measure the objects' masses by using a balance. Record the masses. Compare the masses and the weights. What pattern do you find in your data?

If you travel to Jupiter, you will weigh about 2½ times what you weigh on Earth. On the moon, you will weigh ⅙ as much. Your mass remains the same.

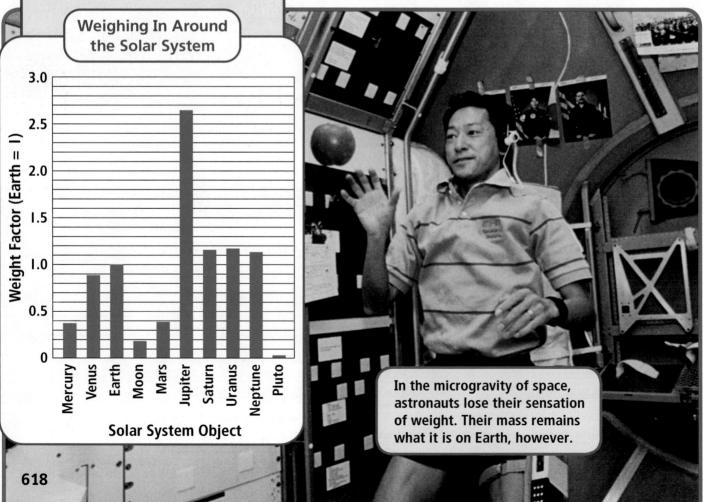

Weighing In Around the Solar System

Weight Factor (Earth = 1) vs. Solar System Object: Mercury, Venus, Earth, Moon, Mars, Jupiter, Saturn, Uranus, Neptune, Pluto

In the microgravity of space, astronauts lose their sensation of weight. Their mass remains what it is on Earth, however.

1. CAUSE AND EFFECT Copy and complete the chart. List one effect of each cause.

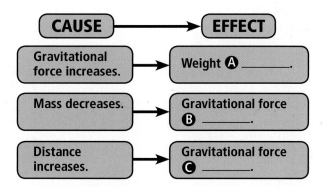

CAUSE	→	EFFECT
Gravitational force increases.	→	Weight **A** _____.
Mass decreases.	→	Gravitational force **B** _____.
Distance increases.	→	Gravitational force **C** _____.

2. SUMMARIZE Write two sentences that tell what this lesson is mainly about.

3. DRAW CONCLUSIONS What are the two masses and the one distance that determine your weight?

4. VOCABULARY Develop a quiz question that tests understanding of each vocabulary term in this lesson. Provide an answer for each question.

Test Prep

5. Critical Thinking Explain why objects weigh less on the moon than they do on Earth.

6. Which unit is used to measure gravity?
   A. meters
   B. meters per second
   C. milligrams
   D. newtons

Links

Writing

Expository Writing
Think of all the facts about gravity you would need to include to teach the subject to a third grader. Write down the facts. Then organize these facts into a **lesson** that you could use to teach the third grader about gravity.

Math

Calculate the Pull of Gravity
Suppose a comet is 1 million km from the sun and is moving away from the sun. When the comet is 2 million km away, the sun's gravitational pull is ¼ of what it had been. When it is 3 million km away, the pull is ⅑ of what it had been. What is the pull of gravity when it is 4 million miles away?

Social Studies

History
Use library resources to find out about the history of roller coasters. Discuss the first wooden coasters, the first metal coasters, and the first looping coasters. Include other events you think are important. Prepare a report for the class that includes drawings.

 For more links and activities, go to www.hspscience.com

North Pole

Kara Sea

Barents Sea

KURSK

ARCTIC OCEAN

Murmansk

Arctic circle

EUROPE

FINLAND

NORWAY

SWEDEN

RUSSIA

Moscow

Raising the Kursk

On August 2, 2000, Russia's latest and most sophisticated submarine, the nuclear-powered *Kursk*, was cruising below the surface of the Barents Sea. Suddenly, two powerful explosions ripped through the sub, tearing a hole in its thick skin.

Before it could surface, the 18,000-ton ship rapidly sank to the seafloor. Moments after the explosion, a huge wall of fire and seawater roared through the sub, killing most of the 118-member crew and trapping others. The entire crew of sailors was lost in that tragedy.

Salvage Work

Immediately after the accident, however, salvage crews and divers were at work. They were trying to raise the submarine and answer questions about why it sank.

Although experts now believe that the explosion occurred when a torpedo accidentally detonated, naval experts wanted to learn in order to prevent another such incident from occurring.

The salvage work was a huge undertaking. Giant equipment and hundreds of people were needed to lift the huge sub from the ocean floor. The task was also hampered by technical problems and bad weather. Divers working on the wreck were 108 meters (354 feet) below the ocean's surface. At that depth, the water is ice cold and the pressure would have harmed the divers had they not been wearing special dive suits.

Success at Last

Their efforts paid off, however, and after more than a year, Russian, Norwegian, and Dutch salvage experts raised the *Kursk*. The salvagers were able to slice off the damaged bow, or nose, of the *Kursk*, where the torpedoes exploded. Workers also drilled holes in the sub's hull so that they could attach 26 steel cables to the vessel.

Salvagers aboard a huge ship on the surface used computer-controlled jacks to pull the sub to the surface with the heavy-duty cables. The sub was then towed to shore, where it was examined.

Now that the sub has been raised, however, some crew members' families would rather have had the sub and the sailors' remains stay on the seafloor.

Think About It

1. Why would it be dangerous to work so far below the ocean's surface?
2. Did gravity make the salvagers' work harder or easier?

Find out more! Log on to
www.hspscience.com

621

MAKING CARS SAFER

Allen Breed was the first person to come up with the idea of using a controlled explosion to deploy air bags.

Breed studied mechanical engineering in college, learning to design, build, and operate machines and engines. Later, Breed did work for the United States military to develop safe ways to set off explosives. While doing that work, Breed thought he could use his skill and knowledge to help protect car drivers and passengers.

By 1968, Breed had invented the air-bag system. When an accident occurs, a sensor triggers a small explosion that instantly inflates the air bags inside a car.

Career   Asphalt Paver Operator

Smooth roads help reduce friction and provide smoother, safer rides. The people who help build these roads are called asphalt paver operators. Paver operators are specially trained on how to safely operate heavy equipment that is used to pave our roads. The paver operator carefully works with a crew to construct the roads and lay the asphalt we drive on.

You Can Do It!

Materials
- string
- spring scale
- brick
- rough board
- soap
- 10 unsharpened round pencils

Quick and Easy Project

Reducing Friction

Procedure

1. Use string to attach a spring scale to a brick.
2. Pull the brick across the board. Record the force you use.
3. Rub the surface of the board with the soap.
4. Repeat Step 2.
5. Line up the pencils on the board. Place the brick on the pencils.
6. Pull the brick across the pencils. Record the force.

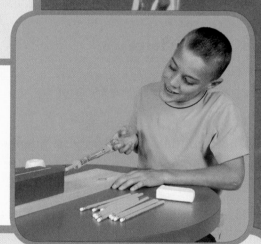

Draw Conclusions

1. When did the brick experience the greatest friction? The least?
2. How do rolling friction and sliding friction compare?

Design Your Own Investigation

Force and Mass

Plan an experiment to investigate how the force needed to pull an object relates to its mass. Use common classroom or household objects and a spring scale. Describe your experiment in writing. Show it to your teacher, and get his or her approval before conducting your investigation.

Review and Test Preparation

Vocabulary Review

Use the terms below to complete the sentences. The page numbers tell you where to look in the chapter if you need help.

velocity p. 599

force p. 600

acceleration p. 600

inertia p. 602

balanced forces p. 606

friction p. 610

gravitational force p. 614

weight p. 618

1. Forces that cancel one another are
   _____ .

2. When you measure the force of gravity on your body, you are measuring your
   _____ .

3. The force that pulls masses together is the
   _____ .

4. The force that prevents or slows motion between objects that are touching is
   _____ .

5. Masses resist changes to their motion because they have _____ .

6. The speed and direction of an object's motion are its _____ .

7. A push or pull is a _____ .

8. An object's change in velocity divided by the time over which the change occurred is _____ .

Check Understanding

Write the letter of the best choice.

9. **CAUSE AND EFFECT** Which two factors affect gravitational force?
   - **A.** acceleration and masses
   - **B.** distance and masses
   - **C.** distance and sizes
   - **D.** volume and masses

10. **COMPARE AND CONTRAST** Which surface would probably offer the least friction if you were to slide a box across it?
    - **F.** brick
    - **G.** carpet
    - **H.** ice
    - **J.** wood

11. An object is floating in a container of water. Which force opposes gravity?
    - **A.** buoyant force
    - **B.** electricity
    - **C.** friction
    - **D.** surface tension

12. Two tug-of-war teams pull with great force on a rope, but there is no motion of the rope. Why not?
    - **F.** Balanced forces act on the rope.
    - **G.** Gravity cancels friction on the rope.
    - **H.** The net force on the rope is not zero.
    - **J.** Unbalanced forces act on the rope.

13. An object is accelerating at a rate of 10 mi/hr per second. After 1 sec, its speed is 10 mi/hr. After 2 sec, its speed is 20 mi/hr. What is its speed after 3 sec?
    - **A.** 10 mi/hr
    - **B.** 20 mi/hr
    - **C.** 30 mi/hr
    - **D.** 100 mi/hr

14. Think about the forces acting on the parachutist. The force of air resistance pushes up. Which is the force pulling down?

   F. friction

   G. gravity

   H. magnetism

   J. surface tension

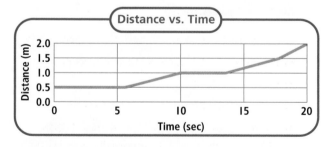

15. Which two factors keep a planet in orbit around the sun?
   A. gravitation and the planet's inertia
   B. gravitation and the planet's weight
   C. gravity and the planet's size
   D. gravity and the sun's inertia

16. Look at the graph below. It shows how a car's distance changed. At what time was the car's acceleration greatest?

Distance vs. Time

(Graph: Distance (m) on y-axis from 0.0 to 2.0; Time (sec) on x-axis from 0 to 20.)

   F. during the first 5 sec
   G. during the second 5 sec
   H. during the third 5 sec
   J. during the fourth 5 sec

Inquiry Skills

17. The planet Jupiter has a greater mass than that of Earth. However, Earth, rather than Jupiter, pulls you to its surface. Analyze and explain these statements.

18. Two identical boulders rolled down a hill. One boulder accelerated at a faster rate than the other boulder. What can you conclude about the forces that acted on the two boulders?

Critical Thinking

19. Can two buses travel at the same speed but with different velocities? Explain.

20. The action at a baseball game can be broken down into the following stages. 1) The pitcher throws the baseball across home plate. 2) The batter hits the ball high into the air. 3) The catcher runs for it and 4) catches the ball.
   Part A Use the concepts and terms you have learned in this chapter to describe the forces and motion at each of these four stages. Include as much detail about force, friction, velocity, gravity, and acceleration as you can.
   Part B Draw a diagram to show the forces involved at one of the stages of the baseball game.

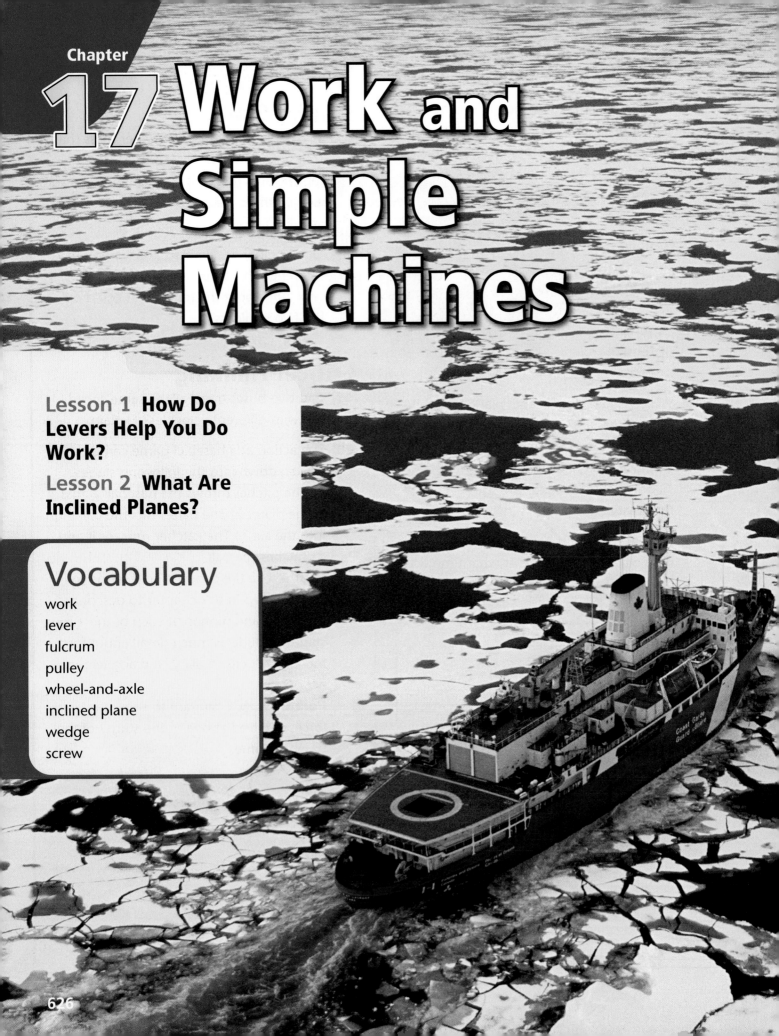

Lesson 1 How Do Levers Help You Do Work?

Lesson 2 What Are Inclined Planes?

Vocabulary

work

lever

fulcrum

pulley

wheel-and-axle

inclined plane

wedge

screw

What do YOU wonder?

This sea of ice makes it difficult for ship travel. The icebreaker, Louis S. St-Laurent, is plowing its way through the ice. The front of the ship is wedge-shaped. It rides up onto the flat of the ice and its weight crushes a section of the ice. Why are icebreakers necessary? Where are they used?

How Do Levers Help You Do Work?

Fast Fact

Balancing the Scales of Justice This famous statue holds scales that represent justice. Justice must be fair and her scales should be balanced. Why do you think the pans in the photo do not look balanced? In the Investigate, you'll have the chance to make your own balance.

Using a Lever

Materials
- 2 metersticks
- metal washers
- metric ruler
- string
- spring scale
- ring stand
- large paper clip
- ring
- tape

Procedure

1 Copy the table.

2 Tie and tape down the string at the 50-cm mark on a meterstick. Hang the meterstick from the ring on the ring stand by using the string.

3 Use the spring scale to measure the total weight of the washers in newtons (N). Record the weight in the table.

4 Bend and tape down the paper clip to hang the washers 25 cm from the middle of the meterstick.

5 Attach the spring scale 25 cm from the middle, opposite the washers. Pull down on the spring scale until the balance is level. Record the force. Use the ruler to measure the distance that the spring scale moved to make the balance level. Record these measurements.

6 Repeat Step 5, but with the spring scale attached 10 cm from the middle of the meterstick and then 40 cm from the middle. In each case, record the force and the distance you moved the scale.

Draw Conclusions

1. What two variables can you identify for balancing the meterstick? Calculate all six products for the load and for the spring scale. Compare products within each column of the table and across columns. What do you notice?

2. **Inquiry Skill** You can control variables in this activity. What would happen if you varied the load position but not the spring-scale position?

Table A

Doing Work with a Lever			
Position of load (cm from the middle)	25 cm	25 cm	25 cm
Force of load (weight in N)			
Distance load moves (cm)			
Force x distance for load			
Position of spring scale (cm from the middle)	25 cm	10 cm	40 cm
Force on spring scale (N)			
Distance spring scale moves (cm)			
Force x distance for spring scale			

Step 5

Investigate Further

Suppose you hooked the spring scale to the very end of the meterstick (50 cm from the middle). Predict how much force you would have to apply to lift the load.

Reading in Science

VOCABULARY

work p. 630
lever p. 632
fulcrum p. 632
pulley p. 634
wheel-and-axle p. 635

SCIENCE CONCEPTS

▶ how levers, pulleys, and wheel-and-axles make work easier

▶ how the work output from a machine relates to the work input

READING FOCUS SKILL

CAUSE AND EFFECT Look for examples of how force affects the work done by a simple machine.

Work

Work is one of those words that everyone uses and everyone understands—right? You work hard at school all day. You work after school when you study or write a report. But are you *really* working? How about when you ride your bike or play kickball? Are you working or are you playing? *Work* is a word that has both an everyday meaning and a scientific meaning. If you use the scientific meaning, you may be surprised at when you're working and when you're not.

A scientist says that **work** occurs when a force causes an object to move in the direction of the applied force. You can push on a heavy chair until you're exhausted. But if the chair doesn't move, you haven't done any work on it. If you push on the chair and it does move, then you've

No Work

▲ The boy doesn't do any work on the large box when he tries to lift it, because that box doesn't move.

Work

▲ The boy does work when he lifts the cans out of the box. He also does work on the box when he lifts it straight up.

No Work

▲ For work to be done, force must be applied in the same direction that the object is moving. When the boy carries the small box, the force exerted on the box is upward, but the motion of the box is forward.

630

This racer is moving along at a rapid speed. He is able to do this because he is using his hands, arms, and shoulders to apply a force to the wheels of his compound machine.

done some work on it. You've used a force to move the chair through a distance. To find out how much work you did, multiply the force you applied to the chair by the distance the chair moved: *work = force × distance.*

The force is measured in newtons (N), and the distance is measured in meters (m). The unit for work is the joule (JOOL) (J). Suppose you push the chair with a force of 100 N. If the chair moves 2 m, you have done 200 J of work.

People do work, and so do machines. Some machines are complex, with many gears, pulleys, wheels, and other parts. These machines are called *compound machines.*

Compound machines are made up of two or more *simple machines.* A simple machine has only a few parts and no more than one movement. Levers, pulleys, and wheel-and-axles are simple machines.

All simple machines make work easier, but they don't reduce the amount of work you need to do to get a job done. The work that you put into a machine is about the same

amount of work that comes out of it. Actually, the amount that comes out is a little less because some of the force needed to make a machine work must overcome the effects of friction.

 CAUSE AND EFFECT A ball rolls downhill. Is work done on the ball? If so, what is the force that does the work?

Insta-Lab

What's the Work?
Use a spring scale to lift some small objects. Record the force used to lift each one. Measure the distance you moved each object, and record it. How much work did you do to lift each object?

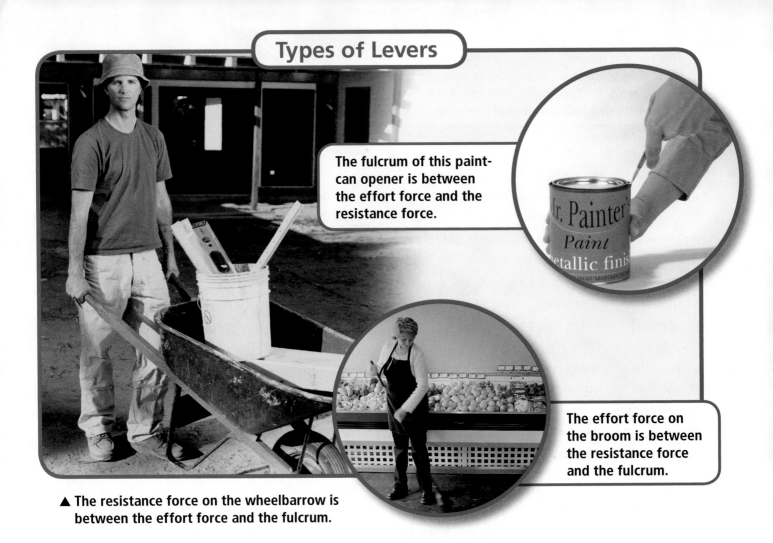

The fulcrum of this paint-can opener is between the effort force and the resistance force.

The effort force on the broom is between the resistance force and the fulcrum.

▲ The resistance force on the wheelbarrow is between the effort force and the fulcrum.

Levers

A simple machine that you may use every day is a lever. You use levers in the form of many common household tools. Scissors, nutcrackers, rakes, can openers, shovels, and seesaws are just a few common devices that each include one or two levers. A **lever** is an arm or rod that turns around a fixed point when a force is applied to it.

The parts of a lever have specific names. The part to which a person or machine applies a force is the effort arm. The fixed point that the *effort arm* moves around is the **fulcrum**. The *resistance arm* is the part of the lever that does work on the load, or the object being moved.

When a lever is used, a force is applied over a distance. The force applied to the lever is the *effort force*. The force that moves the load is the *resistance force*.

To understand how a lever works, think about two children and a playground seesaw. The seesaw can move about the fixed point, or fulcrum. When a child sits down on one end of the seesaw, she applies an effort force. Her side of the seesaw is the effort arm. Her weight moves the effort arm down. The other side of the seesaw, the resistance arm, moves up. It applies a resistance force to the seat on the other end. The child sitting there is the load. The load moves up with the resistance arm.

There are three possible arrangements of the effort force, the fulcrum, and the resistance force. In one arrangement, the fulcrum is between the effort force and the resistance force. The seesaw is an example of this. In another arrangement, the resistance force is between the fulcrum and the effort force. A car jack and a wheelbarrow are examples.

In the third arrangement, the effort force is between the resistance force and the fulcrum. Levers with this arrangement do not increase force. Instead, they increase the speed or distance that a load travels. A broom and a shovel are examples.

Like all simple machines, a lever makes work easier by changing the effort force in strength, direction, or both. Suppose you want to open a paint can. How can you apply the smallest effort force? Remember that *work = force × distance*. If you use a long screwdriver instead of a short one, you can use less effort to pry open the can. The greater length of the effort arm means that you use less force to push down.

You can use the formula for work to see how the girl on the seesaw can lift a heavier partner who is sitting closer to the fulcrum. Remember that in a simple machine the work input, the work done on the machine, is about the same as the work output, the work done by the machine. You can write this as a formula:

$(force × distance)_{effort} = (force × distance)_{resistance}$

Suppose the girl weighs 200 newtons and pushes down over a distance of 1 m. Her work is (200 N) × (1 m) = 200 J. If the other child weighs 400 newtons and is lifted up 0.5 m, the work done on him is (400 N) × (0.5 m) = 200 J. The lighter child lifts the heavier one. How does this happen? The first child makes up for her small input force with a larger input distance.

People often use levers to lift heavy objects. Boulders, cars, and even much heavier objects can be lifted if a lever is long and strong enough. The ancient Greek scientist and mathematician Archimedes (ar•kuh•MEE•deez) discovered the laws of levers and pulleys. He is reported to have said, "Give me a place to stand on, and I will move the Earth." Since he couldn't prove this, he was asked to move a ship. He did so using pulleys.

 CAUSE AND EFFECT What is the effect on the effort force of increasing effort distance?

A piano key is attached to several levers. When someone strikes a key, a series of movements takes place. The movements end when the hammer strikes a string.

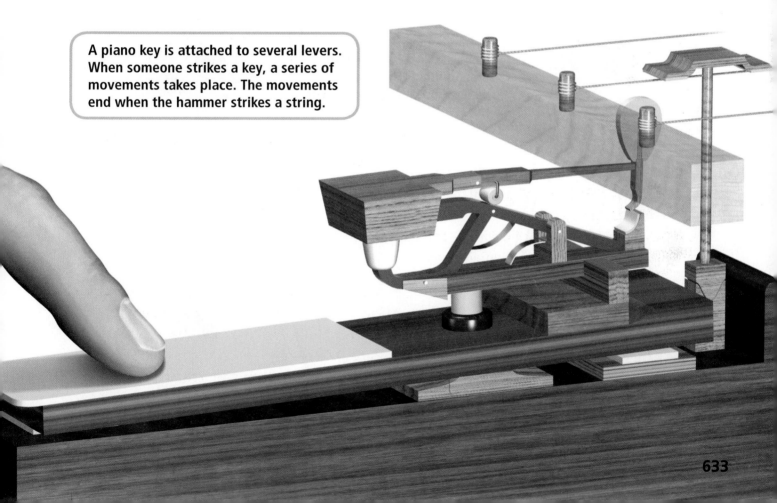

Pulleys

Another kind of simple machine is the pulley. You've probably used pulleys if you live in a house that has Venetian blinds for window coverings. You pull down on a cord, and the blinds go up. You release the cord, and the blinds go down. You may have seen a similar pulley that raises and lowers the flag in front of your school each day. Systems of pulleys are often used to lift large or heavy objects. A **pulley** is a grooved wheel that has a rope or a chain around it. When the rope or chain is pulled, the pulley turns. The rope or chain moves up and down.

A pulley is actually related to a lever. The wheel's center is the fulcrum. The rope or chain applies the effort force. The effort and resistance arms are opposite sides of the pulley wheel.

A single pulley changes the direction of the effort force but not the size of the effort force.

When you pull down on one end of the rope, the load on the other end rises. Your pull is the effort force. The load being lifted is the resistance force. A single, nonmoving pulley makes work easier because it's usually easier to pull down on something than to pull up.

What if you can't lift the load and you need to multiply the effort force? You can make a double pulley by connecting two pulleys. In a double pulley, one pulley is attached to a support and doesn't move. The other pulley is attached to a load. It moves up and down with the load when the rope is pulled.

With a double pulley, the load can move only half as far as the distance that the rope is pulled. But the resistance force is double the effort force.

 CAUSE AND EFFECT What happens when you pull down on one side of a pulley?

A single pulley has only one wheel. It enables you to pull down to lift a load up.

A double pulley has two wheels with a rope wound around them. The double pulley multiplies the effect of the effort force on the load.

The force of the falling water on the water wheel is increased as it is transferred to the axle. The axle turns more slowly than the wheel but with a much larger force. ▶

◀ If you open a sardine can, the outer part of the key moves in a large circle. The key is the wheel. The axle is the long stem of the key.

Wheel-and-Axles

Doorknobs, fishing reels, and the handlebars of bikes and steering wheels of cars are simple machines called wheel-and-axles. A **wheel-and-axle** is made up of a large wheel and a small wheel that turn together. The smaller one is called the axle and is often shaped like a rod. A wheel-and-axle works the same way as a lever, except that the wheel-and-axle turns in a circle.

A wheel-and-axle makes work easier by multiplying the effort force. You apply less effort over a larger distance on the wheel than you would have to apply to move the axle.

Suppose a driver applies a force to turn a car's steering wheel (the "wheel" part of a wheel-and-axle). The steering wheel's motion turns the central steering column (the "axle"). The axle transfers this force to the car's wheels on the road. The steering wheel has a larger radius than the column. So when the driver turns the wheel, it turns a greater distance than the axle. The driver applies a smaller force than would be needed to turn the axle directly. But the force is applied over a greater distance.

Some wheel-and-axles don't increase effort force. They increase the distance through which a force acts. For example, in a Ferris wheel, an effort force turns the axle, which turns the wheel. The seats on the wheel move faster than the axle. Why? The wheel moves through a larger circle, yet the wheel and the axle rotate together. To do this, the wheel must move farther than the axle in the same time.

CAUSE AND EFFECT A screwdriver is a wheel-and-axle. When you turn it, is the result an increase in output force or an increase in distance?

635

More About Machines

Simple machines are almost everywhere. Look around the room you're in right now. How many can you name? Some simple machines enable you to use less force to get work done.

By making your work easier to do, machines give you an advantage over not using them. The term *mechanical advantage* refers to how much a force is increased by using the machine. The smaller the mechanical advantage of a machine, the more force you must use to do work. The greater the mechanical advantage, the less force you must use to do work.

The two-pulley system you just saw has an ideal mechanical advantage (IMA) of 2. Suppose you use the pulleys to lift a crate. You expect your effort force of 100 newtons to produce a resistance force of 200 newtons. The resistance force would actually be a little less. The actual mechanical advantage (AMA) is always less than the IMA. Some of the work you do must go into moving the rope and pulleys. That includes the work to overcome friction. In other words, you always get a little less work out of a machine than you put into it.

Efficiency measures how much work a machine can do compared with how much work must be put into the machine. The efficiency of any machine is always less than 100 percent. This is because there are always forces that must be overcome by the machine, such as friction and wind resistance.

 CAUSE AND EFFECT What causes a typical automobile engine to have an efficiency rating of only about 30 percent?

The Rain Forest Aerial Trams in Costa Rica work on a pulley system.

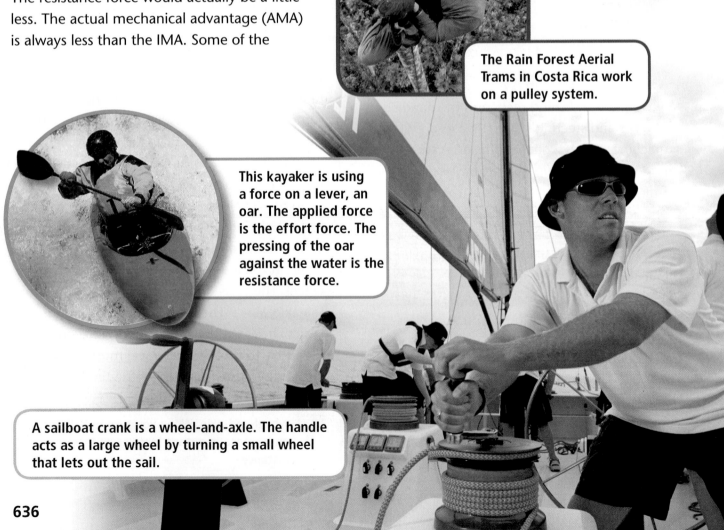

This kayaker is using a force on a lever, an oar. The applied force is the effort force. The pressing of the oar against the water is the resistance force.

A sailboat crank is a wheel-and-axle. The handle acts as a large wheel by turning a small wheel that lets out the sail.

1. CAUSE AND EFFECT Draw and complete this graphic organizer.

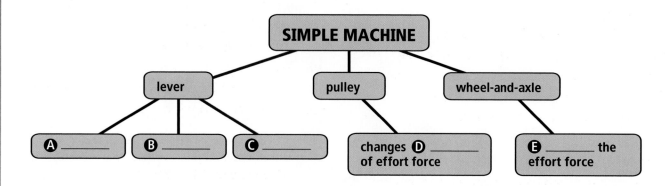

SIMPLE MACHINE

- lever
  - Ⓐ _____
  - Ⓑ _____
  - Ⓒ _____
- pulley
  - changes Ⓓ _____ of effort force
- wheel-and-axle
  - Ⓔ _____ the effort force

2. SUMMARIZE Use the completed graphic organizer to write a lesson summary.

3. DRAW CONCLUSIONS A child rides a tricycle across a lawn. A man pushes on a stalled car but can't move it. Who does work? Why?

4. VOCABULARY Make a crossword puzzle using the vocabulary terms in this lesson.

Test Prep

5. Critical Thinking Why is no more work done with a pulley than without one?

6. How does a lever make work easier?
- **A.** changes load
- **B.** changes effort force
- **C.** changes output
- **D.** changes work

Links

Writing

Persuasive Writing

Write an **advertisement** for a simple machine of your choosing. Describe what type of machine it is, tell how the machine is used, and support the opinion that people should use it.

Math

Use Formulas

A child sits down on a seesaw with an effort force of 320 N and moves down a distance of 0.5 m. How much work does the child do on the seesaw? Write a formula, solve, and give the answer in joules.

Social Studies

Machines Are Simple!

Use the library to research a machine developed before gasoline engines or electric motors. Write a short report describing how the machine worked and how it made life easier. Include illustrations.

 For more links and activities, go to www.hspscience.com

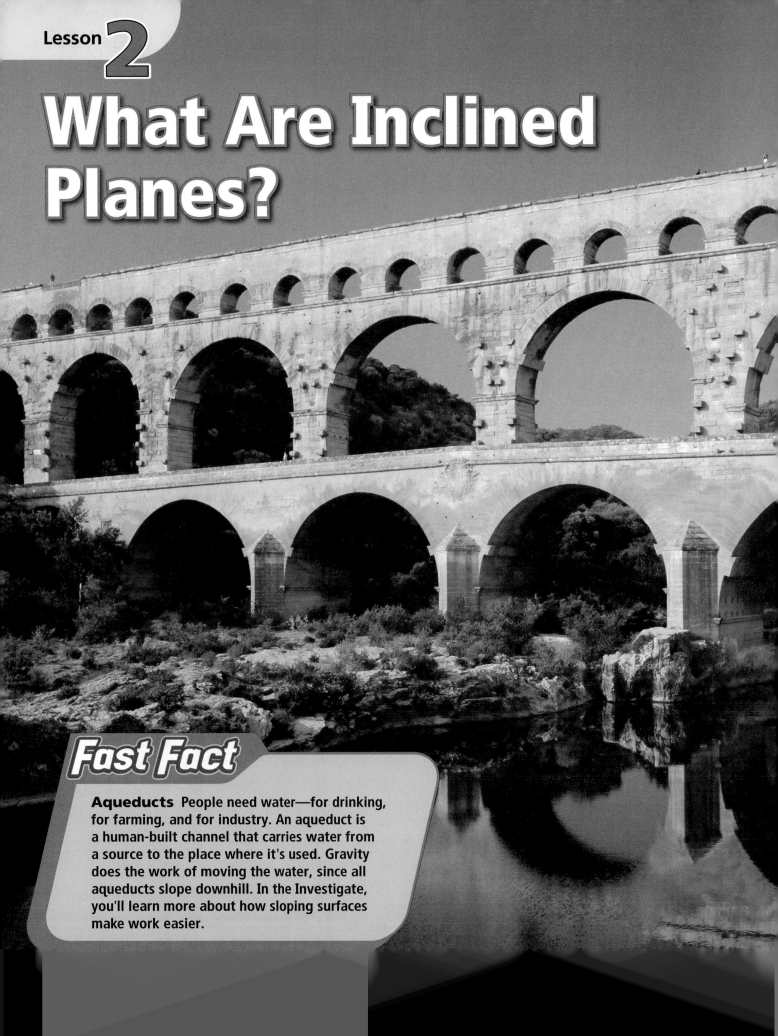

What Are Inclined Planes?

Fast Fact

Aqueducts People need water—for drinking, for farming, and for industry. An aqueduct is a human-built channel that carries water from a source to the place where it's used. Gravity does the work of moving the water, since all aqueducts slope downhill. In the Investigate, you'll learn more about how sloping surfaces make work easier.

Using Ramps

Materials
- several books
- meterstick
- spring scale
- wooden cart
- 1-m board

Procedure

1. Stack several books to a height of about 30 cm.

2. Attach the spring scale to the cart. Using the spring scale, slowly lift the cart to the height of the stack of books. Measure and record the least number of newtons you used and the total distance you lifted the cart to the top of the stack.

3. Use the board to make a ramp to the top of the books. Using the spring scale, pull the cart to the top of the ramp. Record the smallest force you used and the total distance you rolled the cart up the ramp.

4. Use the numbers of newtons and meters to find and record the amount of work you did in Steps 2 and 3 (force × distance = work). Work is expressed in joules.

Draw Conclusions

1. Compare the amounts of work you did using the two different methods to get the cart to the top of the books. Which method required less work?

2. **Inquiry Skill** Do you think you could use less force to get the cart to the top of the books? What is your hypothesis? Plan and conduct a simple investigation to test your hypothesis. Is your hypothesis supported? Do you need to revise the hypothesis and conduct another test?

Step 2

Step 3

Investigate Further

When you pulled the cart up the ramp, some of your force was used to overcome friction. Hypothesize what you could do to reduce the friction of the cart on the board. Try your method to see if it works.

Reading in Science

VOCABULARY
inclined plane p. 640
wedge p. 642
screw p. 644

SCIENCE CONCEPTS
▶ how an inclined plane makes work easier
▶ why wedges and screws are inclined planes

READING FOCUS SKILL
CAUSE AND EFFECT Look for ways inclined planes make work easier.

Inclined Planes

Suppose you're riding in a car with your family, headed for your grandparents' house. You don't think much about the trip, because you've taken it many times before. You realize, though, that the car is climbing uphill. As you look out the window, you see other roads going uphill. Soon you arrive at your grandparents' house. You look out from the front porch and realize that you're on a rather high mountain. Your dad asks if you noticed that the road you were on was like a ramp. As you think about it, you can see that he's right.

A ramp is also known as an inclined plane, and it's the simplest of all the simple machines. An **inclined plane** is any flat, sloping surface. Levers, pulleys, and wheel-and-axles have several parts, but inclined planes have only one.

Inclined planes are used mostly to lift or lower objects. You're probably familiar with many examples. A person in a wheelchair uses an inclined plane to lift the chair plus his or her weight up a curb. Movers use an inclined plane for loading furniture onto or off of a truck. Your parents use ramps every time they get on and off an interstate highway.

An inclined plane can change the amount or the direction of the effort force. Also like other

The ramp spiraling up the floors of the Guggenheim Museum in New York is an inclined plane.

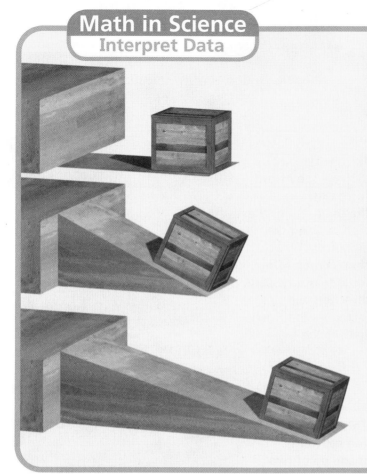

Force	Distance	Work (force × distance)
300 N	1.0 m	300 J
150 N	2.0 m	300 J
100 N	3.0 m	300 J

To get the box up to the loading dock, you could lift it directly, or you could slide it up a ramp. The first ramp lets you use less force over a greater distance to lift the box. The second ramp makes it even easier. Look down the columns of the table. What happens to the amount of force needed? What happens to the distance moved? What happens to the total amount of work?

simple machines, inclined planes can't reduce the total work needed for a particular job. The effort force is decreased by increasing the distance. Lifting is done by using a smaller force over a larger distance.

How might you use an inclined plane in your everyday life? Suppose you need to move a trunk onto the back of a pickup truck. It's too heavy to lift, so what can you do? You might ask a few friends to help you. Or you can get some strong boards and build a ramp. If the boards are short, the ramp will be steep, and you still might not be able to push the trunk onto the truck. What else can you do?

Remember: *work = force × distance*. For a certain amount of work, when the distance you move increases, the force you need to use decreases. If you make a ramp from longer boards, it will be less steep. Lifting the trunk will be easier. The longer ramp increases the distance through which you apply force. As a result, you don't have to push as hard.

A ramp is not just for lifting. Ramps are also helpful for slowing motion. Have you ridden in a car on an interstate highway through very hilly or mountainous areas? You may have noticed very short gravel roads that run off the highway and up a steep hill. These are "runaway truck ramps," designed as escapes for large trucks that are going too fast on downhill slopes. A driver can aim a truck up the ramp. This will slow the truck to a speed at which the driver can get control and stop the truck.

Like other simple machines, inclined planes have been used all over the world for thousands of years. Before there were motorized machines, workers built ramps by piling up dirt. They could then use the ramps to lift the stones and rocks that were used to make tall buildings.

 CAUSE AND EFFECT What's the effect of a gently sloping road on cars going up a mountain?

Examples of Wedges

◀ The sledgehammer delivers the effort force downward to the thick end of the wedge. The other end of the wedge changes the effort force to an outward direction and increases that force to split the log.

This mechanical log splitter is made up of two joined inclined planes. It cuts through wood and splits the wood apart.

Wedge

Wedges

You may have seen wedges being used or even used some yourself. If you have seen someone using an axe to split logs into firewood for a fireplace, you have seen a wedge being used. Have you used a knife to butter your bread or a doorstop to hold a door open? Then you have used wedges. A **wedge** is made up of inclined planes placed back to back. Most wedges—such as a doorstop, an axe, and a woodcutter's wedge—are made up of two inclined planes. A wedge has a thick end and a sharper, narrower end.

When an effort force is applied to the thick end of a wedge, the inclined planes increase this force and change its direction. The sides of the wedge deliver the increased force *outward*.

As the wedge moves through a material, the material separates.

A log-splitting wedge is hammered on its thick end so that it's forced through the log. The wedge's thin edge, where the inclined planes meet, is pushed into the wood, forcing it apart. The hammer's effort force on the thick end of the wedge is directed downward. The inclined planes increase this force and redirect it outward, away from the wedge's surfaces. The wedge pushes the parts of the log apart until finally the log splits.

If you examine a knife blade through a hand lens, you'll observe two inclined planes sloping away from the sharp edge. Once that edge breaks into a material, continued force splits the material apart until it's cut into two pieces.

Although a needle is round, its sharp end is like many inclined planes meeting at a point.

A plow cuts away a layer of soil, lifts the soil, and turns it over. The plow buries leaves and other decaying matter so that they can nourish the soil. ▼

▲ A close-up of this knife blade would show it's made up of two inclined planes joined as a wedge. The sharper the edge, the less effort force is needed.

For more links and activities, go to www.hspscience.com

If the knife becomes dull with use, it won't cut material as well as it did when it was sharper. Then a knife sharpener can be used to restore the knife to its original sharpness.

Wedges are used not only to cut things, but also to lift and push objects. The plow is an ancient kind of wedge used around the world to prepare soil for planting.

A doorstop is a wedge that pushes against a door to hold it open. How does it work? You put the sharp end of the wedge under the door. The wedge pushes upward on the door with a force large enough to lift the door slightly. At the same time, the door applies an equal and opposite force on the doorstop. The force of the door on the doorstop pushes the doorstop hard against the floor. Friction between the doorstop and the floor holds the doorstop in place.

CAUSE AND EFFECT What is the effect on effort force of sharpening a dull knife?

Insta-Lab

Design a Wedge
Design and make a wedge from cardboard. Use scissors *carefully* to cut out cardboard pieces that you need. Use your wedge to cut into a lump of clay. Notice the direction of your effort force. What is the direction of the force of the wedge in the clay?

Screws

Screws are used to fasten things and lift heavy objects. If you look closely at a screw, you see ridges, or *threads.* They form a tiny ramp, or inclined plane. A **screw** is an inclined plane wrapped around a cylinder or a cone.

Like other simple machines, a screw makes work easier by decreasing the force you need to do a job. You apply the reduced force over a larger distance. A screw also changes the direction of the force. As the screw turns around its cylinder, it moves whatever is on the screw threads up or down.

The number of threads per centimeter is a measure of the number of times the inclined plane spirals around 1 cm of the screw. With more threads per centimeter, the slope of the inclined plane is gentler, and less force is needed to turn the screw. Screws with fewer threads per centimeter have a steeper slope to their threads. More force is needed to tighten them.

Screws come in different sizes and shapes for particular jobs. Tiny screws are used in eyeglass frames, cameras, CD players, and small toys. Very large screws are used in screw jacks that lift cars and even houses!

 CAUSE AND EFFECT How does the number of threads per unit of length affect the force needed to turn a screw?

Archimedes invented a device to transport water and irrigate fields. One end of a cylinder containing a screw was placed under water. When the screw was turned, water moved up the threads and flowed out the top of the cylinder.

A wood screw acts as a long, spiraling wedge. As the sharp edges of the threads cut into the wood, the force of the wedge spreads apart the wood fibers. The inclined plane of the threads then slides through the opening.

1. CAUSE AND EFFECT Copy and complete this graphic organizer.

	INCLINED PLANE	WEDGE	SCREW
Description	Ⓐ	Ⓒ	Ⓔ
Effect	Ⓑ	Ⓓ	Ⓕ

2. SUMMARIZE Use the graphic organizer to write a summary of this lesson.

3. DRAW CONCLUSIONS You do 4 joules of work splitting a watermelon. Yet less than 4 joules of work should be required. Why is the work input not equal to the work output?

4. VOCABULARY Write a quiz question and answer for each vocabulary term.

Test Prep

5. Critical Thinking Why does a log splitter enable you to cut wood even though it doesn't reduce the work required?

6. Which simple machine is an inclined plane wrapped around a cone or cylinder?

- **A.** nail
- **B.** pulley
- **C.** screw
- **D.** wedge

Links

Writing

Persuasive Writing

Suppose your city is planning to improve wheelchair access to public buildings. However, some commissioners want to put the project off for a year. Write a **letter** you might send to the newspaper editor expressing your support for doing the project now.

Math

Solve Problems

A worker lifts a chunk of ice weighing 40 newtons through a distance of 1 m. Another worker uses a ramp to lift the ice 1 m. How much work does each person do? Explain.

Health

Levers in the Human Body

Use library resources to research the levers in your body. For example, one lever in your body is your forearm. Illustrate the parts of one "body lever" that you find.

 For more links and activities, go to www.hspscience.com

The Wright Stuff

Wind whipped their faces. Sand swirled, stinging their skin. The steamy August air blowing in from the Atlantic Ocean that summer was hot and sticky.

The brothers Wilbur and Orville Wright were out in the blistering weather in the dunes near Kitty Hawk, North Carolina to find out if the wind-powered glider they had built was airworthy. Once everything was in place, Wilbur lay on his stomach on the glider. Moments later, Orville launched his brother down a ramp and into the air.

An Exact Copy

A century later, scientists have re-created the Wright brothers' 1901 glider. But how did the Wright brothers, who repaired and built

bicycles for a living, manage to make aviation history almost a century ago?

Flight experts aren't sure, because neither the brothers' 1901 glider nor their drawings and notes about their early experiments still exist. So engineers decided to replicate the brothers' experiments and build reproductions of some of Wilbur and Orville's aircraft and engines.

They put the full-scale replica, an exact model of the glider, in a NASA wind tunnel to measure how air flowed over the 1901 craft. A wind tunnel is a tunnel-like chamber where huge fans blow air at an aircraft or other object so engineers can study the effects of airflow on it.

Getting off the Ground

Before the Wrights developed a motorized aircraft, they used gliders to understand how air flows around an aircraft's wings. The upward force of air that allows aircraft to fly is called lift. Without lift, sparrows, eagles, and jet fighters would never get off the ground.

The brothers were disappointed with the 1901 glider's performance. But they used the knowledge gained from that flight to solve the problems of lift. Following the 1901 glider flights, the Wrights built a small-scale

The Wright Brothers, Wilbur and Orville, went from being bicycle shop owners in Dayton, Ohio, to becoming the first people to achieve powered heavier-than-air flight.

wind tunnel to test nearly 200 other wing designs. They learned a lot from those tests and used that information to build and fly the first motorized airplane, in 1903.

"What we continue to find out is that these two brothers were extraordinary engineers," said one expert.

Think About It

1. How do a glider's wings help lift it into the air?
2. Why might it be easier to launch a glider going down an incline?

Milestones in Flight

June 4, 1783 The first large hot-air balloon is launched by the Montgolfier brothers, in Annonay, France.

July 2, 1900 German Count Ferdinand von Zeppelin takes off on the first flight of a rigid metal airship.

Dec. 17, 1903 Orville Wright becomes the first human to fly a motorized aircraft, near Kitty Hawk, N.C.

Sept. 11, 1911–Nov. 5, 1911 Calbraith P. Rogers becomes the first pilot to fly from New York to California.

May 20–21, 1927 Charles Lindbergh makes the first solo nonstop flight across the Atlantic Ocean, from New York to Paris.

June 17–18, 1928 Amelia Earhart becomes the first woman to fly solo across the Atlantic.

Oct. 14, 1947 Chuck Yeager breaks the sound barrier traveling in a jet at almost 700 miles per hour.

Find out more! Log on to
www.hspscience.com

Designing Fun

Travis Kurata loves gadgets. He enjoys designing and building toys from kits and designing things on his computer. Travis also likes theme park rides and hopes someday to design the world's greatest theme park.

In studying theme park rides, Travis has noticed that many rides are like simple machines. A simple machine is a device that makes work easier in some way. Ramps, screws, wedges, and pulleys are examples of simple machines.

Travis has also noticed that a carousel and Ferris wheel are examples of wheel-and-axles. In a wheel-and-axle, a larger disk turns around a smaller cylinder. He has also studied roller coasters. Most roller coasters use a pulley mechanism to lift cars to the top of an incline. Gravity and momentum then cause the cars to move down along the tracks.

You Can Do It!

Quick and Easy Project

Materials
- ring
- ring stand
- pulley
- string (30 cm, 1 m)
- book
- spring scale

How Do Pulleys Make Work Easier?

Procedure

1. Attach the ring to the ring stand. Attach the pulley to the ring. Have your partner steady the ring stand.
2. Tie the short string around the book. Weigh the book by using the spring scale.
3. Tie the long string to the short string you tied around the book. Hang the long string over the pulley. Attach the spring scale to the free end of the string.
4. Place the book flat on the table. Pull the spring scale to lift the book. Record the force required to lift the book off the table.

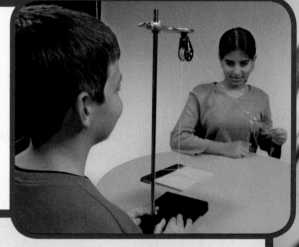

Draw Conclusions

Compare the amount of force needed to lift the book in Step 2 with the amount needed in Step 4. Which amount was less? Why was this so? What do you predict would happen if you added another pulley to your setup? Try it.

Design Your Own Investigation

Make Your Own Simple Machines

Construct a working model of one of the levers and one of the inclined planes discussed in this chapter. Make a lever, a pulley, or a wheel-and-axle; also make an inclined plane, a wedge, or a screw. Use each machine to do work. Find a way to measure the work each time. Compare the machines you constructed with those of your classmates. Perhaps you can display them in the classroom for a short time.

Review and Test Preparation

Vocabulary Review

Use the terms below to complete the sentences. The page numbers tell you where to look in the chapter if you need help.

work p. 630   **wheel-and-axle** p. 635
lever p. 632   **inclined plane** p. 640
fulcrum p. 632   **wedge** p. 642
pulley p. 634   **screw** p. 644

1. A simple machine that enables you to pull down while lifting an object is a _____ .

2. On a lever, the fixed point around which the effort arm moves is the _____ .

3. The result of a force causing an object to move through a distance is _____ .

4. An inclined plane that is wrapped around a cylinder or a cone is a _____ .

5. A simple machine that consists of an effort arm, a resistance arm, and a fulcrum is a _____ .

6. A simple machine with two different-size wheels that move together is a _____ .

7. Inclined planes that are joined and used for splitting make up a _____ .

8. A flat, sloping surface is a simple machine called an _____ .

Check Understanding

Write the letter of the best choice.

9. **CAUSE AND EFFECT** If a simple machine reduces the force required to do a job, how is the distance affected?
   A. It decreases.
   B. It doubles.
   C. It increases.
   D. It does not change.

10. If the friction in a wheel-and-axle could be eliminated, what would its work output be equal to?
    F. the effort force on it
    G. the resistance force on it
    H. the work put into it
    J. the work resistance of it

11. Which of these is the unit of work?
    A. joule
    B. kilogram
    C. meter
    D. newton

12. If you had to lift a heavy object straight up, which would be the best simple machine to use?
    F. inclined plane
    G. pulley
    H. wedge
    J. wheel-and-axle

13. Which ramp reduces the effort force the most?

    A.   **C.**

    B.   **D.**

14. Which simple machine does a log splitter use?
    F. lever
    G. pulley
    H. wedge
    J. wheel-and-axle

15. In a seesaw, what part is located between the effort arm and the resistance arm?
    A. effort force
    B. fulcrum
    C. resistance force
    D. wedge

16. Liam lifts a 10-N box 2 m straight up. Maya pushes the same box up a ramp that measures 5 m horizontally and 3 m vertically. Jim holds the same box but does not move it. Courtney carries the box 5 m. Who does the most work?
    F. Courtney
    G. Jim
    H. Liam
    J. Maya

Inquiry Skills

17. From what you know about friction, draw conclusions about ways to increase the work output of a machine.

18. Suppose you pushed a chair 3 m with a force of 250 N. Use these numbers to find out how much work you did.

Critical Thinking

19. A person holds a barbell over her head for 1 minute but does no work on the barbell. Explain why no work is done.

20. Work is the result of moving an object through a distance in the direction of the applied force.
    Part A How would you find out the amount of work required to move a package up a ramp to a porch?
    Part B Describe a method to find out the work done in moving the package up to the porch in another way. Should the two methods give the same results? Why or why not?

References

Contents

Your Skin

Your skin is your body's largest organ. It provides your body with a tough protective covering. It produces sweat to help control your body temperature. It protects you from disease. Your skin also provides your sense of touch, which allows you to feel pressure, textures, temperature, and pain.

When you play hard or exercise, your body produces sweat, which cools you as it evaporates. The sweat from your skin also helps your body eliminate excess salts and other wastes.

Epidermis
Many layers of dead skin cells form the top of the epidermis. Cells in the lower part of the epidermis are always making new cells.

The skin is the body's largest organ. ▼

Pore
These tiny holes on the surface of your skin lead to your dermis.

Oil Gland
Oil glands produce oil that keeps your skin soft and smooth.

Dermis
The dermis is much thicker than the epidermis. It is made up of tough, flexible fibers.

Sweat Gland
Sweat glands produce sweat, which contains water, salt, and various wastes.

Hair Follicle
Each hair follicle has a muscle that can contract and make the hair "stand on end."

Fatty Tissue
This tissue layer beneath the dermis stores food, provides warmth, and attaches your skin to underlying bone and muscle.

Caring for Your Skin

- To protect your skin and to keep it healthy, you should wash your body, including your hair and your nails, every day. This helps remove germs, excess oils and sweat, and dead cells from the epidermis, the outer layer of your skin. Because you touch many things during the day, you should wash your hands with soap and water frequently.

- If you get a cut or scratch, you should wash it right away and cover it with a sterile bandage to prevent infection and promote healing.

- Protect your skin from cuts and scrapes by wearing proper safety equipment when you play sports or skate, or when you're riding your bike or scooter.

- Always protect your skin from sunburn by wearing protective clothing and sunscreen when you are outdoors in bright sun.

Your Senses

Eyes

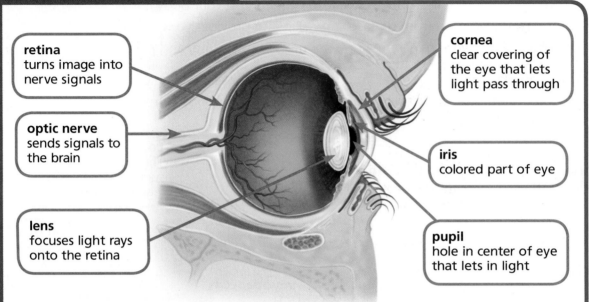

retina
turns image into nerve signals

optic nerve
sends signals to the brain

lens
focuses light rays onto the retina

cornea
clear covering of the eye that lets light pass through

iris
colored part of eye

pupil
hole in center of eye that lets in light

Light rays bounce off objects and enter the eye through the pupil. A lens inside the eye focuses the light rays, and the image of the object is projected onto the retina at the back of the eye. In the retina the image is turned into nerve signals. Your brain analyzes these signals to "tell" you what you're seeing.

Ears

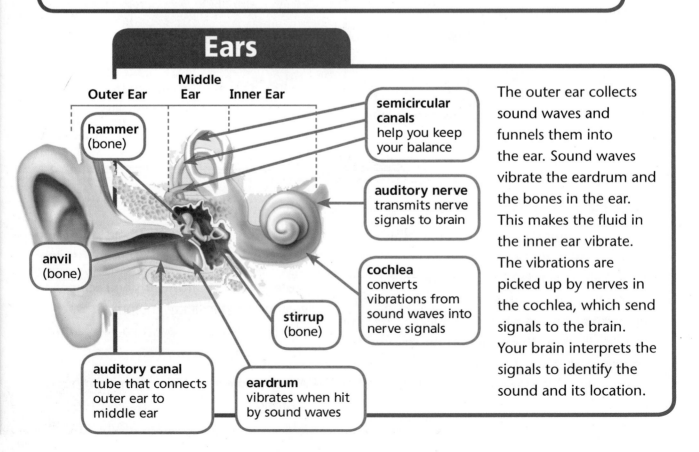

Middle
Outer Ear   Ear   Inner Ear

hammer
(bone)

anvil
(bone)

auditory canal
tube that connects outer ear to middle ear

stirrup
(bone)

eardrum
vibrates when hit by sound waves

semicircular canals
help you keep your balance

auditory nerve
transmits nerve signals to brain

cochlea
converts vibrations from sound waves into nerve signals

The outer ear collects sound waves and funnels them into the ear. Sound waves vibrate the eardrum and the bones in the ear. This makes the fluid in the inner ear vibrate. The vibrations are picked up by nerves in the cochlea, which send signals to the brain. Your brain interprets the signals to identify the sound and its location.

Nose

When you breathe in, air is swept upward to nerve cells in the nasal cavity. The nasal cavity is the upper part of the nose, inside the skull. Different nerve cells respond to different chemicals in the air and send signals to your brain.

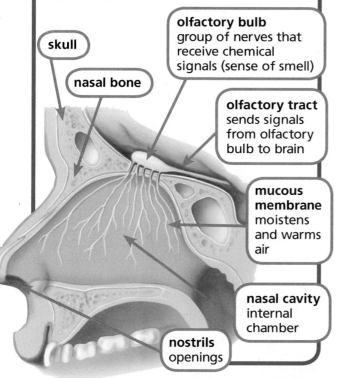

skull

nasal bone

olfactory bulb
group of nerves that receive chemical signals (sense of smell)

olfactory tract
sends signals from olfactory bulb to brain

mucous membrane
moistens and warms air

nasal cavity
internal chamber

nostrils
openings

Skin

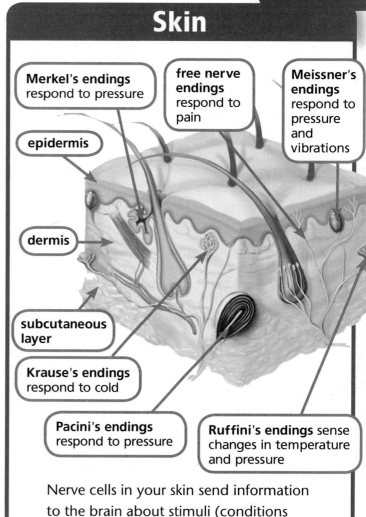

Merkel's endings
respond to pressure

free nerve endings
respond to pain

Meissner's endings
respond to pressure and vibrations

epidermis

dermis

subcutaneous layer

Krause's endings
respond to cold

Pacini's endings
respond to pressure

Ruffini's endings sense changes in temperature and pressure

Nerve cells in your skin send information to the brain about stimuli (conditions around you) that affect the skin.

Caring for Your Senses

- Injuries to these organs can affect your senses.

- Protect your skin and eyes by wearing sunscreen and sunglasses. Protect your ears from loud sounds. Protect your nose from harsh chemicals and your tongue from hot foods and drinks.

Tongue

The tongue is covered with about 10,000 tiny nerve cells, or taste buds, that detect basic tastes in things you eat and drink. Different taste buds respond to different chemicals, and send signals to your brain.

taste buds

Your Digestive System

Your body systems need nutrients from food for energy and for proper cell function. Your digestive system breaks down the food you eat into tiny particles that can be absorbed by your blood and carried throughout your body, so various cells and tissues can use the nutrients.

Digestion begins in your mouth when food is chewed, mixed with saliva, and swallowed. Your tongue pushes the food into your esophagus, which pushes the food down to your stomach with a muscular action, much like the one you use to squeeze toothpaste from a tube.

Your stomach produces gastric juices and mixes them with your food to begin breaking down proteins. Partially digested food leaves your stomach and moves to your small intestine.

Most of the digestive process occurs in your small intestine, where partially digested food is mixed with bile from your liver. This helps break down fats. Your pancreas also produces digestive juices that continue the process of digesting fats and proteins in the small intestine. Your pancreas also produces a special substance called insulin, which helps your body move sugar from your blood into your cells.

As food moves through your small intestine, nutrients are absorbed by the villi and pass into your blood.

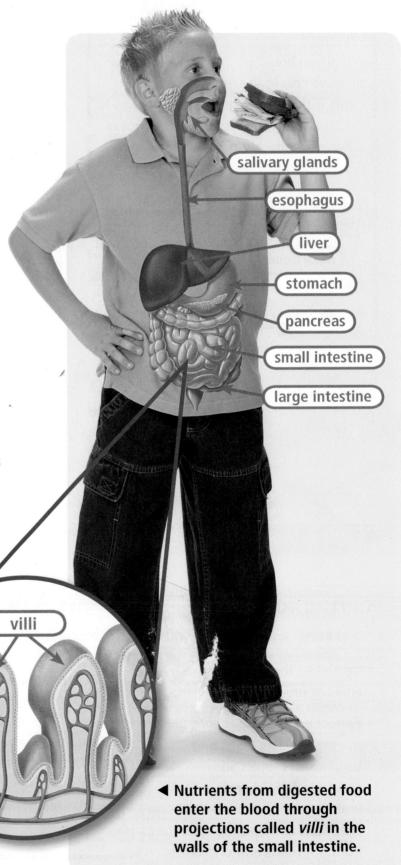

salivary glands

esophagus

liver

stomach

pancreas

small intestine

large intestine

villi

◀ Nutrients from digested food enter the blood through projections called *villi* in the walls of the small intestine.

Specialized Digestive Organs

Your liver produces a fluid called bile that helps break down fats. Bile is stored in your gallbladder. During digestion, the stored bile flows through the bile duct into your small intestine, to help with the digestive process.

Material that is not absorbed by your small intestine passes into your large intestine. This organ absorbs water and vitamins from the undigested materials. The remaining solid wastes are stored by your large intestine until they leave your body.

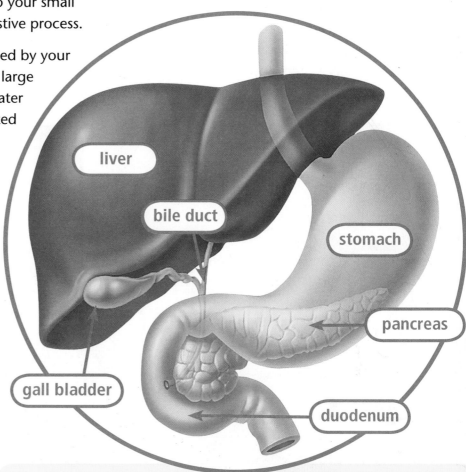

Caring for Your Digestive System

- Drink plenty of water every day. Water helps move food through your digestive system and helps your body replenish saliva, gastric juices, and bile consumed during digestion.

- Eat a variety of foods, choose a well-balanced diet, and maintain a healthy weight.

- Eat plenty of fruits and vegetables. These foods contain essential nutrients and help your digestive system function effectively.

- Chew your food thoroughly before swallowing.

Your Circulatory System

Your body relies on your circulatory system to deliver essential nutrients and oxygen to your organs, tissues, and cells. These materials are carried by your blood. As it circulates, your blood also removes wastes from your tissues. Your circulatory system includes your heart, arteries that carry oxygen-and nutrient-rich blood away from your heart, tiny capillaries that exchange gases and nutrients between your blood and your body's tissues, and veins that carry blood and wastes back to your heart. Your veins have a system of one-way valves that maintains the direction of blood flow within your circulatory system and helps maintain an even distribution of oxygen and nutrients to all parts of your body.

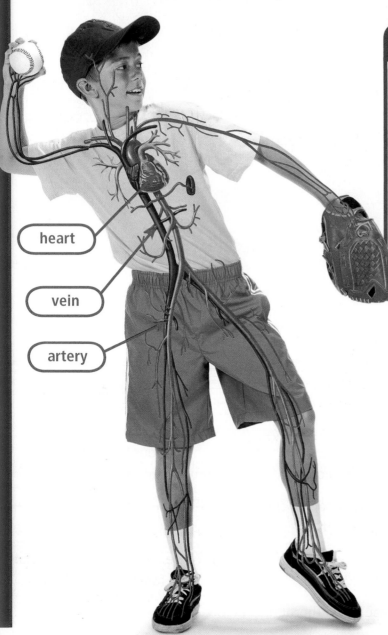

heart

vein

artery

Your Heart

Your heart is a strong, muscular organ that contracts rhythmically to pump blood throughout your circulatory system. When you exercise or work your muscles hard, your heart beats faster to deliver more oxygen-and nutrient-rich blood to your muscles. When you rest, your heartbeat slows. Regular exercise helps keep your heart muscle and the rest of your circulatory system strong.

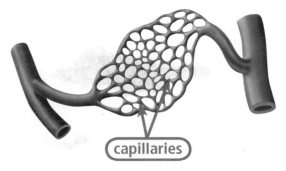

capillaries

▲ Oxygen and nutrients pass from the blood, through capillary walls, and into the cells. Cell wastes pass through capillary walls and into the blood.

Blood Flow and Your Excretory System

Your veins carry blood from your tissues back to your lungs, where carbon dioxide and other waste gases are removed from your red blood cells and expelled when you exhale. Your blood also travels through your kidneys, where small structures called nephrons remove salts and liquid wastes. Urine formed in your kidneys is held in your bladder until it is eliminated. Your liver removes other wastes from your blood, including blood cells. Red blood cells are living tissue, and they live for only 120 days. Specialized cells in your spleen and liver destroy damaged or dead red blood cells.

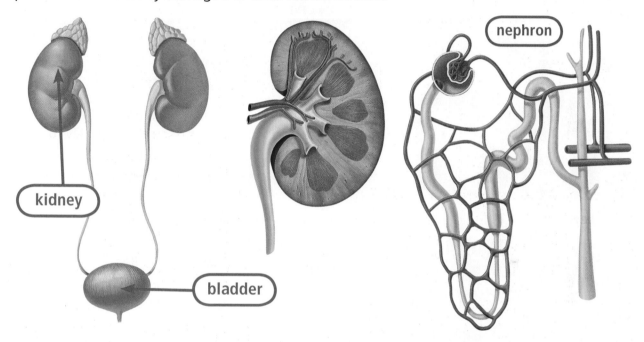

kidney

bladder

nephron

Caring for Your Circulatory System

• Eat foods that are low in fat and high in fiber. Fiber helps take away substances that can lead to fatty buildup in your blood vessels. Eat foods high in iron to help your red blood cells carry oxygen.

• Drink plenty of water to help your body replenish your blood fluid.

• Avoid contact with another person's blood.

• Exercise regularly to keep your heart and blood vessels strong.

• Never smoke or use tobacco. It can strain your heart and damage your blood vessels.

• Don't use illegal drugs or alcohol. They can damage your liver and your heart.

• Follow directions for all medicines carefully. Misuse of medicine can damage your blood's ability to clot after a cut, and can damage your liver and heart.

Your Immune System

A pathogen is an organism or virus that causes illness. An infection is the growth of pathogens in the body. Some pathogens weaken or kill body cells. A disease is an illness that damages or weakens the body so you are not able to do the things you normally do. You may have a sore throat, or you may feel achy or tired, or you may have an unusually high body temperature, or a fever. These are signs that your body is fighting an infection.

Infectious diseases have different symptoms because they are caused by different pathogens. There are four main types of pathogens: viruses, bacteria, fungi, and protozoa.

Diseases Caused by Pathogens

Pathogen	Characteristics	Diseases
Viruses	The smallest pathogens; the ones that cause most infectious diseases	Colds, chicken pox, HIV, infectious hepatitis, influenza (flu), measles, mumps, polio, rabies, rubella (German measles)
Bacteria	One-celled organisms that can—but do not always—cause disease; they make people ill by producing harmful wastes	Strep throat, pertussis (whooping cough), some kinds of pneumonia, salmonella food poisoning, tetanus, tuberculosis (TB), Lyme disease
Fungi	Small, simple organisms like yeasts and molds; they most often invade the skin or respiratory system	Ringworm, athlete's foot, allergies
Protozoa	One-celled organisms somewhat larger than bacteria; they can cause serious diseases	Amoebic dysentery, giardiasis, malaria

There are pathogens all around you. You don't become ill often because your body has a complex system of defenses that prevents most pathogens from entering your body and destroys the ones that get through.

Sometimes pathogens do manage to overcome your body's defenses. When they do, your body's next line of defense is in your blood. Your blood contains white blood cells, which have their own role to play in fighting infection.

Some white blood cells manufacture substances called antibodies. Each antibody is designed to fight a specific kind of pathogen. The antibodies attach themselves to the pathogen and either kill it or mark it to be killed by another kind of white blood cell. When a pathogen enters your body, your immune system produces antibodies to fight it. This process may take several days, during which you may have a fever and feel some other symptoms of the disease. When you have recovered from an illness, your white blood cells remember how to make the antibody needed to fight the pathogen that made you ill. The ability to recognize pathogens and remember how to make antibodies to fight disease is called *immunity*.

You can also develop immunity to certain diseases by getting vaccinations from your doctor that prevent the disease. A vaccine is usually a killed or weakened form of the pathogen that causes a particular disease.

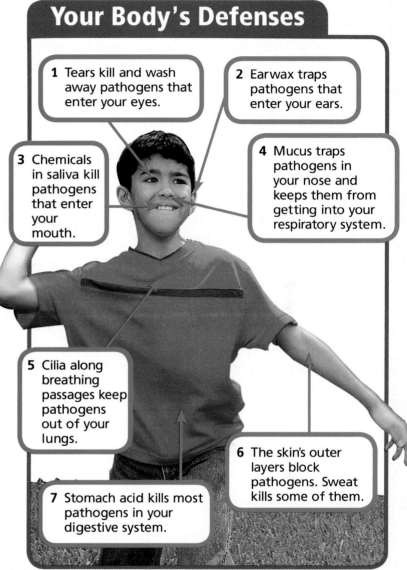

Your Body's Defenses

1 Tears kill and wash away pathogens that enter your eyes.

2 Earwax traps pathogens that enter your ears.

3 Chemicals in saliva kill pathogens that enter your mouth.

4 Mucus traps pathogens in your nose and keeps them from getting into your respiratory system.

5 Cilia along breathing passages keep pathogens out of your lungs.

6 The skin's outer layers block pathogens. Sweat kills some of them.

7 Stomach acid kills most pathogens in your digestive system.

Caring for Your Immune System

- Exercise regularly and get plenty of rest. This helps your body rebuild damaged tissues and cells.

- Eat a healthful, balanced diet. Good nutrition keeps your immune system strong.

- Avoid substances like illegal drugs, tobacco, and alcohol, which can weaken your immune system.

- Wash your hands frequently and avoid touching your eyes, nose, and mouth.

Your Skeletal System

All of the bones in your body form your skeletal system. Your bones protect many vital organs and support the soft tissues of your body. Your skeletal system includes more than two hundred bones that fit together and attach to muscles at joints.

Types of Bones

Your skeleton includes four basic types of bones: long, short, flat, and irregular. Long bones, like the ones in your arms and legs, are narrow and have large ends. These bones support weight. Short bones, found in your wrists and ankles, are chunky and wide. They allow maximum movement around a joint. Flat bones, like the ones in your skull and ribs, protect your body. Irregular bones, like your vertebrae, have unique shapes and fall outside of the other categories.

Types of Joints

Each of the three types of joints is designed to do a certain job.

Ball-and-socket joints like your hips and shoulders, allow rotation and movement in many directions.

Hinge joints, like those between your elbow and knees only move back and forth.

Gliding joints, like those between the vertebrae in your spine or the bones in your wrists and feet, allow side-to-side and back-and-forth movement.

Some joints, like the ones in your skull, do not allow any movement. These flat bones fit tightly together to protect your brain.

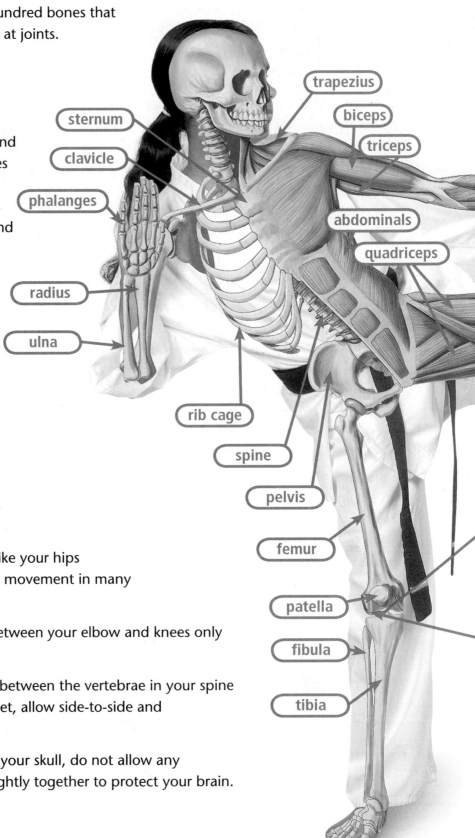

sternum

clavicle

phalanges

radius

ulna

rib cage

spine

pelvis

femur

patella

fibula

tibia

trapezius

biceps

triceps

abdominals

quadriceps

Parts of a Joint

Your bones attach to your muscles and to each other at joints. Your muscles and bones work together to allow your body to move. Joints are made up of ligaments and cartilage. Ligaments are tough, elastic tissues that attach one bone to another. Cartilage is a soft cushioning material at the ends of bones that helps bones move smoothly and absorbs some of the impact when you move. Tendons are dense, cordlike material that joins muscles to bones.

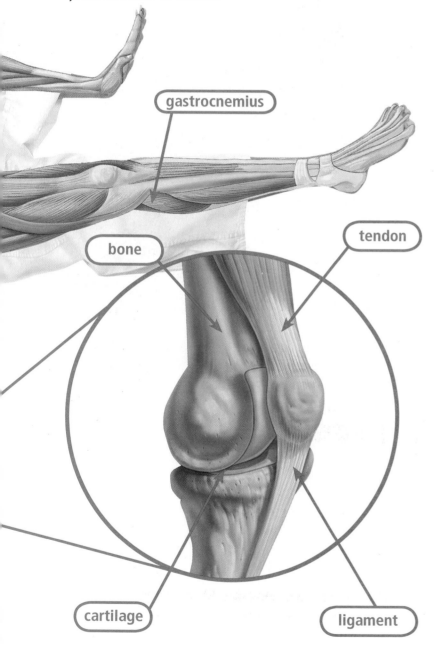

gastrocnemius

bone

tendon

cartilage

ligament

Caring for Your Skeletal System

- Always wear a helmet and proper safety gear when you play sports, skate, or ride a bike or a scooter.
- Your bones are mostly made of calcium and other minerals. To keep your skeletal system strong and to help it grow you should eat foods that are high in calcium, like milk, cheese, and yogurt. Dark green, leafy vegetables like broccoli, spinach, and collard greens are also good sources of calcium.
- Exercise to help your bones stay strong and healthy.
- Always warm up before you exercise.
- Get plenty of rest to help your bones grow.
- Stand and sit with good posture. Sitting slumped over puts strain on your muscles and on your bones.

Your Muscular System

A muscle is a body part that produces movement by contracting and relaxing. All of the muscles in your body make up the muscular system.

Types of Muscle

Your muscular system is made up of three types of muscle. The muscles that make your body move are attached to the bones of your skeletal system. These muscles are called skeletal muscles. A skeletal muscle has a bulging middle and narrow tendons at each end. Tendons are strong flat bands of tissue that attach muscles to bones near your joints. Skeletal muscles are usually under your control, so they are also called voluntary muscles.

Your muscular system includes two other types of muscle. The first of these is called smooth muscle. This specialized muscle lines most of your digestive organs. As these muscles contract and relax, they move food through your digestive system.

Your heart is made of another specialized muscle called cardiac muscle. Your heart's muscle tissue squeezes and relaxes every second of every day to pump blood through your circulatory system. Smooth muscle and cardiac muscle operate automatically. Their contraction is not under your control, so they are also called involuntary muscles.

▼ Skeletal muscle appears striped. It is the kind of muscle that moves bones.

Cardiac muscle forms the walls of the heart. It contracts and relaxes to pump blood through your body. ▶

▲ Smooth muscle lines the walls of blood vessels and of organs such as your esophagus and stomach.

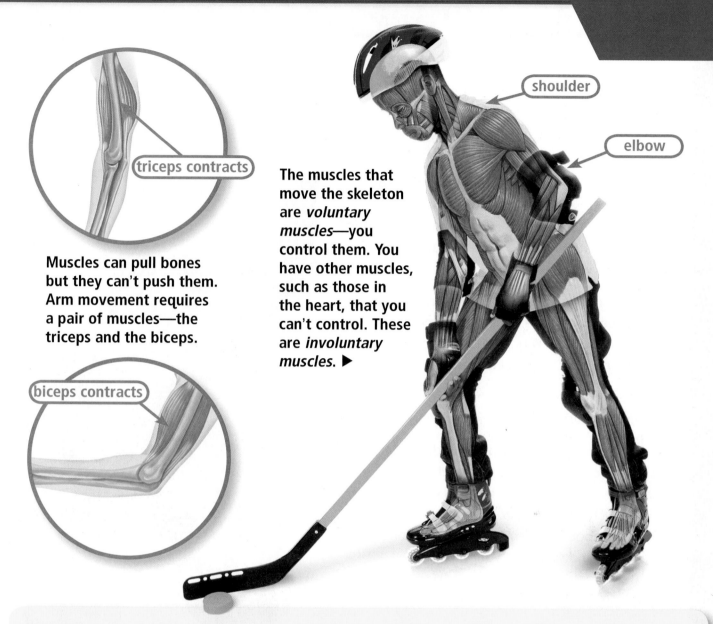

triceps contracts

Muscles can pull bones but they can't push them. Arm movement requires a pair of muscles—the triceps and the biceps.

biceps contracts

The muscles that move the skeleton are *voluntary muscles*—you control them. You have other muscles, such as those in the heart, that you can't control. These are *involuntary muscles*. ▶

shoulder

elbow

Caring for Your Muscular System

- Always stretch and warm your muscles up before exercising or playing sports. Do this by jogging slowly or walking for at least ten minutes. This brings fresh blood and oxygen to your muscles, and helps prevent injury or pain.

- Eat a balanced diet of foods to be sure your muscles have the nutrients they need to grow and remain strong.

- Drink plenty of water when you exercise or play sports. This helps your blood remove wastes from your muscles and helps you build endurance.

- Always cool down after you exercise. Walk or jog slowly for five or ten minutes to let your heartbeat slow and your breathing return to normal. This helps you avoid pain and stiffness after your muscles work hard.

- Stop exercising if you feel pain in your muscles.

- Get plenty of rest before and after you work your muscles hard. They need time to repair themselves and to recover from working hard.

Your Nervous System

Your body consists of a number of different systems. Each of your body's systems plays a different role. The different systems of your body work together to keep you alive and healthy.

Just as a leader directs the work of a group, your nervous system controls your body's activities. Some activities, like the beating of your heart or breathing, are controlled automatically by your nervous system.

Your nervous system allows you to move and to see, hear, taste, touch, and smell the world around you. Your brain also allows you to learn, remember, and feel emotions.

Your nervous system is made up of your brain, your spinal cord, and your nerves.

Your spinal cord is a thick bundle of nerves inside the column of bone formed by your vertebrae. Your nerves are bundles of specialized cells branching from your spinal cord. They send messages about your environment to your brain and send signals to your muscles.

A nerve cell is called a neuron. Signals travel to and from your brain along branching fibers of one neuron to branching fibers of other neurons.

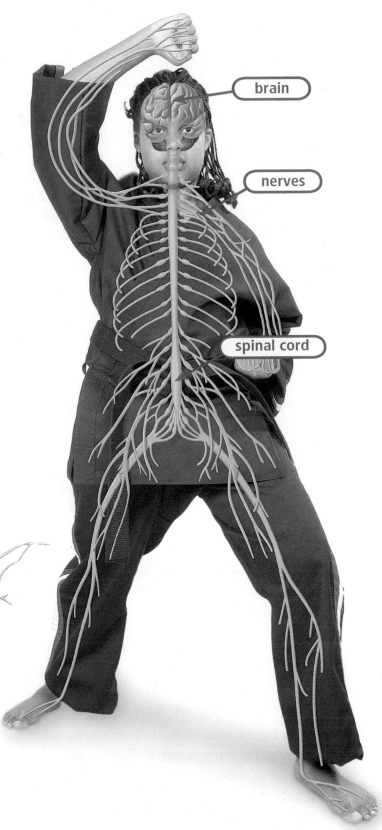

brain

nerves

spinal cord

Your brain contains about 100 billion neurons.
Different areas of your brain control different activities.

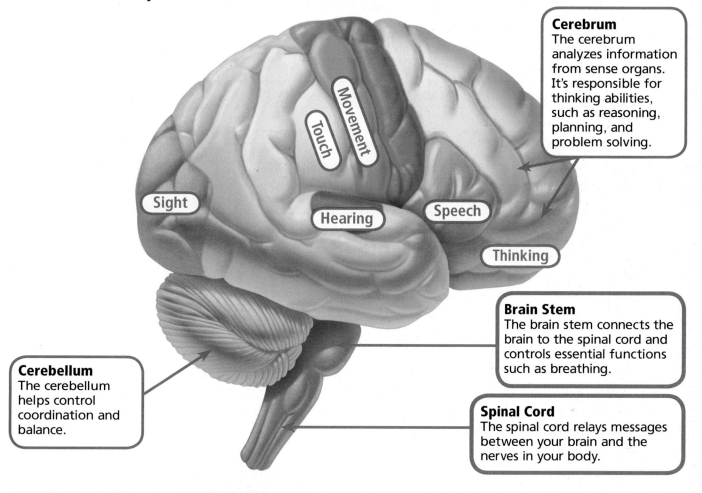

Cerebrum
The cerebrum analyzes information from sense organs. It's responsible for thinking abilities, such as reasoning, planning, and problem solving.

Movement

Touch

Sight

Hearing

Speech

Thinking

Brain Stem
The brain stem connects the brain to the spinal cord and controls essential functions such as breathing.

Spinal Cord
The spinal cord relays messages between your brain and the nerves in your body.

Cerebellum
The cerebellum helps control coordination and balance.

Caring for Your Nervous System

- Don't take illegal drugs, and avoid alcohol. These substances can impair your judgment, which may cause you to react slowly or improperly to danger. They can also damage your nervous system.

- When your doctor prescribes medicines, follow the instructions your doctor gives you. Too much medicine can affect your nervous system. Never take medicine prescribed for someone else.

- Eat a well-balanced diet to be sure your nervous system receives the nutrients it needs.

- Protect your brain and spine from injury by wearing proper safety equipment when you play sports, ride a bike or scooter, or skate.

- Get plenty of rest. Sleep helps keep your mind sharp. Like all of your body's systems, your nervous system requires rest to stay healthy.

Identify the Main Idea and Details

Focus Skill

Many of the lessons in this science book are written so that you can understand main ideas and the details that support them. You can use a graphic organizer like this one to show a main idea and details.

Main Idea: The most important idea of a selection

Detail:
Information that tells more about the main idea

Detail:
Information that tells more about the main idea

Detail:
Information that tells more about the main idea

Tips for Identifying the Main Idea and Details

- To find the main idea, ask—*What is this mostly about?*

- Remember that the main idea is not always stated in the first sentence.

- Be sure to look for details that help you answer questions such as *Who?, What?, Where?, When?, Why?* and *How?*

- Use pictures as clues to help you figure out the main idea.

Here is an example.

Main Idea

All living things are made up of one or more cells. Cells that work together to perform a specific function form tissues. Tissues that work together make up an organ. Each organ in an animal's body is made up of several kinds of tissues. Organs working together form a body system.

Detail

You could record this in the graphic organizer.

Main Idea: All living things are made up of one or more cells.

Detail:
Cells that work together form tissues.

Detail:
Tissues that work together make up an organ.

Detail:
Organs that work together form a body system.

More About Main Idea and Details

Sometimes the main idea of a passage is at the end instead of the beginning. The main idea may not be stated. However, it can be understood from the details. Look at the following graphic organizer. What do you think the main idea is?

Main Idea:

Detail:
Bones make up the skeletal system.

Detail:
The muscular system is made up of voluntary muscles, smooth muscles, and cardiac muscles.

Detail:
Muscles are controlled by the central nervous system.

A passage can contain details of different types. In the following paragraph, identify each detail as a reason, an example, a fact, a step, or a description.

Digestion begins as you chew food. When you swallow, food passes through the esophagus. Gastric juice breaks down proteins. After several hours in the stomach, partly digested food moves into the small intestine. Digestion of food into nutrients is completed in the small intestine. From the small intestine, undigested food passes into the large intestine. In the large intestine, water and minerals pass into the blood and wastes are removed from the body.

Skill Practice

Read the following paragraph. Use the Tips for Identifying Main Idea and Details to answer the questions.

The circulatory, respiratory, digestive, and excretory systems work together to keep the body alive. The circulatory system transports oxygen, nutrients, and wastes through the body. In the respiratory system, oxygen diffuses into the blood and carbon dioxide diffuses out of the blood. The digestive system provides the nutrients your cells need to produce energy. The excretory system removes cell wastes from the blood.

1. What is the main idea of the paragraph?

2. What supporting details give more information?

3. What details answer any of the questions *Who?*, *What?*, *Where?*, *When?*, *Why?* and *How?*

Compare and Contrast

Focus Skill

Some lessons are written to help you see how things are alike or different. You can use a graphic organizer like this one to compare and contrast.

> **Topic:** Name the topic—the two things you are comparing and contrasting.

> **Alike**
> List ways the things are alike.

> **Different**
> List ways the things are different.

Tips for Comparing and Contrasting

- To compare, ask—*How are people, places, objects, ideas, or events alike?*

- To contrast, ask—*How are people, places, objects, ideas, or events different?*

- When you compare, look for signal words and phrases such as *similar, both, too,* and *also.*

- When you contrast, look for signal words and phrases such as *unlike, however, yet,* and *but.*

Here is an example.

Compare

The two basic kinds of energy are kinetic energy and potential energy. Kinetic energy is the energy of motion. Any matter in motion has kinetic energy. However, potential energy is the energy of position or condition. Transformation of energy is the change between kinetic energy and potential energy. The total amount of energy does not change when energy is transformed.

Contrast

Here is what you could record in the graphic organizer.

> **Topic:** Kinetic and Potential Energy

> **Alike**
> Both are basic kinds of energy.
> The total amount of energy stays the same when it changes forms.

> **Different**
> Kinetic energy is the energy of motion.
> Potential energy is the energy of position or condition.

R18

More About Comparing and Contrasting

Identifying how things are alike and how they're different can help you understand new information. Use a graphic organizer to sort the following information about kinetic energy and potential energy.

| kinetic energy | electric energy | thermal energy | mechanical energy | light energy |

| potential energy | elastic potential energy | gravitational potential energy | chemical energy |

Sometimes a paragraph compares and contrasts more than one topic. In the following paragraph, one topic of comparison is underlined. Find a second topic for comparison or contrast.

> **Material that conducts electrons easily is called a conductor. An insulator is a material that does not carry electrons. An electric circuit is any path along which electrons can flow. Some circuits are series circuits. They have only one path for the electrons. Other circuits are parallel circuits, where each device is on a separate path.**

Skill Practice

Read the following paragraph. Use the Tips for Comparing and Contrasting to answer the questions.

> **Within an atom, electrons have a negative charge and protons have a positive charge. Both protons and electrons attract each other. Most objects have equal numbers of protons and electrons. Sometimes, however, electrons are attracted to the protons of another object and rub off. The other object becomes negatively charged.**

1. What are two ways protons and electrons are alike?

2. Explain a difference between protons and electrons.

3. Name two signal words that helped you identify likenesses or differences in this paragraph.

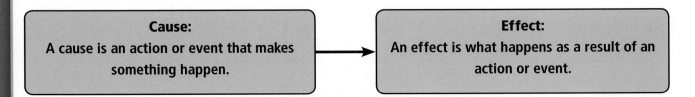

Some of the lessons in this science book are written to help you understand why things happen. You can use a graphic organizer like this one to show cause and effect.

Cause:	**Effect:**
A cause is an action or event that makes something happen.	An effect is what happens as a result of an action or event.

Tips for Identifying Cause and Effect

- To find an effect, ask—*What happened?*

- To find a cause, ask—*Why did this happen?*

- Remember that events can have more than one cause or effect.

- Look for signal words and phrases such as *because* and *as a result* to help you identify causes and effects.

Here is an example.

> Earth's surface is made up of many plates. Plates are rigid blocks of crust and upper mantle rock. Earth's plates fit together like the pieces of a puzzle. Plate movement is very slow. As plates move around, they cause great changes in Earth's landforms. Where plates collide, energy is released, and new landforms are produced. On land, mountains rise and volcanoes erupt.

Here is what you could record in the graphic organizer.

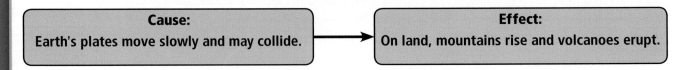

Cause:	**Effect:**
Earth's plates move slowly and may collide.	On land, mountains rise and volcanoes erupt.

More about Cause and Effect

Events can have more than one cause or effect. For example, suppose that example included a sentence that said "On the ocean floor, deep trenches form." You could then identify two effects of Earth's plates colliding.

Cause: Earth's plates move slowly and may collide.	**Effect:** On land, mountains rise and volcanoes erupt.	**Effect:** Deep trenches form on the ocean floor.

Some paragraphs contain more than one cause and effect. In the paragraph below, one cause and its effect are underlined. Find the second cause and its effect.

As Earth's plates pull apart on land, valleys with volcanoes develop. Africa's Great Rift Valley was formed by the African and Arabian plates pulling apart. When plates pull apart under the sea, ridges and volcanoes form. New sea floor is formed at the ridges.

Skill Practice

Read the following paragraph. Use the Tips for Identifying Cause and Effect to help you answer the questions.

When energy is suddenly released in Earth's crust, the ground shakes and an earthquake occurs. The earthquake is a result of plates crushing together, scraping past each other, or bending along jagged boundaries. Because the earth shakes in an earthquake, great damage can occur, such as streets splitting open and bridges collapsing.

1. What causes an earthquake to occur?

2. What are some effects of an earthquake?

3. What two signal words or phrases helped you identify the causes and effects in this paragraph?

Sequence

Some lessons in this science book are written to help you understand the order in which things happen. You can use a graphic organizer like this one to show sequence.

1. The first thing that happened	**2. The next thing that happened**	**3. The last thing that happened**

Tips for Understanding Sequence

- Pay attention to the order in which events happen.

- Remember dates and times to help you understand the sequence.

- Look for signal words such as *first, next, then, last,* and *finally*.

- Sometimes it's helpful to add your own time-order words to help you understand the sequence.

Here is an example.

Time-order words

A substance is buoyant, or will float in a liquid, if its density is less than that of the liquid. Here is a procedure that will show you what it takes for an egg to float in water. First, place an egg in a cup of water. Observe whether or not it floats. Next, remove the egg and stir several spoonfuls of salt into the water. Finally, replace the egg in the water and observe whether or not it floats. By changing the density of the water, you allow its density to become greater than the density of the egg.

You could record this in the graphic organizer.

1. First, place an egg in a cup of water and observe.	**2. Next, remove the egg and stir salt into the water.**	**3. Finally, replace the egg in the water and observe.**

More About Sequence

Sometimes information is sequenced by dates. For example, models of the atom have changed since the late 1800s. Use the graphic organizer to sequence the order of how the model of an atom has changed over time.

| 1. Near the end of the 1800s, Thomson's model of an atom was the first to include subatomic particles. | → | 2. In the early 1900s, Rutherford's model suggested that the atom was made up mostly of empty space. Bohr's model showed different orbits for electrons. | → | 3. Today, the modern model of an atom includes a cloud of electrons around the central positive nucleus. |

When time-order words are not given, add your own words to help you understand the sequence. In the paragraph below, one time-order word has been included and underlined. What other time-order words can you add to help understand the paragraph's sequence?

A person riding a bicycle changes the chemical energy in his or her cells to mechanical energy in order to push the pedals. The energy is transferred from the pedals through the chain to the rear wheel. Finally, the kinetic energy of the turning of the wheel is transferred to the whole bicycle.

Skill Practice

Read the following paragraph. Use the Tips for Understanding Sequence to answer the questions.

First, a flashlight is switched on. Next, the circuit is closed. Then the chemical energy stored in the battery is changed into electric energy. Finally, the electric energy is changed to light in the flashlight bulb.

1. What is the first thing that happened in this sequence?

2. About how long did the process take?

3. What signal words helped you identify the sequence in this paragraph?

Draw Conclusions

(Focus Skill)

At the end of each lesson in this science book, you will be asked to draw conclusions. To draw conclusions, use information from the text you are reading and what you already know. Drawing conclusions can help you understand what you read. You can use a graphic organizer like this.

What I Read List facts from the text.	+	**What I Know** List related ideas from your own experience.	=	**Conclusion:** Combine facts from the text with your own experience.

Tips for Drawing Conclusions

- Ask—*What text information do I need to think about?*

- Ask—*What do I know from my own experience that could help me draw a conclusion?*

- Pay close attention to the information in the text and to your experience to be sure the conclusion is valid, or makes sense.

Here is an example.

> The shore is the area where the ocean and land meet and interact. Waves grind pebbles and rocks against the shore and can cause erosion. The water pressure from a wave can loosen pebbles and small rocks, which outgoing waves carry into the ocean. Longshore currents move sand, pebbles, and shells along the shore.

Here is what you could record in the graphic organizer.

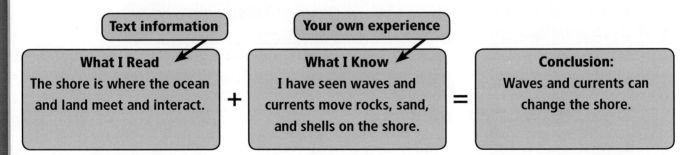

Text information		Your own experience		
What I Read The shore is where the ocean and land meet and interact.	+	**What I Know** I have seen waves and currents move rocks, sand, and shells on the shore.	=	**Conclusion:** Waves and currents can change the shore.

More About Drawing Conclusions

Sensible conclusions based on your experience and the facts you read are valid. For example, suppose the paragraph had ended with the sentence "Human activities can also change the shore." You might have come to a different conclusion about what changes the shore.

What I Read		**What I Know**		**Conclusion:**
The shore is where the ocean and land meet and interact.	**+**	Waves loosen rocks and pebbles. Currents move sand, pebbles, and shells. Structures can be built to prevent erosion.	**=**	Waves, currents, and human activities can change the shore.

Sometimes a paragraph might not contain enough information for drawing a valid conclusion. Read the paragraph below. Think of one valid conclusion you could draw. Then think of one invalid conclusion someone might draw from the given information.

> A jetty is a wall-like structure made of rocks that sticks out into the ocean. Jetties are usually built on either side of an opening to a harbor. Jetties catch sand and pebbles that normally flow down the coast with the current. Jetties can change the shore by building up the beach.

Skill Practice

Read the following paragraph. Use the Tips for Drawing Conclusions to answer the questions.

> Most of the movement of water on the ocean's surface is due to waves. A wave is the up-and-down movement of surface water. On a calm day, ocean waves may only be 1.5 m (5 ft) high or less. However, during a storm, waves can reach heights of 30 m (98 ft).

1. What conclusion did you draw about the height of a wave?

2. What information from your personal experience did you use to draw the conclusion?

3. What text information did you use?

Summarize

At the end of every lesson in this science book, you will be asked to summarize. When you summarize, you use your own words to tell what something is about. In the lesson, you will be given ideas for writing your summary. You can also use a graphic organizer like this one to summarize.

Main Idea: Tell about the most important information you have read.	+	Details: Add details that answer important questions Who?, What?, Where?, When?, Why?, and How?	=	Summary: Retell what you have just read. Include only the most important details.

Tips for Summarizing

- To write a summary, ask—*What is the most important idea of the paragraph?*

- To include details with your summary, ask—*Who?, What?, When?, Where?, Why?* and *How?*

- Remember to use fewer words than the original has.

- Don't forget to use your own words when you summarize.

Here is an example.

Main Idea

Sound waves are carried by vibrating matter. Most sound waves travel through air, but they may also travel through liquids and even some solids. As a sound wave travels, the energy of the wave decreases. The frequency at which the sound wave moves determines the pitch of the sound. The greater the frequency, the higher the pitch. The strength of a sound wave can also be measured. The more energy a sound has, the louder it is.

Details

Here's what you could record in your graphic organizer.

Main Idea: Sound waves are carried by vibrating matter.	+	Details: Pitch is determined by the frequency at which the sound wave moves. The more energy a sound has, the louder it is.	=	Summary: Sound waves are carried by vibrating matter. Pitch is determined by the frequency at which the sound wave moves. The loudness of a sound is determined by how much energy it has.

More About Summarizing

Sometimes a paragraph includes information that would not be included in a summary. For example, suppose a paragraph included a sentence that said "High musical notes have high pitch and high frequency, and low musical notes have low pitch and low frequency." The graphic organizer would remain the same, because that detail is not important to understanding the paragraph's main idea.

Sometimes the main idea of a paragraph is not in the first sentence. In the following paragraph, two important details are underlined. What is the main idea?

> **Air, water, clear glass, and clear plastic are substances which objects can clearly be seen through. Substances that light can travel through are transparent. Substances that are transparent are used to make things like windows and eyeglasses. Some substances are transparent to only certain colors of light. They are described as clear since you can see objects through them, but they have a color.**

Skill Practice

Read the following paragraph. Use the Tips for Summarizing to answer the questions.

> **Light can be absorbed, reflected, or refracted. Sometimes light waves are absorbed when they strike an object. Most objects absorb some colors of light. Other colors of light bounce off objects, or are reflected. These are the colors we see. The change in speed of light causes it to bend. This bending of light waves is called refraction.**

1. If a friend asked you what this paragraph was about, what information would you include? What would you leave out?

2. What is the main idea of the paragraph?

3. What three details would you include in a summary?

Using Tables, Charts, and Graphs

As you do investigations in science, you collect, organize, display, and interpret data. Tables, charts, and graphs are good ways to organize and display data so that others can understand and interpret your data.

The tables, charts, and graphs in this Handbook will help you read and understand data. You can also use the information to choose the best ways to display data so that you can use it to draw conclusions and make predictions.

Reading a Table

A bird-watching group is studying the wingspans of different birds. They want to find out the birds with the greatest wingspans. The table shows the data the group has collected.

Largest Wingspans

Type of Bird	Wingspan (in feet)
Albatross	12
Trumpeter Swan	11
California Condor	10
Marabou Stork	10

Title
Headings
Data

How to Read a Table

1. **Read the title** to find out what the table is about.

2. **Read the headings** to find out what information is given.

3. **Study the data.** Look for patterns.

4. **Draw conclusions.** If you display the data in a graph, you might be able to see patterns easily.

By studying the table, you can see the birds with the greatest wingspans. However, suppose the group wants to look for patterns in the data. They might choose to display the data in a different way, such as in a bar graph.

R28

Reading a Bar Graph

The data in this bar graph is the same as in the table. A bar graph can be used to compare the data about different events or groups.

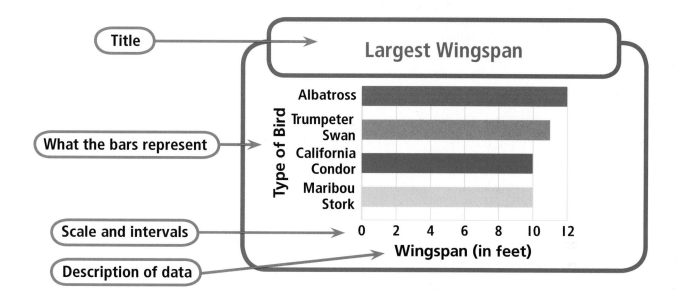

- Title
- What the bars represent
- Scale and intervals
- Description of data

How to Read a Bar Graph

1. **Look** at the graph to determine what kind of graph it is.

2. **Read** the graph. Use the labels to guide you.

3. **Analyze** the data. Study the bars to compare the measurements. Look for patterns.

4. **Draw conclusions.** Ask yourself questions, like the ones in the Skills Practice.

Skills Practice

1. Which two birds have the same wingspan?

2. How much greater is the wingspan of an albatross than the wingspan of a California condor?

3. A red-tailed hawk has a wingspan of 4 feet. Which type of bird has a wingspan that is three times that of the hawk?

4. **Predict** A sixth-grade student saw a bird that had a wingspan that was about the same as her height. Could the bird have been an albatross?

5. Was the bar graph a good choice for displaying this data? Explain your answer.

Reading a Line Graph

A scientist collected this data about how the amount of ice in the Nordic Sea area of the Arctic Ocean has changed over the years.

Nordic Sea Area Ice

Year	Number of Square Kilometers (in millions)
1860	2.8
1880	2.7
1900	2.2
1920	2.4
1940	2.0
1960	1.8
1980	1.5
2000	1.6

Here is the same data displayed in a line graph. A line graph is used to show changes over time.

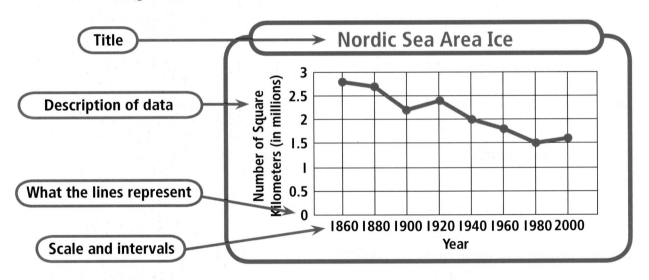

Title

Description of data

What the lines represent

Scale and intervals

How to Read a Line Graph

1. **Look** at the graph to determine what kind of graph it is.

2. **Read** the graph. Use the labels to guide you.

3. **Analyze** the data. Study the points along the lines. Look for patterns.

4. **Draw conclusions.** Ask yourself questions, like the ones in the Skills Practice, to help you draw conclusions.

Skills Practice

1. By how much did the ice in the Nordic Sea area change from 1940 to 1980?

2. **Predict** Will there be more or less than 2.5 million square kilometers of ice in the Nordic Sea area in 2020?

3. Was the line graph a good choice for displaying this data? Explain why.

Reading a Circle Graph

A sixth-grade class is studying U.S. energy sources. They want to know which energy sources are used in the U.S. They classified the different sources by making a table. Here is the data they gathered.

U.S. Energy Sources

Source of Energy	Amount Used
Petroleum	0.38
Natural Gas	0.24
Coal	0.22
Hydroelectric and Nuclear Power	0.12
Other	0.04

The circle graph shows the same data as the table. A circle graph can be used to show data as a whole made up of different parts.

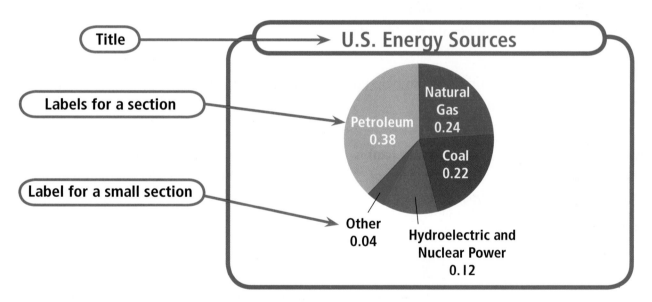

Title

Labels for a section

Label for a small section

U.S. Energy Sources

Petroleum 0.38
Natural Gas 0.24
Coal 0.22
Other 0.04
Hydroelectric and Nuclear Power 0.12

How to Read a Circle Graph

1. **Look** at the title of the graph to learn what kind of information is shown.

2. **Read** the graph. Look at the label of each section to find out what information is shown.

3. **Analyze** the data. Compare the sizes of the sections to determine how they are related.

4. **Draw conclusions.** Ask yourself questions, like the ones in the Skills Practice.

Skills Practice

1. Which source of energy is used most often?

2. **Predict** If wind, geothermal, and solar make up some of the other energy sources, will they be a greater or lesser part of U.S. energy sources in the future?

3. Was the circle graph a good choice for displaying this data? Explain why.

Using Metric Measurements

A measurement is a number that represents a comparison of something being measured to a unit of measurement. Scientists use many different tools to measure objects and substances as they work. Scientists almost always use the metric system for their measurements.

Measuring Length and Capacity

When you measure length, you find the distance between two points. The distance may be in a straight line, along a curved path, or around a circle. The table shows the metric units of **length** and how they are related.

Equivalent Measures
1 centimeter (cm) = 10 millimeters (mm)
1 decimeter (dm) = 10 centimeters (cm)
1 meter (m) = 1000 millimeters
1 meter = 10 decimeters
1 kilometer (km) = 1000 meters

You can use these comparisons to help you understand the size of each metric unit of length.

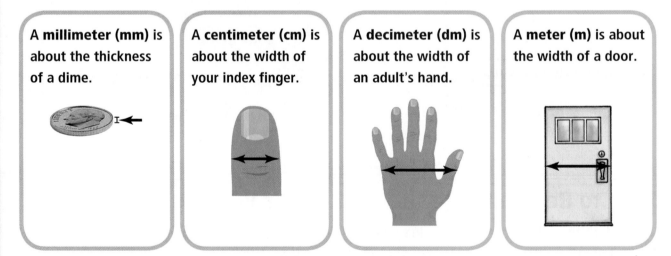

A **millimeter (mm)** is about the thickness of a dime.

A **centimeter (cm)** is about the width of your index finger.

A **decimeter (dm)** is about the width of an adult's hand.

A **meter (m)** is about the width of a door.

Sometimes you may need to change units of length. The following diagram shows how to multiply and divide to change to larger and smaller units.

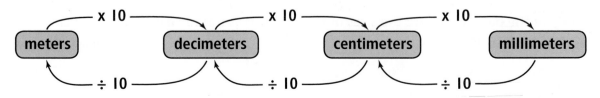

The photos below show the metric units of **capacity** and common comparisons. The metric units of volume are the milliliter (mL) and the liter (L). You can use multiplication to change liters to milliliters. You can use division to change milliliters to liters.

A **milliliter (mL)** is the amount of liquid that can fill part of a medicine dropper.

1 mL

A **liter (L)** is the amount of liquid that can fill a plastic bottle.

1 L

1 L = 1000 mL

To change *larger* units to *smaller* units, you need *more* of the *smaller* units. So, **multiply** by 10, 100, or 1000. To change *smaller* units to *larger* units, you need *fewer* of the *larger units*. So, **divide** by 10, 100, or 1000.

500 dm = ____ cm

Think: There are 10 cm in 1 dm.

500 dm = 500 x 10 = 5000

So, 500 dm = 5000 cm.

4000 mL = ____ L

Think: There are 1000 mL in 1 L.

4000 ÷ 1000 = 4

So, 4000 mL = 4 L.

Skills Practice

Complete. Tell whether you multiply or divide by 10, 100, or 1000.

1. 7 m = _____ cm

2. 4 m = _____ dm

3. 800 _____ = 8 m

4. 9000 mm = _____ m

5. 9 L = _____ mL

6. 6000 mL = _____ L

7. 3000 mL = _____ L

8. 8 _____ = 8000 mL

Measuring Mass

Matter is what all objects are made of. Mass is the amount of matter that is in an object. The metric units of mass are the gram (g) and the kilogram (kg).

You can use these comparisons to help you understand the masses of some everyday objects.

A paper clip is about **1 gram** (g).

A slice of wheat bread is about **20 grams**.

A box of 12 crayons is about **100 grams**.

A large wedge of cheese is **1 kilogram** (kg).

You can use multiplication to change kilograms to grams.

You can use division to change grams to kilograms.

2 kg = ___ g	4000 g = ___ kg
Think: There are 1000 g in 1 kg.	Think: There are 1000 g in 1 kg.
2 kg = 2 × 1000 = 2000 g	4000 ÷ 1000 = 4
So, 2 kg = 2000 g.	So, 4000 g = 4 kg.

Skills Practice

Complete. Tell whether you multiply or divide by 1000.

1. 4000 g = _____ kg

2. 3000 g = _____ kg

3. 7 kg = _____ g

4. 8 _____ = 8000 g

Measurement Systems

SI Measures (Metric)

Temperature

Ice melts at 0 degrees Celsius (°C).
Water freezes at 0°C.
Water boils at 100°C.

Length and Distance

1000 meters (m) = 1 kilometer (km)
100 centimeters (cm) = 1 m
10 millimeters (mm) = 1 cm

Force

1 newton (N) = 1 kilogram x
    1 meter/second/second (kg-m/s^2)

Volume

1 cubic meter (m^3) = 1 m x 1 m x 1 m
1 cubic centimeter (cm^3) =
    1 cm x 1 cm x 1 cm
1 liter (L) = 1000 milliliters (mL)
1 cm^3 = 1 mL

Area

1 square kilometer (km^2) =
    1 km x 1 km
1 hectare = 10,000 m^2

Mass

1000 grams (g) = 1 kilogram (kg)
1000 milligrams (mg) = 1 g

Rates (Metric and Customary)

km/hr = kilometers per hour
m/s = meters per second
mi/hr = miles per hour

Customary Measures

Volume of Fluids

2 c = 1 pint (pt)
2 pt = 1 quart (qt)
4 qt = 1 gallon (gal)

Temperature

Ice melts at 32 degrees
    Fahrenheit (°F)
Water freezes at 32°F
Water boils at 212°F

Length and Distance

12 inches (in.) = 1 foot (ft)
3 ft = 1 yard (yd)
5280 ft = 1 mile (mi)

Weight

16 ounces (oz) = 1 pound (lb)
2000 pounds = 1 ton (T)

Safety in Science

Doing investigations in science can be fun, but you need to be sure you do them safely. Here are some rules to follow.

1. **Think ahead.** Study the steps of the investigation so you know what to expect. If you have any questions, ask your teacher. Be sure you understand any caution statements or safety reminders.

2. **Be neat.** Keep your work area clean. If you have long hair, pull it back so it doesn't get in the way. Roll or push up long sleeves to keep them away from your activity.

3. **Oops!** If you should spill or break something, or get cut, tell your teacher right away.

4. **Watch your eyes.** Wear safety goggles anytime you are directed to do so. If you get anything in your eyes, tell your teacher right away.

5. **Yuck!** Never eat or drink anything during a science activity.

6. **Don't get shocked.** Be especially careful if an electric appliance is used. Be sure that electric cords are in a safe place where you can't trip over them. Don't ever pull a plug out of an outlet by pulling on the cord.

7. **Keep it clean.** Always clean up when you have finished. Put everything away and wipe your work area. Wash your hands.

Visit the Multimedia Science Glossary to see illustrations of these words and to hear them pronounced.
www.hspscience.com

Glossary

As you read your science book, you will notice that new or unfamiliar words have been respelled to help you pronounce them while you are reading. Those respellings are called *phonetic respellings*. In this Glossary you will see the same kind of respelling.

In phonetic respelling, syllables are separated by a bullet (•). Small uppercase letters show stressed syllables.

The boldfaced letters in the examples in the Pronunciation Key below show which letters and combinations of letters are pronounced in the respellings.

The page number (in parentheses) at the end of a definition tells you where to find the term, defined in context, in your book. Depending on the context in which it is used, a term may have more than one definition.

Pronunciation Key

Sound	As in	Phonetic Respelling	Sound	As in	Phonetic Respelling
a	b**a**t	(BAT)	oh	**o**ver	(OH•ver)
ah	l**o**ck	(LAHK)	oo	p**oo**l	(POOL)
air	r**are**	(RAIR)	ow	**ou**t	(OWT)
ar	**ar**gue	(AR•gyoo)	oy	f**oi**l	(FOYL)
aw	l**aw**	(LAW)	s	**c**ell	(SEL)
ay	f**a**ce	(FAYS)		**s**it	(SIT)
ch	**ch**apel	(CHAP•uhl)	sh	**sh**eep	(SHEEP)
e	t**e**st	(TEST)	th	**th**at	(THAT)
	m**e**tric	(MEH•trik)		**th**in	(THIN)
ee	**ea**t	(EET)	u	p**u**ll	(PUL)
	f**ee**t	(FEET)	uh	m**e**dal	(MED•uhl)
	sk**i**	(SKEE)		t**a**lent	(TAL•uhnt)
er	pap**er**	(PAY•per)		penc**i**l	(PEN•suhl)
	f**er**n	(FERN)		**o**ni**o**n	(UHN•yuhn)
eye	**i**dea	(eye•DEE•uh)		playf**u**l	(PLAY•fuhl)
i	b**i**t	(BIT)		d**u**ll	(DUHL)
ing	go**ing**	(GOH•ing)	y	**y**es	(YES)
k	**c**ard	(KARD)		r**i**pe	(RYP)
	kite	(KYT)	z	bag**s**	(BAGZ)
ngk	ba**nk**	(BANGK)	zh	trea**s**ure	(TREZH•er)

abyssal plain [uh•BIS•uhl PLAYN] The vast floor of the deep ocean **(347)**

acceleration [ak•sel•er•AY•shuhn] An object's change in velocity divided by the time it takes for that change to occur **(600)**

acid [AS•id] A substance that turns blue litmus paper red **(512)**

adaptation [ad•uhp•TAY•shuhn] A feature of an organism that helps it survive in its surroundings **(82)**

air pressure [AIR PRESH•er] The force of the weight of air pressing down on a unit of area **(378)**

amplitude [AM•pluh•tood] The distance in a wave from the resting position to the top of the crest or the bottom of the trough **(537)**

angiosperm [AN•jee•oh•sperm] A flowering vascular plant whose seeds are surrounded by a fruit **(126)**

asexual reproduction [ay•SEK•shoo•uhl ree•pruh•DUHK•shuhn] A type of reproduction in which a new organism is formed without the joining of a sperm cell and an egg cell **(121)**

asteroid [AS•ter•oyd] A piece of rock and metal that orbits the sun **(423)**

atmosphere [AT•muhs•feer] The layers of air that surround Earth **(372)**

atom [AT•uhm] The smallest unit of an element that still has the properties of that element **(452)**

atomic number [uh•TAHM•ik NUHM•ber] The number of protons in an atom **(453)**

axis [AK•sis] An imaginary line running through the center of Earth from the North Pole to the South Pole **(406)**

balanced forces [BAL•uhnst FAWRS•iz] Equal forces that act in opposite directions on an object and cancel one another out **(606)**

base [BAYS] A substance that turns red litmus paper blue **(512)**

bedrock [BED•rahk] The bottom layer of soil, made mostly of solid rock **(291)**

biome [BY•ohm] A region of the world defined by its climate and by the types of plants and animals that live there **(174)**

blizzard [BLIZ•erd] A winter storm with strong winds and large amounts of heavy, blowing snow **(394)**

boiling point [BOYL•ing POYNT] The temperature at which a substance changes from a liquid to a gas **(472)**

carbon cycle [KAR•buhn SY•kuhl] The movement of carbon as solids, liquids, or gases through Earth's ecosystems **(204)**

cast [KAST] A model of an organism formed when sediment fills a mold and hardens **(305)**

cell wall [SEL WAWL] A stiff outer layer that surrounds a plant cell, protects it, and gives it its shape **(34)**

chemical change [KEM•ih•kuhl CHAYNJ] A change in which one or more new substances are formed **(504)**

chemical property [KEM•ih•kuhl PRAHP•er•tee] A property that involves the ability of a substance to react with other materials and form new substances **(505)**

chloroplasts [KLAWR•uh•plasts] Organelles, found only in plant cells, in which sugar is made during photosynthesis **(34)**

chromosomes [KROH•muh•sohmz] Structures in the nucleus that contain an organism's genetic information and regulate the cell's activities **(35)**

circuit [SER•kit] A continuous path through which electric charges flow **(580)**

classification [klas•uh•fih•KAY•shuhn] The sorting of things into groups of similar items **(76)**

climate [KLY•muht] The average of all weather conditions in an area over a period of time **(384)**

colloid [KAHL•oyd] A mixture that contains particles that are too small to see **(500)**

comet [KAHM•it] A ball of ice, rock, and frozen gases that orbits the sun **(428)**

community [kuh•MYOO•nuh•tee] All the populations living in an ecosystem **(152)**

competition [kahm•puh•TISH•uhn] The struggle among organisms for limited resources in an area **(166)**

compound [KAHM•pownd] A substance made up of atoms of two or more elements that are chemically combined **(464)**

condensation [kahn•duhn•SAY•shuhn] The process by which water vapor changes into liquid water **(338)**

conduction [kuhn•DUK•shuhn] The transfer of thermal energy that results from the collision of particles **(564)**

conifer [KAHN•uh•fer] A type of gymnosperm whose seeds develop inside a cone **(124)**

conservation [kahn•ser•VAY•shuhn] The careful use of resources so that they will last as long as possible **(196)**

consumer [kuhn•SOOM•er] An organism that eats other organisms **(159)**

continental shelf [kahnt•uhn•ENT•uhl SHELF] A gradually sloping portion of the ocean floor that is made of continental crust **(346)**

continental slope [kahnt•uhn•ENT•uhl SLOHP] The border between continental crust and oceanic crust where the ocean floor drops in depth **(346)**

convection [kuhn•VEK•shuhn] The transfer of thermal energy through the movement of a liquid or a gas **(565)**

coral reef [KAWR•uhl REEF] A large, delicate structure formed by the skeletons of small animals called corals **(358)**

core [KAWR] The layer of Earth that extends from Earth's center to the bottom of the mantle **(231)**

crust [KRUHST] The thin, outermost layer of Earth, which includes both dry land and the ocean floor **(230)**

current [KUR•uhnt] A steady, streamlike movement of ocean water **(348)**

current electricity [KUR•uhnt ee•lek•TRIS•uh•tee] The flow of electric charges through a wire **(572)**

density [DEN•suh•tee] The amount of mass something has in relation to its volume **(488)**

deposition [dep•uh•ZISH•uhn] The dropping or settling of eroded materials **(233)**

diffraction [dih•FRAK•shuhn] The bending of light around the edge of an object **(549)**

diversity [duh•VER•suh•tee] The variety of species in an ecosystem **(154)**

DNA [dee•en•AY] The abbreviation for deoxyribonucleic acid, the chemical that provides detailed instructions for cells **(36)**

dominant [DAHM•uh•nuhnt] Describes a stronger trait that will show up in an organism even if only one factor for it is present **(62)**

earthquake [ERTH•kwayk] A vibration in Earth's crust, caused by the release of energy in a fault **(248)**

eclipse [ih•KLIPS] An event that occurs when one object passes into the shadow of another object **(410)**

ecosystem [EE•koh•sis•tuhm] An area where living things interact with one another and with nonliving things **(151)**

electromagnet [ee•lek•troh•MAG•nit] A temporary magnet that is made by passing an electric current through a coil of wire that surrounds an iron core **(584)**

electromagnetic spectrum [ee•lek•troh•mag•NET•ik SPEK•truhm] All energy waves that travel at the speed of light in a vacuum; includes radio, infrared, visible, ultraviolet, X rays, and gamma rays **(540)**

electron [ee•LEK•trahn] A subatomic particle that orbits an atom's nucleus, has a negative electric charge, and has very little mass **(453)**

element [EL•uh•muhnt] A substance made up of only one kind of atom **(460)**

endangered species [en•DAYN•jerd SPEE•sheez] A species with so few individuals that it could die out **(213)**

energy [EN•er•jee] The ability to cause change in matter **(528)**

energy pyramid [EN•er•jee PIR•uh•mid] A diagram that shows that energy is lost at each level in a food chain **(162)**

epicenter [EP•ih•sent•er] The point on Earth's surface directly above the focus of an earthquake **(249)**

erosion [uh•ROH•zhuhn] The removal and transportation of weathered materials **(232)**

evaporation [ee•vap•uh•RAY•shuhn] The process by which liquid water changes into water vapor **(338)**

extinction [ek•STINGK•shuhn] The loss of an entire species **(213)**

fault [FAWLT] A break in Earth's crust where rocks can slide past each other **(248)**

fern [FERN] A vascular plant that reproduces without seeds **(122)**

first quarter [FERST KWAWRT•er] The phase of the moon when it is one-quarter of the way through its orbit and we see half of the moon lighted **(416)**

focus [FOH•kuhs] The point inside Earth where an earthquake begins **(249)**

food chain [FOOD CHAYN] A sequence of connected producers and consumers **(159)**

food web [FOOD WEB] A group of connected food chains in an ecosystem **(160)**

force [FAWRS] A push or a pull **(600)**

fossil [FAHS•uhl] Any naturally preserved evidence of life **(304)**

fossil fuel [FAHS•uhl FYOO•uhl] An energy-rich resource formed from the buried remains of once-living organisms **(308)**

frequency [FREE•kwuhn•see] The number of vibrations or waves in a given amount of time **(539)**

friction [FRIK•shuhn] A force that acts between any two surfaces in contact with one another and prevents or slows motion **(610)**

front [FRUHNT] The boundary between two air masses that collide **(380)**

fruit [FROOT] The ripened ovary of a flowering plant **(134)**

fulcrum [FUL•kruhm] The fixed point that the effort arm of a lever moves around **(632)**

full moon [FUL MOON] The phase of the moon in which we see the entire moon lighted and it appears bright and round **(416)**

fungus [FUHNG•guhs] An organism that has cell walls but does not have chloroplasts **(84)**

galaxy [GAL•uhk•see] A huge system of stars **(436)**

genes [JEENZ] Pieces of DNA that carry all the information passed from parents to their offspring **(51)**

genus [JEE•nuhs] A group of organisms that share major characteristics and are therefore closely related **(91)**

glacier [GLAY•sher] An immense sheet of moving ice that stays frozen year-round **(234)**

gravitational force [grav•ih•TAY•shuhn•uhl FAWRS] The force that acts between any two masses in the universe and pulls them toward one another **(614)**

gravitropism [gra•VIH•truh•piz•uhm] The growth response of plants to gravity **(114)**

groundwater [GROWND•waw•ter] Water located within the gaps and pores in rocks below Earth's surface **(339)**

gymnosperm [JIM•noh•sperm] A vascular plant that produces seeds that are not surrounded by a fruit **(124)**

habitat [HAB•ih•tat] The part of an ecosystem in which an organism lives **(153)**

heat [HEET] The transfer of thermal energy from warmer objects to cooler ones **(564)**

host [HOHST] The organism that a parasite lives in or on **(168)**

hurricane [HER•ih•kayn] A large, rotating tropical storm system with wind speeds of at least 119 km (74 mi) per hour **(392)**

igneous rock [IG•nee•uhs RAHK] Rock formed when melted rock hardens **(274)**

inclined plane [in•KLYND PLAYN] Any flat, sloping surface used as a simple machine **(640)**

index fossil [IN•deks FAHS•uhl] A fossil of a type of organism that lived in many places during a relatively short time span **(315)**

indicator [IN•dih•kayt•er] A material that indicates whether a substance is an acid or a base **(514)**

inertia [in•ER•shuh] The tendency of matter to resist a change in its state of motion (602)

insulation [in•suh•LAY•shuhn] A substance that conducts thermal energy poorly (566)

intertidal zone [in•ter•TYD•uhl ZOHN] The area of the ocean between the high-tide level and the low-tide level (354)

kinetic energy [kih•NET•ik EN•er•jee] The energy of motion (528)

lava [LAH•vuh] Magma that is exposed at Earth's surface (275)

law of conservation of energy [LAW uv kahn•ser•VAY•shuhn uv EN•er•jee] The rule stating that the total amount of energy in a closed system is always the same—energy cannot be created or destroyed (532)

lever [LEV•er] A simple machine that is an arm or rod that turns around a fixed point (632)

magma [MAG•muh] Melted rock within Earth (274)

mantle [MAN•tuhl] The thick layer of Earth beneath the crust (231)

mass [MAS] The amount of matter something has (488)

mass extinction [MAS ek•STINGK•shuhn] A period in which a large number of species become extinct (323)

melting point [MELT•ing POYNT] The temperature at which a substance changes from a solid to a liquid (472)

metal [MET•uhl] A substance that conducts heat and electricity well and is malleable (461)

metamorphic rock [met•uh•MAWR•fik RAHK] Rock made from igneous or sedimentary rock that has been changed by pressure, high temperature, very hot water, or a combination of these factors (278)

metamorphism [met•uh•MAWR•fiz•uhm] The process by which metamorphic rock is formed (278)

meteor [MEET•ee•er] A piece of rock, smaller than an asteroid, that enters Earth's atmosphere and burns up (426)

mid-ocean ridge [mid•OH•shuhn RIJ] A chain of mountains that runs through the world's oceans (242)

mineral [MIN•er•uhl] A natural, solid substance that has a definite chemical composition and physical structure (266)

mixture [MIKS•cher] A combination of two or more substances that keep their original properties (496)

mold [MOHLD] An impression of an organism formed when sediments harden around the organism (305)

moss [MAWS] A small plant that does not have vascular tissues or true roots, stems, or leaves (120)

natural resource [NACH•er•uhl REE•sawrs] A material that occurs in nature that is essential or useful to people (192)

near-shore zone [neer•SHAWR ZOHN] The area of ocean over the continental shelf that is relatively shallow (356)

neutron [NOO•trahn] A subatomic particle that has the same mass as a proton but no electric charge (453)

new moon [NOO MOON] The phase of the moon in which only a dim outline of its shape is visible (416)

niche [NICH] An organism's role in an ecosystem (153)

nitrogen cycle [NY•truh•juhn SY•kuhl] The movement of nitrogen in different forms from living organisms to the nonliving part of the environment and back (206)

nonmetal [nahn•MET•uhl] A substance that does not conduct electricity and is not malleable (461)

nonvascular plant [nahn•VAS•kyuh•ler PLANT] A plant that lacks tissues for carrying water, food, and nutrients (110)

nucleus [NOO•klee•uhs] The control center of a cell that directs the cell's activities. (35) The center of an atom, usually made of protons and neutrons (453)

opaque [oh•PAYK] Not allowing any light to pass through (550)

open-ocean zone [oh•puhn•OH•shuhn ZOHN] The area of ocean over the continental slope and abyssal plain (356)

organ [AWR•guhn] A structure that contains at least two types of tissue that work together to perform a specific function (42)

parallel circuit [PAIR•uh•lel SER•kit] A circuit in which there is more than one path for the current to follow (582)

parasite [PAIR•uh•syt] An organism that benefits from its relationship with an organism that it lives in or on while the other organism is harmed (168)

periodic table [pir•ee•AHD•ik TAY•buhl] A table that shows the elements arranged by their atomic numbers (462)

pH scale [pee•AYCH SKAYL] A measure of the strength or weakness of acids and bases (514)

phloem [FLOH•em] Plant tissue that carries food from the leaves to other cells (108)

phototropism [foh•TAH•troh•piz•uhm] The growth response of plants to light (114)

physical change [FIZ•ih•kuhl CHAYNJ] A change that does not make a substance into a new substance (490)

physical property [FIZ•ih•kuhl PRAHP•er•tee] A property that describes a substance by itself, such as color, shape, density, or hardness (487)

plasma [PLAZ•muh] A state of matter made up of charged atoms, uncharged atoms, and free electrons (474)

plate tectonics [PLAYT tek•TAHN•iks] The theory that Earth's crust and upper mantle is divided into plates that are always moving (241)

pollination [pahl•uh•NAY•shuhn] The first step of angiosperm reproduction, during which pollen from an anther lands on a stigma of a flower of the same kind (132)

population [pahp•yuh•LAY•shuhn] A group of organisms of the same species living together in an ecosystem (152)

potential energy [poh•TEN•shuhl EN•er•jee] Energy that is due to the position or condition of an object **(528)**

precipitation [pree•sip•uh•TAY•shuhn] Solid or liquid water that falls from the air to Earth **(339)**

producer [pruh•DOOS•er] An organism that makes its own food **(158)**

protist [PROHT•ist] A microscopic organism that may have characteristics of plants, animals, or fungi **(85)**

proton [PROH•tahn] A subatomic particle that has a positive electric charge **(453)**

pulley [PUL•ee] A simple machine that is a grooved wheel that has a rope or a chain around it **(634)**

radiation [ray•dee•AY•shuhn] The transfer of thermal energy as waves **(565)**

reactivity [ree•ak•TIV•uh•tee] The ability of a substance to go through a chemical change **(505)**

recessive [rih•SES•iv] Describes a weaker trait that will show up in an organism only if no factor for the dominant trait is present **(62)**

recycle [ree•SY•kuhl] To process used products into new products by using the materials again **(196)**

reflection [rih•FLEK•shuhn] The bouncing of light off a surface **(546)**

refraction [rih•FRAK•shuhn] The bending of light as it passes from one material to another **(548)**

relative humidity [REL•uh•tiv hyoo•MID•uh•tee] A comparison of the actual amount of water vapor in the air to the amount of water vapor that would be in the air if it were saturated **(379)**

reuse [ree•YOOZ] To use items again after their original use **(197)**

revolution [rev•uh•LOO•shuhn] The movement of one object in an orbit around another object **(406)**

rift [RIFT] A deep valley at the highest part of the mid-ocean ridge, where tectonic plates are moving apart **(242)**

rock cycle [RAHK SY•kuhl] All of the processes that change rock from one type to another **(285)**

rotation [roh•TAY•shuhn] The turning of an object on an axis **(406)**

satellite [SAT•uhl•yt] A body in space that orbits a larger body **(424)**

screw [SKROO] A simple machine that is an inclined plane wrapped around a cylinder or a cone **(644)**

sea-floor spreading [SEE•flawr SPRED•ing] The process, which takes place along the mid-ocean ridge, in which liquid rock rises and becomes solid as two tectonic plates move farther and farther apart **(242)**

sedimentary rock [sed•uh•MEN•ter•ee RAHK] Rock formed when layers of sediment settle and are cemented together **(276)**

series circuit [SIR•eez SER•kit] A circuit in which there is only one path for the current to follow **(582)**

sexual reproduction [SEK•shoo•uhl ree•pruh•DUHK•shuhn] A type of reproduction in which a sperm cell and an egg cell unite to form a single cell **(50)**

solution [suh•LOO•shuhn] A mixture in which all of the substances are evenly distributed **(498)**

species [SPEE•sheez] A single kind of organism that can reproduce among its own kind **(91)**

spore [SPAWR] A structure containing cells that can grow into a new plant without joining with other cells **(121)**

stability [stuh•BIL•uh•tee] The ability of a substance to resist going through a chemical change **(505)**

static electricity [STAT•ik ee•lek•TRIS•uh•tee] The electric charge that builds up on an object that has gained or lost electrons **(570)**

succession [suhk•SESH•uhn] The gradual long-term change of species in an ecosystem **(202)**

suspension [suh•SPEN•shuhn] A mixture that contains particles that are large enough to be seen **(500)**

symbiosis [sim•by•OH•sis] A close relationship between organisms of different species in which one or both of the organisms benefit **(168)**

thermal energy [THER•muhl EN•er•jee] The kinetic energy of the moving particles of a substance or an object **(562)**

third quarter [THERD KWAWRT•er] The phase of the moon when it is three-quarters of the way through its orbit and we see half of the moon lighted **(417)**

thunderstorm [THUHN•der•stawrm] A strong storm with rain, lightning, and thunder **(390)**

tides [TYDZ] The regular rising and falling of the ocean's surface caused mostly by the moon's gravitational "pull" on Earth's oceans **(412)**

tissue [TISH•oo] A group of specialized cells with the same structure and function **(40)**

topsoil [TAHP•soyl] The top layer of soil, made in part from broken-up pieces of lower layers of rock **(291)**

tornado [tawr•NAY•doh] A violently rotating column of air that extends downward from a thundercloud and touches the ground **(391)**

translucent [tranz•LOO•suhnt] Allowing some light to pass through **(550)**

transparent [tranz•PAIR•uhnt] Allowing almost all light to pass through **(550)**

tropism [TROH•piz•uhm] A growth response of a plant toward or away from something in its environment **(114)**

unbalanced forces [uhn•BAL•uhnst FAWRS•iz] Forces that do not cancel one another out **(607)**

vascular plant [VAS•kyuh•ler PLANT] A plant that has transport tissues for carrying water, food, and nutrients to its cells **(108)**

velocity [vuh•LAHS•uh•tee] The speed and direction of a moving object **(599)**

volcano [vahl•KAY•noh] A mountain formed when molten rock is pushed to Earth's surface and builds up **(252)**

volume [VAHL•yoom] The amount of space something takes up **(488)**

water cycle [WAW•ter SY•kuhl] The process by which water moves above, across, and through Earth's crust and ecosystems **(338)**

wave [WAYV] A disturbance that carries energy through matter or space **(536)**

wavelength [WAYV•length] The distance from the middle of the crest of one wave to the middle of the crest of the next wave **(537)**

weathering [WETH•er•ing] The process by which rock is broken down into smaller and smaller pieces **(232)**

wedge [WEJ] A simple machine made of two inclined planes placed back to back **(642)**

weight [WAYT] The measurement of the force of gravity on an object **(618)**

wetland [WET•land] An area of land that is covered by water all or much of the time **(215)**

wheel-and-axle [weel•uhnd•AK•suhl] A simple machine that is a large wheel and a small wheel that are connected and turn together **(635)**

work [WERK] The result that occurs when a force causes an object to move in the direction of the force **(630)**

xylem [ZY•luhm] Plant tissue that carries water and nutrients from a plant's roots to its leaves **(108)**

Unlimited; 268(br), Stone/Getty Images; 269(l), Barry Runk/Stan/Grant Heilman Photography; 269(cl), Joy Spurr/Bruce Coleman, Inc.; 269(c), Joy Spurr/Bruce Coleman, Inc.; 269(cr), E.R. Degginger/Bruce Coleman, Inc.; 269(r), Barry Runk/Stan/Grant Heilman Photography; 269(b), Royalty Free/CORBIS; 270, Peter Arnold/Peter Arnold, Inc.; 272, The Image Bank/Getty Images; 274(t), Dane Johnson/Visuals Unlimited; 274(bl), Doug Sokell/Visuals Unlimited; 274(br), Wally Eberhart/Visuals Unlimited; 275(l), Barry Runk/Grant Heilman Photography; 275(r), Steve McCutcheon/Visuals Unlimited; 276(t), Stan Celestian /Glendale Community College, Arizona; 276(c), Wally Eberhart/Visuals Unlimited; 276(b), Wally Eberhart/Visuals Unlimited; 277(t), Biophoto Associates/Photo Researchers, Inc. ; 277(b), Michael T. Sedam/CORBIS; 278, Stan Celestian/Glendale Community College, Arizona; 279(tl), (tr), Stan Celestian/ Glendale Community College, AZ; 279(b), Joyce Photographics/Photo Researchers, Inc.; 280(b), Dean Conger/CORBIS; 282, Calvin J. Hamilton/Scienceviews.com; 284(tl), Martin Miller/Visuals Unlimited; 284(tr), ALFRED PASIEKA/Science Photo Library/Photo Researchers, Inc. ; 284(bl), Rob & Ann Simpson/ Visuals Unlimited; 284(br), Alfred Paseika/Science Photo Library/Photo Researchers, Inc. ; 285(l), James Randklev/CORBIS; 285(r), ALFRED PASIEKA/Science Photo Library/Photo Researchers, Inc.; 288, Paul A. Souders/CORBIS; 290-291, Jim Foster/CORBIS; 292(l), Jim Richardson/Corbis; 292(r), Franklin D. Roosevelt Library, Hyde Park, New York; 294, 295, Roger Ressmeyer/Corbis; 296, Michelle D Bridwell/Photo Edit; 296(bkgnd), Harcourt Index; 297, Nature Picture Library; 300, Bill Varie/CORBIS; 302, Layne Kennedy/CORBIS; 305(t), Bernhard Edmaier/Photo Researchers, Inc.; 305(cl), Dick Roberts/Visuals Unlimited; 305(cr), Alfred Pasieka/Photo Researchers, Inc.; 305(b), James L. Amos/Photo Researchers, Inc.; 306(t), Tom Bean/CORBIS; 306(b), Virtual Museum of Fossils/Valdosta State University; 307(tl), National Museum of Natural History; 307(tr), SINCLAIR STAMMERS/Science Photo Library/Photo Researchers, Inc.; 307(cl), James L. Amos/CORBIS; 307(bl), Dr. Ann Smith/Photo Researchers, Inc. ; 307(br), Layne Kennedy/CORBIS; 308, Royalty Free/Corbis; 309, Andrew J. Martinez/Photo Researchers, Inc.; 312, Scott Camazine/Photo Researchers, Inc.; 314(t), Albert Copley/Visuals Unlimited; 314(c), Sinclair Stammers/Photo Researchers, Inc.; 314(b), SINCLAIR STAMMERS/Science Photo Library/Photo Researchers, Inc.; 315(both), James L. Amos/Corbis; 316(tl), Visuals Unlimited; 316(bl), MARTIN LAND/Science Photo Library/Photo Researchers, Inc.; 316(r), Natural History Museum, London; 318, James L. Amos/CORBIS; 320(t), Gerald L. Moore; 320(b), Kim Karpeles; 321(t), Nik Wheeler/CORBIS; 321(b), Craig Aurness/CORBIS; 322(t), Louie Psihoyos/CORBIS; 322(b), Chip Clark; 323, Natural History Museum, London; 323(inset), KAJ R. SVENSSON/Science Photo Library/Photo Researchers, Inc.; 324(bl), COLLART HERVE/CORBIS SYGMA; 324(top to bottom), Visuals Unlimited, Natural History Museum, London; COLLART HERVE/CORBIS SYGMA; James Amos/ Corbis; Ken Lucas/Visuals Unlimited; Visuals Unlimited; SINCLAIR STAMMERS/Science Photo Library/Photo Researchers, Inc.; 328, (t) Courtesy, Lisa White; 328(b), Richard Norwiz/Corbis; 329(bg), Ken Lucas/Visuals Unlimited; 331, Bernhard Edmaier/Photo Researchers, Inc.

Unit D

Page 332, Lester Lefkowitz/CORBIS; 333, John Elk III; 334-335, Michael T. Sedam/CORBIS; 336, Jeff Foott/naturepl.com; 338, Yva Momatiuk/John Eastcott/Minden Pictures; 339(l), Craig Tuttle/CORBIS; 339(r), Dan Guravich/CORBIS; 340(t), Creatas (RF)/PictureQuest; 340(c), Tim Davis/Corbis; 340(b), Danny Lehman/CORBIS; 341, Bo Zaunders/CORBIS; 342, Colin Young-Wolff/Photo Edit; 344, IFA/estockphoto/PictureQuest; 347, USGS/Photo Researchers, Inc.; 348, Los Alamos National Lab/Photo Researchers, Inc. ; 349, Jeff Greenberg/Photo Edit; 350(t), ALEXIS ROSENFELD/Science Photo Library/Photo Researchers, Inc.; 350(c), Creatas (RF)/PictureQuest; 350(b), John B. Boykin/CORBIS; 352, Peter Pinnock/ PictureQuest; 354(l), Constantinos Petrinos/naturepl.com; 354(r), Brandon Cole; 355(t), Lynn M. Stone/naturepl.com; 355(b), Danita Delmont/Alamy; 356, Doug Perrine/naturepl.com; 357, Eric Riesch/fishid.com; 358-359, CHRIS NEWBERT/Minden Pictures; 358(inset), Alexis Rosenfeld/ Photo Researchers, Inc.; 360(t), Science VU/Visuals Unlimited; 360(b), Science VU/C. Wirsen, WHOI/Visuals Unlimited; 360(inset), B. Boonyaratanakornkit & D.S. Clark, G. Vrdoljak/EM Lab, U of C Berkeley/Visuals Unlimited; 362, AP/Wide World Photos; 363, AP/Wide World Photos; 364, (t) AP/Wide World Photos, 364(b), Courtesy the Browne Family; 365(bg), Thomas Wiewandt; Visions of America/Corbis; 367(l); Lynn M. Stone/naturepl.com; 367(r), CHRIS NEWBERT/Minden Pictures; 368-369, Corbis; 370, Science Photo Library/Photo Researchers; 376, Jon Davies/Jim Reed Photography/Science Photo Library/Photo Researchers; 379(t), Mark Baker/AP/Wide World Photos; 379(inset), courtesy of Fairmount Weather Systems, United Kingdom; 380, John A. Day; 381, VAUGHAN FLEMING/Science Photo Library/Photo Researchers, Inc. ; 382(top row) John A. Day; 382(cl), WeatherStock; 382(cr), John A. Day; 382(c), Richard Hamilton Smith/Corbis; 382(bl), (bc), John A. Day; 382(br), Visuals Unlimited; 384(t), NOAA/Science Photo Library/Photo Researchers; 384(b), Vince Streano/Corbis; 386, Warren Faidley/Weatherstock; 388(tr), Jim Reed/Science Photo Library/Photo Researchers; 388(tl), Jim Reed/Corbis; 388(b), Simon Fraser/Science Photo Library/ Photo Researchers; 389(l), British Antarctic Survey/Science Photo Library/Photo Researchers; 389(c), Corbis; 389(r), Paul Seheult; Eye Ubiquitous/Corbis; 390, Jim Reed/Corbis; 391(all), Warren Faidley/Weatherstock; 393(l), NOAA/Science Photo Library/Photo Researchers; 393(r), NOAA/Science Photo Library/Photo Researchers; 394(t), Mark Lennihan/AP/Wide World Photos; 394(c), Charlie Neibergall/AP/Wide World Photos; 394(b), NOAA; 396, Luiz Marigo/Peter Arnold; 398, (t), (c), NASA; 398(b) Brownie Harris/Corbis; 399, S. Cazenave/Age Fotostock America, Inc.; 402-403, Frank Zullo/Photo Researchers, Inc. ; 404, Georg Gerster/Photo Researchers, Inc. ; 408-409(all), Gabe Palmer/CORBIS; 410, G.ANTONIO MILANI/SPL/Photo Researchers, Inc. ; 411(t), Science Photo Library/Photo Researchers, Inc; 411(b), Fred Espenak/Science Photo Library/Photo Researchers, Inc.; 412(both), Andrew J. Martinez/Photo Researchers, Inc.; 414, ImageState/Alamy Images; 416, JPL/NASA; 420, JPL/NASA; 423, American Museum of Natural History; 426(t), JPL/NASA; 426(bl), NASA/SPL/Photo Researchers, Inc. ; 426(br), Galen Rowell/CORBIS; 427(t), JPL/NASA; 427(b), American Museum of Natural History; 428, Jerry Lodriguss/Photo Researchers, Inc. ; 430, Nigel Sharp, Rich Reed, Dave Dryden, Dave Mills, Doug Williams, Charles Corson, Roger Lynds and Arjun Dey/NOAO/WIYN/NSF; 434, Space Telescope Science Institute/NASA/ SPL/Photo Researchers, Inc.; 435(l), NASA, NOAO, ESA, the Hubble Helix Nebula Team, M. Meixner (STScI), and T.A. Rector (NRAO); 435(r), NOAO; 437(tl), NOAO; 437(tr), Jean-Charles Cuillandre (CFHT), Hawaiian Starlight, CFHT/NASA; 437(cl), NOAO; 437(cr), JEAN-CHARLES CUILLANDRE/ CANADA-FRANCE- HAWAII TELESCOPE/Science Photo Library/Photo Researchers, Inc.; 437(bl), (br), NOAO; 440, 441, NASA; 442, AP/Wide World Photos; 443, NOA.

Unit E

Page 446, Thomas Alva Edison Memorial Tower and Menlo Park Museum; 447, AP/Wide World Photos; 448-449, Jorma Luhta /Nature Picture Library; 450, PATRICE LOIEZ, CERN/Science Photo Library/Photo Researchers, Inc.; 453(t), ANDREW MCCLENAGHAN/Science Photo Library/Photo Researchers, Inc.; 453(b), COLIN CUTHBERT/Science Photo Library/Photo Researchers, Inc.; 454, SCIENCE PHOTO LIBRARY/Photo Researchers, Inc.; 455(t), Science Photo Library/Photo Researchers, Inc.; 455(b), Frances Evelegh/Science Photo Library/Photo Researchers, Inc.; 458, Corbis; 460(l), Charles D. Winters/Photo Researchers, Inc.; 460(c), Charles D. Winters/Photo Researchers, Inc.; 460(r), ANDREW LAMBERT PHOTOGRAPHY/Science Photo Library/Photo Researchers, Inc.; 461(t), MICHAEL & PATRICIA FOGDEN/Minden Pictures; 461(b), Jerry Lodriguss/Photo Researchers, Inc.; 462(t), Charles D. Winters/Photo Researchers, Inc.; 462(b), Edward R. Degginger/Bruce Coleman, Inc.; 463(t), Astrid & Hanns-Frieder Michler/Photo Researchers, Inc.; 463(b), Corbis; 464(t), Corbis; 464(bl), MARTYN F. CHILLMAID/Science Photo Library/Photo Researchers, Inc.; 464(bc), Visuals Unlimited; 464(br), ANDREW LAMBERT PHOTOGRAPHY/Science Photo Library/Photo Researchers, Inc.; 465, Ed Degginger/Bruce Coleman, Inc.; 466, Angelo Cavalli/Getty Images; 468, AlaskaStock; 470, Gunter Marx/www. guntermarx-stockphotos.com; 472(l), Corbis; 472(r), Royalty Free/Corbis; 473, Charles D. Winters/ Photo Researchers, Inc. ; 474, E.R. Degginger/Bruce Coleman, Inc.; 476, Gusto/Photo Researchers; 477(t); Picture Quest, 477(b), Biophoto Assoc/Photo Researchers; 478(t), Corbis, 478(b), Philippe Psala/Photo Researchers; 479(bg), E. Gebhardt/AGE Fotostock; 482-483, Spectrum Stock, Inc.; 484, Greg Probst/Corbis; 486, Alan Schein Photography/Corbis; 487(tr), Masterfile; 487(b), Tim Davis/ CORBIS; 489(bg), Lew Robertson/Corbis; 489(tl), Bill Howes/Corbis; 489(tr), Photo Researchers, Inc.; 489(cl), Lawrence Lawry/Science Photo Library/Photo Researchers, Inc.; 489(bl), Paul A. Souders/CORBIS; 489(br), Sheila Terry/SPL/Photo Researchers, Inc.; 491(t), View Stock/Alamy Images; 491(b), Digital Vision/Media Bakery, LLC; 492(t), Phil Schermeister/CORBIS; 492(b), Gabe Palmer/CORBIS; 494, Ed Degginger/Color-Pic; 496(l), Royalty-Free/CORBIS; 496(r), Scott T. Smith/ CORBIS; 497(l), Michael S. Yamashita/CORBIS; 497(r), courtesy, Arkansas Media Room, Crater of Diamonds State Park; 498(t), Science Photo Library/Photo Researchers, Inc. ; 498(b), Dwight R. Kuhn; 499(l), Science Photo Library/Photo Researchers, Inc.; 499(r), Erich Lessing/Art Resource, NY; 500(t), Foodpix; 500(b), Craig Aurness/CORBIS; 502, Photowood Inc./CORBIS; 504, Patrick Ward/CORBIS; 505(l), Royalty-Free/CORBIS; 505(r), Andrew Lambert Photography/Science Photo Library/Photo Researchers, Inc.; 506(b), Andrew Lambert Photography/Science Photo Library/ Photo Researchers, Inc. ; 507(b), Science Photo Library/Photo Researchers, Inc. ; 508(t), David Cavagnaro/Visuals Unlimited; 508(b), Nathan Benn/CORBIS; 510, Adam Jones/Photo Researchers, Inc.; 512(c), Tom Prettyman/PhotoEdit; 512(r), Foodpix; 513(r), Royalty-Free/Corbis; 516(t), Bruno Morandi/Age Fotostock America, Inc.; 518, AP/Wide World Photos; 519, Sanford Agliolo/Corbis; 520(b), Peter Falkner; 521(bg), Neal & Molly Jansen/Age Fotostock America, Inc.; 523, Foodpix; 524-525, David Parker/SPL/Photo Researchers, Inc. ; 526, George H. H. Huey/CORBIS; 529(t), AP/ Wide World Photo; 529(b), Bruce Coleman, Inc.; 530, Otto Rogge/CORBIS; 532, DiMaggio/Kalish/ CORBIS; 534, Brian Bielmann/Age Fotostock America, Inc.; 536-537, Linda Svendsen/Panoramic Images; 538, Teri Bloom Photography; 539(t), David Lawrence; 539(tc), Pedro Coll/Age Fotostock America, Inc.; 539(bc), AP Photo/University of Illinois, James Appleby; 539(b), Craig Tuttle/ CORBIS; 540, Lester Lefkowitz/CORBIS; 540(inset), VOLKER STEGER/Science Photo Library/ Photo Researchers, Inc. ; 541(tr), NASA/Science Photo Library/Photo Researchers,Inc.; 541(tl), DR JEREMY BURGESS/Science Photo Library/Photo Researchers, Inc. ; 541(b), Dr. Jeremy Burgess/ Science Photo Library/Photo Researchers, Inc. ; 542(t), NASA; 544, Gregory G. Dimijian/Photo Researchers, Inc. ; 546, James Lund/Corbis; 547(tl), Royalty-Free Corbis; 547(tr), Grant Heilman Photography; 547(b), Getty Images; 548(tr), Barry Runk/Stan/Grant Heilman Photography; 548(b), Steve Percival/Photo Researchers, Inc. ; 549, Jose Fusta Raga/Corbis; 552, 553, AP/Wide World Photos; 554(t), Bettmann/Corbis; 554(b), Getty Images; 555(bg), Getty Images; 558-559, Tony McConnell/Science Photo Library/Photo Researchers, Inc.; 560, Sheldan Collins/CORBIS; 562(t), Paul A. Souders/CORBIS; 562(b), Jim Sugar/CORBIS; 564(l), Owaki - Kulla/CORBIS; 564(r), JIM REED/Science Photo Library/Photo Researchers, Inc.; 565(l), David Young-Wolff/PhotoEdit; 565(r), Michael S. Yamashita/CORBIS; 566(t), Ken Redding/Corbis; 566(b), Mark E. Gibson/CORBIS; 568, David Taylor/Science Photo Library/Photo Researchers, Inc.; 571, James Sparshatt/CORBIS; 574, Bettmann/CORBIS; 575, Alamy Images; 576(t), Joseph Sohm; ChromoSohm Inc./CORBIS; 576(b), ATTAR MAHER/CORBIS SYGMA; 578, Tibor Bognar/Corbis; 581(t), Phil Banko/CORBIS; 581(b), Jose Luis Pelaez, Inc./CORBIS; 583(b), SETBOUN/CORBIS; 584(l), JEREMY WALKER/Science Photo Library/Photo Researchers, Inc.; 586, 587, Wavegen; 588(l), NASA; 588(r), Peter Falkner.

Unit F

Page 592, Kevin Fleming/CORBIS; 593, TRAPPER FRANK/CORBIS SYGMA; 594-595, Getty Images; 596, Ian Shaw/Alamy; 598(t), Rob C. Nunnington/ Gallo Images/CORBIS; 598(c), S. Carmona/ CORBIS; 598(b), Tom Brakefield/CORBIS; 602(all), TRL Limited/Science Photo Library/Photo Researchers, Inc.; 604, Jeff Greenberg/Omni-Photo Communications; 606(t), Clay Perry/CORBIS; 606(b), AP/The Potomac News; 607(t), AlaskaStock; 607(b), Paul A. Souders/CORBIS; ; 608(t), Warren Morgan/CORBIS; 608(c), ALEX BARTEL/Science Photo Library/Photo Researchers, Inc.; 608(b), Science Photo Library/Photo Researchers, Inc. ; 612, Cedar Point; 614(t), Tom Stewart/ CORBIS; 614(b), Allsport Concepts/Getty Images; 615(t), Simon Fraser/Science Photo Library/Photo Researchers, Inc. ; 615(inset), Animals Animals; 618, NASA/Science Photo Library/Photo Reseearchers, Inc.; 620, AP/Wide World Photos; 621, Reuters/Newscom; 622(t), Hillary Mitchell, 622(b), Mitch Woinarowicz/Image Works; 623(bg), Richard T. Nowitz/Corbis; 625, ALEX BARTEL/Science Photo Library/Photo Researchers, Inc.; 626-627, Paul Nickien/National Geographic/Getty Images; 628, Royalty Free/Corbis/PictureQuest; 631, Rafael Winer/Corbis; 632(l), The Image Bank/Getty Images; 632(b), RF BrandXPictures/Getty Images; 635(t), Hubert Stadler/CORBIS; 635(b), Tom Payne/Alamy; 636(tl), Frans Lanting/Minden Pictures; 636(tr), Alaska Stock/Alamy Images; 636(bl), Tony Wayrynen/ NewSport/Corbis; 636(br), Mike Powell/The Image Bank/Getty Images; 638, Robert Harding World Imagery/Getty Images; 640, David Buctow/CORBIS SABA; 642(l), GP Bowater/Alamy; 642(r), David Frazier Photolibrary; 643(t), Corbis RF; 643(b), Stephen Saks Photography/Alamy; 644(l), Alan Towse/ Ecoscene/CORBIS; 644(r), Royalty-Free/CORBIS; 646, Bettmann/Corbis; 647, AP/Wide World Photos; 648(t), Peter Falkner; 648(b), Monsoon Images/Picturequest; 649(bg), Michael Mullan/CORBIS; 651(t), David Frazier Photolibrary; 651(b), Dennis MacDonald/Photo Edit.

Health Handbook

R8(t), CNRI/Science Photo Library/Photo Researchers; R8(tc), A. Pasieka/Photo Researchers; R8(bc), CNRI/Science Photo Library/Photo Researchers; R8(b), Custom Medical Stock Photo. R12(t), Sercomi/Photo Researchers; R12(c), Custom Medical Stock Photos; R12(b), Science Photo Library/Photo Researchers.

Back End Sheets

(page 1) (t) Matt Meadows/Peter Arnold, Inc.; (br) Kjell B. Sandved/Visuals Unlimited; (bg) Jeff Lepore/Photo Researchers; (page 2) (t) Ed Reschke/Peter Arnold, Inc.; (b) Premaphotos/Animals Animals-Earth Scenes; (bg) Jeff Lepore/Photo Researchers; (page 3) (t) Greg Neise/Visuals Unlimited; (c) J. Brackenbury/Peter Arnold, Inc.; (b) JH Pete Carmichael/The Image Bank/Getty Images; (bg) Jeff Lepore/Photo Researchers.

All other photos © Harcourt School Publishers.

Harcourt Photos provided by the Harcourt Index, Harcourt IPR, and Harcourt photographers; Weronica Ankarorn, Victoria Bowen, Eric Camden, Doug Dukane, Ken Kinzie, April Riehm, and Steve Williams.

DIET 7-8 grasshoppers per square meter, spread over 4 hectares (10 acres), eat as much in one day as a cow!

SENSES A grasshopper's ears are on its legs or abdomen (belly).

BELIEVE IT OR NOT Each year some kinds of grasshoppers cause $80,000,000 in crop damage.

SOUND These pegs are found only on the male grasshoppers. They are used to make the familiar chirping sound.